This modern text is designed to prepare you for your future professional career. While theories, ideas, techniques, and data are dynamic, the information contained in this volume will provide you a quick and useful reference as well as a guide for future learning for many years to come. Your familiarity with the contents of this book will make it an important volume in your professional library.

EX LIBRIS

Personnel/
HUMAN RESOURCE
MANAGEMENT

A DIAGNOSTIC APPROACH

Personnel /

HUMAN RESOURCE
MANAGEMENT

A DIAGNOSTIC APPROACH

George T. Milkovich
John W. Boudreau

both of Cornell University
with the assistance of Carolyn Milkovich

1988 Fifth Edition

BUSINESS PUBLICATIONS, INC.
Plano, Texas 75075

Acquisitions editor: John R. Weimeister
Developmental editor: Rhonda K. Harris
Production editor: Lynne Basler
Copyediting coordinator: Jean Roberts
Production manager: Bette Ittersagen
Designer: Paula Lang
Artist: Mary Jo Szymnanski
Calligrapher: John Thoeming
Compositor: Weimer Typesetting Co., Inc.
Typeface: 10½/13 Caledonia
Printer: Arcata Graphics/Hawkins

ISBN 0-256-05963-2
Library of Congress Catalog Card No. 87–72391

Printed in the United States of America

1 2 3 4 5 6 7 8 9 0 K 5 4 3 2 1 0 9 8

American managers are being urged to change how they manage employees. Competing in a worldwide economy, the difficulties U.S. firms experience are blamed, at least in part, on managers' human resource practices. Critics characterize current practices as obstacles to the flexibility and innovation required to successfully compete.

Managers are urged to do more than simply rethink their relationships with employees. Solutions are prescribed. Advice includes simplifying organizational structures and hierarchies—flat structures with few layers are in, and anything that hints of hierarchy is out; compensation linked to the value of what people do in their jobs is out, and pay tied to what people are, their skills and needs is in. Top-down autocratic supervisory styles are out, and supervisors acting as team leaders or facilitators who build trust among employees and managers are in. Multiskilled, flexible employees are desired, specialists are not. Adversarial relations with unions that in the past have led to strikes and work stoppages need to be replaced with cooperation, teamwork, and the search for mutuality of interest.

But on what is this advice based? And does it pay off? Are we in danger of replacing one set of managerial myths with other, more contemporary myths? Were managers simply misguided when they originally adopted the now conventional approaches to managing human resources? Or were these conventional approaches the rational responses to the conditions and objectives at the time? Perhaps some current practices have outlived their usefulness. But by advocating wholesale change, we run the risk of simply replacing them with trendier practices.

The organization's human resources should be managed with the same care and logic as its financial, capital, and raw material resources. Yet, it is typical for human resource management to be regarded as a "soft" management function, demonstrating little impact on an organization's bottom line. This is unfortunate because the potential returns from effective human resource management decisions can match and even surpass the returns from these other management functions.

Prescriptions abound, systematic decision making does not. And that's what this book is all about—a diagnostic, decision-making approach to human resource management. This book approaches the study and practice of human resource management from one basic premise—*decisions about human resources make a difference.* Human resource decisions affect the fairness and equity of employment relationships, the attitudes and behaviors of employees, and the ultimate efficiency and effectiveness of organizations.

This book undertakes three tasks: First, to examine the current theoretical and research developments related to human resources management, because it is this theory and research that suggests how human resource decisions achieve their objectives. Extensive and up-to-date references after each chapter support these theoretical frameworks.

The second task is to examine the current state of human resource practices. Current practices illustrate new innovations as well as established approaches to human resource management. They show how the theory can be used in practical ways. We draw on practices actually used by a wide variety of employers, focusing on those that should be readily transferable to various job settings.

Our third task is to provide students with opportunities to develop their own decision-making skills. We have included a series of cases drawn from situations faced by actual human resource managers. By using the concepts and techniques in the chapters to analyze and evaluate these cases, students can develop skills that can be transferred to future jobs. A personal-computer–based case book is also available with more extensive case situations illustrating how to harness the power of PCs as tools for human resource decision making.

ACKNOWLEDGMENTS

Several colleagues shared their ideas with us. Marick Masters, *Texas A&M University*; Richard Lutz, *University of Akron*; Anne S. Tsui, *Duke University*; Marc Singer, *James Madison University*; Steve Motowidlo, *Penn State University*; James Rush, *University of Western Ontario*; Gerald Ferris, *Texas A&M University*; Tom Bergmann, *University of Wisconsin—Eau Claire*; Judy Olian, *University of Maryland—College Park*; Francis Gallagher, *Bloomsburg State College*; Alan Cabelley, *Portland State University*; Linda Krefting, *Texas Tech University*; Joanne Loomba, *California State University—Hayward*; R. Kelley, *Governors State University*; James Bitter, *University of Northern Colorado*; and Solomon Montoya, *St. John's University*.

contents

Personnel/

HUMAN RESOURCE
MANAGEMENT

A DIAGNOSTIC APPROACH

chapter

one

THE DIAGNOSTIC APPROACH

CHAPTER OUTLINE

Remember your first day at work? When you signed the required personnel forms that day, you became part of an employer's human resources. Although plant, equipment, and financial assets are also resources required by organizations, employees—the human resources—are particularly important. This is so for at least two reasons: First and foremost, human resources influence the efficiency and effectiveness of organizations. People design and produce the goods and services, control quality, market the products, allocate financial resources, and set overall strategies and objectives for the organization. Without effective people it is simply impossible for an organization to achieve its objectives.

Second, human resources are also a major expense or cost of doing business. For some organizations, such as General Foods Corporation and Texaco, wages, benefits, training, and the like can range from approximately 20 to 30 percent of total operating expenses. For others, such as H & R Block, Inc., and Citicorp, labor expenses can be over 50 percent of operating expenses. Exhibit 1–1 shows some of these variations.

What often goes unrecognized, however, is the profound effect that human resources have on productivity. A single human resource management program might train 100 engineers. If each engineer stays with the organization for seven years, this training program will affect 700 person-years of productivity. If the training produces an average of only $1,000 worth of improved engineering productivity per person in each year, this single program is worth $700,000 to the organization. Imagine the impact of ongoing human resource programs affecting thousands of person-years of productivity. Clearly, the impact of human resource management decisions rivals (and may often exceed) the impact of decisions managing other organizational resources such as finances, plant/equipment, inventories, and marketing.

Human resources are unique. Beyond their vital contributions to an organization's efficiency and productivity, they demand fairness and equity. Civil rights and labor laws, as well as minimum wage and pension

**EXHIBIT 1–1
Labor Costs as a Percent of
Total Operating Expenses**

General Foods Corp.	18%
Black & Decker Mfg. Co.	27
Armco	32
Johnson & Johnson	36
USAir	38
Kaiser Steel	41
Citicorp	51
Bank of New York	53
H & R Block, Inc.	57

Note: Use caution in interpreting these figures. Most organizations adopt accounting conventions unique to their organizations. These data only illustrate the magnitude of differences among organizations.

Source: 1986 annual reports.

regulations reflect governmental attempts to ensure fair treatment of employees. Job retraining, employment security provisions, dispute resolution, and job posting practices all illustrate some employers' efforts to ensure fair treatment of employees. Human resources are vital not only because they play a major role in shaping and achieving any organization's objectives, but also because these human beings deserve fairness and justice.

A sense of inequity among employees affects their attitudes and behaviors. Absenteeism, low motivation, lack of concern for the quality of products or services, withholding suggestions for improvements, lack of commitment, and even sabotage may result. These attitudes and behaviors affect costs, productivity, profits, and, hence, the market value of the firm's stock. Equitable treatment in employment relationships may indirectly affect efficiency—but equity also stands alone as an important objective of human resources management.

Managing human resources is a central concern of every manager in any organization. For example, a plant manager trying to profitably manufacture personal computers needs to coordinate electronic components (the raw materials), production designs, and financial budgets. This coordination depends on effective human resource management. Even though a human resource professional may be on the staff to offer advice and expertise to all of them, the designer, the purchaser, and the financial officer actually manage the human resources. In small businesses, such as boutiques or service stations where managers make all the decisions, they also manage human resources, usually without the support of a human resources professional. Public sector organizations also manage human resources. For instance, city managers must deliver police and fire protection, sanitation, and social services to a public that often feels the quality of service is too low and the taxes too high. This requires effective human resource management, too. Whether in the public or private sector, or in local, national, or international markets, effective management of human resources is a critical part of any manager's job.

Recently, a number of developments have combined to make the effective management of human resources even more important, and more complex. These developments include the drastic changes occurring in the nature of work performed, changes in workers available to perform the work—their expectations, values, ages, and skills—as well as the changing nature of organizations. One of the most important trends is the changing nature of work. Work has become more varied and dynamic. Changing technologies and shortened product life cycles dictate changes in the tasks required to produce goods and the skills necessary to perform those tasks. Consequently, employers are seeking more flexible employees capable of learning new skills as work requirements change.

Today's workers have higher expectations about the work they are willing to perform, a desire for involvement in managing their jobs, and a wish to share in the financial gains achieved by the organization.[1] Demographics of the population and labor force are also changing.[2] Women's increased participation in the work force, dual-career families, single-parent families, the influx of immigrants and undocumented workers, and the aging of the labor force are all examples of demographic changes that affect the nature of the work force.[3]

As a result, employers can no longer afford to view workers as interchangeable economic units, if they ever did. Pegging people into static, narrowly defined jobs that offer little discretion with even less regard for their needs serves neither the employer nor the employee.

Not only are workers changing but organizations are also changing.[4] Government regulation of the employment relationship, economic competition on a global scale, and a host of other factors have forced this change. Rigidly bureaucratized organizations which require layer on layer of approval for decisions are threatened by those that are more agile in responding to change. New organization forms, more decentralized business units, and employee work teams with greater autonomy and control over their work are evolving. For example, General Motors Corporation and Ford Motor Company, like many firms, have agreed with their employees to form work teams and change production methods to improve product quality and reduce costs. In the process, entire layers of middle management and staff have been cut from assembly plants.[5]

A DIAGNOSTIC APPROACH TO HUMAN RESOURCE MANAGEMENT

The changing nature of work, workers, and organizations are trends that require rethinking traditional approaches to human resource management. This book is about meeting those challenges. It provides theoretical and technological knowledge; it also offers a model to aid the process of making decisions about human resources. These two veins, the knowledge required (what to do) and the process (how to do it), run throughout the book. The next section presents an overview of this knowledge/process approach to human resource management.

Human Resource Management: Decisions and Constituents

Human resource managers make decisions that affect the relationships between employees and employers. How many employees to hire, at what levels of skill and experience, who to promote to which jobs, who to train in which skills, how much to pay, and how to handle dissatisfied employees are examples of these decisions. To achieve organizational goals, managers must make decisions regarding human resources and consider the interrelationships among these decisions. Rates of pay, for example, affect firms' ability to hire and promote. They also affect employees' willingness to join firms, to take on the training and extra responsibilities involved in a promotion, or to vote to certify a union for collective bargaining. So the effects of decisions can be very complex.

The goals of human resource management can also be complex. Many constituencies or interested parties are involved. These constituencies (e.g., stockholders, executives, regulatory agencies, unions, employees, and managers) hold the employer accountable for achieving objectives that they consider important. For example, stockholders expect personnel decisions to increase the value of the firm. They may support a decision to link executives' pay closely to the market value of a firm's stock or reduce unit labor costs. Some regulatory agencies and employees, on the other hand, may have different interests. They may feel that who gets hired and promoted and how people are paid affect the equity and fairness in American society. These constituencies expect personnel decisions to be consistent with broader social objectives. And, of course, individual employees directly affected by human resource decisions are a critical constituency, as are the managers who make the decisions.

Definition

Human resource management is a series of decisions that affect the relationship between employees and employers; it affects many constituencies and is intended to influence the effectiveness of employees and employers.

The Diagnostic Process

Exhibit 1–2 illustrates the diagnostic process used in this book. It includes four basic phases: (1) assess and analyze human resource conditions, (2) set objectives based on the assessment, (3) choose a course of action from alternatives generated to achieve the objectives, and (4) evaluate the results. Results provide feedback to undertake the process again.

This diagnostic process applies to any number of situations. For instance, think of a particularly effective physician you may have visited. The physician's general objective is to maintain or improve your health. With this in mind, he or she first diagnoses your health problems or improvement opportunities, perhaps by examining your medical history, interviewing you regarding your symptoms, or conducting laboratory tests. This assessment and analysis phase results in several more specific health objectives, which probably differ in their importance or priority. Drawing on technical knowledge, the physician next considers alternative treatments to address the objectives. Then the doctor chooses a treatment based on the priorities of the various health objectives, the knowledge of the physician, and your own preferences.

If the treatment fails to yield the desired results, the doctor analyzes information on its effects. After combining this analysis with the original assessment of your state of health, the physician considers a new or revised treatment. This process of assessing the situation, setting objectives, choosing among alternatives, and monitoring results continues throughout your relationship with the physician. Sometimes, a crisis causes one objective to take precedence (e.g., to stop the bleeding), and the physician weighs alternatives and makes choices rapidly based on limited information. At other times, the objectives may be more broad (e.g., to reduce cholesterol or reduce blood pressure) and the doctor considers alternatives with more deliberation.

EXHIBIT 1-2
A Diagnostic Approach to Human Resource Management

ASSESS HUMAN RESOURCE CONDITIONS	SET HUMAN RESOURCE OBJECTIVES	CHOOSE AND APPLY HUMAN RESOURCE ACTIVITIES	EVALUATE RESULTS
EXTERNAL CONDITIONS	EFFICIENCY	Planning	EFFICIENCY
Economic Conditions	Organization	Staffing	EQUITY
	Employee	Development	
Government Regulations	EQUITY	Employee/Union Relations	
Unions	Organization	Compensation	
ORGANIZATIONAL CONDITIONS	Employee		
Nature of the Organization			
Nature of the Work			
EMPLOYEE CONDITIONS			
Abilities			
Motivation			
Interests			

An Example

Human resource management falls within the same generic process. Consider the situation where productivity in a certain manufacturing unit has declined. First, the manager assesses the situation (i.e., a gap exists between what product quality should be and what it is). The manager gathers and analyzes information on equipment malfunctions, raw material quality, and production histories to better identify the nature of the gap, and to suggest possible causes. Perhaps the manager can trace the gap to the employees (e.g., inappropriate work behaviors, frequent absenteeism, omission of certain tasks). If this is the case, then the gap becomes a human resource management issue because it stems from the relationship with employees. A manager who diagnoses a gap between certain correct work behaviors and current behaviors identifies several alternative remedies. Possible options include training current employees in the appropriate way to perform the job, linking the appropriate behaviors to pay, selecting employees who have better qualifications, or even redesigning the job to better fit employee behaviors. Based on the available information, the priorities attached to different outcomes, and any evidence regarding the effectiveness of different alternatives, the manager could choose one or more options to address the situation. After the options are implemented, the programs' effects on the quality gap become additional information. To choose the best option, the manager weighs relative costs, feasibility, and chances of success. More often than not, the choice of treatment, like the physician's, is based on the manager's knowledge of human resources management and on personal experience rather than a complex cost-benefit analysis.

A Proactive Perspective

In addition to simply reacting to a problem after it occurs, managers must also anticipate and prevent issues from arising. They must be proactive. Suppose the top management of a business machine manufacturer concludes that declining sales of electric typewriters will result in the need for fewer engineers than the number currently employed. The plant's human resource manager could diagnose the situation and decide to let naturally occurring turnover combine with a hiring freeze to solve the engineer surplus. However, life is seldom that simple. If electric typewriter sales are declining, top management may also decide to enter the electronic typewriter and word processor business. This combination of strategic market decisions has a cascading effect on human resource decisions. Perhaps considerable engineering talent and new ideas will be required to design these new products. Many current engineers may not possess the skills to design and manufacture electronic typewriters and word processors. Obsolete engineers can be retrained, encouraged to take advantage of an early retirement program, or even offered help in seeking employment with other firms. At the same time, engineers with different expertise need to be hired. This example is not hypothetical; it is part of Smith Corona's human resource management plan. If, as is often the case, the company's marketing strategy shifts, then the manager needs to adjust the human resource decisions accordingly.

However, human resource conditions also affect the decision to pursue a particular strategy. For example, research by two IBM physicists has led to remarkable breakthroughs in superconductivity. You can be sure that IBM has already mapped out product development plans based on these employees' abilities and interests—human resource conditions.

Applying the Process to Human Resource Management

The study of human resource management involves theoretical and technical knowledge as well as understanding the diagnostic process used. As Exhibit 1–2 shows, the diagnostic model integrates these two basic characteristics: the diagnostic process and the content, or the technical knowledge that makes up human resource management.

The four phases of the diagnostic process are at the top of the model. They are:

Assess Human Resource Conditions.

Set Human Resource Objectives.

Choose and Apply Human Resource Activities.

Evaluate Results.

Under each of these four phases is the overall framework for the content. The diagnostic model provides an overview and integration of the content and technical knowledge of human resource management—the subject matter of the rest of this book.

ASSESS HUMAN RESOURCE CONDITIONS

The human resource conditions to be assessed fall into three broad categories: external conditions, organizational conditions, and employee conditions.

External Conditions

The external environment influences and restricts an organization's strategies, activities, and ultimately its effectiveness. This amalgam of societal, cultural, political, and economic factors relevant to the organization and its employees includes economic conditions, government regulations and union expectations.

Economic Conditions

Changing economic conditions directly influence all operations of any organization, including its human resource activities. Management decisions to hire additional people, to lay off current employees, or to grant a cost-of-living wage increase are all decisions influenced by economic conditions. Economic conditions also directly influence employees. For example, high unemployment rates make many employees reluctant to leave their present jobs, and thus reduce turnover. Or workers squeezed by inflation may ask for extra hours of work to increase the size of their paychecks. Thus, data on the economic environment organizations face are relevant to human resource decisions.

Government Regulations

Laws reflect a society's response to social, political, or economic problems. A growing share of business decisions—one estimate is as many as half— are shaped by the government.[6] The human resource laws and regulations of federal, state, and local governments, and the courts' interpretation of these laws, have become increasingly important to employers. Equal employment opportunity legislation and employment-at-will decisions are especially significant examples. These laws require a total reexamination of every single personnel policy and program to ensure compliance. Pension and benefit regulations, health and safety guidelines, and immigration laws also shape decisions regarding human resources.

Union Expectations

Unions form for several reasons; too often the reason is poor management of human resources.[7] In many cases, unions have forced employers to adopt sound human resource programs. However, the presence of a union reduces employers' flexibility in designing human resource programs. Therefore, many organizations wish to maintain or achieve a union-free status. Union strategies and their organizing and negotiating priorities are important factors in an organization's external conditions.

Organization Conditions

The second component to be assessed is organization conditions. The organization's internal environment is made up of many factors. Two of the key ones are discussed here, but our list is not exhaustive.

Nature of the Organization

Several factors make up the nature of the organization; its strategies and objectives, financial situation, technology, and culture are examples. Chapter Four examines them in depth. To demonstrate the model in Exhibit 1–2, briefly consider the strategy of the organization. Texas Instrument, Inc.'s decision to leave, and IBM's decision to enter, the personal computer market reflect different strategic directions for those companies. Information about the organizations' business strategies shapes human resource decisions. Companies deploy their organizational resources—financial, material, and human resources—in a manner consistent with these strategic directions; therefore, human resource activities must be designed and administered consistent with these strategies. USX's decision to concentrate on three steel products where it had unique competitive advantages—steel sheet for auto makers, seamless pipe for energy exploration, and plates and beams for construction—has human resource implications.[8] To accomplish this strategy, managers closed plants producing other steel products. USX's human resources were severely disrupted. Some employees, both steelworkers and managers, were permanently laid off. Others were retrained to operate new equipment and facilities. Perhaps pay plans based on profit sharing, cost reduction, or product quality will also be designed.

Nature of the Work

The work at Iowa Beef Processors differs from the work at the New York Metropolitan Museum of Art. While each organization requires human resources, the differences in the work require designing and choosing different human resource management systems. Nature of the work is the second aspect of the organization considered in the model. The work to be performed influences the skill and training required, the compensation and rewards systems that can be offered, the manner in which the jobs can be designed, and other human resource activities.

Employee Conditions

Information about the nature of employees is critical for setting objectives and shaping human resource decisions. Information can be obtained on each individual and on the work force as a whole. Each employee has unique experiences, skills, abilities, needs, and motivations. Individual differences relevant to human resource management include possession of highly sought-after skills, career preferences, or performance characteristics. Relevant work force data, its demographics, include average experience, wages, and performance levels. Information on work force demographics is important for several reasons; experienced work forces tend to have lower turnover rates than those with younger, less experienced workers. Similarly, a younger work force values pensions and deferred compensation differently than an older work force; differences in expectations and values may also exist. So the diagnostic process assesses employee conditions, as well as organization and external conditions.

Management analyzes information in these categories to set objectives for human resource management.

SET HUMAN RESOURCE OBJECTIVES

The second phase of the diagnostic process in Exhibit 1–2 is setting objectives. The information gathered in the first phase by assessing the external, organizational, and employee conditions confronting the organization not only suggests what current conditions are, but also what future conditions may be. This information is useful in setting human resource objectives. Desired conditions and discrepancies between the desired conditions and actual or likely future conditions also affect objectives. Human resource objectives establish targets and priorities for reducing the discrepancies. The two categories of objectives are efficiency and equity.

Efficiency and equity objectives may reflect either organization or employee considerations. A basic premise underlying human resource management is that organization objectives are affected by the culmination of the behaviors and attitudes of individual employees.

Efficiency

Every organization operates by combining resources (raw materials, data, technology, and human resources) in a way that produces marketable products or services. If we think of the resources as inputs and the products/services as outputs, then efficiency refers to the comparison between inputs and outputs. Efficient organizations maximize outputs while minimizing inputs. Managers' decisions regarding human resources affect an organization's efficiency by employing the work force in the most efficient manner.

Analysts consider efficiency as a ratio, such as the labor cost per unit produced; or as a difference, such as the total revenue from selling one unit, minus the total labor cost of producing it. Typical measures of human resource efficiency include organization-level outcomes (such as market share, return on investment, and quality of public service), which are affected by employee-level behaviors (such as job performance, unit labor cost, attendance, accident costs, and employee separations).

Equity

Equity refers to the perceived fairness of both the procedures used to make human resource decisions and the ultimate decisions themselves. The rules and procedures used to decide pay increases, hiring, layoffs or promotions, as well as the effects of those decisions, come under scrutiny from several constituents. Employees; managers; government regulatory agencies, such as the Equal Employment Opportunity Commission; and the larger society judge the equity of employment decisions.

Measures of fairness or equity are less well developed than efficiency measures. Like efficiency, however, equity may be measured from the perspective of the organization or the employee: From the perspective of the organization, equity indicators include balance (or lack of it) in minority and female work force representation. Public perceptions include whether the organization is a good place to work or operates as a good community citizen. And, union perceptions weigh how fairly the organization deals with labor issues. At the employee level, equity is usually measured through attitude surveys; behaviors such as grievances, absenteeism, and separations may also reflect employee equity perceptions.

Integrating Efficiency and Equity

Efficiency and equity are interrelated. For example, many organizations believe that fair and equitable employment policies enable them to operate more efficiently because such policies increase employees' willingness to accept retraining or relocation or to offer productivity improvement suggestions without fear of losing their jobs. On the other hand, efficiency and equity are not always maximized by the same decisions. For example, layoffs designed to retain younger employees with more up-to-date skills may seem unfair to senior employees who feel that their long-term investment in the organization should be worth greater consideration. Although other management functions (such as marketing, finance, and operations) also face questions of efficiency and equity, some of the most vivid, important, and exciting issues fall squarely within the employment relationship. Finding a balance is one of the most critical challenges for human resource management.

So establishing human resource objectives is the second phase of the diagnostic approach. Human resource objectives establish the goals and priorities for human resource management decisions and activities. Properly formulated, they can serve as standards for evaluating those decisions. They can also suggest which activities are most appropriate for achieving the objectives.

CHOOSING AND APPLYING HUMAN RESOURCE MANAGEMENT ACTIVITIES

The third phase in the diagnostic approach is human resource activities. These are the programs designed in response to the human resource objectives and managed to achieve those objectives. Each of these activities contains numerous alternatives from which managers choose. We have identified five activities.

Planning

Planning activities focus on the future; *how* an organization should move from its current human resource condition to achieve its human resource objectives. Planning establishes the links between the organization's overall strategies and its human resource strategies. It is concerned with how to integrate all human resource decisions into a coherent overall human resource strategy. Additionally, managers face decisions about how to structure the human resources management function, such as whether to employ specialists rather than generalists in various human resource activities, whether to centralize or decentralize the human resource function, and the function's role in the organization.

Staffing

Staffing activities determine the composition of an organization's human resources. Issues addressed include: How many people should we employ? Which skills, abilities, and experiences do we require? When and how should people be redeployed, recruited, or laid off? How do we select the correct individuals in each case?

Development

Employee development and training activities are among the most common and costly methods of achieving human resource objectives. These activities aim to help employees learn new skills or refine existing skills. Development activities can also affect employees' attitudes. For example, newly hired employees typically undergo an orientation session soon after joining the organization. Although this orientation involves some training in job skills, another purpose is to make the employee feel part of the organization. Descriptions of the unique advantages of working for the organization, and a chance for employees to voice their own concerns and questions regarding their new jobs are attempts to influence employee attitudes. Employee development activities represent a powerful tool for human resource decision makers to enhance the efficiency and equity of the organization, especially when they are integrated with activities in other areas such as staffing and compensation. Human resource managers must decide which skills or knowledge areas need development and which methods are most effective for helping employees acquire skills and knowledge.

Employee/Union Relations

Employee relations activities promote harmonious relationships among managers and employees. The relationship with unions, including collective bargaining and contract administration, is the most visible aspect of employee relations. A basic decision is to establish a policy regarding unions; some employers actively pursue nonunion (or union-free) status, others adopt a cooperative policy, and still others maintain an aggressively adversarial relationship. For some managers, employee relations means reducing manager and employee hostilities or at least keeping employee dissatisfaction to a tolerable murmur. For others, it means designing and managing human resource activities to ensure fair and equitable treatment of all employees. Employment security provisions, grievance procedures, provisions for child care and drug counseling may all be part of employee relations activities. Employee relations also include health and safety activities to reduce accidents and health hazards and to promote the physical and mental health of employees.

Compensation

Compensation includes the rewards and returns for employees' expertise and services. Compensation decisions include determining: How to position the organization's pay level relative to its competitors' pay level. How to ensure fair and equitable internal pay differences among employees. How large a pay increase employees should receive and whether it should be based on individual performance, work team performance, or the profits of the organization. And, which forms compensation should take (cash, incentives, bonuses, health and medical benefits, or pensions). Challenging work assignments, the sense of personal accomplishment, and other intrinsic aspects of work are rewards or compensation, too.

These, then, are the five major human resource activities listed in the diagnostic approach: planning, staffing, development, employee/union relations, and compensation. How these activities are designed and managed depends on the previous two phases of the model: the human resource conditions the organization faces, and the human resource objectives it has established. Managers' decisions regarding all of these activities make up the organization's human resource strategy and shape its ability to achieve its objectives. Evaluating how well the organization's human resource objectives are accomplished is the fourth and final phase of the model.

EVALUATING RESULTS

Striving to achieve objectives through human resource activities makes little sense unless management evaluates the results of those choices and applications. Identifying the contribution of sound human resource management requires evaluating results. Evaluation is driven by the objectives established in the second phase: efficiency and equity. Similar to objectives, evaluation can focus on both organization and employee indicators.

Evaluation determines the effects of human resource activities. Did they help the organization to achieve its human resource objectives? For example, organization efficiency might be evaluated by comparing the unit labor cost after a staffing or training program to the unit labor cost before the program. Agencies may evaluate organization equity by comparing the proportion of minorities and females attained by a more aggressive recruiting activity to affirmative action objectives. At the employee level, managers may evaluate efficiency by comparing performance ratings or absenteeism rates occurring after implementing a behavior-based reward system to those that occurred before. To evaluate employees' perceptions of equity, managers may examine responses to satisfaction or opinion surveys.

Finally, just as objectives reflect the variety of constituencies interested in the employment relationship, management must measure and present evaluation results in a way that satisfies the important constituencies. Managers, employees, unions, and regulatory agencies may all require different evidence to convince them that human resource management decisions and activities make a difference.

THE BOOK PLAN

The organization of this book parallels the diagnostic model. Part One, the next section, describes external, organizational, and employee conditions relevant to human resource decisions. We discuss assessment techniques such as environmental scanning, job design and analysis, and performance appraisal. Part Two examines how to set human resource objectives and evaluate the results. The book then goes into detail about the human resource activities, including planning, staffing, development, employee/union relations, and compensation. It is useful to keep the diagnostic model in mind as you progress throughout the book. The model provides a framework for both the process and technical knowledge that makes up human resource management and serves as a guide for the book.

WHO MANAGES HUMAN RESOURCES?

As we have already pointed out, every organization, no matter its size, needs to manage its human resources. Very small organizations do not hire a person who specializes in human resource management. The owners or operating managers can do it. As organizations increase in size and complexity, however, the operating manager's work is divided up and some of it becomes specialized. Human resource management is one such function, as is accounting or marketing.

Interaction between the Operating Manager and the Human Resource Professional

With two managers—operating managers and human resource specialists—making decisions, the potential for conflict exists when the responsibility for specific decisions is blurred. Additionally, operating and human resource managers may have different orientations or even different objectives. For example, an operating manager may wish to minimize costs by paying only the minimum wage necessary to attract sufficient workers to do the job at minimum levels of competence. On paper, the operating manager's plan looks good. Over time, however, resentful workers may take out their frustrations on product quality and equipment; inferior goods or services may drive away formerly loyal customers. Eventually, profits may plummet, but by then the short-sighted operating manager may have moved on to a new location. In contrast, human resource managers ought to have the long-term needs of the employees and the organization in mind, and try to ensure efficient and equitable decisions.

The potential conflict between personnel people and operating managers is most manifest where the decisions must be joint efforts, as on such issues as discipline, physical working conditions, termination, transfer, promotion, and employment planning. Operating managers are *the* managers of human resources. They are the ones responsible for the effective utilization of all the organization's resources. Yet the human resource professional, similar to the financial or marketing or engineering professional, must advise and counsel to make certain that the human resource decisions are correct under the specific circumstances. Ideally, the human resource professionals and operations managers will complement each other rather than compete.

Human Resource Staffing Ratios

Several studies have examined human resource staffing ratios, that is, the number of human resource specialists hired for every 1,000 employees.

EXHIBIT 1–3
Personnel Staff Ratios (number per 100
employees on company payroll)*

Human Resource Management Professionals	Median Number
All companies (418)	0.6
By industry	
Manufacturing (213)	0.6
Nonmanufacturing (110)	0.8
Finance (55)	0.8
Nonbusiness (95)	0.4
Health care (51)	0.4
By size	
Up to 250 employees (73)	0.9
250–499 employees (91)	0.6
500–999 employees (83)	0.5
1,000–2,499 employees (98)	0.4
2,500 or more employees (73)	0.4

Note: Figures in parentheses indicate the number of companies providing data in each category.

*Does not include peripheral staff, such as guards and cafeteria workers, who may be on personnel department payroll. In companies with a medical facility as part of the personnel department, doctors and nurses are included as professional/technical staff.

Source: ASPA/BNA Survey No. 49, "Personnel Activities, Budgets and Staff 1985–1986," *Bulletin to Management,* June 5, 1986.

The median ratio as seen in Exhibit 1–3 is 6 specialists per 1,000 employees, or 1 human resource professional for every 167 employees.[9]

Based on the diagnostic model, we expect to find human resource staffing ratios vary under different environmental, organizational, and employee conditions. Ratios do vary by industry, from the highest in financial service firms (8 specialists per 1,000 employees) to the lowest in health care (4 per 1,000 employees). Smaller firms have higher rates than larger firms, probably reflecting economies of scale. Nonunion companies tend to have higher ratios, 10 or more professionals per 1,000 employees. The staffing ratio tends to diminish with increasing unionization. American Management Associations found that human resource ratios were higher in firms with greater percentages of professional, engineering, and managerial workers than nonprofessional, production workers.[10]

Why do some industries and firms devote more resources to human resource management than others? Why do professional/engineering/

EXHIBIT 1–4
IBM Human Resource Philosophy

"IBM people are our greatest asset—increased efficiency cannot be paid for by debiting our traditional respect for the individual—there can and need be no compromise on that. The management of people remains paramount."

JOHN OPEL

---

managerial employees have more resources devoted to them than production/blue-collar workers? One answer may be that certain employees require greater resources to recruit, train, and pay than others. Other employers take the position that more resources devoted to human resource activities will improve overall organization efficiency. Exhibits 1–4 and 1–5 show IBM's human resource philosophy and some of their human resource programs. Little systematic research has studied the effects of human resource staffing ratios and resource deployment on organizations.

The Role of the Human Resource Manager

In 1987 there were almost half a million people employed in personnel work in the United States.[11] About 60 percent of them work in the private sector, 30 percent in the public sector, and the remaining 10 percent in the not-for-profit sector (hospitals, libraries, or voluntary organizations). And the future looks bright.

The human resource function has been moving toward greater education and professionalism. College training includes courses in personnel management, human resource planning, equal employment opportunity, compensation administration, training, recruiting, staffing, labor law, and collective bargaining. Those who wish to become more specialized may join an association like the American Society for Personnel Administrators (ASPA), attend meetings, read professional journals (see the Appendix at the end of this chapter) or seek accreditation (see Appendix).

Human resource professionals are well paid. According to recent surveys, the average cash salary of the head of human resource management at large firms is $117,000.[12] The average pay for an employment interviewer (a typical entry-level job for an inexperienced employee with a bachelor's degree in human resource management) is $20,300. Salaries differ by geographic region, by human resource specialty, and by industry (pharmaceutical firms and chemical firms average the highest, public service and banks average the lowest).

EXHIBIT 1–5
IBM's Human Resource Policies Focus on the Employee and Programs Are Designed to Increase Each Employee's Involvement

IBM Vice President Walton E. Burdick commented on a number of the specific policies IBM is using to manage its U.S. work force, now numbering about 200,000.

Compensation: ". . . everyone employed by IBM is salaried. All employees were placed on salary in 1958, and at the same time, all time clocks in the company were removed. . . . Today, employees fill out weekly time sheets that are verified by their managers."

Benefits: "All of IBM's benefit programs are noncontributory. . . . The benefit programs provide wide coverage and we try to be as innovative as possible."

The Line Manager: "We try to maintain a very close employee and manager relationship. We give the manager full human resource responsibility, including merit evaluation and salary."

Training for Managers: "To enable managers to function well in this environment, we provide them with a broad base of management training. In addition, we require all managers, at all levels, to have 40 hours of specific management training each year."

Opinion Surveys: "Opinion surveys, routinely conducted about once a year in most units, are an anonymous process that allows employees to express their opinions on anything about the business, including top management."

Performance Appraisal: "There is a long tradition of individual treatment in IBM. I mentioned the merit system earlier. . . . The appraisal and counseling program is an integral part of that. This program requires that managers and employees sit down and develop objectives, and that employees be evaluated against these objectives at least annually."

Flexible Hours: "We announced in 1981 that individualized work schedules—popularly known as flextime—would be extended to the entire IBM Corporation, about 200,000 in the U.S. . . . Employees are enthusiastic, and management and employees both have seen this program as a current and tangible manifestation of our commitment to respect for the individual."

Quality Circles: "At present, we have in operation over 1,000 excel circles—commonly known as quality circles. Their numbers are increasing, consistent with the company's continuing emphasis on quality. This approach is an excellent way for employees to participate in job-related decisions that affect them."

Manager's Expense Fund: "Our managers are expected to be concerned with their people. To support their human relations efforts, managers are provided with funds for personalized gestures or recognition—or concern—such as a gift for a hospitalized employee."

SUMMARY

Human resource management is a fascinating and important subject. The fascination lies in the fact that it involves people and decisions involving people at work. It is important because human resources *are* the organization. Human resources make the decisions, set the objectives, and design, assemble, and sell the products.

The basic premise underlying the study of human resource management and this book is that decisions about how people are managed make a difference. These decisions about human resources involve both process and content. The process refers to how decisions get made and includes assessing human resource conditions, setting objectives, choosing and applying programs, and reviewing the results obtained.

The diagnostic model offers a framework combining the content or technical knowledge in the field with the process. In our model, conditions in the external environment, the organization, the nature of the work as well as employees affect human resource decisions and their effectiveness in achieving objectives. Objectives include organizational efficiency and equity. These objectives then become the standards for evaluating the results of decisions.

We should emphasize that the diagnostic model in Exhibit 1–2 is not static. Changing conditions, such as society's expectations, technology, and employees' interests, dictate ongoing assessment and flexible decision making. Nor do the relationships always proceed in one direction. Human resource activities can affect external conditions (such as changing the labor market by attracting more candidates), and organization conditions (such as identifying strategic directions best suited to the skills and motivations of employees), as well as employees. Managing such a dynamic process is what makes human resource decisions so important and challenging.

APPENDIX/Specialization and Professionalization

Human resource managers advance their knowledge of the field by reading professional journals. These include:

1. Journals for the human resource manager:
   American Federationist
   Administrative Management
   Employment Benefit Plan Review
   Labor Law Journal
   Monthly Labor Review

> *The Personnel Administrator*
> *Personnel*
> *Personnel Journal*
> *Public Personnel Management*

2. Scholarly journals. The following is a list of publications written for both scholars and executives. Reading these requires more technical training than do the preceding journals.

> *Academy of Management Journal*
> *Academy of Management Review*
> *Human Relations*
> *Human Organization*
> *Human Resources Management*
> *Industrial Relations*
> *Industrial and Labor Relations Review*
> *Journal of Applied Psychology*
> *Organizational Behavior and Human Performance*
> *Personnel Psychology*

In addition, several companies offer management information services. The best known of these are the Bureau of National Affairs (BNA), Commerce Clearing House (CCH), and Prentice-Hall Services.

Accreditation

The American Society of Personnel Administrators (ASPA) has set up the ASPA Accreditation Institute to offer executives the opportunity to be accredited as specialists (in functional areas such as employment, placement and planning, or training and development) or as generalists (multiple specialties). This institute is a nonprofit organization formed for the purpose of accrediting human resource professionals.

Accreditation is based on mastery of a body of knowledge, as demonstrated by passing a comprehensive written examination, and on varying amounts of full-time professional experience in the field, as practitioners, consultants, educators, or researchers. Individuals must currently be serving in roles appropriate to the accreditation they seek. Accreditation can be changed or upgraded as roles change and experience accumulates. A generalist must pass examinations in five areas to demonstrate broad knowledge, whereas the specialist is expected to possess greater in-depth knowledge. Information and application materials are available from the Personnel Accreditation Institute, American Society of Personnel Ad-

EXHIBIT 1–6
Specialties of the Personnel Administration and Industrial Relations Field as Defined by the American Society of Personnel Administrators

1. **Staffing:** Screening, interviewing, recruitment, testing, personnel records, job analysis, job description, staffing tables, promotion, transfer, job enlargement, etc.
2. **Personnel Maintenance:** Counseling, personnel appraisal inventories, turnover, health services and accident prevention, employee benefits and services, etc.
3. **Labor Relations:** Group relationships with organized or unorganized employees; negotiations, contract administration, grievances, arbitration, third-party involvement, mutual aid pacts, etc.
4. **Training/Development:** Job training, supervisor and foreman training, manager and executive development, pre-employment and special-purpose training, retraining, etc.
5. **Compensation:** Wage and salary surveys, incentive pay plans, profit sharing, stock ownership, financial and nonfinancial rewards, job enrichment, wage and salary controls, etc.
6. **Employment Communications:** House organ, employee handbook, rumor control, listening, attitude, morale and expectations surveys, feedback analysis, etc.
7. **Organization:** Structural design, planning and evaluation, innovation, utilization of formal and informal reducing conflict, overcoming resistance to organizational change, etc.
8. **Administrator:** Explanation and interpretation of options—authoritative, consultative, participative, self-management styles, assistance in change, etc.
9. **Personnel Policy and Planning:** Defining organizational goals, policy guidelines and strategies; identifying, translating, and complying with public manpower policy; forecasting manpower needs, selecting optional courses, etc.
10. **Review, Audit, Research:** Program reporting recording; evaluation of policies and programs. Theory testing, innovation, experimentation, cost/benefit studies, etc.

Source: *Personnel Administrator,* January 1984.

ministrators, 606 North Washington St., Alexandria, Virginia 22314, (763) 548–3440. Exhibit 1–6 lists the areas of specialty as defined by ASPA.

DISCUSSION AND REVIEW QUESTIONS

1. Define human resource management and tell why it is important in an organization.
2. Which environmental conditions influence human resource management?
3. What are the major phases in the diagnostic processes?
4. Describe the interaction of operating and human resource managers in making decisions.

5. Which basic objectives do human resource decisions seek to affect? What data measure these results?

NOTES AND REFERENCES

1. Some writers make the case that work will be more complex. Yet others argue it will be greatly simplified, except for a small portion of jobs; "Work in the 21st Century," *Personnel Administrator*, December 1983, the entire issue; and Martin L. Weitzman, *The Share Economy: Conquering Stagflation* (Boston: Harvard University Press, 1984).
2. Valerie A. Personick, "A Second Look at Industry Output and Employment Trends Through 1995," Bureau of Labor Statistics, *Monthly Labor Review*, November 1985, pp. 27–40.
3. Donald L. Huddle, Arthur F. Corwin, and Gordon J. MacDonald, *Illegal Immigration: Job Displacement and Social Costs* (Washington, D.C.: The American Immigration Control Foundation, 1985); Arland Thornton and Deborah Freedman, "The Changing American Family," *Population Bulletin* 38, no. 4 (October 1983), pp. 12–27.
4. New York Stock Exchange, *People and Productivity: A Challenge to Corporate America* (New York Stock Exchange, 1982).
5. Pat Choate and J. K. Linger, *The High-Flex Society* (New York: Alfred A. Knopf, 1986).
6. Joseph T. Nolan, "Political Surfing When Issues Break," *Harvard Business Review*, January–February 1985, pp. 78–87.
7. Seymour Martin Lipset and William Schneider, *The Confidence Gap: Business, Labor and Government in the Public Mind* (New York: Free Press, 1983); AFL–CIO Committee on the Evolution of Work, *The Changing Situation of Workers and Their Unions* (Washington, D.C.: AFL–CIO, February 1985).
8. "The Toughest Job in Business: How They're Remaking U.S. Steel," *Business Week*, February 25, 1985, pp. 50–56.
9. *Bulletin to Management*, ASPA/BNA Survey No. 49, "Personnel Activities, Budgets, and Staff 1985–86" (Washington, D.C.: Bureau of National Affairs, June 5, 1986).
10. James N. Baron, Frank R. Dobbin, and P. Devereaux Jennings, "War and Peace: The Evolution of Modern Personnel Administration in U.S. Industry," *American Journal of Sociology*, September 1986, pp. 350–83.
11. *Salaries and Bonuses in Personnel/Industrial Relations Functions* is available for $150 from Abbott, Langer & Associates, 548 First St., Crete, Illinois 60417.
12. *1987 ASPA/Hansen Human Resource Management Compensation Survey* (Deerfield, Ill.: Mercer-Meidinger-Hansen, 1987).

THE DIAGNOSTIC MODEL

ASSESS HUMAN RESOURCE CONDITIONS	SET HUMAN RESOURCE OBJECTIVES	CHOOSE AND APPLY HUMAN RESOURCE ACTIVITIES	EVALUATE RESULTS
EXTERNAL CONDITIONS	EFFICIENCY	Planning	EFFICIENCY
Economic Conditions	Organization	Staffing	EQUITY
Government Regulations	Employee	Development	
Unions	EQUITY	Employee/Union Relations	
	Organization	Compensation	
ORGANIZATIONAL CONDITIONS	Employee		
Nature of the Organization			
Nature of the Work			
EMPLOYEE CONDITIONS			
Abilities			
Motivation			
Interests			

Part

one

Assessing Conditions

*P*art One assesses the relevant factors that influence human resource management. The diagnostic model on this page groups these factors into three categories: external, organization, and employee conditions. This grouping provides a framework for Part One. Chapters Two and Three assess external conditions: Chapter Two discusses economic influences, legal requirements, and union expectations. Chapter Three elaborates on equal employment opportunity requirements, an external factor that affects every human resource decision.

Moving from the external to the internal environment, the next chapter assesses the characteristics of the organization. It also discusses how the objectives of the organization may be linked with human resource activities.

Chapter Five assesses the nature of work itself—how tasks, behaviors, responsibilities and outcomes are assigned to different jobs, and how jobs relate to each other.

Chapters Six and Seven focus on the individual employee. Chapter Six discusses various theories of human behavior, and ties these theories to work outcomes, such as absenteeism, turnover, and productivity. Chapter Seven discusses the process for assessing individuals' performance.

chapter

two

EXTERNAL CONDITIONS

CHAPTER OUTLINE

Demand for labor was so keen that an employee could quit a job in the morning and have employment in another organization at noon. The term "five day worker" or "floater" came into use to describe the undependable work force. Labor turnover was enormous. One organization's average yearly employment was 14,300, but 50,448 employees left in that year.[1]

It was evident that such turnover was an expensive indulgence. Some sort of program that would insure a stable, experienced work force was badly wanted. After a series of studies, human resource programs were designed to increase work force stability. These included profit sharing, training programs to insure employees could use the modern technology, a department store, legal aid (with six full-time lawyers to give employees legal advice), medical and dental facilities (with a staff of 12), and employee athletic and musical programs. While demand for labor continued unabated, the turnover and absenteeism dropped dramatically following the onset of these programs.[2]

The success story of a human resource manager in California's Silicon Valley, competing for computer and software design engineers in the 1980s? No, it was the Ford Motor Company's experience between 1913 and 1920 in Detroit.

Ford found that conditions in the external environment in 1913 affected their employees' work behaviors as well as management's ability to achieve organization objectives. High demand for labor and the unmet needs and expectations of new workers were external conditions that led Ford to instigate programs to be run by a department of sociology, a forerunner to the modern human resource management function. The department's activities ranged from forecasting future availability of labor in Detroit to visiting workers' homes to discuss their needs and behaviors.[3]

Improved human resource management is often a direct response to external pressures. In fact, Jacoby argues that personnel programs first arose as a result of widespread labor unrest and union pressures in the 1920s and 1930s.[4] He states that "according to various surveys, the proportion of large firms with personnel departments rose markedly during 1919 to 1935. The proportion of the industrial work force covered by personnel departments shot up from 20 percent in 1929 to about 70 percent by 1935."[5] Other researchers point to data which show that government regulations plus the role of personnel professionals in insuring compliance with regulations also hastened the growth and importance of human resource management departments.

The rigor with which civil rights, equal employment opportunity (EEO), and occupational safety regulations are enforced affects the resources employers allocate to related human resource programs. For example, many employers believe that enforcement is less rigorous in the

1980s than in the 1970s.[7] Therefore, they fold specialized equal employment responsibilities into responsibilities for overall employee relations. One the other hand, enforcement may be as rigorous, but now the laws have been clarified. With reduced uncertainty about what is required or forbidden, organizations may not find it necessary to allocate the same level of expertise to meeting these legal responsibilities. Whatever the reason, an understanding of external influences is necessary to be an effective manager.

EXTERNAL CONDITIONS AND THE DIAGNOSTIC MODEL

The diagnostic model shows three key sources of external pressures on human resource management:

Economic pressures

Governmental regulations

Union influences

Assessing External Conditions

Exhibit 2–1 lists some of the techniques used to diagnose the nature of relevant external pressures.

Specialists conduct most of the analysis for specific human resource activities. For example, staffing and recruiting activities require searches to assess conditions in the external labor market. They also conduct wage and benefit surveys to determine competitive pay rates.

One procedure shown in the exhibit, environmental scanning, assesses economic, governmental, and union trends. Because of its flexibility, it illustrates how managers may diagnose external conditions.

Environmental Scanning

External environmental scanning (EES) for general business purposes is reasonably well developed, but human resource management applications are less common, and there is virtually no research.

Most formal (and probably most informal) EES applications follow some variant of the process shown in Exhibit 2–2. This process includes monitoring, screening, conducting issues research, communicating, and developing plans.

The Trend Analysis Program (TAP) of the American Council of Life Insurance illustrates the general process.[8] TAP has been in effect for more

EXHIBIT 2–1
Techniques to Diagnose External Conditions for Key Human Resource Programs

Device	External Conditions Analyzed	Human Resource Programs
External environmental scanning	Economic conditions Governmental regulations Societal values Union expectations and power	Human resource planning
Salary and benefit surveys	Economic conditions: Wages and benefits paid by competitors in labor and product markets	Compensation and benefits
Recruiting and availability analysis	Economic conditions: Availability of required skills and experience Availability of protected groups (women and minorities)	Recruiting Affirmative action planning
Labor settlement surveys	Union expectation and power: Recent contract settlement provisions	Labor relations

EXHIBIT 2–2
The External Environmental Scanning Process

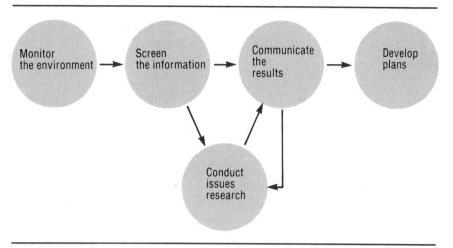

Source: G. Milkovich, L. Dyer, T. Mahoney, "HRM Planning," in *Human Resources Management in the 1980's,* ed. Stephen J. Carroll and Randall S. Schuler (Washington, D.C.: Bureau of National Affairs, 1983), pp. 2–18. Copyright © 1983 by The Bureau of National Affairs, Inc. Reprinted by permission.

than a decade. Monitoring is done by 100 life insurance executives who voluntarily read publications in four general areas: economic and business conditions, governmental/political trends, social developments, and technological and scientific trends. The readers identify relevant articles, abstract them, and forward them, along with comments, to two screening committees. The first committee reviews submissions and identifies trends and patterns. The second committee reviews and expands on the work of the first and directs the preparation of trend reports.

Preparation of trend reports often involves research to supplement the available material. Completed trend reports are made available to member companies who assume responsibility for communicating and integrating the material into planning processes. Trend reports have usually been on subjects of broad interest to organization planners, but a few have focused exclusively on human resource issues.

Monitoring the Environment

Similar to an early warning system, monitoring involves gathering intelligence about the organization's environment with emphasis on patterns and discontinuities.[9] Honeywell, Inc., a typical example, concentrates on several major topic areas, such as work force demographics, economic conditions, technological developments, work force social trends, legal and

EXHIBIT 2–3
Environmental Scanning: Trends and Implications

Trends	*Implications*
Work Force Demographics	
1. Rising female and declining male work force participation.	• Long-term shift on work roles and responsibilities between sexes.
	• Women take on attributes of men in the workplace (e.g., lifetime job patterns).
	• Men will take more risks with their careers.
	• Women become more loyal and willing to sacrifice other activities for work.
	• Change in corporate culture due to women management styles.
	• Greater pressure on organization for family concerns for working parents.
2. Immigration accounts for an increasingly high percentage of net population growth.	• Increase in cultural diversity to the general population.
	• Increase in entrepreneurial behavior and values.
	• Increase in problems with education, unemployment, crime, welfare, and housing by cultural grouping.
	• Ability of organizations to use the cultural knowledge of immigrants to their advantage.
3. United States trains the world's engineers; U.S. science and engineering students increasingly taught by foreign-born faculty.	• Increase in hiring of foreign born to find engineers with advanced degrees.
	• Engineers will be more compatible with corporation's international business.
	• Differences in culture and language could cause problems but may contribute to a broadening of a company's culture.
	• Education and supply of engineers will become a factor in agreements with foreign companies.
	• Foreign faculty may reshape U.S. engineering education and R&D.
Economic Conditions	
1. Unemployment rate continues at around 7 percent, greater job flexibility develops to stabilize the work force.	• Employees will be able to reduce work force costs by a variety of management innovations (e.g., two-tiered wage scales, contract employment).
	• Shortage of workers will be regional in nature.
	• Shortage of workers will be skill specific.
	• Labor negotiations will be cooperative where there is a job loss, intransigent where skills are critical.
	• Job flexibility appears a more appropriate goal than job security.

EXHIBIT 2–3 *(concluded)*

Trends	Implications
2. An increasingly volatile climate of corporate restructuring.	• Restructuring may represent the breaking of a compact and leave a legacy of distrust and poor morale by long-term employees. • Younger employees may see restructuring as an opportunity. • Requires integration of differing corporate cultures. • Ability to retain an effective work force. • Employees, unions, and governments will seek a larger role in the restructuring of jobs or relocation of work sites.
3. The pattern of occupations and the structure of the work force continue to change.	• Filling jobs at the entry level from a scarce supply. • Ability to compete effectively for employees with critical skills. • Need to find new ways of promoting and rewarding the coming glut of experienced prime-age workers. • Need to determine the range of skills required for evaluating, hiring, and training the information worker. • Information workers will use expanded access to computers and other sources in order to find a satisfactory match between skills, employer, and location.

Source: Abstracted from *The Future of Work and Workers in the American Corporation*, a report prepared by Joseph F. Caotes, Inc., New York, for the Environmental Scanning Association, a compendium of 18 Fortune 500 firms. Uncopyrighted.

regulatory matters, and regional/metropolitan characteristics.[10] Exhibit 2–3 shows part of a report on trends of significance for human resource management. The items included have not been analyzed for importance or relevance to any particular employer. Nor are they discussed in depth. It's almost like a headline news service. Someone else must screen the information and conduct additional research on items of particular interest.

Screening the Information

Monitoring tends to turn up more information than is useful. Further, the information tends to come in bits and pieces, whereas planners and decision makers need to be aware of patterns, that is, trends and discontinuities in the environment. Screening separates the wheat from the chaff and begins to organize the information around issues. Screening is sometimes done by one or a few members of a scanning staff group, or it can be done by a committee.

Issues Research

Issues research further investigates topics identified during the monitoring process. Its purpose is to assess probable implications for human resource management in the context of known business plans. For example, legislation on illegal immigration may be a topic of great interest for Sunkist, but less so for Weyerhaeuser. Sunkist may anticipate greater impact of any changes in such legislation than Weyerhaeuser, and so would research the topic in greater depth.

Communication

Even the most sophisticated monitoring and analysis are of no avail unless the results are transmitted to managers on a timely basis and in an understandable and usable form.

The variety of communications approaches ranges from annual written reports to abstracts and seminars. The effectiveness of these various approaches can only be guessed. A common complaint about written reports is that they are less specific than required in drawing out the human resource implications of enviornmental conditions.

Develop Plans

Many employers do not simply react to environmental trends; they attempt to influence them. A particularly good example is legislative trends. Exhibit 2–4 shows some of the regulatory issues Motorola, Inc. judged to be critical for 1988–90. Motorola evaluates each trend on three factors: (1) its impact on Motorola, (2) the probability of regulatory action occur-

EXHIBIT 2–4
Motorola, Inc.: Anticipated Employment Regulatory Issues for 1988–1990

	Impact on Motorola	Probability of Action	Position
1. Drug testing—protection from Title VII litigation.	Highest	Medium	Lead
2. Comparable worth.	Highest	Medium	Resist
3. Training—focus on retraining incentive for current workers.	High	Medium	Lead
4. Occupational disease notification and prevention.	High	High	Resist/ modify

ring, and (3) the recommended position Motorola management should take on the issue. On two issues Motorola has decided to take the lead in trying to influence. For two other issues, it will resist or try to modify.

Although a variety of procedures can diagnose external conditions, EES monitors the overall trends across the entire external environment. Next, we discuss recent trends in the external conditions identified in the diagnostic model: economic conditions, government regulations, and union influences.

ECONOMIC CONDITIONS

Many economic factors have an impact on human resource objectives and decisions; three basic ones are (1) the makeup of the population and the labor force, (2) labor market conditions, and (3) product/service market conditions.

Population and the Labor Force

According to the United States Census Bureau, the population of our country in 1986 was approximately 243 million: 120 million males and 123 million females.[11]

There is a difference between the population and the labor force. Only part of the population is eligible to work. People over 16 years who are not institutionalized in prisons or hospitals are counted as eligible to work. Those eligible can be further subdivided into (1) the labor reserve, or those not working for economic gain even though they are eligible to work (some homemakers, college students, and retirees); and (2) those in the total labor force (Exhibit 2–5). The total labor force is made up of members of the armed forces and the civilian labor force (CLF); the CLF, in turn, is composed of the unemployed and the employed.

Simply stated:

Population = All the people; Those eligible to work + Those ineligible to work because of age or institutionalization.

Eligible to work = Labor reserve + Total labor force.

Total labor force = Armed forces + Civilian labor force.

Civilian labor force = Unemployed + Employed.

The proportion of people eligible to work who do work is the labor force participation rate (LFPR).

$$\text{LFPR} = \frac{\text{Total labor force}}{\text{Labor reserve} + \text{Total labor force}}$$

EXHIBIT 2–5
United States Labor Force Defined 1986 (in thousands)

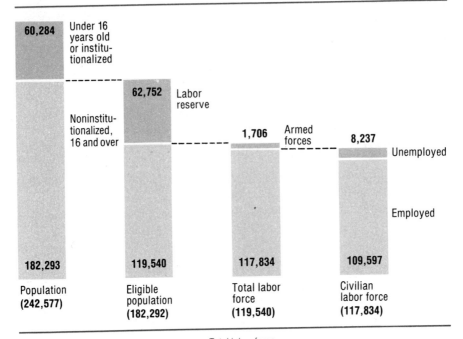

Note: Labor force participation rate $= \dfrac{\text{Total labor force}}{\text{Eligible population}}$

$= \dfrac{119,540}{182,292} \times 100 = 66\%$

Sources: "Estimates of the Population of the United States," U.S. Department of Commerce, Bureau of the Census, Current Population Reports: Population Estimates and Projections Series P–25 # 1002; *Statistical Abstract of the United States*, U.S. Department of Commerce, Bureau of the Census, March 1987.

The Changing Face of the Civilian Labor Force

When you read the word *employee*, do you picture a white male? The labor force is changing. Women, Hispanics, and Asian immigrants are joining the labor force in increasing numbers; white males are no longer the overwhelming majority they used to be.[12] Additionally, the labor force is graying, as the age profile of the nation changes.[13]

Trend 1—Shortage of Young Workers. Owing to past fluctuations in the birthrate, there are many more people at some ages than others. Exhibit 2–6 compares the population-age profile in 1970 with projections for 1990. Because of low birthrates in the 1960s and 70s, the absolute number

EXHIBIT 2–6
Profile of the Population by Age Groups
(figures rounded off, in millions)

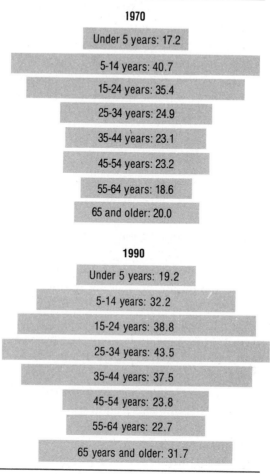

1970

Under 5 years: 17.2

5-14 years: 40.7

15-24 years: 35.4

25-34 years: 24.9

35-44 years: 23.1

45-54 years: 23.2

55-64 years: 18.6

65 and older: 20.0

1990

Under 5 years: 19.2

5-14 years: 32.2

15-24 years: 38.8

25-34 years: 43.5

35-44 years: 37.5

45-54 years: 23.8

55-64 years: 22.7

65 years and older: 31.7

Source: U.S. Bureau of Census Report, *Projections of the Population of the United States by Age, Sex, and Race,* 1987.

of younger people has fallen.[14] From 1970 to 1980 the number of people in the 5–14 age group fell from 41 to 35 million; it is projected to decline to around 32 million by 1990. Yet the total population increased at the same time.

Trend 2—Middle Age Bulge. The population's changing age profile resembles a pig in a python. A baby boom in the 40s and 50s resulted in an age bulge which is slowly moving through the population. Nearly one third of the U.S. population is crammed into a 20-year period.[15] In Exhibit 2–6 note the increase in the 25–34 age bracket: 25 million people in 1970, 37.1 million in 1980, and 43 million by 1990.

Trend 3—Increased Employment of Older Workers. Because of that age bulge resulting from the baby boom, the American CLF is aging and will continue to do so into the 1990s.

Trend 4—The Increasing Role of Women. The upward trend in the labor force participation of women, as shown in Exhibit 2–7, is expected to continue.[16] In 1975, 46 percent of all U.S. women were in the labor force, 54 percent were by 1985, and by 1995, 60 percent will be. This compares to 78 percent in 1975, 76 percent in 1985, and 67 percent by 1995 for men.

As Exhibit 2–7 shows, the participation rates of women are becoming more like men's at all age groups. A growing proportion of women are returning to work soon after having children. In 1975, 31 percent of all new mothers returned to work within one year of giving birth; by 1990 the proportion is likely to be over 50 percent. These changes are attributed to three factors: an increase in mothers who are the sole support of their families, more women are postponing having children until later in life, and the increased investment of women in their careers.[17] Further, over 65 percent of U.S. families have two or more wage earners. In sum, women are starting to work outside the home earlier in life, and returning to work sooner after children arrive. Their attachment to the work force is becoming more permanent.

Trend 5—Significant Influx of Immigrants and Illegal Aliens. America's biggest import is human resources. About 450,000 arrive legally each year and perhaps another 1,500,000 illegally. Immigration now appears to be as important as birthrates in shaping the U.S. population; it represents a major factor in the labor supply.[18] Between 1980 and 1985, the immigrants admitted to the United States surpassed the totals of any similar period since 1925.

Trend 6—Quality of the Work Force. Americans of both sexes and all ages enjoy high and growing levels of educational attainment. At the same time, a nationwide survey by the U.S. Department of Education reported that 17 million to 21 million adults are illiterate.[19] Many of these illiterates are refugees and immigrants unable to understand or speak English who need jobs. Nearly 13 percent of a sample (3,400 people, age 20 and over) failed the literacy test shown in Exhibit 2–8. Functional illiteracy—defined as the inability to use reading skills to cope with everyday life—is apparently an increasing problem. One study found that 14 percent of adults could not fill out a bank check and 38 percent could not match

EXHIBIT 2–7
Labor Force Participation Rates
of Men and Women
Aged 16 and over, 1975–1995

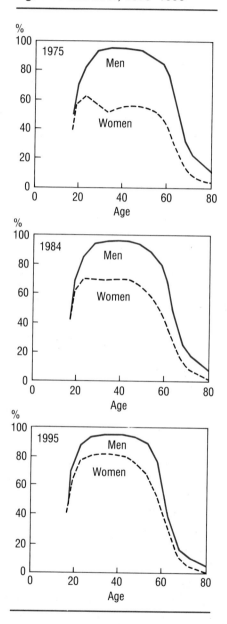

EXHIBIT 2–8
A Literacy Test

Here are questions from the U.S. Department of Education test on literacy. Choose a synonym for the italicized word or phrase.

1. Persons may receive benefits if they are *eligible.*
   a. qualified
   b. complete
   c. single
   d. logical
2. We cannot see you today. *When can you return?*
   a. When was the last time you came?
   b. Who should you call when you come?
   c. On what date can you come again?
   d. Are those the papers you can return?
3. *Enter* your Social Security number here.
   a. Find
   b. Check
   c. Show
   d. Write
4. You may request a review of the decision made on the application or recertification for assistance and *may request a fair hearing concerning any action affecting receipt or termination of assistance.*
   a. will get the service
   b. must help the worker
   c. must sign the application form
   d. have a right to an appeal

personal qualifications with job requirements in help wanted ads.[20] According to this study "approximately one fifth of U.S. adults are functionally incompetent." Blue Cross of Massachusetts discovered that of its clerical workers tested for promotion, 50 percent read below a median 12th grade level. And at the Hydra-matic Division of General Motors Corporation, some 22 percent of employees said they needed training in "understanding simple words, signs, and labels" and 31 percent needed help in "understanding basic written directions, charts, and instructions."[21]

Implications for Human Resource Management

Age profile qualifications ultimately influence human resource management since these trends form the basis for any employer's external supply of human resources. Thus, the CLF and its trends directly affect managers' human resource decisions.

Future chapters discuss the implications of these and other trends for specific human resource decisions. Here we illustrate just a few: Shortages of younger workers are already being experienced by some employers.

Fast-food chains, retailers, and hotels are struggling to fill entry level jobs.[22] Typically low paying, these require little experience. Some firms are responding to the shortage by offering higher wages, improved benefits, better training, and career opportunities. Others have turned to retired workers who are interested in part-time jobs to supplement retirement incomes.[23]

The increased role of women in the labor force is affecting every human resource decision. It has increased interest in equal opportunity, pay discrimination, day-care benefits, and flexible work schedules.[24] Pressures springing from unchecked immigration resulted in the Immigration Reform and Control Act of 1986, which requires employers to verify workers' citizenship status and levies financial penalties for violations.

Industry is just beginning to feel the effects of the aging of the labor force. Increased costs will be the main effect on human resource decisions. For example, men aged 50 to 64 submit an average of $1,897 a year in medical expense claims that are reimbursed by their employers' health insurance plans. This is more than triple the claim rate of men aged 20 to 35. Women 50 to 64 submit $1,867 a year, 51 percent more than their younger counterparts.[25] The implications go beyond costs: aging work forces require additional training as the nature of the work changes in response to competition and new technology. They require flexible training programs to prevent obsolescence, phased retirements, and job redesign to accommodate changing physical needs and simultaneously capitalize on workers' experience. (As textbook authors age, many argue—perhaps wistfully—that older workers' experience and productivity more than offset these adjustments.)

Finally, some managers see the illiteracy trend as a societal problem—certainly not one that directly affects their human resource decisions. But managers at Onan Corporation, an electrical generator manufacturer, ran into it head on when they built a new $50 million plant. Newly hired employees could not handle the new technology; the reading and computational requirements were beyond them. Perhaps this problem simply reflects poorly on Onan's selection decisions and says nothing of illiteracy. Nevertheless, Onan instituted a training program with basic reading, math, and computer numeric control classes to overcome the problems.

Labor Market Conditions

Labor market pressures is a second economic condition in the diagnostic model. Exchanges between employers and potential employees occur in the labor market. Information is exchanged about opportunities, skills, and requirements. When parties reach an agreement acceptable to all participants, a formal or implied contract is executed, and employees are allocated to job opportunities at various rates of pay.[26]

An employer must be aware of conditions in the labor market. But it is not necessary or feasible to know about every single exchange. So we use the concept of relevant labor market. These three factors usually define the relevant labor market:

Occupation (qualifications and skills required).

Geography (distances employees are willing to relocate or commute).

Other employers that compete with similar products and services.

These three factors define the part of the labor market that is of interest to a particular employer. So the exchanges of greatest interest to employer A involve nearby employers seeking to hire people with qualifications similar to those employer A seeks. Human resource professionals conceive of labor markets in terms of all three factors. The skills and qualifications required in an occupation are important because they regulate the mobility of people among occupations. This includes licensing and certification requirements as well as training and education. Accountants, for example, cannot do the work of dentists.

Qualifications interact with geography to further narrow the scope of the relevant labor markets (see Exhibit 2–9). Those skills possessed by degreed professionals (accountants, engineers, physicians) are recruited nationally; others (technicians, craft workers, and operatives) are recruited regionally, and still others (office workers) locally. As the importance and complexity of the qualifications increase, the geographic limits also increase.

However, the geographic scope of a market is not fixed. It changes in response to workers' willingness to relocate or commute certain distances.[27] This propensity to move may, in turn, be affected by personal and economic circumstances as well as the pay level offered by an employer. Configurations of local markets can even be shaped by the availability of convenient public transportation. Additionally, the geographic limits may not be the same for all in a broad skill group. All MBAs (not a homogeneous group) do not operate in a national market; some firms recruit them regionally, others nationally.

In addition to the occupation and its geography, the industry in which the organization competes for labor and sells its products/services is also important.[28] Industry affects the employer's ability to pay and the particular skills required.

Although labor market conditions do affect human resource decisions, the exact nature of their effect cannot be specified without further information on the organization, its employees, its strategies, and its objectives.

EXHIBIT 2–9   Relevant Labor Markets, by Geographic and Employee Groups

Geographic Scope	Employee Groups/Occupations					
	Production	Office and Clerical	Technicians	Scientists and Engineers	Managerial Professional	Executive
Local: Within relatively small areas such as cities or MSAs (Metropolitan Statistical areas; e.g., the Dallas metropolitan area)	Most likely	Most likely				
Regional: Within a particular area of the state or county or several states (e.g., Greater Boston area)	Only if in short supply or critical	Only if in short supply or critical	Most likely	Likely	Likely	
National: Across the country				Most likely	Most Likely	Most likely
International: Across several countries				Only for critical skills or those in very short supply	Only for critical skills or those in very short supply	Sometimes

RELEVANT MARKET

Source: George T. Milkovich and Jerry Newman, *Compensation* (Plano, Tex.: Business Publications, 1987).

Product/Service Market Conditions

Changes in the product/service markets in which an organization operates is an additional aspect of economic conditions to consider.

Increased Worldwide Competition

International competition in domestic and foreign markets is, perhaps, the key market condition affecting human resource management.[29] Private sector employers are being forced to take action to improve their profitability. This often entails the introduction of automated equipment and financial restructuring, as well as human resource decisions (e.g., reductions in force, retraining, or wage reductions).

Conditions in a firm's markets directly affect not only its ability to pay but also the quantity and quality of people employed.[30] Any organization must, over time, receive enough revenues to cover expenses, including those for human resource programs. Thus, an employer's ability to pay employees is constrained by its ability to compete in the product market and generate sales revenues.

In effect, the product market puts a lid on the maximum pay level that an employer can set.[31] If the employer pays at a level that jeopardizes its profitability, then it has two options. It can try to pass on the higher pay level through price increases, or it can hold prices fixed and allocate a greater share of total revenues to cover labor costs.

Consider the U.S. auto makers' recent experiences.[32] For many years auto makers passed on increased pay levels to consumers in the form of increased car prices. Even though competition among the Big Three existed, all three passed on the pay increases. But then the product market changed: The level of competition from Japan and Korea reduced U.S. auto makers' ability to pass on pay increases. In response, some auto workers were forced to take pay cuts, accept smaller wage increases, and agree to work rule changes intended to improve productivity. Many other auto workers had no such choices—they lost their jobs.

So an employer's ability to finance higher pay levels through price increases depends on the product market conditions. Employers in highly competitive markets are less able to raise prices without loss of revenues.

International product competition has additional implications for human resource management. To compete on a global scale, many companies have established manufacturing and distribution facilities in other countries. At these facilities they must manage human resources in a style consistent with the cultural, social, and legal conditions of the host countries.[33]

Demand for a firm's products (along with productivity, plant capacity, inventory levels) directly affects managers' staffing decisions. This occurs for managers in public as well as in profit-making organizations. Consider a city government, a symphony, or even a college. Changes in demand for services (e.g., increased enrollments) eventually affect the people employed (professors, teaching assistants). Consequently, managers making personnel employment forecasts use product demand and productivity data to decide how many employees possessing which skills and experience are required.

Inflationary Pressures

Inflation is the rate of change in the prices we pay for goods and services. Its most direct effect on human resource decisions is on cost-of-living adjustments (COLAs) to wages and pension plans.[34]

Although inflation has been at reasonably low levels for the last few years, it still has a cumulative effect, perhaps more serious than we realize. Between 1980 and 1985 the cumulative inflation rate was 30 percent. This means that if you made $30,000 in 1985, your real income in 1980 dollars would only be $23,059. Inflation also influences human resources in indirect and less obvious ways. Inflation indirectly affects the real costs of interviewing, recruiting, and training employees. Hence, increased funding for training and recruiting may be necessary simply to keep up with inflation and may not represent any increase in real terms. One estimate of the employer's total investment per professional employee (degreed managerial/technical) after two years is over $100,000, and may be $1 million over a 20-year career.[35] Obviously, estimating the total expenditures over a 20-year career depends on assumptions regarding inflation.

Technological Changes

Technological change is one of the most powerful forces influencing the way companies manage employees. It has altered jobs, created new skills while making others obsolete, altered the relationship between unions and management, and changed the need for employees to learn and be trained.

> We are approaching a historic moment in American economic development. Sooner or later, perhaps well before the record books close on the 1980s, the number of professional, managerial, and technical workers will exceed the number of blue-collar workers. When that moment comes, it will mark the end of an era that began in the early days of the 20th century, when manual workers succeeded farm workers as the most numerous group among the employed.
>   The census data for 1910 were the first to record that historic milestone—the number of blue-collar workers is given there as 14.2 million, the number of farm workers, 11.5 million.

Now, three quarters of a century later, the blue-collar pre-eminence is giving way to the quintessential workers of the new economy—the professional, managerial, and technical workers, who are projected to have the most rapid expansion among occupational groups up to the mid-90s. In the 1980s, so far, their count has increased by more than 5.5 million, or 24 percent, the largest rise among the broad occupation groupings. Only sales occupations come close.[36]

Exhibit 2–10 shows in greater detail how technology has changed America's work force. In 1940 for example, 9.5 million, or 23 percent, of the labor force worked in agriculture. In 1980 this figure had dropped to 4 percent—about 3 million people. The job loss in agriculture was compensated for by an increase in service occupations. Three and a half million people, 9 percent of the labor force, were in service industries in 1940; by 1980 almost 18 million people, 19 percent of the labor force, were in this classification.[37] Changes in technology influence the nature of the work performed and, consequently, the qualifications and skills required to perform it. One effect of technological change on the skills required has been described as "the skills twist":[38] The demand for highly trained technical skills and relatively lower level operator skills both increase, while the need for intermediate skills decreases.

Speculation about the effects of robots has led some soothsayers to claim that robots will make workers obsolete.[39] The Robot Institute of America, an industry trade association, predicts that there will be 75,000 to 100,000 robots in U.S. factories by 1990.[40] But a survey of users and manufacturers of robots concludes that robots are likely to replace 440,000 workers by 1990, of which all but 5 percent would be retained rather than dismissed.[41]

EXHIBIT 2–10
The Changing Nature of Work

Sector	1940	1980	1990
Agriculture	23%	4%	2%
Nonagriculture	79	96	98
Construction	3	5	6
Finance	4	6	7
Government	10	17	15
Manufacturing	26	22	20
Mining	2	1	1
Services	9	19	26
Transportation/ public utilities	7	6	4
Wholesale/retail trade	16	22	19

Source: U.S. Department of Labor Bureau of Labor Statistics, *Handbook of Labor Statistics,* June 1985.

The president of the International Association of Machinists union agrees.[42] He argues that the replacement of human skills with computerized machinery will occur slowly; shortages of skilled workers will remain the most pressing human resource problem. Affected unions will likely seek job security and retraining guarantees in their labor contracts. Some unions seek to be involved in investment decisions that could cause the displacement of workers.[43]

So, assessing relevant economic conditions is important for effective human resource management. The expertise required to do this involves determining which particular conditions are relevant, and then forecasting their effects.

GOVERNMENT INFLUENCES: LAWS, REGULATIONS, AND POLICIES

Governments are major players in the management of human resources because their laws and regulations have a direct effect. Examples are readily apparent: the Fair Labor Standards Act specifies a minimum wage for the nation, although states may require higher minimums than the national standard. The Wagner Act established the National Labor Relations Board, which oversees collective bargaining. The Civil Rights Act established the Equal Employment Opportunity Commission to deal with allegations of discrimination. Later chapters discuss these specific laws and their effects. The influence of Equal Employment Opportunity law on human resource management is so pervasive that the next chapter is devoted entirely to the topic.

Assessing trends in government is not a simple task. Federal, state, and local jurisdictions are all involved and often move in somewhat different directions. The current development of comparable worth bills is a case in point. These bills generally require that jobs within an organization that are *comparable* in their value should be paid the same, whether or not their job content is equal. The issue most frequently arises in setting pay for clerical workers in relationship to pay for blue-collar jobs.[44] Lawmakers in Minnesota, New York, and Washington have passed different forms of comparable worth legislation. While some states are considering legislation, others have rejected it, and the federal government seems to be avoiding it.[45] The comparable worth laws in the three states pertain only to public sector employers. In California, however, where a proposal included private sector employers, the bill was defeated, in part by active lobbying by private sector employers. Major employers with nationwide facilities usually scan these developments through various professional associations as well as their internal staffs.

Naturally, governments are more than sources of laws and regulations; their policies affect both the supply and demand for human resources. Governments affect the demand for human resources in several ways: as major employers, as consumers of goods and services, and through their fiscal and monetary policies. Similarly, they affect the supply of labor. As employers, they compete for labor; as regulators, they set licensing standards (e.g., lawyers, teachers, physicians, and hairstylists). Through appropriating funds for education and training programs and by controlling curriculum standards, they also affect the skills possessed by potential employees. The problems with employees' illiteracy referred to earlier may be traced to past educational policies. And government support for job training programs affects employers' training decisions. For example, the Bank of America used California state funding to retrain and place employees it otherwise may have laid off.

The Regulatory Process: Human Resource Constraints

Human resource programs must comply with laws and regulations. By understanding the regulatory process, managers can better comply with the intent of legislation.[46] Problems in society often instigate a pressure for legislative action. When enough support develops—often as a result of compromises and trade-offs—laws are passed. Once passed, agencies must enforce the laws through rulings, regulations, inspections, and investigations. Management responds to enforcement by auditing and/or altering personnel practices, defending lawsuits, and lobbying for policy change.

The manner in which managers perceive regulations differs. Some view the regulatory process as a constraint—bureaucratic burdens that create inflexibility and limit freedom to make decisions. Others see the regulatory process as an opportunity for initiatives to influence the policy itself.

The Regulatory Process: Human Resource Initiatives

Human resource managers may play an active role in influencing the regulatory process to balance social needs with needs to produce workable legislation and maintain management flexibility. Many employers lobby through their governmental relations units or through a consortium of employers such as Business Roundtable or American Society of Personnel Administrators.

Employers also influence interpretation of legislation by defending their practices in the courts. Because this is a costly procedure, it is not one that many employers seek.

UNIONS' POWER AND STRATEGIES

Employees form unions because they feel it is in their best interest to deal as a group with management.[47] Collectively, employees have more power to protect their interests. For managers, the presence of a union means many human resource decisions must be negotiated with a third party. These decisions are frequently negotiated within organizations even when unions are not present. Conflicting views and priorities are not limited to union relations; however, union power and interests clearly constrain managers' freedom to make human resource decisions.

Historically, American unions' interests have focused on particular issues in the employment relationship: wages and benefits, work hours and schedules, job security, and work rules. In contrast, European unions arose as part of a class struggle. From the beginning, European unions formed political parties and were more directly involved in national politics.[48] Chapters Sixteen and Seventeen say more about collective bargaining. At this point, we consider unions in broad terms, as one of many external factors influencing human resource objectives and the decisions managers make.

In 1987 unions represented just under 18 percent of the U.S. nonfarm labor force, down from its peak strength of about 35 percent in the 1940s. Declines have continued into the 1980s.[49] As Exhibit 2–11 shows, between 1980 and 1984 slippages in the ranks have been the greatest among manufacturing occupations (a decline from 30 percent to 24 percent) and the least among government workers (35.9 percent to 35.7 percent).

Shifting Union Strategies

In the 1980s a host of factors have pressured American unions and management. Worldwide competition, relatively higher labor costs, and problems with productivity and product quality all combined to change the face of union-management relations.[50] Severe business conditions, coupled with declining membership, forced many unions to adopt new strategies. Exhibit 2–12 shows some of these. Shifting from the usual adversarial relationship with management, some unions are emphasizing mutual interests and participation in quality of work life and productivity improvement programs.[51] Other aspects of the new strategies include recognizing that the success of any organization is a shared concern, reaching out for nonunion workers through new associate memberships, and stressing innovative approaches to organizing new members.[52] One example of new organizing approaches is the increased emphasis on family and women's issues at the bargaining table. More and more unions are bargaining for,

EXHIBIT 2–11
Slippage in the Ranks of Union Membership (in thousands)

	1980			1984		
	Total Number of Workers	Members of Unions*	Percent of Employed in Unions	Total Number of Workers	Members of Unions*	Percent of Employed in Unions
All private and public wage and salary workers	87,480	20,095	23.0%	92,194	17,340	18.8%
All private workers	71,424	14,332	20.1	76,361	11,684	15.3
Manufacturing†	27,590	8,428	30.5	27,081	6,508	24.0
Service workers	43,834	5,904	13.5	49,281	5,176	10.5
Government workers	16,056	5,764	35.9	15,833	5,656	35.7

*Includes members of a labor union or employee association similar to union.

†Includes agricultural workers.

Source: Bureau of Labor Statistics.

EXHIBIT 2–12
Shifting Union Strategies

From	→	To
Emphasis on adversarial relations and differences with managers.		Emphasis on mutual interest and areas for cooperation.
Managers are responsible for business success.		Labor shares responsibilities for business success.
Political insiders become union officials.		Emphasis on participation in union affairs by members.
Traditional organizing tactics.		Reaching out to nonunion employees; emphasizing common interests; using innovative approaches to target and organize employees.

lobbying, and going to court to press for child care, maternity and parental leave, pay equity, and flexible work schedules. By emphasizing family and women's issues, unions are simply recognizing the increased participation rates of women and the other work force trends discussed earlier.

Union Concessions

Economic conditions and declining membership pressures have also forced some unions to agree to concessions.[53] Exhibit 2–13 summarizes some of these concessions. Cutting crew sizes, redefining jobs, adjusting seniority and hours of work, and agreeing to smaller wage increases were all intended to help save members' jobs mainly by reducing unit labor costs.

Public sector unions such as the National Education Association (NEA) and the American Federation of State, County, and Municipal Employees (AFSCME) have not faced as serious economic and membership pressures. Thus, they have not been forced into similar concessions.[54]

EXTERNAL EFFECTS ON HUMAN RESOURCE MANAGEMENT

In this chapter we have seen that external pressures on the management of human resources may spring from several factors. These include (1) economic conditions (e.g., trends in the makeup of the labor force or shifts in the degree of competitiveness in product markets), (2) government policies and regulations (e.g., public funding for workers' retraining,

EXHIBIT 2–13

Unions Are Granting These Major Changes in Work Rules. . . .

		. . .in These Industries
Job assignments	Cutting size of crews; enlarging jobs by adding duties; eliminating unneeded jobs	Steel, autos, railroads, meatpacking, airlines
Skilled maintenance and construction	Combining craft jobs such as millwright, welder, rigger, and boilermaker; allowing journeymen to perform helpers' duties; permitting equipment operators to run more than one machine	Autos, rubber, steel, petroleum, construction
Hours of work	Giving up relief and wash-up periods; allowing management more flexibility in scheduling daily and weekly hours; working more hours for the same pay	Autos, rubber, steel, meatpacking, trucking, airlines (pilots), textile
Seniority	Restricting use of seniority in filling job vacancies, 'bumping' during layoffs, and picking shifts	Autos, rubber, meatpacking, steel
Wages	Restricting pay to hours worked rather than miles traveled	Railroads, trucking
Incentive pay	Reducing incentives to reflect changing job conditions	Rubber, steel
Team work	Allowing team members to rotate jobs; permitting pay for knowledge instead of function; allowing management to change crew structure to cope with new technology	Autos, auto suppliers, steel, rubber

Source: *Business Week*, May 16, 1983, p. 100.

enforcement of equal employment laws, passage of immigration laws), and (3) unions' power and strategies. Shifts in societal values and major jolts, such as armed conflicts, also can play a role.

A basic premise of this book is that environmental conditions are directly related to human resource strategies and decisions. Examples have been offered throughout this chapter. The passage of the Civil Rights Act and subsequent court decisions shaped the equity objectives and affirmative action strategies adopted by employers. The advent of computer-assisted manufacturing technology and just-in-time inventory systems caused managers to emphasize teamwork, flexible work forces, and retraining.

Research provides further supporting evidence.[55] From a historical perspective, the waves of immigrant laborers in the early 1900s, the passage of significant labor legislation in the 1930s, labor regulations imposed during World War II, and the civil rights laws of the 60s and 70s were major environmental changes. The research also shows that the importance of personnel activities shifted in response to these changes. Expertise in human resource management becomes critical during periods of serious labor shortages, strong union threats, significant government regulations and/or serious competitive pressures.[56] The importance of specific areas of expertise, such as labor relations or EEO, increases or declines in response to changes in external threats. When faced with these pressures, organizations tend to hire people with expertise in human resource management and allocate resources to them.

BEYOND ORGANIZATION WALLS

Another basic premise of this book is that human resource decisions can also shape factors in the external environment. Lobbying the regulatory process is the obvious example. Other examples are less apparent. Many employers work closely with technical schools and universities to affect the education and training of future employees and customers. Employer initiatives to help improve the literacy rate and math skills are examples.[57] So are major grants of computer hardware and software to engineering and business schools. Even corporate support of community cultural and civil organizations is an initiative to shape the organization's human resource environment.

SUMMARY

External conditions set the stage for the management of human resources. They influence the decisions organizations make; the decisions in turn influence these conditions. Although the nature of the external conditions can be discussed in general terms, it is sometimes difficult to discuss specifics. This is so for several reasons.

First, the external conditions are interrelated, and constantly changing. For example, we have classified relevant conditions as economic, governmental, and union influence in our diagnostic model. Yet economic changes not only affect organizations, they also affect unions, government, and all of society. So as one factor changes, the others inevitably change, too.

Second, organizations differ, and they are constantly changing, too. So, while an aging work force affects all organizations, repercussions are very different. A technologically mature industry may experience a burdensome labor bill and little opportunity for career advancement for younger employees. Such an organization may decide to sweeten retirement packages to create more turnover at the top. A rapid-growth organization may hire those retired workers to cut the lead time required to obtain experienced employees. So the same external condition may have very different implications among organizations.

Human resource managers also take initiatives to affect the external conditions facing them. They may take actions to avoid unions, to modify regulations from government agencies, or to improve the quality of the finance department in the local college.

DISCUSSION AND REVIEW QUESTIONS

1. Why is it important for human resource managers to keep track of external forces?
2. Which devices do organizations use to scan the external environment and to which personnel programs are they related?
3. What is the difference between the population and the civilian labor force?
4. Which major economic forces influence human resource management decisions?
5. Select two of the major trends in the makeup of the labor force; explain how these trends might affect human resource decisions made by managers.

NOTES AND REFERENCES

1. *Essays on American Industrialism: Selected Papers of Samuel Levin*, ed. Mark L. Kahn (Detroit, Mich.: Wayne State University, 1973), pp. 39–40.
2. Ibid., pp. 40–41.
3. Ibid., pp. 33–65.
4. Sanford M. Jacoby, "Industrial Labor Mobility in Historical Perspective," *Industrial Relations*, Spring 1983, pp. 261–82.

5. Ibid., p. 262.
6. Thomas A. Kochan, Harry C. Katz, and Robert B. McKersie, *The Transformation of American Industrial Relations* (New York: Basic Books, 1986); and James N. Baron, Frank R. Dobbin, and P. Devereaux Jennings, "War and Peace: The Evolution of Modern Personnel Administration in U.S. Industry," *American Journal of Sociology*, September 1986, pp. 350–83.
7. *Bulletin to Management*, ASPA/BNA Survey No. 43, "Status of Human Resources Programs. Mid-Year 1983" (Washington, D.C.: Bureau of National Affairs, August 1983); Steven Langer, "Budgets and Staffing: A Survey, Part II," *Personnel Journal*, June 1982, pp. 464–68.
8. George Milkovich, Lee Dyer, and Thomas Mahoney, "HR Planning," chap. 2 in *Human Resources Management in the 1980s*, ed. S. J. Carroll and R. S. Schuler (Washington, D.C.: Bureau of National Affairs, 1983), pp. 2-1, 2–28.
9. Also see R. B. Frantzreb, ed. "Environmental Scanning," *Manpower Planning* 3, no. 11 (1980), the entire issue; J. A. Sheridan, "The Relatedness of Change: A Comprehensive Approach to Human Resource Planning in the Eighties," *Human Resource Planning* 4, no. 2 (1982), pp. 11–17; J. A. Sheridan and J. O. Monaghan, "Environmental Issues Scanning: Starting a Self-Sustaining Research Program," *Human Resource Planning* 5, no. 2 (1982), pp. 57–69; J. K. Brown, *This Business of Issues: Coping with the Company's Environments* (New York: The Conference Board, 1979); David A. Aaker, "Organizing a Strategic Information Scanning System," *California Management Review* 25, no. 2 (1983), pp. 76–83.
10. Frantzreb, "Environmental Scanning," p. 3.
11. *Projections of the Population of the United States: 1983 to 2080, Current Population Reports*, Series P–25, No. 952 (Washington, D.C.: Bureau of the Census, 1984).
12. C. B. Leon, "Occupational Winners and Losers: Who They Were during 1971–80," *Monthly Labor Review*, June 1982, pp. 30–34; Richard Freeman, "The Work Force of the Future: An Overview," in *Work in America: The Decade Ahead*, ed. Clark Kerr and Jerome Rosow (New York: Van Nostrand Reinhold, 1979); Jerome M. Rosow, "Personnel Policies for the 1980s," in *Industrial Relations and Personnel Policies and Prospects for the Future* (Minneapolis: Industrial Relations Center, University of Minnesota, 1979); Kerr and Rosow, *Work in America*; George Strauss, "Key Personnel Issues for the Eighties," in *Personnel Management*, ed. K. Rowland and S. Ferris (Boston: Allyn & Bacon, 1981); Howard N. Fullerton, Jr., "The 1995 Labor Force: BLS' Latest Projections," *Monthly Labor Review*, November 1985, pp. 17–25; Oxford Analytica, *America in Perspective* (Boston: Houghton Mifflin, 1986).
13. Robert L. Clark, "Aging and Labor Force Participation," in *Aging and Technological Advances*, ed. Pauline K. Robinson, Judy Livingston, and James E. Birren (New York: Plenum Press, 1985), pp. 39–54; Herbert S. Parnes, *Policy Issues in Work and Retirement* (Kalamazoo, Mich.: W. E. Upjohn Institute for Employment Research, 1983); John Bussey, "An Older Work Force Burdens Big Producers in the Basic Industries," *The Wall Street Journal*, March 8, 1987, pp. 1, 21.
14. George T. Silvertri, John M. Lukasiewitz, and Marcus E. Einstern, "Oc-

cupational Employment Projections through 1995," *Monthly Labor Review,* November 1983, pp. 37–50.

15. Fullerton, "The 1995 Labor Force"; Judith Dobrzynski, "Spreading the Entrepreneurial Spirit," *Business Week,* September 1, 1986, p. 31.

16. Kingsley Davis, "Wives and Work: Consequences of the Sex Role Evolution," *Population and Development Review,* September 1984, pp. 397–417; Kingsley Davis and Peitronella van den Oever, "Demographic Foundations of New Sex Roles," *Population and Development Review,* September 1982, pp. 495–511; Willard L. Rodgers and Arland Thornton, "Changing Patterns of First Marriage in the United States," *Demography,* May 1985, pp. 265–79; Thomas J. Espenshade, "Marriage Trends in America: Estimates, Implications, and Causes," *Population and Development Review,* June 1985, pp. 193–245.

17. See J. Gregory Robinson, "Labor Force Participation Rates of Cohorts of Women in the United States: 1890–1979," presented at the 1980 Annual Meeting of the Population Association of America; Claudia Goldin, "The Changing Economic Role of Women: A Quantitative Approach," *Journal of Interdisciplinary History,* Spring 1983, pp. 707–33.

18. Vernon M. Briggs, Jr., *Immigration Policy and the American Labor Force* (Baltimore, MD: The Johns Hopkins University Press, 1984), p. 1. Marion F. Houstoun, "Aliens in Irregular Status in the United States: A Review of Their Numbers, Characteristics, and Role in the U.S. Labor Market," *International Migration,* 1983, pp. 372–414.

19. Paula Duggan, *Literacy at Work* (Washington, D.C.: Northeast-Midwest Institute, 1985).

20. Ibid.

21. Sylvia Nasar, "America's Poor: How Big a Problem?" *Fortune,* May 26, 1986, pp. 74–79; Ann P. Bartel and Frank Lichtenberg, "The Comparative Advantage of Educated Workers in Implementing New Technology: Some Empirical Evidence" (Working paper, Columbia University Graduate School of Business, March 1986).

22. William Serrin, "Growth in Jobs since '80 Is Sharp, but Pay and Quality Are Debated," *New York Times,* June 7, 1986, pp. 1, 32; Sylvia Nasar, "Jobs Go Begging at the Bottom," *Fortune,* March 17, 1986, pp. 33–35.

23. JoAnn Lee and Tanya Clemons, "Factors Affecting Employment Decisions about Older Workers," *Journal of Applied Psychology* 70, no. 4 (1985), pp. 785–88.

24. Jeanne M. Brett and James D. Werbel, *The Effect of Job Transfer on Employees and Their Families* (Washington, D.C.: Employee Relocation Council, 1980); Sandra L. Burud, Pamela R. Aschbacher, and Jacquelyn McCroskey, *Employer-Supported Child Care* (Boston: Auburn House Publishing, 1984); S. J. Smith, "New Worklife Estimates Reflect Changing Profile of Labor Force," *Monthly Labor Review,* March 1982, pp. 15–20; A. S. Grossman, "More than Half of All Children Have Working Mothers," *Monthly Labor Review,* February 1982, pp. 41–43.

25. Stephen Greenhouse, "Health Plans Are Feeling a Little Peaked," *New York Times,* August 24, 1986, p. E5; David A. Wise, "Labor Aspects of Pension Plans," *NBER Reporter,* Winter 1984–85, pp. 23–25; and Bussey, "An Older Work Force Burdens Big Producers."

26. For a more extended discussion of labor markets see Arne L. Kalleberg and Aage B. Sorensen, "The Sociology of Labor Markets," *Annual Review of Sociology*, 1979, pp. 351–79; Ronald G. Ehrenberg and Robert S. Smith, *Modern Labor Economics* (Glenview, Ill.: Scott, Foresman, 1982), or Robert J. Flanagan, Robert S. Smith, and Ronald G. Ehrenberg, *Labor Economics and Labor Relations* (Glenview, Ill.: Scott, Foresman, 1984).

27. David Petersen, "Availability in Local Labor Markets" in *Perspectives on Availability*, ed. K. McGuiness (Washington, D.C.: Equal Employer Advisory Council, 1978); see also F. Krzystofiak and J. Newman, "Evaluating Employment Outcomes: Availability Models and Measures," *Industrial Relations* 21, no. 3 (1982), pp. 227–93.

28. John T. Dunlop, "The Task of Contemporary Wage Theory," in *New Concepts in Wage Determination*, ed. George W. Taylor and Frank C. Pierson (New York: McGraw-Hill, 1975); Thomas A. Mahoney, *Compensation and Reward Perspectives* (Homewood, Ill.: Richard D. Irwin, 1979); George T. Milkovich and Jerry M. Newman, *Compensation*, 2nd ed. (Plano, Tex.: Business Publications, 1987).

29. D. Q. Mills, *The New Competitors* (New York: John Wiley & Sons, 1985).

30. See, for example, Milkovich and Newman, *Compensation*, chap. 6; also see James Walker, *Human Resources Planning* (New York: McGraw-Hill, 1980).

31. Walter A. Fogel, "Job Rate Ranges: A Theoretical and Empirical Analysis," *Industrial and Labor Relations Review*, July 1964, pp. 584–97.

32. Harry C. Katz, *Shifting Gears* (Cambridge, Mass.: MIT Press, 1985).

33. "If You Can't Beat 'Em, Buy 'Em: Takeovers Arrive in Japan," *Business Week*, September 29, 1986, pp. 80–83; Edwin Dean, Harry Boissevain, and James Thomas, "Productivity and Labor Cost Trends in Manufacturing, 12 Countries," *Monthly Labor Review*, March 1986, pp. 3–10.

34. Jerry Newman, "The Consumer Price Index: Issues and Understanding" (paper presented at the American Compensation Association National Conference, October 22, 1981); Alan S. Blinder, "The Consumer Price Index and the Measurement of Recent Inflation," in *Brookings Papers on Economic Activity*, 2nd ed., ed. William C. Brainard and George L. Perry (Washington, D.C.: Brookings Institution, 1980); Janet L. Norwood, "Two Consumer Price Indexes," *Monthly Labor Review*, March 1981, pp. 58–61.

35. Henry L. Dahl, "Measuring the Human ROI," *Management Review*, January 1979, pp. 44–50.

36. Samuel M. Ehrenhalt, "Work Force Shifts in 80s," *New York Times*, August 15, 1986, p. 26.

37. Pat Choate, *Retooling the American Work Force* (Washington, D.C.: Northeast-Midwest Institute, 1982); Sar A. Levitan and Clifford M. Johnson, *Second Thoughts on Work* (Kalamazoo, Mich.: W. E. Upjohn Institute for Employment Research, 1982); Peter George, *The Emergence of Industrial America* (Albany: State University of New York Press, 1982).

38. Pat Choate and J. K. Linger, *The High-Flex Society* (New York: Alfred A. Knopf, 1986).

39. Fred K. Foulkes and Jeffrey L. Hirsch, "People Make Robots Work," *Harvard Business Review*, January–February 1984, pp. 94–102; Robert Ayres and Steve Miller, "Industrial Robots on the Line," *Technology Review*, May–June 1982, p. 43; "Changing Technology: Managing an Organization

for Successful Robot Installation" (report by the Human Resource Council of the Construction Group, Westinghouse Electric Corporation, Pittsburgh, 1982), p. 16; Testimony during Joint Economic Hearing on Robotics and Unemployment before the Joint Economic Committee of Congress on March 18, 1983, as reported in *1983 Daily Labor Report*, no. 54, F–1 (Washington, D.C.: Bureau of National Affairs, March 18, 1983).

40. Sar A. Levitan and Clifford M. Johnson. "The Future of Work: Does It Belong to Us or to the Robots?" *Monthly Labor Review*, September 1982, pp. 10–14; H. Allan Hunt and Timothy L. Hunt, *Human Resource Implications of Robotics* (Kalamazoo, Mich.: W. E. Upjohn Institute for Employment Research, 1983); George L. Whaley, "The Impact of Robotics Technology upon Human Resources Management," *Personnel Administrator*, September 1982, pp. 61–71.

41. Foulkes and Hirsch, *"People Make Robots Work,"* p. 94.

42. Levitan and Johnson, *"The Future of Work,"* p. 14.

43. "A Work Revolution in U.S. Industry," *Business Week*, May 16, 1983, pp. 100–110; Daniel B. Cornfield, ed., *Workers, Managers, and Technological Change* (New York: Plenum Press, 1987).

44. Helen Remick, ed., *Comparable Worth and Wage Discrimination* (Philadelphia: Temple University Press, 1984).

45. Alice Cook, "Comparable Worth: Recent Developments in Selected States," *Proceedings of the 1983 Spring Meeting of the Industrial Relations Research Association*, Honolulu, March 1983, pp. 494–504.

46. Ann Bartel and Lacy Glenn Thomas, "Predation through Regulation" (Working paper, Columbia University, February 1986); James Ledvinka, *Federal Regulation of Personnel and Human Resource Management* (Boston: Kent Publishing, 1982).

47. Richard B. Freeman and James L. Medoff, *What Do Unions Do?* (New York: Basic Books, 1984); John A. Fossum, *Labor Relations*, rev. ed. (Plano, Tex.: Business Publications, 1982).

48. Freeman and Medoff, *What Do Unions Do?*

49. Kochan, Katz, and McKersie, *The Transformation of American Industrial Relations*.

50. Audrey Freedman, *The New Look in Wage Policy and Employee Relations* (New York: The Conference Board, 1985).

51. Harry C. Katz, Thomas A. Kochan, and Mark Weber, "Assessing the Effects of Industrial Relations Systems and Efforts to Improve the Quality of Working Life on Organizational Effectiveness," *Academy of Management Journal* 28 (1985), pp. 509–26; T. Kochan, H. Katz, and N. Mower, *Worker Participation and American Unions: Threat or Opportunity?* (Kalamazoo, Mich.: W. E. Upjohn Institute for Employment Research, 1984).

52. Cathy Trost, "Three Labor Activists Lead a Growing Drive to Sign Up Women," *The Wall Street Journal*, January 29, 1985, pp. 1, 16.

53. Peter Cappelli, "Concession Bargaining and the National Economy," *Proceedings of the Thirty-Fifth Annual Meeting of the Industrial Relations Research Association, 1982* (Madison, Wis.: IRRA, 1983), pp. 362–71.

54. "Troubles of U.S. Labor Unions Eased in 1986," *New York Times*, February 15, 1987, p. 16.

55. Alan D. Meyer, "Adapting to Environmental Jolts," *Administrative Science Quarterly* 27 (December 1982), pp. 515–37.
56. Charles O'Reilly and John C. Anderson, "Personnel/Human Resource Management in the U.S.: Some Evidence of Change" (Working paper, University of California, Berkeley, Graduate School of Management, 1982).
57. Irwin Ross, "Corporations Take Aim at Illiteracy," *Fortune*, September 29, 1986, pp. 48–54.

chapter

three

EXTERNAL CONDITIONS: EQUAL EMPLOYMENT OPPORTUNITY

CHAPTER OUTLINE

Shortly after Paul Johnson applied for a promotion to dispatcher in Santa Clara County (California), he was pleased to learn that he had earned the highest score on the selection test. When Diane Joyce, who scored fourth, got the job, Johnson sued the county for reverse discrimination. He claimed he had been discriminated against because of his sex.[1]

The county said that both Johnson and Joyce were qualified, even though her score was lower. She got the job as part of an affirmative action plan designed to achieve a work force that reflected the race and sex composition of the county's population. The county had never been legally required to have an affirmative action plan, nor did it ever acknowledge any past discrimination, even though none of the county's 238 skilled jobs were held by women.

The Justice Department sided with Johnson, alleging that hiring preferences could be used only by employers who admitted past discrimination. To give preference to people who were not personally victims of discrimination violated Title VII of the Civil Rights Act, which outlaws discrimination on the basis of sex and race.

But the Supreme Court rejected this view. Employers who had not necessarily discriminated against women and minorities can still give preference to integrate previously segregated job categories.

Legal rights of various employees can conflict. And many of these conflicts involve EEO. For instance, Memphis's contract with their firefighters' union specified promotions and layoffs based on seniority. In a court-ordered consent decree, the city also agreed to an affirmative action plan for minority employees. When budgetary problems forced layoffs, however, the affirmative action decree and the union contract were in conflict. A district court ordered the city to keep less senior minorities on the staff, so whites with greater seniority were laid off. This action was consistent with the affirmative action decree but not with the union contract. The Supreme Court ruled that in this case, the seniority system could *not* be ignored.[2] Unless minorities could prove they had been actual victims of discrimination, seniority rights prevailed over affirmative action.

These cases reflect how complex managing EEO and affirmative action is today. They are part of a stream of cases beginning in the 1960s in which the courts and the country explored how equal opportunity and affirmative action should be implemented.

Equal opportunity influences every personnel decision from recruiting, hiring, upgrading, layoffs, and retirement to compensation, training, performance evaluation, and labor relations. There is not a single decision in human resource management that is not affected. Because its effects are so pervasive, it merits a separate chapter as an external condition influencing human resource management.

THE NEED FOR EQUAL EMPLOYMENT OPPORTUNITY (EEO)

The Civil Rights Act of 1964 became law almost three decades ago. In the 1960s most employers and unions ignored EEO legislation. No one was quite sure how it would be enforced or how it would affect personnel practices.[3] Equal employment opportunity seemed to direct managers to prepare minorities and women to take advantage of job opportunities and to remove the informal barriers which prevented them from doing so. This approach focused on good faith efforts.

The 1970s saw the emphasis shift to affirmative action policies requiring a proactive approach: seeking out minorities and women to actively and affirmatively share job opportunities. Agencies argued that affirmative efforts were necessary to overcome past discrimination.

Definition

Affirmative action is the activities employers use to ensure that current decisions and practices enhance the employment, upgrading, and retention of minorities and women. Such actions go beyond refraining from practices that discriminate.

Issues in the 1980s

By the late 70s most employers and unions were sensitive to their roles in achieving equal employment opportunity. The change in employers' and unions' approaches to EEO was due to many factors. Employers recognized that huge supplies of skilled, talented people had been systematically excluded from employment opportunities. These underutilized people represented wasted human resources. There was also a growing awareness of how costly discriminatory practices could be—not only in back-pay awards, but also in the loss of government contracts and poor public relations.[4] Nothing rivets corporate attention like a multimillion dollar lawsuit!

The eighties brought an increasing awareness of conflicting claims between those seeking jobs and promotions and those with seniority-based claims. Court orders prescribing promotions and entrance to training programs for minorities frequently conflicted with seniority-based systems.[5] Reductions in work force in reverse order of hire, which favored seniority, were likely to result in layoffs of recently hired minorities, thus negating the effects of affirmative action plans. These conflicts focused attention on three issues (1) reverse discrimination, (2) the use of general goals versus specific quotas, and (3) the difference between an individual who has been directly victimized by discrimination and one who belongs to a group which historically has suffered discrimination. These issues remain to be sorted out by the courts today.[6]

Although EEO and affirmative action (AA) are accepted and progress has been made, signs of inequality persist. The next section examines two of these signs, occupational attainment and the earnings gap.

Occupational Attainment

The distribution of ethnic and sex groups among occupations remains uneven, with women concentrated in clerical jobs and blacks and Hispanics in semiskilled and unskilled occupations.[7] Exhibit 3–1 shows the uneven occupational attainment among ethnic and sex groups. In 1986, 29 percent of working women worked in clerical (administrative support) occupations, and over half of all blacks and Hispanics were in semiskilled and unskilled occupations. Compare these data to the distribution of all employees— fewer than one fifth in clerical, and one third in semiskilled and unskilled occupations. However, there has been a marked change in some occupations. For example, in 1970 5 percent of lawyers were women, compared to 14 percent in 1980 and 18 percent in 1986. Exhibit 3–2 shows some of the change (or lack of it) in occupational attainment for women and minorities over a 10-year period.

Earnings Gap

Not only are the races and sexes unevenly distributed among occupations, but there is also a gap in their earnings.[8] The median weekly earnings of women working full-time in 1986 is approximately 69 percent of men's.[9] This gap exists for black and Hispanic men and women, too. Even in traditionally female occupations, such as clerical, men's earnings have

EXHIBIT 3–1

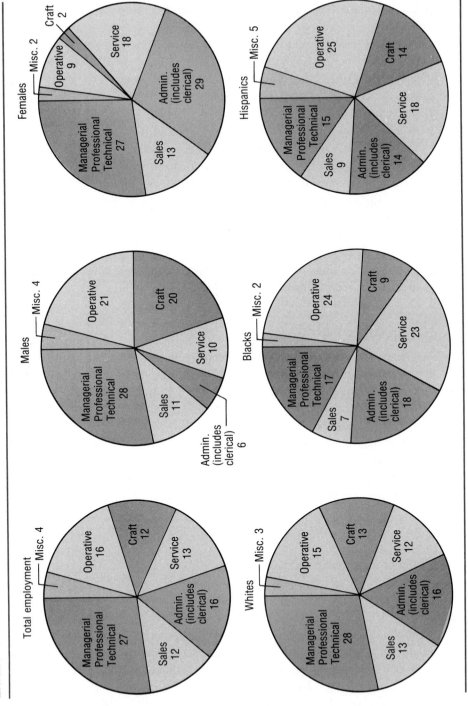

EXHIBIT 3–2

Change over a Decade (women and nonwhites in selected jobs as a percent of all workers in those jobs)

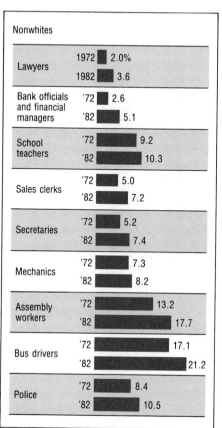

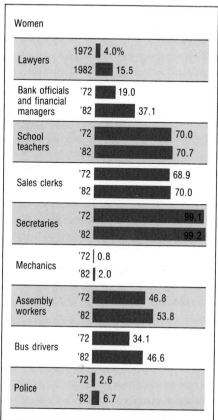

Source: Bureau of Labor Statistics.

been consistently higher than women's. Among blacks, the earnings gap between women and men is narrowing. In 1955 black women earned about 55 percent of what black men made, while in 1980 they earned 74 percent as much as black males. Despite this gain, black women remain at the bottom of the earnings scale. Even though black men have made progress in narrowing the gap between their earnings and those of white males, Exhibit 3–3 shows that the percent of black males who are participating in the labor market has declined substantially.[10] This drop has occurred at all age and educational levels.

We cannot attribute the fact that there is not an equal distribution among occupations and wages solely to discriminatory personnel practices.

EXHIBIT 3–3
The Worsening Economic Plight of
Black Men

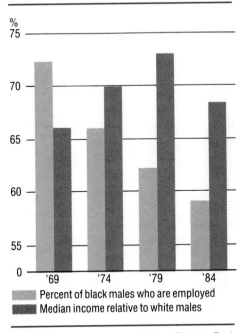

■ Percent of black males who are employed
■ Median income relative to white males

Data: Labor Department, Federal Reserve Bank
of Boston.

Other factors such as educational attainment, personal interests and preferences, and work patterns also play a role. Nevertheless, the existence of differences creates pressures in society for change. One instrument for this change is to ensure that personnel decisions do not discriminate.

A DIAGNOSTIC APPROACH TO EEO

Laws that regulate personnel decisions to ensure equal opportunity stem from society's concerns for fair treatment of its members. Yet organizations and human resource managers are not passive; they often act to shape their environment. Employers may testify before legislative committees or take disputes to the courts to clarify interpretations of laws.

Economic conditions play a key role in the success of any EEO efforts. Improved sales and earnings create job opportunities which are essential to the progress of minorities and women. In addition to hiring new workers, expanding organizations can promote workers more rapidly and create additional vacancies to fill. It is a lot more difficult to change the composition of the internal work force if a company is not hiring new people, or is laying off workers.

In addition to considering the external environment, managers must also examine human resource actions inside their organizations. One personnel executive observed:

> When we began to look into our own practices (in the early 1970s) we were horrified. We found we had just as much of a corporate blind spot with regard to jobs women might qualify for as we ever had with regard to jobs blacks should be hired to do.
>
> It had never occurred to us, for example, that women might be willing and able to do many skilled craft jobs, many sales representatives' jobs, and many of our professional and managerial jobs. Most of our local employment people simply assumed that women should only be considered for light assembly jobs or for office and clerical jobs. Some even maintained separate lists of job openings for men and for women.[11]

THE LAWS: WHAT IS DISCRIMINATION?

On the face of it, equal employment opportunity and discrimination seem so simple and intuitive that their definitions would be obvious to all. Yet considering the enormous volume of regulatory paperwork and the continuing litigation, these concepts are anything but simple in the real world. In fact, the Civil Rights Act provided no definition for discrimination, leaving the task to courts and regulatory agencies.

Exhibit 3–4 gives a brief description of some of the U.S. laws and executive orders that prohibit discrimination. Understanding these laws is a necessary part of managing human resources. They are part of the context in which personnel decisions are made. Thus, we look at several of them in more detail.

Title VII of the Civil Rights Act of 1964

Title VII prohibits discrimination on the basis of sex, race, color, religion, or national origin in any employment condition, including hiring, firing, promotion, transfer, compensation, and admission to training programs.[12] Title VII was amended in 1972 and 1978. The 1972 amendments strengthened enforcement and expanded coverage to include employees of government and educational institutions, as well as private employers of more than 15 persons. The pregnancy amendment of 1978 made it illegal to discriminate because of pregnancy, childbirth, or related conditions.[13]

EXHIBIT 3–4
Employment Discrimination Legislation

Law	Prohibits	Covers
Title VII of the 1964 Civil Rights Act	Discrimination or segregation based on race, color, religion, sex, or national origin	Private employers with 15 or more employees; federal, state, and local governments; unions and apprenticeship committees; employment agencies
Equal Pay Act of 1963	Sex differences in pay for substantially equal work	Private employers (state and local governments uncertain)
Executive Order 11478 (1969)	Discrimination based on race, color, religion, sex, national origin, political affiliation, marital status, or physical handicap	Federal government
Executive Orders 11246 and 11375 (1965)	Discrimination based on race, color, religion, sex, or national origin (affirmative action required)	Federal contractors and subcontractors
Age Discrimination in Employment Act of 1967	Age discrimination against those between the ages of 40 and 70	Private employers with 20 or more employees, unions with 25 or more members, employment agencies, apprenticeship and training programs (state and local governments uncertain)
Rehabilitation Act of 1973; Executive Order No. 11914 (1974)	Discrimination based on physical or mental handicap (affirmative action required)	Federal contractors, federal government
Vietnam-era Veterans Readjustment Act of 1974	Discrimination against disabled veterans and Vietnam-era veterans (affirmative action required)	Federal contractors, federal government
State laws	Similar to Title VII	Vary by state; passed in about 85 percent of states

Defining Discrimination

Since 1964 the courts have ruled that several different behaviors by employers and unions are unlawful under Title VII. These fall into two basic behaviors: disparate treatment, and disparate impact. Exhibit 3–5 contrasts the two behaviors.[14]

Disparate Treatment. Disparate treatment includes practices in which an organization treats protected group members less favorably than others, either openly or covertly. Under this definition, a practice is unlawful if it applies different standards to different employees. For example, rejecting women but not male job applicants even though both have school-age children (different standards). Under the unequal treatment definition, the employer is permitted to impose any requirements if they are imposed on all employees alike.

However, simply prohibiting disparate treatment does not ensure that all groups will be equally affected. Even though many common job requirements are applied to all groups equally, they may have adverse impact on certain groups. For example, some blacks may be less able to meet educational requirements and less likely to attain a passing score on employment tests. The disparate treatment definition of discrimination allows requirements that minorities are less likely to meet than whites—even if those requirements have no relationship to the job in question. Permitting such requirements to exist threatened to leave blacks and other minorities in the same disadvantaged status that prevailed prior to Title VII. Thus, courts and government agencies have adopted a more stringent definition of discrimination—disparate impact.

EXHIBIT 3–5
Discriminatory Behavior

Disparate Treatment	Disparate Impact
Impact on individual claimants, not classwide	Impact is classwide on all similarly situated employees
Intent to discriminate may be inferred	Discriminatory intent need not be present
Group statistics not useful	General statistical impact may show discrimination
Different standards for different individuals or groups	Same standards have differing consequences
Individual actions scrutinized	Business practices, not individual actions examined
Employer can justify actions by absence of discrimatory intent and exercise of reasonable business judgment	Employer can justify impact only through business necessity

Disparate Impact. Personnel practices that have a differential effect on certain groups are illegal under the disparate impact definition, unless the differences can be justified as necessary to the safe and efficient operation of the business, or are work-related. The major case which established this interpretation of Title VII is *Griggs* v. *Duke Power Co.* In this case the Court struck down employment tests and educational requirements that screened out a greater proportion of blacks than whites. The requirements in question were that applicants be high school graduates and score above a certain level on a general intelligence test. The requirements were imposed "on the Company's judgment that they generally would improve the overall quality of the work force." But the court concluded that

> The evidence shows that employees who have not completed high school or taken the tests have continued to perform satisfactorily and make progress in departments for which the high school and test criteria are now used. The promotion record of present employees who would not be able to meet the new criteria thus suggests the possibility that the requirements may not be needed even for the limited purpose of preserving the avowed policy of advancement within the Company.
>
> Good intent or absence of discriminatory intent does not redeem employment procedures or testing mechanisms that operate as "built-in headwinds" for minority groups and are unrelated to measuring job capacity.[15]

The standards were certainly applied equally: both whites and blacks had to pass them. The practices were prohibited because (1) they had the consequence of excluding blacks disproportionately and (2) they were not related to the jobs in question.

Under the disparate impact definition of discrimination, whether or not the employer intended to discriminate is irrelevant.[16] Thus a personnel decision can, on its face, seem neutral. If the results of it are unequal, however, the employer must demonstrate that the decision is either work-related or a business necessity.

The courts have also ruled that *every* personnel action must meet these standards. In *Connecticut* v. *Teal*, the employer had used a multistage promotion process. Applicants provisionally promoted to supervisory positions had to pass written tests and receive satisfactory performance ratings and supervisor recommendations to receive permanent promotion to the positions. Failure to pass the test precluded an applicant from further consideration, no matter how outstanding the work record may have been. When blacks failed the test in greater proportions than whites, the employer applied an affirmative action program so that the net outcome of the promotion process (i.e., bottom-line figure) was more favorable to blacks than to whites. But the Court said this bottom-line result did not protect the employer from charges of discrimination at an earlier stage of the process. The U.S. Supreme Court said,

> [a] job-related test that has a disparate racial impact . . . is "used to discriminate" within the meaning of Title VII, whether or not it was "designed or intended" to have this effect and *despite an employer's efforts to compensate for its discriminatory effect* (italics added).[17]

In other words, even if the final outcome of the promotion process was equal for all race and sex groups, if one stage of the process has disparate impact, that stage must be shown to be job-related. Every single step of the hiring/promotion process must be job-related if it has disparate impact; equality of bottom-line results is not enough.

Exceptions to Title VII

Several specific exceptions to the definitions of discrimination have emerged from the courts' interpretations of Title VII. Among these are work-related requirements, bona fide occupational qualifications, seniority systems, and preferential quota systems.

Job-Related. Even if an employment practice has disparate impact on the groups covered by Title VII, an employer can successfully defend its use by showing that it is job-related. It may sound easy for a company to show that its practices are job-related—if they were not, why would the company continue to use them? In fact, employers have had a difficult time defending their practices in court. Courts have held employers to a very demanding standard of job-relatedness or business necessity. For example, the U.S. Supreme Court has said that employers wishing to defend tests that have unequal impact must follow the *Uniform Guidelines on Employee Selection*, issued by the Equal Employment Opportunity Commission.[18] The guidelines require the employer to undertake extensive, expensive research.

Nevertheless, if an employment practice serves a legitimate need, and if there is no alternative that has less of an adverse impact, it may be worthwhile for the organization to try to defend that practice.

Bona Fide Occupational Qualifications (BFOQ). In circumstances where race, religion, sex, or national origin is "reasonably necessary to the normal operations of the particular business or enterprise," such factors may be used in employment decisions. In the late 1960s and early 70s, state laws protected women from certain occupations considered in earlier periods to be too dangerous, too dirty, or inconvenient. But the courts (*Rosenfeld* v. *Southern Pacific*) decided these "protective laws" were in conflict with Title VII and thus null and void.[19] Some employers also thought that BFOQ exceptions precluded hiring men for jobs that women supposedly performed better. The most celebrated example of this reasoning was the *Diaz* v. *Pan American Airways* decision, in which the court ruled that an airline could not limit its employment of flight attendants to women.[20] At the time, the idea of a male flight attendant was unheard of, but the court ruled against the airline. Today, the notion of male flight attendants is well accepted. BFOQ is still recognized in cases of age discrimination, especially where public safety is involved. For example, it is legal to set an upper age limit for admission to police, firefighting, and bus driver training programs. But sex as a BFOQ is not very common.

Seniority System Exception. To be considered bona fide, a seniority system must have a nondiscriminatory purpose behind its creation. So long as a seniority system was not conceived out of an intent to discriminate, it is not unlawful under Title VII, even though it may result in restrictions of employment opportunities. As we saw in the Memphis firefighters case, sometimes a seniority system can have unequal impact. If blacks were not hired into an employer's work force until recently, a seniority system that bases promotions on seniority would have an unequal impact on black promotions, and one that bases layoffs on a "last hired, first fired" rule would adversely affect black employment when the work force is reduced.[21]

In *Teamsters* v. *United States* the Supreme Court stated:

> The seniority system in this case is entirely bona fide. It applies equally to all races and ethnic groups. To the extent that it "locks" employees . . . it does so for all. . . . the seniority system did not have its genesis in racial discrimination and it was negotiated and has been maintained free from any illegal purpose.[22]

In the 1984 Memphis case, the Supreme Court ruled that an employer may not be ordered to ignore a seniority system when making layoffs, even if the effect will be to reduce the number of women or minorities hired under a court-mandated affirmative action plan. Although individuals who can demonstrate that they have been actual discrimination victims may be awarded artificial seniority, "mere membership in the disadvantaged class is insufficient to warrant a seniority award."[23]

So the courts are free to award artificial seniority (seniority that would have been attained by an individual were it not for illegal discrimination) for individual victims of discrimination, but seniority systems are not illegal.

Preferential-Quota System Exception. Virtually everyone has read about "quota systems and preferential treatment."[24] In essence, such systems set aside a portion of opportunities for groups who have been discriminated against. The objective is to overcome the long history of discrimination that has relegated certain groups to a lower-economic status. The systems do so by instituting employment preferences for members of such groups. For example, a specific share (say, 20 percent) of openings in a training program may be set aside for minorities or women.

Quota systems are a source of controversy. Claims of reverse discrimination reverberate across the country. The chairman of the U.S. Commission on Civil Rights said:

> Affirmative action with its goals and preferences is a bankrupt policy. It has not provided opportunity for those whom it was intended to help. It has delegitimized minority achievement because we really don't know who makes it without it. Minorities who have worked harder than many whites in similar positions are looked at with jaundiced eyes because it is believed that they received their position because of minority preference rather than achievement. [25]

However, the U.S. Supreme Court has consistently ruled that employers can voluntarily give *temporary* preference to qualified members of underrepresented protected groups. In the first such case, *Weber* v. *Kaiser Aluminum and Chemicals,* an employer and union had collectively bargained access to an in-plant training program that was required to attain higher-paying jobs. Separate lists of black and white workers eligible to receive the training were maintained. Fifty percent of the openings in the training program were reserved for blacks. The result was that qualified blacks experienced shorter waits for training than qualified whites. The court ruled such a plan was legal, noting that

> the plan does not unnecessarily trammel the interests of the white employees. The plan does not require the discharge of white workers and their replacement with new black hires. . . . Nor does the plan create an absolute bar to the advancement of white employees; half of those trained in the program will be white. Moreover, the plan is a temporary measure; it is not intended to maintain racial balance, but simply to eliminate a manifest racial imbalance. Preferential selection of craft trainees at the plant will end as soon as the percentage of black skilled craft workers in the plant approximates the percentage of blacks in the local labor force. [26]

Additional cases since *Weber,* including the *Johnson* case discussed in the beginning of this chapter, have upheld affirmative action plans, providing they are "narrowly tailored" to correct serious imbalances among race and sex groups in a comparison to their availability. [27]

Thus, Title VII permits unequal impact of personnel decisions if the practice is a job-related business necessity, or is defensible as a bona fide occupational qualification, as the result of a seniority system, or as a preferential quota system designed to overcome past discrimination.

Title VII has a very broad intent, and has had profound impact on the workplace. A narrower discrimination law, but one with equal impact, has been the Equal Pay Act.

The Equal Pay Act of 1963

This law is technically an amendment to the Fair Labor Standards Act (see Chapter Eighteen). Passed after nearly two years of congressional debate, the Equal Pay Act (EPA) forbids wage discrimination:

> between employees on the basis of sex when employees perform equal work on jobs in the same establishment requiring equal skill, effort, and responsibility and performed under similar working conditions. . . . Pay differences between equal jobs can be justified when that differential is based on (1) a seniority system; (2) a merit system; (3) a system measuring earnings by quality or quantity of production; or (4) any factor other than sex.[28]

Thus, the EPA embodies for women the "equal work" definition of pay discrimination. Pay discrimination against minorities is covered under Title VII. In fact, both women and minorities can bring suit over pay discrimination under Title VII. Equal work is defined by *four factors:* (1) equal skill, (2) equal effort, (3) equal responsibility, and (4) equal working conditions. However, the EPA permits pay differences between men and women engaged in equal work if there are also differences (1) in seniority, (2) in quality of performance, (3) in quality or quantity of production, or (4) some factor other than sex.

Although the definition of equal work contained in the Equal Pay Act and the exceptions are relatively specific, numerous cases have required the courts to interpret the law. Some important issues raised include:

- How equal is equal?
- What is meant by equal skill, effort, responsibility, and working conditions?

Definition of Equal

Schultz v. *Wheaton Glass Company* provided some guidelines to define equal work in 1970.[29] Wheaton Glass Company maintained male and female job classifications for selector packers in its production department. The female job class carried a pay rate 10 percent below that of the male job class. The company claimed that the male job class included additional tasks that justified the pay differential, such as shoveling broken glass, opening warehouse doors, and doing heavy lifting. The plaintiff claimed that the extra tasks were infrequently performed, and not all men did them. Did the additional tasks performed by some members of one job class render the jobs unequal? The court decided not, and ruled that the equal work standard required only that jobs be *substantially* equal, not identical. The extra duties performed by some of the men did not justify paying all of the men 10 percent more than the women. The concept "equal pay for substantially equal work" has been recognized in cases following *Schultz v. Wheaton Glass Company.*

Factors Defining Equal Work

The Department of Labor provides these definitions of the four factors that define equal work.[30]

> Skill—Experience, training, education, and ability as measured by the performance requirements of a particular job.
>
> Effort—(Mental or physical) the amount or degree of effort, not type of effort, actually expended in the performance of a job.
>
> Responsibility—The degree of accountability required in the performance of a job.
>
> Working conditions—The physical surroundings and hazards of a job, including dimensions such as inside versus outside work, heat, cold, poor ventilation.

The courts have consistently held that overall time, effort, or skill required must be substantially greater in one of the jobs to support any claim of unequal work, and that all of the higher-paid workers must actually perform the additional tasks to justify any pay differential.[31] Hence, any system of valuing jobs must specify these distinctions. We return to the discussion of pay discrimination and the idea of equal pay for jobs of "comparable" value (as contrasted with *substantially similar*) in the chapters about compensation.

Executive Order 11246

Executive Order 11246 requires that all firms with government contracts of $100,000 or more and 100 or more employees must agree not to discriminate and to take affirmative action to ensure equal opportunity in employment. Many employers voluntarily act affirmatively to rectify the effects of past practices, or to anticipate and avoid future problems.

Age Discrimination in Employment Act

Organization downsizing resulting in layoffs and the early retirement of older workers has increased interest in age discrimination. In recent years, age discrimination complaints have grown at a faster rate than any other discrimination issue.[32] Congress enacted the Age Discrimination in Employment Act (ADEA) in 1967 to protect persons between the ages of 40 and 70 against arbitrary discrimination in employment practices. ADEA's prohibitions are similar to those of Title VII. Its purpose is to "promote employment of older persons on their ability rather than age; to prohibit arbitrary age discrimination in employment; to help employers and workers find ways of meeting problems arising from the impact of age on employment." A subsequent amendment which took effect in 1987 removed the upper age boundary. The law forbids: mandatory retirement based on age (with some exceptions), limiting or classifying employees in any way that would adversely affect their status because of age, reducing any employee's wage rate to comply with the act, or discriminating in compensation or terms of employment because of age.

Public safety employees such as police and firefighters are exempt from the law until 1994. The exemption provides time to study whether tests can be developed to adequately evaluate job-related mental or physical fitness. If such tests are feasible, then these measures would be used in lieu of age to evaluate individual qualifications to continue work.

Practices which would otherwise be prohibited are permissible if (1) age is a bona fide occupational qualification, (2) the differentiation is on reasonable factors other than age, (3) the employer is observing a bona fide seniority or benefit plan, (4) the employer is disciplining or discharging an employee for just cause, or (5) the employee is a top executive or policymaker.

Employers face a particularly complex set of issues in attempting to diagnose age discrimination. For example, when promotion rates of older and younger workers are compared, older workers tend to have lower rates.[33] This may be due to differences in job opportunities available—older, more senior workers tend to be in higher-level positions where fewer promotion possibilities exist. Or, older workers may have reached a job level that matches their competence. Or, there may, indeed, be age discrimination.

Vocational Rehabilitation Act

The Rehabilitation Act of 1973 prohibits discrimination on the basis of physical or mental handicap. Employers with federal contracts of over $2,500 are required to take affirmative action for the employment and promotion of qualified handicapped individuals.

In many ways, this law is similar to Title VII but there are significant differences. One major difference is that affirmative action plans for the handicapped, unlike those for women and minority groups, need not set specific numerical hiring goals based on population figures. A second important difference is that although neither plan requires the hiring of unqualified workers, employers of the handicapped must take steps to reasonably accommodate workers with disabilities so that they can hold

EXHIBIT 3–6

IF YOU ARE BEING HARASSED . . .

1. DON'T QUIT YOUR JOB. It won't solve anything, and you'll be out of a paycheck. Quitting may also work against you if you file an EEOC complaint, for the company will be under no pressure to negotiate. If the harassment intensifies because of your complaint, that only strengthens your case.

2. ACT QUICKLY. The best defense to harassment is a strong offense. Confront the harasser. Tell him his behavior is offensive to you, and ask him to stop.

3. GET SUPPORT FROM YOUR CO-WORKERS. Make sure the men and women who work with you are aware of the situation and your efforts to remedy it. Many men find sexual harassment as offensive as women.

4. RIDICULE THE HARASSER. Public exposure of sexual harassment can be the most effective way of stopping it. You may ask the harasser, "Does it make you feel like a big man to pick on a woman?" Or, "Do you speak to your wife like that? Maybe I'll have to call her and ask."

5. USE YOUR UNION GRIEVANCE PROCEDURE. Union women have more protection than their non-union sisters, under an anti-discrimination clause that is part of most contracts. Contact your union representative immediately and consider filing a grievance.

6. NOTIFY THE COMPANY, whether your harasser is a supervisor or a co-worker. If you don't your employer can claim ignorance and deny responsibility for the behavior. *Put it in writing, and keep a copy!*

7. KEEP A DIARY. Include dates, times, names of witnesses. Write exact quotes, if possible. The more evidence, the better.

8. FIND OTHER VICTIMS. If you can build evidence that the harasser has abused other women, or that harassment has been condoned by management, your case will be strengthened.

Source: Marat Moore and Connie White, *Sexual Harassment in the Mines* (Oak Ridge, Tennessee: Coal Employment Project, no date).

specific acts complained of were authorized or even forbidden by the employer and regardless of whether the employer knew or should have known of their occurrence.[37]

A nonprofit organization that helps women obtain and keep jobs in the coal mining industry offers the advice in Exhibit 3–6 to those who feel they are victims of harassment.

EVALUATING EEO PERFORMANCE

Many employers face the legal enforcement of EEO and AA regulations with a mixture of resignation and despair, feeling little can be done to minimize the threat of legal action. To some, the government and its reg-

jobs they otherwise could not perform. Reasonable accommoda
include redesigning jobs, constructing ramps, installing phones
cial adaptations, installing elevators to all floors, and examining
and promotion opportunities for jobs from which the handicap
have been excluded but for which they are qualified.

The appropriate treatment of employees with acquired imm
ciency syndrome (AIDS) is a growing policy concern. Experts ad
ployers to treat AIDS as an employee disability and to
discriminating against employees who have the disease. Other pr
measures include training supervisors about the company's position
issue, reviewing related policies on personal leave, disability pla
health insurance for consistency with the policy on AIDS and re
safety procedures in settings such as hospital laboratories where a
exposure, however slight, may exist.[34] Chapter Fifteen contains
discussion of this sensitive topic.

Sexual Harassment

Government agencies issue a variety of guidelines intended to int
the equal employment opportunity law and executive orders.
guidelines are frequently the subject of considerable interest and co
versy, because they are the rules used to implement the law's intent.
example of federal guidelines deals with sexual harassment as a viol
of Title VII of the Civil Rights Act. These guidelines hold that the
ployer is responsible for the actions of its employees, and define se
harassment:

> Unwelcome sexual advances, requests for sexual favors, and other verb;
> physical conduct of a sexual nature constitute sexual harassment w
> (1) submission to such conduct is made either explicitly or implicitly a t
> or condition of an individual's employment, (2) submission to or reject
> of such conduct by an individual is used as the basis for employment de
> sions affecting such individual, or (3) such conduct has the purpose or eff
> of substantially interfering with an individual's work performance or cre
> ing an intimidating, hostile, or offensive working environment.[35]

A 1986 Supreme Court case, *Meritor Savings Bank* v. Vinson confirn
this definition.[36]

According to the guidelines, "sexual harassment can take many form
which involve verbal or nonverbal behavior that is subtle and therefor
difficult to recognize. While no conscious intent to harass may be in
volved, behavior acceptable in a social setting may be inappropriate in the
workplace." Under these guidelines, an employer is liable for the sexual
harassment acts of its supervisors and agents "regardless of whether the

ulations seem arbitrary, punitive, and chaotic—more susceptible to the artistry of an attorney than to the problem-solving skill of a human resources manager.

Yet, in the final analysis, all human resource decisions and actions must achieve results. EEO actions are no different. The next section discusses a basic approach to evaluate an employer's EEO performance. It may seem overly involved and quantitative. However, managing equal employment opportunity is not unlike managing other activities. Whether they are used to evaluate the management of financial resources or human resources, performance measures serve to indicate progress, highlight potential problem areas, and suggest areas for future directions. The results-oriented approach to EEO helps to focus management's attention and to suggest future actions.

Every major human resource activity (staffing, compensation, training, labor relations) needs to be evaluated for its EEO implications. Here, however, we discuss how to evaluate only the overall employment patterns of an organization. We examine the EEO implications for specific human resource activities in the appropriate chapters.

EEO analysis has four steps:

1. *Analyze the work force* to determine representation (percentage) of minorities and women in each job group in the organization.
2. *Analyze availability* in the relevant labor force to determine the proportion of minorities and women qualified and interested in the job opportunities.
3. *Establish EEO goals* by comparing the present work force to availability. Goals are the percentages of job opportunities to be shared with women and minorities to increase their representation in jobs in which they are underrepresented, where their percentage in a job is less than their percentage in the relevant availability.
4. *Prepare EEO programs* specifying how the EEO goals are to be achieved and a proposed timetable for achievement.

The EEO work force analysis is relatively straightforward and objective. It simply involves determining representation rates, the proportions of employees in each job group who are members of various race and sex groups. Work force analysis may also focus on how employees flow into and through the organization by calculating hiring and promotion rates, the percentage of race and sex groups hired or promoted into specific job groups. Exhibit 3–7 shows part of an EEO form often used as part of this analysis.

If certain employee groups are scarce in a group of jobs, such as in the Santa Clara Transportation Agency's laborers, drivers, and dispatchers,

EXHIBIT 3-7
Part of an EEO Form

Section D - EMPLOYMENT DATA

Employment at this establishment — Report all permanent, temporary, or part-time employees including apprentices and on-the-job trainees unless specifically excluded as set forth in the instructions. Enter the appropriate figures on all lines and in all columns. Blank spaces will be considered as zeros.

JOB CATEGORIES	OVERALL TOTAL (SUM OF COL. B THRU K) A	MALE					FEMALE				
		WHITE NOT OF HISPANIC ORIGIN B	BLACK NOT OF HISPANIC ORIGIN C	HISPANIC D	ASIAN OR PACIFIC ISLANDER E	AMERICAN INDIAN OR ALASKAN NATIVE F	WHITE NOT OF HISPANIC ORIGIN G	BLACK NOT OF HISPANIC ORIGIN H	HISPANIC I	ASIAN OR PACIFIC ISLANDER J	AMERICAN INDIAN OR ALASKAN NATIVE K
Officials and Managers	700	572	10	1	3		105	7		2	
Professionals	261	198	6	2	1		51	2		1	
Technicians	71	40	3	1			30				
Sales Workers	40	35					2				
Office and Clerical	544	30	1				502	10		1	
Craft Workers (Skilled)	5	5									
Operatives (Semi-Skilled)	4	3					1				
Laborers (Unskilled)	2						2				
Service Workers	19	9	2				8				
TOTAL	1646	892	22	4	4		701	19		4	
Total employment reported in previous EEO-1 report	1696	904	31	4	3		732	16		5	1

(The trainees below should also be included in the figure for the appropriate occupational categories above)

Formal On-the-job trainees												
White collar	27	17	3				7					
Production												

1. NOTE: On consolidated report, skip questions 2-5 and Section E.

2. How was information as to race or ethnic group in Section D obtained?

   1 ☐ Visual Survey   3 ☐ Other—Specify..........

   2 ☒ Employment Record

3. Dates of payroll period used - 2/28/87

4. Pay period of last report submitted for this establishment   2/29/84

5. Does this establishment employ apprentices?

   This year?   1 ☐ Yes   2 ☒ No

   Last year?   1 ☐ Yes   2 ☒ No

what does this tell us? How great is the extent of any underrepresentation? What should the sex and race composition have been? The answer is found in availability analysis.

Availability Analysis

Availability analysis determines the proportions of employees in the relevant labor force who are members of various race and sex groups and who are *qualified* and *interested* in specific job opportunities.[38] Availability is the standard against which actual representation, hiring, and promotion rates are compared for evidence of discrimination. The availability of specific skills in each race and sex category is presumed to reflect approximately what the race and sex composition of the employer's work force would be were it not for discrimination.

Unfortunately, determining availability involves considerable judgment. Hence, the results are open to controversy.[39] Data provided by the Bureau of the Census are often too broad, and typically only serve as a starting point. Further refinements may be based on geographical factors (commuting patterns), information on enrollments in local trade schools or other training institutions, or any other factors that appear to affect the supply of labor. Availabilities are merely estimates.

Measuring Availability

Exhibit 3–8 gives some alternative measures of availability and the assumptions that underlie each measure. Let us use the job of arc welding at the Pontiac Fiero Plant in Detroit, Michigan, as an example. Not everyone in the entire U.S. population, the first category in the exhibit, is qualified to be an arc welder in an auto plant, nor is the entire civilian labor force, the second category. So we narrow the relevant availability to those qualified. But all those qualified may not be available or interested—some may already be employed, others may live in California and not wish to relocate. The next step may be to narrow availability to applicants, and consider the percentage of minorities and women who actually apply for jobs as arc welders. Each time we move to a narrower category in the exhibit, the numbers become more specific. But how much narrowing of the definition of availabilities is reasonable? For example, do we assume that only those who actually apply for the welder's job and can demonstrate that they can weld should be included in an availability estimate? In doing so, we have limited our estimate to welders actively seeking employment, which may not reflect the actual subpopulation of minority and women welders. Some people may not be aware of the job opportunity, or may be discouraged from applying due to past discrimina-

EXHIBIT 3–8
Assumptions Characterizing Alternative Availability Estimates

Alternative Labor Pools	Assumptions		
	Available	Interested	Qualified
Population	All persons are equally available for employment.	Job interests are equally distributed across population.	All persons possess requisite job skills.
Civilian labor force	Both employed and unemployed are available; excludes disabled, institutional inmates, retirees, housewives, young children, and those in the Armed Services.	Persons not working or not looking for work are not interested; interests are equally distributed across those in the civilian labor force.	All persons in the civilian labor force possess requisite job skills.
Qualified labor force	Both employed and unemployed are available.	All persons employed or looking for employment are equally interested.	Persons employed or looking for employment in the occupational categories which correspond to employer's job group possess necessary skills.
Applicants	Those who apply are available for employment.	Only those who apply are interested, and interests are equally distributed.	All applicants possess the necessary skills.
Qualified applicants	Those who apply are available for employment.	Only those who apply for employment are interested, and interests are equally distributed.	Only applicants possessing the necessary skills are qualified.

Source: Patricia Snider, "External Data for Affirmative Action Planning," *Human Resources Planning* 2, no. 1 (1979), p. 8.

tion. Additionally, we have ignored those who are interested in becoming welders and who could gain the necessary skill within a reasonable time period. This group is called *qualifiable,* and estimating their numbers and whether to include them is an additional complication. Clearly, there is no best approach to estimating availabilities. All availability statistics have limitations. Recognizing the limitations allows an employer to make a best estimate that is useful and workable.

Utilization Analysis

For each job or job group, utilization analysis compares the representation, hiring, and/or promotion rates of minorities and women to their relevant availability. This comparison may produce three outcomes:

1. *Underutilization*—the representation, hiring, and/or promotion rate is below the relevant availability.
2. *Parity*—the representation, hiring, and/or promotion rate is approximately equal to the relevant availability.
3. *Overutilization*—the representation, hiring, and/or promotion rate is above the relevant availability.

Underutilization is usually regarded as the most serious outcome, but overutilization can signal possible reverse discrimination against whites or males.

For parity, how equal is approximately equal? How much must the representation, hiring, or promotion rate fall below availability to indicate a problem? There is no simple answer. Courts and regulatory agencies have adopted several tests, including: (1) whether the difference in rates is statistically significant (not due to chance); (2) whether the representation, hiring, or promotion rate is less than four fifths of the availability; and (3) whether the representation, hiring, or promotion rate is zero.[40]

Programming to Achieve Goals

Human resource managers must diagnose the causes of underutilization. In this way they know which practices must be changed to increase representation of women and minorities.[41]

An Illustration

Exhibit 3–9 shows IBM's affirmative action planning processes. This exhibit requires the following definitions:

1. Availabilities—the percentage of women and minorities that should be found in each job category in each facility.
2. Utilization rates—the adequacy of current representations of women and minority in each facility. The percentage of anticipated opportunities (i.e., vacancies) in each job category in each facility that must go to women and/or minority candidates during the plan year.
3. Timetables—where utilization rates are inadequate, the year in which full utilization (parity) can be expected to occur.

EXHIBIT 3–9
Model of the IBM Affirmative Action Planning Process

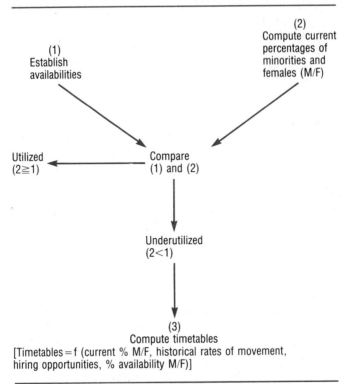

Source: Lee Dyer and N. O. Heyer, "Human Resource Planning at IBM: A Field Study" (Working Paper, Cornell University, 1984).

At IBM, availabilities for each job category in each facility are established in the following way: First, analysts use three-year historical data to determine the proportion of opportunities (vacancies) that are filled from external or internal sources. Second, they establish the percentage of women and minorities in each source from published data for external labor markets and personnel records for internal sources. Third, they combine the first two pieces of information to determine goals for women and minority groups for each job category in each facility.

Analysts determine utilization rates by comparing the percentage of women and minorities actually employed against availability. Where underutilization occurs, they set timetables and goals. All managers in a facility must indicate: (1) the number of opportunities they expect to have in each job group, and (2) the estimated number that they can fill with women and minorities. Annual goals become targets for managers, and progress is monitored on a quarterly basis.

Affirmative action programs do work. IBM established its equal opportunity department in 1968, in compliance with Executive Order 11246. Whereas in 1962, IBM had 750 black employees, by 1968 the figure was 7,251, and that figure more than doubled to 16,546 in 1980. Similarly, in 1971 IBM had 429 blacks, 83 Hispanics, and 471 females working as officials and managers. By 1980 there were 1,596 blacks, 436 Hispanics, and 2,350 females in such positions. Starting with a small representation of females and minorities in 1962 (13 percent and less than 2 percent respectively), by 1980 IBM had significantly integrated its work force (22 percent female and 14 percent minority).[42]

SETTLING DISPUTES

The courts are not the only interpreters of EEO laws; several governmental agencies also interpret and enforce the laws. Regulatory agencies are an important factor in the organization's external environment. Compliance agents often make site visits and require explanations of firms' EEO performance.

Equal Employment Opportunity Commission (EEOC)

The lead agency in most EEO matters is the Equal Employment Opportunity Commission (EEOC). The EEOC has several responsibilities. It interprets the law through guidelines that have the effect of law. Guidelines dealing with sexual harassment as a violation of Title VII are an example. EEOC also processes discrimination charges and files lawsuits in federal court on behalf of alleged victims of discrimination. Enforcement of the Age Discrimination Act, Equal Pay Act, and Title VII of the Civil Rights Act all fall within EEOC jurisdiction.

EEOC's Major Activities

EEOC's major activity is the processing of charges made by those who believe they are victims of discrimination. EEOC interviews each complainant to determine whether the complaint falls within the coverage of legislation. If it does, then the charge is turned over to the state or local fair employment practice agency. If there is no agency with adequate powers in the state, EEOC investigates by interviewing the parties concerned with the alleged discrimination and collecting facts that might have a bearing on the charge. Ordinarily, those investigators are the first EEOC personnel with whom the employer comes into contact.

Conciliation

If there appears to be some truth to the accusations against the employer, EEOC attempts to bring about an out-of-court agreement between the employer and the charging party. This process is called *conciliation*. If the employer and EEOC accept the settlement, then the matter ends. But if conciliation efforts fail, the complainant and/or EEOC may file in federal district court.

The EEOC itself cannot order a remedy or impose a settlement. It can only negotiate settlements with employers, or failing that, turn to the courts.[43]

EEO-1 Reports

All employers subject to Title VII with 100 or more employees must submit to EEOC a form (EEO-1) such as the one shown in Exhibit 3–7. This form reports employment by sex and race for each of several broad job classifications. Multiple-establishment enterprises must file a report for each establishment of 50 or more employers. These data indicate, at least initially, whether an employer is complying with Title VII.

The EEOC has moved away from quotas and statistics to achieve "broad social goals," and is concentrating on ending specific employer behavior that discriminates against specific victims.[44] Yearly court filings have tripled since the early 1980s.[45] The commission's Voluntary Assistance Program provides seminars for employees. By dialing a toll-free number (800-USA-EEOC) employees can learn not only about their rights, but also how to file charges against employers.

Office of Federal Contract Compliance (OFCCP)

The Office of Federal Contract Compliance is that part of the Department of Labor which administers affirmative action plans required under Executive Order 11246. OFCCP issues its own guidelines and goals for compliance. Its regulations stress that goals are "not rigid quotas which the contractor must achieve regardless of employment circumstance," but rather are "targets to be affirmatively pursued." Like EEOC, OFCCP appears to be moving away from reliance on quotas and statistics, and is encouraging innovation and flexibility in hiring and training programs.

Organizations: Internal Resolution Procedures

Whether required by a union contract or not, most employers agree that some sort of internal grievance process is desirable for all personnel issues, but especially for EEO issues.[46] Supervisors who have open communication with their workers may avoid or satisfy many complaints, grievances, and even lawsuits.

Three elements are necessary to successfully deal with EEO disputes: The first is a published policy advising employees how to bring a complaint within the organization. Such a policy should also include the company's stance on sexual harassment and equal opportunity. The system must be flexible enough so that in cases of sexual harassment, the offender, who may be the immediate supervisor, is not the organization's representative with whom the victim must file the complaint.

Second, every complaint lodged should be thoroughly investigated. Investigators may be the human resource staff, other employees, or neutral parties.

Third, employees must be kept informed on the investigation's progress. If an investigation is inconclusive, accusing employees should be informed and advised of their alternatives or opportunities to present further evidence. If cause is found for the complaint, then disciplinary action applied in other offenses should be required.

But if internal resolution does not work, what are the options? A discrimination suit can be resolved by coming to an agreement with the person involved, or going through a formal trial. If the EEOC is involved, management's options are reduced. EEOC may try to negotiate an agreement both before and after a suit is filed, or it may seek court orders requiring specific actions. Court remedies typically include back pay awards, changes in hiring/promotion or other job practices, and attorneys' fees and legal costs. Exhibit 3–10 outlines the main features of a settlement to which an insurance company recently agreed. The advantage of negotiating a settlement is that many of the required behaviors—for example, installing a performance evaluation system—are what good personnel practice would dictate.[47]

Supervisors

The supervisor may play the most important role in an organization's EEO program. The supervisor translates much policy into action, and the supervisor's actions often determine whether employees believe they are being treated fairly.

When EEO goals require changes in procedures, problems may arise in getting supervisors to buy into the need for these changes. Occupational role stereotyping, societal sexism, and sexual harassment have sometimes made it difficult for organizations to implement affirmative action programs.[48] Male supervisors and co-workers may be unable to objectively appraise the work performance of women or accept their

EXHIBIT 3–10
United States Fidelity and Guaranty Company (USF&G)
EEO Settlement Agreement

Who Will Benefit from the Agreement?—More than 20,000 minorities and women who were employed by the company between February 18, 1974, and August 31, 1981—or who applied for employment—can expect to receive cash payments. In its scope, the agreement covers employees from the professional to the clerical levels of the company.

The Amount of Money Involved.—The payments to be made under the agreement total $3.5 million. The money is distributed by use of a backpay distribution formula. The amount going to any given individual is based on job tenure, education, job grade, prior experience, the job applied for, length of service, and race and sex. The formula is intended to vary individual awards according to the likelihood and extent of harm caused by the company's alleged race and sex discrimination.

Affirmative Action Measures.—The USF&G agreement requires the company to implement affirmative action measures to ensure the hiring and advancement of minorities and women. The company is required to establish affirmative action goals, monitor compliance, post jobs, train minorities and women for supervisory positions, offer career counseling, and set up a performance appraisal program. The company agreed in a separate provision to make a good-faith effort to achieve its employment goals for minorities and women for five years beginning with the effective date of the agreement.

occupational competence. If this is the case, the organization must communicate to the supervisor why changes are necessary and how they can benefit the organization. Most managers pay attention to the criteria on which their own job performance ratings are based. Therefore, a good way to get managers to help implement EEO policy is to review their performance on the basis of their unit's EEO behavior.

Unions

Executive Order 11246 also requires that unions lend a hand in employers' affirmative action efforts. A nondiscrimination clause is included in virtually all collective bargaining agreements. Affirmative action efforts are often constrained, however, by the seniority provisions found in many contracts. One alternative is *inverse seniority* where, in a layoff situation, the most senior person is allowed to elect a temporary layoff with substantial compensation and the right to return to work at some future time. This alternative to the "last hired, first fired" allows the employer to temporarily reduce the work force and still retain the minorities and women who may have lower seniority. However, the inducement to get senior employees' cooperation may be very costly, and is not a long-term solu-

EXHIBIT 3–11
A Guide to Legal Remedies

	Description	Benefits	Filing to Settlement	Problems
State and federal EEOC	Enforcement agencies for implementation of state and federal civil rights laws.	Reinstatement, back pay, or financial settlement. Free.	6 months to 1 year, or longer.	EEOC has a huge backlog; may push complainant to accept financial settlement in exchange for dropping complaint.
Title VII—1961 Civil Rights Act	Federal legislation prohibiting sex discrimination in employment; must file with EEOC first.	Monetary compensation for back pay, lost benefits, job reinstatement.	2–3 years.	Applies to workplace with at least 15 employees. Must prove discrimination. Must hire attorney. Trial by judge, not jury.
State civil rights laws	Similar to Title VII, but vary from state to state.	Varies; can include jury trial and compensatory damages.	1–3 years.	Some states have no civil rights laws. Law varies widely from state to state.
Union grievance procedure	Breach of union contract allows employee to file grievance which union processes through grievance procedure to arbitration.	Financial compensation for employment losses, reinstatement to job if employee has been fired.	Varies from union to union, company to company. Can be settled in weeks or may require arbitration—up to a year.	Few women/minorities are unionized. Union contract may not be interpreted to cover sexual harassment. Male-dominated unions may be unresponsive.

Adapted from *Stopping Sexual Harassment, A Handbook.* (Detroit, Mich.: Labor Education and Research Project, 1980).

tion. Clearly, a combined effort is required by both employers and unions to attain affirmative action goals.

Unions' attitudes and actions to equal employment vary as much as employers' attitudes and actions.[49] Construction unions have contributed to the shortage of women in that industry, by their control over hiring. The AFL-CIO's unlawful racial practices in the 1930s and 1940s, including segregating members by race and racial discrimination in collective bargaining activities, may have contributed to the unions' lack of success in organizing in the South and its subsequent erosion of membership.[50]

At the other extreme, unions in industries with a large percent of women members, especially those in the public sector, have been on the forefront of women's issues.[51] Many unions have championed equal opportunity and the comparable worth concept discussed in later chapters about pay.

The Employee

Discrimination and harassment are against the law. But is the law the best way to deal with the problem? Litigation costs money, and can take years. Many employees find that union grievance procedures are faster and more effective. Many women and minorities have found that unions offer a faster, easier route to complaint resolution than the courts. Union support on a complaint may help decrease the imbalance in power between an aggrieved employee and employer. Additionally, the Supreme Court has upheld an employee's right to still file a complaint if the result of the grievance procedure is unsatisfactory.[52] Exhibit 3–11 lists some options to complaining about an unpleasant work situation, as well as the problems with various approaches.

SUMMARY

Equal employment opportunity affects all human resource decisions. In one sense, EEO legislation and regulations simply require employers to adopt sound human resource practices. The treatment employees receive must be based on work and business factors rather than race or sex. This not only makes good business sense but also ensures compliance with the law.

Dispute continues over whether we as a nation have made any progress at eliminating employment discrimination. Although differences in occupational attainment and earnings among race and sex groups remain, some studies suggest progress has been made. Yet unexplained differences remain and some of this is the result of discriminatory practices in the workplace.

There are no magical cures for these problems, but one proposition that does seem to go a long way is *involvement*. Too often, EEO is treated as the exclusive province of the personnel department. If this can be changed by involving operating managers in planning and goal setting, attainment of EEO objectives should increase.

To make EEO programs work, top management must not only communicate its desires but also build EEO effectiveness into the reward system for managers. The goal is to make the EEO program ethical, workable, and in full compliance with the law.

General Electric Company requires its managers to report their progress in achieving EEO goals. Their degree of goal achievement in EEO affects their compensation, as does their progress in cost control. This system has helped General Electric meet its EEO goals. This kind of communication and control system is more likely to achieve courtproof EEO systems than memos or other such means.

In sum, top managers must get involved in EEO programs to make sure that the enterprise is, in fact, an equal employment opportunity employer and that the EEO–AA program meets the letter as well as the spirit of the law.

Over the last 20 years approaches to EEO have matured. Even though some managers still view it as an infringement on their "right to manage," many go beyond accepting it and view it as good business practice. The threat of costly lawsuits probably remains a major factor ensuring that some employers provide equal opportunity to all. Society continues to debate whether Congress intended EEO to mean equal opportunities or equal results. Human resource professionals have an important role in that debate.

DISCUSSION AND REVIEW QUESTIONS

1. What does *availability* mean? Why is it so important in EEO analysis to define relevant availability?
2. Compare and contrast equality of opportunity and equality of results.
3. How would you recognize discriminatory employment behavior? What are the two basic definitions?
4. Compare reverse discrimination and affirmative action.
5. How are EEO disputes settled?

NOTES AND REFERENCES

1. *Johnson v. Transportation Agency, Santa Clara County, California*, No. 85–1129 (March 25, 1987).
2. *Firefighters Local 1784 v. Stotts*, 104 Sup. Ct. 2576 (1984).
3. Uncertainty accompanied passage of the original EEO legislation, too. See, for example, George T. Milkovich, "The Emerging Debate" in *Comparable Worth: Issues and Alternatives*, ed. E. R. Livernash (Washington, D.C.: Equal Employment Advisory Council, 1978).
4. John F. Wymer III, "Compensatory and Punitive Damages for Sexual Harassment," *Personnel Journal*, March 1983, pp. 181–83; Nancy Fisher Chudacoff, "New EEOC Guidelines on Discrimination Because of Sex: Employer Liability for Sexual Harassment under Title VII," *Boston University Law Review* 61, no. 2 (March 1981); pp. 535–62; Samuel E. Bodily, "When Should You Go to Court?" *Harvard Business Review*, May–June, 1981, p. 103.
5. Conflict between seniority and EEO was an issue in *Teamsters v. United States*, 431 U.S. 324 (1977); and *Boston Fire Fighters Union, Local 718 v. Boston Chapter, NAACP*, No. 82–185 (May 16, 1983); *Williams v. City of New Orleans*, 18 FEP Cases 345 (E.D. La. 1976).
6. G. T. Milkovich and R. Broderick, "Pay Discrimination: Legal Issues and Implications for Research," *Industrial Relations* 21, no. 3 (1982), pp. 309–17; "EEOC Says It Is Discontinuing the Use of Numerical Quotas," *Human Resource Management Ideas and Trends*, February 21, 1986, p. 25, 30–32; David L. Kirp, Mark G. Yudof, and Marlene Strong Franks, *Gender Justice* (Chicago: University of Chicago Press, 1986); *Further Improvements Needed in EEOC Enforcement Activities*, HRD 81–29 (Washington, D.C.: U.S. Government Accounting Office, 1981); Finis R. Welch, "Affirmative Action and Its Enforcement," *American Economic Review* 71 (May 1981), pp. 127–33; *Women in the American Economy*, Current Population Reports Special Series P–23, No. 146 (Washington, D.C.: Superintendent of Documents, U.S. Government Printing Office, 1987).
7. P. England and S. D. McLaughlin, "Sex Segregation of Jobs and Male-Female Income Differentials," in *Discrimination in Organizations*, ed. R. Alverez, K. Lutterman, and Associates (San Francisco: Jossey-Bass, 1979); and U.S. Department of Labor, Women's Bureau, *The Earnings Gap between Women and Men* (Washington, D.C.: U.S. Government Printing Office, 1979); J. M. Abowd and M. R. Killingsworth, "Sex Discrimination and the Male-Female Wage Differential," *Industrial Relations* 22, no. 3 (1983), pp. 387–413; G. J. Borjas, "The Measurement of Race and Gender Wage Differentials: Evidence from the Federal Sector," *Industrial and Labor Relations Review* 37, no. 1 (1983), pp. 79–82; Andrea Beller, "The Impact of Equal Opportunity Policy on Sex Differentials in Earnings and Occupations," *AEA Papers and Proceedings* 72, no. 2 (1982), pp. 171–82; and G. Johnson and G. Solon, *Pay Differences between Women's and Men's Jobs* (Cambridge, Mass.: National Bureau of Economic Research, 1984).
8. H. Remick, ed., *Comparable Worth and Wage Discrimination* (Philadelphia: Temple University Press, 1984); D. J. Treiman and H. I. Hartmann,

ed., *Women, Work, and Wages* (Washington, D.C.: National Academy of Science, 1984).

9. Council of Economic Advisers, *1987 Annual Report* (Washington D.C.: U.S. Government Printing Office, 1987).

10. R. B. Freeman, "Have Black Labor Market Gains Post-1964 Been Permanent or Transitory?" (Working Paper 751, National Bureau of Economic Research, 1981); Thomas Sowell, *Markets and Minorities* (New York: Basic Books, 1981); James P. Smith and Finis R. Welch, *Closing the Gap: Forty Years of Economic Progress for Blacks* (Santa Monica, Calif.: The Rand Corporation, 1986).

11. William B. Chew, "An Agenda for the Future," in *Industrial Relations and Personnel Policies and Prospects for the Future* (Minneapolis: Industrial Relations Center, University of Minnesota, 1979).

12. For an excellent and detailed review of the EEO laws and litigation, see Ruth G. Shaeffer, *Nondiscrimination in Employment—And Beyond*, Report No. 782 (New York: The Conference Board, 1980). For even more extensive analysis, see Bureau of National Affairs, *Fair Employment Practices Manual*, 1984; a general discussion of EEO laws and regulations is in James Ledvinka, *Federal Regulations of Personnel and Human Resources Management* (Boston: Kent Publishing, 1982).

13. *General Electric Co.* v. *Gilbert*, 429 U.S. 125 (1977). But see *Cleveland Board of Education* v. *Lafleur*, 414 U.S. 632, 5 FEP 1253 (1974); and *Holthaus* v. *Compton & Sons, Inc.*, 514 F.2d 651, 10 FEP 601 8th Circuit (1975); also see Ruth Shaeffer, *Nondiscrimination and Beyond*.

14. B. L. Schlei and P. Grossman, *Employment Discrimination Law* (Washington, D.C.: Bureau of National Affairs, 1980); David C. Baldis and James W. L. Cole, *Statistical Proof of Discrimination* (New York: McGraw-Hill, 1980).

15. *Griggs* v. *Duke Power Co.*, 401 U.S. 424 (1971).

16. Bureau of National Affairs, *Fair Employment Practices Manual, Federal Laws*; Bureau of National Affairs, *Fair Employment Practices Summary*.

17. *Connecticut* v. *Teal*, 112 SCT 2525, U.S. Sup. Ct. 29 EPD, 32, 870 (1982).

18. *Uniform Guidelines on Employee Selection Procedures*, 29 Code of Federal Regulations, Part 1607; *Federal Register* 43, no. 166 (1978), pp. 38295–309.

19. *Rosenfeld* v. *Southern Pacific Company*, 9th Cir. 444 F.2d 1219 (1971).

20. *Diaz* v. *Pan American World Airways, Inc.*, 5th Cir., 422 F.2d 385 (1971).

21. Marcia Graham, "Seniority Systems and Title VII: Reanalysis and Redirection," *Employee Relations Law Journal* 9, pp. 81–102; Michael E. Gordon and William A. Johnson, "Seniority: A Review of Its Legal and Scientific Standing," *Personnel Psychology* 35, no. 2 (1982), pp. 255–80.

22. *Teamsters* v. *United States*, 431 U.S. 324 (1972).

23. *Firefighters Local 1784* v. *Stotts*, 104 U.S. 2576 (1984).

24. B. Rosen and T. H. Jerdee, "Coping with Affirmative Action Backlash," *Business Horizons* 22 (1979), pp. 15–20; W. B. Reynolds, "The Justice Department's Enforcement of Title VII," *Labor Law Journal* 34, no. 5 (1983), pp. 259–65; Thomas I. Chacko, "Women and Equal Employment Opportunity: Some Unintended Effects," *Journal of Applied Psychology* 67, no. 1 (1982), pp. 119–23.

25. Clarence M. Pendleton, Jr., Chairman's address to the National Equal Employment Conference, 1983. Reported in *The Wall Street Journal*, June 21, 1983, p. 1.

26. *Weber v. Kaiser Aluminum and Chemical Corp.*, 415 F. Sup. 761, 12 CCH *Employment Practices Decisions* 91 11,115, S.D. La. (1976).

27. *Equal Employment Advisory Council Perspectives on Availability* (Washington, D.C., 1978); Pat Snider, "External Data for Affirmative Action Planning," in *Affirmative Action Planning*, ed. George Milkovich and Lee Dyer (New York: Human Resources Planning Society, 1979); F. Krzystofiak and Jerry Newman, "Evaluating Employment Outcomes: Availability Models and Measures," *Industrial Relations* 21, no. 3 (1982), pp. 277–93.

28. Peyton K. Elder and Heidi D. Miller, "Fair Labor Standards Act: Changes of Few Decades," *Monthly Labor Review* 93 (1970), pp. 10–16. For detailed discussion of Equal Pay Act and its implications for personnel decisions, see George Milkovich and Jerry Newman, *Compensation*, 2nd ed. (Plano, Tex.: Business Publications, 1987); E. Cooper and G. V. Barrett, "Equal Pay and Gender: Implications of Court Cases for Personnel Practices," *Academy of Management Review* 9, no. 1 (1984), pp. 84–94.

29. *Schultz v. Wheaton Glass Co.*, 421 F.2d 259, 3rd Cir. (1970).

30. U.S. Department of Labor, *Equal Pay for Equal Work under the Fair Labor Standards Act* (Washington, D.C.: U.S. Department of Labor, 1971).

31. Cooper and Barrett, "Equal Pay and Gender." Also see Randall Filer, "Male-Female Wage Differences: The Importance of Compensating Differentials," *Industrial and Labor Relations Review*, April 1985, pp. 426–37.

32. "ADEA Update: Case Law and Cost as Defense," *Personnel Administrator*, February 1985, pp. 116–19.

33. N. B. Smith and L. P. Leggette, "Recent Issues on Litigation under the Age Discrimination in Employment Act," *Ohio State Law Journal*, vol. 41549 (1982), pp. 350–65; James Madett, *Promotions, Age and Discrimination* working paper, MIT, 1984; Stephen J. Cabot, "Living with the New Amendments to the Age Discrimination in Employment Act," *Personnel Administrator*,
January 1987, pp. 53–54; Robert P. Pritchard, Scott E. Maxwell, and W. Carl Jordan, "Interpreting Relationships between Age and Promotion in Age—Discrimination Cases," *Journal of Applied Psychology* 69, no. 2 (1984), pp. 199–206; and JoAnn Lee and Tanya Clemons, "Factors Affecting Employment Decisions about Older Workers," *Journal of Applied Psychology* 70, no. 4 (1985), pp. 785–88.

34. Vigdor Grossman, *Employing the Handicapped Persons: Meeting EEO Obligations* (Washington, D.C.: Bureau of National Affairs, 1979), and *Fair Employment Practices* 421:361; 421:651 (Washington, D.C.: Bureau of National Affairs, 1978); "Justice Department on AIDS Discrimination," *Fair Employment Practices*, June 26, 1986, p. 76.

35. Donne E. Legerwood and Sue Johnson-Dietz, "Sexual Harassment: Implications for Employer Liability," *Monthly Labor Review* 104, no. 4 (April 1981), pp. 45–47; Michael Marmo, "Arbitrary Sex Harassment Cases," *The Arbitration Journal* 35, no. 1 (March 1980), pp. 35–40; Mary P. Rowe, "Dealing with Sexual Harassment," *Harvard Business Review*, May–June 1981, pp. 42–46; Robert W. Schupp, Joyce Windham, and Scott Draugn,

"Sexual Harassment under Title VII: The Legal Status," *Labor Law Journal*, April 1981, pp. 238–52; M. Moore and C. White, *Sexual Harassment in the Mines, Bringing the Issue to Light* (Oakridge, Tenn.: Coal Employment Project, 1983); George M. Sullivan and William A. Nowlin, "Critical New Aspects of Sex Harassment Law," *Labor Law Journal*, September 1986, pp. 617–24; Robert L. Simison and Cathy Trost, "Sexual Harassment at Work Is a Cause for Growing Concern," *The Wall Street Journal*, June 24, 1986, pp. 1, 17; "Sexual Harassment—Already a Major Concern—May Become an Even Higher Priority in 1986," *Human Resources Management Ideas and Trends*, January 24, 1986, pp. 9–12.

36. *Meritor Savings Bank* v. *Vinson*, Sup. Ct. 40 FEP Cases 1826 (1986).

37. D. D. Bennett-Alexander, "Protection of the Individual Employee and the Bottom Line Defense," *Labor Law Journal*, November 1983, pp. 704–10; *Connecticut* v. *Teal* 112 Sup. Ct. 2525, 29 EPD 32, 820 (1982).

38. *Equal Employment Advisory Council Perspectives on Availability* (Washington, D.C., 1978); Pat Snider, "External Data for Affirmative Action Planning," in *Affirmative Action Planning*, ed. George Milkovich and Lee Dyer (New York: Human Resources Planning Society, 1979); *Fair Employment Practices*, OFCCP Rules Revision, no. 467 (Washington: Bureau of National Affairs, 1983).

39. D. Atwater, R. J. Niehaus, and J. A. Sheridan, "Labor Pool for Antibias Program Varies by Occupation and Job Market," *Monthly Labor Review*, September 1981, pp. 43–50.

40. James Ledvinka, *Federal Regulation of Personnel and Human Resource Management* (Boston: Kent Publishing, 1982).

41. For example, the underrepresentation of women may be attributed to a host of factors including the company's reputation and a location that is considered unsafe. Once potential causes are diagnosed, then programs may be designed to increase the representation of women. Flexible work schedules, day-care programs, or providing escorted transportation are options. Without knowing the cause, however, managers may attempt to increase the representation of women by lowering the requirements for women. Such a move increases the risk of reverse discrimination charges, and also contributes to morale problems inside the company.

42. Richard T. Seymour, "Why Executive Order 11246 Should Be Preserved," *Employee Relations Law Journal* 11, no. 4 (1986), pp. 568–84.

43. Peter Feuille and David Lewin, "Equal Employment Opportunity Bargaining," *Industrial Relations* 20, no. 3 (1981), pp. 322–34; J. S. Leonard, "Antidiscrimination or Reverse Discrimination: The Impact of Changing Demographics, Title VII and Affirmative Action on Productivity," Working Paper No. 1240, Cambridge, Mass.: National Bureau of Economic Research, 1983; William A. Webb, "The Mission of the Equal Employment Opportunity Commission," *Employee Relations Law Journal* 34, no. 7 (1983) pp. 387–93.

44. "Courts' Ruling for Sears and against the EEOC Further Confirms the Trend Away from Numerical Quotas," *Human Resources Management Ideas and Trends*, March 21, 1986, pp. 41–45; Steve Weiner, "Sears's Costly Win in a Hiring Suit," *The Wall Street Journal*, March 18, 1986, p. 35.

45. "New Focus for EEOC," *BNAC Communicator* 7, no. 1 (Spring 1987),

p. 1; Joseph N. Cooper, "New Directions within OFCCP," *Labor Law Journal,* January 1986, pp. 3–5.

46. J. D. Coombe, "Peer Review: The Emerging Successful Application," *Employee Relations Law Journal* 9, no. 4 (Spring 1984), pp. 659–71; J. D. Coombe and George D. Jones, "Peer Reviews: A Concept for the 80s," *Employee Relations Today* 176 (Summer 1983), p. 10; *Fair Employment Practices, Dispute-Resolution Options: Ombudsman and Arbitration* (Washington, D.C.: Bureau of National Affairs, 1984).

47. "EEOC and General Motors Sign," *Fair Employment Practices Manual* (Washington, D.C.: Bureau of National Affairs, November 3, 1983), pp. 3–4.

48. B. Rosen and T. H. Jerdee, "Influence of Sex Role Stereotypes on Personnel Decisions," *Journal of Applied Psychology* 59 (1974), pp. 9–14; W. J. Bigoness, "Effect of Applicant's Sex, Race, and Performance on Employers' Performance Ratings: Some Additional Findings," *Journal of Applied Psychology* 61 (1976), pp. 80–84; V. E. Schein, "Sex Role Stereotyping, Ability, and Performance: Prior Research and New Directions," *Personnel Psychology* 31 (1978), pp. 259–68; J. Gliedman and W. Roth, *The Unexpected Minority: Handicapped Children in America* (New York: Harcourt Brace Jovanovich, 1980); L. A. Krefting, and A. P. Brief, "The Impact of Applicant Disability on Evaluation Judgments in the Selection Process," *Academy of Management Journal* 19 (1976), pp. 675–80; Stephan J. Motowidlo, "Sex Role Orientation and Behavior in a Work Setting," *Journal of Personality and Social Psychology* 42, no. 5 (1982), pp. 935–45; G. T. Fairhurst and B. K. Smavely, "Majority and Token Minority Group Relationships: Power Acquisition and Communications," *Academy of Management Review* 8, no. 2 (1983), pp. 292–300; David E. Bloom and Mark R. Killingsworth, "Pay Discrimination Research and Litigation: The Use of Regression," *Industrial Relations* 21, no. 3 (1982), pp. 318–40; John E. Hunter and Frank L. Schmidt, "Ability Tests: Economic Benefits versus the Issue of Fairness," *Industrial Relations* 21, no. 3 (1982), pp. 293–309; J. N. Cleveland and F. J. Landy, "The Effects of Person and Job Stereotypes on Two Personnel Decisions," *Journal of Applied Psychology* 68, no. 4 (1983), pp. 609–19.

49. Marvin D. Dunnette and Stephan J. Motowidlo, "Estimating Benefits and Costs of Antisexist Training Programs in Organizations," *Woman in the Work Force,* ed. H. John Bernardin (New York: Praeger Publishers, 1982), chap. 7.

50. Herbert Hill, "The AFL and the Black Worker: Twenty-Five Years after the Merger," *The Journal of Intergroup Relations,* Spring 1982, pp. 5–79.

51. Richard Freeman and Jonathan Leonard, *Union Maids: Unions and the Female Workforce* (Cambridge, Mass.: National Bureau of Economic Research, 1985); *Ourself: Women and Unions* (Washington, D.C.: Food and Beverage and Trades Department, AFL-CIO, 1981); American Federation of State, County and Municipal Employers, *You've Come a Long Way—Maybe* (Washington, D.C.: AFL-CIO, 1984).

52. Lisa Portman, Joy Ann Grune, and Eve Johnson, "The Role of Labor," in *Comparable Worth and Wage Discrimination,* ed. H. Remick (Philadelphia: Temple University Press, 1984).

four

ORGANIZATION CONDITIONS

CHAPTER OUTLINE

TRW, Inc., manufactures products ranging from microelectronic guidance systems for NASA to auto brakes for General Motors to zippers for Levi's jeans.[1] To compete effectively in such diverse markets, TRW is organized into three sectors: Electronics and Defense, Automotive World Wide, and Industrial and Energy. Each of these sectors is further subdivided into divisions and plants located throughout the United States and the world. The organization's conditions in the three sectors differ; so do many of their human resource programs. For example, the Electronics and Defense sector must recruit and retain electrical engineers and computer software specialists. These skills are currently enjoying a very high demand and escalating salaries. Thus, Electronics and Defense is operating under highly competitive labor market conditions. At the same time, the other two sectors have experienced less dependable markets and stiff foreign competition. Layoffs, retrenchment, changes in work rules, relocation and modernizing of plants and equipment, and controlled wage increases (even wage concessions) have been typical personnel actions in these sectors. So in one company different business units face different conditions. Some units are going after an increased share of expanding product markets; other units are regrouping to preserve their share of stable markets; still others are trying out new ventures with new ideas and products.

Contrast TRW to Jack's Auto Repair. Jack's pumps gas, services cars, and does minor repair work. Jack has a two-bay station, but as cars get more complex, it is getting harder and harder to keep up on the equipment and expertise needed to repair them. The regional marketing representative for the oil company suggested that Jack drop the repair-service part of the business and convert his garage into a convenience store. But Jack has no experience in marketing, purchasing, and inventorying convenience items. He is better at mechanics than mathematics. What business should Jack be in—auto service and repair or gasoline and other convenience items?

Jack's and TRW have something in common. No matter the size or complexity, differences in organization conditions influence human resource decisions. And in turn, human resources influence the nature of the organization. The demand for TRW's varied products translates into the need to employ diverse skills in TRW's work force. TRW's ability to successfully compete in its many markets depends, at least in part, on the ability of its employees to design, produce, and sell products. Similar relationships between product demand, human resources, and ability to compete are also present in small organizations.

ORGANIZATION CONDITIONS AND THE DIAGNOSTIC APPROACH

Which characteristics of organizations affect human resource decisions? Although they are probably limitless, this chapter discusses four key factors: financial conditions, technological change, culture and philosophy, and organization strategies.

Financial Conditions

An organization's financial condition is all too often ignored in models of human resource management. The ability to pay, the portion of wages that are fixed, funding for retraining workers and for all personnel activities are all affected by an organization's financial condition and its cash flow.[2] Examples of the importance of the employer's financial status are all around us. The current interest in a "shared economy" in which a portion of employee wages are tied to profits is one example.[3] Highly profitable periods bring larger bonuses, unprofitable periods yield no wage increases. The effect is to make a portion of wages a variable rather than a fixed cost; this offers employers greater financial flexibility. The effect on employees is greater uncertainty by placing more of their earnings at risk.

Chief executive officers are fond of proclaiming "Employees are our most important asset." Nonetheless, many manage as if employees are the most important expense. Expenditures on human resources ought to be evaluated as benefits as well as costs. More often than not, personnel expenses are treated as costs without attention to their returns.

Translating the benefits of many personnel decisions into dollar terms is difficult and requires technical knowledge.[4] Evaluating personnel decisions according to their effects on human resource objectives, their costs, and their benefits lies at the core of the diagnostic approach. This approach is applied through the book.

Technological Change

Technology can be defined as the processes and techniques used to generate goods and services. Investment in technology is reinventing how American organizations generate goods and services. Purchase of factory automation systems alone doubled to 18 billion between 1980 and 1985 and is expected to double again by 1990.[5] Automation systems include computer-integrated-manufacturing, computer-aided design, robotics, and just-in-time inventory systems. Technological change is a permanent feature of U.S. organizations that influences personnel decisions.

Despite all the dollars spent by American companies on technological changes, a persistent and troubling gap often exists between the hoped for results of the new technology and the managers' ability to put it to work effectively. General Electric Company (GE) discovered that it is important for the employees, as the users of technological innovations, to develop "ownership" of it. In their state-of-the-art dishwasher manufacturing plant, GE managers discovered that by involving employees in the installation and design of the new manufacturing system, the installation time and the quality of the products improved. Even more important were the training sessions that permitted employees to transfer their knowledge from the old operation to the new process. Even though the expenditures on the new system were originally justified through cost savings, innovative human resource management boosted the savings and productivity gains.

Culture and Philosophy

Experts have written volumes about the importance of corporate culture and philosophy in achieving employee and organization effectiveness.[6] Culture refers to the values, beliefs, and traditions shared by all members in an organization.[7] Despite the currency of the term, debate exists about such fundamental issues as what corporate culture really is, how it changes, and whether that change emanates from the top or the bottom of an organization. To some, the culture of an organization is the bedrock which gives it identity and stability. It is best reflected in day-to-day practices. To others, culture is a force that drives an organization to its goals. An example might be the eight principles shown in Exhibit 4–1.[8] According to Peters and Waterman, organizations that exemplify "excellence" exhibit these principles. Although such principles are appealing to managers, more rigorous research has yet to document the effects of these attributes of excellence.[9]

Still, a lot of managers believe culture is important to their success and is related to human resource management. A survey reported that 97 percent of the organizations agreed that corporate culture was important to their business success (though the survey sponsor neglected to report how many organizations were in the survey).[10] Exhibits 4–2 and 4–3 are examples of IBM's and Johnson & Johnson's corporate philosophies toward human resources. Their personnel programs are designed to be consistent with and supportive of these philosophies. Hence, IBM emphasizes individual merit pay, internal grievance ("speak up") programs for airing dissatisfactions, a generous benefits program, a minimum of 40 hours of

EXHIBIT 4–1
Eight Attributes of Excellent Companies

1. Bias for Action	"Getting on with it." "Not paralyzed by analysis."
2. Close to Customer	"Learn from customers." "Get product ideas from customers; provide highest quality service."
3. Autonomy and Entrepreneurship	"Foster many leaders and innovators through the organization."
4. Productivity through People	"Treat employees as the root source of quality and productivity gain." "Respect for the individual."
5. Hands-On Value Driven	"Basic philosophy of an organization has more to do with its achievements than do technological or economic resources, organization structure, or innovation."
6. Stick to the Knitting	"Never acquire a business you cannot run."
7. Simple Form, Lean Staff	"The underlying structural forms and systems in excellent companies are elegantly simple."
8. Simultaneously Tight–Loose Properties	"Excellent companies are both centralized and decentralized." "Autonomy down to the shop floor but centralized about a few guiding core values."

Source: Adapted from Thomas J. Peters and Robert H. Waterman, Jr., *In Search of Excellence* (New York: Harper & Row, 1983).

EXHIBIT 4–2
IBM Principles

Respect for the individual
Customer service
Excellence
Effective management leadership
Obligation to stockholders
Fair deal for suppliers
Corporate citizenship

human resource training for all new managers, and other programs designed to instill the IBM philosophy in all employees. Johnson & Johnson's Credo covers four constituencies: its customers, its employees, the communities in which it is located, and the stockholders.

Strategies

Strategy refers to an organization's basic directions, its long-term perspective, in other words, its major deployment of resources.[11] An example is U.S. Steel's dramatic decision in the face of foreign competition to focus

EXHIBIT 4–3

Our Credo

We believe our first responsibility is to the doctors, nurses and patients,
to mothers and all others who use our products and services.
In meeting their needs everything we do must be of high quality.
We must constantly strive to reduce our costs
in order to maintain reasonable prices.
Customers' orders must be serviced promptly and accurately.
Our suppliers and distributors must have an opportunity
to make a fair profit.

We are responsible to our employees,
the men and women who work with us throughout the world.
Everyone must be considered as an individual.
We must respect their dignity and recognize their merit.
They must have a sense of security in their jobs.
Compensation must be fair and adequate,
and working conditions clean, orderly and safe.
Employees must feel free to make suggestions and complaints.
There must be equal opportunity for employment, development
and advancement for those qualified.
We must provide competent management,
and their actions must be just and ethical.

We are responsible to the communities in which we live and work
and to the world community as well.
We must be good citizens — support good works and charities
and bear our fair share of taxes.
We must encourage civic improvements and better health and education.
We must maintain in good order
the property we are privileged to use,
protecting the environment and natural resources.

Our final responsibility is to our stockholders.
Business must make a sound profit.
We must experiment with new ideas.
Research must be carried on, innovative programs developed
and mistakes paid for.
New equipment must be purchased, new facilities provided
and new products launched.
Reserves must be created to provide for adverse times.
When we operate according to these principles,
the stockholders should realize a fair return.

Johnson & Johnson

on specialized steel products and to phase out those that foreign steel firms sell at lower prices.[12] Acquiring Marathon Oil Company also represented a strategic decision—a shift from reliance on basic steel to a greater diversification. In 1980 steel products accounted for 80 percent of total revenues at U.S. Steel; by 1986 steel accounted for less than 30 percent.[13] Oil and gas from the Marathon acquisition accounted for over 55 percent. Perhaps, the decision to change its name from U.S. Steel to USX reflects the dramatic strategic shift. Other examples of organizational strategies include Holiday Inns, Inc.'s decision to open gambling casinos in Atlantic City, and Jack's decision to purchase a McDonald's franchise rather than repair autos.

Strategic decisions involve choices, and these choices shape human resource decisions. USX's choices to reposition itself in specialty steels and to acquire Marathon involved major redeployment of human resources. The effects were dramatic: 150 steel plants were closed; 100,000 employees were laid off or retired; and employees are learning to compete with new products in new markets.

Just as an organization's strategies shape human resource decisions, so, too, do human resource decisions affect strategic choices. Perhaps, the most clear-cut examples are the selection of chief executives and top managers. Since these people are so involved in formulating strategies, changes in their ranks can have significant effects. US West, one of the "Baby Bells," has an ambitious strategy involving the marketing of a wide range of new voice and data communication equipment and services. However, US West developed its existing pool of executive talent to lead a traditional telephone company, not a risk-taking entrepreneurial enterprise. US West's ability to implement its new business strategy may be constrained by its previous human resource decisions.

Strategic Levels: Corporate, Unit, or Functional

Strategic decisions occur at three levels in the organization: the total organization, the unit, and the function.[14] The total organization refers to corporate decisions. Managers at this level decide what the organization's business should be. Unit-level decisions focus on parts of the organization, often called profit centers, lines of business, or business units (TRW's three sectors are examples). Managers at this level decide how to compete in their specific markets. Functional decisions involve particular components of the organization, such as marketing, finance, and, of course, human resources. At this level, managers adopt a strategy that will help their function contribute to the achievement of corporate and unit objectives. So the strategic issues addressed by managers at each level differ as Exhibit 4–4 shows. All organizations, even small ones like Jack's Auto Repair,

EXHIBIT 4–4
Issues at Three Strategic Levels

Strategic Level	Issue
Corporate	What business(es) should we be in?
Business units	How do we compete?
Functions	How do we contribute to business unit and corporate objectives?

must decide whether they want to fix cars or sell groceries or even hamburgers (What business should we be in?). They must choose which specific products and services to offer (How do we compete?) and decide whether to hire new employees with required skills or to train present employees to do new jobs, and how to deal with unions (How can we contribute to the unit and corporate objectives?).

Strategic Types: Diversification and Market Share

Within organization levels strategies are classified in a variety of ways. At the corporate level analysts classify an organization by how diversified or integrated its product lines are.[15] (Exhibit 4–4: What businesses should we

EXHIBIT 4–5
Characteristics of Business Strategic Types

Strategy	Characteristics
Start-up	High financial risk
	Limited management team cohesiveness
	No organization, systems, or procedures in place
	No operational experience base
	Endless workload: multiple priorities
	Generally insufficient resources to satisfy all demands
	Limited relationship with suppliers, customers, and environment
Turnaround	Time pressure for "results": need for rapid situational assessment and decision making
	Poor results, but business is worth saving
	Weak competitive position
	Eroded morale: low-esteem cohesion
	Inadequate systems: possible weak or bureaucratic organizational infrastructure
	Strained and eroded relationships with suppliers, customers, and environment
	Lack of appropriate leadership: period of neglect
	Limited resources: skills shortages: some incompetent personnel

EXHIBIT 4–5 *(continued)*

Strategy	*Characteristics*
Extract profit rationalize existing business	"Controlled" financial risk
	Unattractive industry in long term: possible need to invest selectively, but major new investments not likely to be worthwhile
	Internal organizational stability
	Moderate-to-high managerial technical competence
	Adequate systems and administrative infrastructure
	Acceptable to excellent relationships with suppliers, customers, and environment
Dynamic growth in existing business	Moderate-to-high financial risk
	New markets, products, technology
	Multiple demands and conflicting priorities
	Rapidly expanding organization in certain sectors
	Inadequate managerial technical financial resources to meet all demands
	Unequal growth across sectors of organization
	Likely shifting power bases as growth occurs
	Constant dilemma between doing current work and building support systems for the future
Redeployment of efforts in existing business	Low-moderate, short-term risk; high long-term risk
	Resistance to change: likely bureaucracy in some sections
	High mismatch between some organization skill sets, technology, people versus needs created by redefined strategy
	Likelihood of lack of strategic planning for some historical period—highly operational orientation to executive team
Liquidation divestiture of poorly performing business	Weak competitive position, unattractive industry, or both
	Likely continuance of poor returns
	Possible morale problems and skills shortages
	Little opportunity for turnaround or redeployment due to unsatisfactory "payback"
	Need to cut losses and make tough decisions
New acquisitions	Acquisitions may fall into one of the above situations. In addition, the following conditions characterize a recent acquisition situation:
	Pressure on new management to "prove themselves"
	Existing management ambivalent defensive about change
	Fundamental need to integrate acquired company with parent at some levels

Source: Reprinted from "Strategic Selection—Matching Executives to Business Conditions," by M. Gerstein and H. Reisman, SLOAN MANAGEMENT REVIEW 24, no. 2 (1983), pp. 33–49, by permission of the publisher, copyright © 1983 by the SMR Association. All rights reserved.

be in?) Firms like McDonald's or IBM where a large portion of revenues are accounted for by single or related product lines are said to be integrated. More diversified firms, like TRW or General Electric (with over 40 business units), are in multiple lines of businesses, none of which account for the lion's share of corporate revenues.

At the business unit level (Exhibit 4–4: How do we compete?) business strategies are expressed in relative market share. Exhibit 4–5 defines seven strategic types in more detail: start-up, turnaround, profit, growth, redeployment, liquidation, and acquisition.[16]

What does all this have to do with human resources management? As depicted in Exhibit 4–6, the decisions managers make about their human resources need to be related to the characteristics of the organization and to the conditions in the external environment. So the financial, technological, cultural, and strategic characteristics of the organization, coupled with relevant environmental forces, are directly related to the choices managers make regarding human resources. The pattern exhibited in these choices becomes the human resources strategy of the organization.

STRATEGIC HUMAN RESOURCE MANAGEMENT

Definition

The *human resource strategy* of an organization refers to its fundamental approach toward its employees; the pattern of human resource decisions made by managers reflect strategies and are directly related to organizational and environmental conditions. The approaches to the separate human resource activities are integrated to provide a unified pattern to the employment relationship which is consistent with organization conditions and strategies.

This definition focuses attention on three things: (1) the choices managers make regarding the employment relationship, (2) the effects of environmental pressures on the organization and on human resources, and (3) the relationship between organization conditions and managers' decisions regarding human resources. Human resource strategy positions the organization in relation to the pressures in its environment and guides managers' personnel decisions.

Exhibit 4–7 describes an example of a human resource strategy recommended for manufacturing firms.[17] The strategy here specifies a job

EXHIBIT 4–6
Conditions Affecting Strategic Human Resource Management

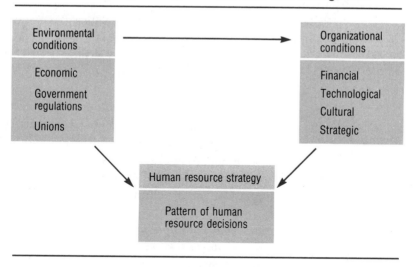

EXHIBIT 4–7
Human Resource Strategies for Manufacturing Firms

Management philosophy: Treat employees as valued contributing members of the team; individuals desire challenging jobs and seek responsibility and autonomy.

Job design: Work is multiskilled and performed by teamwork where possible. Encourage relatively flat organizational structures with few reporting levels; employees' suggestions are valued.

Training and security: Employees are valued resources and are constantly retrained in new skills.

Wages: Pay is based on skills acquired. Group incentives and profit sharing plans tie effort and performance to pay.

Labor relations: Emphasis is on mutual interests. Management shares information about business. Labor shares responsibility for making the firm succeed.

design approach, the nature of training and employment security, the basis for pay determination, and an approach to labor relations. The pattern or overall approach integrates the employer's approach to the employment relationship. Many believe that adopting this specific strategy results in more effective employees and organizations. The actual payoffs from such a strategy, however, remain to be studied.

Organizational Conditions and Human Resource Strategies

Miles and Snow were among the first to study the relationship between organization conditions and human resource management.[18] They classify organizations as three basic types, shown at the top of Exhibit 4–8. These three types are defined primarily by their approaches to product/service markets. Briefly, they are:

Defenders: Organizations operating in a few stable product markets. Managers are highly expert in their limited areas of operation but tend not to search for new product opportunities. Primary attention is on improving the efficiency of existing operations. Examples may include units of larger firms, such as Honeywell's residential division, which produces climate control devices (thermostats and air cleaners) or Lincoln Electric, which produces generators.

Prospectors: Organizations that continually search for new product and market opportunities and regularly take risks. Managers of these organizations tend to be creators of change and uncertainty, to which their market competitors must respond. The emphasis is on research and development, and on being first on the market with unique products, rather than on efficiency. An example in the computer industry seems to be Apple Computer, Inc., which tries to introduce new and innovative personal computers before its competitors do, or Hewlett-Packard Company, which concentrates on technically unique products.

Analyzers: Organizations that operate in many product markets, some relatively stable, others changing. Managers in the stable areas operate routinely and efficiently through formalized structures and activities. In the more dynamic areas, managers watch competitors for new ideas, then rapidly adopt the most promising. Examples include Merck and Company; Texas Instruments Incorporated; and 3M Company.

Snow and Miles state that this typology is most useful when applied to business unit and functional levels of organizations rather than to corporate-level decisions.[19]

Contingent Human Resource Strategies

A major point in the diagnostic approach is that human resource decisions are related to the nature of the organization. As shown in the bottom half of Exhibit 4–8, each of Miles and Snow's three organizational types has a different approach to the human resource decisions listed in our diagnostic model. On one hand, a "defender" organization tends to design formal planning activities, hire new employees into entry-level jobs, promote from within for higher-level jobs, and focus on internal pay relationships

EXHIBIT 4–8
Organization Types and Human Resource Management Activities

Organizational Characteristics	Type A (Defender)	Type B (Prospector)	Type C (Analyzer)
Typical company	Lincoln Electric	Hewlett-Packard	Texas Instruments
Product-market strategy	Limited, stable product line; predictable markets	Broad, changing product line; changing markets	Stable and changing product line; predictable and changing markets
Research and development	Limited mostly to product improvement	Extensive; emphasis on "first-to-market"	Focused; emphasis on "second-to-market"
Production	High volume/low cost; emphasis on efficiency and process engineering	Customized; prototypical emphasis on effectiveness and product design	High volume/low cost; emphasis on process engineering
Marketing	Limited mostly to sales	Focused heavily on market research	Extensive marketing campaigns
Human Resource Management Activities			
Basic role	Maintenance	Entrepreneurial	Coordination
Human resource planning	Formal; extensive	Informal; limited	Formal; extensive
Recruitment, selection, and placement	Make	Buy	Make and buy
Training and development	Skill building	Skill identification and application	Skill building and application
Compensation	Internal pay relationships; internal equity	External pay relationships; external competitiveness	Internal consistency and external competitiveness, a blend
Performance appraisal	Process-oriented; focus on training needs, individual/group performance	Results-oriented; focus on staffing needs, division/corporate performance	Mostly process-oriented; training and staffing needs, individual/group/division performance

among employees. "Prospectors," on the other hand, seek more entrepreneurial managers who may hire experienced employees at all job levels in
the organization, tolerate only limited formal planning procedures, emphasize specific and technical training, and ensure that pay rates are competitive with those paid by competing employers.

The State of Knowledge

Before leaving this section on strategic human resource management, let
us consider the state of knowledge in the field. This requires a note of
caution. Research about which specific human resource strategies fit the
various organization and environmental conditions is not well developed.
Research suggests that differences in the nature of organizations, particularly in the product market strategies each pursue, are related to human
resource strategies.[20] We can even describe which personnel activities
seem to fit with different organization conditions. But that is all that we
can do—describe the strategies that different organizations have adopted.
The field is not advanced enough to prescribe. Studies of the payoffs of
various human resource strategies under different environmental and organization conditions have yet to be conducted.

MERGERS AND ACQUISITIONS

Corporate mergers and acquisitions serve as classic illustrations of how
personnel practices that serve well under one set of organization conditions simply do not fit under another set. Merger activities are occurring
more frequently than at any time in U.S. history.[21] In 1986 alone, over
2,700 mergers and acquisitions were recorded.[22] The most common reasons for these combinations are to increase market share, enter new markets, and acquire technology or economics of scale. Yet some argue that
from one third to one half of all mergers fail to realize their intended
objectives. Many disappointments are due to unanticipated human resource problems.

The merger of INA Corporation and Connecticut General, two insurance firms, is a case in point. Exhibit 4–9 contrasts the two firms. From a
financial perspective, the merger made sense. INA was in the cyclical
property and casualty insurance business. Connecticut General's business
centered in the more stable life and health insurance and pension markets.
Each had evolved very different human resource strategies. As Exhibit
4–9 summarizes, INA was more free wheeling, emphasized risk taking and
hired people at all levels of the firm. Connecticut General, on the other
hand, developed people from within, and used a very formal planning and

EXHIBIT 4–9
Merger of Connecticut General and INA Corporation

	Connecticut General	INA
Product markets	Group life, health, pensions	Property and casualty
	Steady growth	Boom/Bust cycles
Management style	"The process"; goals and timetables	Smart risk taking; free wheeling
Staffing and development	Promote from within; grow our own	Hire experienced talent
Pay	Based on job level, individual merit; liberal benefits	Based on market pressures, performance bonuses; lean benefits
Employee relations	Part of CG family; company store, bus, bowling alley	Respect employee independence and privacy

goal-setting process. A merger of the two complementary sets of products seemed to make sense. But the initial result was chaos—the two very different cultures with different human resource strategies clashed. A case at the end of Part 1 offers an opportunity to analyze this merger in greater detail.

At present, personnel issues become salient in the postacquisition phase, after the merger decisions have been approved. Many argue that the human resource implications need to be considered earlier in the preacquisition phase to help ensure its success.

HUMAN RESOURCE DEPARTMENTS: STRUCTURES AND STAFFS

In this chapter we have discussed the relationship between organizational conditions and human resource management without considering the human resource department itself. As a management specialty, human resource departments are designed to support the operation of the organization. Consequently, structural arrangements for personnel departments vary widely—reflecting the wide variety of organizations they support. Two factors in the design of personnel departments deserve special attention, the extent of decentralization, and the effects of the decentralization on staffing patterns within the personnel function.

Centralized—Decentralized

An important issue related to structuring the function revolves around centralized or decentralized. Decentralization means that separate organization units design and administer their own human resource activities. This contrasts with centralization, which locates the design and administration responsibility in a single corporate unit. Some firms, such as IBM, 3M Company, Merck & Company, and General Mills, have relatively large corporate staffs who formulate human resource strategies and design activities. Exhibit 4–10 shows a centralized human resource management structure. Administration of human resource activities falls to those working in various units, often personnel generalists. Generalists handle all personnel activities, rather than specializing in planning, staffing, training, labor relations, or compensation.

Highly decentralized organizations, such as TRW, employ small corporate human resource staffs (professionals) whose primary responsibility is managing personnel systems for executive and corporate staff. These professionals operate in a purely advisory capacity to other organization units. The units in turn may employ their own human resource specialists (e.g., compensation or staffing specialists) and generalists. Exhibit 4–11 shows TRW's decentralized human resource structure. Each sector, Automotive World Wide (AWW), Electronics and Defense (E&D), and Industrial and Energy (I&E) has its own human resource staff plus generalists located in the subunits. The relationship of these sector staffs to corporate is advisory only (dotted line). The primary reporting relation (solid line) is to the sector line managers.

Another structural variation, found at Honeywell, Inc. and the reorganized AT&T, treats the corporate human resource function as internal consultants. As such, the human resource professionals must market and "sell" their products and services to the operating units. Certain activities, such as benefit plans and corporate profit sharing, remain under control of the corporate group. The responsibility for other activities, such as recruiting, hiring, pay, and training, is delegated to the units. The unit managers may decide to adopt corporate's services, design their own, or even use outside consultants.

Decentralizing certain aspects of personnel administration has considerable appeal. Pushing these responsibilities (and expenses) closer to the units and managers affected by them may help ensure that decisions are related to the organizational objectives. However, decentralization is not without dilemmas. Problems occur in treating employees consistently across units. So, too, do problems of designing human resource activities

EXHIBIT 4–10 Merck's Centralized Human Resource Structure

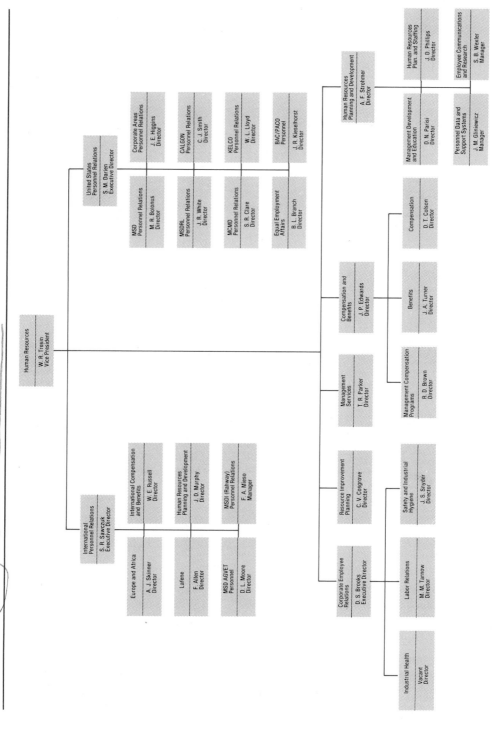

EXHIBIT 4–11
TRW's Decentralized Human Resource Structure

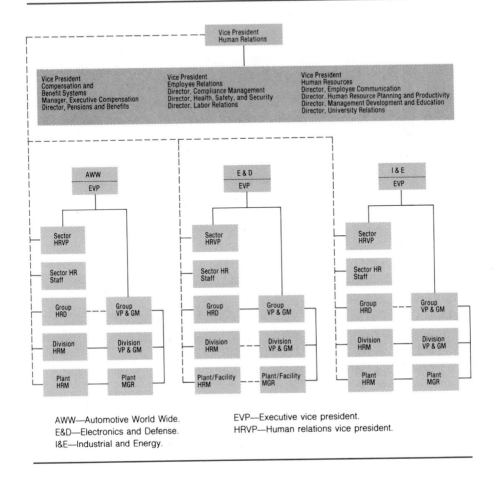

AWW—Automotive World Wide.
E&D—Electronics and Defense.
I&E—Industrial and Energy.

EVP—Executive vice president.
HRVP—Human relations vice president.

that support a unit's objectives but run counter to the overall corporate objectives.

The answer to these and related problems of decentralization lie in developing a set of corporate principles or guidelines that all must meet. For example, a decentralized employer would permit different personnel activities to be adopted by the units as long as the plans could be shown to be (1) job related, (2) business related, (3) acceptable to managers and employees, (4) cost-effective, and (5) able to withstand legal challenge.

Generalist—Specialist

Human resource professionals can be either specialists or generalists. Specialists possess the technical knowledge and experience related to particular activities; compensation, benefits, staffing, and labor relations are examples. Generalists, like general managers, have a working knowledge of most aspects of human resource management. They possess breadth but not the depth of technical knowledge of a specialist. Corporate levels tend to retain specialists while generalists handle business unit and individual facilities. Consequently, highly decentralized organizations employ more generalists with a lean staff of specialists providing support at the corporate level. Highly centralized firms, on the other hand, are more likely to have larger portions of specialists on their staffs.

SUMMARY

Organizations adopt different approaches to human resources: Some promote from within, while others hire experienced people; some seek cooperative relations with unions, while others aggressively avoid them. Some offer employment security and retraining, others do not; and some base pay on group performance and profit sharing, while others use individual performance schemes. These differences are not simply the result of varying environmental conditions. Even though pressures in external environment, economic forces, government regulations, and union pressures affect human resource decisions, organization factors also play a significant role. To better understand differences in human resource decisions, we need to assess differences in organizations as well as environmental conditions.

With a diagnostic approach, managers assess the conditions of the organization before they make human resource decisions. We analyzed four important conditions in this chapter: financial, technological, cultural, and strategic.

Strategies are integrated patterns of decisions made about employees. Strategic human resource management links pressures from the external environment, discussed in the previous two chapters, with the conditions faced within the organization.

We turn next to discuss another feature of organizations that is important when making personnel decisions: the nature of the work that is done in the organization.

DISCUSSION AND REVIEW QUESTIONS

1. Why is a strategic perspective considered so pivotal in human resource decision making?
2. Reread the seven business strategies discussed in Exhibit 4–5. Develop human resource strategies for each of them. How do your human resource strategies for a business following a turnaround strategy differ from those following growth or emerging strategies?
3. Which human resource issues would you consider during a preacquisition phase of a merger?
4. Discuss the skills, abilities, and experiences you believe are required for a human resource professional. Does this make any difference if the firm is centralized or decentralized or if the job is for a specialist or a generalist?
5. What are some key human resource issues at each strategic level?

NOTES AND REFERENCES

1. TRW Human Relations Strategic Corporate Plan (Cleveland, Ohio: TRW Corporate Human Resources Department, 1987).
2. To pursue more rigorous economic analysis see Robert Flanagan, Robert Smith, and Ronald G. Ehrenberg, *Labor Economics and Labor Relations* (Glenview, Ill.: Scott, Foresman, 1984).
3. Martin L. Weitzman, *The Share Economy: Conquering Stagflation* (Boston: Harvard University Press, 1984).
4. J. W. Boudreau, "Effects of Employee Flows on Utility Analysis on Human Resource Productivity Improvement Programs," *Journal of Applied Psychology* 68 (1983), pp. 396–407; J. W. Boudreau, "Economic Considerations in Estimating the Utility of Human Resource Productivity Improvement Programs," *Personnel Psychology* 36 (1983), pp. 551–57; W. F. Cascio and V. Silbey, "Utility of the Assessment Center as a Selection Device," *Journal of Applied Psychology* 64 (1979), pp. 107–18; Ira T. Kay and Martin Leshner, *Human Resource Costs and Business Strategy: Striving for Competitive Advantage in the Pharmaceutical Industry* (New York: The Hay Group, 1986); and Lyle M. Spencer, Jr., *Calculating Human Resource Costs and Benefits* (New York: John Wiley & Sons, 1986).
5. George L. Whaley, "The Impact of Robotics Technology upon Human Resource Management," *Personnel Administrator*, September 1982, pp. 61–71; Dorothy Leonard-Barton and William A. Kraus, "Implementing New Technology," *Harvard Business Review*, November–December 1985, pp. 102–10; "High Tech to the Rescue," *Business Week*, June 16, 1986, pp. 100–104; and *Computerized Manufacturing Activities: Employment, Education, and the Workplace* (Washington, D.C.: U.S. Congress, Office of Technology Assessment, 1987).
6. Melissa A. Berman, ed., *Corporate Culture and Change* (New York: The Conference Board, 1986); Terence E. Deal and Allan A. Kennedy, *Corporate Cultures* (Reading, Mass.: Addison–Wesley Publishing, 1982); Jay B. Barney, "Organizational Culture: Can It Be a Source of Sustained Compet-

itive Advantage?" *Academy of Management Review*, July 1986, pp. 656–65; Manfred F. R. Kets de Vries and Danny Miller, "Personality, Culture, and Organization," *Academy of Management Review*, April 1986, pp. 266–79; and Sally J. Blank, "Hershey: A Company Driven by Values," *Personnel*, February 1987, pp. 46–51.

7. M. Davis, "Corporate Culture and Human Resource Management," *Human Resource Planning* 6, no. 3 (1983), pp. 17–35; Berman, *Corporate Culture and Change;* Andrew M. Pettigrew, "On Studying Organizational Cultures," *Administrative Science Quarterly*, December 1979, pp. 570–81.

8. Thomas J. Peters and Robert H. Waterman, Jr., *In Search of Excellence*, (New York: Harper & Row, 1983).

9. John Pfeffer, "Schlock for Sale: A Review of *In Search of Excellence*," *Science '84*, 2, no. 6 (1984), p. 18.

10. Howard Schwartz and Stanley M. Davis, "Matching Corporate Culture and Business Strategy," *Organizational Dynamics*, Summer 1981, pp. 36–48.

11. Gloria deBejar and George Milkovich, "Human Resource Strategy at the Business Level" (paper presented at National Academy of Management Meetings, Chicago, August 1986); C. W. Hofer and D. Schendel, *Strategy Formulation: Analytical Concepts* (St. Paul, Minn.: West Publishing, 1978); H. Mintzberg, "Patterns in Strategy Formulation," *Management Science* 24 (1978), pp. 934–48; Lee Dyer, "Strategic Human Resources Management and Planning," in *Research in Personnel and Human Resources Management*," vol. 3, ed. K. M. Rowland and F. R. Ferris (Greenwich, Conn.: JAI Press, 1985), pp. 1–30; and Richard E. Walton and Gerald I. Susman, "People Policies for the New Machines," *Harvard Business Review*, March–April 1987, pp. 98–106.

12. "The Toughest Job in Business: How They're Remaking U.S. Steel," *Business Week*, February 25, 1985, pp. 50–56.

13. USX Annual Report, 1986.

14. George Milkovich, "Human Resource Strategy and Evaluation: Introduction," *Industrial Relations* 23, no. 2 (1984), pp. 151–55; Lee Dyer, "Studying Human Resource Strategy: An Approach and an Agenda," *Industrial Relations* 23, no. 2 (1984), pp. 156–69; John W. Boudreau, "Decision Theory Contributions to HRM Research and Practice," *Industrial Relations* 23, no. 2 (1984), pp. 198–217.

15. R. P. Rumelt, *Strategy, Structure, and Economic Performance* (Boston: Harvard Business School, 1974); and M. Leontiades, *Strategies for Diversification and Change* (Boston: Little, Brown, 1980).

16. R. S. Schuler and I. C. MacMillan, "Gaining Competitive Advantage through Human Resource Management Practices," *Human Resource Management*, Fall 1984, pp. 241–55; R. S. Schuler, "Personnel and Human Resource Management Choices and Corporate Strategy," in *Readings in Personnel and Human Resource Management*, ed. R. S. Schuler and S. A. Youngblood (St. Paul, Minn.: West Publishing, 1987); Kim Cameron and Raymond F. Zammuto, "Matching Managerial Strategies to Conditions of Decline," *Human Resource Management Journal* 22, 1984, pp. 359–76; F. K. Foulkes, *Strategic Human Resource Management* (Englewood Cliffs, N.J.: Prentice Hall, 1986).

17. D. Q. Mills, *The New Competitors* (New York: Free Press, 1985).

18. R. E. Miles and C. C. Snow, *Organizational Strategy, Structure, and Processes* (New York: McGraw-Hill, 1978).
19. C. C. Snow and R. E. Miles, "Organizational Strategy, Design, and Human Resource Management" (paper presented at National Academy of Management meetings, Dallas, 1983).
20. deBejar and Milkovich, "Human Resource Strategy at the Business Level"; Dyer, "Strategic Human Resources Management and Planning."
21. David Robino and Kenneth DeMeuse, "Corporate Mergers and Acquisitions: Their Impact on HRM," *Personnel Administrator*, November 1985, pp. 33–44; and M. L. Marks, "Merging Human Resources: A Review of Current Research," *Mergers and Acquisitions* 2, no. 17 (1982), pp. 38–44.
22. Robert W. Swaim, "Mergers—The Personnel Squeeze," *Personnel Journal*, April 1985, pp. 34–40; Michael C. Jensen, "Takeovers: Folklore and Science," *Harvard Business Review*, November–December 1984, pp. 109–21; and David B. Jemison and Sim Sitkin, "Corporate Acquisitions: A Process Perspective," *Academy of Management Review* 11, 1 (1986), pp. 145–63.

chapter

five

THE NATURE OF WORK

CHAPTER OUTLINE

VII. Summary

> I put on my hard hat, change into my safety shoes, put on my safety glasses, go to the bonderizer. They rake the metal, they wash it, they dip it in a paint solution, and we take it off. My arms get tired about the first half hour. After that, they don't get tired any more until maybe the last half hour at the end of the day.
>
> Interview with steelworker, *Working*, by Studs Terkel[1]

> Everything that happens in the market I see instantaneously. I have a machine in front of me that records and memorizes every transaction that takes place in the entire day. I watch 18 million, 20 million shares pass the tape. I look at every symbol, every transaction. I would go out of my mind, but my eye has been conditioned to screen maybe two hundred stocks and ignore the others. I pick up with my eyes Goodrich, but I don't see ITT. There are over 3,200 symbols. I drop the other 3,000. Otherwise I'd go mad. I really put in an enormously exhausting day.
>
> Interview with stockbroker, *Working*, by Studs Terkel[2]

Work is a coat of many colors. It requires different tasks to be performed, different qualifications to perform it, and different pay offered to those who perform it. This variety is what makes work so difficult to define. A common definition is "purposeful effort." But a wag responds, "If work is purposeful effort, what is golf?"[3]

This chapter examines the nature of work and its role in the management of human resources; it also discusses alternative approaches to job design and job analysis.

A DIAGNOSTIC APPROACH TO ASSESSING WORK

Work is a critical concept in human resources management. The skills and experience required to perform work influence the education and training people seek. Work influences the pay employees receive, and thus their economic well-being. Many people find status and personal fulfillment in their work. So the nature of work interacts with the environment, other conditions in the organization, and individual employees—all human resource conditions found in our diagnostic model.

External Conditions

Technology plays a key role in the changing nature of work.[4] Computer-assisted design eliminates tedious drafting; laser copiers eliminate keyboarding routine information; robots lessen the risk of exposure to dangerous organisms or chemicals in the laboratory or factory. Many of the dirty, dangerous, and boring aspects of work are eliminated through new technology. Many employees are wary of new technologies, however, fearing high tech threatens their job security.[5] Greater employee autonomy and participation in decisions that affect how work is structured can help allay these fears. Under such conditions, employees and organizations have greater flexibility in adapting to continuing changes in work.[6]

Government regulation, another external factor, also affects the nature of work. Safety regulations, wage and hour limitations, even EEO pressures affect how work is done. For example, as part of its affirmative action efforts, AT&T redesigned its outside crafts jobs so that women could perform them more readily.[7] Their research found problems with an extension ladder that was hard for women to handle and a safety harness used by workers in climbing telephone poles. Also, AT&T restructured a particularly grueling training program by spreading the hard physical labor over a longer period of time—to benefit men as well as women.

Union restrictions have both a positive and a negative effect on the way work is done.[8] On the positive side, unions have long led the fight for safer conditions and shorter hours. On the other hand, many work rules written into union contracts have hindered the introduction of technological changes required to increase efficiency.

Organizational Conditions

An organization's basic decisions about technology, goods, or services delineate the nature of work in that particular plant. Allegheny Ludlum, for example, sells specialty steel that it produces from raw steel made from iron ore. Allegheny has many options. It can buy partially finished steel and finish it to customers' specifications, or it can buy iron ore to smelt in its own furnace. Many factors go into Allegheny's decision on which business strategy to pursue, but whatever decision it makes determines the nature of the work done at Allegheny. All organizations face similar issues. The strategies and objectives that managers choose affect the work to be performed.

Individual Conditions

Sometimes it is difficult to distinguish between the work and the person performing it. For example, even though Ray Charles and Billy Joel sing the same song, they do it very differently. When it hires a marketing manager, or a financial vice president, or a professor to utilize the unique talents of a specific individual, an organization fully anticipates that this individual will structure the work somewhat differently than another individual.

Employees at all levels affect the nature of the work performed.[9] Experienced employees may adopt shortcuts. Employees in close proximity may swap tasks with co-workers. Indeed, work may change in response to factors of which the managers may not even be aware.

ASSESSING WORK

We started this chapter with two people describing their work. They discuss the tasks they perform, the abilities required, and the rewards (or lack of them) for doing the work. These are the same three types of information that human resource managers typically use to assess work.

Definition

The *nature of work* includes:
1. The content—tasks, behaviors, duties, relationships, responsibilities.
2. The qualifications required to perform it—skills, abilities, experience.
3. The returns and rewards for performing it—pay, promotions, and intrinsic satisfaction.

Content

Work content typically focuses on either the specific *tasks* done—the purpose of each task, and what each task accomplishes—or on some specific *behavior* that occurs (e.g., advising, negotiating, writing, lifting, assembling).

Qualifications

Qualifications describe the skills and abilities, the personality makeup, and the experience and knowledge required to perform the work satisfactorily. Data about these qualifications are necessary to perform recruiting, selecting, compensating, and training activities. Data on work qualifications also help ensure compliance with EEO regulations. It would be impossible to match individuals with work without details on the precise qualifications required for different jobs.

Rewards and Returns

The rewards and returns from work are either *extrinsic* or *intrinsic*. Extrinsic rewards are external to the individual and relatively concrete. Examples include pay, benefits, promotions, praise, and pleasant working conditions. Intrinsic rewards are more conceptual—less observable to others—and to some extent less controllable by others. Examples include feelings of accomplishment, freedom, or autonomy in the work.[10]

Caution must be exercised, however, because people do not always agree on what is intrinsically and extrinsically rewarding. "Past experiences, present roles, expectations, may result in different perceptions and definitions of the same work."[11] People with differing educations, backgrounds, aspirations, or reference groups may see the content, qualifications, and rewards of work differently. Do you think the steelworker would enjoy being a stockbroker? Or vice versa?

The three aspects that usually assess work are content, qualifications, and rewards. These data in turn are used in two procedures, job design and job analysis. Job design assigns job content and responsibilities to members of the organization. Job analysis collects information about jobs and the relationships among jobs so that human resource decisions can be made in a systematic way.

JOB DESIGN

Definition

Job design integrates work content (tasks, functions, relationships), the rewards (extrinsic and intrinsic), and the qualifications required (skills, knowledge, abilities) for each job in a way that meets the needs of employees and the organization.

The design of jobs has a critical impact on organization and employee objectives. From the organization's perspective, the way tasks and responsibilities are grouped can affect productivity and costs.[12] Jobs that are not satisfying or are too demanding are difficult to fill. Boring jobs may experience higher turnover. For an employee, motivation and job satisfaction are affected by the match between job factors (content, qualifications, and rewards) and personal needs. Therefore, the thoughtful design of jobs can help both the organization and its employees achieve their objectives.

Four Techniques

These four job designs affect the degree of specialization and the psychological dimensions of work:

Work Simplification. This approach leads to very specialized jobs. In work simplification, the complete job (such as making a car) is broken down into small subparts, usually consisting of a few operations. This is done so that less well-trained and less well-paid employees can do these jobs. Many small jobs can also be performed simultaneously, so that the complete operation can be done more quickly.

Job Rotation. In job rotation, the employees take turns performing several work-simplified jobs. Job rotation provides more flexible work assignments, makes it easier to staff unpleasant or heavier jobs, and reduces the boredom and monotony of work-simplified jobs.

Borg-Warner Corporation uses job rotation at its drive chain assembly plant. For instance, an employee may be qualified to operate both a chain assembly machine and a forklift. If the plant manager needs the forklift operated, the employee is assigned to do it, but is paid at the higher assembly operator rate. The advantage of this system to the organization is a flexible, better trained work force. However, employees are paid at the highest job rate for which they qualify. Higher average wages may be offset because fewer employees are required. The advantage to the employee is the potential for high wages plus increased motivation and satisfaction resulting from the job rotation.[13]

Job Enlargement. Job enlargement is the opposite of work simplification. In contrast to the work-simplified job consisting of three operations, the job enlargement approach expands until a meaningful component or part is completed by one person. The theory is that whole jobs reduce boredom (through more variety) and give more meaning to work. Critics say that enlargement often simply assigns more tasks to employees without affecting their motivation.[14]

Job Enlargement

Two operations	Basic tasks JOB 1 Five operations	Two operations

← ————————————— **Increased** ————————————— →

In the preceding diagram, Job 1 has five operations. To enlarge its scope, four operations could be added: two from the job that precedes it and two from the job that follows. Enlargement serves to increase variety, lengthen cycle time, provide the task with more wholeness and identity, and increase the knowledge necessary to perform it.

Job Enrichment. Job enrichment increases the responsibility of the workers and gives them more autonomy and control. Enrichment increases the *vertical scope* of a job, as shown for Job 2 in the following diagram. For instance, an employee might be expected not only to perform certain operations on the product but also to order the materials necessary for these operations and inspect them for quality control purposes. Essentially, this enrichment takes some of the authority from supervisors (or other departments) and adds it to the job. Thus it can increase an employee's authority, responsibility, and autonomy. The advantages claimed for job enrichment include greater intrinsic rewards available to employees, which in turn reduce absenteeism and turnover.[15]

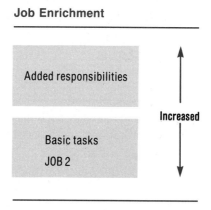

Job Enrichment

Added responsibilities

Basic tasks

JOB 2

Increased

How does job enrichment differ from job enlargement? The key difference is control. Job enlargement does not increase employees' discretion over what they do or how or when they do it. It merely provides a greater variety in tasks to relieve the monotony of overspecialized jobs. However, it does at least create the possibility that employees can be proud of what they produce. Job enrichment, on the other hand, gives employees greater responsibility and control of their work. By increasing employee authority, managers hope to increase employees' feelings of personal achievement, competency, and satisfaction. Theory suggests that such feelings increase employee motivation as well as productivity.[16]

Job Design Theories

Exhibit 5–1 shows how these job design techniques relate to various job design theories. Even though the theories are listed in historical order, from scientific management to sociotechnical, this does not mean that the older theories are no longer useful. As the diagnostic model emphasizes, the utility of alternative techniques depends on the particular situation. And as the exhibit points out, each theory has advantages and disadvantages.

Scientific Management

First outlined by Frederick W. Taylor in 1911, "scientific management" emphasized the production process of work.[17] Taylor's writings have been the basis for many jobs and organizations since that time.

Taylor's early experiences as chief engineer at the Midvale Iron Company in Pennsylvania influenced his understanding of the goals of job design. After studying the technical aspects of the production process, the individual, and the groups employees form, he calculated standards and specific methods based on the systematic organization of this information.

Taylor's methods emphasized the following components:

- Narrow range of tasks that made up a job.
- Very specific job descriptions.
- Systematic routing and scheduling of work.
- Close supervision.

The core of the approach rested with the reduction of each job to its most essential elements (job simplification) to be performed under close supervision.

Taylor's scientific management principles were an early systematic effort at job design. By focusing on the close supervision and setting standards that contained little flexibility, many managers abused his system. The hated "foreman" or "drive" system arose, in which standards were rigidly enforced, with little regard for employees' physical needs and safety, much less their psychological needs.[18] Dissatisfaction, alienation, and frustration resulted. The human relations movement identified these problems.

Human Relations

The human relations movement was in large part a reaction against the dehumanizing aspects of scientific management carried to an extreme. Rather than emphasizing the production needs of the organization, the human relations movement looked at jobs from the perspective of the individual worker.[19] The movement grew out of studies done by E. Mayo in

EXHIBIT 5-1

Job Design Theory	Techniques	Advantages	Disadvantages
Scientific management	Work simplification	Creates jobs that are safe, simple, reliable. Minimizes the mental demands on employees.	Boring, demeaning.
	Job rotation	Increases organization flexibility.	Jobs may still be boring.
	Job enlargement	Can reduce waiting time between tasks, enhance organization flexibility, reduce support staff needs.	May lose the advantages of work simplification without offsetting the disadvantages.
Human relations	Work groups	Recognizes importance of social needs of employees.	Gives little technical guidance.
Job characteristics	Job enrichment	Creates jobs that "engage" the employee, boost motivation, satisfaction, production.	Costly. Accident/error potential increases. May require additional employees. Control still rests with managers.
Sociotechnical	Work teams	Gives employees a great deal of control over jobs. Most successful in new plants, where technology allows this approach. Facilitates introduction of new technology.	Requires compatible organization design, careful structuring of teams. Relationships among teams must be managed. Some work may still be boring. A lot of time devoted to nonproduction issues.

the early 1920s, now referred to as the Hawthorne Studies.[20] The Hawthorne Studies mark a critical turning point, away from an excessive emphasis on the technical aspects of job design and toward a recognition of the social needs of workers and how these needs affect performance. The original goal of the Hawthorne Studies at the Western Electric Company's Hawthorne plant in 1924 was to test how variations in working conditions affected productivity. The striking conclusions were that variations in the work environment (lighting, ventilation, temperature) were less important than the social interaction with co-workers.[21]

The researchers began to discover that workers spontaneously organized the work environment, established standards, and enforced sanctions among themselves. Economic incentives, which scientific management theories had viewed as the key motivation for workers, were now viewed as secondary to the need for social solidarity provided in work groups. Social and emotional needs of workers, if cultivated and controlled, seemed to lead to higher productivity. The human relations movement advocated job design as a way to direct social solidarity needs toward stable, predictable forms that achieved organization objectives. It touted supportive work groups and nonauthoritarian supervisors as keys to increasing workers' motivation. Quality circles and other worker participation programs are recent applications of these ideas.[22]

Job Characteristics

The Hackman-Oldham model of job design (Exhibit 5–2) is a more recent approach to job design.[23] This model identifies specific job characteristics that can potentially motivate workers. These characteristics are:

1. Skill variety	The degree to which the job requires a variety of different activities in carrying out the work and uses a number of an individual's skills and talents.
2. Task identity	The degree to which the job requires completion of a "whole" and identifiable piece of work—that is, doing a job from the beginning to end with a visible outcome.
3. Task significance	The degree to which the job has a substantial impact on the lives or work of other people—whether in the immediate organization or in the external environment.
4. Autonomy	The degree to which the job provides substantial freedom, independence, and discretion to the individual in scheduling the work and in determining the procedures to carry it out.

EXHIBIT 5–2
Job Characteristics Model

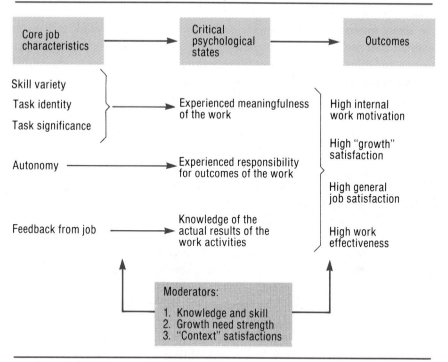

Source: J. R. Hackman and G. R. Oldham, *Work Redesign* (Reading, Mass.: Addison-Wesley Publishing, 1980), p. 90. Used by permission.

5. Feedback   The degree to which carrying out the work activities required by the job results in the individual's obtaining direct and clear information about the effectiveness of his or her performance.

The first three job characteristics influence whether or not an individual feels the work is important. Autonomy influences whether an individual feels personally responsible for good or poor performance; and feedback provides the individual with knowledge of the results of the work. The "moderators" at the bottom of the model account for individual differences in the way workers respond to jobs. Moderators explain why individuals react differently to jobs that theoretically should be motivating.

The Hackman-Oldham model's primary emphasis is on the intrinsic rewards of a job; these rewards are thought to enhance motivation. The model focuses on the interaction between the individual and the job. Unfortunately, it is very difficult for managers to apply, because of its reliance on psychological states that may or may not exist. Moderator variables—the variance in individual reactions to a job situation—may play too great a role.

These three job design approaches vary in that the first focuses on the organization and its technology, the second on the employee, and the third on the job. Rarely are all three levels integrated. To overcome these difficulties, some organizations have switched from assessing jobs and individuals in those jobs to work group design—the design of autonomous work teams that assume responsibility for a set of tasks.[24] Instead of specifying tasks for individual jobs, the sociotechnical approach specifies broader tasks for an employee group.

Sociotechnical Approach

Under this approach, the unit of analysis for assessing work is not the job; it is the work team. Members of the team do not have "jobs" in the traditional sense. Rather, they have roles to play in accomplishing the primary task of the team. These roles can change, according to the particular qualifications of the team members, or their preferences (individual responses to characteristics of the tasks). The team has the authority to assign roles among themselves in any way they choose. Thus, the manager's responsibility is not to design jobs that are intrinsically motivating. Instead, the manager seeks to form work teams whose members possess the qualifications to accomplish the task, are compatible, and whose objectives correspond to those of the organization.[25]

THE WORK TEAM

> ### Definition
> A *work team* is a set of two or more people who are interdependent with one another for the accomplishment of a purpose and who communicate and interact with one another on a more or less continuous basis. In many cases (but not always) they work closely together physically. The team assumes responsibility for deciding how it will accomplish its primary task.

Informal work groups can probably develop in any work setting. The hallmark of the sociotechnical approach is that the *teams are purposely designed with regard to primary task content, qualifications, and rewards/returns associated with completing the primary task.*

Organization Advantages

What do teams do for organizations? Along with the supervisor, they help orient and socialize new employees and teach the tasks. Teams may also make it easier to introduce new technologies. Many advanced technologies are only feasible with work teams, since shorter lead times mean that any problem requires a faster solution, and the information for a correct solution may rest with another member of the team.[26]

Unfortunately, work teams, as with any work group, can also have negative effects when team members pressure others to restrict production at artificially low levels. This effect was first documented in the Hawthorne studies mentioned previously: The work group decided on production quotas and ridiculed any group member who tried to exceed the quota. The group was able to enforce its norms in spite of a pay system based on output. Thus, the influence of the group can be powerful.

Employee Advantages

Effective work teams seem to do a lot for employees. Teams support members against arbitrary demands by outsiders, thus giving employees more control over their work lives and a greater sense of power and dignity.[27]

Effective work teams also offer friendship and acceptance—a feeling of belonging. It is difficult to get such a feeling in most large organizations. The U.S. military employs millions, General Electric hundreds of thousands, and the University of California thousands. A feeling of belonging within organizations of this size is enhanced by membership in small work teams. One of the biggest advantages of the work team approach is the control that it gives employees over how they accomplish their assignments. In effect, employees assume the role of job designers.

Saturn: An Illustration

Exhibit 5-3 describes General Motors Corporation's planned work organization at its Saturn plant in Tennessee. The work units or teams are the smallest unit of organization. These are groups of production workers. The next ring is the business-unit team, composed of production workers, technicians, engineers, and staff specialists. The specialists serve as advisers to the business-unit team leaders. The exhibit illustrates that the work team approach affects the entire organization design. As with all job design methodologies, the organization of work must be congruent with other organization systems.[28]

In summary, job design arranges the content, qualifications, and rewards of work to enhance employee motivation and organizational efficiency. Several alternative approaches to job design are feasible.[29] Job

EXHIBIT 5-3
The Saturn Plant: A New Subculture for General Motors

General Motors hopes that its new Saturn plant in Tennessee, slated to open in 1988, will manufacture cars in a new way — using a business-unit, participative-management structure. James Lewandowski, vice president-human resources for the Saturn Corporation, describes some difficult aspects of managing that enormous transition from traditional GM culture to an entirely different one: adapting to the new structure, designing the pay system, and establishing staffing guidelines.

Structure

"We like to use the image of the planet Saturn and its rings to describe the organization of the Saturn plant," says Lewandowski. (See diagram.) "If you split the planet in half and opened it up, you'd see a series of concentric circles around a core. The new plant will be set up that way."

Saturn's Rings

The smallest circle in the rings concept will be the work-unit module —groups of production workers and other employees who work together every day. The next ring, the business-unit team, really creates the essential core of Saturn, Lewandowski explains. Business-unit teams are led by the business-unit managers, or team leaders. Each team is responsible for the production and operation of an entire business unit, which may be quite large.

"We're staffing these units now with production workers and technicians, engineers, training professionals, labor-relations people, negotiators, union people, and so on," says Lewandowski. "All sides of the enterprise are represented, and they'll all be involved from day one in all the decisions. The specialists, however, are there as advisors, not as supervisors or administrators." In consultation with these specialists and the production technicians, the business-unit team leaders will actually make the day-to-day decisions.

The next circle is the manufacturing advisory committee, with representatives drawn from business-unit teams and some functional specialists, including human-resource people. That group reaches a consensus about running the whole plant, the collection of individual business units. Finally, the largest circle is the strategic advisory committee, which draws some of its membership from the interior circles. Union representatives also sit on this committee, along with Bill Hoglund, Saturn's president, his staff, and Lewandowski. This group, as its name implies, deals with issues of strategy for the entire Saturn Corporation.

"But these are not self-contained boxes or layers built up vertically," Lewandowski stresses. "They're really circles within circles, and there's a lot of overlap. Some people in the small circles also work with the people in the larger ones. There are no rigid barriers separating these rings."

analysis, our next topic, collects information on job content and qualifications in a systematic manner. This information then serves as input for other human resource activities, including job design. Whether job analysis or job design comes first probably depends on which information is already available. For example, we cannot talk about assessing jobs until the organization's tasks have been divided into jobs—job design.[30] But the detailed information collected in job analysis may result in an organization's redesigning its jobs to improve productivity and motivation.

JOB ANALYSIS

> ### Definition
> *Job analysis* is a systematic process of collecting data and making certain judgments about all of the important information related to the nature of a specific job. Results of job analysis serve as input for many human resource activities.

Job analysis usually collects information about specific tasks or what a person does.[31] A group of tasks performed by one person makes up a position. Identical positions make a job, and broadly similar jobs combine into an occupation.[32] Exhibit 5–4 summarizes these terms.

EXHIBIT 5–4
Job Analysis Terminology

Task	Smallest unit of analysis, a specific statement of what a person does: for example, operates an Apple II terminal, answers the telephone.
Position	Next level of analysis, *a group of tasks* performed by *one* person: for example, all tasks done by a computer operator or secretary.
Job	Many positions, all with the same basic tasks and with several people performing them.
Occupation	Grouping of jobs with broadly similar content, for example, managerial, technical, crafts.
Job descriptions	Systematic summary of the information collected in the job analysis.
Job specifications	The minimum skills, knowledge and abilities required to perform the job.

Source: E. J. McCormick, "Job and Task Analysis," in *Handbook of Industrial and Organizational Psychology*, ed. M. D. Dunnette, © 1976, John Wiley & Sons, Inc. Reprinted by permission.

Why Analyze Jobs?

Job analysis is a basic tool in human resource management because information about the work performed serves so many purposes. Exhibit 5–5 lists some of the uses, in addition to job design, of data gathered through job analysis. Some common uses of job analysis data include:

1. Training program—Information gathered about qualifications and job content permits tailoring training programs to actual qualifications required to perform the jobs, rather than to some hypothetical ones dreamed up by managers.[33]
2. Job-related interviews and recruitment—Job analysis can tell a trained interviewer which requirements are necessary for success on the job.[34] This communication can pay off two ways: it can allow the interviewer to better assess the fit between the candidate and the job, and it can allow candidates to decide if they are really interested.
3. Test development, selection, and validation—Tests chosen or developed on the basis of measuring information related to actual job content and qualifications have a greater chance of being useful in hiring decisions as well as in complying with equal employment regulations.[35]
4. Performance evaluation—Basing evaluations on job analysis information helps ensure that they are job-related.[36]
5. Compensation—Job analysis is often a first step in evaluating jobs for pay purposes.[37]

EXHIBIT 5–5
Uses of Job Analysis Information

Function	Job Analysis		Result
	Information		
Job design	Tasks, qualifications, rewards, expected results	→	Organization structure
Recruitment and selection	Required qualifications	→	Selection and promotion standards
Training and development	Tasks, behaviors	→	Training programs
Performance appraisal	Behavior standards or expected results	→	Performance appraisal criteria
Compensation	Tasks, abilities, behaviors	→	Similarities and differences in the work; job descriptions

6. **EEO**—Job analysis data can be helpful in establishin~~g~~ are work related.[38] The courts have affirmed the importa~~nce~~ ysis. A review of court decisions on EEO concludes:

> A well-done job analysis is an important step in both comp~~iling and~~ defending against actions brought under these laws. This m~~ay seem auto-~~ matic . . . To a great many employers, unfortunately, it does ~~not~~ appear to be clear. Until these employers understand the implications of job analysis to equal employment opportunity, they will be "aiming in the dark."[39]

In spite of its importance, many employers do not use job analysis.[40] Reasons cited frequently include the time and expense. Consequently, it is important that the reasons for conducting job analysis be well thought out and properly understood. Those authorizing the activity and those carrying it out need to be fully aware of the time and cost commitment, as well as the nature of any changes that may result based on job analysis results.

Too often, job analysis is assigned to the newest hire in the personnel department, a person who has had little opportunity to understand an organization's culture and work, and lacks the authority to secure the organization's commitment to the process.

Job Descriptions

To make it useful for other human resource activities, job analysis data are summarized into the standard format of a job description sheet.[41] The job description typically contains three sections, which identify, define, and describe the job.

1. *Identify the job.* Analysts identify a job by its title, the number of people in the organization who hold this job, whether or not it is exempt from Fair Labor Standards Act coverage, the department or work site, and the job number.
2. *Define the job.* This summary section reflects the purpose of the job: why the job exists, what constitutes satisfactory job performance, and how it fits in with other jobs and overall organization objectives.
3. *Describe the job content.* What are the major duties of this jobholder? What specific work is performed? How closely supervised is this job? How much discretion does jobholder enjoy? Which controls limit the actions of the jobholder? Content may also include the training and experience qualifications for the job.

Appendix A at the end of this chapter contains sample job descriptions.

Which Data to Collect?

Deciding which information to collect depends on two factors: existing data and the purpose of the analysis. As more purposes are served by job analysis, the greater the variety of data necessary. For example, job design requires information on how differences in the work structure and content affect motivation and performance. For recruiting and selection decisions, the specific behaviors and abilities required to perform a job are of interest. Pay decisions are based on information about similarities and differences in the skill, effort, responsibility, and working conditions among jobs. With the aid of computers, it is feasible to collect and analyze vast amounts of job-related data.[42] But the key issue is to make certain that the data collected serve the purposes of the job analysis.

Analysts collect three basic categories of job information: task data, behavioral data, and abilities data. Job analysis methodologies emphasize various categories, as the next section explains.

Task Data

Work data involve the elemental units of works, subparts of a job called tasks, with emphasis on the purpose of each task. Exhibit 5–6 contains an excerpt from a job analysis questionnaire that collects task data. Although the aspect of work is "communication," the questionnaire describes it in terms of actual tasks; for example, "read technical publications," and "consult with co-workers." The other distinguishing characteristic is the emphasis on the output, or objective of the task, "read technical publications to keep current on industry," and "consult with co-workers to exchange ideas and techniques." Task data reveal the actual work performed and its purpose or outcome.[43]

Behavioral Data

This approach describes jobs by the behaviors that occur. Exhibit 5–7 shows such behavioral observations, again concerned with "communications." This time, the questions focus on verbs that describe human behavior, such as advising, negotiating, or persuading. Exhibit 5–7 is from the Position Analysis Questionnaire (PAQ), developed by McCormick and associates.[44] PAQ groups work information into seven basic factors: Information Input, Mental Processes, Work Output, Relationships with Other Persons, Job Context, Other Job Characteristics, and General Dimensions. These seven general processes describe similarities and differences among jobs rather than specific aspects unique to each job.[45] The communications behavior in Exhibit 5–7 is part of the "Relationships with Other Persons" factor.

EXHIBIT 5–6
Job Analysis Questionnaire Using Task Data (excerpt)

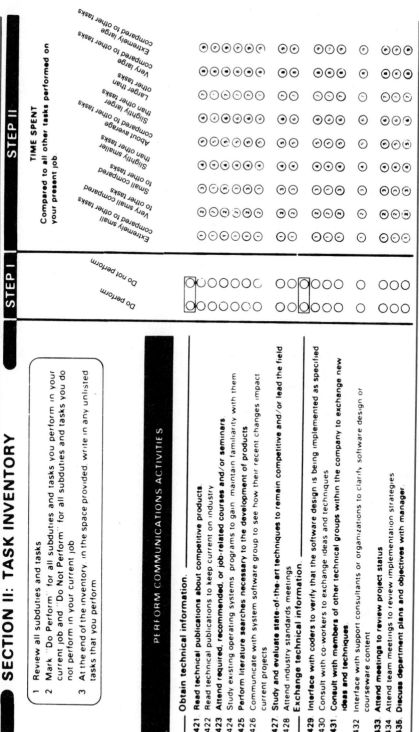

EXHIBIT 5–7
Job Analysis Questionnaire Using Behavioral Data (excerpt)

Section 4 Relationships with Other Persons

This section deals with different aspects of interaction between people involved in various kinds of work.

Code Importance to this Job (1)	
N	Does not apply
1	Very minor
2	Low
3	Average
4	High
5	Extreme

4.1 Communications

Rate the following in terms of how *important* the activity is to the completion of the job. Some jobs may involve several or all of the items in this section.

4.1.1 Oral (communicating by speaking)

99 _____ Advising (dealing with individuals in order to counsel and/or guide them with regard to problems that may be resolved by legal, financial, scientific, technical, clinical, spiritual, and/or other professional principles)

100 _____ Negotiating (dealing with others in order to reach an agreement or solution, for example, labor bargaining, diplomatic relations, etc.)

101 _____ Persuading (dealing with others in order to influence them toward some action or point of view, for example, selling, political campaigning, etc.)

102 _____ Instructing (the teaching of knowledge or skills, in either an informal or a formal manner, to others, for example, a public school teacher, a machinist teaching an apprentice, etc.)

103 _____ Interviewing (conducting interviews directed toward some specific objective, for example, interviewing job applicants, census taking, etc.)

104 _____ Routine information exchange: job related (the giving and/or receiving of *job-related* information of a routine nature, for example, ticket agent, taxicab dispatcher, receptionist, etc.)

105 _____ Nonroutine information exchange (the giving and/or receiving of *job-related* information of a nonroutine or unusual nature, for example, professional committee meetings, engineers discussing new product design, etc.)

106 _____ Public speaking (making speeches or formal presentations before relatively large audiences, for example, political addresses, radio/TV broadcasting, delivering a sermon, etc.)

4.1.2 Written (communicating by written/printed material)

107 _____ Writing (for example, writing or dictating letters, reports, etc., writing copy for ads, writing newspaper articles, etc.; do *not* include transcribing activities described in item 4.3, but only activities in which the incumbent creates the written material)

4.1.3 Other Communications

108 _____ Signaling (communicating by some type of signal, for example, hand signals, semaphore, whistles, horns, bells, lights, etc.)

109 _____ Code communications (telegraph, cryptography, etc.)

Source: PAQ Services, Inc., Logan, Utah. Copyright © 1969 by Purdue Research Foundation, West Lafayette, Indiana 47906.

EXHIBIT 5–8
Job Analysis Questionnaire Using Ability Data (excerpt)

WRITTEN COMPREHENSION

This is the ability to understand written sentences and paragraphs.

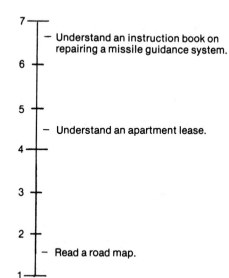

Requires understanding complex or detailed information *in writing*, containing unusual words and phrases and involving fine distinctions in meaning among words.

7 — Understand an instruction book on repairing a missile guidance system.

6

5

— Understand an apartment lease.

4

3

Requires understanding short, simple *written* information containing common words and phrases.

2

— Read a road map.

1

ORAL COMPREHENSION

This is the ability to understand spoken English words and sentences.

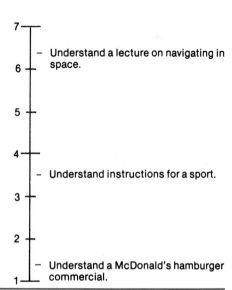

Requires understanding complex or detailed information, *presented orally*, containing unusual words and phrases and involving fine distinctions in meaning among words.

7

— Understand a lecture on navigating in space.

6

5

4

— Understand instructions for a sport.

3

Requires understanding short, simple, *spoken* information containing common words and phrases.

2

— Understand a McDonald's hamburger commercial.

1

Source: AT&T.

Abilities Data

Abilities data capture the knowledge and skill a worker must possess for satisfactory performance.[46] These abilities underlie the behavior that occurs on the job. The taxonomy developed by E. A. Fleishman includes (1) psychomotor abilities, (2) physical proficiency abilities, and (3) cognitive abilities, and forms the foundation for abilities-based job analysis.[47] AT&T, in conjunction with the Communication Workers of America and other unions, has developed a set of 16 abilities required in nonmanagerial work.[48] "Expression" and "Comprehension," their first two factors, probably correspond most closely to the communication aspect we looked at with task data and behavioral data. Exhibit 5–8 shows their scale for assessing the degree of an ability required in a job.

Thus, analysts describe the communication aspect of a job by assessing the degree of understanding and use of spoken and written sentences required to perform that job. This assessment can be done with or without reference to specific tasks or behaviors in a job.

Although the communication scales shown in Exhibits 5–6, 5–7, and 5–8 illustrate the shades of differences in task, behavior, and ability data, these three represent different views of work. They vary in the way they describe a job. Thus, it is not surprising that varying approaches to job analysis may yield different results. One study examined seven foreman jobs in a chemical processing plant using all three types of job analysis data.[49] Using the same statistical procedures on all three data sets, they found that different data sets yielded different results. In other words, the data collected affect the results. Their recommendation is sound advice for human resource managers: the purpose of the analysis dictates the nature of the data to collect. Thus, if you intend to design training programs, according to Exhibit 5–5, you'll probably need to collect task and behavioral data. If you need to develop an equitable pay structure, then all three types of data may be useful.

How to Collect Data

Exhibit 5–9 categorizes the most common methods of job analysis data collection. Appendix B in this chapter describes procedures for collecting data and includes a questionnaire. Significant advances in the practice of job analysis collecting and analyzing job information have occurred in the past few years.[50] Basically these include techniques to quantify the data and computerize the analysis. Such developments help minimize errors in data collection and, insofar as possible, increase the chances that the jobs are analyzed on work-related factors. To review the state of the art, next we discuss two job analyses—conventional and quantitative.

Conventional Job Analysis

Conventional procedures vary in specific details, but generally an analyst uses a questionnaire, in conjunction with interviews of job incumbents and supervisors.[51] Then the analyst transfers the data collected to a summary job description. Often both job incumbents and supervisors are given an opportunity to modify and approve (sign off) the description.

EXHIBIT 5–9
Methods of Data Collection

Method	Descriptions	Characteristics
Questionnaire	Using standardized form, jobholders and/or supervisors describe the work. Data can be gathered either through mailed survey or through individual interview.	Variations include combining questionnaire with individual or group interview. As with all questionnaires, responses may be incomplete or difficult to interpret, a limitation minimized by combining with interviews. Standard format eases mathematical analysis. Interviews, however, may be time-consuming, and become more difficult with workers at multiple locations.
Checklist	Jobholders and/or supervisors check items on a task inventory that apply to their particular job. Checklist can be tailor-made or purchased.	Depends on recognition rather than recall. Cheap, easy to administer and analyze. However, care must be taken that all significant aspects of work are included in the list.
Diary	Jobholders record activities as they are performed.	Has the advantage of collecting data as events occur, but it is often difficult to obtain continuous and consistent entries. Obtained data is not in a standardized format.
Observation	Analyst records perceptions formed while watching the work being done by one or more jobholders.	The absence of preconceived structures or artificial constraints can lead to richer data. Each job can be studied in any depth desired. However, validity and reliability of data can be a problem, and the relative emphasis of certain work aspects is dependent on the acuteness of the analyst's perceptions. Also, the observation of employee behavior by an analyst influences the behavior.
Activity sampling	Observations are made at random intervals.	
Activity matrix	Respondents identify time spent in relation to tasks and products or services.	Data collected is amenable to quantitative analysis, and is highly adaptable to other human resource management needs; however, another job analysis procedure must be used initially to develop the matrix.
Critical incidents	Behaviorally oriented incidents describe key job behaviors. Analyst determines degree of each type of behavior present or absent in each job.	Analysis clearly based on concrete behavior. Scales require some expertise to develop.

Functional Job Analysis

Probably the most detailed conventional procedure is functional job analysis (FJA), a refinement of Department of Labor methodology developed in the 1930s. Although common in the public-sector, few private-sector employers have adopted it. Nevertheless, anyone undertaking job analysis for the first time would be well advised to consult the Department of Labor's *Handbook for Analyzing Jobs.* Exhibit A–1 in the appendix is written from information developed with conventional job analysis.

Key features of the FJA approach are the assumptions that all jobs involve relationships of *data, people,* and *things;* and that the analyst can arrange these relationships according to their complexity. (See Exhibit 5–10.) For example, the simplest relationship to people requires taking instructions or serving. The most complex people relationship is mentoring (serving as a role model or counselor).

S. A. Fine and other advocates of FJA see it as the cornerstone for all human resource systems.[52] Critics, however, complain that the typical essay descriptions of job activities are not adequately descriptive of the jobs in question.

Quantitative Job Analysis

Quantitative job analysis is a result of efforts to reduce reliance on the limitations of the analyst. Conventional job analysis requires the analyst to

EXHIBIT 5–10
Worker Function Scales of Functional Job Analysis

	Data	People	Things
Higher level	Synthesizing	Mentoring	Precision working, setting up
	Coordinating		
	Innovating	Negotiating	Manipulating, operating-controlling, driving-controlling
	Analyzing	Supervising	
	Computing	Consulting, instructing, treating	
	Compiling		
		Coaching, persuading, diverting	Handling, feeding-offbearing, tending
	Copying	Exchanging information	
Lower level	Comparing	Taking instructions-helping, serving	

Source: Adapted from: S. A. Fine and Wretha A. Wiley, *An Introduction to Functional Job Analysis: A Scaling of Selected Tasks from the Social Welfare Field* (Kalamazoo, Mich.: W. E. Upjohn Institute for Employment Research, 1971).

understand the work performed and to translate it into description sheets. Descriptions vary among analysts. Certain safeguards, such as multiple approvals by supervisors and incumbents can help minimize that difficulty, but they cannot eliminate it.

Quantitative job analysis (QJA) involves the detailed assessment—the quantification—of the tasks and behavioral traits involved in a job. QJA is more systematic, relies on computers for analysis, and is less subject to error than conventional job analysis. It is also more costly to develop.[53]

Inventories are the core of QJA. An inventory is essentially a structured questionnaire listing the task and behavior attributes relevant for the group of jobs being analyzed. Exhibits 5–6 and 5–7 are taken from quantitative job analysis inventories.

Position Description Questionnaire (PDQ)

Exhibit 5–6 shows Control Data Corporation's Position Description Questionnaire. The item scales show that a task is measured by time spent doing it in comparison to other tasks. Other measures could be degree of importance and prior experience required. The person presently holding a job would be the one most likely to fill out one of these inventories.

Position Analysis Questionnaire (PAQ)

The most publicly available example of a QJA is Exhibit 5–7's Position Analysis Questionnaire (PAQ). PAQ uses degree of importance as its measure. Some users caution that the PAQ has a high reading comprehension level and complex instructions, which make it difficult for some employees to complete the questionnaire without assistance.[54]

A major limitation of all QJA is cost. One study reported an installation that required a full-time project director who combined managerial and communications skills with a personnel background, knowledge of the work in the organization, and knowledge of data management and computer principles; three to seven job analysts; and a system analyst.[55] For one task inventory, an inexperienced project staff required 44 weeks to move from defining the scope of the inventory and identifying job families to production of management reports. So considerable time and money are required for any job analysis, with or without computer assistance. Efforts continue to improve QJA procedures and minimize the expense and effort involved. In comparison, the PAQ or conventional job analysis is relatively inexpensive.

Advantages of Quantitative Job Analysis

In spite of its limitations, the practice of job analysis has been upgraded with the development of quantitative job analysis. At least four factors are operating to increase its use: First, as more employers use it, the technology becomes better understood and simpler to apply. Second, sound information about the nature of work and the requirements to perform it is the basic foundation of effective human resource decision making. Third, challenges from employees, courts, and EEO agencies to verify the work-relatedness of personnel decisions require sound job analysis. And fourth, QJA lends itself to user-friendly computer applications.

IS JOB ANALYSIS USEFUL?

Job analysis procedures, whether conventional or quantitative, involve a high degree of judgment. Analysts compare job analysis methods, particularly the reliability, validity, acceptability, and usefulness of methods.

Reliability

Reliability is the consistency of the results obtained. The assessment of job content and qualifications should be the same regardless of who is involved (supervisors, incumbents, analysts, consultants) and the methods used. Several studies have compared employee-supervisor agreement of work content.[56] They present a mixed picture. Employees and supervisors often differ in how they view the distribution of time among tasks, the skills required to perform the work, and the difficulties of the tasks performed. So the results may vary, depending on the source of the data. Other studies have found that different analysts using the same quantitative methods on the same jobs get the same results.[57]

Conventional job analysis does not usually lend itself to formal reliability analysis because of the narrative and unstructured output.[58] This imprecision makes reliability a serious issue for conventional methods.[59] Whichever method is adopted, it should be used independently by analysts, supervisors, and subordinates; and they should investigate and resolve any differences.

Consistent (reliable) job information does not necessarily mean that it is accurate, comprehensive, or free from bias. To find out if the results are accurate, we need to consider its validity.

Validity

Research on estimating the validity of job analysis is particularly difficult, since there is almost no way of showing the extent to which the results are accurate portraits of the work. The most promising approach may be to examine the convergence of results among multiple sources of job data (analysts, incumbents, supervisors) and multiple methods. A common approach to increase the accuracy of a job analysis is to require the jobholder and the manager to mutually sign off on the results. Although signing off may reflect their acceptance, it may also reflect their desire to get rid of the analyst and get back to performing the job rather than analyzing it.

Acceptability

The acceptability of the results of job analysis by the employees and managers remains a critical test. No matter how well the rest of the human resource management system is administered, if jobholders are dissatisfied with the initial data collected and the process for collecting it, they are not likely to feel the results are internally equitable.

Traditional job analysis is not always well accepted by the parties involved because of its potential for subjectivity. One writer says, "We all know the classic procedures. One (worker) watched and noted the actions of another . . . at work on (the) job. The actions of both are biased, and the resulting information varied with the wind, especially the political wind."[60] Nonetheless, the acceptability of quantitative job analysis is also mixed. Control Data's Executive Position Questionnaire, developed over a four-year period, ran into several problems, which led most managers to refuse to use it.[61] Among the problems analysts faced were:

1. *Employee/Manager understanding.* The statistical methods used were difficult to understand so many managers were unable to communicate the results to employees. Consequently, an antagonistic climate developed and the credibility of the system deteriorated.
2. *Behaviorally oriented versus "scope" data.* Omitting "scope" data (e.g., size of budgets, total payroll, contribution to organizational objectives) caused managers to feel that the questionnaire did not accurately analyze their jobs.
3. *Abstract and ambiguous factors.* The nature of the data collected (e.g., analyze subordinates' weaknesses and strengths) was perceived to be too abstract and ambiguous. Results were considered too subjective and open to personal interpretation.

Usefulness

Researchers recognize the necessity of judging the usefulness of job analysis methods according to the purpose of the analysis.[62] If there is a need for uniform job data at many locations, does the method provide it? Can the method provide documentable evidence of the work-relatedness of the pay structure? Are subtle differences among jobs unique to the organization adequately assessed? Are both the typist and the vice president of marketing convinced that the method fairly describes their jobs? These challenges to job analysis provide criteria to judge a method's usefulness. Some advocates get so taken with their statistics and computers that they ignore the role that human judgment must continue to play in job analysis. As M. D. Dunnette states,

> I wish to emphasize the central role played in all these procedures by human judgment. I know of no methodology, statistical technique or objective measurement that can negate the importance of, nor supplement, rational judgment as an important element in the process of deriving behavior and task information about jobs and of using that information to develop or justify human resource programs.[63]

Quantitative and more systematic approaches to job analysis do not remove the judgment; they only permit us to become more systematic in the way we judge.

SUMMARY

Continuing our examination of organization factors that influence human resource management, this chapter has concentrated on assessing the nature of work and how this work affects employees as well as organizations. The *content* (duties, tasks, behaviors, functions, responsibilities), the *qualifications* required to perform it (skills, abilities, experience), and *returns and rewards* for performing it (pay, promotions, challenging work) constitute the nature of work.

Job design is concerned with alternative arrangements of the content, rewards, and qualifications. Alternate techniques include simplification, rotation, enlargement, and enrichment. These techniques are applied within an overall approach to job design. Scientific management is the oldest approach. Currently, work teams using a sociotechnical model is a popular approach; however, any job design approach is limited by the technology of the workplace.

Job analysis assesses the content of jobs. Its results provide input for a variety of human resource activities, including job design. Although job analysis is a basic assessment process, not all organizations do it. Job analysis can be tedious, time-consuming, and expensive. Recent advances in computerizing the process may eliminate some of these drawbacks, but not all of them. Computerization raises the possibility of collecting a great deal of job information for a variety of purposes. Unfortunately, the amount of data may outrun its usefulness. Informed human judgment can never be omitted from the work assessment process.

The basic premise of this chapter is that the nature of work plays a critical role in the management of human resources. Job analysis and job design are important tools in the process of matching the nature of the individual with the nature of the work. This matching process helps achieve employee and organizational objectives.

APPENDIX A / Sample Job Descriptions

EXHIBIT A–1
Job Description for a Personnel Manager

166.117-018 Manager, Personnel (professional and kindred)
    Plans and carries out policies relating to all phases of personnel activity. Recruits, interviews, and selects employees to fill vacant positions. Plans and conducts new employee orientation to foster positive attitude toward company goals. Keeps record of insurance coverage, pension plan, and personnel transactions, such as hires, promotions, transfers, and terminations. Investigates accidents and prepares reports for insurance carrier. Conducts wage survey within labor market to determine competitive wage rate. Prepares budget of personnel operations. Meets with shop stewards and supervisors to resolve grievances. Writes separation notices for employees separating with cause and conducts exit interviews to determine reasons behind separations. Prepares reports and recommends procedures to reduce absenteeism and turnover. Contracts with outside suppliers to provide employee services, such as canteen, transportation, or relocation service. May keep records of hired employee characteristics for governmental reporting purposes. May negotiate collective bargaining agreement with *business representative labor union* (professional and kindred).

Source: U.S. Department of Labor, *Dictionary of Occupational Titles,* 4th ed. (Washington, D.C.: U.S. Government Printing Office, 1977).

EXHIBIT A–2

Johns-Manville   **Professional/Managerial**
Job Description

Job Title: DIRECTOR, EMPLOYEE BENEFITS

Job Number:

Reports To (Job Title): V. P., EMPLOYEE RELATIONS

Division/Staff Responsibility: EMPLOYEE RELATIONS

Location: DENVER GHQ

I. Organization—Attach Chart
Number of People Supervised and Functionally Directed

Salaried Direct: Exempt _____1_____ Non-Exempt _____1_____

Salaried Workforce: Exempt _____ Non-Exempt _____4_____

Hourly: Direct _____ Workforce _____

Functionally Directed _____

II. Position Summary
A. Position Objective

Direct the design, implementation and administration of all corporate salaried, hourly and retiree benefit programs, both domestic and foreign.

B. Position Functions

1. Direct the development and implementation of policies, improvements and modifications to all Corporate Employee Benefit Programs for salaried, hourly and retirees.
2. Provide procedures and policy interpretation necessary for the uniform administration of all benefit programs.
3. Direct personnel at GHQ, Plants, Mines and Regional Offices in uniform application and administration of employee benefit programs.
4. Establish and direct employee and management informative benefits communication programs.
5. Recommend and establish benefit plans unique to foreign nationals employed by wholly or partially owned overseas subsidiaries.
6. Advise and recommend modifications to benefit plans based on surveys and federal, state, dominion, provincial and foreign legislation.

_____   _____
Description Prepared by   Date

_____   _____
Line Approver   Date

(If additional space is needed, please use back of form.)

Job Analysis Report

Date 2-23-86

Job Analyst C. Davis

1. Job Title Executive Secretary

2. Department General Headquarters

3. No. incumbents 2   Interviewed 2

4. Relation to other jobs:

   Promotion: From Secretary-D   To Executive Secretary

   Transfer: From Administrative Assistant   To Executive Secretary

   Supervision received From President and/or Chairman of the Board.

   Works under minimal supervision.

   Supervision given Regularly to other clerical personnel.

5. Summary of Job:

   Personal Secretary to President and/or Chairman of the Board. Performs variety of secretarial and clerical duties including transcribing dictation, filing, routing mail, as well as answering telephone and written inquiries. Exercises discretion in handling confidential and specialized information, screening telephone calls and letters, arranging meetings, and handling inquiries during superior's absence.

6. Equipment used: Typewriter, word processor, dictaphone and telephone.

Working conditions:

   Hazards (list): N/A

   Work space and quarters: Office environment

Noise exposure: None

Lighting: Good

Temperature: Regulated office environment

Miscellaneous: —

Job training:

A.   Required experience: (include other jobs)
Four years of secretarial-stenographic experience or the equivalent.

B.   Outside educational courses:

Time in semesters/quarters

Vocational courses: Typing, stenography
2 semesters

High school courses: Graduate
6-8 semesters

College courses:
None

Continuing education required:
None

C.   In-house training courses:

Time in months

Courses   Basic and Advanced Word Processing
1/2 month

Task Statement Worksheet

Task Statement: Opens and organizes mail addressed to superior.

1.   Equipment used   —

2.   Knowledge required   Must be well versed on superior's responsibilities, how superior's job fits into overall organization.

3.   Skills required   —

4.   Abilities required   Discretion. Organization skills.

5. Time spent and frequency of task performance (hourly, daily, monthly)
Time varies by assignment. Daily frequency.

6. Level of difficulty/consequence of error
Relatively easy, little effect of error.

Task Statement: Establishes, maintains, and revises files.

1. Equipment used   Typewriter, word processor.

2. Knowledge required   Understanding of organization and responsibilities of superior.

3. Skills required   Typing and word processing, filing.

4. Abilities required   Ability to organize and categorize information.

5. Time spent and frequency of task performance (hourly, daily, monthly)
One hour spent daily.

6. Level of difficulty/consequence of error   Relatively easy, but moderate to serious consequences if information mishandled.

APPENDIX B / Procedures for Gathering Job Information

Overview

A combination of on-site observations, interviews, and pre-interview preparation and study develops the necessary job information.

Data Sources

Sources of information for developing the job description include:

- Existing documents, such as job briefs, previously developed task lists, and training manuals.
- On-site observations of work operations.
- Interviews with first-level supervisors and job incumbents.

General Procedures

1. Develop preliminary job information.
   a. Review existing documents to develop an initial "big-picture" familiarity with the job: its main mission, its major duties or functions, work flow patterns.
   b. Prepare a preliminary list of duties to serve as a framework for conducting the interviews.
   c. Make a note of major items which are unclear, ambiguous, or need clarification during the data-gathering process.
2. Conduct an initial tour of the work site.
   a. The initial tour familiarizes the job analyst with the work layout, the tools and equipment used, the general conditions of the workplace, and the mechanics associated with the end-to-end performance of major duties.
   b. The initial tour is particularly helpful in those jobs where a firsthand view of a complicated or unfamiliar piece of equipment saves the interviewee the thousand words required to describe the unfamiliar or technical.
   c. For continuity, the first-level supervisor-interviewee should be the designated guide for the job site observations.
3. Conduct interviews.
   a. The interviewees are considered subject matter experts because they perform the job (in the case of job incumbents) or are responsible for getting the job done (in the case of first-level supervisors).
   b. The first interview should be conducted with the first-level supervisor who is in a better position than the jobholders to provide an overview of the job and how the major duties fit together.

c. The job incumbent to be interviewed should represent the *typical* employee who is knowledgeable about the job (not the trainee who is just learning the ropes nor the most outstanding member of the work unit).

d. For scheduling purposes, no more than two interviews should be conducted per day, each interview lasting no more than three hours.

4. Conduct a second tour of the work site.

   a. The second tour of the work site is designed to clarify, confirm, and otherwise refine the information developed in the interviews.

   b. As in the initial tour, the same first-level supervisor-interviewee should conduct the second walk-through.

5. Consolidate job information.

   a. The consolidation phase of the job study involves piecing together into one coherent and comprehensive job description the data obtained from several sources: supervisor, jobholders, on-site tours, and written materials about the job.

   b. Past experience indicates that one minute of consolidation is required for every minute of interviewing. For planning purposes, at least five hours should be set aside for the consolidation phase.

   c. A subject matter expert should be accessible to the job analyst as a resource person during the consolidation phase. The supervisor-interviewee fills this role.

   d. Check your initial preliminary list of duties and questions—all must be answered or confirmed.

6. Verify job descriptions.

   a. The verification phase involves bringing all the interviewees together for the purpose of determining if the consolidated job description is accurate and complete.

   b. The verification process is conducted in a group setting. Typed or legibly written copies of the job description (narrative description of the work setting *and* list of task statements) are distributed to the first-level supervisor and the job incumbent interviewees.

   c. Line by line, the job analyst goes through the entire job description and makes notes of any omissions, ambiguities, or needed clarifications.

   d. Collect all materials at the end of the verification meeting.

DISCUSSION AND REVIEW QUESTIONS

1. What did the Hawthorne experiments tell us about group influences on individual productivity?

2. Contrast the perspectives of scientific management and human relations.

3. Applying the diagnostic model, which factors should an organization consider in designing jobs?
4. What is the critical advantage of quantitative job analysis over conventional approaches? Why is this important?
5. If human judgment is central to job analysis, why bother doing it?

NOTES AND REFERENCES

1. Studs Terkel, *Working: People Talk about What They Do All Day and How They Feel about What They Do* (New York: Pantheon Books, a Division of Random House, 1974), Copyright 1972, 1974 by Studs Terkel.
2. Ibid.
3. H. G. Heneman, Jr., "Work and Nonwork: Historical Perspectives," in *Work and Non-Work in the Year 2001*, ed. M. Dunnette (Monterey, Calif.: Brooks/Cole Publishing, 1973).
4. "Getting Man and Machine to Live Happily Ever After," *Business Week*, April 20, 1987, pp. 61–62; G. L. Whaley, "The Impact of Robotics Technology upon Human Resource Management," *Personnel Administrator*, September 1982, pp. 61–71; Ann P. Bartel and Frank Lichtenberg, "The Comparative Advantage of Educated Workers in Implementing New Technology," *The Review of Economics and Statistics*, February 1987, pp. 1–11; and M. Denny and M. Fuss, "The Effects of Factor Prices and Technological Change on the Occupational Demand for Labor: Evidence from Canadian Telecommunications," *Journal of Human Resources* 17, no. 2 (1983), pp. 161–76.
5. Georgia T. Chao and Steve W. J. Kozlowski, "Employee Perceptions on the Implementation of Robotic Manufacturing Technology," *Journal of Applied Psychology* 71, no. 1 (1986), pp. 70–76.
6. Pat Choate and J. K. Linger, *The High-Flex Society* (New York: Alfred A. Knopf, 1986).
7. Phyllis A. Wallace, ed., *Equal Employment Opportunity and the AT&T Case* (Cambridge, Mass.: MIT Press, 1976).
8. Richard Freeman and James Medoff, *What Do Unions Do?* (New York: Basic Books, 1984).
9. Charles O'Reilly, G. N. Parlette, and J. Blum, "Perceptual Measures of Task Characteristics: The Biasing Effects of Differing Frames of References and Job Attitudes," *Academy of Management Journal* 123, no. 1 (1980), pp. 118–31.
10. George H. Dreher, "Individual Needs or Correlates of Satisfaction and Involvement with a Modified Scanlon Plan Company," *Journal of Vocational Behavior*, August 1980, pp. 89–94; Joseph E. Champoux, "The World of Non-Work: Some Implications for Job Redesign Efforts," *Personnel Psychology*, Spring 1979, pp. 61–75; Andrew Weiss, "The Effect of Job Complicity on Job Satisfaction: Evidence from Turnover and Absenteeism" (National Bureau of Economic Research Working Paper Series, 1985); Seymour Adler, Richard Skou, and Nat Salvemini, "Job Characteristics and Job Satisfaction: When Cause Becomes Consequence," *Organizational Behavior and Human Decision Processes* 35 (1985), pp. 266–78.
11. O'Reilly et al., "Perceptual Measures of Task Characteristics."

12. Marvin Dunnette and Edwin Fleishman, eds. *Human Performance and Productivity* (Hillsdale, N.J.: Lawrence Erlbaum, 1982); John W. Kendrick, *Improving Company Productivity* (Baltimore: The Johns Hopkins University Press, 1984).

13. G. Douglas Jenkins, Jr., and Nina Gupta, "The Payoffs of Paying for Knowledge," *Labor-Management Cooperation Brief*, August 1985; Henry Tosi and Lisa Tosi, "Knowledge-Based Pay: Some Propositions and Guides to Effective Use" (Working paper, University of Florida, 1984); Edward E. Lawler III, "The New Pay," in *Current Issues in Human Resource Management*," ed. Sara L. Rynes and George T. Milkovich (Plano, Tex.: Business Publications, 1986).

14. S. W. Kozlowski and B. M. Hults, "Joint Moderation of the Relation between Task Complexity and Job Performance for Engineers," *Journal of Applied Psychology* 71 (1986), pp. 196–202.

15. David J. Cherrington and J. Lynn England, "The Desire for an Enriched Job as a Moderator of the Enrichment-Satisfaction Relationship," *Organizational Behavior and Human Performance*, February 1980, pp. 139–59; and Kae H. Chung and Monica F. Ross, "Differences in Motivational Properties between Job Enlargement and Job Enrichment," *Academy of Management Review*, January 1977, pp. 113–21.

16. Sam Bacharach and Stephen Mitchell, *Job Reference Manual* (Ithaca, N.Y.: Organization Analysis and Practice, 1983).

17. Frederick W. Taylor, "On the Art of Cutting Metals," *Transactions of the American Society of Mechanical Engineers* 28 (1907); F. W. Taylor, *Principles of Scientific Management* (New York: Harper & Row, 1911).

18. Edwin A. Locke, "The Ideas of Frederick W. Taylor: An Evaluation." *Academy of Management Review* 7, no. 1 (1982), pp. 14–25; Taylor, *Scientific Management*.

19. Gary J. Blau and Ralph Katerberg, "Toward Enhancing Research with the Social Information Processing Approach to Job Design," *Academy of Management Review* 7, no. 4 (1982), pp. 543–51; A. Carey, "The Hawthorne Studies: A Radical Criticism," *American Sociological Review* 32, no. 2 (1976), pp. 295–308; J. R. Hackman and G. R. Oldham, *Work Redesign*, (Reading, Mass.: Addison-Wesley Publishing, 1979).

20. E. Mayo, *The Human Problems of an Industrial Civilization* (New York: Macmillan, 1933).

21. Gary L. Cooper, "Humanizing the Work Place in Europe: An Overview of Six Countries," *Personnel Journal*, June 1980, pp. 488–91.

22. Stephen H. Fuller and Berth Jonsson, "Corporate Approaches to the Quality of Work Life," *Personnel Journal*, August 1980, pp. 645–48.

23. Hackman and Oldham, *Work Redesign*.

24. Bernard Bass, "Individual Capability, Team Performance, and Team Productivity," In *Human Performance and Productivity*.

25. T. R. Mitchell, J. R. Larson, and S. G. Green, "Leader Behavior, Situational Moderators, and Group Performance: An Attributional Analysis. *Organizational Behavior and Human Performance* 18 (1977), pp. 254–68.

26. Richard E. Walton and Gerald I. Susman, "People Policies for the New Machines," *Harvard Business Review*, March–April 1987, pp. 98–106; M. E. Shaw, *Group Dynamics: The Psychology of Small Group Behavior*, 3rd ed. (New York: McGraw-Hill, 1981).

27. G. R. Salancik and J. Pfeffer, "A Social Information Processing Approach to Job Attitudes and Task Design," *Administrative Science Quarterly* 23 (1978), pp. 224–53.

28. K. Roberts and W. Glick, "The Job Characteristics Approach to Task Design: A Critical Review," *Journal of Applied Psychology* 66 (1981), pp. 193–217.

29. Yitzhak Fried and Gerald Ferris, "The Validity of the Job Characteristics Model: A Review and Meta-Analysis," *Personnel Psychology*, Summer 1987, pp. 287–322.

30. Michael A. Campion and Paul W. Thayer, "Development and Field Evaluation of an Interdisciplinary Measure of Job Design," *Journal of Applied Psychology* 70 (1985), pp. 29–43.

31. E. J. McCormick, *Job Analysis: Methods and Applications* (New York: AMACOM, 1979); George T. Milkovich and Jerry Newman, *Compensation*, 2nd ed. (Plano, Tex.: Business Publications, 1987); Stephen E. Bennis, Ann Holt Belenky, and Dee Ann Soder, *Job Analysis* (Washington, D.C.: Bureau of National Affairs, 1983).

32. E. J. McCormick, "Job and Task Analysis," in *Handbook of Industrial and Organizational Psychology*, ed. M. Dunnette (Chicago: Rand McNally, 1976).

33. Kenneth N. Wexley and Gary P. Latham, *Developing and Training Human Resources in Organizations* (Glenview, Ill.: Scott, Foresman, 1981).

34. M. D. Dunnette, L. M. Hough, and R. L. Rosse, "Task and Job Taxonomies as a Basis for Identifying Labor Supply Sources and Evaluating Employment Qualifications," *Human Resources Planning* 2, no. 1 (1979), pp. 37–51.

35. K. Perlman, "Job Families: A Review and Discussion of the Implications for Personnel Selection," *Psychological Bulletin* 82, no. 1 (1980), pp. 1–28; Duane Thompson and Toni Thompson, "Court Standards for Job Analysis in Test Validation," *Personnel Psychology* 35 (1982), pp. 865–74.

36. Richard Henderson, *Performance Appraisal: Theory to Practice* (Reston, Va.: Reston Publishing, 1980); H. John Bernardin and Richard Beatty, *Performance Appraisal* (Boston: Kent Publishing, 1984).

37. Milkovich and Newman, *Compensation;* Ronald C. Page, "The Use of Job Content Information for Compensation and Reward Systems" (paper presented at Academy of Management Conference, August 1982, New York); Walter W. Tornow, "An Integrated Personnel Approach to Job Analysis and Job Evaluation" (paper presented at Conference on Job Analysis, Institute of Industrial Relations, University of California, Berkeley, February 1979).

38. Clement J. Berwitz, *The Job Analysis Approach to Affirmative Action* (New York: John Wiley & Sons, 1975).

39. John Lacey, "Job Evaluation and EEO," *Employee Relations Law Journal* 7, no. 3 (1979), pp. 210–17.

40. Milton L. Rock, ed., *Handbook of Wage and Salary Administration* (New York: McGraw-Hill, 1984).

41. Alfred R. Brandt, "Describing Hourly Jobs," in *Handbook of Wage and Salary Administration*, ed. Milton L. Rock (New York: McGraw-Hill, 1984).

42. Ernest J. McCormick, "Job Information: Its Development and Applica-

tions," in *Handbook of Personnel and Industrial Relations*, ed. D. Yoder and H. G. Heneman, Jr. (Washington, D.C.: Bureau of National Affairs, 1979).

43. Ramon J. Aldag, Steve H. Barr, and Arthur P. Brief, "Measurement of Perceived Task Characteristics," *Psychological Bulletin* 90, no. 3, pp. 415–31; Page," The Use of Job Content Information."

44. McCormick, "Job Information"; McCormick, *Job Analysis* (New York: AMACOM, 1979); McCormick, "Job and Task Analysis," in *Handbook of Industrial and Organizational Psychology*, ed. M. D. Dunnette (Chicago: Rand McNally, 1976). The PAQ is distributed by the Purdue University Book Store, 360 West State Street, West Lafayette, Indiana 47906.

45. R. C. Mecham, E. J. McCormick, and P. R. Jeanneret, *Technical Manual for the Position Analysis Questionnaire (PAQ) System* (Logan, Utah: PAQ Services, 1977).

46. E. T. Cornelius III, T. J. Carron, and M. M. Collins, "Job Analysis Models and Job Classification," *Personnel Psychology* 32 (1979), pp. 693–708; also see R. W. Lissitz, J. L. Mendoza, C. J. Huberty, and V. H. Markos, "Some Ideas on a Methodology for Determining Job Similarities/Differences," *Personnel Psychology* 32 (1979), pp. 517–28; and JoAnn Lee and Jorge L. Mendoza, "A Comparison of Techniques which Test for Job Difference," *Personnel Psychology* 34 (1981), pp. 731–48.

47. E. A. Fleishman, *Structure and Measurement of Physical Fitness* (Englewood Cliffs, N.J.: Prentice-Hall, 1964); E. A. Fleishman, "Toward a Taxonomy of Human Performance," *American Psychologist* 30 (1975), pp. 1017–32; E. A. Fleishman, "Evaluating Physical Abilities Required by Jobs," *The Personnel Administrator* 24 (1979), pp. 82–92; E. A. Fleishman, "On the Relation between Abilities, Learning, and Human Performance," *American Psychologist* 27 (1972), pp. 1017–32.

48. Ronnie Staw and Lorel Foged, "The Limits of Job Evaluation to Achieve Comparable Worth" (paper presented at Atlantic Economic Conference, Montreal, Canada, October 11–14, 1984).

49. Cornelius, Carron, and Collins, "Job Analysis Models"; and Jack E. Smith and Milton D. Hakel, "Convergence among Data Sources, Response Bias, and Reliability and Validity of a Structured Job Analysis Questionnaire," *Personnel Psychology* 32, no. 4 (1979), pp. 677–92.

50. M. J. Wallace, "Methodology, Research Practice, and Progress in Personnel and Industrial Relations," *Academy of Management Review* 8, no. 1 (1983), pp. 6–13.

51. U.S. Department of Labor, Manpower Administration, *Handbook for Analyzing Jobs* (Washington, D.C.: Government Printing Office, 1972); S. A. Fine and W. W. Wiley, *An Introduction to Functional Job Analysis*, monograph no. 4 (Kalamazoo, Mich.: W. E. Upjohn Institute for Employment Research, 1971).

52. Fine and Wiley, *Functional Job Analysis*.

53. Frank Krzystofiak, Jerry M. Newman, and Gary Anderson, "A Quantified Approach to Measurement of Job Content: Procedures and Payoffs," *Personnel Psychology*, Summer 1979, pp. 341–57.

54. Ronald A. Ash and S. L. Edgell, "A Note on the Readability of the Position Analysis Questionnaire (PAQ)," *Journal of Applied Psychology* 60 (1975), pp. 765–66; John R. Roark and John H. Burnett, "Objective Methods of

Job Analysis," in *Handbook of Wage and Salary Administration*, ed. Milton L. Rock (New York: McGraw-Hill, 1984).

55. J. J. N. Gambardella and W. G. Alvord, "Ti-CODAP: A Computerized Method of Job Analysis for Personnel Management," report prepared for Prince Georges County, Maryland, April 1980.

56. H. H. Meyer, "Comparison of Foreman and General Foreman Conceptions of the Foreman's Job Responsibility," *Personnel Psychology* 12 (1959), pp. 445–52; A. P. O'Reilly, "Skill Requirements: Supervisor-Subordinate Conflict," *Personnel Psychology* 26 (1973), pp. 75–80; J. T. Hazel, J. M. Madden, and R. E. Christal, "Agreement between Worker-Supervisor Descriptions of the Worker's Job," *Journal of Industrial Psychology* 2 (1964), pp. 71–79; and R. Likert, *New Patterns of Management* (New York: McGraw-Hill, 1961). Also see Paul R. Sackett, Edwin T. Cornelius III, and Theodore J. Carron, "A Comparison of Global Judgment versus Task-Oriented Approaches to Job Classification," *Personnel Psychology* 34 (1981), pp. 791–804.

57. Edwin T. Cornelius III, Angelo S. DeNisi, and Allyn Blencoe, "Expert and Naive Raters Using the PAQ: Does It Matter?" *Personnel Psychology* 37 (1984), pp. 453–64; Smith and Hakel, "Convergence among Data Sources."

58. George T. Milkovich and Charles J. Cogill, "Measurement as an Issue in Analysis and Evaluation of Jobs," in *Handbook of Wage and Salary Administration*, ed. Milton L. Rock (New York: McGraw-Hill, 1984).

59. Roark and Burnett, "Objective Methods of Job Analysis." For an example of the statistical analysis on PAQ results, see R. D. Arvey, S. E. Maxwell, R. L. Gutenberg, and C. Camp, "Detecting Job Differences: A Monte Carlo Study," *Personnel Psychology* 34 (1981), pp. 709–30.

60. E. M. Ramras, "Discussion," *Proceedings of Division of Military Psychology Symposium: Collecting, Analyzing, and Reporting Information Describing Jobs and Occupations*, 77th Annual Convention of the American Psychological Association, Lackland Air Force Base, Texas, September 1969, pp. 75–76.

61. Luis R. Gomez-Mejia, Ronald C. Page, and Walter W. Tornow, "A Comparison of the Practical Utility of Traditional, Statistical, and Hybrid Job Evaluation Approaches," *Academy of Management Journal* 25, no. 4 (1982), pp. 790–809.

62. Ronald A. Ash and Edward L. Levine, "A Framework for Evaluating Job Analysis Methods," *Personnel* 57, no. 6 (November-December 1980), pp. 53–59; E. L. Levine, R. A. Ash, and N. Bennett, "Exploratory Comparative Study of Four Job Analysis Methods," *Journal of Applied Psychology* 65 (1980), pp. 524–35; and R. A. Ash, E. L. Levine, and F. Sistrunk, "The Role of Jobs and Job-Based Methods in Personnel and Human Resources Management," *Research in Personnel and Human Resources Management* 1 (1983), pp. 45–84. Edward L. Levine, Ronald A. Ash, Hardy Hall, and Frank Sistrunk, "Evaluation of Job Analysis Methods by Experienced Job Analysts," *Academy of Management Journal* 26, no. 2 (1983), pp. 339–48.

63. M. D. Dunnette, L. M. Hough, and R. L. Rosse, "Task and Job Taxonomies as a Basis for Identifying Labor Supply Sources and Evaluating Employment Qualifications," in *Affirmative Action Planning*, ed. George T. Milkovich and Lee Dyer (New York: Human Resource Planning Society, 1979), pp. 37–51.

chapter

six

EMPLOYEE CONDITIONS: INDIVIDUAL DIFFERENCES

CHAPTER OUTLINE

Individual differences determine which individuals are suited for different organizational roles, respond to organizational rewards, and profit from training activities. Virtually all human resource activities consider individual differences in setting objectives and evaluating results. Individual differences can create immense opportunities for improved productivity. Research on manufacturing jobs suggests that high performers are often 20 percent more productive than average performers, and 44 percent better than poor performers.[1] Performance differences in jobs with even more individual discretion (such as managerial positions) are probably even larger. For example, U.S. Army researchers recently estimated that it would take only 9 tanks commanded by superior tank commanders to accomplish the same task as 17 tanks commanded by average tank commanders.[2] Nuclear power plant operators who fall asleep on the job pose serious threats not only to the organizations they work for, but to the larger society as well.[3] Given identical job requirements, organizational conditions, and external environments, individual differences can lead to very different outcomes.

Think about all the ways individuals differ. We can observe differences in gender, height, and weight, as well as eye, skin, and hair color. When individuals engage in certain physical tasks such as lifting weights, we can measure their strength, speed, and stamina. When individuals engage in certain mental tasks such as paper and pencil tests, we can measure their knowledge, comprehension, mathematical ability, verbal ability, and ability to read a language. When individuals interact with equipment or machinery, we can measure their ability to drive, operate a drill press, or hang glide. If we observe individuals over time, we can measure their behavior patterns, job changes, and physical aging. Some individual differences are apparent to only one person, such as features that make people attractive or unattractive to you. Some individual differences are affected by environment, such as whether they have received hang-gliding training. Other individual differences are genetic and do not respond to the environment (except in very extreme cases), such as gender or eye color.

Unlike raw materials or financial instruments, one cannot simply order employees with particular characteristics. People are complete packages of distinct individual features. So the task of human resource managers is more complex than managing raw materials or finance. If human resource activities, such as selection or compensation, attend to only one feature, they may risk disaster if other features also are affected. For example, in the southern United States Duke Power Company's selection system required a high school diploma in an attempt to improve the intelligence of its work force. Because this requirement excluded virtually all blacks from the job, the company paid substantial legal penalties.[4] Unlike raw materials (steel girders or silicon chips), one cannot test a sample of human beings to the breaking point to ensure their adequacy before hiring. The human resource decision maker must choose which of the infinite individual differences affects future performance. Some characteristics are obviously important for some jobs but not for others. For instance, vision is critical for selecting truck drivers, but perhaps less critical for selecting radio dispatchers. Some characteristics, such as eye color, may seldom be relevant to the employment relationship. Of the infinite number of individual differences, how does a human resource manager decide which to attend to and which to ignore?

Similar to assessments of external or organizational conditions, or assessments of job requirements and specifications, the individual differences discussed in this chapter represent information that can support decisions about human resource activities. This chapter presents theories about individuals that have proved useful in making human resource decisions to achieve efficiency and equity.

No person is an island; individuals form groups and interact with each other at work. For example, a baseball team built solely on younger stars is usually not as effective as one built on a mixture of veterans and younger players. The Cincinnati Reds baseball team needs both Eric Davis (a 24-year-old player with great potential) and Dave Parker (a 35-year-old veteran). The sum of a work group can be more than its individual parts. Therefore, human resource management must consider not only each individual's characteristics, but how individuals work together in work groups and how they interact through supervisory relationships. This chapter explores the nature of individual differences, theories to explain individual reactions to employment relationships, and the impact of supervisory relationships on human resource management.

HUMAN RESOURCE DECISIONS AND THE MATCHING PROCESS

As Exhibit 6–1 shows individual differences in behaviors and attitudes resemble a matching process. Human resource activities match individuals and jobs. Individuals bring particular *skills/knowledge/aptitudes* and *needs/values* to the employment relationship. As discussed in Chapter Five, jobs have certain *content* or duties, tasks, behaviors, functions, and responsibilities necessary for satisfactory performance. They also have *returns* or results of membership and performance, such as pay, status, and social relationships. The worker-job match affects efficiency and equity.

EXHIBIT 6-1
The Matching Process (matching process for individual work behaviors)

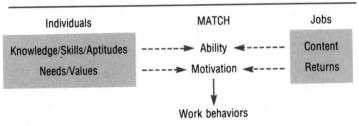

Matching process for individual work attitudes

Regarding efficiency, the match between the individual's skills/knowledge/ aptitudes and the job's content determines the individual's ability to accomplish work behaviors such as performance, attendance, and tenure. The match between the individual's needs/values, behaviors, and the job's returns determines the individual's motivation to engage in the work behaviors. Regarding equity, the match between the individual's needs/ values and the job's returns affects the individual's work attitudes, such as job satisfaction.

Definition

Abilities are capabilities to engage in some behavior. Abilities derive from *knowledge* (awareness of information, techniques, or facts), *skills* (proficiency at basic tasks necessary for achieving more complex behaviors), and *aptitudes* (potential abilities that have not yet been fully developed or applied).

Definition

Attitudes are emotions or feelings. They derive from relationships between perceived outcomes and individual *values* (perceptions of what is desired and important) and *needs* (perceptions of what is required).

> **Definition**
>
> *Motivation* is the drive that energizes, sustains, and directs a person's behavior. Motivation derives from perceived relationships between behaviors and the fulfillment of *values* and/or *needs*.

ABILITY, MOTIVATION, AND EMPLOYEE WORK BEHAVIORS

What leads one employee to perform a job better than another? What causes some employees to come to work reliably and regularly, while others are frequently absent? What causes some employees to work for decades for an employer, while others leave after a short time? Three general factors affect employees' work behaviors: First is individual *ability*. Everyone has heard stories of the super salesperson or super engineer who, when promoted to management, turned out to be mediocre or worse. Skills, aptitudes, and knowledge that are well suited to one job may be useless in another. Second is the complex dimension of *motivation*, resulting from the match between the individual's needs/values and job outcomes, as well as the perceived link between engaging in work behaviors and obtaining the desired outcomes. Why are some people highly motivated by sales commissions, while others fail to work hard for such rewards? Unlike ability, motivation cannot be measured, only inferred by observing behavior; it can fluctuate among individuals and over time in the same individual. The third factor affecting employee work behaviors is *conditions beyond the individual's control*. For example, a salesperson may not perform well because a fire destroyed inventories, making it impossible to meet orders. In this chapter, our primary concern is with individual differences, one of several factors affecting employee work behaviors.

Motivation interacts with ability to affect individual work behaviors.[5] Imagine that you encountered an accident victim who would die without an emergency tracheotomy (an incision and tube through the windpipe to allow breathing). Your motivation to perform the task would likely be quite high. However, without the knowledge and skills required, you would not have the ability to perform the operation. Similarly, nearly all seven-year-olds have the required ability to pick up and put away their toys. Yet, any parent can attest that the motivation to do so is often sadly lacking, and no performance occurs. A simple model suggests that performance equals ability times motivation ($P = A \times M$); but the precise nature of the ability/motivation/performance relationship is unclear.[6]

Ability

For years, psychologists and others have recognized the existence of individual differences in ability.[7] Psychologists categorize various kinds of ability as:[8]

> *Mechanical ability*—Ability to visualize how parts fit together into a whole; comprehension of mechanical relationships.
>
> *Motor coordination ability*—The ability to move the body effectively to perform physical tasks.
>
> *Intellectual ability*—General intelligence or reasoning; verbal and numerical ability.
>
> *Creative ability*—Innovative and artistic ability; aesthetic judgment.

That abilities influence job performance is generally well accepted. In fact, recent studies of abilities suggest that they may be related to job performance even in quite different jobs (more about this in Chapter Eleven on selection).[9]

Using Abilities in Human Resource Activities

Two human resource activities—staffing and training—most strongly rely on individual ability differences to increase the match between individuals and jobs.

   Staffing. Staffing activities move people into, through, and out of the organization. Determining which individuals to hire, promote, transfer, or lay off often requires indicators of their ability to accomplish the job requirements. Measuring abilities and predicting future behaviors from those abilities is an important purpose of staffing activities.

   Training. Training activities provide experiences and learning opportunities in hopes of changing the abilities of individuals to better match job requirements. Obviously, trainers must carefully consider employees' abilities before training to ensure matching training to the employees' learning ability. After the training, trainers must ensure that the abilities developed through training match the job requirements. Because selection predictions are not perfect, some employees may not perform as well as predicted. One way to correct such situations is to provide training for those employees who need additional strength in certain abilities.

Motivation

Many psychologists agree that goal-directed behavior is important.[10] Knowing why behavior occurs and why it is directed toward one of countless possible goals allows considerable progress in improving an employee's job performance. For example, one auto assembly worker makes the appropriate welds in a timely fashion as cars pass on the line. Another worker expends considerable energy in finding ways to beat the system. As a result, welds are missed; coat hangers are welded to parts of the body and are virtually undiscoverable until an owner takes the car in with complaints about an "irritating rattle." These two employees work on the same line, with similar environments; each receives the same pay and works the same hours. Yet their behavior is obviously directed to entirely different goals.

The following theories shed some light on this and countless other motivation problems experienced in the real world. We discuss these theories as they bear on job performance; they also have relevance for other work behaviors such as absenteeism and turnover.

Content Theories

Content theories emphasize *what* motivates people rather than *how* people are motivated. The key variable in these theories is needs.[11] The two most well-known content theories include the work by Abraham Maslow,[12] and by Frederick Herzberg, Bernard Mausner, and Barbara Snyderman.[13]

Maslow. As Exhibit 6–2 shows, Maslow's theory is based on a hierarchy of five needs; each need is assumed to motivate behavior in varying degrees.[14] Maslow argues that lower-level needs in the hierarchy take precedence: behavior is directed toward satisfying these needs sufficiently to make the next higher order need dominant. For example, illegal aliens entering the United States may first direct their behavior toward obtaining necessary food to satisfy the physiological needs of themselves and their families. If they obtain jobs that ensure consistent satisfaction of that need, the security need becomes dominant. Higher-order needs become progressively more important as lower-order needs are satisfied.

EXHIBIT 6-2
Maslow's Hierarchy of Needs

1. Physiological needs	The need for food, water, and air.
2. Safety needs	The need for security, stability, and the absence from pain, threat, or illness.
3. Social needs	Need for affection, belongingness, love.
4. Esteem needs	Need for personal feelings of achievement or self-esteem and also a need for recognition or respect from others.
5. Self-actualization needs	Need to become all one is capable of becoming, to realize one's own potential, or achieve self-fulfillment.

Source: George T. Milkovich and Jerry M. Newman, *Compensation*, 2nd ed. (Plano, Tex.: Business Publications, 1987), p. 277.

One of the major problems with this approach is that it is extremely difficult to identify which needs are prepotent at any given time. Without this information, it is virtually impossible to determine how a work environment should be structured to improve performance. For example, research indicates that needs vary by age, geographic location (urban/rural), socioeconomic status, and sex, to name a few. There is even speculation that the needs of the general population have been shifting over time toward a greater concern for such higher-level needs as autonomy and self-actualization.[15]

Herzberg. Herzberg's theory appears very similar to Maslow's.[16] He argues that two factors are present across organizations: hygienes and motivators (see Exhibit 6–3). Hygiene factors include such things as company policy, administration, supervision, salary, interpersonal relations, and working conditions. Motivators are represented by opportunities for advancement, achievement, responsibility, and recognition. It might be argued that Maslow's theory has gravitated in the same direction as Herzberg's. If most lower-order needs are generally satisfied in our affluent society, then individual needs that are prepotent in Maslow's framework include esteem and self-actualization.[17] As conceived by Maslow, these needs are very similar to Herzberg's conception of advancement, achievement, and recognition. Because these factors are prepotent, they assume responsibility for a great deal of the goal direction of individuals. In Herzberg's terms they become the motivators, the factors that can lead to job satisfaction if met by the organization.[18]

Process Theories

Process theories of motivation focus on *how* people are motivated. They certainly recognize the role of content theories in examining the needs and reinforcers that are part of the motivational process. They also attempt to explain how this process operates.

Expectancy Theory. The motivation theory most studied over the last two decades is *expectancy*, or VIE theory. VIE is an acronym for valence

EXHIBIT 6–3
Herzberg's Two Factors

Hygiene Factors (content)	Motivating Factors (content)
Company policies	Feelings of accomplishment
Pay	
benefits	
Supervision	Feelings of achievement
Working conditions	Recognition
Job security	Personal growth

EXHIBIT 6–4
A Composite Expectancy-Valence Model

Force to expend specific level of effort	Expectancy that specific level of effort will/will not accomplish task	Valence of task goal accomplish-ment/failure	Instrumentality of task accomplishment/ failure for job outcomes	Valence of job outcomes	Instrumentality of job outcomes for need satisfaction	Valence of "basic" needs

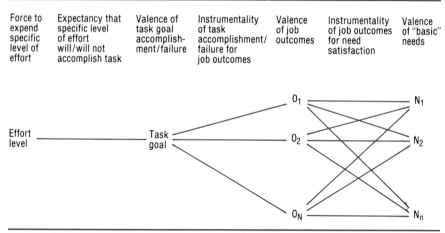

Note: For purposes of simplicity this schematic portrays only one level of effort and one level of success on one task goal. A similar set of relationships exists for alternative levels of effort and alternative tasks or alternative levels of success.

Source: John P. Campbell and Robert Pritchard, "Motivation Theory in Industrial and Organizational Psychology," in *Handbook of Industrial and Organizational Psychology,* ed. Marvin Dunnette, © 1976, John Wiley & Sons, Inc. Reprinted by permission.

(V), instrumentality (I), and expectancy (E). Based on earlier works,[19] John Campbell and Richard Pritchard present a composite of the important variables in the VIE theory.[20] Exhibit 6–4 summarizes the model.

Effort. The variable explained by the model is effort, which is a result of the perceived force to expend energy in a certain way. Individuals always face choices among ways to expend energy. For example, as you read this, you may or may not be exerting effort to take notes.

Expectancy. Will effort lead to behaviors? Expectancy is an individual's estimated probability that exerting a specific level of effort will accomplish or fail to produce the desired behavior or task. The question here is, "If I try, will I accomplish the task or behavior?" Probabilities represent numbers between 0 percent and 100 percent, and the higher the probability of effort producing task accomplishment, the higher the possible force to expend that effort. For example, if you frequently take notes while reading, the probability (expectancy) is high that exerting note-taking effort will result in useful notes. If you have never taken notes while reading, this probability is lower.

Valence. The second factor in this model is the valence (or value) of the task, job outcome, or satisfied need. The question here is "if I did accomplish the task, receive the job outcome, or satisfy a need, how much would I value that?" Different individuals may place quite different values on these things. Maslow's theory suggests that satisfying prepotent needs has greater valence than satisfying nonprepotent needs. For example, in deciding to take notes, you might consider how much you value taking good notes, how much you value the higher test grades (if any) such notes would lead to, and how much you value satisfying your need for achievement with higher test grades (if they do satisfy this need).

Instrumentality. Although accomplishing a task or behavior, such as taking notes, can have intrinsic value in and of itself, individuals also consider the extrinsic rewards that result from performing the task or behavior, such as pay, promotions, or good grades.[21] Instrumentality reflects this link. The question is, "If I did accomplish the task or behavior, what is the probability that I would receive outcomes; and if I received those outcomes, what is the probability they would satisfy my needs?" Similar to expectancies, instrumentalities represent probabilities; higher instrumentalities mean higher potential effort levels. For example, in deciding to take notes, you might consider whether the notes actually would help you increase your course grade, and whether a higher course grade would satisfy your need for achievement.

VIE theory explains why students expend more effort in courses related to their career goals: Such effort leads to better studying, better studying is instrumental to getting jobs, and jobs are related to satisfying needs for income, security, and status. In an employment setting, VIE theory suggests that pay motivates performance if employees perceive that their effort can accomplish job tasks, that those tasks are instrumental to receiving increased pay, and that the increased pay is sufficient to satisfy their needs.

Equity Theory. "Being stuck in traffic is bad, but seeing cars moving freely in the lane next to you is infuriating." Receiving a raise from $4.00 to $5.00 per hour after one year on the job may seem great, until you find out that new employees are getting $5.50. Perceptions of what we receive and what we want are affected by what we think others are getting, and what they must do to get it.

J. Stacey Adams argues that individuals compare their inputs and outcomes to those of relevant other persons in determining whether they are equitably (fairly) treated.[22] Stated another way, the comparison process is a comparison of ratios:

$$\frac{\text{Person's outcomes}}{\text{Person's inputs}} \quad \begin{matrix}\text{compared} \\ \text{to}\end{matrix} \quad \frac{\text{Other's outcomes}}{\text{Other's inputs}} \rightarrow \begin{matrix}\text{Employee} \\ \text{Behavior}\end{matrix}$$

Varying Perceptions. This model suggests that individuals consider the ratio of the outcomes or rewards they receive to the inputs they provide, and compare their ratio to their perceptions of the ratio for some relevant other person or group. When the two ratios are unequal, an individual is motivated to reduce the perceived inequity. A key in this explanation is the word *perceived*. Perceived inequities can result when individuals consider as inputs factors that others might consider irrelevant. For example, a physically attractive salesperson might consider attractiveness a relative input and expect to be compensated higher than a less attractive individual, other things equal. Yet the organization may consider this an irrelevant input for pay purposes, pay the two individuals equally, and never realize that it is perceived as an inequitable exchange.

Perceptions and Performance. The possible impact of perceived inequity on motivation and subsequent performance is pointed out by Adams.[23] People can (1) cognitively distort their or others' inputs and/or outcomes, (2) attempt to change their or others' inputs and/or outcomes, (3) change the comparison person, or (4) reduce their involvement in the exchange relationship. Several of these consequences have implications for work behavior. For example, consider a company that has a union representing all blue-collar workers. If nonunionized clerical workers do not receive raises commensurate with those obtained by unionized workers, one possible outcome could be efforts by clerical workers to form their own union. If clerical workers use the unionized blue-collar workers as relevant others and perceive that rewards for the two groups are out of balance, given inputs, the clerical workers could view unionization as a way to improve outcomes and reestablish equity.

Individual Motivation in Human Resource Decisions

What does all of this discussion of ability, motivation, and performance have to do with human resource management? A goal of designing human resource management activities is to maximize employee effectiveness through high levels of performance. Thus, human resource management programs must act on employees' abilities and motivation.

Influencing employees' motivation is more difficult than influencing employees' abilities through staffing or training. According to expectancy theory, employees are motivated if they believe: (1) that exerting increased effort leads to rewarded behaviors, and (2) that achieving certain behaviors leads to desired outcomes. Equity theory suggests that employees exert effort to the extent that they believe it can reduce perceived inequities compared to some other person or group. Thus, expectancy and equity theories suggest that motivation results not only from factors under the organization's control, such as reward levels and work rules linking behaviors and rewards, but also from factors not under the organization's control, such as importance attached to rewards, perceptions of the work outcomes received by others, and social rewards provided by co-workers. Human resource activities such as job design and compensation establish a framework that links employee behaviors and rewards. There is no guarantee, however, that employees perceive the system in the way that it is designed, nor that the rewards considered important by the designers are also important to the employees.

EMPLOYEES' ATTITUDES

Human resource decision makers are concerned with the feelings and emotions employees have toward their work for at least two reasons: First, employee attitudes seem related to employee behaviors such as attendance and length of service;[24] and, though supporting evidence is limited, there is a common belief that positive attitudes contribute to increased employee performance.[25] Second, independent of its effects on behaviors related to efficiency, equity is one of the major objectives of human resource management. Interest groups such as governments, unions, and communities judge the equity of human resource activities, but one of the most important interest groups is an organization's own employees. Therefore, many employers take great pride and devote substantial effort to ensure that employees perceive them as good employers.

Job Satisfaction

Though employee attitudes go by names such as morale, opinions, or job involvement and are measured in many ways, industrial psychologists have devoted great effort to defining and measuring job satisfaction.

Definition

Job satisfaction is a pleasurable or positive emotional reaction to a person's job experiences.[26]

Content of Job Satisfaction

Analysts measure job satisfaction primarily through questionnaires. These questionnaires typically address satisfaction with various facets of the job, as well as provide an overall satisfaction score for each employee. The *Job Descriptive Index* (JDI) measures satisfaction with five job facets: (1) work itself, (2) supervision, (3) pay, (4) promotion opportunity, and

EXHIBIT 6–5
Job Satisfaction Facets from the MSQ

Ability utilization	Moral values
Achievement	Recognition
Activity	Responsibility
Advancement	Security
Authority	Social service
Company policies and practices	Social status
Compensation	Supervision—human relations
Co-workers	Supervision—technical
Creativity	Variety
Independence	Working conditions

(5) co-workers.[27] The *Minnesota Satisfaction Questionnaire* (MSQ) measures satisfaction with the 20 work facets in Exhibit 6–5.[28] Analysts compute overall measures of individual satisfaction by summing the individual facet satisfaction levels, or by asking individuals a specific question about their overall satisfaction.

Process of Job Satisfaction

Why do individuals differ in their job satisfaction? What processes operate to influence satisfaction with the various facets of work? Edwin Locke has proposed a *discrepancy theory* of job satisfaction.[29] This theory states that satisfaction is affected by two factors: First, individuals' values that define what they want or desire as well as the importance of the desire. Second, perceptions that define how much individuals believe they are receiving. The discrepancy between desired and perceived work facets, as well as the importance of the facet, determines the level of satisfaction. Exhibit 6–6 illustrates this, showing how satisfaction with pay and temperature relates to each facet and the importance attached to each facet by individuals.

Pay satisfaction rises as pay increases because an individual can probably never have too much pay, so the discrepancy is always getting smaller as pay rises. Other work facets that might show this similar pattern would be fringe benefits and status.

In contrast, temperature satisfaction rises and then falls as temperature increases because there is an ideal temperature level, and both positive and negative differences from it cause less satisfaction. Work facets that might show this pattern include supervisory attention, interactions with co-workers, and variety in job duties.

Equity theory also helps to explain individual differences in work attitudes, by suggesting how individuals decide how much of a work facet

EXHIBIT 6–6
Satisfaction Functions Illustrating Discrepancy Theory

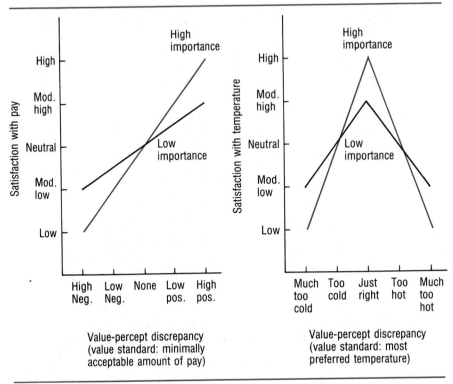

Adapted from Edwin A. Locke, "The Nature and Causes of Job Satisfaction," in *Handbook of Industrial and Organizational Psychology*, ed. Marvin D. Dunnette (Chicago: Rand McNally, 1976).

they desire, or feel would be equitable. Individuals may consider the ratio of the work outcomes and inputs for others, compare that ratio to the levels of inputs the individual provides, and judge what the appropriate level of their own work outcomes should be. The importance of the work facet may also be partially determined by the importance of the equity perception to the individual.

Specialized Attitude Information

The MSQ and JDI may not provide information specific to organizational objectives. Therefore, many organizations develop their own opinion or morale surveys to tap employees' attitudes in areas of particular interest. Sears Roebuck & Co. has used attitude questionnaires and interviews since 1938.[30] IBM has used regular employee attitude surveys since the late 1950s.

Attitude surveys typically contain mixtures of multiple-choice questions and open-ended questions allowing employees to write in their responses. Some of the questions are core or standard items included in all surveys. Others may reflect issues relevant only to a particular location (such as the introduction of new technology), or only at a particular time. Exhibit 6–7 shows a hypothetical example of a managerial attitude survey report with several typical questions and hypothetical survey results.

Implementing Specialized Attitude Measures

Attitude surveys can provide useful information when they are designed to support human resource decisions, but they can be harmful if not carefully used. As with all information used to make decisions, attitude surveys are more valuable if they improve important decisions and obtain information at low cost. It is important that organizations carefully consider the purposes of attitude information before using surveys. Attitude data can serve at least six purposes:

1. Identification of trends in employee morale and the degree and trends of specific employee opinions by skill and organizational units.
2. Identification and analysis of key issues that may be common throughout the business units or functions.
3. Feedback to management regarding administration of policies, practices, programs, and the effectiveness of business operations.
4. Feedback to managers as a basis for improving working relationships with their subordinates.
5. A process that ensures timely planning and implementation of appropriate corrective actions.
6. Conducting research.

Once employees have been surveyed, they likely expect to receive at least information on survey results and any plans or decisions based on the results. Organizations should administer surveys to those employee groups best suited to provide useful information. For example, employee groups affected by layoffs may provide the most useful information about layoff attitudes. Guarantees of anonymity may be useful in obtaining honest responses (for instance, guarantees that no one sees the opinion forms except data processing personnel). Answer sheets are destroyed after processing, and individual responses are combined with others in computing statistics. Companies should consider survey results in context. There is no "best" level of employee attitudes. Therefore, such results should be monitored over time and/or compared to the attitude levels of similar groups of employees in other locations or organizations. Exhibit 6–7 provides comparisons between the department, function and location.

EXHIBIT 6–7
Hypothetical Specialized Attitude Questionnaire Results

PDQ, Incorporated
Opinion Survey Results—Location XYZ—February 1987
Department 1102, Function B, Manager T. W. Post, Building A431
Confidential

	Average	Percent Giving This Response				
		1	2	3	4	5

1. How would you rate PDQ as a company to work for compared with other companies?
   1—One of the best 2—Above average 3—Average 4—Below average 5—One of the worst

	Average	1	2	3	4	5
Department 1102	1.89	33	44	22		
Function B	1.95	22	61	17		
Location XYZ	1.83	34	49	17		

2. If you have your way, will you be working for PDQ five years from now?
   1—Certainly 2—Probably 3—Not sure 4—Probably not 5—Certainly not

	Average	1	2	3	4	5
Department 1102	1.56	44	56			
Function B	2.32	20	44	23	10	3
Location XYZ	2.38	18	43	24	10	4

3. Do you feel pressure for increasing your output above what you think reasonable?
   1—A great deal 2—Quite a bit 3—Some 4—A little 5—No pressure

	Average	1	2	3	4	5
Department 1102	4.56			11	22	67
Function B	3.40	9	17	26	21	27
Location XYZ	3.40	10	16	26	20	28

4. In recent months have job pressures or requirements interfered with your personal or family life?
   1—Yes, very often 2—Quite often 3—Sometimes 4—A little 5—No pressure

	Average	1	2	3	4	5
Department 1102	3.89			22	67	11
Function B	3.04	14	15	38	21	13
Location XYZ	3.09	13	14	37	23	13

5. How effective is the appraisal program in letting you know what you should do to improve your performance?
   1—Very efficient 2—Quite 3—Somewhat 4—Not too 5—Not at all efficient

	Average	1	2	3	4	5
Department 1102	3.00		33	33	33	
Function B	2.94	4	25	37	27	
Location XYZ	3.17	4	24	34	27	11

Using Employees' Attitude Information in Human Resource Decisions

The discrepancy theory of satisfaction suggests that human resource activities affect employee attitudes through their effects on employee values and perceptions. The objective aspects of jobs (such as pay levels, upward mobility, supervisor attention, and interactions with co-workers) affect employee attitudes. Discrepancy theory also suggests that individual reactions to work can be different, even when the objective work characteristics are the same. First, individuals may place different importance levels on work facets. Employees with children may place greater importance on opportunities for health insurance, college tuition support, and day-care centers. Younger employees may place importance on upward mobility, while older employees may be more concerned with pension benefits. Second, individuals may differ in the amount of any work facet that they prefer. New employees may prefer a great deal of guidance and attention from supervisors, while experienced employees may find such attention distracting or unnecessary. Third, individuals may differ in the amount of a work facet they perceive themselves as receiving. Some employees may make an effort to become quite well informed about the amount and value of their fringe benefits, while others may be completely unaware of them.

Individual values are relatively fixed, and are probably most readily changed through staffing activities. Organizations that provide realistic information about pay and benefit levels, working conditions, supervision, and promotion opportunities may find that they attract applicants whose values better fit the available work outcomes. Discrepancy theory suggests that such individuals will experience smaller discrepancies between what they desire and what they perceive they are getting, and thus may be more satisfied.

Compared to employee values, employee perceptions are more easily altered by human resource activities, especially communication activities. For example, employees often underestimate the amount and value of their fringe benefit levels; careful communication efforts, however, may help them see the true value of such rewards. Discrepancy theory suggests that such communication can increase employee satisfaction because employees perceive the level of fringe benefits as being closer to their desired level. As noted earlier, the supervisor plays a key role in such communication and, therefore, in shaping the attitudes of the work force.

SUPERVISION

One of the most important influences on employee motivation is the supervisor. Supervisors enhance motivation by helping employees see the link between the requirements of the organization, such as performance standards, and employees' behaviors. Supervisors can communicate the relationships between jobs, employees, and work groups, and thus influence the comparisons used when employees consider the equity of the employment relationship. Supervisors enhance attitudes by helping employees more accurately perceive the value of the job's returns to satisfying their needs.

The supervisor or manager is directly involved in many of the most significant human resource management activities. The supervisor and the work group constitute the social environment within which the individual learns the norms and expectations for production. A favorable and constructive social environment is conducive to positive individual motivation and productivity.[31] A negative social environment inhibits motivation, which has an unfavorable impact on performance. The success of the entire human resource management system depends on how thoughtfully and fairly the supervisor manages it.[32]

Leadership Styles

Leadership is a mutual process. Not only do leaders affect workers, but workers also affect leaders. Additionally, other organization factors such as the organization objectives, finances, technology and culture, and the nature of the work—all factors in our diagnostic model—affect leadership.[33]

Considerable effort was once spent trying to identify which personality characteristics determined a successful leader.[34] Such information would be helpful in selecting supervisors. One group classified leaders by their decision-making style:

Authoritarian—The leader makes decisions alone and tells subordinates what they are to do.

Democratic—The leader actively involves subordinates in the decision-making process, sharing problems, soliciting input, and sharing authority.

Laissez-faire—The leader avoids making decisions whenever possible and leaves it up to subordinates to make individual decisions with little guidance either from the leader or from the rest of the group.

Research on the effectiveness of alternative leadership styles produced some interesting results. For example, individuals under democratic leadership were more satisfied, had higher morale, were more creative, and had better relationships with their superiors.[35] However, the quantity of output produced by workers was highest under the autocratic leadership style, slightly lower under democratic leadership, and lowest under laissez-faire leadership.

Most researchers now agree that no single leadership style is universally associated with effectiveness.[36] Rather, a *contingency approach* is advocated. A contingency approach recognizes that effective leadership depends on the circumstances. The nature of the organization, work, and employees all affect what is required of leaders. Effective leadership requires a match between the circumstances and the supervisor.

Effective supervisors are able to adapt their style of relating to employees to the employees' abilities and motivation. They encourage employee participation in key decisions in the work unit. And they help develop effective work groups.

SUMMARY

The basic premise of this chapter is that differences in employees play a key role in managing human resources. Understanding and utilizing these differences in personnel decisions helps achieve employee and organizational objectives.

The concept of individual differences is incorporated into the design and administration of many personnel activities. Selecting employees with required skills, granting larger pay increases to superior performers, promoting only those employees with the greatest potential, tailoring training programs to individual needs, and offering health insurance options with the flexibility to meet each employee's needs are all examples.

Having examined theories about individual differences, and how human resource activities affect basic individual reactions such as motivation and attitudes, the next chapter examines the results of motivation and attitudes: job performance and attendance.

DISCUSSION AND REVIEW QUESTIONS

1. Differentiate abilities from aptitudes. If you were trying to fill an assembly line job, what kind of abilities would you look for in a prospective employee? How would these abilities differ from those you would seek in a person to fill the plant manager's position?

2. Suppose you are a human resource specialist. Why would it be important for you to understand employee motivation? Explain motivation to work in terms of the expectancy theory. Give some practical applications of the theory you could use to motivate employees.

3. Suppose your attitude survey suggests a sudden drop in employees' satisfaction with pay. Using discrepancy theory, suggest which individual factors might cause this result. Suggest human resource actions that might increase pay satisfaction.
4. If you worked for a small company considering starting its first attitude survey, what advice would you give them?
5. What is the supervisor's role in affecting employee performance?

NOTES AND REFERENCES

1. Frank L. Schmidt and John E. Hunter, "Individual Differences in Productivity: An Empirical Test of Estimates Derived from Studies of Selection Procedure Utility," *Journal of Applied Psychology* 68 (1983), pp. 407–14.
2. N. Kent Eaton, Hilda Wing, and K. J. Mitchell, "Alternate Methods of Estimating the Dollar Value of Performance," *Personnel Psychology* 38 (1985), pp. 27–40.
3. Ronald A. Taylor, "Nuclear-Power Industry Gets a Wake-Up Call," *U.S. News & World Report*, April 13, 1987, p. 14.
4. *Griggs* v. *Duke Power Co.*, 401 U.S. 424 (1971).
5. Abraham Korman, *The Psychology of Motivation* (Englewood Cliffs, N.J.: Prentice-Hall, 1974); David McClelland, *The Personality* (Hinsdale, Ill.: Dryden Press, 1951); Victor Vroom, *Work and Motivation* (New York: John Wiley & Sons, 1964); Clayton Alderfer, *Existence, Relatedness, and Growth* (New York: Free Press, 1972); J. W. Atkinson, *An Introduction to Motivation* (New York: American Book, 1964); John Campbell and Robert Pritchard, "Motivation Theory in Industrial and Organizational Psychology," in *Handbook of Industrial and Organizational Psychology*, ed. M. D. Dunnette (Chicago: Rand McNally, 1976); *Motivation & Society: A Volume in Honor of David C. McClelland*, ed. Abigail J. Stewart (San Francisco: Jossey-Bass, 1982).
6. Campbell and Pritchard, "Motivation Theory"; Michael E. Cavanaugh, "In Search of Motivation," *Personnel Journal*, March 1984, pp. 76–80.
7. Bernard Bass, "Individual Capability, Team Performance and Team Productivity," in *Human Performance and Productivity*, eds. M. D. Dunnette and E. A. Fleishman (Hillsdale, N.J.: Lawrence Erlbaum, 1982).
8. C. N. Cofer and M. H. Appley, *Motivation: Theory and Research* (New York: John Wiley & Sons, 1964).
9. John E. Hunter, *The Dimensionality of the General Aptitude Test Battery and the Dominance of General Factors over Specific Factors in the Prediction of Job Performance* (Washington, D.C.: U.S. Employment Service, 1982).
10. Edwin Locke, "The Motivational Effect of Knowledge of Results: Knowledge or Goal Setting?" *Journal of Applied Psychology* 51, no. 2 (1967), pp. 324–29.
11. Edward Lawler III, *Pay and Organization Effectiveness: A Psychological View* (New York: McGraw-Hill, 1971).
12. Abraham Maslow, *Motivation and Personality* (New York: Harper & Row, 1954).

13. Frederick Herzberg, Bernard Mausner, and Barbara Snyderman, *The Motivation to Work* (New York: John Wiley & Sons, 1959).

14. Maslow, *Motivation and Personality*.

15. Theodore Roszak, *The Making of a Counter-Culture: Reflections on the Technocratic Society and Its Youthful Opposition* (Garden City, N.Y.: Doubleday Publishing, 1969).

16. Herzberg et al., *The Motivation to Work*.

17. Maslow, *Motivation and Personality*.

18. Herzberg et al., *The Motivation to Work*.

19. V. H. Vroom, *Work in Motivation* (New York: John Wiley & Sons, 1964); G. Graen, "Instrumentality Theory of Work Motivation: Some Experiential Results and Suggested Modifications," *Journal of Applied Psychology*, monograph 53, no. 2 (1969), pp. 1–25.

20. Campbell and Pritchard, "Motivation Theory."

21. See, for example, E. Deci, "Notes on the Theory and Metatheory of Intrinsic Motivation," *Organizational Behavior and Human Performance* 15, no. 1 (1975), pp. 130–45.

22. J. Stacey Adams, "Inequity in Social Exchange," in *Advances in Experimental Social Psychology*, ed. Leonard Berkowitz (New York: Academic Press, 1965); J. Stacey Adams, "Toward an Understanding of Inequity," *Journal of Abnormal and Social Psychology* 67, no. 3 (1963), pp. 442–636.

23. Ibid.

24. Edwin A. Locke, "The Nature and Causes of Job Satisfaction," in *Handbook of Industrial and Organizational Psychology*, ed. Marvin D. Dunnette (Chicago: Rand McNally, 1976).

25. Ibid.; M. M. Petty, Gail W. McGee, and Jerry W. Cavender, "A Meta-Analysis of the Relationships between Individual Job Satisfaction and Individual Performance," *Academy of Management Review* 9, no. 4 (1984), pp. 712–21.

26. Locke, "Nature and Causes of Job Satisfaction."

27. Pat C. Smith, L. M. Kendall, and Charles L. Hulin, *The Measurement of Satisfaction in Work and Retirement* (Chicago: Rand McNally, 1969).

28. D. J. Weiss, R. V. Dawis, G. W. England, and L. H. Lofquist, *Manual for the Minnesota Satisfaction Questionnaire* (Minneapolis: Minnesota Studies in Vocational Rehabilitation, 1967).

29. Locke, "Nature and Causes of Job Satisfaction."

30. Sanford Jacoby, "Employee Attitude Testing at Sears, Roebuck and Company, 1938–1960." (Working paper, Graduate School of Management, University of California at Los Angeles, 1986).

31. H. Peter Dachler and Bernhard Wilpert, "Conceptual Dimensions and Boundaries of Participation in Organizations: A Critical Evaluation," *Administrative Science Quarterly*, March 1978, pp. 1–39; Ben Graham, Jr., and Parvin Titus, *The Amazing Oversight* (New York: AMACOM, 1979); "Eric Trist on the Quality of Working Life," *Labour Gazette*, August 1977, pp. 365–71; Joseph W. McGuire, "The 'New' Egalitarianism and Management Practice," *California Management Review*, Spring 1977, pp. 21–29.

32. Daniel C. Feldman and Hugh J. Arnold, *Managing Individual and Group Behavior in Organizations* (New York: McGraw-Hill, 1983).

33. S. R. Rhodes and Mildred Doering, "An Integrated Model of Career Mo-

tivation," *Academy of Management Review* 8, no. 4 (1983), pp. 631–40; Manuel London, "Toward a Theory of Career Motivation," *Academy of Management Review* 8, no. 4 (1983), pp. 620–31; Robert Oliver, *Career Unrest: A Source of Creativity* (New York: Center for Research in Career Development, Columbia University, 1981). See, for example, R. M. Stoghill, *Handbook of Leadership: A Survey of Theory and Research* (New York: Free Press, 1984); R. Tannenbaum, R. Weschler, and F. Massarik, *Leadership & Organization* (New York: McGraw-Hill, 1961); G. Yukl, *Leadership & Organizations* (Englewood Cliffs, N.J.: Prentice-Hall, 1981); F. E. Fiedler, *A Theory of Leadership Effectiveness* (New York: McGraw-Hill, 1967); also see V. H. Vroom and P. W. Yetton, *Leadership & Decision Making* (Pittsburgh: University of Pittsburgh Press, 1973).

34. K. Lewin, R. Lippitt, and R. K. White, "Patterns of Aggressive Behavior in Experimentally Created Social Climates," *Journal of Social Psychology* 10 (1939), pp. 271–99.

35. Yukl, *Leadership*.

36. See especially Fiedler, *Leadership Effectiveness*.

chapter seven

EMPLOYEE CONDITIONS: PERFORMANCE AND ATTENDANCE

CHAPTER OUTLINE

V. Summary
  Appendix / Bank of America Employee Booklet on Performance
  Planning, Coaching, and Evaluation

Former New York Yankees pitching coach Johnny Sain knows the importance of evaluating performance systematically:

> I keep a notebook of my pitchers and grade them poor, fair, good, and excellent. If you don't keep looking at the book over a period of time, you will remember only the excellent performances, and you will be unfair to the staff as a whole. Their positions change all the time as to who is the best starting pitcher at the moment, or who is the best stopper now when he is needed. Many times after a pitcher works I will ask him to grade himself or have the pitchers grade each other. Then I will tell them how I graded them. That way each individual is working to be No. 1.[1]

Sain appears to be aware of the important considerations involved in designing and managing performance assessment. Because performance assessment is often called performance appraisal and performance evaluation, we use these terms interchangeably. Performance assessments have many uses, including motivating employees—"each individual is working to be No. 1"—and providing information for staffing decisions—which pitcher to use and under which circumstances. Such assessments also can pinpoint training needs, such as more practice with runners on base, and support compensation decisions, such as the salary a baseball club is willing to negotiate with a particular pitcher.

The first decision is what to assess. For pitchers, Sain probably assessed long-run outcomes or earned runs per inning pitched; specific behaviors, such as the average speed of their fast balls; and situation-specific outcomes, such as early-inning versus late-inning performance, or pitching with runners on base. Choosing assessment criteria requires considering how employee behaviors contribute to organizational objectives.

A second decision is who should do the performance assessment. Even though Sain obviously does a good deal of assessment himself, he also relies on peer assessment and self-assessment. Each assessor may provide very different valuable information.

A third decision is which assessment procedure to use. Sain's notebook allows frequent evaluation and provides examples of specific pitching incidents to use in discussions with the pitchers. It also documents the work relatedness of decisions for EEO purposes. Sain's evaluation procedures are tailored to fit the organization, the job, and the individuals involved, both as evaluators and evaluatees.

The fourth decision is how performance assessments should be communicated to those assessed. Sain discusses his ratings with his pitchers, apparently providing specific instructions on how to improve. Communication can be immediate or it might wait until lots of performance incidents have been collected and a pattern discerned.

All human resource managers face the task of assessing performance. Just as Johnny Sain did, they must design assessment systems that provide information to support other human resource decisions, but also fit the organization well enough to be used correctly by assessors and minimize organizational costs. This chapter discusses one of the most important human resource conditions—individual performance and its assessment. However, it is not enough that employees perform well when they are on the job. It is also important that they come to work reliably and avoid absenteeism. So, this chapter also explores how to assess attendance and its costs and benefits for the organization.

Definition

Employee performance is the degree to which employees accomplish job requirements. *Performance assessment* is the process that measures employee performance. It involves deciding (1) what to assess, (2) who should make the assessments, (3) which assessment procedure to use, and (4) how to communicate assessment results.

Definition

Attendance is how often employees are available for work. It is the opposite of *absenteeism*.

A DIAGNOSTIC APPROACH TO PERFORMANCE ASSESSMENT

Similar to assessing external and organizational conditions and individual differences, performance assessment provides information for human resource decisions. It also represents one of the most important interactions between supervisors and individuals, because it can enhance or diminish the effects of other human resource management activities.

External Conditions

Government regulations significantly influence the design of performance assessment systems.[2] Since the passage of EEO legislation, employers often must demonstrate that they do not discriminate against minorities or women in their decisions about promotions, pay raises, training, and staffing. Because performance information is so critical to these decisions, government requirements have indirectly encouraged more objective and rigorous performance assessment systems.[3]

Unions profoundly affect performance assessment, frequently opposing it because they believe assessment systems produce biased results. In fact, a recent BNA survey showed that 84 percent of companies with non-unionized production employees had a formal production-employee assessment system, but only 42 percent of those with unionized production employees had a formal system.[4]

Organizational Conditions

Larger organizations may devote more resources to performance assessment and require more standardized information for large-scale planning and evaluation. Larger firms are also more likely to conduct appraisals regularly and more frequently.[5] Organizations with a tradition of communication and/or trust may be more able to obtain accurate performance information and discuss it with employees.

In many organizations, formal and informal assessment systems exist side by side. Informally, supervisors often discuss how well an employee is doing on the spur of the moment. Formal performance assessment is an activity designed to regularly and systematically assess employee performance on specified criteria. Formal systems are the main focus of this chapter. However, the formal and informal systems must complement one another. A formal system must recognize that daily informal assessment and feedback occurs all the time.

Work

The choice of a performance assessment method often reflects the nature of the work, the type of employees, and the abilities of the supervisors using the process. For example, production jobs and top management jobs are much less likely to have a formal performance assessment program than clerical, professional, and supervisory jobs.[6] Personnel decisions in blue-collar jobs are often influenced by seniority as well as performance.[7]

Employee Characteristics

For most people, assessments can be very important. If this process is badly handled, unwanted turnover can increase, morale decline, and productivity drop. If employees lack confidence in the fairness of the assessment process, the link between performance and the evaluation is broken. So the degree of trust among employees and supervisors also influences the design of performance assessment systems. As we shall see, combining feedback about past performance with setting specific future performance goals can be a powerful performance motivator.[8]

Setting Objectives for Performance Assessment

Performance assessment not only provides information to support other human resource activities, but it also provides a communication channel between employees and the organization, helping to clarify what each expects from the other.[9] Therefore, the assessment's objectives should reflect both of these purposes. Performance information is valuable to the extent that its results improve decisions, that the improvements are valuable to the organization, and that the process of gathering the information is efficient and costs no more than the value of the information provided.

A performance evaluation helps meet the needs of employers and employees by:

- Giving employees the opportunity to indicate the direction and level of their ambition.
- Giving managers the opportunity to indicate interest in employees' development. This interest can help retain ambitious, capable employees instead of losing them to competitors.
- Identifying areas where specific training is needed or desired and available.
- Providing encouragement to the employee who has been trying to perform well.
- Providing a means for communicating and documenting dissatisfaction with unacceptable employee performance and efforts to improve it.[10]

Because the pitfalls of performance evaluation are so numerous and the possible negative effects so serious, some suggest abandoning the whole process. Nathan Winstanley believes that many companies would be better off with no formal appraisals, particularly where managers are untrained in its use.[11] Many of the uses previously listed can be met other ways. For example, firms can base pay on skill level, seniority, or myriad factors that do not necessarily have to include performance. Indeed, many union contracts specify pay levels based on the job and seniority.[12] Performance may be improved through communication and training, rather than evaluation systems.[13] However, others argue that the need to ensure and document the work relatedness of development, reward, staffing, and

EXHIBIT 7–1
How Organizations Use Performance Assessment Information

	Nonexempt			Exempt			
Performance appraisals are used for	Production (119)	Office Clerical (232)	Professional Technical (222)	Professional Technical (225)	Supervisors (first-level) (238)	Middle Management (228)	Top Management (167)
• Determining wage/salary adjustments	78%	86%	86%	87%	87%	87%	87%
• Making promotion decisions	75	79	79	79	80	80	80
• Developing communication between supervisors and subordinates	72	73	74	72	72	71	71
• Determining training and development needs	70	71	72	72	72	72	70
• Human resources planning	31	37	38	40	40	42	44
• Developing skills inventories or other employee information systems	21	20	21	20	20	20	21
• Determining order of layoff/work force reductions	17	16	17	14	13	13	13
• Other	1	2	2	3	3	4	2

Source: The Bureau of National Affairs, Inc., "Performance Appraisal Programs," *Personnel Policies Forum, Survey no. 135* (1983), p. 12.

other personnel decisions can only be met by a formal system.[14] Winstanley's opinions should serve as a warning that "ready, fire, aim!" is not the way to proceed in performance evaluation.

Nonetheless, performance assessment is a common feature of organizations. Exhibit 7–1 shows the percentages of companies with appraisal programs for different employee groups reporting various uses for their assessments. Clearly, performance assessment supports many human resource activities affecting both efficiency and equity.

CRITICAL PERFORMANCE ASSESSMENT DECISIONS

Designing and implementing a performance assessment system requires considering four decisions:

1. What to assess, which employee behaviors or job outcomes to observe and measure.
2. Who should make the assessments, which of the various people with an opportunity to observe the behaviors or results should provide the assessment.
3. Which assessment procedure to use, the techniques include ranking, keeping diaries, or using checklists.
4. How to communicate assessment results, which communication system can best serve both the employee being assessed and the assessor and accomplish organizational objectives as well.

What Should be Assessed

Performance assessments can consider behaviors (how the employee does the job), results (how well the employee accomplished job requirements), or some combination of them. Some results are sometimes quite measurable. For example, supermarkets using computerized checkout systems often have records of every register entry made by every employee during every shift. Such information could measure the accuracy, speed, and volume of items processed by checkout clerks. In many jobs, however, results are not so measurable. For example, even though checkout clerks may also stock shelves, greet customers, train new employees, and clean displays, none of these results are reflected on the computerized checkout printout. Moreover, measuring only results may provide insufficient information or reduce employees' motivation and satisfaction. Behaviors can show whether poor results reflect inadequate employee skills, lack of effort, or conditions beyond employees' control. Usually both behaviors and results are measured.[15]

Tailor Criteria to Organizational Objectives

The criteria must be tied to the organizational objectives. If an organization's objective is cost-effective production, it requires cost data or output data to evaluate performance. Because such measures are typically available on a unit level (e.g., team or department productivity) rather than for an individual, it may make sense to evaluate performance on a group or team basis.[16] When group performance is measured, then perhaps pay and training decisions ought to be tied to those group measures, too.[17] Similar to other human resource management systems, performance assessment should be congruent with available information and projected uses.

Tailor Criteria to the Job

The criteria for evaluating employees' performance on the job should arise from the job itself.[18] Job analysis and the resulting job description is the basis for developing an evaluation instrument. The basic job description merely defines the tasks that make up the job and may indicate the skill required. Performance assessment requires additional information on the scope of responsibility and accountability. Performance standards should be feasible and, insofar as possible, measurable.[19] The description should take into account the tasks to be performed, and what is, and is not, under the employees' control.

Tailor Criteria to Employees' Needs

In addition to satisfying the employer's needs, performance assessment must address the needs of those being evaluated if it is to be successful. Certainly employees are interested in how the organization evaluates their performance (if it does), but most are also interested in their future prospects with an employer. By assessing and discussing performance, the employer communicates something about an employee's potential for promotion and development.[20] Performance evaluation interviews also provide the opportunity for employees to communicate how they feel about their jobs, their work groups, and their interest in future training or promotions.[21] Research has found that unrealized expectations for promotions and training can lead to absenteeism and turnover.[22] The impression of restricted promotion and training opportunities can lead to turnover and expressed dissatisfaction.

Multiple Criteria

Because success on the job is due to a number of factors, multiple criteria are necessary to measure performance completely.[23] The multiple criteria can be added together statistically or combined into a single multifaceted measure. Exhibit 7–2 shows some multiple criteria that may evaluate a salesperson's performance.

How do you weight the importance of multiple criteria? For example, if the salesperson being evaluated on both number of calls (effort) and sales dollars (results) is high on one and low on the other, what is the person's overall rating? Various criteria may be weighted according to their importance. Relative importance may be a topic of negotiation between employer and employee. Stephen Carroll and Craig Schneier provide some alternative weighting methods (see Exhibit 7–3).[24] Because some methods are very statistical, they may not be well understood or accepted. They may require more time and effort to calculate than they pay back to the organization in the form of more accurate evaluations.[25]

A BNA study found that for white-collar workers, the following criteria were used: quality of work (93 percent of the participating firms used it), quantity of work (90 percent), job knowledge (85 percent), and attendance (79 percent).[26] Other criteria were: initiative (87 percent), cooperation (87 percent), dependability (86 percent), and need for supervision (67 percent). These last four factors are personal characteristics that might assess potential for promotion or development.

EXHIBIT 7–2
Multiple Criteria Used in an Evaluation Report for Salespeople

Objectives Set	Period Objective	Accomplish-ments	Variance
1. Number of sales calls	100	104	104%
2. Number of new customers contacted	20	18	90
3. Number of wholesalers stocking new product 117	30	30	100
4. Sales of product 12	10,000	9,750	92.5
5. Sales of product 17	17,000	18,700	110
6. Customer complaints/service calls	35	11	30
7. Number of sales correspondence courses successfully completed	4	2	50
8. Number of sales reports in home office within one day of end of month	12	10	80

EXHIBIT 7–3
Methods for Weighting Subcriteria

1. Judgment	Experts judge the relative importance of each subcriterion to overall job performance or success on the job.
2. Reliability	Subcriteria on which multiple judges agree most regarding their ratings are weighted highest.
3. Predictability	Subcriteria which are most closely related or highly correlated with overall performance are weighted highest.
4. Factor analysis	A statistical technique reduces the number of subcriteria into a more meaningful, somewhat mutually exclusive set, with weights determined by statistical properties.
5. Correlation	Weights are determined by the degree to which subcriteria are correlated with, and hence in a sense redundant with, other subcriteria.
6. Dollar value	Weights are assigned relative to the dollar value of each subcriterion to job success or to the organization's effectiveness.
7. Equality	All subcriteria are weighted equally.

Source: Stephen J. Carroll and Craig E. Schneier, *Performance Appraisal and Review Systems* (Glenview, Ill.: Scott, Foresman, 1982), p. 34. Copyright © 1982 by Scott, Foresman and Company. Reprinted by permission.

Who Should Assess Performance?

Even a well-designed performance assessment system can cause problems if the evaluators are not suited to it. Potential performance assessors include the supervisors (one or more supervisory levels above), peers (employees at the same level, often working on the same task or process), subordinates, or even the employees themselves. Moreover, one is not limited to a single appraiser. By far, the most common system is to have the employee's immediate supervisor provide the performance assessment, usually reviewed by a higher-level manager or the personnel department.[27] The usefulness of a performance assessor will depend on the opportunity to observe relevant work behaviors, the ability to translate those behaviors into performance ratings, and the motivation to provide useful performance ratings.

Opportunity to Observe

Not all performance raters have ample opportunity to observe the person being rated. Although the immediate supervisor may usually be quite familiar with employee's work, peers, subordinates, or the employee may also provide useful and unique information. For example, for employees working in teams, the best observers of individual contributions, group dynamics, and interpersonal skills may be the team members themselves.[28]

Ability to Translate Observations into Useful Ratings

Several studies have examined the effectiveness of rater training in reducing rating errors, but in many of them it is difficult to tell whether the change in rating behavior reflected greater accuracy or just substituted one inaccurate rating pattern for another.[29] "Frame of reference" training attempts to identify raters who tend to adopt different rating standards and methods from most other raters, and help the "idiosyncratic" raters understand and use the more common standards.[30]

Motivation to Provide Useful Performance Information

Expectancy theory (see Chapter Six) suggests that performance appraisers are motivated to provide useful ratings to the extent that they believe their effort will produce appropriate ratings that lead to desired outcomes and fulfill their needs. A large portion of variability in ratings may be due to the motivation, or lack of motivation, of raters.[31] Motivation can be affected by raters' trust in the assessment process, requirements that raters justify their ratings, and training to handle the negative outcomes of assessments (ratees' fury at low performance ratings). Treating performance assessment as an important part of managerial performance ratings and linking rewards to assessment quality can also increase motivation.

Which Assessment Technique to Use?

Performance assessment techniques fall into four categories:

1. Rating, in which assessors evaluate employees on separate characteristics.
2. Ranking, in which supervisors compare employees to each other.
3. Critical incidents, in which assessors log statements that describe a range of actual job behaviors and evaluate whether they constitute effective or ineffective behavior.
4. Other methods in which the criteria for evaluation may vary, such as management by objectives (MBO).

Exhibit 7–4 shows the percent of companies using various performance assessment techniques.

Rating

Graphic Rating Scale. The most widely used performance evaluation technique is a graphic rating scale. It is also one of the oldest. In this

EXHIBIT 7–4
Performance Assessment Technique Usage

	Nonexempt			Exempt			
Methods used in performance evaluation process for each employee group	Production (119)	Office Clerical (232)	Professional Technical (222)	Professional Technical (225)	Supervisors (first-level) (238)	Middle Management (228)	Top Management (167)
• Rating scale	67%	67%	65%	55%	56%	50%	46%
• Essay	48	53	55	60	59	63	61
• Checklist	40	34	35	28	28	25	21
• Critical incident	18	18	19	19	19	18	19
• Management by objectives (MBO)	11	22	24	44	44	49	56
• Ranking	10	7	9	8	7	8	7
• Other	3	3	3	4	3	4	4

Source: The Bureau of National Affairs, Inc., "Performance Appraisal Practices," *Personnel Policies Forum, Survey No. 135* (1983), p. 6.

EXHIBIT 7–5
Typical Graphic Rating Scale

Name _____	Dept. _____			Date _____	
	Out-standing	*Good*	*Satis-factory*	*Fair*	*Unsatis-factory*
Quality of work Thoroughness, (neatness and accuracy of work) Comments:	□	□	□	□	□
Knowledge of Job Clear understanding of the facts or factors pertinent to the job Comments:	□	□	□	□	□
Personal qualities Personality, appearance, sociability, leadership, in- tegrity Comments:	□	□	□	□	□
Cooperation Ability and willingness to work with associates, supervisors, and sub- ordinates toward com- mon goals Comments:	□	□	□	□	□
Dependability Conscientious, thorough, accurate, reliable with re- spect to attendance, lunch periods, reliefs, etc. Comments:	□	□	□	□	□
Initiative Earnestness in seeking increased responsibili- ties. Self-starting, unaf- raid to proceed alone? Comments:	□	□	□	□	□

technique, the evaluator uses a graph such as that shown in Exhibit 7–5 and rates employees on each of the characteristics listed. The number of characteristics rated varies from a few to several dozen.

The evaluator marks descriptive words ranging from unsatisfactory to outstanding. After assigning a score of five for outstanding and zero for unsatisfactory, evaluators can compute total scores. In some plans, more important traits are more heavily weighted; in others, evaluators may be asked to explain each rating with a sentence or two.[32]

Two modifications to graphic rating scales have attempted to make them more effective. One is Blanz and Ghiselli's *mixed standard scale.*[33] Instead of just rating a trait such as initiative, the evaluator chooses one of three statements to describe the trait, such as:

1. This person is a real self-starter, always takes the initiative and never requires stimulation from the supervisor (best description).
2. Although this person generally shows initiative, an occasional prod from the superior is required to get the work done.
3. This person has a tendency to sit around and wait for directions (poorest description).

After each description the rater places either a check mark indicating the employee fits the description, a plus sign meaning the employee is better than the statement, or a minus sign because the employee is poorer than the statement. This gives a wider range of possible scores.

The second modification is to add *behavioral* or *benchmark* statements to describe different levels of performance.[34] For example, an excerpt from the U.S. Air Force's officer evaluation scale is given in Exhibit 7–6. Part A shows part of the evaluation scale for job knowledge, which is only one of the factors evaluated. Part B describes the standards for evaluating job knowledge. The complete evaluation form contains many such factors and standards.

Checklists. Another individual rating technique is the checklist. In its simplest form, the checklist is a set of adjectives or descriptive statements. If the rater believes that the employee possesses a trait listed, the rater checks the item; if not, the rater leaves it blank. A rating score from the checklist equals the number of checks. A more sophisticated checklist, shown in Exhibit 7–7, contains statements describing work behaviors. The rating score equals the number of positive statements checked.

Forced Distribution. The forced-distribution technique is similar to grading on a curve. The evaluator rates employees in some fixed distribution among performance levels, such as 10 percent in unsatisfactory, 20 percent in fair, 40 percent in satisfactory, 20 percent in good, and 10 percent in outstanding. One reason forced distribution was developed was to try to alleviate such problems as inflated ratings and the tendency to rate everyone in the middle of the scale. On the other hand, if all the people in a department are outstanding performers, forcing their manager to rate some of them as good, satisfactory, fair, or even unsatisfactory seems a misuse of the evaluation system. Forced distributions are most suitable

EXHIBIT 7–6
Excerpts from U.S. Air Force's Officer Evaluation Graphic Rating Scale

A. Performance Factor

	Not Observed or Not Relevant	Far below Standard	Below Standard	Meets Standard	Above Standard	Well above Standard
1. Job knowledge (depth, currency, breadth) Specific example: What has the officer done to actually demonstrate depth, currency, or breadth of job knowledge in the performance of duties? Consider both quality and quantity of work.	0	☐	☐	☐	☒	☐

B. Standards for Rating Job Knowledge

Far below Standard
1. Has serious gaps in technical/professional knowledge
Knows only most rudimentary phases of job
Lack of knowledge affects productivity
Requires abnormal amount of checking

Below Standard
Technical/professional knowledge is inadequate for the job
Must be assigned only routine duties and monitored regularly
Requires close supervision

Meets Standard
Demonstrates adequate technical/professional knowledge required for the job
Searches out facts and arrives at sound solutions to problems
Broad knowledge of related jobs and functions
Conversant with significant job-related developments

Above Standard
Possesses keen insight and the ability to evolve it into practical solutions
Keeps informed of important developments in related fields
Can handle difficult situations effectively
Broad knowledge of related missions
Rarely requires guidance or assistance

Well above Standard
Possesses superb technical/professional knowledge
Sufficiently well versed in the job to discuss and implement improved methods resulting in savings in manpower or material
Maintains and increases professional/technical knowledge
Actively pursues new ideas and developments and their relation to the overall mission
Recognized authority in the field

EXHIBIT 7–7
Statement Checklist

Position: PROGRAM AUDITOR
Job Dimension: DATA ASSEMBLY/ORGANIZATION

———— 1. Unable to separate important from irrelevant information.
———— 2. Omits important information from workpaper summaries.
———— 3. Cross-indexes so as to facilitate referencing of reports.
———— 4. Produces workpaper summaries which can be readily transformed into a report.
———— 5. Requires excessive amount of instruction to produce summaries.
———— 6. Unable to reduce data to manageable form.
———— 7. Offers a number of alternative methods of data display.
———— 8. Clearly defines issues to be summarized and explains their relevance to job objectives.

Source: Stephen J. Carroll and Craig E. Schneier, *Performance Appraisal and Review Systems* (Glenview, Ill.: Scott Foresman, 1982). Copyright © 1982 by Scott, Foresman and Company. Reprinted by permission.

where there are large numbers of employees and wide variations in performance levels.

Ranking

Ranking employees according to relative performance is the simplest, fastest, easiest to understand, and the least expensive performance evaluation technique. Ranking simply involves ordering employees from highest to lowest in performance.

The two ways of ranking are alternation ranking and paired comparison. *Alternation ranking* involves ordering the employees alternately at each extreme. Exhibit 7–8 illustrates this procedure in which all the employees are considered. Agreement is reached on who is the highest performer, then the lowest performer. Evaluators alternate between the next highest performer and the next lowest performer, and so on, until all employees have been ranked.

The *paired comparison ranking* technique involves comparing all possible pairs of employees. The number of pairs to compare can be calculated: $(n) \times (n - 1) \div 2$. Five people result in $[(5 \times 4) \div 2]$ or 10 paired comparisons; 50 employees $[(50 \times 49) \div 2] = 1,225$ comparisons. A simple way to do paired comparison is to set up a matrix as shown in Exhibit 7–9, designating in each cell the higher performer of the two employees being compared. The employee with the highest total of "more valuable" rankings becomes the highest-ranked employee, and so on. Some evi-

EXHIBIT 7–8
Alternation Ranking

Employees to be ranked: Bob, Carol, Ted, Alice, Mary, Michael, Matthew, Sarah, George, Carolyn

    1. Sarah (highest)
    2. Carol (next highest)
    3.
    4.
    5.
    6.
    7.
    8.
    9. Alice (next lowest)
  10. Bob (lowest)

EXHIBIT 7–9
Paired Comparison Ranking

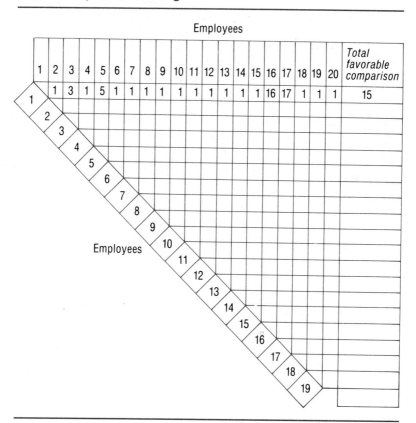

dence suggests that the alternation ranking and paired comparison methods produce similar results more consistently than simple ranking.

Ranking is seldom the recommended approach.[35] The criteria on which employees are ranked are usually so crudely defined (if they are specified at all) that the evaluations become subjective opinions that are difficult if not impossible to explain and justify in work-related terms. Furthermore, evaluator(s) using this method must be knowledgeable about every single employee under study. The numbers alone make this task formidable—50 employees require 1,225 comparisons—and as turnover and new hires occur, it is difficult to remain knowledgeable about all employees. Some organizations try to overcome this difficulty by ranking employees within single departments and merging the results. However, without greater specification of the criteria on which the rankings are based, merging ranks is a major problem. Even though ranking is simple, fast, and inexpensive, in the long term it may be more costly. Since the results are difficult to explain and to defend, costly solutions are often required to overcome the problems the ranking method has created.

Critical Incidents

Several evaluation techniques use descriptions of actual observed behavior as scale anchors.

Critical Incident Technique. Operating managers and employees prepare statements describing very effective and very ineffective behavior in a job. These are the *critical incidents*.[36] These statements are combined into categories. Exhibit 7–10 lists a few examples.

After developing the categories and statements of effective and ineffective behavior, the evaluator prepares a log for each employee. During the evaluation period, the evaluator records examples of critical (outstandingly good or bad) behaviors in each of the categories, and uses a log to evaluate the employee at the end of the period. The log is also very useful for the evaluation interview, because the evaluator can be specific in making positive and negative comments.

EXHIBIT 7–10
Critical Incidents for Residence Hall Adviser

October 1: As adviser was on way to class, a resident approached adviser asking for assistance. Adviser took a few moments to determine the nature of the problem, then arranged an appointment with student for 4 P.M. that same day (effective behavior).

November 13: Adviser discovered that two of her advisees had failed midterm examinations. Adviser took no action (ineffective behavior).

The critical incident technique has spawned a number of other evaluation formats. Although they differ in details, they all begin with actual job behaviors, independently rated as effective or ineffective; these behaviors serve as scale anchors.

Behaviorally Anchored Rating Scales. Behaviorally anchored rating scales (BARS) are a variant on standard rating scales, in which the various scale levels are anchored with behavioral descriptions directly applicable to jobs being evaluated (see Exhibit 7–11).[37] By anchoring scales with concrete behaviors, firms adopting a BARS format hope to make evaluations less subjective.

These are the basic steps in developing a behaviorally anchored rating scale:

1. Supervisors of a group of employees performing similar jobs are asked to identify those broad sets of job activities that make up the job. For programmer/analysts, examples of such "performance dimensions" might be coding and documentation.
2. The same supervisors generate a set of critical incidents that represent actual examples of very good and very poor performance on the dimension.
3. Each member of a second, independent group of supervisors then rates each incident on a good-bad continuum and also identifies that dimension to which each incident belongs.

EXHIBIT 7–11
Behaviorally Anchored Rating Scale for Residence Hall Adviser

Performance dimension

   Concern for individual dorm residents: attempts to get to know individual dorm residents and responds to their individual needs with genuine interest. This resident adviser could be expected to:

Rating scale

(1)	(2)	(3)	(4)	(5)
Recognize when a floor member appears depressed and ask if person has problem he/she wants to discuss.	Offer floor members tips on how to study for a course he/she has already taken.	See person and recognize him/her as a floor member and say "hi."	Be friendly with a floor member; get into discussion on problems, but fail to follow up on the problem later on with student.	Criticize a floor member for not being able to solve his/her own problems.

4. The designer then identifies that set of incidents that was systematically associated by the second group with the original performance dimension.

5. The resultant set of performance dimensions, each with a set of ordered and scaled incidents, is referred to as BARS.

Variations on BARS. The use of BARS has led to further refinements and distinctions. Behavioral Observation Scales (BOS), for example, require that the raters assess the frequency of behavior. Behavior Discrimination Scales (BDS) also require rating frequency of a behavior, but the actual frequency is compared to the frequency of opportunities to exhibit the behavior and the frequency expected for each performance level. Thus, BDS claims to also assess the consistency of performance.[38]

There are numerous other variations of BARS.[39] Although they all offer advantages, there is no compelling evidence demonstrating the superiority of one technique over others.[40] Thomas DeCotiis compared BARS with traditional techniques such as graphic rating scales. He found that none of the measurements was satisfactorily resistant to errors. DeCotiis concludes: "It may be time to quit hedging about the efficacy of behavioral scaling strategies and conclude that they offer no clear-cut advantages over more traditional and easily developed methods of performance evaluation."[41]

Unspecified Criteria

The essay evaluation technique does not specify the criteria being used. The management by objectives technique varies the criteria with the individual job, rater, ratee, and time period.

Essay Evaluation. In the essay technique of evaluation, the evaluator describes the strong and weak aspects of the employee's behavior. The essay may be combined with another form, such as a graphic rating scale. In this case, the essay elaborates on some of the ratings, or discusses aspects not on the scale. The essay can be open-ended, but in most cases guidelines specify the topics to cover and the purpose of the essay.

Management by Objectives. Another individual evaluation technique in use today is management by objectives (MBO). In this system, the supervisor and employee to be evaluated jointly set objectives in advance for the employee to try to achieve during a specified period. The technique encourages, if not requires, them to phrase these objectives primarily in quantitative terms. The evaluation consists of a joint review of the degree of achievement of the objectives. Exhibit 7–2 is an example of MBO objectives.

This technique has become popular because of the high degree of employee involvement, but it can produce serious problems when it is used to change basic job requirements in each appraisal and objective-setting period. Over time, MBO may change fundamental job requirements, producing performance standards that no longer reflect the original purpose.[42]

How Should Performance Assessment Results Be Communicated?

The biggest hazard in performance assessment may be the employee's reaction to the assessment.[43] Evaluators can provoke hostile responses from employees even while conveying favorable results. Imagine how you would feel if your professor said to you, "Well, you *finally* got a decent grade on a test." Work relationships are inevitably personal relationships. Discussing performance has the potential to disrupt these relationships and evoke an emotional response.[44] Even though there is substantial evidence that performance feedback and setting explicit performance goals can increase goal achievement,[45] it is unlikely that an annual performance assessment interview can provide sufficiently timely or specific feedback to accomplish this. Exhibit 7–12 shows how aspects of the appraisal can improve subsequent job performance. The appraisal interview itself is important, and assessors should ensure participation, and produce both future performance targets and agreed-on indicators of achievement. However, just as important is proper preparation by both the subordinate and superior, as well as a written follow-up to ensure mutual understanding.

ASSESSING ATTENDANCE/ABSENTEEISM

Assessing employees' performance involves monitoring not only how they perform while at work, but also how often they come to work. Even the best performing employees become less valuable if they fail to attend reliably. Absenteeism assessment measures the work time lost when employees do not come to work. The formula for absence used by the Bureau of National Affairs (BNA) is:

$$\frac{\text{Worker days lost through job absence during the month}}{(\text{Average number of employees}) \times (\text{Number of workdays in month})}$$

BNA does not include absences for jury duty, scheduled disciplinary time off, long-term disabilities (after the first four days), or excused absences scheduled in advance.[46] Because absence data should support decision making, however, organizations might wish to adopt different measures to fit their own needs. Decisions about controlling absence through motiva-

EXHIBIT 7–12
Factors Contributing to the Effectiveness of Performance Assessment Interviews

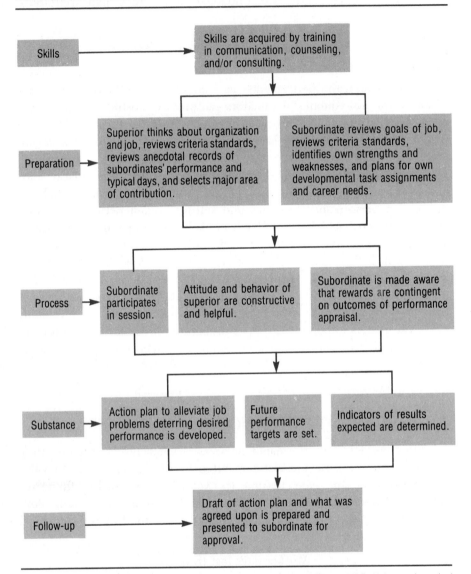

Source: Craig E. Schneier and Richard W. Beatty, "Combining BARS and MBO: Using an Appraisal System to Diagnose Performance Problems." Reprinted from the September 1979 issue of *Personnel Administrator,* copyright 1979, The American Society for Personnel Administration, 606 North Washington Street, Alexandria, Virginia 22314.

tion can focus only on absences completely under employees' control, thus excluding jury duty. Decisions involved in planning work force size must account for typical lost time by considering the total lost work time caused by absenteeism.

Absence rates vary with the job, industry, and economic conditions. BNA reports quarterly absence statistics. For example, the absence rate for 1986 averaged 1.8 percent per month, with higher rates in larger companies and nonprofit organizations.[47]

Exhibit 7–13 shows a model of employee attendance. It suggests that attendance is a function of both the ability and motivation to attend, and is affected by on-the-job as well as off-the-job factors. Thus, reducing ab-

EXHIBIT 7–13
Major Influences on Employees' Attendance

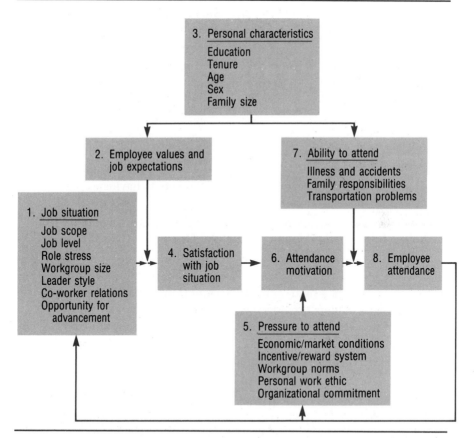

Source: Richard M. Steers and Susan R. Rhodes, "Major Influences on Employee Attendance: A Process Model," *Journal of Applied Psychology 63*, no. 4 (1978), p. 393. Copyright 1978 by the American Psychological Association. Reprinted by permission of the author.

sence requires that human resource managers not only take a broad view of its causes in any particular situation, but also devise programs to address those causes. Organizations can discipline absent employees, verify medical excuses, and better communicate rules regarding excusable absences. They can also reward good attendance records.[48]

EVALUATING PERFORMANCE AND ABSENTEEISM ASSESSMENT

The discussion so far has focused on how human resource personnel conduct performance and absenteeism assessments and what affects them. But how do assessments improve human resource management? First, performance and absenteeism information can support decisions, by helping to set human resource objectives, choose human resource activities, and evaluate results. Second, the assessment and communication process affects employee behaviors directly, regardless of how the information is used to make decisions. This section discusses how performance and absenteeism assessments accomplish both purposes, and suggests that performance and absenteeism have substantial monetary consequences for organizations.

Efficiency

Information contributes to efficiency to the extent that it supports decisions, and to the extent that its assessment affects behaviors.

Does Performance/Absenteeism Information Support Decisions?

Reward Decisions. When evaluation data helps determine pay increases, promotions, demotions, or terminations, there must be some common denominator for comparisons among many individuals. Frequently, this implies a numerical rating of performance. The various ranking and rating methods provide such numerical ratings.

Reward decisions addressing absenteeism are more potent if they address behaviors under individuals' control, so information for rewards should reflect absences that represent employees' choices, not unavoidable instances.

Training/Career Development Decisions. Does the technique communicate the goals and objectives of the organization to the employee? Is feedback to employees a natural outgrowth of the evaluation format that identifies employee development needs and communicates them readily?[49] Does it communicate what we wish? These are some of the issues addressed in designing evaluations for the purpose of developing employees.

For career development, an important question is whether performance assessments identify performance factors that could be enhanced through experience in future jobs. Absenteeism information can also support training. For example, training in better time management and organization may reduce absences due to employees waiting until the last minute before work to arrange for babysitters or other obligations.

Staffing Decisions. Applicants predicted to perform well can be monitored through performance evaluation. As with the reward criteria, though, evaluations typically need to be quantitative to permit the statistical manipulations that may be required for validating decisions.[50]

For internal staffing (moving people between jobs), performance ratings become the predictors of future job performance, and quantitative information is important to statistically assess this predictability. Absenteeism is a tempting criterion to compare to applicant characteristics. It is usually relatively easy to observe and record. However, companies must ensure that absence data reflects legitimate factors that could be affected by selection and be alert to possible EEO issues. For example, single parents may be absent more frequently and may more often be women, but this does not justify screening out single parents and reducing the number of women hired.

Assessment Errors and Biases

Errors and biases reduce the usefulness of performance assessment. Investigations of errors and biases focus on several factors.

Reliability. Inter-rater reliability assesses the extent of agreement between raters evaluating the same individual or group of individuals. If the performance factors and scales to measure them are accurately defined and unambiguous, raters have a common foundation for evaluating employees, and this improves inter-rater reliability.

Content Validity and Rating Errors. Content validity refers to the degree to which a measure reflects the content (behaviors, outcomes, responsibilities) of a specific job.

The most frequently described rating errors include halo, leniency, severity, and central tendency errors.[51] Positive halo occurs when a rater evaluates an employee based on a positive general attitude toward the individual, elevating ratings on performance criteria for reasons other than actual job performance. Negative halo involves the opposite phenomenon, downgrading an individual on multiple performance criteria because of negative data on one criteria. In contrast to halo errors, the remaining three errors affect a total group rather than a single individual. The best way to illustrate these errors is to view Diagram 1 as a true indicator of the performance of individuals. Relative to these scores, Diagrams 2, 3, and 4 reflect the ratings distributions with leniency, severity, or central tendency errors, respectively.

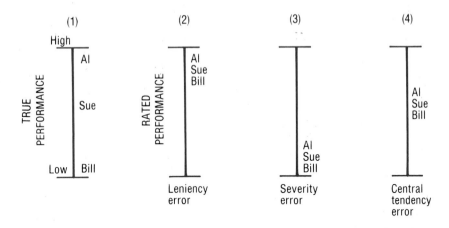

By far the most common of these three errors is the leniency error. By being lenient in rating subordinates, a supervisor avoids the unpleasant feedback and possible criticisms that may result from low evaluations.

Assessment Costs

M. A. Jones conducted a systematic assessment of evaluation costs in one application.[52] Exhibit 7–14 shows the costs from development stages through maintenance. Notice that the earliest costs were for job analysis before any evaluation was done. Cost per rating is approximately $34. Is this cost reasonable? That depends on how good an evaluation results from it, and how effectively the organization uses evaluation results as inputs to other human resource decisions. Further cost and benefit studies are necessary to compare techniques and to judge the utility of the whole evaluation system.[53]

Gathering absenteeism data is probably less expensive than assessing performance, but the more elaborate and detailed the technique, the more costly it will be. Again, cost justification depends on how the information is used and how valuable are the decision improvements it supports.

Comparisons and Combinations of Performance Assessment Methods

Exhibit 7–15 summarizes the "track record" of the different evaluation methods. Ranking and essays do not fare too well, while MBO and BARS

EXHIBIT 7–14
Cost Estimates of the Elements in a Performance Appraisal System

Cost Element	1975–1977	1977–1978
Operating costs		
DP production	$ 11,406.00	$ 3,483.00
DP develop and enhancement	41,688.00	14,643.00
Keypunch (hardware)	0.00	385.00
Paper (OPM)	1,691.00	179.00
Paper (agency)	N/D	637.00
Mailing and distribution		
(postage and messenger)	500.00	6,583.00
Training workshops (5 hrs.)	0.00	23,492.00
Total operations cost	$ 55,285.00	$ 49,402.00
Operations cost per rating	$ 0.00	$ 9.31
Manpower costs		
Job knowledge experts (time)	$ 15,072.00	$ 0.00
Job analyst (time)	21,887.00	0.00
Clerical support (OPM)	10,179.00	6,786.00
Professional coordinator (1)	0.00	7,223.00
Rater time	0.00	80,696.00
Ratee time	0.00	29,783.00
Clerical processing (Agency)	1,000.00	4,353.00
Consultant	25,480.00	1,500.00
Manpower totals	$ 73,618.00	$130,341.00
Manpower cost per rating	$ 0.00	$ 24.55
Grand totals	$128,903.00	$179,743.00
Cost per rating		$ 33.86

Source: M. A. Jones, "Estimating Costs in the Development and Implementation of a Performance Appraisal System" (paper presented at the first annual Scientist-Practitioner Conference in Industrial-Organizational Psychology, Old Dominion University, Norfolk, Va., 1980).

seem to fare better. This should not be too surprising. Ranking and essays require little development time, but they also permit supervisors to evaluate subordinates on what can be vague and totally different performance criteria. At the other extreme is management by objectives. The very process of establishing work objectives requires individualized attention to relevant job criteria. However, in a review of 185 studies of the effects of MBO on productivity and/or job satisfaction, Jack Kondrasuk found the research support for MBO "inversely related to research design sophistication."[54] There are a lot of unsubstantiated testimonials for the method's effectiveness, but not enough research to tell us under which conditions it is the best evaluation method. And the same holds true for most evaluation methods.

EXHIBIT 7–15
Performance Assessment Techniques

	Employee Development	Rewards	Staffing	Practicality	Validity	Comparison Scale
Graphic rating scales	Average—general problem areas identified. Some information on extent of developmental need is available, but no feedback on necessary behaviors/outcomes.	Average—ratings valuable for merit increase decisions and others. Not easily defended if contested.	Average—validation studies can be completed, but level of measurement contamination unknown.	Good—inexpensive to develop and easy to use.	Average—content validity is suspect. Rating errors and reliability are average.	Adjective descriptors.
Essay	Unknown—depends on guidelines for inclusions in essay as developed by organization or supervisors.	Poor—essays not comparable across different employees considered for merit or other administrative actions.	Poor—no quantitative indices to compare performance against employment test scores in validation studies.	Average—easy to develop but time-consuming to use.	Unknown—unstructured format makes studies of essay method difficult.	Unknown.
Management by objectives	Excellent—extent of problem and outcome deficiencies are identified.	Poor—MBO not suited to merit income decisions. Level of completion and difficulty of objectives hard to compare across employees.	Poor—nonstandard objectives across employees and no overall measures of performance make validity studies difficult.	Poor—expensive to develop and time-consuming to use.	Good—high content validity. Low rating errors.	Expected job outcomes.

Method					
Adjective checklist	Average—general problem areas identified for employee, but little information on extent of problem or behaviors/outcomes necessary to change evaluation.	Average—adjective rankings can be tallied for merit decisions.	Good—checklists equated for social desirability may yield relatively uncontaminated performance data.	Average—expensive to develop.	Good—usually good content validity and equating items for social desirability reduces rating errors.
Behaviorally anchored rating scales	Good—identifies extent of problem and behavioral needs.	Good—BARS good for making administrative decisions. Defensible for EEO because job-relevant.	Good—validation studies can be completed and measurement problems on BARS less than many other criterion measures.	Average—expensive to develop but easy to use.	Good—high content validity. Some evidence of inter-rater reliability and reduced rating errors.
Ranking: Paired comparison. Forced distribution	Poor—ranks typically based on overall performance, with little thought given to feedback on specific performance dimensions.	Poor—comparisons of ranks across work units to determine merit raises are meaningless.	Average—validation studies can be completed with rankings of performance.	Good—inexpensive source of performance data. Easy to develop and use in small organizations and in small units.	Average—good reliability but poor on rating errors, especially halo.

Adjective descriptors.

Expected job behaviors.

Other employees.

Source: Adapted from George Milkovich and Jerry Newman, *Compensation*, 2nd ed. (Plano, Tex.: Business Publications, 1987), p. 341.

No single evaluation technique will be entirely appropriate across all jobs for all purposes in an organization. Michael Keeley suggests that the choice of technique largely depends on the nature of the work. He argues that tasks can be ordered along a continuum from those that are very routine in nature to those for which the appropriate behaviors are largely unspecified. Exhibit 7–16 depicts such a continuum. Behavior-based evaluation procedures that define specific performance criteria are only appropriate for the highly routine tasks.[55] Behaviorally anchored rating scales fall into this category. The behavioral anchors define specific performance expectations and specify different levels of employee performance.

However, when tasks become less routine, it becomes more difficult to specify the behavior that must occur to accomplish a goal. Rather, varying behaviors are both feasible and appropriate to reach a final goal. Under these circumstances, Keeley argues that technique should focus on evaluating the extent to which the final goal is accomplished—*what* is accomplished, rather than *how* it was accomplished. Thus, for such tasks a management-by-objectives method would be appropriate. As long as the assessor can specify the final accomplishment or output, performance can be evaluated in relation to that output without specifying or evaluating the behavior used to produce the output. The focus is exclusively on the output, not on behavior.

At the other extreme of the continuum are tasks so uncertain in nature that it is difficult to specify either expected output, or successful behavior. For this type of task, judgment-based evaluation procedures are most appropriate, such as essays or even checklists. Raters make subjective estimates about the levels of employees' performance. The extent of the uncertainty for both *what* was done, and *how*, makes this evaluation very subjective, and may well explain why so many people are uncomfortable participating in it.

Does Performance/Absenteeism Make any Difference?

Increasing evidence suggests that individual differences in performance are much greater than might have previously been suspected. Because human resource decisions are often directed at changing individual performance levels, researchers have recently devoted more attention to estimating the dollar value of individual differences among groups of employees with the same job title. Even though these methods are exploratory and have not yet been validated, there is evidence that in manufacturing jobs with observable outputs good performers perform 20 percent better than average performers, and 44 percent better than poor performers.[56] In jobs with even more discretion, and even more critical outcomes (such as upper-level management jobs where decisions often in-

EXHIBIT 7–16
Interaction between the Nature of Work and Performance Assessment Techniques

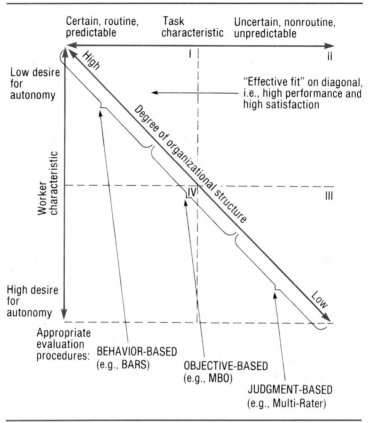

volve millions of dollars), individual differences are likely to be even more important. A review of these studies suggested that the yearly value of the difference in performance between average and superior performers has almost always been above 40 percent of the average salary level for the job, and has often been over 100 percent of average salary.[57] Thus, in a job where average salary is $50,000 per year, good performers may be worth between $20,000 and $50,000 (or more) per year more than average performers. In just five years, the benefits of having even one superior performer instead of one average performer could amount to between $100,000 and $250,000! Imagine the effects of training, rewarding, or selecting hundreds of employees over time. Though these numbers are hypothetical, even if they are optimistic by a factor of 10, performance differences and the decisions that affect them can be quite important.

Not only is performance assessment important for supporting human resource activities, but also the assessment and communication method itself can actually produce substantial dollar benefits. One hypothetical demonstration suggested that introducing performance feedback for 500 managers could produce a $5.3 million return in each year.[58] A more recent application of performance feedback to fast-food servers (involving setting more explicit serving standards and using a scale to weigh servings) suggested that profits would be doubled.[59]

Absenteeism can be very costly. Dan Dalton suggests that a 5 percent absenteeism rate for an organization with 200 regular operational employees earning $6 per hour could be worth $300,000 per year, including salary and benefits paid for nonwork time as well as extra full-time employees to fill in for absent ones.[60] When absenteeism information supports decisions that successfully reduce it, the organization may reap substantial benefits.

Equity

Because performance assessment supports so many human resource decisions, it is a highly visible and important activity to several interest groups concerned with the equity and fairness of the employment relationship.

Legal Liabilities, EEO, and Performance Assessment

Legal considerations require employers to closely examine performance assessment and feedback systems. Poorly handled performance assessments open the door for legal suits. For example, when John Chamberlain, a manager of manufacturing engineering at Bissell, Inc., was informed that performance problems caused him not to receive a wage increase, he was not told that he was in danger of termination. When this employee of 23 years was subsequently fired for poor performance and attitude (which had been discussed with him in his performance appraisal interviews), he successfully sued Bissell, Inc. for $61,354.[61]

EEO legislation focuses on the equity of performance assessment and the role it plays in staffing and reward decisions. In staffing, performance assessments are selection tests just like predictors. In reward decisions, assessments may produce unequal pay for some protected groups doing equal work.

Reviewing 66 cases dating back to 1976, Holley and Feild concluded that employers should be careful to design and administer evaluation systems that minimize the chances of discrimination.[62] That is, if the majority of women and minorities receive less than satisfactory ratings, and the majority of white males are rated satisfactory or better, then a closer look at the system is in order. Second, the design of the system must be based on complete, accurate, and current job analysis. Third, raters must be provided clearly written instructions. Fourth, raters must provide feedback and discussion to ratees. Finally, raters should also receive training in the evaluation process.

Wayne Cascio has come up with what he calls legal and operational imperatives for designing a workable evaluation system.[63] His legal imperatives include:

1. The system must have a clear link between performance standards and organizational goals.
2. The system must be able to separate effective from ineffective workers.
3. The system must be reliable (recall our previous discussion of reliability).

Cascio's operational imperatives include:

1. The system must be acceptable to users.
2. The system must be practical and not interfere with normal operations.

What will be the probable thrust of future EEO cases dealing with performance appraisal? If performance evaluations continue to be treated as if they are tests, we can predict these trends: First, the courts will require that performance standards be related to the job being evaluated.[64] The standards on which performance is to be rated must be derived from an accurate job analysis. Second, it is also likely the courts will insist that performance evaluations be as free as possible from errors based on subjective judgments (e.g., halo, leniency, severity, central tendency).

A third possible requirement for performance evaluation may be that the entire process be empirically validated, that is, proof that where evaluations are used as a basis for promotions, the performance ratings predict actual performance on the job after promotion. If this requirement is mandated, current practices have to be dramatically altered. In a survey of company practices, not one of 217 companies that used evaluation results to make promotion decisions had analyzed whether the ratings were, in fact, a good predictor of job performance after promotion.[65]

Recent reviews summarizing results from many studies suggest a significant tendency for black raters and white raters to give higher ratings to members of their own races. This tendency is not affected by the assessment technique, assessment purpose, or by training assessors, but is somewhat lower in situations where the percentage of blacks is higher.[66] Performance ratings also relate to the ratee's age, with ratings based on objective performance outcomes increasing with age and supervisory ratings declining slightly with age. Age, however, accounted for only a small percentage of performance variance.[67] Although it is premature to conclude that these results indicate bias, they do suggest the need to consider the effects of performance assessment on the employment opportunities of protected groups.

SUMMARY

Individual differences in performance and absenteeism greatly affect human resource and organizational objectives. Performance information is valuable because it can improve important decisions. However, this potential value can be lost if the system is not acceptable to those who must use it. Moreover, the assessment and communication process has the potential to support those objectives or cause substantial problems in reaching them. Though a great deal of attention is often paid to finding the right assessment technique, the assessment process should first consider the purpose of gathering performance information. Then, evaluators must make four decisions in designing the appraisal process, including (1) what to assess, (2) who should make the assessments, (3) which assessment procedure to use, and (4) how to communicate assessment results. As we have seen, each of these decisions determines the success or failure of performance assessment.

APPENDIX / Performance Evaluation Guide

PERFORMANCE PLANNING, COACHING, AND EVALUATION: GUIDE FOR EMPLOYEES

Introduction

The Performance Planning, Coaching, and Evaluation (PPC&E) process is important to all employees at Bank of America. While it helps achieve the business goals of your unit, the process also supports your growth and development. PPC&E helps you know:

- What your manager expects of you.
- How well you are doing during the review period.
- How closely your results match your plan at the end of the review period.

Your participation is the key to the success of PPC&E. Once you know what your manager expects during the review period, you are responsible for carrying out the plan.

During the review period, your manager should communicate and work with you to help you achieve your performance goals. At the end of the review period, your manager should formally evaluate your performance and review it with you. Your performance during the year will become the basis for your future pay.

Use the *PPC&E Guide for Employees* when you want to review the steps in the process. It, however, is only a guide. Your manager may modify the process depending on the situation.

Performance Planning

Overview

Your manager should work with you to develop a performance plan for you based on the goals for your unit. Then, he or she should sit down with you to discuss it and answer questions you may have.

Preplanning

Before or during your performance planning session, you and your manager may discuss what he or she expects from you during the review period. With that in mind, think about:

- How you will contribute during the performance period.
- Any additional responsibilities you can assume.
- Activities you might pursue for self-development.

Developing Objectives

An *objective* is a statement of intent. It states what your manager expects you to accomplish, how well, and by when. Objectives are important tools for helping you understand the key results expected of you during the review period.

Quality objectives typically have these characteristics:

Traceable. Related to the unit goals as determined by your manager.

Results-Oriented. Aimed at achieving results. Results can be the outcome of activities or they can be tangible products. Activities themselves are *not* results.

Specific. Written in specific terms. Each objective should state the result(s) that you intend to achieve.

Measurable. Include a means for measuring your performance. This measurement can be based on the *quantity* of results you produce and/or the *quality* of those results.

Time-Bound. Include target dates, specific times by which you intend to achieve the planned results.

The Performance Planning Session

During the performance planning session, you and your manager should:

1. Discuss:

   - Each objective and its importance in your plan.
   - How your accomplishment of each objective will be measured.
   - Your major ongoing responsibilities. *Ongoing responsibilities* are those activities that are part of your job but are not specific objectives for the review period.
   - Any developmental activities that you will undertake during the review period. *Developmental activities* are activities you plan to undertake to improve your current skills or prepare yourself for new responsibilities. You should be an active participant in planning developmental activities.
   - How you will make the plan work.

2. Sign and date the plan.

   Although your performance plan should describe your major objectives and responsibilities, it is not all inclusive. You may have significant duties not included in your plan.

Your Role in Planning

Be sure to offer your ideas, comments, and suggestions for developing the performance plan.

Your responsibility: Once your performance plan is established, it is up to you to carry out objectives and other responsibilities specified in the plan. Your manager should work with you throughout the review period to help you succeed by coaching you on your performance. You should approach your manager, however, any time you need help.

Coaching

Overview

Once you begin to put your performance plan into action, your manager should observe and talk with you about your performance. There are two types of coaching—informal and formal. Each has a specific role in the PPC&E process.

Informal Coaching

Informal coaching is the ongoing communication your manager has with you about your performance. On an informal basis, your manager may:

- Observe your performance.
- Ask you questions and listen to your answers.
- Give you feedback about:
  —Excellent performance.
  —Performance that is meeting your objectives.
  —Performance that is not meeting your objectives.
- Keep you informed of changes in unit objectives or the business environment that could have an impact on your results.

Formal Coaching

Formal coaching provides you and your manager with the opportunity to meet and discuss your performance. Your manager should hold periodic formal coaching sessions with you, preferably once each quarter during the review period.

At the formal coaching session, your manager may:

- Assess the results of your performance to date, comparing them to the performance plan.
- Give positive feedback on your performance that meets or exceeds your objectives.
- Develop with you ideas on how your performance can be maintained or improved.
- Discuss with you any significant new assignments. These *unplanned activities* are activities you undertake which are not part of the original plan.
- Revise your performance plan, as appropriate, if the circumstances under which it was developed have changed.
- Let you know if your performance level has changed.

Your Role in Coaching

During coaching:

- Listen carefully to your manager's assessment of your progress.

- Discuss your own view of your performance, if it is different from your manager's.
- Be prepared to discuss issues or clarify misunderstandings with your manager as they come up.

Good communication between you and your manager throughout the review period can help you keep your performance on target and your manager informed about how you are doing.

Evaluation

Overview

During your performance evaluation, your manager should:

- Rate the results of your performance.
- Document the evaluation on the PPC&E form.
- Review with you and summarize the results of your performance.

If you and your manager developed an effective performance plan and communicated throughout the review period, the evaluation should confirm and summarize what you have already discussed.

When Evaluations Occur

Generally, you will be evaluated once a year, either at the beginning of the calendar year or on the anniversary of your date of hire, most recent promotion, or transfer. You may receive an evaluation earlier if you:

- Are new to the bank.
- Are promoted to a new position.
- Transfer to a new unit.
- Have shown a marked change in performance, either up or down, since your last evaluation.

Your manager may also evaluate you if he or she is leaving the unit.

The Evaluation Session

In the evaluation session, your manager should discuss your evaluation with you. Be open to discussion. Ask questions to clarify your understanding of the evaluation.

During the session, you and your manager should:

1. Discuss your results and ratings for:

   - Objectives.
   - Ongoing responsibilities.
   - Developmental accomplishments (not rated).
   - Unplanned activities, if any.

See last section for rating definitions.

Unsatisfactory performance is job performance that is rated "Met Some Not All" (MSNA) or "Did Not Meet" (DNM). Your performance cannot be rated unsatisfactory twice in a row.

If your overall rating is "MSNA":

- You are performing at an unsatisfactory level.
- Your manager should set a period for you to improve your performance to a "Met" level.
- If you do not improve to "Met" within the period, you will be:
  —Terminated.
  OR
  —Demoted/reassigned if your manager believes you can contribute in an available job.

If your overall rating is "DNM":

- You are performing at an unsatisfactory level.
- Your manager should put you on an appropriate measured assignment. You will need to improve your performance to "Met" by the end of the assignment or you will be:
  —Terminated.
  OR
  —Demoted/reassigned if your manager believes you can contribute in an available job.

Note: In some cases, unsatisfactory performance on a critical objective or responsibility may mean immediate termination or demotion/reassignment without any measured assignment or probationary period.

2. Discuss your strengths and suggested improvements.
3. Sign and date the form. Your signature indicates that you have seen the completed evaluation form but does not necessarily imply agreement with the evaluation. If you disagree with your evaluation, you may contact Personnel Relations.

Note: If you wish to comment on your evaluation, do so in the space provided on the back of the form.

Your New Performance Plan

Your evaluation marks the beginning of a new review period. You and your manager should develop a new plan that encourages growth for you while continuing to meet unit objectives.

In Conclusion

Your participation in the PPC&E process ensures that you will have the opportunity to be a more effective employee. By understanding what is expected of you and then achieving the results outlined in your plan, you will more fully contribute to the achievement of your unit's goals and the goals of the company.

Rating Definitions*

Far Exceeded (FE): The employee has far exceeded acceptable levels of performance in completing objectives and responsibilities. The employee accomplishes the overall job with excellence, demonstrating creativity where appropriate. The employee anticipates, quickly responds to, and sometimes initiates priority changes within the job. The employee contributes the highest quality work in a timely manner and requires very little guidance from the manager.

Exceeded (E): The employee has exceeded acceptable levels of performance in completing objectives and responsibilities. The employee usually accomplishes the overall job with excellence, demonstrating creativity where appropriate. The employee responds to priority changes within the job and usually anticipates such changes. The employee contributes high quality work in a timely manner and requires little guidance from the manager.

Met (M): The employee has met acceptable levels of performance in completing objectives and responsibilities. Where appropriate, the employee sometimes demonstrates creativity. The employee usually responds to priority changes within the job and can sometimes anticipate such changes. The employee contributes good quality work in a timely manner and requires periodic guidance from the manager.

Met Some Not All (MSNA): The employee has met some but not all acceptable levels of performance in completing objectives and responsibilities. The employee's performance is marginal and needs improvement in order to receive a "Met" rating. The employee often responds slowly to priority changes within the job and generally does not anticipate such changes. Work is often accomplished by relying on others to solve problems. The employee usually requires considerable guidance or supervision to complete work.

Did Not Meet (DNM): The employee overall did *not* meet acceptable levels of performance in completing objectives and responsibilities. The employee generally does not respond to priority changes within the job nor anticipate such changes. Work is accomplished by relying on others to solve problems. The employee's work may contain repeated errors or poor results, and may not be completed in a timely manner. The employee requires detailed guidance and more than an appropriate amount of supervision to complete work.

*Employee performance need not meet all criteria to fall within a given rating.

DISCUSSION AND REVIEW QUESTIONS

1. List the four critical performance assessment decisions. How can decisions in one of the four areas affect decisions in the others?

2. What are the four main categories of evaluation methods? Give an example of each, along with its advantages and disadvantages. For reward purposes, which method would be best to evaluate a professor? A dormitory dietitian? A high school principal? A stonemason? Give reasons for your answer. Would your answer be different if the evaluations were for developmental purposes? How?

3. Suppose you were about to conduct a performance assessment interview with a fellow student who promised to take notes for you, but did a poor job. How would you use the factors listed in Exhibit 7–12 to improve the interview?

4. Using Exhibit 7–13, discuss why a monthly lottery of $10 for those with perfect attendance might reduce absenteeism. Discuss conditions under which it might fail to reduce absenteeism.

5. Considering the relative advantages and disadvantages of assessment techniques indicated in Exhibit 7–15, and the most common use of assessment information suggested by Exhibit 7–1, does the usage pattern shown in Exhibit 7–4 seem logical? Why or why not?

NOTES AND REFERENCES

1. John P. Campbell, Marvin D. Dunnette, Edward E. Lawler III, and Karl E. Weick, Jr., *Managerial Behavior, Performance, and Effectiveness* (New York: McGraw-Hill, 1970), p. 118.

2. Kenneth L. Sovereign, *Personnel Law* (Reston, Va.: Reston Publishing, 1984).

3. W. F. Cascio and H. J. Bernardin, "Implications of Performance Appraisal Litigation for Personnel Decisions," *Personnel Psychology* 34, no. 2 (1981), pp. 211–26; David C. Martin, "Performance Appraisal, 2: Improving the Rater's Effectiveness," *Personnel*, August 1986, pp. 28–33.

4. Bureau of National Affairs, "Performance Appraisal Programs," *Personnel Policies Forum, Survey No. 135*, February, 1983.

5. Bureau of National Affairs, "Employee Performance: Evaluation and Control," *Personnel Policies Forum, Survey No. 108*, February 1975.

6. Bureau of National Affairs, "Performance Appraisal Programs."

7. Paul Osterman, ed., *Internal Labor Markets* (Cambridge, Mass.: MIT Press, 1984).

8. Mark P. Edwards, "Productivity Improvement through Innovations in Performance Appraisal," *Public Personnel Management*, Spring 1983, pp. 13–14.

9. Cynthia Fisher and Joe Thomas, "The Other Face of Performance Appraisal," *Human Resource Management*, Spring 1982, pp. 24–26.

10. L. L. Cummings and D. P. Schwab, "Designing Appraisal Systems for Information Yield," *California Management Review*, Summer 1978, pp. 18–25.
11. Nathan B. Winstanley, "Performance Appraisal: Another Pollution Problem?" *The Conference Board Record*, September 1972, pp. 59–63.
12. John Fossum, *Labor Relations*, rev. ed. (Plano, Tex.: Business Publications, 1982).
13. Gary P. Latham and Kenneth N. Wexley, *Increasing Productivity through Performance Appraisal* (Reading, Mass.: Addison-Wesley Publishing, 1981).
14. H. John Bernardin and Richard W. Beatty, *Performance Appraisal: Assessing Human Behavior at Work* (Boston: Kent Publishing, 1983); Wexley and Latham, *Developing and Training*.
15. Robert L. Heneman, "The Relationship between Supervisory Ratings and Results-Oriented Measures of Performance: A Meta-Analysis," *Personnel Psychology* 39 (1986), pp. 811–26.
16. Peggy Lanza, "Team Appraisals," *Personnel Journal*, March 1985, pp. 47–51.
17. Charles J. Hobson and Frederick W. Gibson, "Capturing Supervisor Rating Policies: A Way to Improve Performance Appraisal Effectiveness," *Personnel Administrator*, March 1984, pp. 59–68.
18. Erich P. Prien, Mark A. Jones, and Louise M. Miller, "A Job-Related Performance Rating System," *Personnel Administrator*, January 1978, pp. 1–17.
19. E. T. Cornelius, M. D. Hakel, and P. R. Sackett, "A Methodological Approach to Job Classification for Performance Appraisal Purposes," *Personnel Psychology* 32 (1979), pp. 283–97.
20. W. I. Sauser, "Evaluating Employee Performance Needs, Problems and Possible Solutions," *Public Personnel Management*, January–February 1984, pp. 12–18.
21. Douglas Cederblom, "The Performance Appraisal Interview: A Review, Implications, and Suggestions," *Academy of Management Review*, April 1982, pp. 219–27.
22. Ronald J. Burke, William Weitzel, and Tamara Weir, "Characteristics of Effective Employee Performance Review and Development Interviews: Replication and Extension," *Personnel Psychology* 32 (1978), pp. 903–19.
23. F. J. Landy, J. L. Farr, and R. R. Jacobs, "Utility Concepts in Performance Measurement," *Organizational Behavior and Human Performance* 30 (1982), pp. 15–40.
24. Stephen J. Carroll and Craig E. Schneier, *Performance Appraisal and Review Systems* (Glenview, Ill.: Scott, Foresman, 1982).
25. S. M. Danzig, "What We Need to Know about Performance Appraisals," *Management Review*, January 1980, pp. 20–27.
26. Bureau of National Affairs, "Employee Performance: Evaluation and Control," *Personnel Policies Forum*, February 1975. Bureau of National Affairs, "Performance Appraisal Programs."
27. Peggy Lanza, "Team Appraisals."
28. H. John Bernardin and Richard W. Beatty, *Performance Appraisal: Assessing Human Behavior at Work* (Boston: Kent Publishing, 1984).

29. H. John Bernardin and M. R. Buckley, "A Consideration of Strategies in Rater Training," *Academy of Management Review* 6 (1981), pp. 205–12.
30. Bernardin and Beatty, "Performance Appraisal"; H. John Bernardin, R. L. Cardy, and J. Abbott, "The Effects of Rater Training and Cognitive Complexity on Psychometric Error in Ratings" (paper presented at the national meeting of the Academy of Management, 1982); H. J. Bernardin, R. L. Cardy, and J. J. Carlyle, "Cognitive Complexity and Appraisal Effectiveness: Back to the Drawing Board?" *Journal of Applied Psychology* 67 (1982), pp. 151–60.
31. Bernardin and Beatty, "Performance Appraisal," pp. 267–68.
32. F. J. Landy and J. L. Farr, "Performance Rating," *Psychological Bulletin*, April 1980, pp. 72–107.
33. F. Blanz and E. E. Ghiselli, "The Mixed Standard Scale: A New Rating System," *Personnel Psychology* 25 (1972), pp. 185–99.
34. V. L. Huber, "An Analysis of Performance Appraisal Practices in the Public Sector: A Review and Recommendations," *Public Personnel Management Journal*, November 1983, pp. 258–67.
35. "Performance Appraisal Pitfalls," in *Fair Employment Practices: Summary of Latest Developments*, October 20, 1983 (Washington, D.C.: Bureau of National Affairs).
36. Patricia Smith, "Behaviors, Results, and Organizational Effectiveness," in *Handbook of Industrial and Organizational Psychology*, ed. M. Dunnette (Chicago: Rand McNally, 1976).
37. George Rosinger, Louis B. Myers, Girard W. Levy, Michael Loar, Susan Morhman, and John R. Stock, "Development of a Behaviorally Based Performance Appraisal System," *Personnel Psychology*, Spring 1982, pp. 75–88; Richard W. Beatty, Craig Schneier, and James Beatty, "An Empirical Investigation of Perceptions of Ratee Behavior Frequency and Ratee Behavior Change Using Behavioral Expectation Scales (BES)," *Personnel Psychology* 30 (1977), pp. 647–58; K. R. Murphy, C. Martin, and M. Garcia, "Do Behavioral Observation Scales Measure Observation?" *Journal of Applied Psychology* 67 (1982), pp. 652–67; J. S. Kane and H. J. Bernardin, "Behavioral Observational Scales and the Evaluation of Performance Appraisal Effectiveness," *Journal of Applied Psychology* 35 (1982), pp. 635–41.
38. J. S. Kane and E. E. Lawler III, "Performance Appraisal Effectiveness: Its Assessment and Determinants," in *Research in Organizational Behavior*, ed. B. Staw (Greenwich, Conn.: JAI Press, 1979).
39. Jeffrey Kane, "Performance Distribution Assessment: A New Breed of Appraisal Methodology," in Bernardin and Beatty, *Performance Appraisal*; H. J. Bernardin, "Behavioral Expectation Scales versus Summated Scales: A Fairer Comparison," *Journal of Applied Psychology* 62 (1977), pp. 422–27; H. J. Bernardin and J. S. Kane, "A Second Look at Behavioral Observation Scales," *Personnel Psychology* 33 (1980), pp. 809–14; G. P. Latham, C. H. Fay, and L. M. Saari, "The Development of Behavioral Observation Scales for Appraising the Performance of Foremen," *Personnel Psychology* 32 (1979), pp. 299–311; and G. P. Latham, C. Fay, and L. M. Saari, "BOS, BES, and Baloney: Raising Kane with Bernardin," *Personnel Psychology*, Winter 1980, pp. 815–22.

40. P. O. Kingstrom and A. R. Bass, "A Critical Analysis of Studies Comparing Behaviorally Anchored Rating Scales (BARS) and Other Rating Formats," *Personnel Psychology* 34 (1981), pp. 263–89; H. J. Bernardin and P. C. Smith, "A Clarification of Some Issues Regarding the Development and Use of Behaviorally Anchored Rating Scales," *Journal of Applied Psychology* 66 (1981), pp. 458–63.

41. Thomas A. DeCotiis, "An Analysis of the External Validity and Applied Relevance of Three Rating Formats," *Organizational Behavior and Human Performance* 19 (1977), pp. 247–66.

42. Jeffrey S. Kane and Kimberly A. Freeman, "MBO and Performance Appraisal: A Mixture That's Not a Solution, Part 1." *Personnel* 63, no. 12 (December 1986), pp. 26–36; Jeffrey S. Kane and Kimberly A. Freeman, "MBO and Performance Appraisal: A Mixture That's Not a Solution, Part 2." *Personnel* 64, no. 2 (February 1987), pp. 26–32.

43. John F. Kikoaki and Joseph A. Litterer, "Effective Communication in the Performance Appraisal Interview," *Public Personnel Management*, Spring 1983, pp. 33–42; Douglas Cederblom, "The Performance Appraisal Interview"; R. J. Burke and D. S. Wilcox, "Characteristics of Effective Employee Performance Reviews and Development Interviews," *Personnel Psychology* 22 (1980), pp. 291–305.

44. E. Kay, H. H. Meyer, and S..R. P. French, "Effects of Threats in a Performance Appraisal Interview," *Journal of Applied Psychology* 49 (1965), pp. 311–17.

45. Anthony J. Mento, Robert P. Steele, and Ronald J. Karren, "A Meta-Analysis of Goal Setting and Feedback," *Organizational Behavior and Human Decision Processes*, 39 (1987), pp. 52–83.

46. Bureau of National Affairs, "Quarterly Report on the Employment Outlook, Job Absence, and Turnover" (Washington, D.C.: Bureau of National Affairs, 1986).

47. Ibid.

48. L. M. Schmitz and Herbert G. Heneman III, "The Effectiveness of Positive Reinforcement Programs in Reducing Employee Absenteeism," *Personnel Administrator* 25, no. 9 (1980), pp. 87–93.

49. D. R. Ilgen and J. M. Feldman, "Performance Appraisal: A Process Focus," *Research in Organizational Behavior*, January 1983, pp. 141–47.

50. M. D. Dunnette and W. C. Borman, "Personnel Selection and Classification Systems," *Annual Review of Psychology* 30 (1979), pp. 477–525.

51. W. H. Cooper, "Ubiquitous Halo," *Psychological Bulletin* 90 (1981), pp. 218–44; Charles L. Hulin, "Some Reflections on General Performance Dimensions and Halo Rating Error," *Journal of Applied Psychology* 67, no. 2 (1982), pp. 165–70.

52. M. A. Jones, "Estimating Costs in the Development and Implementation of a Performance Appraisal System" (paper presented at the first annual Scientist-Practitioner Conference in Industrial-Organizational Psychology, Norfolk, Va.: Old Dominion University, 1980).

53. H. J. Bernardin, B. B. Morgan, and P. S. Winne, "The Design of a Personnel Evaluation System for Police Officers," *JSAS Catalog of Selected Documents in Psychology* 10 (1980), pp. 1–280.

54. Jack N. Kondrasuk, "Studies in MBO Effectiveness," *Academy of Management Review* 6, no. 3 (1981), pp. 419–30.

55. Michael Keeley, "A Contingency Framework for Performance Evaluation," *Academy of Management Review*, July 1978, pp. 428–38.

56. Frank L. Schmidt and John E. Hunter, "Individual Differences in Productivity: An Empirical Test of Estimates Derived from Studies of Selection Procedure Utility," *Journal of Applied Psychology* 68 (1983), pp. 407–14.

57. John W. Boudreau, "Utility Analysis in Human Resource Management Decisions," in *Handbook of Industrial and Organizational Psychology*, 2d ed., ed., Marvin D. Dunnette (Chicago: Rand McNally, in press).

58. Frank J. Landy, James L. Farr, and Rick R. Jacobs, "Utility Concepts in Performance Measurement," *Organizational Behavior and Human Performance* 30 (1982), pp. 15–40.

59. Beth C. Florin-Thuma and John W. Boudreau, "Performance Feedback Utility Effects on Managerial Decision Processes," *Personnel Psychology*, 1988.

60. Dan R. Dalton, "Absenteeism and Turnover: Measures of Personnel Effectiveness," in *Applied Readings in Personnel and Human Resource Management*, ed. Randall Schuler, James M. McFillen, and Dan R. Dalton (New York: West Publishing, 1981).

61. David C. Martin, "Performance Appraisal 2: Improving the Rater's Effectiveness," *Personnel*, August 1986, pp. 28–33.

62. H. S. Feild and W. H. Holley, "The Relationship of Performance Appraisal System Characteristics to Verdicts in Selected Employment Discrimination Cases," *Academy of Management Journal* 25, no. 2 (1982), pp. 392–406.

63. Wayne F. Cascio, "Scientific, Legal and Operational Imperatives of Workable Performance Appraisal Systems," *Public Personnel Management*, Winter 1982, pp. 367–75.

64. Michael Schuster and Christopher Miller, "Performance Appraisal and the Age of Discrimination in Employment Act," *Personnel Administrator*, March 1983, pp. 48–58; R. G. Wells, "Guidelines for Effective and Defensible Performance Appraisal Systems," *Personnel Journal*, October 1982, pp. 776–82.

65. Robert I. Lazer, "The Discrimination Danger in Performance Appraisal," in *Contemporary Problems in Personnel*, ed. W. Hammer and F. Schmidt (Chicago: St. Clair Press, 1977).

66. Kurt Kraiger and J. Kevin Ford, "A Meta-Analysis of Ratee Race Effects in Performance Ratings," *Journal of Applied Psychology* 70 (1985), pp. 56–65.

67. David A. Waldman and Bruce J. Avolio, "A Meta-Analysis of Age Differences in Job Performance," *Journal of Applied Psychology*, 71 (1986), pp. 33–38.

PART ONE CASES

There are several types of cases at the end of each part in this book. Ithaca's Own is an integrated case that allows you to consider several human resource issues in a single organization. Therefore, Ithaca's Own reappears throughout the book. In addition, a number of cases are set in other organizations.

In solving these cases, try to follow the diagnostic approach used in this textbook. Consider factors in the external environment (product and labor market conditions, government regulations, union influences), organization conditions (business strategy, culture, nature of the work), nature of the individual employees, and the overall objectives of the organization.

We hope you enjoy working these cases and discussing possible solutions with other students and your instructor. We also hope they increase your knowledge and interest in human resource management.

▶ ITHACA'S OWN
CASE 1: STRATEGIES, STRUCTURE, AND STAFF

Ithaca's Own, Inc., founded in 1978, was begun as a small regional enterprise that specialized in "health and natural food" products. Since 1978, I-O has experienced reasonable growth. Last year its total revenues exceeded $10.2 million and its net income was about $1.7 million. Today it can be said that I-O is unique in an industry dominated by giants such as General Mills, Kellogg, and General Foods. I-O's advantage, according to its founder and chief executive officer (CEO), lies in its ability to innovate based on its research and development capabilities. For example, I-O's Research and Development Group developed an entire line of freeze-dried fruit snacks (Apple Bits and Bites is an example) to compete with candies and confections; other products developed by I-O are its Cayuga Coolers (a fruit-base drink) and a growing list of prepared products for microwave ovens (Cornell Quickie is a big seller). I-O markets these products to wholesale distributors as well as to institutions and restaurants.

During a recent interview with a national trade publication, the CEO described I-O as "an aggressive, technical-research–oriented enterprise whose competitive advantage lies in its relatively small size (approximately 410 employees) and its flexibility." Discussing the strategic thrust for the future, the CEO said, "Ithaca's Own will become a think tank for new consumer-oriented food products—I-O's principal product will be R&D— to generate new products, develop new production and marketing approaches, and to sell these products and processes to other firms, or perhaps spin them off as manufacturing affiliates."

Organization of Ithaca's Own

Ithaca's Own is organized functionally (Exhibit 1). The staff-support functions are performed in the Administrative Services Group reporting to the CEO through a vice president–administrative services. Operations has three groups, Research and Development, Production, and Marketing. The Human Resource Management (HRM) Department was added just six months ago.

EXHIBIT 1
Organization Chart of Ithaca's Own

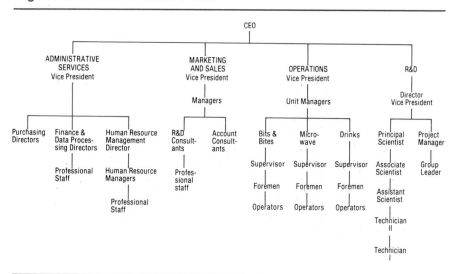

While I-O has sold several of its new products to other firms, it decided to retain three basic products to manufacture and market on its own. These three are the freeze-dried Bits and Bites, microwave products, and cooler drinks. Under the current business plan, these product lines are to be sold or established as affiliates of I-O. The R&D function remains the key to the firm's success. Currently R&D has a dual-career progression ladder, one for technical-research personnel and another for managers and project leaders. Marketing is organized in a somewhat similar manner with market researchers on one career track and sales-account personnel on the other. Currently the sale-account jobs mainly involve marketing I-O manufactured products to wholesalers and institutional customers. The market researchers focus on new-product development and designing marketing strategies for them.

Work Flow

The general flow of work is as follows—someone, typically in marketing research or R&D, initiates an application for a new idea. The application is reviewed by a "new products" team, consisting of management representatives from Marketing, Operations, and R&D. If the new idea is approved, further development in R&D and marketing is usually required. Once the product development is reasonably well along, Operations assigns it to a unit to develop a production process or fit it into an existing process. Prototypes or pilot products are developed and tested in the labs, among consumer samples, and then it is trial-marketed. At any point in the development process, Ithaca's Own may sell the product (complete with market testing data and recommended production processes) to other firms rather than go into full-scale production. However, as noted earlier, it does have full-scale production of its original products.

Briefly stated, the work flow is: product idea, product development and market testing, production process development, unit-process sale.

Employment at Ithaca's Own

I-O is not currently, nor ever has been, unionized. Two years ago, however, organizers from the Teamsters attempted to organize the hourly employees in the Operations department. Although the attempt was unsuccessful, first-line supervisors believe another organizing campaign is likely.

I-O draws its work force primarily from the local area, and because it is one of the few industries in the Ithaca area, I-O has experienced few problems in meeting its employment needs. Recently, however, as I-O continues to grow, certain functions are becoming more difficult to staff. In particular, professional and managerial positions are becoming increasingly more difficult to fill. For the first time, the management of I-O is considering extending its recruiting efforts beyond the local area.

The organization has never been involved in a lawsuit regarding its human resource policies, although no formal analysis of these policies has ever been conducted. Documentation consists of employee portfolios which include information such as the incumbent's name, position, number of absences, hiring date, sex, age, and date of termination, where applicable. A separate file is maintained for each employee by Administrative Services, and to date no effort has been made to compile and analyze this data for the work force as a whole. Accident rates are also documented. I-O has never been inspected for safety compliance, and internal safety audits are conducted on what can best be described as an ad hoc basis. While I-O considers itself an equal opportunity employer, no formal affirmative action plan exists.

The Human Resource Management Function

Growth and diversification at I-O necessitated the establishment of a Human Resource Management (HRM) department six months ago. Four HRM generalists have been hired, one to address the needs of each functional area, and a director of human resources (also a generalist), to coordinate activities. The director reports to the vice president—administrative services. (See Exhibits 1 and 2 for organizational charts.)

I-O has what is generally considered an "emergent" approach to strategic human resource planning. Specifically, I-O has made its recent human resource decisions in an ad hoc manner; consequently, if any strategy exists it must be inferred from these decisions.

I-O Human Resource Budget Allocation

Exhibits 3 and 4 offer some information on I-O's employment plan for the next period as well as data on their human resource budget allocations over the past few years. Exhibit 3 indicates the human resource programming expenditures. I-O's total labor costs include salaries and benefits plus these programming expenditures on human resource activities. In Exhibit 3, 25 percent of I-O's human resource programming budget was allocated to the R&D group compared to 5 percent to Administrative Services. Note also that the 25 percent allocation to R&D was distributed across nine activities, with staffing receiving the largest share: 45 percent.

EXHIBIT 2
Administrative Services

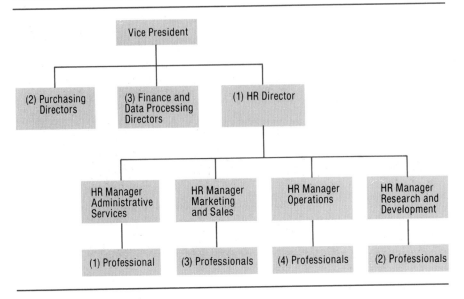

Discussion Questions

You have been brought in as a consultant to advise Ithaca's Own top management regarding HRM issues. I-O top management has asked you to consider three major issues:

A. Considering what you know about organization and environmental conditions facing I-O,
   1. What, if any, strategies or patterns "emerge" from I-O's recent human resource decisions? Examine the budget allocations shown in Exhibit 3. How do these relate to the CEO's stated direction?
   2. What recommendations would you make to I-O with respect to the reallocation of its human resource efforts? Discuss how these recommendations may be more consistent with I-O's business directions and environmental conditions.
B. Consider organizational structure and staffing in the human resource management department (refer to Exhibits 1 and 2).
   1. If a basic tenet of this book is correct—every manager is a manager of human resources—then what is the justification for employing human resource professionals?
   2. Is the current department structure consistent with I-O business strategy? For example, consider the Human Resource Depart-

EXHIBIT 3
Human Resource Strategic Programming—Budget Allocation (percents)

Strategic Programming	Functions			
	R&D	Operations	Marketing	Administrative Services
Total of Ithaca's Own (100%)	25%	60%	10%	5%
Training and development	15	40	30	20
Managerial	5	15	10	10
Technical	10	10	10	10
Skill-Craft	—	15	10	—
Staffing	45	10	30	20
Recruiting	35	10	20	10
Succession charting	5	—	5	5
Career planning	5	—	5	5
Performance evaluation	10	15	10	20
Compensation design	10	10	10	20
Equal Employment Opportunity	10	15	10	10
New programs	10	10	10	10
	100%	100%	100%	100%

EXHIBIT 4
Human Resource Requirements and Turnover

	Current Year Employment	Planned Year Forecasted Requirements	Estimated Turnover	Surplus/ (Shortage)
R&D:				
Principal scientist	10	7	0	3
Associate scientist	50	43	3	4
Assistant scientist	70	65	3	2
Manager	10	10	2	(2)
Group leader	20	23	4	(7)
Technician	30	32	4	(6)
Secretary and clerical	3	2	0	1
Total	193	182	16	(5)
Operations:				
Manager	3	3	2	(2)
Supervisor	9	8	1	0
Foremen	35	31	2	2
Operators	60	72	10	(22)
Secretary and clerical	3	2	1	0
Total	110	116	16	(22)
Marketing and sales:				
Managers	3	5	0	(2)
R&D consultants	10	6	2	2
Account consultants	8	11	1	(4)
Professional	30	38	2	(10)
Secretary and clerical	15	17	5	(7)
Total	66	77	10	(21)
Administrative services:				
Human resource managers and director	5	5	0	0
Purchasing director	2	2	1	(1)
Finance and data processing director	3	4	2	(3)
Human resource professionals	10	10	1	(1)
Finance professionals	10	8	0	2
Secretary and clerical	11	9	4	(2)
Total	41	38	8	(5)

ment's relationship with Operations. Explore the advantages and disadvantages of alternative organization structures. Does having personnel report directly to general managers of each Operations unit have merit? Do you feel it is appropriate to assign generalists to each functional area? Would it be preferable to hire human resource managers with functional specialties (i.e., staffing, compensation, training)?

3. What challenges/opportunities do you foresee facing the department in the upcoming year? Specifically, what factors in the external environment are affecting I-O? What factors in the internal environment? Select one aspect of the external environment and explain how changes in this area may affect the role and/or importance of the HRM function. Which HRM activity(s) would be involved? How would you adjust the allocation of the personnel budget to accommodate to that change?

C. Finally, what three or four pieces of additional data would you recommend collecting to better diagnose Ithaca's Own? Be specific about how you would use these data in your analysis.

▶ ITHACA'S OWN
CASE 2: EQUAL EMPLOYMENT OPPORTUNITY

The establishment of the human resource management function has placed I-O in a better position to take proactive, or preventive, measures with regard to compliance with equal employment opportunity regulations. Specifically, as I-O continues to grow, top management has become concerned that its employment practices may eventually come under review by compliance agents. The human resource management director has decided to examine I-O's status concerning the proportion of men and women currently employed and make further recommendations for the planned year's recruiting cycle.

Able Lee, HR manager for Operations, has analyzed the male/female work force composition for each position at I-O. He presented his results in Exhibits 1 and 2. Able then grouped positions by functions that are recruited from common sources. At this point, however, he is not sure whether the pattern of men and women employed at I-O is a problem or not. As a human resource professional assisting Able Lee, it is your job to identify potential problem areas related to EEO.

Any analysis includes both a comparison of percentages of minority and sex subgroups (only sex is relevant in this exercise), as well as comparison of subgroup utilization rates relative to their availability in the labor market. There are three possible outcomes of the analysis:

1. Underutilization—the percentage of minorities or women within a job group is below their percentage in the relevant availability.
2. Parity—the percentage of a protected group is equal to their percentage in the relevant availability.
3. Overutilization—the percentage of a protected group is above their percentage in the relevant availability.

EXHIBIT 1
Current Year Pattern of Employment of Women by Functions

	Current Year Employment	Number Female	Percent Female
R&D:			
Principal scientists	10	4	40%
Associate scientists	50	8	16
Assistant scientists	70	15	21
Manager	10	2	20
Group leader	20	3	15
Technicians	30	10	33
Secretary and clerical	3	2	67
Total	193	44	23
Operations:			
Managers	3	0	0
Supervisors	9	4	44
Foremen	35	0	0
Operators	60	30	50
Secretary and clerical	3	2	67
Total	110	36	33
Marketing and sales:			
Managers	3	1	33
R&D consultants	10	3	30
Account consultants	8	2	25
Professionals	30	9	30
Secretary and clerical	15	13	87
Total	66	28	42
Administrative services:			
Purchasing director	2	0	0
Finance and data processing director	3	0	0
Human resource managers and director	5	1	20
Human resource professionals	10	4	40
Finance professional	10	3	30
Secretary and clerical	11	11	100
Total	41	19	46

Relevant Availability

You have been provided with the report on Equal Employment Indicators from the 1980 Census of Population for Tompkins County, New York, the geographic/political area in which I-O is located (Exhibits 3 through 10). These data will be your starting point to determine relevant availability for I-O.

EXHIBIT 2
Current Year Employment of Women by Job Groups

	Total	Number Female	Percent Female
Group 1:			
Principal scientists	10	4	40%
Associate scientists	50	8	16
Assistant scientists	70	15	21
Total	130	27	21
Group 2:			
Managers, R&D	10	2	20
Managers, operations	3	0	0
Supervisors, operations	9	4	44
R&D consultants	10	3	30
Total	32	9	28
Group 3:			
Managers, marketing and sales	3	1	33
Purchasing directors	2	0	0
Professionals, Marketing and Sales	30	9	30
Total	35	10	29
Group 4:			
Human resource managers and director	5	1	20
Human resource professionals	10	4	40
Total	15	5	33
Group 5:			
Technicians, R&D	30	10	33
Group leader, R&D	20	3	15
Operator, operations	60	30	50
Total	110	43	39
Group 6:			
Finance and data processing director	3	0	0
Account consultants	8	2	25
Finance professionals	10	3	30
Total	21	5	24
Group 7:			
Secretary and clerical, all departments	32	28	88

Assignment

Your report should cover the following:

A. *Analysis of Current Representation*

Do you see any potential problems with the current pattern of employment of women at I-O (without considering the availability data)? (Exhibit 1) Be specific with regard to positions where possible problems may exist. What can you say if anything, about I-O's EEO behavior from this analysis?

B. *Conduct an Availability Analysis*

1. To determine the relevant availability, match each job group at I-O with an occupation (or group of occupations) from the census data (Exhibit 3). The census occupation(s) you choose will serve as a reference point for determining the relevant availability of women for a particular job group at I-O. Since your utilization analysis will be based on this match, select a census occupation(s) that has similar skills/abilities requirements as the I-O job group you are examining. For example, a technical job group at I-O may be best matched with a technically oriented census occupation. You will soon discover that matching job requirements on only job title is a tricky business. Note that a preliminary matching has already been done for each job group. For example, a set of "possible census occupation matches" has been identified for each job group (Exhibits 4 through 10).

   After indicating your job match decision, discuss any difficulties you uncover with regard to the matching process. Specifically, is there an exact match for each job group at I-O within the census data? Does the census data provide you with enough information to make a match? Based on your job match decision, what is I-O's status with respect to utilization for each job group?

2. For each of I-O's job groups, select an alternative census occupation that could be used as a job match. For example, you might consider chemistry teachers in addition to chemists as a match for I-O's scientific job group. Would choosing an alternative job match change your conclusions about I-O's utilization status? In general, how does the census occupation chosen as a reference point for relevant availability affect the conclusions one may draw about I-O's EEO behavior? What other sources of data could be used to construct a utilization analysis?

C. *Recommendations*

1. Based on these analyses, what would you recommend I-O do next concerning EEO compliance?

   a. Collect more data? Specifically, what additional data?

   b. Recruit more women? In what job groups? Do you have enough information to warrant this, or would it be a premature decision?

   c. Which job groups are "high risk" with regard to possible EEO scrutiny?

EXHIBIT 3
1980 Census Data for Tompkins County, New York (introduction)

Abstract	This report, based on the 1980 Census Equal Employment Opportunity (EEO) Special File, provides information on the civilian labor force by sex and racial/ethnic categories for 514 detailed occupational categories. The information is designed to be used for planning EEO/Affirmative Action programs.
Geographic coverage	Areas covered by this Report include Tompkins County, New York.
Race/Hispanic origin	Census data on race and Hispanic origin were obtained through self-identification. In this report, "Total Minority" is defined as Total minus White not Hispanic. "Remaining Races" is defined as Total less White, Black, Native American and Asian and Pacific Islander. Persons of Hispanic origin may be of any race.
Symbols used in tables	A dash "—" represents zero or a percent which rounds to less than 0.1. The three-dot symbol ". . ." indicates data suppressed by the Census Bureau or a composite item one or more of whose components contained such suppressions.

Sources: U.S. Department of Labor, Employment and Training Administration, Census of Population, 1980. Equal Employment Opportunity Special File/prepared by the Bureau of the Census, Washington, D.C.: The Bureau (producer and distributor), 1982. Technical Documentation/prepared by the Data User Services Division, Bureau of the Census, Washington, D.C.: The Bureau, 1982.

EXHIBIT 3 *(concluded)*
Equal Employment Indicators
Summary Occupations by Sex and Race/Ethnicity

Summary Occupations	Total	White Not Hispanic	Total Minority
Universe: Total civilian labor force			
Total, all occupations	42,016	39,691	2,325
Percent	100.0	94.5	5.5
Executive, administrative, and managerial	4,092	3,932	160
Professional specialty	9,247	8,493	754
Technicians and related support	2,630	2,429	201
Sales occupations	3,178	3,077	101
Administrative support, including clerical	7,147	6,759	388
Service occupations	6,631	6,206	425
Farming, forestry and fishing	1,125	1,099	26
Precision production, craft and repair	3,669	3,586	83
Machine operators, assemblers, inspectors	2,378	2,264	114
Transportation and material moving	952	917	35
Handlers, equipment cleaners, helpers, laborers	967	929	38
Universe: Male civilian labor force			
Total male, all occupations	22,921	21,625	1,296
Percent	100.0	94.3	5.7
Executive, administrative, and managerial	2,656	2,573	83
Professional specialty	5,214	4,759	455
Technicians and related support	1,549	1,402	147
Sales occupations	1,524	1,483	41
Administrative support, including clerical	1,665	1,570	95
Service occupations	3,033	2,781	252
Farming, forestry and fishing	946	925	21
Precision production, craft and repair	3,364	3,285	79
Machine operators, assemblers, inspectors	1,278	1,228	50
Transportation and material moving	895	860	35
Handlers, equipment cleaners, helpers, laborers	797	759	38
Universe: Female civilian labor force			
Total female, all occupations	19,095	18,066	1,029
Percent	100.0	94.6	5.4
Executive, administrative, and managerial	1,436	1,359	77
Professional specialty	4,033	3,734	299
Technicians and related support	1,081	1,027	54
Sales occupations	1,654	1,594	60
Administrative support, including clerical	5,482	5,189	293
Service occupations	3,598	3,425	173
Farming, forestry and fishing	179	174	5
Precision production, craft and repair	305	301	4
Machine operators, assemblers, inspectors	1,100	1,036	64
Transportation and material moving	57	57	—
Handlers, equipment cleaners, helpers, laborers	170	170	—

*Because there are so few people in this category in Tompkins County, it is not included in later exhibits.

Black Not Hispanic	Asian/PI Not Hispanic	Native American Not Hispanic*	Remaining Races Not Hispanic*	Hispanic All Races
935	749	44	40	557
2.2	1.8	0.1	—	1.3
65	52	—	—	43
238	364	5	17	130
34	121	6	—	40
49	27	8	—	17
192	78	7	—	111
190	77	—	17	141
16	10	—	—	—
46	6	12	3	16
59	7	6	—	42
19	7	—	—	9
27	—	—	3	8
470	443	31	30	322
2.1	1.9	0.1	0.1	1.4
24	35	—	—	24
87	247	5	17	99
25	84	—	—	38
29	2	8	—	2
45	5	—	—	45
108	56	—	7	81
16	5	—	—	—
46	2	12	3	16
44	—	6	—	—
19	7	—	—	9
27	—	—	3	8
465	306	13	10	235
2.4	1.6	—	—	1.2
41	17	—	—	19
151	117	—	—	31
9	37	6	—	2
20	25	—	—	15
147	73	7	—	66
82	21	—	10	60
—	5	—	—	—
—	4	—	—	—
15	7	—	—	42
—	—	—	—	—
—	—	—	—	—

EXHIBIT 4
Job Group 1 and Possible Census Occupation Matches

Group 1	Total	Number Female	Percent Female
Principal scientists	10	4	40%
Associate scientists	50	8	16
Assistant scientists	70	15	21
Total	130	27	21

EXHIBIT 4 *(concluded)*
Equal Employment Indicators
Detailed Occupations by Sex and Race/Ethnicity

		Universe:

Detailed Occupations by 1980 Census Occupation Code		Total
078 Biological and life scientists	Total	102
	%	100.0
	Female	18
	%	17.6
083 Medical scientists	Total	26
	%	100.0
	Female	9
	%	34.6
087 Dietitians	Total	45
	%	100.0
	Female	35
	%	77.8
073 Chemists, except biochemists	Total	26
	%	100.0
	Female	6
	%	23.1
033 Supervisors, food preparation and service occupations	Total	199
	%	100.0
	Female	91
	%	45.7
015 Managers, medicine and health	Total	30
	%	100.0
	Female	20
	%	66.7

| | Civilian Labor Force | | | |
White Not Hispanic	Total Minority	Black Not Hispanic	Asian/PI Not Hispanic	Hispanic All Races
90	12	6	6	—
88.2	11.8	5.9	5.9	—
12	6	—	6	—
11.8	5.9	—	5.9	—
26	—	—	—	—
100.0	—	—	—	—
9	—	—	—	—
34.6	—	—	—	—
45	—	—	—	—
100.0	—	—	—	—
35	—	—	—	—
77.8	—	—	—	—
20	6	—	6	—
76.9	23.1	—	23.1	—
6	—	—	—	—
23.1	—	—	—	—
194	5	—	5	—
97.5	2.5	—	2.5	—
91	—	—	—	—
45.7	—	—	—	—
30	—	—	—	—
100.0	—	—	—	—
20	—	—	—	—
66.7	—	—	—	—

EXHIBIT 5
Job Group 2 and Possible Census Occupation Matches

Group 2	Total	Number Female	Percent Female
Managers, R&D	10	2	20%
Managers, Operations	3	0	0
Supervisors, Operations	9	4	44
R&D consultants	10	3	30
Total	32	9	28

EXHIBIT 5 (concluded)
Equal Employment Indicators
Detailed Occupations by Sex and Race/Ethnicity

		Universe:
Detailed Occupations by 1980 Census Occupation Code		Total
(019) Managers and administrators, n.e.c., salaried*	Total	1,849
	%	100.0
	Female	612
	%	33.1
633 Supervisors: production occupations	Total	451
	%	100.0
	Female	67
	%	14.9
073 Chemists, except biochemists	Total	26
	%	100.0
	Female	6
	%	23.1
688 Food batchmakers	Total	20
	%	100.0
	Female	4
	%	20.0
224 Chemical technicians	Total	32
	%	100.0
	Female	11
	%	34.4
056 Industrial engineers	Total	82
	%	100.0
	Female	15
	%	18.3
363 Production coordinators	Total	109
	%	100.0
	Female	41
	%	37.6
048 Chemical engineers	Total	7
	%	100.0
	Female	—
	%	—

*n.e.c. = not elsewhere classified.

	Civilian Labor Force			
White Not Hispanic	Total Minority	Black Not Hispanic	Asian/PI Not Hispanic	Hispanic All Races
1,768	81	29	27	25
95.6	4.4	1.6	1.5	1.4
564	48	29	—	19
30.5	2.6	1.6	—	1.0
445	6	—	—	6
98.7	1.3	—	—	1.3
67	—	—	—	—
14.9	—	—	—	—
20	6	—	6	—
76.9	23.1	—	23.1	—
6	—	—	—	—
23.1	—	—	—	—
20	—	—	—	—
100.0	—	—	—	—
4	—	—	—	—
20.0	—	—	—	—
26	6	—	6	—
81.2	18.7	—	18.7	—
5	6	—	6	—
15.6	18.7	—	18.7	—
74	8	—	—	8
90.2	9.8	—	—	9.8
15	—	—	—	—
18.3	—	—	—	—
104	5	—	—	5
95.4	4.6	—	—	4.6
41	—	—	—	—
37.6	—	—	—	—
7	—	—	—	—
100.0	—	—	—	—
—	—	—	—	—
—	—	—	—	—

EXHIBIT 6
Job Group 3 and Possible Census Occupation Matches

Group 3	Total	Number Female	Percent Female
Manager, marketing and sales	3	1	33%
Purchasing director	2	0	0
Professionals, marketing and sales	30	9	30
Total	35	10	29

EXHIBIT 6 *(concluded)*
Equal Employment Indicators
Detailed Occupations by Sex and Race/Ethnicity

		Universe:

Detailed Occupations by 1980 Census Occupation Code		Total
005 Administrators and officials, public administration	Total	70
	%	100.0
	Female	42
	%	60.0
007 Financial managers	Total	127
	%	100.0
	Female	29
	%	22.8
013 Managers, marketing, advertising and public relations	Total	172
	%	100.0
	Female	25
	%	14.5
009 Purchasing managers	Total	10
	%	100.0
	Female	—
	%	—
197 Public relations specialists	Total	62
	%	100.0
	Female	15
	%	24.2
256 Advertising and related sales occupations	Total	34
	%	100.0
	Female	9
	%	26.5
029 Buyers, wholesale and retail trade except farm products	Total	85
	%	100.0
	Female	34
	%	40.0

Civilian Labor Force				
White Not Hispanic	Total Minority	Black Not Hispanic	Asian/PI Not Hispanic	Hispanic All Races
70	—	—	—	—
100.0	—	—	—	—
42	—	—	—	—
60.0	—	—	—	—
127	—	—	—	—
100.0	—	—	—	—
29	—	—	—	—
22.8	—	—	—	—
172	—	—	—	—
100.0	—	—	—	—
25	—	—	—	—
14.5	—	—	—	—
10	—	—	—	—
100.0	—	—	—	—
—	—	—	—	—
—	—	—	—	—
62	—	—	—	—
100.0	—	—	—	—
15	—	—	—	—
24.2	—	—	—	—
34	—	—	—	—
100.0	—	—	—	—
9	—	—	—	—
26.5	—	—	—	—
57	28	10	—	18
67.1	32.9	11.8	—	21.2
34	—	—	—	—
40.0	—	—	—	—

EXHIBIT 7
Job Group 4 and Possible Census Occupation Matches

Group 4	Total	Number Female	Percent Female
Human resource managers and directors	5	1	20%
Human resource professionals	10	4	40
Total	15	5	33

EXHIBIT 7 *(concluded)*
Equal Employment Indicators
Detailed Occupations by Sex and Race/Ethnicity

		Universe:
Detailed Occupations by 1980 Census Occupation Code		Total
027 Personnel, training, and labor relations specialists	Total	121
	%	100.0
	Female	49
	%	40.5
305 Supervisors: financial records processing	Total	33
	%	100.0
	Female	29
	%	87.9
316 Interviewers	Total	19
	%	100.0
	Female	19
	%	100.0
389 Administrative support occupations, n.e.c.*	Total	199
	%	100.0
	Female	147
	%	73.9
163 Counselors, educational and vocational	Total	334
	%	100.0
	Female	210
	%	62.9
338 Payroll and timekeeping clerks	Total	44
	%	100.0
	Female	36
	%	81.8
008 Personnel and labor relations managers	Total	83
	%	100.0
	Female	45
	%	54.2

*n.e.c. = not elsewhere classified.

		Civilian Labor Force		
White Not Hispanic	Total Minority	Black Not Hispanic	Asian/PI Not Hispanic	Hispanic All Races
121	—	—	—	—
100.0	—	—	—	—
49	—	—	—	—
40.5	—	—	—	—
33	—	—	—	—
100.0	—	—	—	—
29	—	—	—	—
87.9	—	—	—	—
19	—	—	—	—
100.0	—	—	—	—
19	—	—	—	—
100.0	—	—	—	—
199	—	—	—	—
100.0	—	—	—	—
147	—	—	—	—
73.9	—	—	—	—
280	54	38	8	8
83.8	16.2	11.4	2.4	2.4
192	18	18	—	—
57.5	5.4	5.4	—	—
44	—	—	—	—
100.0	—	—	—	—
36	—	—	—	—
81.8	—	—	—	—
83	—	—	—	—
100.0	—	—	—	—
45	—	—	—	—
54.2	—	—	—	—

EXHIBIT 8
Job Group 5 and Possible Census Occupation Matches

Group 5	Total	Number Female	Percent Female
Technicians, R&D	30	10	33%
Group leader, R&D	20	3	15
Operator, operations	60	30	50
Total	110	43	39

EXHIBIT 8 (continued)
Equal Employment Indicators
Detailed Occupations by Sex and Race/Ethnicity

		Universe:
Detailed Occupations by 1980 Census Occupation Code		Total
073 Chemists, except biochemists	Total	26
	%	100.0
	Female	6
	%	23.1
363 Production coordinators	Total	109
	%	100.0
	Female	41
	%	37.6
785 Assemblers	Total	718
	%	100.0
	Female	530
	%	73.8
216 Engineering technicians, n.e.c.*	Total	496
	%	100.0
	Female	235
	%	47.4
637 Machinists, except apprentices	Total	190
	%	100.0
	Female	13
	%	6.8
224 Chemical technicians	Total	32
	%	100.0
	Female	11
	%	34.4

*n.e.c. = not elsewhere classified.

| | Civilian Labor Force | | | |
White Not Hispanic	Total Minority	Black Not Hispanic	Asian/PI Not Hispanic	Hispanic All Races
20	6	—	6	—
76.9	23.1	—	23.1	—
6	—	—	—	—
23.1	—	—	—	—
104	5	—	—	5
95.4	4.6	—	—	4.6
41	—	—	—	—
37.6	—	—	—	—
686	32	16	7	9
95.5	4.5	2.2	1.0	1.3
503	27	11	7	9
70.1	3.8	1.5	1.0	1.3
482	14	—	10	4
97.2	2.8	—	2.0	0.8
233	2	—	—	2
47.0	0.4	—	—	0.4
185	5	5	—	—
97.4	2.6	2.6	—	—
13	—	—	—	—
6.8	—	—	—	—
26	6	—	6	—
81.2	18.7	—	18.7	—
5	6	—	6	—
15.6	18.7	—	18.7	—

EXHIBIT 8 *(concluded)*
Equal Employment Indicators
Detailed Occupations by Sex and Race/Ethnicity

		Universe:
Detailed Occupations by *1980 Census Occupation Code*		*Total*
873 Production helpers	Total	30
	%	100.0
	Female	17
	%	56.7
203 Clinical laboratory technologists and technicians	Total	43
	%	100.0
	Female	30
	%	69.8
425 Crossing guards	Total	9
	%	100.0
	Female	7
	%	77.8
233 Biological technicians	Total	92
	%	100.0
	Female	42
	%	45.7
115 Chemistry teachers	Total	46
	%	100.0
	Female	13
	%	28.3
216 Engineering technicians, n.e.c.*	Total	496
	%	100.0
	Female	235
	%	47.4
747 Pressing machine operators	Total	13
	%	100.0
	Female	7
	%	53.8
734 Printing machine operators	Total	98
	%	100.0
	Female	45
	%	45.9
797 Production testers	Total	28
	%	100.0
	Female	13
	%	46.4
634 Tool and die makers, excluding apprentices	Total	72
	%	100.0
	Female	—
	%	—
688 Food batchmakers	Total	20
	%	100.0
	Female	4
	%	20.0

*n.e.c. = not elsewhere classified.

	Civilian Labor Force			
White Not Hispanic	Total Minority	Black Not Hispanic	Asian/PI Not Hispanic	Hispanic All Races
30	—	—	—	—
100.0	—	—	—	—
17	—	—	—	—
56.7	—	—	—	—
43	—	—	—	—
100.0	—	—	—	—
30	—	—	—	—
69.8	—	—	—	—
9	—	—	—	—
100.0	—	—	—	—
7	—	—	—	—
77.8	—	—	—	—
85	7	7	—	—
92.4	7.6	7.6	—	—
42	—	—	—	—
45.7	—.	—	—	—
44	2	—	2	—
95.7	4.3	—	4.3	—
13	—	—	—	—
28.3	—	—	—	—
482	14	—	10	4
97.2	2.8	—	2.0	0.8
233	2	—	—	2
47.0	0.4	—	—	0.4
7	6	—	—	—
53.8	46.2	—	—	—
7	—	—	—	—
53.8	—	—	—	—
98	—	—	—	—
100.0	—	—	—	—
45	—	—	—	—
45.9	—	—	—	—
28	—	—	—	—
100.0	—	—	—	—
13	—	—	—	—
46.4	—	—	—	—
72	—	—	—	—
100.0	—	—	—	—
—	—	—	—	—
—	—	—	—	—
20	—	—	—	—
100.0	—	—	—	—
.4	—	—	—	—
20.0	—	—	—	—

EXHIBIT 9
Job Group 6 and Possible Census Occupation Matches

Group 6	Total	Number Female	Percent Female
Finance and data processing director	3	0	0%
Account consultants	8	2	25
Finance professionals	10	3	30
Total	21	5	24

EXHIBIT 9 *(continued)*
Equal Employment Indicators
Detailed Occupations by Sex and Race/Ethnicity

Universe:

Detailed Occupations by 1980 Census Occupation Code		Total
023 Accountants and auditors	Total	206
	%	100.0
	Female	98
	%	47.6
026 Management analysts	Total	12
	%	100.0
	Female	5
	%	41.7
034 Business and promotion agents	Total	11
	%	100.0
	Female	—
	%	—
007 Financial managers	Total	127
	%	100.0
	Female	29
	%	22.8
009 Purchasing managers	Total	10
	%	100.0
	Female	—
	%	—
338 Payroll and timekeeping clerks	Total	44
	%	100.0
	Female	36
	%	81.8
197 Public relations specialists	Total	62
	%	100.0
	Female	15
	%	24.2
166 Economists	Total	83
	%	100.0
	Female	28
	%	33.7

| | Civilian Labor Force | | | |
White Not Hispanic	Total Minority	Black Not Hispanic	Asian/PI Not Hispanic	Hispanic All Races
202	4	4	—	—
98.1	1.9	1.9	—	—
94	4	4	—	—
45.6	1.9	1.9	—	—
12	—	—	—	—
100.0	—	—	—	—
5	—	—	—	—
41.7	—	—	—	—
11	—	—	—	—
100.0	—	—	—	—
—	—	—	—	—
—	—	—	—	—
127	—	—	—	—
100.0	—	—	—	—
29	—	—	—	—
22.8	—	—	—	—
10	—	—	—	—
100.0	—	—	—	—
—	—	—	—	—
—	—	—	—	—
44	—	—	—	—
100.0	—	—	—	—
36	—	—	—	—
81.8	—	—	—	—
62	—	—	—	—
100.0	—	—	—	—
15	—	—	—	—
24.2	—	—	—	—
83	—	—	—	—
100.0	—	—	—	—
28	—	—	—	—
33.7	—	—	—	—

EXHIBIT 9 *(concluded)*
Equal Employment Indicators
Detailed Occupations by Sex and Race/Ethnicity

		Universe:
Detailed Occupations by *1980 Census Occupation Code*		*Total*
383 Bank tellers	Total	163
	%	100.0
	Female	133
	%	81.6
229 Computer programmers	Total	264
	%	100.0
	Female	79
	%	29.9
386 Statistical clerks	Total	104
	%	100.0
	Female	61
	%	58.7
065 Operations and systems researchers and analysts	Total	21
	%	100.0
	Female	6
	%	28.6
255 Securities and financial services sales occupations	Total	32
	%	100.0
	Female	10
	%	31.2
337 Bookkeepers, accounting, and auditing clerks	Total	798
	%	100.0
	Female	699
	%	87.6
308 Computer operators	Total	58
	%	100.0
	Female	32
	%	55.2
276 Cashiers	Total	663
	%	100.0
	Female	528
	%	79.6
016 Managers, properties and real estate	Total	84
	%	100.0
	Female	17
	%	20.2

| | Civilian Labor Force | | | |
White Not Hispanic	Total Minority	Black Not Hispanic	Asian/PI Not Hispanic	Hispanic All Races
157	6	4	2	—
96.3	3.7	2.5	1.2	—
131	2	—	2	—
80.4	1.2	—	1.2	—
234	30	—	20	10
88.6	11.4	—	7.6	3.8
67	12	—	12	—
25.4	4.5	—	4.5	—
85	19	8	2	9
81.7	18.3	7.7	1.9	8.7
61	—	—	—	—
58.7	—	—	—	—
16	5	5	—	—
76.2	23.8	23.8	—	—
6	—	—	—	—
28.6	—	—	—	—
32	—	—	—	—
100.0	—	—	—	—
10	—	—	—	—
31.2	—	—	—	—
780	18	12	—	6
97.7	2.3	1.5	—	0.8
687	12	12	—	—
86.1	1.5	1.5	—	—
58	—	—	—	—
100.0	—	—	—	—
32	—	—	—	—
55.2	—	—	—	—
641	22	7	—	15
96.7	3.3	1.1	—	2.3
513	15	—·	—	15
77.4	2.3	—	—	2.3
84	—	—	—	—
100.0	—	—	—	—
17	—	—	—	—
20.2	—	—	—	—

EXHIBIT 10
Job Group 7 and Possible Census Occupation Matches

Group 7	Total	Number Female	Percent Female
Secretaries and clericals (all departments)	32	28	88%

EXHIBIT 10 (continued)
Equal Employment Indicators
Detailed Occupations by Sex and Race/Ethnicity

		Universe:
Detailed Occupations by 1980 Census Occupation Code		Total
319 Receptionists	Total	288
	%	100.0
	Female	273
	%	94.8
359 Dispatchers	Total	53
	%	100.0
	Female	30
	%	56.6
326 Correspondence clerks	Total	—
	%	100.0
	Female	—
	%	—
329 Peripheral equipment operators	Total	92
	%	100.0
	Female	48
	%	52.2
335 File clerks	Total	65
	%	100.0
	Female	48
	%	73.8
378 Bill and account collectors	Total	43
	%	100.0
	Female	29
	%	67.4
327 Order clerks	Total	64
	%	100.0
	Female	49
	%	76.6
336 Records clerks	Total	61
	%	100.0
	Female	35
	%	57.4
313 Secretaries	Total	1,634
	%	100.0
	Female	1,610
	%	98.5

	Civilian Labor Force			
White Not Hispanic	Total Minority	Black Not Hispanic	Asian/PI Not Hispanic	Hispanic All Races
270	18	—	9	9
93.7	6.2	—	3.1	3.1
255	18	—	9	9
88.5	6.2	—	3.1	3.1
53	—	—	—	—
100.0	—	—	—	—
30	—	—	—	—
56.6	—	—	—	—
—	—	—	—	—
—	—	—	—	—
—	—	—	—	—
92	—	—	—	—
100.0	—	—	—	—
48	—	—	—	—
52.2	—	—	—	—
65	—	—	—	—
100.0	—	—	—	—
48	—	—	—	—
73.8	—	—	—	—
36	7	7	—	—
83.7	16.3	16.3	—	—
22	7	7	—	—
51.2	16.3	16.3	—	—
64	—	—	—	—
100.0	—	—	—	—
49	—	—	—	—
76.6	—	—	—	—
61	—	—	—	—
100.0	—	—	—	—
35	—	—	—	—
57.4	—	—	—	—
1,557	77	39	9	22
95.3	4.7	2.4	0.6	1.3
1,533	77	39	9	22
93.8	4.7	2.4	0.6	1.3

EXHIBIT 10 *(concluded)*
Equal Employment Indicators
Detailed Occupations by Sex and Race/Ethnicity

		Universe:
Detailed Occupations by 1980 Census Occupation Code		*Total*
275 Sales counter clerks	Total	20
	%	100.0
	Female	8
	%	40.0
446 Health aides, except nursing	Total	94
	%	100.0
	Female	78
	%	83.0
304 Supervisors: computer equipment operators	Total	44
	%	100.0
	Female	17
	%	38.6
385 Data-entry keyers	Total	95
	%	100.0
	Female	86
	%	90.5
387 Teachers' aides	Total	234
	%	100.0
	Female	140
	%	59.8
315 Typists	Total	271
	%	100.0
	Female	271
	%	100.0
347 Office machine operators, n.e.c.*	Total	6
	%	100.0
	Female	6
	%	100.0
379 General office clerks	Total	890
	%	100.0
	Female	701
	%	78.8

*n.e.c. = not elsewhere classified.

		Civilian Labor Force		
White Not Hispanic	Total Minority	Black Not Hispanic	Asian/PI Not Hispanic	Hispanic All Races
20	—	—	—	—
100.0	—	—	—	—
8	—	—	—	—
40.0	—	—	—	—
94	—	—	—	—
100.0	—	—	—	—
78	—	—	—	—
83.0	—	—	—	—
44	—	—	—	—
100.0	—	—	—	—
17	—	—	—	—
38.6	—	—	—	—
92	3	—	—	3
96.8	3.2	—	—	3.2
83	3	—	—	3
87.4	3.2	—	—	3.2
204	30	23	—	7
87.2	12.8	9.8	—	3.0
132	8	8	—	—
56.4	3.4	3.4	—	—
236	35	18	17	—
87.1	12.9	6.6	6.3	—
236	35	18	17	—
87.1	12.9	6.6	6.3	—
6	—	—	—	—
100.0	—	—	—	—
6	—	—	—	—
100.0	—	—	—	—
808	82	42	28	12
90.8	9.2	4.7	3.1	1.3
633	68	37	28	3
71.1	7.6	4.2	3.1	0.3

▶ CONSOLIDATED DEFENSE MANUFACTURING

CDM is a large firm producing devices primarily purchased by the Department of Defense of the United States. With the approval of the U.S. government, CDM does sell some of the devices to foreign governments such as the Federal Republic of Germany and Australia.

CDM is considering bidding on a new contract to make an improved version of its product for the U.S. Army. This would be a large contract and would require additional hiring of several hundred skilled workers to produce the devices.

These workers (tool and die workers, machinists, etc.) are thought to be in short supply. Before CDM bids on the contract, top management has asked for the advice of its management as to feasibility of the project. Thus the financial people are working with production people on a minimum bid. The production people are projecting their needs for plant and equipment.

Discussion Question

You have been asked to recommend whether the personnel are available and at what cost. Several production sites are feasible: Hartford, Connecticut; Milwaukee, Wisconsin; and Birmingham, Alabama. Your recommended site and projected personnel availability are expected in 30 days. Where do you begin? Which kinds of data would you need for each potential site?

▶ STOESS YARN, INC.

Stoess Yarn Company has a plant in Charlestown, South Carolina. The jobs in the plant are relatively simple and require only a small amount of training. The intelligence and mechanical ability necessary to do the job effectively are minimal.

Recently the Equal Employment Opportunity Commission had a complaint about the Charlestown plant. After investigating, the commission required the firm to file an affirmative action program. It noted:

> Although Charlestown area has a black population of at least 40 percent, the distribution of blacks at the plant is as follows: top management—none; middle management and staff—none; supervisory management—1 percent; and employees management—6 percent.
>
> We require that Stoess hire and retain two black top managers and staff, five black middle managers, nine black supervisors, and 150 black nonsupervisory employees.

EXHIBIT 1
Seniority Distribution of Stoess Employees

Positions	Years Seniority (in percent)					
	<5	6–10	11–15	16–20	21–25	>25
Top managers	0	0	7	32	28	33
Middle managers	0	5	13	29	29	23
Supervisory managers	2	16	20	27	23	12
Nonsupervisory employees	20	29	26	18	6	1

We also note that although the employees are 74 percent women, there are only three female supervisors, and there are no female middle or top managers.

We require that Stoess hire and retain five female top managers, 11 female middle managers, and 16 female supervisors.

The sales trend for Stoess has been downward. The marketing department is projecting no sales increase next year. In fact, Stoess had furloughed 15 employees each month prior to the EEOC visit.

The seniority distribution of the present Stoess employees is given in Exhibit 1. The number of employees involved in the study was top management, 15; middle management and staff, 35; supervisory management, 50; and nonsupervisory employees, 175.

Discussion Question

You are Charles Tedrowe, personnel manager of Stoess. Draw up your plan to meet with the EEOC and develop an implementation plan that would reach the EEOC goals.

THE DIAGNOSTIC MODEL

ASSESS HUMAN RESOURCE CONDITIONS	SET HUMAN RESOURCE OBJECTIVES	CHOOSE AND APPLY HUMAN RESOURCE ACTIVITIES	EVALUATE RESULTS

EXTERNAL CONDITIONS
 	
  Economic Conditions
 	
  Government Regulations
 	
  Unions
 	
ORGANIZATIONAL CONDITIONS
 	
  Nature of the Organization
 	
  Nature of the Work
 	
EMPLOYEE CONDITIONS
 	
  Abilities
 	
  Motivation
 	
  Interests
	EFFICIENCY
	
	  Organization
	
	  Employee
	
	EQUITY
	
	  Organization
	
	  Employee
		Planning
		
		Staffing
		
		Development
		
		Employee/Union Relations
		
		Compensation
			EFFICIENCY
			
			EQUITY

Part two

Setting Objectives

art Two may well be the most important part of the book. Throughout the book, we discuss the need to set objectives for the human resource activities and to weigh the results of activities against these objectives. Setting objectives is a major component of our diagnostic model, Exhibit Two. Objectives flow from the assessment of conditions the organization faces (Part One), and an assessment of where the organization would like to be. Objectives serve to direct and guide managers' decisions. The results of these decisions need to be evaluated, and compared to the objectives. Setting objectives and evaluating results keep the train on the right track.

Chapter Eight introduces the human resource planning process and discusses two phases: (1) how organizations go about setting objectives, and (2) various approaches to evaluating results. Chapter Nine continues the discussion, giving special attention to employment planning.

chapter

eight

SETTING OBJECTIVES AND EVALUATING RESULTS

CHAPTER OUTLINE

The setting is an executive conference room. The top officers of a large bank are participating in the annual planning meeting. Each functional vice president presents the department's budget for next year after a review of the past year's accomplishments.

Vice President for Marketing Martha Renstrom, who has just completed her budget request, had her advertising budget cut for the next year. Last year, return on assets and profits were down at the bank.

Andrew Major, vice president for personnel, speaks next.

Andrew: Well, folks, I'm not going to take much of your time. It's been a long day. You know what we do for the bank. We hire, train, and pay the employees, provide benefits, career planning, EEO, and so on. Personnel is not asking for any major increases. My budget is simply last year's budget adjusted upward 8 percent for inflation. Any questions?

Martha: Wait a minute, Andy. My budget just got cut and here you come asking for 8 percent more than last year. I suppose we have to have a personnel department. But why shouldn't my advertising budget be increased and your budget cut? After all, advertising brings customers into the bank and helps us make money. What *specifically* does personnel do for this bank's profit and loss statement? How *specifically* does personnel help us reach our goals of growth and profitability?

Martha's questions are to the point. If Andy's personnel department has set specific objectives and evaluated results against those objectives, he will have some answers. If not, the lack of evidence may cause the bank's top officers to conclude (perhaps mistakenly) that human resource activities contribute little to the organization's "real" goals.

THE DIAGNOSTIC APPROACH AND HUMAN RESOURCE PLANNING

This chapter introduces human resource planning and explores two critical phases of it:

How managers set human resource objectives.

How managers evaluate human resource activities.

Definition

Human resource planning is the *process* by which management determines how the organization should move from its current human resource conditions to its desired human resource conditions.

This definition is deceptively simple. It assumes that we can answer four basic questions shown in Exhibit 8–1. These questions form the four phases of the planning process and are the same four phases used in the diagnostic process through the book.

1. *Where are we now?* (Assessing conditions) Answering this question has been the subject of Part One of this book—assessing human resource conditions. It involved (*a*) scanning the external conditions, the threats

EXHIBIT 8–1
Human Resources Planning: Four-Phase Process

Question		*Diagnostic Process*
1. Where are we now?	1.	*Assessing human resource conditions*—scan external conditions, analyze internal organization conditions, and evaluate employees.
2. Where do we want to be and how do we contribute?	2.	*Set human resource objectives*—efficiency and equity, including productivity, costs, compliance, performance, absenteeism, and turnover.
3. How do we achieve these objectives?	3.	*Choose human resource activities*—design and administer personnel programs: staffing, training, labor relations, and compensation activities.
4. How did we do?	4.	*Evaluate results.*

and opportunities facing the organization; *(b)* assessing the internal organization environment including its business strategies, culture, technological changes, and changing nature of the work; and *(c)* assessing the work force and employees, their skills and abilities, their work behaviors such as performance, absenteeism, and turnover and their satisfaction with their work. The focus is on using this information to set human resource objectives.

2. *Where do we want to be and how do we contribute?* (Set objectives) The answer to this question requires setting objectives that are consistent with the overall strategies and mission of the organization. Broadly conceived, these involve concerns for efficiency and equity. Human resource planning ensures that human resource decisions are tailored to the organization purposes.

3. *How do we get from where we are to where we want to be?* (Choose actions) Answering this question is the heart of human resource decision making. Managers choose among alternative approaches to achieve the objectives. Alternatives may be designed to increase unit productivity and employee performance, to reduce labor costs, to ensure compliance with legislation and regulations, and/or to resolve any current or anticipated problems that employees may face.

4. *How effective were our actions?* (Evaluate results) Answers here evaluate the results of the personnel activities, to assess if the actions taken did accomplish the human resource objectives set earlier.

Human Resource Planning: The Integrating Link

The purpose of human resource planning is to provide linkages—to ensure that the human resource decisions that managers make are integrated and directed toward achieving objectives. Exhibits 8–2 and 8–3 present examples of two companies' human resource objectives and the decisions directed toward achieving them. In Merck & Company's case, Exhibit 8–2, the highest priority is ensuring that Merck has the management talent required to achieve its business objectives. Key activities in Merck's plan included training all new supervisors, recruiting from colleges, and succession planning.

Human Resource Management: Collection of Activities for Maintenance and Control

Without planning, personnel management runs the risk of becoming simply a collection of activities, similar to those described in each separate chapter of this book. Personnel management without planning consists of

EXHIBIT 8–2
Merck's Corporate Human Resource Objectives

Detailed Action Plans (1982–1986) in Support of Strategic Priorities

Summary of Priorities:

1. Satisfy the long-term *Management Requirements* of the Company at all levels.

2. Continued concentration on improved and effective *Employee Relations* at all levels of the Company.

3. Continue to focus on *Affirmative Action*, with emphasis on developing a total environment conducive to equal employment opportunity.

4. Expanded use of various media for continued development and implementation of *Employee Communications*.

5. Continued emphasis on the importance of the *Supervisor* at all levels of the organization by providing training and communications support of our strategy of cooperation and understanding.

6. Develop new and more effective ways to accommodate *Employee Participation* in joint problem-solving areas and in appropriate policy/practice development.

7. Continue development and implementation of programs and policies which will strengthen *Employee Identification and Commitment* to the Company and its business goals and objectives.

8. Review and expand employee *Compensation and Reward Systems* to assure that they are truly motivating high performance. Merchandise the programs to assure their acceptance at all levels of the organization.

9. Continue development and expansion of the broad-based *Employee Health and Safety Program*, focused on health and well-being both on and off the job.

10. Develop innovative approaches to *Organization Design* and to *Job Design & Scheduling* to improve productivity.

Key Action Plans in Support of Strategic Priorities:

Priority #1. Satisfy the long-term *Management Requirements* of the Company at all levels

The long-term survival of the Company will depend in large measure on the availability of outstanding management talent at all levels of the organization. During the last few years, Human Resource planning and training & development efforts have been markedly expanded to meet growing present and future needs. Emphasis has been placed on management and supervisory programs to assure adequate numbers of personnel for leadership positions requiring strong skills in planning, communicating, problem resolution, coaching, and training others.

We will need to continue to emphasize and expand the wide variety of activities required to develop effective leaders for the future:

- Recruitment, selection, & placement.
- Succession planning.
- Individual career planning and development.
- Identification of high potential management talent at all levels.
- Inter-divisional exchange of high potential employees.

Supporting Action Plans:

a. Continue strong emphasis on Human Resource planning and development activities which include recruitment of people with strong management potential,

EXHIBIT 8–2 (concluded)

succession planning, individual career planning, and identification of high potential management talent throughout the Company.

> Timetable: 1981 & continuing   Cost: To be determined

b. Develop programs to require *minimum skills training* for all *new* supervisory and managerial personnel.

> Timetable: 1982–1983   Cost: To be determined

c. Expand our college recruiting program as a high-priority source of new talent.

> Timetable: 1981 & continuing   Cost: Budgeted

d. Implement a Senior Management Briefing Program to provide orientation on key issues, information on new management techniques, and reviews of materials and approaches being used in the supervisory and management development programs throughout the Company. Program will include leading outside authorities in the management and organization planning/development field.

> Timetable: 1981–1982   Cost: $20,000

e. In anticipation of loss of Human Resources people to other companies, possibly to other functions and to general turnover, continue the program of regular recruitment of high potential individuals.

> Timetable: 1981 & continuing   Cost: Budgeted

Source: Merck & Co., Inc.

rather discrete efforts, such as recruiting; monitoring EEO performance; and designing and administering labor relations, compensation, and training programs. Each of these activities focuses on a specific set of goals (attracting applicants, meeting EEO goals, controlling labor costs) and draws on a subset of theories and research related to specific problems. Under such a view, personnel/human resource management tends to be primarily a maintenance and control function. It is less likely to focus on the overall objectives of employee and organization effectiveness.

Human Resource Management: Integrated System for Achieving Results

In the diagnostic approach, human resource planning directs the personnel manager to ensure that personnel activities are integrated into a system greater than the sum of its parts, thus assisting the organization to effectively employ its human resources. Managers evaluate recruiting, labor relations, and all personnel activities to assess how well they help organizations and employees achieve their objectives. Human resource planning also helps the personnel function become more than a loose collection of separate activities. It ensures that activities are integrated with each other and with the overall organization objectives.

EXHIBIT 8–3
Ontario Hydro's Corporate Policy—Human Resources Planning

1. The corporation shall forecast its human resources requirements as a necessary part of other forecasts.
2. Managers at all levels shall engage in human resources planning as an integrated and supporting part of work program planning.
3. The corporation shall consider future as well as present requirements when filling positions.
4. Managers at level X-1 shall recommend succession plans for level X and shall provide assistance to prepare candidates to meet position requirements.
5. Human resources planning for senior management positions at levels 2 and 3 shall be conducted and monitored by a policy and administration committee appointed by the president.
6. The policy and administration commitee shall establish policy and procedures for forecasting of needs; identification of target jobs, nomination, assessment, succession planning, development and selection of candidates for positions at levels 2 and 3 as part of the senior management resources plan.
7. Employees shall have the primary responsibility for their own career development.
8. The corporation shall provide assistance to employees in individual career planning to the extent permitted by work priorities.
9. The corporation shall include consideration of the identified career aspirations, interests, and personal constraints on career mobility of potential candidates for positions in planning for its human resources requirements.

Source: James Rush and L. Bourne, "Human Resource Planning at Ontario Hydro: A Field Study" (London, Ontario: Western Ontario University, 1983).

As noted, the previous chapters examined the first phase of human resource planning and the diagnostic approach: Assessing the conditions that are relevant to human resources management. The remainder of this chapter explores the two other phases that are crucial to ensure that human resources management is effective:

How managers set human resource objectives.

How human resource activities are evaluated.

THE DIAGNOSTIC APPROACH TO SETTING OBJECTIVES AND EVALUATING RESULTS

Several options exist for setting human resource objectives and evaluating activities. In reviewing these options, we illustrate a systematic approach to human resource objectives and evaluation.

Definition

The *objectives* of human resource management identify the discrepancies between desired or required conditions and present or anticipated conditions, establish the priorities for reducing the discrepancies, and specify the measurements that indicate effectiveness.

Businesses have long realized the importance of setting objectives and evaluating results in human resource management (HRM).[1] One survey found that more than 80 percent of responding companies formally evaluated their personnel function. Yet, human resource objectives may be irrelevant, and evaluation may fail to support organizational goals. As later chapters illustrate, companies often evaluate human resource activities on very limited objectives that are not directly related to productivity or profits.[2] Writers still commonly admonish human resource managers to attend to the costs, benefits, and bottom-line implications of their decisions.[3] It is difficult even to imagine such a reminder for managers of financial, marketing, and raw material resources.

Definition

Evaluation measures the effects of human resource management activities and decisions in reducing important discrepancies between desired or required conditions and present or anticipated conditions. It provides information for revising and establishing new objectives.

Evaluation serves many purposes. It can:

Improve the operation of activities by providing data on the activities' costs and results.

Assist personnel and operating managers to decide which personnel activities to continue, modify, or drop.

Help ensure that personnel activities are related to achieving the organization's strategies and objectives.

Help ensure that employees, managers, and other HRM constituents are aware and satisfied with the decisions and services provided.

Help justify personnel activities and formulate budgets.

Is It Future or Past?

The emphasis on identifying gaps between actual and desired conditions implies both a proactive (forward-looking) and a reactive (backward-looking) approach. In setting health care objectives by diagnosing a patient's conditions, the physician not only examines the current condition and immediate problems, but also forecasts anticipated future health conditions and establishes desired future health goals. Similarly, human resource managers do more than put out the fires by reacting to gaps between current conditions and previously set goals. They forecast future trends and influences to identify desired or required future conditions, such as imminent new legislation, or an anticipated need for additional computer programmers. They also establish objectives that bring human resources in line with those desires or requirements. By anticipating problems before they arise, managers ensure that efficient and equitable activities are available. For example, long-term planning allows employee surpluses to be remedied by attrition and retirement rather than layoffs.

Exhibit 8–2 shows the role of objectives and evaluation in the diagnostic model. Derived from an analysis of conditions, objectives are either efficiency related or equity related. Human resource activities are chosen to address the objectives, and then the objectives come into play again when results are evaluated.

Why discuss evaluation here, even before you have read about human resource activities? There are two reasons: First, setting objectives and evaluating results are closely related. In fact, they are two sides of the same coin. The purpose of objectives is to establish standards and benchmarks for subsequent evaluation. Without objectives, evaluation is impossible. Evaluation also affects objectives. It is pointless to establish objectives that cannot be measured or cannot be affected by activities. So, setting objectives implies considering how results will eventually be compared to them.

The second reason for addressing objectives and evaluation at this point is more fundamental. The basic premise of this textbook is that *human resource decisions make a difference*. Objectives and evaluation are the tools for recognizing and communicating that difference. The nature of objectives and evaluation reflect not only how managers think about human resource management, but also how the organization regards it. Human resource managers are the stewards of one of the most potentially valuable resources available to an organization—its people. The effects of human resource management should be planned and evaluated just as the effects of other management functions are planned and evaluated. The key is an appropriate system for setting objectives and evaluating results.[4]

Thus, the concepts and techniques discussed in this chapter represent a way of thinking about human resources that shows why the activities and techniques exist and how they fit together. Objectives and evaluation are so fundamental that every subsequent chapter in this book addresses objective-setting and evaluation issues specific to each human resource activity. In this chapter, we develop the general concepts underlying objective-setting and evaluation.

The Role of Assessing Conditions

Exhibit 8–4 depicts the relationship between assessments of conditions and human resource objectives. Previous chapters have already discussed assessing external, organizational, and employee conditions. These assessments produce information, such as labor market trends, legislative requirements, organizational strategies, and employee attitudes, or performance levels. The objective-setting process uses the information to identify discrepancies that are important enough to direct activities.

Some information describes desired or required human resource conditions, such as appropriate female and minority representation levels, production or market share targets, and desired employee attitudes or performance levels. Other information describes actual or anticipated human resource conditions, such as actual accident rates, female and minor-

EXHIBIT 8–4
The Role of Assessing Conditions in Setting Human Resource Objectives

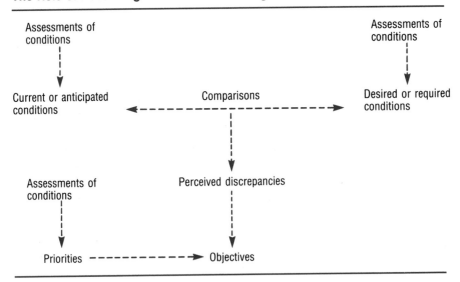

ity representation rates, production and market share levels, and attitude or performance levels.

The differences between the desired or required conditions and the actual or anticipated conditions represent discrepancies. However, human resource management cannot, and should not, address every discrepancy. Priorities must be based on the magnitude of the discrepancy and on the importance attached to the discrepancy by relevant constituents. For example, if actual performance levels are only 1 percent below desired levels, this may be too small to be an objective. However, if performance levels are under close scrutiny by top management, and they consider a 1 percent deviation significant, then the discrepancy can quickly become a formal objective.

Assessments also structure the priorities different constituencies attach to the various conditions and discrepancies. For example, manufacturing supervisors may place prime importance on meeting production targets, while regulatory agencies may place primary importance on bringing minority and female representation rates into parity with availability (see Chapter Three).

Whether they be staff professionals, line supervisors, or executives, human resource managers must consider the nature and magnitude of the discrepancies, the priorities attached to them by various constituents, and translate this information into human resource objectives.

Measuring Discrepancies and Setting Priorities

The chapters on assessing organizational conditions vividly demonstrate the many, varied interest groups within and outside the organization who judge the efficiency and equity of human resource activities. Inside groups include employees, line managers, top management, and the legal staff, while outside groups are government agencies, communities, and potential job applicants. Moreover, each of these groups is likely to adopt a somewhat different set of goals and objectives on which to make judgments.

This chapter discusses alternative approaches to establishing objectives and evaluating results. Even though most authors approach evaluation as distinct from objectives, the two clearly go hand in hand. Any evaluation method implies certain objectives. For example, if an organization measures performance levels, the implication is that performance discrepancies are the possible target of human resource activities. Therefore, we discuss both the objectives and the evaluation procedures implied by the alternative approaches.

SETTING OBJECTIVES AND EVALUATING EFFICIENCY

Human resource management decisions, similar to decisions in other management areas, can be based on efficiency. Efficiency-based evaluations reflect how human resource activities use scarce resources and produce valued returns.

Quantity, Quality, and Cost Applied to Human Resource Decisions

Any management activity enhances efficiency by affecting one or more of three variables—quantity, quality, and cost.[5] For example, applying a new production technology may affect the quantity of units produced, it may increase their quality, and it incurs costs to develop or purchase the technology. Exhibit 8–5 depicts an example, which we examine in some detail.

Quantity

Referring to the number of employees and time periods affected by a human resource decision or activity, quantity is the "leverage" of human resource activities. Exhibit 8–5 depicts the leverage for a training program. The program is applied for five years and trains the existing 200-person work force in the first year. After that, five trained employees leave each year. The 25 new employees who join the work force each year are trained using the program—a gain of 20 employees. Therefore, the program puts 200 trained employees into the work force in the first year, 220 in the second year, 240 in the third year, and so on. By training 300 people, the organization reaps 1,200 person-years of productivity effects over the five years. When human resource decisions affect the productivity of employees for many years, they can quickly amass large leverage values.

Quality

The effects of a human resource decision on employee quality reflect two factors: First, they reflect any enhancements in employee service value to the organization, such as increased sales or better-quality production. Second, they reflect any additional service costs required to maintain and improve the enhanced employee value, such as increased inventories to support increased sales or higher productivity-based pay. The difference between enhanced employee service value and increased employee service cost is the net increase in employee value for the program. Thus, the effect of human resource activities on quality is the average increase in net employee value, per employee, per year. Though this concept is very difficult to measure, perfect precision usually is not necessary.

EXHIBIT 8–5
Cost-Benefit Analysis for a Training Program

Computing Quantity/Leverage

Year	Trained Employees Added to the Work Force	Trained Employees Leaving the Work Force	Net Increase in Trained Employees in the Work Force	Total Trained Employees in the Work Force
1	200	0	200	200
2	25	5	20	220
3	25	5	20	240
4	25	5	20	260
5	25	5	20	280
Total person-years of productivity affected				1,200

Estimating Program Quality

Supervisors estimate the dollar value of the expected increase in employee service value from the training program, on a per person, per year basis, less the increased service costs that would have to be incurred to maintain that increased service value. The estimates of net value ranged from a low of $1,000 to a high of $10,000 per person-year.

Computing Program Costs

Year	Start-Up Costs	Ongoing Program Costs	Total Costs
1	$500,000	$100,000	$ 600,000
2	0	100,000	100,000
3	0	100,000	100,000
4	0	100,000	100,000
5	0	100,000	100,000
Total program costs over 5 years			$1,000,000

Computing Total Program Returns

Total program returns = (Program quality × leverage) − Program costs

Program Quality	Leverage	Program Costs	Total Program Returns
$ 833/Person-year	1,200	$1,000,000	$ 0
1,000/Person-year	1,200	1,000,000	$ 200,000
10,000/Person-year	1,200	1,000,000	$11,000,000

Adapted from John W. Boudreau, "Utility Analysis: A New View of Strategic Human Resource Management," in *ASPA/BNA Handbook of Human Resource Management*, vol. 1, chap. 4, ed. Lee D. Dyer (Washington, D.C.: The Bureau of National Affairs, Inc., 1988).

In Exhibit 8–5, assume that the most pessimistic managers said the training program could produce an increase in net value averaging at least $1,000 per person-year, while the most optimistic managers said it could increase net value as much as $10,000 per person-year.

Cost

The cost of a human resource activity refers to the value of the resources implementing that decision. These resources include the out-of-pocket expenses to develop and carry out the decision and the value of employees' time as participants, administrators, or in-house instructors. Relevant costs include those to develop and establish the activity as well as those to keep it going.

In Exhibit 8–5, this training program requires building a state-of-the-art system of training studios, capable of receiving closed-circuit audio-video transmissions of live training broadcasts and communicating with the instructors through a remote two-way audio system. Costs to build, maintain, and staff the studios as well as to develop and carry out the training decision would be $1 million for the five-year program, with half spent in the first year to build the studios.

Total Program Returns

The organization depicted in Exhibit 8–5 faces the decision of whether to spend $1 million to train 300 employees over five years, a cost of $3,333 per trainee. However, this cost level is misleading. Because of the leverage factor, the training program need only produce an average increase in net employee value of $833 per trainee, per year to cover its costs (that is, $1 million divided by 1,200). This is the break-even value of quality improvement.[6] If it produces the conservatively estimated $1,000 average increase in net employee value per person-year, the total return will be $200,000 ($1.2 million less the $1 million cost), for a 20 percent return on the original $1 million investment. If it produces the optimistic $10,000 average increase in net employee value per person-year, the total return of $11 million ($12 million minus the $1 million cost) is a 1,100 percent return on investment.

This relatively simple analysis can be enhanced to account for financial/economic investment considerations. It can also apply to recruitment, selection, internal staffing, compensation, and combinations of human resource activities or programs.[7] Chapter 7 discusses an application to performance feedback.

Such an analysis is very typical for new plants, stock or bond offerings, or new marketing programs, but it is rare for human resource management. Yet, the preceding analysis is no hypothetical example, but the actual analysis used by a major manufacturing organization to justify its investment in an audio-video network training program. This Quantity-Quality-Cost framework is useful in comparing different approaches to setting objectives and evaluating results.

Audits of Processes, Activities, and Procedures

Audits are reviews to determine if key personnel policies and procedures are in place and followed.[8] Exhibit 8–6 shows an audit checklist used to interview operating managers regarding the objectives and effectiveness of human resource activities. Audit methods do not actually measure quantity, quality, and cost. Rather, they describe how well key personnel procedures are being followed, or whether work is being performed as expected. They can provide a general impression of human resource activity effects, and perhaps suggest areas for further attention. For example, one recent study gathered data from archives, such as separation percentages, payroll complaints per employee, and compensation increases. This study also considered executive surveys, such as rankings of the function on planning, EEO climate, and employee relations, as well as employee surveys indicating satisfaction with various employment factors. These data were analyzed to determine which factors related to overall organizational performance, executive and employee satisfaction, and personnel budget allocation per employee.[9] However, interpreting audit results can be difficult.[10] Audits do not necessarily tell which activities or decisions might enhance achievement of objectives, nor whether the original planned activities were appropriate.

Quantity-Based Approaches to Objectives and Evaluation

Some of the most commonly used human resource management effectiveness indexes show how many employees are affected by human resource activities. Exhibit 8–7 provides examples of such quantity-based indexes for different human resource management activities. Comparisons of these indexes over time, or to a stated objective, or even to some industry standard aid many organizations with interpretation.

Although quantity-based indexes may be interesting, they provide useful information on only one aspect of the effects of the activities. They tell little about the activities' effects on costs or productivity. For example, companies may increase their job applicants by paying exorbitant salaries, recruiting less qualified applicants, or spending huge sums on recruiter travel and entertainment. Even though the quantity-based index may show improvement, these are not necessarily appropriate decisions for enhancing organizational efficiency. Objectives and evaluations based only on quantity run the risk of producing shortsighted decisions. In Exhibit 8–5, knowing that 300 people will be trained, or that 5 people leave each year is insufficient to determine whether the training investment is worthwhile.

EXHIBIT 8-6
An Illustration of a Personnel Audit (an interview with the operating manager)

1. What would you say are the objectives of your plant?
2. As you see it, what are the major responsibilities of managers?
3. Have there been any important changes in these over the last few years in the plant?
4. Are there any personnel responsibilities on which you think many managers need to do a better job?
5. What are some of the *good* things about employee relations in this plant?
6. Do you feel there are any important problems or difficulties in the plant? Causes? How widespread? Corrective measures?
7. Do you have any personnel goals for the year?
8. Overall, how well do you feel the personnel department does its job? Changes the department should make?

Community relations

9. What are managers expected to do about community relations? Is there plant pressure? Reaction to pressures?
10. What have you done about community relations? Do you encourage subordinates to participate in them? What are your personal activities?

Safety and medical

11. Who is responsible for safety in your area? Role of group leaders and lead men?
12. What things do you do about safety? Regular actions? Results achieved?
13. Do you have any important safety problems in your operation? Causes? Cures? How widespread?
14. What does the safety specialist do? How helpful are those activities?
15. Are there any other comments or suggestions about safety you would like to make?

16. Have you any comments about the dispensary? Employee time involved? Types of service offered? Courtesy?

Communication

17. How do you keep your people informed? What are your regular communication activities? Particular problems?
18. How do you go about finding out information from employees? Channels and methods? How regularly are such channels used? How much information is passed on to employee superiors? How much interest do supervisors show? Does personnel provide information?
19. Has the personnel department helped improve communication in the plant? What assistance is needed? Nature of assistance provided?
20. Has the personnel department helped you with your own communication activities?

Communication channels available

21. What improvement is needed in these?
22. Are there any other comments about communication you'd like to make? Any changes or improvements you'd especially like to see?

Manpower planning

23. What kind of plans do you have for meeting the future manpower needs of your own component? Indicate plans for hourly, nonexempt. How far do plans extend into the future?
24. What does your manager do about planning for future manpower needs? How is this planning related to your own planning?
25. What part does the personnel department play in planning for the future manpower needs of your component? Of the plant as a whole?

Personnel development

26. How is the training of employees handled in your group? (on-the-job training) Who does it? Procedures followed?

27. What changes or improvements do you think should be made in the training of employees? (on-the-job training) Why?

28. What changes or improvements do you feel are needed in the amount or kind of classroom training given here? Why?

29. Have you worked with your subordinates on improving their current job performance? Inside or outside regular appraisal? Procedure? Employee reaction? Results? Improvements needed?

30. Have you worked with subordinates on plans for preparing for future job responsibilities? Inside or outside regular appraisal? Procedure? Employee reaction? Results? Improvements needed?

31. What does personnel do to help you with your training and development problems?

32. Do you have any other comments on personnel development or training?

Personnel practices

33. How are employees added to your work group? New employees, for example. (*Probe*: Specify exempt, nonexempt, hourly. Procedure followed? How are decisions made? Contribution of personnel? Changes needed and reasons? Transfers?)

34. How is bumping or downgrading handled? (*Probe*: Specify nonexempt or hourly. Procedure followed? How are decisions made? Contribution of personnel? Changes needed and reasons?)

35. How are promotions into or out of your group handled? (*Probe*: Specify exempt, nonexempt, hourly. Procedure followed? How are decisions made? Contribution of personnel? Changes needed and reasons?)

36. Do you have any problems with layoffs? (*Probe*: Nature of problems? Possible solutions? Contribution of personnel?)

37. How do you handle "probationary" periods? (*Probe*: Specify hourly, nonexempt, exempt. Length of period? Union attitude? How handled?)

38. How are inefficient people handled? (*Probe*: Specify hourly, nonexempt, exempt, How do you handle? How do other supervisors handle? Frequency?)

Salary administration—Exempt

39. What is your responsibility for exempt salary administration? (*Probe*: Position evaluation? Determining increases? Degree of authority?)

40. How do you go about deciding on salary increases? (*Probe*: Procedure? Weight given to merit? Informing employees? Timing?)

41. What are your major problems in salary administration? (*Probe*: Employee-centered? Self-centered? Plan-centered?)

42. Has the personnel department assisted you with your salary administration problems? How? (*Probe*: Administrator's role? Nature of assistance? Additional assistance needed and reasons?)

Salary administration—Nonexempt

43. What is your responsibility for nonexempt salary administration? (*Probe*: Nature of plan? Position evaluation? Changes needed and reasons?)

44. How has the personnel department helped in nonexempt salary administration? (*Probe*: Specify personnel or other salary administrators. Nature of assistance? Additional assistance needed and reasons?)

Source: Reprinted by permission from "Auditing PAIR," by Walter R. Mahler, in *ASPA Handbook of Personnel and Industrial Relations*, ed. D. Yoder and H. Heneman, p. 2–103. Copyright © 1979 by The Bureau of National Affairs, Inc., Washington, D.C. 20037.

EXHIBIT 8–7
Quantity-Based Indexes for Different Human Resource
Management Activities

Planning
  Average tenure of the work force
  Average age of the work force
  Accuracy of predicted employee acquisitions, separations, and movements
    between jobs
  Extent to which nonpersonnel managers use human resource planning
    information
Staffing
  Number of job applicants per job opening
  Number of vacancies filled per season
  Number of internal job candidates
  Number of relocated current employees
Development
  Number trained
  Number of training programs delivered
  Number of employees currently fully qualified for their jobs
  Number of trainees divided by number of employees
Employee/union relations
  Number of grievances or complaints filed
  Number of suggestions offered
  Number of employee questions received and answered
Compensation/fringe benefits
  Number of employees participating in bonus plan
  Number of employees participating in employee stock ownership plan

Cost-Based Approaches to Objectives and Evaluation

Cost-based approaches reflect the costs of the resources required to develop, implement, and maintain human resource activities. Exhibit 8–8
depicts several cost-based evaluation indexes for different human resource
activities.[11] Some indexes reflect actual dollar costs, while others reflect
time or personnel resources used by a human resource activity.

Work Analysis and Budgeting

Work analysis and budgeting examine how time and money resources are
allocated among human resource activities.

Work analysis is typically performed by using work sampling techniques. Stephen Carroll describes the technique as "observations made at
random intervals of what the personnel professional is doing with the purpose of providing a basis for inferences about the various elements that
comprise his (her) total work activity."[12] Exhibit 8–9 reports some of Carroll's findings. It shows that if the objectives of the department included

EXHIBIT 8–8
Cost-Based Indexes for Different Human Resource Management Activities

Planning
    Payments to external consultants/advisers
    Administrative costs of preparing forecasts and plans
    Value of managerial time spent in planning
    Computer and other data processing time
Staffing
    Recruiting cost per recruit generated
    Recruiting and selection cost per job offer accepted
    Cost of selection test development and application
    Cost of managerial assessment center development and application
    Cost of administrative support for internal job posting system
Development
    Training program cost per trainee
    Training program cost per hour of delivered training
Employee/union relations
    Administrative costs for processing grievances and complaints
    Costs of personnel and support for safety inspections
    Costs of union negotiations, such as travel, lodging, and time off the job
    Average time to respond to an employees' question/grievance/complaint
Compensation
    Average compensation/benefit costs per employee
    Compensation/benefit costs divided by total revenues

emphasis on benefits and staffing, then their activities were consistent with those objectives, since 50 percent of the time was spent on them. However, if the objectives emphasized training activities, then the department's actual activities are not consistent with the training emphasis, and reexamination is in order.

Budgeting is, at best, a cost-control device rather than an objective-setting and evaluation approach. Yet, back in the 1950s Dale Yoder pointed out that the basic concern in budgeting includes benefits as well as costs.[13] Accordingly, human resource activities are evaluated by the percentage of the department budget allocated to each and the dollars per employee expended through each activity. The percentage allocated to each activity reflects the strategic directions of the personnel department and the dollars expended per employee within each activity reflects the magnitude of effort. These two indexes along with total expenditures can describe the human resource activity strategy. Changes in the directions and magnitude are assessed over time as well as compared with other personnel activities.

The Bureau of National Affairs periodically surveys employers' personnel budgets. Exhibit 8–10 shows the wide variation in the strategic direc-

EXHIBIT 8–9
Percentage of Total Work Time Spent on Various Employee Functions by Personnel Department Members

Type of Function	Five Clerical Workers		Four Personnel Department Managers		Total Staff in Department	
	Number of Observations	Percentage of Total Work Time	Number of Observations	Percentage of Total Work Time	Number of Observations	Percentage of Total Work Time
Administration of the department	60	05%	214	22%	274	13%
Staffing	88	08	196	20	284	14
Training	0	00	5	01	5	00
Labor relations	72	06	122	13	194	09
Wage and salary administration	117	10	46	05	163	08
Benefits and services	490	43	257	27	747	36
Research, audit, and review	76	07	35	04	111	05
Personal activities	43	04	61	06	104	05
Insufficient data*	197	17	22	02	219	10
Total	1,143	100%	958	100%	2,101	100%

* These observations could not be classified because two participants failed to explain adequately the purpose of some of their activities.

Source: Stephen J. Carroll, Jr., "Measuring the Work of a Personnel Department." Reprinted by permission of the publisher from *Personnel*, July–August 1960, p. 55. Copyright © 1960 by the American Management Association, Inc. All rights reserved.

EXHIBIT 8–10
Personnel Budgets—1986

	Range of Budgets Reported				
	Low	First Quartile	Median	Third Quartile	High
Total budget: 1986					
All companies (258)	$ 40,000	$ 255,500	$ 520,000	$ 1,519,145	$ 66,000,000
By industry					
Manufacturing (118)	40,000	250,000	484,000	1,247,905	66,000,000
Nonmanufacturing (66)	96,827	459,703	1,279,366	3,250,000	21,462,654
Finance (34)	96,827	395,135	1,100,000	2,103,204	16,940,675
Nonbusiness (74)	73,000	218,930	339,038	625,000	14,900,000
Health care (41)	81,879	261,712	437,198	828,364	14,900,000
By size					
Up to 250 employees (20)	40,000	107,000	165,975	200,000	962,119
250–499 employees (50)	40,000	160,000	223,000	405,500	1,000,000
500–999 employees (52)	76,022	250,000	412,619	599,598	3,665,556
1,000–2,499 employees (77)	73,000	370,000	665,000	1,800,000	14,997,159
2,500 or more employees (59)	297,200	1,200,000	2,319,000	5,808,000	66,000,000
Cost per employee: 1986					
All companies (258)	40	305	593	1,022	9,621
By industry					
Manufacturing (118)	50	414	678	1,145	9,621
Nonmanufacturing (66)	93	519	809	1,434	5,510
Finance (34)	202	600	985	1,618	5,510
Nonbusiness (74)	40	203	282	451	2,685
Health care (41)	104	216	272	498	2,685
By size					
Up to 250 employees (20)	200	632	790	1,667	9,621
250–499 employees (50)	140	431	667	951	2,666
500–999 employees (52)	82	385	593	958	5,414
1,000–2,499 employees (77)	40	235	432	1,115	9,089
2,500 or more employees (59)	50	222	443	1,009	3,687

Note: Figures in parentheses indicate number of companies in each category providing figures.

Adapted from ASPA-BNA Survey No. 49, Personnel Activities, Budgets and Staffs (Washington, D.C.: The Bureau of National Affairs, Inc., 1986).

tions and magnitude of effort expended. For example in 1986, the lowest expenditure on programming was $40,000, compared to a high of over $66 million; some employers spend only $40 per employee on personnel activities (for an entire year!), whereas others expend almost $10,000 per employee. Even though the accuracy of these data may be suspect due to the survey techniques, they do reflect the wide budget variations. Experts have done little research about the factors that may explain these differences. The diagnostic model suggests specific organizational and external conditions that affect them. We expect a firm's business strategy, for example, to significantly affect expenditures on personnel activities. A new, emerging firm is more likely to emphasize recruiting experienced personnel over training and development activities, for example.

As an important factor in determining human resource activities' contributions to organizational efficiency, program costs inevitably direct attention to the resources used by activities rather than the benefits produced. Objectives and evaluations based on costs alone provide no information to show what the costs (investments) produce. When companies view human resource management as a cost center rather than a productive investment, reducing human resource activities may become a tempting cost-cutting measure even when it is not an efficient decision.

In the training example, the $1 million cost of the audio-video network seemed exorbitant to many managers within and outside of the training function. Based on costs alone, it is quite likely that such a program would never have received serious consideration, and the organization would likely have rejected a potentially productivity-enhancing opportunity. Costs and resource allocations alone are not sufficient to reflect the efficiency contributions of human resource activities.

Quality-Based Approaches to Objectives and Evaluation

Several human resource objective-setting and evaluation methods focus on the quality of the work force, but this is one of the most complex and difficult variables to measure. Chapter Seven showed the complexity of assessing employee performance. Imagine how much more complex the task of evaluating work force value in dollar terms comparable to the costs of resource commitments. Nonetheless, evaluating the efficiency contribution of human resource activities requires attention to the activities' effects on work force quality. Several approaches have emerged to accomplish this.

Performance and Behavior Rates

Perhaps the most common approach involves simply recording employees' work behaviors. Exhibit 8–11 suggests several typical behavioral indexes.

EXHIBIT 8–11
Behavior-Based Indexes for Different Human Resource
Management Activities

Average employee performance ratings
Sales/production levels per employee, or per time period
Number of separations per time period
Proportion of the work force separating (turnover rate) per time period
Average tenure of current employees
Number of absences during the past month
Proportion of absences to total work days in the month (absenteeism rate)
Number/rate of grievances/complaints
Number/rate of accidents
Number/rate of disciplinary actions or rule infractions

Employee performance and behaviors can be recorded and compared to standards similar to information on quantity and cost. Trends over time produce useful information about changes in employee behaviors. However, it is difficult to use such information alone to make decisions about human resource activities, because the information fails to reflect the consequences of the employee behaviors. How much value does an increase in sales or units produced imply? How much does absenteeism cost? Do employee separations mean the loss of valuable employees, or do they reflect the removal of lower-valued employees to be replaced with higher-valued employees?

Behavioral Costing

One approach to placing a value on employees' behavior is to determine the costs of inappropriate behaviors. This approach has been termed *behavioral costing*.[14] Its roots can be traced to early attempts at Human Resource Accounting (HRA) in the 1970s.[15] HRA attempted to place an asset value on human resources by estimating the costs of acquiring them (similar to the logic used to value capital assets). Although this concept has not proved particularly useful, several of the methods are useful for measuring the costs of employee separations, acquisitions, and development. Some have applied this concept to employee behaviors other than separation and acquisition, including absenteeism, accidents, tardiness, grievances, and smoking.[16] Exhibit 8–12 depicts the dollar implications of several employee behaviors.

By measuring the costs of employees' inappropriate behaviors, behavioral costing can provide a much-needed index of the monetary effects of human resource activities that reduce such behaviors. Managers can explore questions such as "What is the value of an employee counseling

EXHIBIT 8–12
Estimated Costs of Behavior at XYZ Corporation (1972–1975)

Behaviors and Performance	Period 1 (1972–1973)		Period 2 (1973–1974)		Period 3 (1974–1975)	
	Estimated Cost per Incident	Estimated Total Cost	Estimated Cost per Incident	Estimated Total Cost	Estimated Cost per Incident	Estimated Total Cost
Absenteeism*						
Absences	55.36	$ 286,360	53.15	$ 510,453	62.49	$ 431,494
Leave days	—	—	55.04	687,229	61.64	821,795
Accidents*						
OSHA reported	727.39	194,213	698.31	229,046	1,106.52	240,115
Minor	6.64	21,122	5.71	38,331	6.45	35,856
Revisits	6.64	11,992	5.71	14,018	6.45	13,081
Tardiness*†‡	4.86	56,920	—	—	—	—
Turnover*						
Voluntary	120.59	18,089	131.68	33,973	150.69	18,083
Involuntary	120.59	14,230	131.68	21,859	150.69	18,686
Grievances	32.48	1,851	34.44	1,378	56.10	2,300
Quality below standard‡‡	19,517	663,589	19,517	573,800	19,517	409,857
Production below standard§	22,236	266,838	22,236	335,764	22,236	255,714
Total costs§§#		$1,535,204		$2,445,851		$2,246,971

* Costs associated with absenteeism, leave days, accidents, turnover and grievances during the last four months of this period are projections. Product quality and production below standard are actual figures.

† Rates and costs for salaried personnel are assumed to be the same as those for hourly employees (period 1: salaried absence costs—$41,669; salaried accident costs—$11,638; salaried tardiness costs—$9,641; salaried turnover costs—$1,829).

‡ Average tardiness time was 27 minutes.

‡‡ The costs of rejects and scrap was 3.4 percent of total sales for period 1. Each .1 reduction is valued at $19,517 per incident. Period 2 costs were 2.94 percent of total sales; period 3 costs were 2.1 percent of total sales. A constant dollar equivalency of $19,517 was used in periods 2 and 3 to discount inflation. Nondiscounted cost was $613,970 ($29,237 per incident); in period 3, nondiscounted cost was $677,015 ($23,028 per incident).

§ Plant productivity for period 1 was 88 percent of standard. The production below standard rate is 12 percent; thus, a reduction of 1 percent is valued at $22,236 per incident. Plant productivity in periods 2 and 3 was 84.9 percent and 88.5 percent of standard, respectively. A constant dollar equivalency of $22,236 was used in periods 2 and 3 to discount inflation. Nondiscounted cost of production below standard in period 2 was $400,567 ($26,528 per incident); in period 3, nondiscounted cost was $405,938 ($25,299 per incident).

§§ The total cost in period 1 is $1,470,427 for hourly personnel; $64,777 for salaried personnel.

The total cost is reflected in standard labor dollars. The estimated cost in real dollar equivalents in period 1: $1,688,724 or 10.4 percent of sales; in period 2: $2,690,436 or 8.45 percent of sales; in period 3: $2,471,668 or 10.61 percent of sales.

Source: Reprinted from B. A. Macy and P. H. Mirvis, "A Methodology for Assessment of Quality of Work Life and Organizational Effectiveness in Behavioral-Economic Terms," Administrative Science Quarterly, June 1976, pp. 212–16. © The Administrative Science Quarterly.

program that prevents two absences per month?" or "If this new compensation program prevents five separations per year, how much do we save?"

However, human resource management activities are not just designed to prevent employees' inappropriate behaviors; they are designed to encourage *appropriate* behaviors, whose impact may be felt in improved productivity, not reduced costs. In addition, some apparently costly employee behaviors actually produce organizational benefits, such as when turnover brings in new blood or grievances lead to suggestions for improvements. A cost-focused approach suggests reducing such behaviors, when they may actually be beneficial.

Dollar-Valued Employee Performance

Placing a dollar value on differences in employees' performance or service to the organization is a valuable basis for objectives and evaluation.[17] However, it has proved to be fraught with problems. Chapter Seven suggested the issues and problems involved in assessing employee performance with abstract ratings and comparative scales. Imagine how much more complex and difficult attaching dollar values to employee performance is. HRA focused on this issue, proposing to estimate the current and discounted future value of the organization's human assets, including such factors as the probability of promotions, separations, and deaths as well as the projected future salary levels of employees.[18] More recently, research focused on the value of differences in employee value, usually the difference between high, low, and average performers. Several estimation methods have emerged; generally, they suggest that the difference between high and average performers may be greater than 40 percent of annual average salary. Some of the methods are very complex and require difficult judgments. None have produced convincing evidence of greater validity or accuracy.[19]

Such accuracy, however, may not be necessary. In many cases, even crude estimates of improvements in employee value are useful. Typically, the necessary levels of performance differences are well below even the most conservative dollar value performance estimates.[20] For example, in Exhibit 8–5, it did not really matter that some managers felt the quality increase would be worth $1,000 per person-year while others felt it would be worth $10,000 per year. Either value justified the program.

Still, measuring performance differences alone is not sufficient for setting objectives and evaluating results. Such measures fail to reflect the costs and quantities of employees affected by human resource activities.

Integrative Approaches

Human resource managers can and do combine the preceding approaches. This can be a sound policy because, as we have seen, each objective and evaluation approach has unique purposes and advantages. The objective-setting and evaluation methods discussed next reflect an explicit integration between the quantity, quality, and cost components. They take a broader, more integrated view of the evaluation and objective-setting process.

Utility Analysis

The training example presented in Exhibit 8–5 illustrates this approach. Utility analysis attempts to set objectives and evaluate the results of specific human resource activities based on their costs and benefits. Early applications focused on external selection, such as deciding whether to invest in improved testing; the approach has also been applied to performance feedback, training, recruitment, turnover, and internal staffing.[21] We discuss applications to these areas in the appropriate activities chapters. These models can set objectives and evaluate individual activities as well as combinations of activities. They are also quite useful in considering the cost implications of research findings regarding the effectiveness of human resource activities.[22] However, they make statistical and economic assumptions that may not be satisfied in all situations.[23] They also are most appropriate when facing a relatively well-defined set of activity options.

Return on Investment Approaches

These approaches focus on the human resource function at the unit or organizational level, rather than on the objectives and evaluation of individual human resource activities. They address four questions:

1. How much is the investment in human resources?
2. What return are we getting on this investment?
3. What are optimum staffing levels?
4. How can we improve the return on investment in human resources?[24]

Various indexes can show the overall resources used and outputs produced. Exhibit 8–13 presents several examples. These approaches have

EXHIBIT 8–13
Return on Investment Indexes for Different Human Resource Management Activities

Sales dollars divided by total employee compensation
Net profits divided by total employee compensation and benefits
Return on equity divided by total personnel expenses
Total assets divided by total number of employees
Total yearly profits divided by the investment in human resources

the advantage of stating objectives and evaluating results in terms similar to those used to report financial results. Nonetheless, their global nature can also be a drawback because it can be very difficult to identify the causes of improvements or reductions in performance. Such identification is essential for evaluating past decisions and forecasting the effects of future decisions. One variant on this approach is to examine standard unit-level productivity outcomes, such as production levels, total sales, frequency of defects or repairs, over time to determine if changes in these outcomes coincide with the introduction of human resource activities.[25]

SETTING OBJECTIVES AND EVALUATING EQUITY

Objective-setting and evaluation methods for equity results are less well developed. Chapter Seven described how attitude and opinion surveys can assess employees' equity perceptions. To the extent that absenteeism and separations are related to equity, setting objectives and evaluating these results reflects equity considerations. One of the most important areas of equity objectives and evaluation is compliance with regulations and laws. Chapters Two and Three described several compliance indicators, such as comparisons between representation rates and availability. Some objectives relate to both efficiency and compliance, such as adherence to safety procedures and accident rates.

Reputational Approach

The premise of the reputational approach is that their reputation with their constituents or clients determines the effectiveness of personnel units and their activities.[26] Anne Tsui, in her research on personnel effectiveness, observes that a personnel department has multiple constituencies.[27] These may include functional executives (the top position in personnel), line executives (top positions in the business operations), operating managers (middle level and supervisors), all nonmanagerial employees, and external clients (unions, EEO agents, etc.).

According to Tsui, the value of personnel units, and by implication their policies and actions, is defined in terms of "reputation effectiveness," by which she means the judgments of the users of personnel services.[28] Whatever patterns emerge, effective units are most likely to satisfy the critical demands of their most important constituents and in turn contribute the most to organization effectiveness.

One study surveyed line executives responsible for profit and cost for an entire plant or major unit, operating managers responsible for a partic-

EXHIBIT 8–14
Reputation of the Human Resource Department on Three Evaluation Criteria

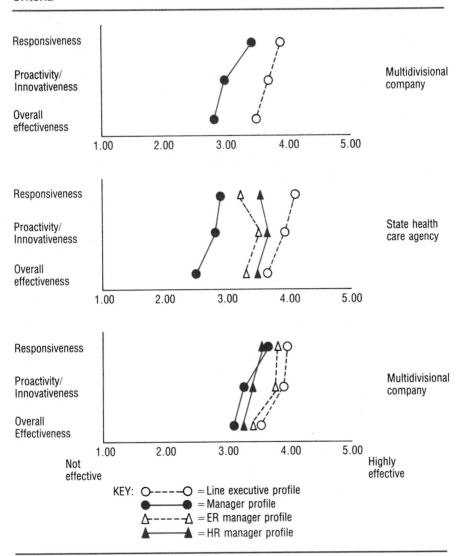

KEY: O----O = Line executive profile
●——● = Manager profile
△----△ = ER manager profile
▲——▲ = HR manager profile

Adapted from Anne S. Tsui, "Defining the Activities and Effectiveness of the Human Resource Department: A Multiple Constituency Approach," *Human Resource Management* 26, no. 1 (Spring 1987), pp. 35–69.

ular production process or client service, and employee relations managers who were staff members responsible for advice and counsel on labor/union relations. The study included human resource managers, who are the plant or corporate executives responsible for advice and counsel on general human resource issues, at two corporations and a state health care agency. The study sought opinions about each human resource department's reputation for (1) responsiveness (quick answers to questions, cooperation, objectivity, and neutrality); (2) proactivity and innovativeness (innovative policies, evaluation against goals, and quality of support to line and top management); and (3) overall effectiveness. Exhibit 8–14 shows the results. These results might indicate that line executives generally have the highest opinion of the human resource department, while operating managers have the lowest. Responsiveness seems to be highly rated, while overall effectiveness is rated lower. This approach also reflects a mixture of efficiency and equity.

Objectives and evaluation based on efficiency have an underlying cost-benefit framework, reflecting resources used and returns produced. Equity objectives and evaluation, however, have no such general framework. Nonetheless, such objectives and evaluation are important for effective human resource management, and they must be integrated with efficiency objectives.

REALITY IS MORE COMPLEX

Clearly, reaching consensus on all but the most objectively measured discrepancies, and deciding which discrepancies are most important is more of an art than a science.[29] The discussion of various objective-setting and evaluation methods does not imply that human resource managers simply set their objectives, choose and implement the activities, and then rigidly and rationally evaluate the results. A "fudge factor" based at least in part on intuition and irrationality comes into play.[30] For example, projected budget levels may imply a maximum hiring level of 10 new engineers, even though the demand for engineers may range between 7 and 10. Somehow the human resource manager must decide on the appropriate hiring goal, which might involve splitting the difference, taking the higher number to be safe, or taking the lowest number to avoid overstaffing.

Personal experience tells the human resource manager that actual decisions are often subject to politics, unfounded but dearly held beliefs, and limited ability to comprehend all the relevant facts. A good deal of research confirms that these things do affect decisions.[31] Emerging research suggests that not only can expert intuition be understandable, but it can also be modeled using computers.[32] Systematic models are useful even when objectives and results are affected by intuition, emotion, and irrationality. Models, though incomplete, are more consistent than unstructured human judgment. Humans learn from their experience—though not always very efficiently—whereas models can be modified to reflect observed results, too. Though human judgments made quickly and with little information may seem cheaper than objectives and evaluations made by gathering and analyzing information, the payoff from more correct decisions can be enormous.[33] For example, recall the $11 million payoff identified with using a systematic cost-benefit model in the training example.

The point is that careful objective setting and evaluation is even more important when decisions are subject to irrational influences. Even though objectives and evaluative information never offer perfect or complete answers, they do offer a framework for making systematic decisions about human resource activities, and for effectively communicating the results of those activities to others. The stock market, consumer behavior, and even production technology are not perfectly predictable, and decisions in these areas are often influenced by irrationality. This does not stop financial, marketing, and production managers from using systematic models to set objectives, evaluate results, and communicate their accomplishments in specific production levels or profit contributions. There is no reason human resource management should adopt less effective objective-setting and evaluation methods.

HUMAN RESOURCE INFORMATION SYSTEMS

Obviously, the large amount of information available to set objectives and evaluate results implies the need for a systematic approach to gathering, processing, and using data. Therefore, a Human Resource Information System (HRIS) is a key component of human resource management.

Definition

An *HRIS* is a systematic procedure for collecting, storing, maintaining, retrieving, and validating certain data needed by an organization about its human resources, personnel activities, and organization unit characteristics.[34]

Information systems can be as informal as the payroll records and time cards of a small boutique or restaurant, or they can be as extensive and formal as the computerized human resource data banks of major manufacturers, banks, and governments. HRISs can support planning with information for labor supply and demand forecasts; staffing with information on equal employment, separations, and applicant qualifications; and development with information on training program costs and trainee work performance. HRISs can also support compensation with information on pay increases, salary forecasts, and pay budgets; and labor/employee relations with information on contract negotiations and employee assistance needs. In every case, their purpose is to provide information that is either required by human resource constituents, or supports human resource decisions.

The Purposes of Human Resource Information

Analysts gather and record some information simply because it is required by law or regulation. For example, government and regulatory agencies require EEO-1 forms describing minority and female representation (see Chapter Three), as well as pay and benefit information related to unemployment compensation, pension funds, or wage and hour laws. Organizational constituents insist that other information be gathered and recorded. For example, corporate management may require budgets for compensation, staffing activities, and training programs. Such information can, and often does, support human resource management decisions; however, such support is not necessary to justify its usefulness. It is gathered because it is required.

Analysts gather and record the vast majority of information presumably because it supports human resource management decisions. Information gathered for this purpose must satisfy three requirements:

1. It must improve one or more decisions. That is, it must cause a less appropriate decision to be rejected, and a more appropriate decision to be made. Information has little value if the same decisions could be made with or without it.
2. The decision improvements must affect important consequences. Information has little value if it affects inconsequential decisions.
3. The cost of gathering and using the information must not exceed its expected value in changing important decisions.

To illustrate the first requirement, consider the role of performance assessments when collective bargaining agreements stipulate that decisions about hiring, pay, and promotion are based on seniority. Performance assessment information is less valuable under such agreements than where decisions about these activities can be altered in response to performance differences.

To illustrate the second requirement, consider the role of selection information when work is paced by assembly lines or governed by rigid control and monitoring. Selection tests providing information on applicants' qualifications are less valuable for such work because the rigid control and pacing leaves little chance for different employees to affect important work outcomes.

To illustrate the third requirement, consider centralized computerized information systems. Because these systems provide faster, more efficient information processing, they are often costly and complicated. The key to their value is the difference they make in human resource decisions. Often a simpler or more decentralized system would serve better—perhaps based on personal computers rather than centralized mainframe computers. It is important for human resource managers to keep these requirements in mind as they design and modify information systems.

HRIS Design Process

No best approach to the design process has emerged. Exhibit 8–15 shows the process used by TRW, Inc. to design their fairly common system. The first and most important step involves specifying the system requirements. These specifications are the heart of the system and include such decisions as the type of data to collect, the amount of data to collect, how to collect it, and when to collect it.[35]

The next step in TRW's design process is the business system design. It involves answering questions about who will use the system, how will they access it, how will it be updated, and so on. Technical design includes software system development and programming. Then the system is tested at certain locations and evaluated.

EXHIBIT 8–15
An Illustration of an HRIS Design Process

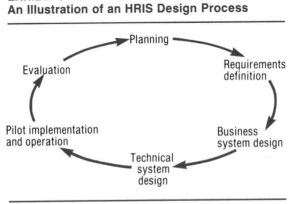

Source: TRW Task Force Report on employee Information System 1983.

Information Requirements

Many attempts to develop an HRIS start and stop at trying to determine the data requirements. Typically, a newly hired personnel specialist's first assignment is to visit all possible users and find out their data needs. An enormous wish list can result, containing so many items that the project is crushed by its own weight. Exhibit 8–16 lists typical data elements for an HRIS in alphabetical order.

    An alternative approach is to tackle one area at a time, by developing flexible, expandable modular systems. Exhibit 8–17 illustrates this modular approach. Each human resource activity develops a module which draws on a core data set. Exhibit 8–18 illustrates the compensation module from such a system.

Basic Components of an HRIS

It is convenient to consider these three major functional components in any HRIS:[36]

Input Function. The input function provides the capabilities needed to enter personnel information into the HRIS. This includes the procedures required to collect the data, such details as who collects data, when, and how data is processed need to be specified.

Data Maintenance Function. After the data are processed by the input function, they enter the data maintenance function. It updates and adds the new data to the existing database.

Output Function. The most visible function of an HRIS is the output generated. It can take many forms. These may range from a standard report to special reports. The output reports are the crucial links to the users. The decision maker must be able to use the output if the HRIS is to be an effective tool. Interested readers should consult references to this chapter for more detailed discussions.

Common Mistakes

After 15 years of building and installing computer-based HRISs, A. J. Walker reported the "10 most common mistakes." These mistakes are listed in Exhibit 8–19. Many seem self-evident but deserve some com-

EXHIBIT 8–16
Typical Data Elements in a Human Resource Information System

Address (work)
Address (home)
Birthdate
Birthplace
Child support deductions
Citizenship
Claim pending (description)
Claim pending (outcome)
Claim pending (court)
Claim pending (date)
Date on current job
Department
Dependent (sex)
Dependent (number of)
Dependent (relationship)
Dependent (birthdate)
Dependent (name)
Discipline (appeal date)
Discipline (type of charge)
Discipline (appeal outcome)
Discipline (date of charge)
Discipline (outcome)
Discipline (hearing date)
Division
Driver's license (number)

Garnishments
Grievance (type)
Grievance (outcome)
Grievance (filing date)
Handicap status
Health plan coverage
Health plan (no. dependents)
Injury date
Injury type
Job location
Job preference
Job position number
Job title
Job location
Leave of absence start date
Leave of absence end date
Leave of absence type
Life insurance coverage
Marital status
Marriage date
Medical exam (date)
Medical exam (restrictions)
Medical exam (blood type)
Medical exam (outcome)
Miscellaneous deductions

Salary change type
Salary
Salary range
Schools attended
Service date
Service branch
Service discharge type
Service ending rank
Service discharge date
Sex
Sick leave used
Sick leave available
Skill function (type)
Skill subfunction (type)
Skill (number of years)
Skill (proficiency level)
Skill (date last used)
Skill (location)
Skill (supervisory)
Social Security number
Spouse's employment
Spouse's date of death
Spouse's name
Spouse's birthdate
Spouse's sex

Driver's license (state)
Driver's license (exp. date)
Education in progress (date)
Education in progress (type)
Educational degree (date)
Educational degree (type)
Educational minor (minor)
Educational level attained
Educational field (major)
EEO—1 code
Emergency contact (phone)
Emergency contact (name)
Emergency contact (relation)
Emergency contact (address)
Employee weight
Employee number
Employee code
Employee status
Employee height
Employee date of death
Federal job code
Full-time/part-time code

Name
Organizational property
Pay status
Pension plan membership
Performance rating
Performance increase ($)
Performance increase (%)
Phone number (work)
Phone number (home)
Prior service (term. date)
Prior service (hire date)
Prior service (term. reason)
Professional license (type)
Professional license (date)
Race
Rehire code
Religious preference
Salary points
Salary compa ratio
Salary (previous)
Salary change date
Salary change reason

Spouse's Social Security
number
Start date
Stock plan membership
Supervisor's name
Supervisor's work address
Supervisor's work phone
Supervisor's title
Termination date
Termination reason
Training schools attended
Training schools (date)
Training schools (field)
Training schools completed
Transfer date
Transfer reason
Union code
Union deductions
United Way deductions
Vacation leave available
Vacation leave used
Veteran status

Reprinted by permission of the publisher from "A Matter of Privacy: Managing Personnel Data in Company Computers," Donald Harris, *Personnel*, February 1987, p. 37. © 1987 American Management Associations, New York. All Rights Reserved.

EXHIBIT 8–17
A Modular Approach to HRIS

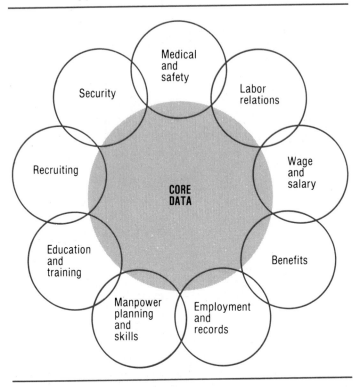

ment. The first—being all things to all people, all at once—is a common error. Automated procedures can produce an almost infinite variety of complex reports and graphics and can be made to interface with financial, marketing, and other information systems.[37] Yet ensuring that the reports actually aid the user to manage more effectively is often overlooked. Walker suggests keeping the HRIS simple in design and output, and user-friendly.[38] He estimates that it takes a minimum of two or three years to put an HRIS into operation from conception to installation. This may be a conservative estimate for more complex systems, because the TRW Employee Information System Project, which began in 1980, was not piloted at a few sites until 1984.

The Role of Personal Computers in the HRIS

One of the most apparent developments in human resources is the increasing use of microcomputers or personal computers (PCs) as part of the HRIS. Extraordinary increases in power and price reductions have made

EXHIBIT 8–18
An HRIS Compensation Module

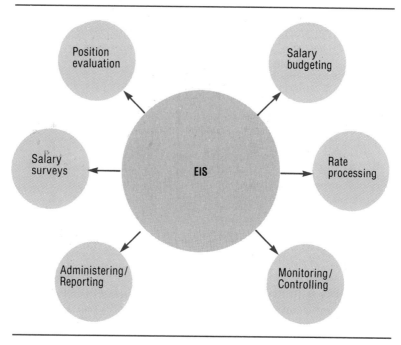

PCs commonplace in large and small organizations. New software programs for managing human resources with PCs are appearing at a rapid rate in virtually every activity.[39] By using a modem, PC operators can tap into on-line databases to retrieve the latest updates on labor law, personnel policies, research studies, business developments, and regulations.[40]

Some companies have avoided the expense of purchasing specialized software by developing in-house personal computer applications to streamline many activities, such as job applicant tracking, compensation budgeting, and employee benefits communication. These in-house applications frequently use general business software packages. One survey found that 1–2–3® from Lotus® was the most popular off-the-shelf software package used.[41] A companion supplement to this textbook contains cases and exercises to help you learn how to use 1–2–3® with personal computers to support human resource decisions.[42]

The Issue of Security and Privacy

Corporation and public-sector information systems are accumulating more and more information about individuals. Access to computerized informa-

EXHIBIT 8–19
Ten Most Common Mistakes in Developing
a Computer-Based HRIS

1. Being all things to all people, all at once.
2. No personnel expertise on the project team.
3. Separate systems for each personnel activity.
4. Too much complexity.
5. Insufficient operating management support.
6. No participation in design.
7. Technical marvels, but not "user-oriented."
8. Loose design project control.
9. Promising savings that don't occur.
10. Building, when you can buy.

Source: A. J. Walker, "The 10 Most Common Mistakes in Developing Computer-Based Personnel Systems," *Personnel Administrator*, July 1980, pp. 39–42.

tion continues to expand through personal computers, electronic mail, and decentralized databases. This has prompted federal and state governments to enact legislation protecting privacy and allowing individuals access to their personal information in government files.[43] Human resource managers should consider carefully which individuals need access to information, as well as whether that access should include reading the information, writing or changing the information, or both. Exhibit 8–20 presents a matrix that might be used to plan and describe access to personal information.

SUMMARY

Human resource planning serves as a mechanism for ensuring that human resource management is integrated and objective related. It involves finding answers to four questions that reflect the phases of our diagnostic approach: (1) How do we assess our human resource condition? (2) How do we set our human resource objectives? (3) What is the best approach for reaching these objectives? and (4) How do we evaluate how we did? The two crucial questions addressed in this chapter involve setting objectives and evaluating results. The rest of the book is taken up with detailed discussions of the alternative activities of human resource management.

Objectives and evaluation are essential to systematic human resource decisions, and effectively communicating the results of those decisions to constituents. Effective goal setting and objectives form the basis for effective human resource management, which is just as essential as managing the financial, marketing, and production resources. Moreover, objectives and evaluation go hand in hand—the objectives determine how

EXHIBIT 8–20
Information Access Matrix

Employee name	Employee address	Employee phone number	Employee SSN	Employee education	Employee salary history	Employee medical	Employee pension	
11	11	11	11	11	11	11	11	Personnel
01	01	01	01	00	00	00	01	Accounting
00	00	00	00	00	00	00	00	Marketing
00	00	00	00	00	00	00	00	Purchasing
11	11	11	11	11	11	11	11	DBA
10	10	10	10	10	10	10	10	Maintenance
10	10	10	10	10	10	10	10	Programmers
10	10	10	10	10	10	10	10	Operations
01	01	01	00	00	00	00	00	Clerical

Legend
01—Read   00—No access
11—Read and write   10—Write only

*Reproduced from Ken S. Brathwaite, *Data Administration: Selected Topics of Data Control* (New York: John Wiley & Sons, 1985).

activities are evaluated, and the evaluative information determines how objectives are set and modified. Although the real-world task of setting objectives and evaluating results is complex and subject to rational and irrational influences, systematically considering both efficiency and equity is not only possible, but essential.

Human resource information systems (HRISs) manage the array of available human resource information. Keeping in mind the three factors that determine the value of information, such systems can become valuable foundations for more systematic objectives and evaluations.

Objective-setting and evaluation are among the least developed phases of human resource planning. However, we are making important advances; the framework presented here will help you understand and use them.

DISCUSSION AND REVIEW QUESTIONS

1. Distinguish between objectives and evaluation. What role does assessing conditions play in both? What does it mean to say they go hand-in-hand?

2. Define the terms *quantity, quality,* and *cost* applied to human resource activities. Why is it usually necessary to consider all three in setting objectives or evaluating efficiency? Under which conditions would objectives and evaluation based on only one of them be sufficient?

3. How are objectives and evaluations of equity different from those for efficiency? How are they similar? Is equity or efficiency more likely to be affected by intuition and irrationality? Are systematic approaches to objective-setting and evaluation appropriate under conditions of irrationality or uncertainty?

4. Which three requirements must information satisfy to support decisions? How can each of the three components of an HRIS assist in satisfying the requirements? How could they be used to determine whether a computerized (as opposed to a noncomputerized) HRIS is appropriate?

5. Why is the data security issue so important? What are the advantages and disadvantages of using personal computers from a data security perspective?

NOTES AND REFERENCES

1. Paul Sheibar, "Personnel Practices Review: A Personnel Audit Activity," *Personnel,* March–April 1974, pp. 211–17; Malathi Bolar, "Measuring Effectiveness of Personnel Policy Implementation," *Personnel Psychology,* Winter 1970, pp. 463–80; Michael Gordon, "Three Ways to Effectively Evaluate Personnel Programs," *Personnel Journal,* July 1972, pp. 498–504; J. Fitz-enz, "Quantifying the Human Resources Function," *Personnel,* March–April 1980, pp. 41–52.

2. Sara L. Rynes and John W. Boudreau, "College Recruiting in Large Organizations: Practice, Evaluation, and Research Implications," *Personnel Psychology* 39 (1986), pp. 729–57; Sara M. Freedman, Robert T. Keller, and R. Montanari, "The Compensation Program: Balancing Organizational and Employee Needs," *Compensation Review* 2 (1982), pp. 47–53.

3. J. F. Gow, "Human Resource Managers Must Remember the Bottom Line," *Personnel Journal,* April 1985, pp. 30–32; Jac Fitz-Enz, *How to Measure Human Resources Management* (New York: McGraw–Hill, 1984); Robert L. Desatnik, *The Business of Human Resource Management* (New York: John Wiley & Sons, 1983); Lyle M. Spencer, Jr., *Calculating Human Resource Costs and Benefits* (New York: John Wiley & Sons, 1986); Harish Jain and Victor Murray, "Why the Human Resources Management Function Fails," *California Management Review* 26, no. 4 (Summer 1984), pp. 95–110.

4. Daniel J. Koys, Steven Griggs, and Steven C. Ross, "Developing a Framework to Assess Human Resource Department Effectiveness" (Working paper 85–116; Marquette University, 1985); Brian D. Steffy and Steven D. Maurer, "The Dollar-Productivity Impact of the Human Resource Func-

tion: Conceptualization and Measurement," (Working Paper 86–07, University of Minnesota Industrial Relations Center, 1986).

5. John W. Boudreau, "Utility Analysis: A New View of Human Resource Management Decision Making," Chapter 4 in *ASPA/BNA Handbook of Human Resource Management*, vol. 1, ed. Lee D. Dyer (Washington, D.C.: Bureau of National Affairs, 1988).

6. John W. Boudreau, "Decision Theory Contributions to HRM Research and Practice," *Industrial Relations* 23 (1984), pp. 198–217.

7. John W. Boudreau, "Utility Analysis: A New View of Human Resource Management"; John W. Boudreau, "Economic Considerations in Estimating the Utility of Human Resource Productivity Improvement Programs," *Personnel Psychology* 36, pp. 551–57; John W. Boudreau, "Effects of Employee Flows on Utility Analysis of Human Resource Productivity Improvement Programs," *Journal of Applied Psychology* 68 (1983), pp. 396–407; John W. Boudreau, "Decision Theory Contributions to HRM Research and Practice," *Industrial Relations* 23 (1984), pp. 198–217.

8. Walter R. Mahler, "Auditing PAIR," in *ASPA Handbook of Personnel and Industrial Relations*, ed. D. Yoder and H. Heneman, Jr. (Washington, D.C.: Bureau of National Affairs, 1979), pp. 2–103; Geneva Seybold, *Personnel Audits and Reports to Top Management*, Studies in Personnel Policy 191 (New York: The Conference Board, 1964); Sheibar, "Personnel Practices Review."

9. Luis R. Gomez-Mejia, "Dimensions and Correlates of the Personnel Audit as an Organizational Assessment Tool," *Personnel Psychology* 38 (1985), pp. 293–308.

10. Sheibar, "Personnel Practices Review."

11. See also Fitz-enz, *How to Measure Human Resources Management*.

12. Stephen J. Carroll, Jr., "Measuring the Work of a Personnel Department," *Personnel*, July–August 1960, pp. 49–56.

13. Dale Yoder, *How Much Do Personnel Activities Cost: 1954 Budget Study*, Reprint Series No. 15 (Minneapolis: University of Minnesota); H. G. Heneman, Jr., *Personnel Audits and Manpower Assets* (Minneapolis, University of Minnesota Industrial Relations Center, 1967).

14. Wayne F. Cascio, *Costing Human Resources: The Financial Impact of Behavior in Organizations*, 2nd ed. (Boston: Kent Publishing, 1987).

15. E. Flamholtz, "Replacement Cost as a Surrogate Measure of Human Resource Value: A Field Study" (AIS working paper No. 74–1, July 1973, mimeographed); E. Flamholtz, "Human Resource Accounting: Measuring Positional Replacement Costs," *Human Resource Management*, Spring 1972, pp. 8–16; Eric G. Flamholtz, *Human Resource Accounting*, 2nd ed. (San Francisco: Jossey–Bass, 1985). R. Likert, *The Human Organization: Its Management and Value* (New York: McGraw-Hill, 1967); R. Likert and D. G. Bowers, "Organizational Theory and Human Resource Accounting," *American Psychologist*, September 1969, pp. 585–92; James A. Craft, "Resource Accounting and Manpower Management: A Review and Assessment of Current Applicability," *Journal of Economics and Business* 1 (1980), pp. 42–50.

16. Barry A. Macy and Philip H. Mirvis, "A Methodology for Assessment of Quality of Work Life and Organizational Effectiveness in Behavioral-

Economic Terms," *Administrative Science Quarterly*, June 1976, pp. 212–26; Cascio, *Costing Human Resources*; Fitz-enz, *How to Measure Human Resources Management*.

17. Hubert E. Brogden and E. K. Taylor, "The Dollar Criterion—Applying the Cost Accounting Concept to Criterion Construction," *Personnel Psychology* 3 (1950), pp. 133–54. Likert and Bowers, "Organizational Theory and Human Resource Accounting."

18. Flamholtz, *Human Resource Accounting*; B. Lev and A. Schwartz, "On the Use of the Economic Concept of Human Capital in Financial Statements," *The Accounting Review* 71 (1971), pp. 103–12; P. Ogan, "A Human Resource Value Model for Professional Service Organizations," *The Accounting Review* 51 (1976), pp. 302–20.

19. Cascio, *Costing Human Resources*; Wayne F. Cascio and Robert Ramos, "Development and Application of a New Method for Assessing Job Performance in Behavioral/Economic Terms," *Journal of Applied Psychology* 71 (1986), pp. 20–28; Tom Janz and Marvin Dunnette, "An Approach to Selection Decisions: Dollars and Sense," in *Perspectives on Performance in Organizations*, ed. J. Richard Hackman, et al. (New York: McGraw-Hill, 1977).

20. John W. Boudreau, "Utility Analysis for Human Resource Management Decisions," in *Handbook of Industrial and Organizational Psychology*, ed. M. D. Dunnette (Chicago: Rand McNally, in press); John W. Boudreau, "Decision Theory Contributions to HRM Research and Practice."

21. John W. Boudreau, *Utility Analysis: A New View of Strategic Human Resource Management*"; Frank L. Schmidt, John E. Hunter, Robert C. McKenzie, and Tressie W. Muldrow, "Impact of Valid Selection Procedures," *Journal of Applied Psychology* 64 (1979), pp. 490–97. Frank L. Schmidt, John E. Hunter, and Kenneth Pearlman, "Assessing the Economic Impact of Personnel Programs on Work-Force Productivity," *Personnel Psychology* 35 (1982), pp. 333–47; Frank J. Landy, James L. Farr, and R. R. Jacobs, "Utility Concepts in Performance Measurement," *Organizational Behavior and Human Performance* 30 (1982), pp. 15–40; John W. Boudreau and Sara L. Rynes, "Role of Recruitment in Staffing Utility Analysis," *Journal of Applied Psychology* 70 (1985), pp. 354–66; John W. Boudreau and Chris J. Berger, "Decision-Theoretic Utility Analysis Applied to External Employee Movement," *Journal of Applied Psychology* 70 (1985), pp. 581–612; John W. Boudreau, "Utility Analysis Applied to Internal and External Employee Movement" (Working paper, NYSSILR–Cornell University, 1987).

22. E. A. Locke, D. B. Feren, V. M. McCaleb, K. N. Shaw, and A. T. Denny, "The Relative Effectiveness of Four Methods of Motivating Employee Performance," in *Changes in Working Life*, ed. K. D. Duncan, M. M. Gruneberg, and D. Wallis (New York: John Wiley & Sons, 1980); Richard A. Guzzo, Richard D. Jette, and Raymond A. Katzell, "The Effects of Psychologically Based Intervention Programs on Worker Productivity: A Meta-Analysis," *Personnel Psychology* 38 (1985), pp. 275–91.

23. Brian Becker, "Utility Analysis of Human Resources Programs: Some Caveats," (Working paper, State University of New York at Buffalo, 1986).

24. Henry L. Dahl and Kent S. Morgan, "Return on Investment in Human Resources," in *White Collar Productivity*, ed. R. N. Lehrer (New York: McGraw-Hill, 1983).

25. Mark A. Frohman, "Human Resource Management and the Bottom Line: Evidence of the Connection," *Human Resource Management* 23, no. 3 (1984), pp. 315–35.

26. Terry Connelly, E. J. Conlon, and S. J. Deutsch, "A Multiple Constituency Approach of Organizational Effectiveness," *Academy of Management Review* 5, no. 2 (1980), pp. 211–18; Michael Keeley, "Impartiality and Participant-Interest Theories of Organizational Effectiveness," *Administration Science Quarterly* 29, no. 1 (1984), pp. 1–26; Michael Hitt, R. D. Ireland, B. W. Keats, and A. Vianna, "Measuring Subunit Effectiveness," *Decision Sciences*, January 1983, pp. 87–102; Michael Keeley, A Social Justice Approach to Evaluation, *Administrative Science Quarterly*, June 1978, pp. 272–92.

27. Anne S. Tsui, "A Tri-partite Approach to Research on Personnel Department Effectiveness," *Industrial Relations*, Spring 1984, pp. 188–97.

28. Ibid.

29. Lee Dyer, "Bringing Human Resources into the Strategy Formulation Process," *Human Resources Management*, Fall 1984, pp. 10–21.

30. Howard S. Friedman, "A Guide from the Perplexed," *Newsweek*, May 5, 1986, p. 8.

31. Daniel Kahhneman and Amos Tversky, "On the Psychology of Prediction," *Psychological Review* 80 (1973), pp. 237–51; Kevin McKean, "Decisions, Decisions, Decisions," *Discover*, June 1985, pp. 22–31; Bernard M. Bass, *Organizational Decision Making* (Homewood, Ill.: Richard D. Irwin, 1983); Ronald N. Taylor, *Behavioral Decision Making* (Glenview, Ill.: Scott, Foresman, 1984).

32. Herbert A. Simon, "Making Management Decisions: The Role of Intuition and Emotion," *Academy of Management Executive*, February 1987, pp. 57–64.

33. Hillel J. Einhorn and Robin M. Hogarth, "Decision Making: Going Forward in Reverse," *Harvard Business Review*, January–February 1987, pp. 66–70.

34. This definition is adapted from A. J. Walker, *HRIS Development* (New York: Van Nostrand Reinhold, 1982).

35. Walker, *HRIS Development;* also see Lyman Seamans, Jr., "Establishing the Human Resource System Data Base," *Personnel Administrator*, November 1977, pp. 44–49; V. Ceriello, "A Guide for Building a Human Resource Data System," *Personnel Journal*, September 1978, pp. 496–503; Mary Jo Lavin, "HRDIS: A Computerized Human Resource Development Information System," *Human Resource Planning*, 14, no. 1 (1981), pp. 25–35; William B. Miller, "Building an Effective Information Systems Function," *MIS Quarterly*, June 1980, pp. 21–30.

36. Sidney H. Simon, "The HRIS: What Capabilities Must It Have?" *Personnel*, September–October 1983, pp. 36–49.

37. A. J. Walker, "The 10 Most Common Mistakes in Developing Computer-Based Personnel Systems," *Personnel Administrator*, July 1980, pp. 39–42.

38. Ibid.
39. Margaret Magnus, "Microcomputer Software Guide," *Personnel Journal*, April 1986, pp. 53–68.
40. Patricia Teets, "Need HR Information Fast? Try Online Data Base Services," *Computers in Personnel*, Fall 1986, pp. 21–25.
41. David C. Mahal, "Personal Computing in Human Resources—1986," *HR/PC*, 2, no. 1 (November–December 1986), pp. 1–50.
42. John W. Boudreau and George T. Milkovich, *Personal Computer (PC) Exercises in Personnel/Human Resource Management: A Diagnostic Decision-Making Approach* (Plano, Tex.: Business Publications, 1988).
43. Donald Harris, "A Matter of Privacy: Managing Personal Data in Company Computers," *Personnel*, February 1987, pp. 34–43.

chapter nine

EMPLOYMENT PLANNING

CHAPTER OUTLINE

General Electric Company is in a dizzying array of businesses. It makes toasters, turbines, televisions, light bulbs, robots, and CAT scanners. It even mines coal, explores for oil, makes synthetic diamonds, and has a huge financial investment business. It employs 400,000 people. Some 25,000 have "manager" in their titles.[1] As part of managing all its businesses, GE managers must decide how many people to employ, which skills they must possess, and when they will be required. In fact, all managers, not only those in GE, face these questions. Finding the answers is the role of employment planning and that is the subject of this chapter.

A DIAGNOSTIC APPROACH TO EMPLOYMENT PLANNING

The human resource needs of an organization flow from the strategic and human resource decisions made by top management. Exhibit 9–1 illustrates the relationship of strategic management decisions and employment

EXHIBIT 9–1
Interaction between Strategic Organization Decisions, Strategic Human Resource Decisions, and Employment Planning

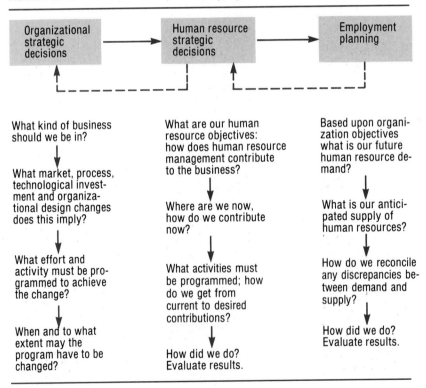

Organizational strategic decisions	Human resource strategic decisions	Employment planning
What kind of business should we be in?	What are our human resource objectives: how does human resource management contribute to the business?	Based upon organization objectives what is our future human resource demand?
What market, process, technological investment and organizational design changes does this imply?	Where are we now, how do we contribute now?	What is our anticipated supply of human resources?
What effort and activity must be programmed to achieve the change?	What activities must be programmed; how do we get from current to desired contributions?	How do we reconcile any discrepancies between demand and supply?
When and to what extent may the program have to be changed?	How did we do? Evaluate results.	How did we do? Evaluate results.

planning. Management assesses factors in the external and internal environment; this involves analyzing the strategic opportunities and risks facing the organization as well as setting objectives. Strategic human resource management involves identifying the human resource implications of the organization's strategic decisions.[2] Employment planning is a part of the overall human resource plan. It focuses on the numbers of employees and the qualifications required to achieve the organization's objectives. In the total overall human resource plan (see Chapter Eight), employment plans are integrated with other human resource activities including compensation, training, and employee relations. Before we examine the decisions and techniques involved in employment planning, the conditions affecting it need to be considered.

Definition
Employment planning estimates the future demand for employees, both in quality and quantity; compares the expected demand with the current work force; and determines the employee shortages or surpluses based on the organization's strategies and objectives.[3]

External Conditions

Economic conditions affect employment planning. Shortages of critical skills may cause longer lead times to hire or train the needed personnel and hence make planning more important. Surpluses in the labor market shorten the time required to hire personnel, and so planning does not need to be done as far ahead since people with the skills required are readily available. But surpluses in the external labor market adversely affect employers who face the prospect of laying off employees and who are concerned about them. Witness the case of Eastman Kodak Company.[4] For decades Kodak had a reputation as one of America's most employee-centered employers. Faced with unparalleled foreign competition, Kodak's revenue growth declined and its market share was no longer uncontested. It faced increased uncertainty and risk. As a result, in moves completely out of character, Kodak reduced its work force and postponed pay increases. Exhibit 9–2 shows the actions Kodak managers took in an eight-month period. The laid-off employees faced a soft external labor market; there were more workers than available jobs. So Kodak attempted to soften the blow to employees by setting up intensive career planning workshops, résumé and interviewing seminars, and even retraining activities. The employment staff sought jobs for workers facing the prospect of being laid off. All employers are not as employee oriented—many simply

EXHIBIT 9–2
Kodak's Employment Plan Actions in the Face of Economic Decline (1983)

January 4	Offered early retirement programs. Some 5,000 employees accepted.
January 10	Laid off 1,100 employees.
June 6	Laid off an additional 1,600 employees.
June 6	Announced it would not hire college students for routine summer jobs.
July 30	Postponed merit raises until following year.
August 8	Expanded program offering extended vacations without pay to employees.

Source: E. N. Berg, "Shrinking a Staff, the Kodak Way," *New York Times*, September 4, 1983, p. 84.

dismiss workers. This illustration shows how competitive economic conditions affect the employment planning process. The exact effects are contingent on many factors, including the commitment of the firm to its employees.

Government Regulations

Regulations and laws clearly affect employment planning. Perhaps the most obvious case is the equal employment opportunity laws. Recall from Chapter Three that equal opportunity and affirmative action require detailed analysis of how job opportunities are shared with women, minorities, and older workers.[5] In fact, affirmative action is really the application of employment planning to special employee groups protected under the law.

Regulations most often constrain the alternative actions that a manager may take. For example, minimum wage legislation prohibits reducing hourly wages below $3.35, and child labor laws restrict the hours that those 16 years and younger may work, thereby limiting the hiring options.

Unions

Unions may also exert an important influence on employment planning. Union-management agreements may regulate hiring, promotion, transfer, and layoff actions. Seniority provisions and "bumping rights" in many contracts need to be tied into employment plans. Faced with the need to reduce the work force, many employers have joined with unions to assist employees facing permanent layoffs. Similar alliances have occurred to cope with the impact of plant closings. The contract between the Communications Workers of America (CWA) and AT&T specifies the joint efforts to be made to assist employees affected by plant closings. The parties formed a new jointly administered corporation, the Alliance for Employee Growth and Development, funded by AT&T, to train and place workers. Assistance includes psychological counseling, testing and placement services, internal transfer assistance, and retraining.

Organization Conditions

Organization conditions are the primary factors affecting employment planning. The demand for labor is derived from the demand for the organization's products and services and the technology employed. Hence, employment planning requires information from production, marketing, and finance. Anticipated production volume, expectations about sales, or plans to invest in new facilities or to close down plants all affect employment plans.

Anticipated decisions reflected in the plans of other functions of the organization affect employment plans. Planning is an attempt by managers to cope with these uncertainties and risks.[6] So we would expect employment planning to be most important during periods of great change and turbulence, such as rapid expansion, diversification, or any strategic changes. When a manager is faced with stable, highly predictable, future conditions, the need for and the potential contribution of employment planning seems smaller. Herein lies a contradiction and a dilemma for personnel professionals. For this chapter shows that some of the techniques for employment planning depend on sound historical data and accurate estimates of the future.[7] Often it seems that employment planning is easiest to apply in those stable and certain situations where its payoffs are likely to be the smallest.

Employee Conditions

The nature of the work and the qualifications required also significantly affect the design of employment planning. For example, the number of employees required for unskilled work need not be specified three to five years ahead, since unskilled labor is usually easily obtainable and relatively inexpensive. But requirements for critical technical and managerial positions may need to be forecasted years ahead because these skills take longer to develop and/or recruit.[8]

So employment planning depends on assessing many factors: first and foremost, the nature of the organization's conditions, but also the external conditions such as government regulations, the presence of unions, the nature of the work, and the employees.

EMPLOYMENT PLANNING

Simply stated, mployment planning is planning how to staff the organization with effective human resources.

Reasons for Employment Planning

Many organizations do more talking than actual planning for employment.[9] Yet more and more of them seem to be moving to formal planning systems as they discover that unsystematic approaches are inefficient in meeting their employment needs. Some common reasons for formal employment planning are to achieve:[10]

More Efficient and Equitable Use of People at Work. Employment planning precedes other personnel activities. How could a manager schedule recruiting or downsizing not knowing how many people were needed? How could anyone effectively hire or lay off employees not knowing the kinds of people needed for job openings? How large an orientation or outplacement program is necessary? When? Careful analysis of many human resource activities shows that their efficiency depends on answers to questions about how many people with which talents are required.

More Effective Employee Development and Greater Sense of Fairness to Employees. The employees of organizations with good employment planning systems have a better chance to participate in planning their own careers and to share in training and development experiences. Thus, they are more likely to feel their talents are important to the employer, and they have a better chance to be placed in jobs that use these talents. Perhaps more crucial is that good employment planning permits employers to anticipate oncoming surpluses, and avoid or minimize layoffs through retraining and redeployment. Consequently, sound employment planning affords employers the opportunity to treat employees more fairly and equitably.

More Effective EEO Planning. Strong equal employment opportunity regulations require effective human resource programs. Employment planning should focus managers' attention on the treatment of minorities and women. Further, data collected routinely during employment planning is required for government reports to ensure compliance with EEO. Consequently, employment planning should enhance an employer's ability to comply with government regulations.

Three Phases of Analysis

The goal of employment planning is to get the right numbers and types of employees doing the right work at the right time. As Exhibit 9–3 indicates, employment planning involves three basic phases of analysis:

EXHIBIT 9–3
Employment Planning Process: Three Phases

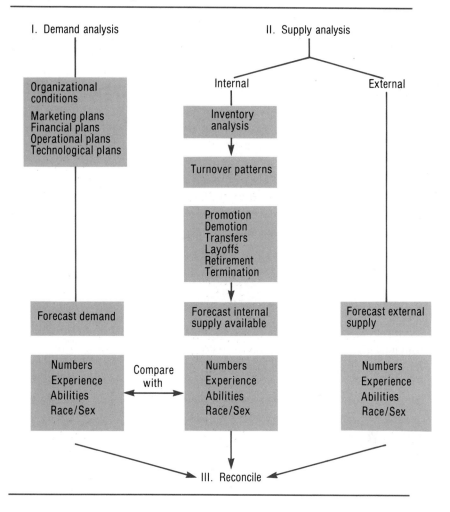

1. Forecasting human resource demand.
2. Analyzing human resources available.
3. Reconciling any discrepancy between demand and supply by designing human resource activities.

The next section describes the state of knowledge and practice in each phase; first we'll turn to forecasting the demand for human resources.

FORECASTING THE DEMAND FOR HUMAN RESOURCES

There are several approaches to demand forecasting. The headquarters can forecast the total demand for the entire organization (top-down approach), or individual units can forecast their own requirements which are then added up to get total demand (bottom-up approach), or these two approaches can be combined.[11]

Demand forecasting, like any process of predicting the future, is an art.[12] Employment planners must use their heads as well as models and formulas. The most perplexing problem in demand forecasting is to estimate the relationship between the demand for human resources and the output—goods and services—produced by the organization. Exhibit 9–4 shows the basic model for estimating demand for employees. The future demand for employees is derived from the anticipated demand for the products, the financial performance objectives of the organization, and a productivity factor. In practice, the difficulty lies in getting good measures of each of these variables.

Estimating Organization Performance

Several different measures of an organization's demand for products or its financial performance are used in employment planning. The 3M Company, for example, uses gross sales revenues.[13] State Farm Insurance Companies use insurance policies-in-force.[14] Upjohn Company uses return on investment, and other firms use estimated production volumes or value added (the difference between the cost of raw materials and the price of the final product).[15]

EXHIBIT 9–4
Demand and Supply Forecasting Process

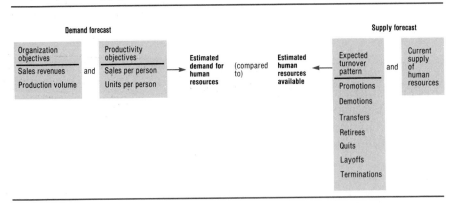

In practice it seems that the best measures to use in starting employment planning are those used in the financial, manufacturing, and marketing plans. This ensures that the employment plan is better integrated with the business plans. These data are usually readily available. The estimated revenues and production forecasts are typically generated in the overall business planning process and serve as inputs to the employment forecasts.

Productivity

As discussed in the last chapter, analysts measure productivity at various levels: organization, unit, product line, or whichever level seems logical. In general, productivity is the output produced per unit of input.[16] Measuring output has been previously discussed. Human resource inputs are measured in the number of employees, person-hours, or costs.

What difference does the measurement of productivity make? Look at Exhibit 9–5, which contrasts several different measures of productivity.

The factors chosen to measure productivity focus our effort. In sales revenue per number of employees, productivity is dollar sales related to each employee. Contrast that with dollar sales generated for each dollar in compensation paid, or with units produced per hours worked. The measures used shift our attention. The one to use depends on which factors (wages, hours, number of employees) we are trying to affect and control.

Research literature tells us little about which measures are most commonly used. Nor is much known about the effects of using various alternatives. Yet our experience suggests that firms which focus on controlling

EXHIBIT 9–5
Productivity Measures for Human Resource Demand Forecasts

Measure	Definition	Focus
Sales revenues per number of employees	Dollar sales associated with each employee	Sales and number of employees; treats each employee identically
Sales revenues per wage bill	Dollar sales associated with each dollar paid in wages	Sales and costs of labor; recognizes different experience and skills receive different pay
Sales revenues per person-hour	Dollar sales associated with each hour worked	Sales and hours worked; used in manufacturing units
Production units per person-hour	Units produced per hour worked	Production and hours; used in manufacturing

the numbers of employees, such as 3M, use sales per person. Others that focus on return on investments and costs, such as Upjohn Company and Honeywell, Inc., use a sales-to-wage-bill ratio.[17] Any productivity measures should be consistent with the organization's strategic objectives; for example, profits or revenue growth.

Next we illustrate an actual employee forecast. Such forecasts usually involve the number of employees and the mix of qualifications required.

An Illustration

Employee Forecasts: Numbers Required

The employees required for a future plan period is a function of the estimated sales revenue (or production estimate) for that period and the productivity goal. In the example in Exhibit 9–6 the current year's revenues were $120 million; productivity was determined by dividing $120 million by the current work force, 857 employees, to get revenue of $140,000 per person. During the plan year, managers made two forecasts. They based the first on the current year's productivity figure, and the second on a productivity improvement goal of 7 percent ($140,000 $\times$ 107 percent = $149,800 per employee). With the improved productivity, 1,001 employees ($150 million $\div$ 149,800 = 1,001) are required, which is 70 less than without the productivity improvement goal. If the average wage bill (pay plus benefits) is $20,000 per employee, then the savings generated by the productivity improvement equals $1.40 million ($20,000 $\times$ 70).

Other approaches to demand forecasting are more complex, but the basic concepts remain—demand for employees is derived from revenue or production targets and productivity objectives.[18]

EXHIBIT 9–6
Human Resource Demand Forecast

	Current Year	Plan Year Estimate: No Change in Productivity	Plan Year Estimate: 7 Percent Productivity Improvement
Revenue	$120 million	$150 million	$150 million
Present Employees	857		
Productivity (Revenue per Employee)	$140,000	$140,000	$149,800
Employees Required		1,071	1,001

EXHIBIT 9–7
Employment Forecast: Skills Mix

Work Force Category	Current Year		Plan Year Forecast	
	Number	Percent	Expected number	Percent
Total employees	857	100%	1,000	100%
Executive	8	1	10	1
Manager—Supervisor	128	15	150	15
Professional and staff specialist	171	20	200	20
Scientist— Engineer	214	25	250	25
Office	86	10	100	10
Production— Maintenance	250	29	290	29

Employee Forecasts: Skills Mix

The mix or combination of skills and experience required is more difficult to forecast. Many employers simply use the same distribution of skills that they have during the current period. Exhibit 9–7 shows the proportion of employees in each skill or job category during the current period. The forecasted total number of employees derived above is simply allocated according to the current proportions. Then, managers use their best judgments for any redeployment of employees.

Managers address the question of skill mix in others ways, too. Some employers estimate support staff needs (accountants, human resource professionals) as a function of the number of a critical skill required.[19] For example, in firms in which engineering talent is critical, such as at Hewlett-Packard Company or Rockwell International, the number of engineers required becomes the determinant of the level of clerical, accounting, and other support personnel. The ratio may be 1 support employee for every 20 engineers.

Regardless of the approach, the results of the demand forecasts serve as inputs to managers. They may be adjusted by managers with more intimate knowledge to fit the needs of a particular organization.[20]

Productivity Goals

Productivity is one of the key efficiency objectives of human resource management. Exhibit 9–8 shows there are really five basic strategies for improving productivity.[21] We can design programs that will either raise

EXHIBIT 9–8
Five Basic Strategies to Improve Productivity

$$\text{Productivity} = \frac{\text{Outputs}}{\text{Inputs}}$$

Strategy	Description	HRM Example
1.	Increase output faster than inputs	Increase sales or production faster than adding employees or person-hours
2.	Increase output while holding input stable	Increase sales or production while keeping the work force numbers constant; no net additions to staff; replace exits
3.	Decrease inputs faster than output	In a declining situation reduce the work force faster than the decline in production or sales revenues
4.	Maintain output with reduced inputs	Maintain sales or production with fewer employees
5.	Increase output with reduced inputs	Improve sales and production with a reduced work force

the numerator (output) more quickly than the denominator (input) or lower the denominator more quickly than the numerator.

Recall the earlier discussion about Kodak's experience. It faced declining revenues (numerator), so it reduced employees (denominator) and delayed the salary increases for one year (denominator). In the example in Exhibit 9–6, revenues (numerator) and number of employees (denominator) both increased, but not in the same proportion.

In sum, improving productivity is a key objective of human resource management. This is so for several reasons: First, the productivity goal plays a key role in determining the number of employees required. Second, productivity is directly linked to achieving the organization's goals. Third, the desire to improve productivity focuses the human resource professional's attempts to design programs. Hence, improved productivity should benefit the organization as well as employees.

Tailoring Tools to the Situation

A wide variety of forecasting techniques is available for use in employment planning. Exhibit 9–9 describes some of these; the interested reader

EXHIBIT 9–9
Statistical Techniques to Project Future Labor Supplies

Name	Description
1. Markov analysis	Projects future flows to obtain availability estimates through a straightforward application of historical transition rates. Historical transition rates are derived from analyses of personnel data concerning losses, promotions, transfers, demotions, and, perhaps, recruitment.
2. Simulation (based on Markov analysis)	Alternative (rather than historical) flows are examined for effects on future human resource availabilities. Alternative flows reflect the anticipated results of policy or program changes concerning voluntary and involuntary turnover, retirement, promotion, etc.
3. Renewal analysis	Estimates future flows and availabilities by calculating: (1) vacancies as created by organizational growth, personnel losses, and internal movements out of states and (2) the results of decision rules governing the filling of vacancies. Alternative models may assess the effects of changes in growth estimates, turnover, promotions, or decision rules.
4. Goal programming	Optimizes goals—in this case a desired staffing pattern—given a set of constraints concerning such things as the upper limits on flows, the percentage of new recruits permitted in each state, and total salary budgets.

Source: Adapted from Lee Dyer, "Human Resource Planning," in *Personnel Management,* ed. K. Rowland and G. Ferris (Boston: Allyn & Bacon, 1982).

should pursue the references to this chapter.[22] The techniques range from sophisticated quantitative models to the use of qualitative managerial judgments. However, researchers have yet to specify the conditions under which specific techniques work better than others.

Experience does suggest the following "tricks of the forecasting trade."

Time Horizon: Most managers want forecasts to extend as far into the future as possible. Yet too long a period increases the complexity and costs, while diminishing the accuracy. Human resource demand forecasts typically cover one- to five-year periods but those beyond three years are seldom used in practice.

Technical Know How: Many techniques require computer and mathematical skills; not all human resource professionals have sharpened these skills, so additional technical expertise may be sought.

Costs: Most of the costs of forecasting occur in the beginning during the developmental, design phase. Assembling the data in a useful and accessible form is an often overlooked cost.

Quality of Data: Before selecting a technique, consider the quality and availability of the data. More often than not, organizations simply do not have the data required by more sophisticated techniques. And much of the financial, marketing, and production data required may not be readily available to human resource professionals without cooperation from other functions.[23]

Usefulness of Results to Managers: The results of the forecasts need to be communicated in a form that decision makers can readily use. Voluminous, spiral-bound reports only occupy shelf space.[24]

Some evidence suggests that the particular proclivities of the manager influence the techniques used. It is sort of like children with a hammer—once they learn to use the tool, they apply it to everything. P. F. Buller and W. R. Maki report the historical evolution from design to implementation, evaluation, and ultimate disuse of a forecasting model at Weyerhaeuser.[25] They present the model's life cycle (see Exhibit 9–10) and offer the following reasons for the decline in the model's use:

- Weyerhaeuser's human resources requirements stabilized.
- The personnel department shifted its orientation from an organizational to an individual/developmental approach.
- The leadership changed; the designer of the model was promoted.

EXHIBIT 9–10
Weyerhaeuser Experience: History of Utilization of the Employment Planning Model*

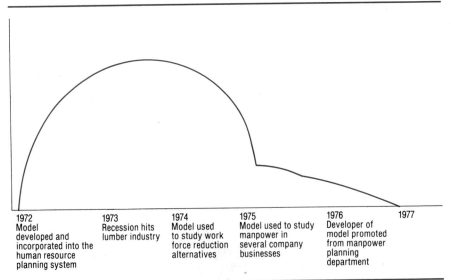

1972	1973	1974	1975	1976	1977
Model developed and incorporated into the human resource planning system	Recession hits lumber industry	Model used to study work force reduction alternatives	Model used to study manpower in several company businesses	Developer of model promoted from manpower planning department	

* This graph was constructed from subjective assessment of the authors. At its peak the model was used on a weekly, sometimes daily, basis. In 1976 the model was used on a quarterly, then semiannual, basis.
Source: P. F. Buller and W. R. Maki, "A Case History of a Manpower Planning Model," *Human Resource Planning* 4, no. 3 (1981), p. 132.

Buller and Maki observed that "A given model may outlive its usefulness. The personnel professional shouldn't foster the use of a model if a particular problem no longer warrants it."[26]

What is intriguing about the Weyerhaeuser experience is the questions it raises. What effects do changing economic and organizational circumstances have on the employment planning techniques used? And what difference does changing the techniques make on the results obtained?

Probably the best piece of advice for an employment planner is to be familiar with several techniques and don't be afraid to try out different ones to fit the circumstances.

Prediction Accuracy versus Objectives Achieved

How do we judge a forecasting model? Some research into employment forecasting focuses on the accuracy of the results.[27] That is, the results of a forecast are compared to the actual employment behavior of the organization. Results of such studies have been very disappointing, suggesting that relying on historical relationships to predict future employment needs is not a very fruitful endeavor.

However, the emphasis on accuracy of forecasts may be misplaced. The models may have a greater payoff in helping managers achieve productivity goals. For example, if productivity is treated as a human resource objective, then the required human resources are simply derived from it. Under this view, the productivity goal and the resulting employment forecasts become a control device or goal rather than a prediction. For example, 3M may set its productivity figures at $120,000 sales revenues per person and no employee can be added to the work force unless anticipated sales revenue permits. The emphasis is on goals and control rather than predictive accuracy. No one claims that such a goal is optimal—all that is claimed is that the productivity goal is achieved. And employment levels are controlled to guarantee that result.

Keeping Employment Forecasts in Perspective

We have emphasized that employment planning procedures need to be designed to fit the circumstances. All too often employment planning is limited in scope. In many cases, the business plans from which they are derived are not sufficiently developed. Even in cases where they are, the human resource variables may be difficult to define and quantify. Think about the nature of employment planning. It is to translate one set of estimates (future sales or production) into another set of estimates (future numbers and skills of employees required). Often this seems like constructing a structure on shifting sand.

Another problem faced in demand forecasting is that its output is expressed as the right number and right types of employees in the right place at the right time. But the human resource objectives of efficiency and equity are broader than simply the right numbers. They include labor costs, achievement of safe working conditions, and employee satisfaction.[28]

Nevertheless the process of determining employment needs still has value beyond the numbers obtained. In many organizations it alerts top management to the human resource implications of financial, manufacturing, and marketing plans and directs their attention toward the management of those resources. Witness Dahl and Morgan's suggestions to managers of Upjohn's 17 profit centers.[29] Before adding employees to the work force, Upjohn managers were asked the following questions:

1. What purposes does the new position serve?
2. Which alternatives were considered to accomplish the same purposes?
3. If the position is filled, what are the projected five-year costs?
4. What impact will this position have on:
   a. Maintenance or improvement of sales?
   b. Maintenance or improvement of earnings?
   c. Improved utilization of people?

We have now examined the first phase of employment planning: demand forecasting. Next we turn to the second phase: analysis of the supply of human resources.

FORECASTING HUMAN RESOURCE SUPPLY

Analysis of the available human resource supply focuses on such issues as: How many people, with which qualifications and interests, do we currently employ? How many of these do we estimate will be available during the planning period?

As shown in Exhibit 9–3, supply analysis considers two sources of human resources, external (available in labor markets) and internal (available in the organization). Managers analyze these sources not only for the numbers of people available but also for other characteristics, including their abilities, interests, and work experience. Supply analysis begins with an internal inventory of human resources.[30] This is a count of the numbers of people and skills currently employed.

The next step is to project the current supply into the future. This is done to estimate which human resources will be available internally during the plan year. As Exhibit 9–4 shows in the box labeled turnover patterns, the current internal supply undergoes changes. Some workers are promoted, retire, or transfer. Forecasting future supplies involves estimating this movement in the work force and adjusting the projected supply accordingly.[31]

Turnover Rates as an Objective

Many employment planners establish specific rates of turnover (or patterns of mobility) as an objective. Subsequently, personnel programs are designed to achieve the objective. Looking again at Kodak, it designed early retirement programs to encourage older, experienced, and more expensive employees to leave.[32] It also designed layoffs and instituted a recruiting freeze. Other firms may attempt to reduce the loss of employees who are highly skilled and high performers. The point is that specific turnover rates can be established as human resource objectives, just as productivity improvement rates are. Whether to seek increased or decreased turnover rates depends on the circumstances faced by the organization.[33]

Human Resource Supply Estimates

As Exhibit 9–4 shows, once the expected turnover rates are established, they are combined with the current supply of employees to determine the expected future supply of human resources. Sound simple? For a small employer, it is relatively easy to know how many employees there are, what they do, and what they can do. A grocery store may be operated by the owners, who have to plan for two part-time helpers. When they expect turnover (one part-time employee is going to graduate from college and take a new job in June) they know they need a replacement. Sources of supply could include their own children, converting their other part-time helper into a full-time employee, or calling the school's employment office for possible applicants.

It is quite a different situation with an organization employing hundreds at numerous locations.[34] To analyze their supply of human resources, these organizations must know how many full-time and peripheral workers they have, and where. They must also know which skills and experiences the employees who leave take with them.

Supply Analysis Techniques

A range of tools for analysis of internal supplies are available.[35] We examine four: skills inventories, replacement/succession charts, Markov models, and organization profiles.

Skills Inventories

A skills inventory in its simplest form is a list of the names, certain characteristics, and skills of the people working for the organization.[36]

Many organizations introduced skills inventories when computers became available for this purpose. Most organizations do have the information in one form or another, but frequently it is buried in personnel folders, and time and effort are needed to get at it. Good skills inventories enable organizations to determine quickly and expeditiously what kinds of people with specific skills are presently available. This information is useful whenever an employer decides to expand and accept new contracts or to change strategies. It is also useful in planning for training, management development, EEO compliance, promotion, transfer, and related personnel activities.

Replacement and Succession Charts

Managers use replacement or succession charts to analyze and project the supply of managerial talent available.

Replacement planning is typically implemented by using charts based on organization charts. Those charts provide a "snapshot" of key positions in the organization and the availability of replacements in the current work force. Replacement charts document judgments about employees' knowledge, skills, and abilities. This aids decision making when informal knowledge is less complete.[37]

Replacement charts and skills inventories provide data used for internal staffing decisions; we discuss these in greater detail in Chapter Thirteen, Internal Staffing.

Transitional Matrixes

A third, somewhat more advanced, tool used for the analysis and projection of human resource supplies is transitional probability matrixes.[38] Basically such tables show the movement (promotions, demotions, transfers, hires, and turnover) of employees into, through, and out of the organization.

Exhibits 9–11 and 9–12 illustrate the usefulness of this technique. There are three basic features of a transitional matrix:

1. *"State" definitions:* States may be salary grades, performance levels, or other characteristics to be analyzed. They represent the way the planner has divided the organization. For example, in Exhibits 9–11 and 9–12 the letters A to J represent positions in the organization's job hierarchy, with A at the top of the organization and J at the bottom.

EXHIBIT 9–11
Descriptive Use of Transitional Probability Matrix (internal human resources movement)*

	Job States†	A	B	C	D	E	F	G	H	I	J	Exit	Total
Time I	A	1.00										—	1.00
	B	.15	.80									.05	1.00
	C		.16	.76	.04							.04	1.00
	D		.01	.23	.73							.03	1.00
	E					.85	.05					.10	1.00
	F					.25	.65	.05				.05	1.00
	G						.40	.50	.03			.07	1.00
	H						.02	.15	.75			.08	1.00
	I								.20	.50		.30	1.00
	J										.50	.50	1.00
	Recruit level				.10				.20	.30	.40	—	1.00

Time II across the top.

Organizational career I — (near E)
Organizational career II — (near C/D)
Organizational career III — (near J)

* Cell entries are proportions.
† A to J are different jobs arranged hierarchically.

EXHIBIT 9–12
Interpreting the Transitional Probability Matrix

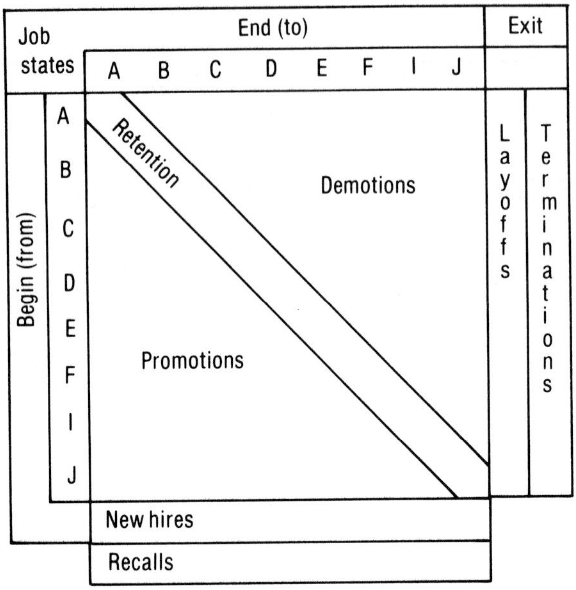

2. *Time interval:* The matrix represents the movement of employees in a
time period. The vertical axis (Time I) shows the job structure (A
through J) at Time I, the beginning of the time period. The horizontal
axis (Time II) shows the structure at the end of the time period. The
time period analyzed may be one day, one month, one year, or a decade; it is established at the discretion of the planner.
3. *Cell entries:* The entries in the cells of the matrix indicate the proportion of the individuals moving from one position at Time I to another
position at Time II. For example, cell AA (1.00) tells us that all the
people who were in position A at Time I were still there at Time II.
Cell BA indicates that 15 percent of the individuals in position B in
Time I have moved up to position A at Time II.

All the cells in the diagonal represent the probability of remaining in
the same job, and off-diagonals represent promotions and demotions.
These proportions were calculated by placing the number of employees in
a job at the beginning of the time period in the denominator and the
number who move from the job to another job at the end of the period in
the numerator. For example, consider position B. Suppose that at the be-

ginning of the period (Time I, vertical axis) 100 people were employed as Bs. At Time II (horizontal axis) we find that of these original 100 people employed in B, 15 went up to A (Cell BA), 80 remained in B (Cell BB), and 5 have left the organization. By calculating the proportion we see that 15 percent (15/100) of those who started in B moved up to A, 80 percent (80/100) remained in B, and 5 percent (5/100) left.

What can the transitional probability matrix tell us? First, we can analyze the movement or staffing patterns during the period. For example, we can identify career patterns in the organization. A career pattern in our example is DCBA. A is its top job and D is the entry-level job. Another career pattern has E at the top and I as the entry job. But for job J, people just come into position J and stay (50 percent during this period) or leave (50 percent left). It appears that there is no possibility of promotion in job J. Through these analyses we can identify "dead-end" positions (J, E, and A) and entry-level positions (people come into the organization at D, H, I, J), perform turnover analysis, and study the rate of employee movement through the organization.

To see how a matrix works, let us assume that we wanted to eventually be in job A. Where would we have to enter this organization? Options are to enter at D, H, I, or J. Based on data from this period, the only way to get to A is to start at job D; the other careers are "dead-ended" before getting to A.

Forecasts and Simulations

So far we have illustrated how a matrix describes the employer's current behavior.[39] Matrixes can also simulate the expected future supply of personnel by projecting the employer's current behavior into the future. Simulating the future tells what the employer can expect if it continues to hire, move, and lose people in the future at the same rate that it currently hires, moves, and loses people. Exhibit 9–13 illustrates forecasting and simulation uses. The calculations can all be performed by a micro-computer.[40]

A simulation requires three basic pieces of data:

1. The numbers of employees in each position at the beginning of the period (Time I).
2. The matrix that reflects the expected staffing patterns of employees. This matrix can be based on past history, or it can represent hypothetical staffing rates that we plan to apply in the future. In other words, the matrix can calculate "what would happen if"?
3. The number of time periods into the future we wish to project the current supply.

EXHIBIT 9–13
Forecasting and Simulation Use of Transitional
Probability Matrixes (Markov Analysis)

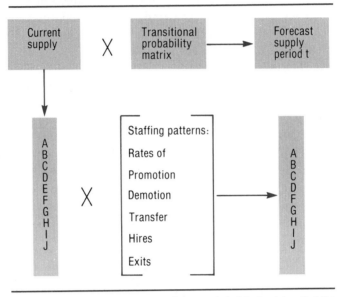

Note: t represents the number of time periods into the future that the current supply is being forecast.

By causing the current supply of personnel to move according to the staffing patterns reflected in the matrix, we can forecast the supply of personnel in a future period. In other words, this tool helps answer the question: given our current supply of personnel and our staffing plans (promotions, demotions, transfers), what is our expected supply of personnel in our planning period?

Turning back to the employment planning process in Exhibit 9–3, we see that the forecasted supply of personnel available is an important component of an employment plan. If the forecast supply of human resources available differs from the human resources required, then corrective action to reconcile this difference is necessary (Phase III).

Analysts have reported on several actual applications of matrixes including ones at AT&T, Merck, and Weyerhaeuser.[41] H. G. Heneman III and M. G. Sandver argue that the uses of matrixes may have been oversold, especially in terms of the accuracy of the forecasts.[42] However, a matrix's greatest potential lies not in forecasting but in description and simulation. They have been applied to testing the cumulative effects of differing recruiting and training programs, and to staffing and budgeting problems in the several organizations. One of the greatest uses to date has been in affirmative action and equal employment analysis.[43] In this case, an employer could calculate what percentage of workers in each job or job category are minorities or women, and how staffing patterns might be adjusted to change the percentages in a future time period.

Work Force Profiles

Another type of supply analysis, work force profiles, examines the distribution of employees by organization level. The profiles in Exhibit 9–14 depict the proportion of the organizations' work force at each level. All organizations do not have the same profiles, but if one firm's profile differs significantly from its competitors', it does raise the question of why the organizations are staffed so differently. Caution is required here: *Level* is a poorly defined term; some firms report 5 levels, while others claim to have 11 or more.

Tom Peters, the author of *In Search of Excellence*, opines "that 7 levels of management seems too high and 11 is downright dispiriting."[44] He points to the data in Exhibit 9–15 in which the sales and earnings growth of "lean" companies (those with the fewest management levels, 7.2) are compared to "fat" companies (the most levels, 11.1). All the 26 "lean" companies outperformed the "fat" ones. But this analysis is akin to looking at the relationship between sunspots and the weather. Sunspots alone do not determine the weather. And although overstaffing is not likely to be the road to sales and earnings growth, neither is fewer organization levels per se. Other probable factors include quality of products, marketing, productivity of employees—the list goes on. Nevertheless, the work force profile offers an approach which permits comparisons of work force distribution.

We have now examined the first two phases of the employment planning process, analysis of demand and supply; the third phase is programming strategies to reconcile differences.

DESIGNING PROGRAMS

Several managerial decisions have to be made once the demand and supply of people have been forecast and compared. Exhibit 9–16 presents a more detailed scheme of the personnel programming considerations.

Actions with No Difference in Supply and Demand

Sometimes the demand for employees and the projected supply match, but this is rare. More frequently, if the total supply is correct, there are variances in subgroups. Thus, even though the total employment level required and the total available match, the distribution of employees

EXHIBIT 9–14
Human Resource Profiles by Organization Level (six-company comparison)

Company B

1	Top management	0.1%
2		0.2%
3		0.7%
4		6.2%
5		35.2%
6		57.7%

Company T

Top management	0.1%
Senior staff and group exec.	0.2%
Senior group staff and division president	0.6%
Division senior staff and mid-management	14.0%
Supervisory	11.2%
Non-management	74.2%

Company D

Top management	0.3%
Section managers	4.9%
Subsection managers	17.4%
Unit managers	30.4%
Sub-unit managers	27.5%
Individual contributors below sub-unit	19.5%

Company U

Top management	0.1%
Unit heads	0.3%
Others on executive payroll	7.1%
Other exempt employees	92.5%

Company E

Top management	0.1%
Department	0.7%
Division	1.7%
District	6.0%
Second	23.2%
First	68.2%

Company V

Top management	0.2%
Division management	1.6%
Section management	16.6%
Group management	81.6%

EXHIBIT 9–15
Are Fewer Organization Levels Better?

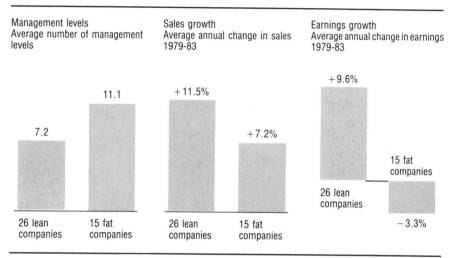

Management levels Average number of management levels	Sales growth Average annual change in sales 1979-83	Earnings growth Average annual change in earnings 1979-83

Adapted from T. Peters and N. Austin, *A Passion for Excellence* (New York: Harper & Row, 1985).

among different positions, with various skills, or in various plant locations may not match. The balancing process may involve transfers, promotions, demotions, and even retraining employees.

Actions with a Shortage of Employees

When employment specialists compare demand to supply and find that the supply of workers is less than the demand, several actions are possible. If the shortage is small and employees are willing to work overtime, it can be filled with present employees. If the shortage is of higher-skilled employees, training and promotions of present employees, together with recruitment of lower-skilled workers, is a possibility. Previous employees who may have been laid off can be recalled. Additional employees can be hired, or some of the work can be subcontracted.

Actions under Surplus Conditions

Deciding what to do with surplus employees is one of the most difficult decisions that managers must make, because the employees who are considered surplus are seldom responsible for the conditions leading to the surplus. The surplus may be caused by poor business decisions, such as a poorly designed or marketed product, or to declining market conditions.

Some employers go to great lengths to avoid laying off surplus employees.[45] Often this seems to be a matter of the organization's policies and culture rather than any economic analysis. Encouraging older employ-

EXHIBIT 9–16
Actions to Reconcile Differences

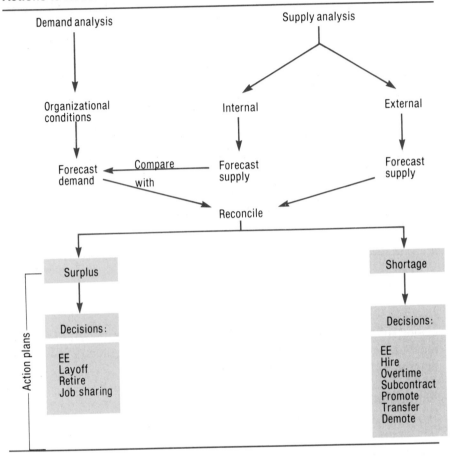

ees to take early retirement is a common strategy to reduce a surplus.[46] Monsanto Company's program is typical.[47] They offered employees who were at least 55 years old and whose age plus years of service added up to 80 or more the option to retire. Incentives were paid in cash and ranged from 50 percent to 140 percent of annual salary depending on the number of years at Monsanto, base salary, and eligibility for social security. Motorola Inc. used a different approach—work sharing to save jobs. In one facility, production had to be reduced by 20 percent. The company asked 100 workers to work four days a week instead of five. According to Motorola, this saved the jobs for 20 employees in that facility. The employees who accepted this work-sharing program participated in the decision-making process.

The decision to undertake major work force reductions has become more common.[48] It has become such an important option in the staffing process that an upcoming chapter is devoted to it.

INNOVATIVE HUMAN RESOURCE OPTIONS

Many employers have developed innovative approaches to cut costs and yet avoid work force reductions. One way to look at the situation is to change the issue: Rather than reducing the work force, the real issue is reducing costs.

Reducing Costs without Reducing People

One approach is to consider the factors that go into determining labor costs. The simplified model in Exhibit 9–17 depicts some of these. All the factors in the model—employees, hours worked, average wage per hour, benefits—are either fixed or variable. Traditionally, the number of employees and the hours worked were considered variable, with the result that employees were laid off and hired as the need occurred. Reducing costs without reducing employees simply requires designing programs which make the factors other than the number of employees variable. Upcoming chapters examine these options in greater detail, so we only introduce the idea here.

Variable Compensation. The most obvious way to reduce costs is to reduce the wage rates paid to employees. These drastic actions used by employers whose survival is threatened can have costly consequences. Turnover of top performers, dissatisfaction leading to lower-quality products, absenteeism, and difficulties in attracting quality employees are possible. Organizations that plan ahead build the required flexibility into their

EXHIBIT 9–17
Fixed versus Variable Factors in Total Labor Costs: Reducing Labor Costs without Reducing People

Total labor costs	=	Number of employees	×	Hours worked	× (	Average wage/ hour	+	Benefits)
		↑		↑		↑		↑
Decisions:		Staffing		Staffing		Compensation		Compensation

compensation systems so as to avoid these consequences. Several options are possible. For example, a portion of the wages can be made contingent on the firm's performance.[49] Gainsharing, profit sharing, and incentive plans are examples. Performance improvements, such as reduced costs, increase revenues or profits that are shared with employees through bonuses. During periods of peak organization performance, employees receive their basic wages plus bonuses. Conversely, during economic downturns the employees receive the base pay, sans bonuses. Hence, a portion of compensation varies with the organization's performance.

Variable Benefits

Designing programs that make benefit costs variable is more difficult. One approach is to make some benefits contributory. That means employees must pay some portion of the costs. Another approach is linked to staffing decisions—part-time employees typically are not covered by all benefits, so increasing the part-time portion of the work force reduces benefit costs.

Variable Schedules

The hours worked can also vary—reduced overtime and Motorola's program to reduce the length of the workweek are examples.

Variable Staffing: Core and Contingent Employees

Some employers have adopted two categories of employees: core and peripheral, or contingent workers. Permanent full-time employees form the core work force. Contingent workers are part-time, temporary, leased, and subcontracted employees.[50] Exhibit 9–18 illustrates contingent work force programs used by several firms. Contingent employees offer employers flexibility; during downswings they can reduce the contingent work force, providing a protective buffer to the core employees and reducing costs. The contingent workers, however, bear the costs of the reduction. For retirees who are not interested in permanent employment or those who work for temporary firms this may not be a hardship. But for those who are seeking to become core employees, theirs is a less attractive lot.

Other Programs

There are additional ways for firms to reduce costs. For example, in 1987 Digital Equipment Company (DEC) shifted its manufacturing from a single-product assembly line with high labor costs to one based on product groups that used highly automated, flexible manufacturing, and much less labor. DEC faced a surplus of 5,000 in its 33,000 work force. It conducted a skills inventory to determine which skills were available in current employees. This inventory was matched to the skill requirements generated

EXHIBIT 9–18
Variable Staffing: Contingent Work Force

Temporary workers	**Dunhill of New England** is a personnel supply firm based in Springfield, Massachusetts. Since the last recession, it has seen a boom in the use of its temporary employees by a wide variety of firms, for both long- and short-term assignments. Among its clients is Digital Equipment Corp., which uses temps regularly. Digital, which has a no-layoff policy for its regular employees, has used temps rather than hire regular staff for some operations.
Temporary workers	**Jobs Unlimited** is a temporary employee supply firm in San Jose, California, serving a variety of employers in and around Silicon Valley. Specializing in professional and technical employees for high-tech firms, Jobs Unlimited has had to cope with downturns in the high-tech sector.
Temporary workers	**Grumman Corp.**, the military, space, and civilian equipment manufacturer, uses temporary employees for engineering and other jobs. In July 1986, some 1,150 "job shoppers" were working alongside 21,000 regular employees at Grumman's Bethpage, New York, operations. The firm says job shoppers have proved to be skilled project workers, provide a measure of job security for regular employees, and sometimes become regular employees.
On-call workers	**The Travelers Corp.** in 1981 instituted an on-call worker pool made up of its own retirees to staff temporary assignments at its Hartford, Connecticut, headquarters. A quick success with the insurance firm and retirees alike, the 650-person pool now includes retirees of other companies. On a typical work day, the company estimates, about 175 retirees can be found working at the 10,000-employee Travelers headquarters.
Employee leasing	**White Memorial Otolaryngology Foundation,** a Los Angeles–area medical office concern, "leases" its entire office staff—from nurses to office managers—from an employee leasing firm. For a set fee, the leasing firm handles payroll and personnel functions and provides employees with a complete compensation package.
Subcontracting	**American Airlines** created a wholly owned subsidiary in the Caribbean island nation of Barbados to perform data entry work previously done in Tulsa, Oklahoma, by American Airlines employees. Satellite technology allowed the switch. American reports that the arrangement has reduced its costs by almost half, due to lower labor costs and higher productivity. No airline employees lost jobs due to the work transfer, American says.

Source: *The Changing Workplace: New Directions in Staffing and Scheduling* (Washington, D.C.: The Bureau of National Affairs, Inc., 1986).

by its demand forecasts. Surplus skills were assemblers, material planners, supervisors, and middle managers. Skill shortages occurred in designers, programmers, analysts, and sales. DEC launched a mass retraining effort; over 100 production supervisors decided to become sales personnel. By August of 1987, 4,500 of the surplus had been redeployed. And DEC plans to retrain 2,500 employees every year to ensure future flexibility.[51]

SUMMARY

Planning directs attention to designing several options to achieve objectives. Although employment planning tends to focus on staffing options, other factors in the human resource system can also be variable. Programs can be designed in compensation and training as well as staffing. Planning provides the frame of reference and the lead time necessary to consider these alternatives.

Planning is a useful means of preparing for future risks and uncertainty. It permits the systematic judgment needed to achieve human resource objectives. The precise techniques and procedures used must be tailored to fit the context. To adopt a completely ad hoc and reactive stance seems foolhardy. The real danger with planning is that managers become so ossified and bureaucratic that they fail to take advantage of unforeseen opportunities.

DISCUSSION AND REVIEW QUESTIONS

1. Compare the human resources planning discussed in Chapter Eight with employment planning. Which questions does each address?
2. Why should managers bother with employment planning?
3. Compare and contrast alternative demand forecasting techniques. Under which conditions would you consider using each?
4. What are the two major sources of supply of human resources?
5. Which programming options are available when an employer is overstaffed? Understaffed?

NOTES AND REFERENCES

1. General Electric Company annual report, 1983.
2. J. R. Gailbraith and D. A. Nathanson, *Strategy Implementation: The Role of Structure and Process* (St. Paul Minn.: West Publishing, 1978); Robert M. James, "Effective Planning Strategies," *Human Resource Planning* 2, no. 1 (1980), pp. 1–10; Richard F. Vancil, "Strategy Formulation in the

Complex Organizations," *Sloan Management Review*, Winter 1976; James W. Walker, *Human Resources Planning* (New York: McGraw-Hill, 1980); Mary A. Devanna, C. Fombrun, and N. Tichy, "Human Resource Management: A Strategic Approach," *Organizational Dynamics*, Spring 1981; J. A. Craft, "A Critical Perspective on Human Resource Planning," *Human Resource Planning* 3, no. 2 (1980), pp. 39–52.

3. Eric Vetter, *Manpower Planning for High Talent Personnel* (Ann Arbor: University of Michigan, Bureau of Industrial Relations, 1967).

4. E. N. Berg, "Shrinking a Staff, the Kodak Way," *New York Times*, September 4, 1983, p. 4.

5. Richard J. Niehaus, "Computer-Assisted Manpower Planning Using Goal Programming," Research Report no. 32 (Washington, D.C.: Dept. of Navy Office of Civilian Manpower, 1977); J. W. Merck and K. Hall, *A Markovian Flow Model: The Analysis of Movement in Large Scale Systems* (Santa Monica, Calif.: Rand Corporation, 1971).

6. George Milkovich and Thomas Mahoney, "Human Resources Planning and PAIR Policy," in *ASPA Handbook of Personnel and Industrial Relations*, eds. D. Yoder and H. Heneman, Jr. (Washington, D.C.: Bureau of National Affairs, 1979); Lee Dyer, "Human Resource Planning," in *The Management of Personnel/Human Resources: New Perspectives*, ed. K. Rowland and G. Ferris (Boston: Allyn & Bacon, 1982).

7. George Milkovich, Lee Dyer, and Tom Mahoney, "HRM Planning," chap. 2 in *Human Resource Management in the 1980s*, ed. Stephen J. Carroll and Randall S. Schuler (Washington, D.C.: Bureau of National Affairs, 1983); John Edwards, Chris Leek, Ray Loveridge, Roger Lumley, John Mangan, and Mick Silver, eds., *Manpower Planning* (New York: John Wiley & Sons, 1983); G. G. Alpander, *Human Resources Management Planning* (New York, AMACOM, 1982); James F. Bolt, "Management Resources Planning: Keys to Success," *Human Resource Planning* 5, no. 4 (1982), pp. 185–97; D. M. Atwater, E. S. Bres III, R. J. Niehaus, and J. A. Sheridan, "An Application of Integrated Human Resources Planning Supply-Demand Models," *Human Resources Planning* 5, no. 1 (1982), pp. 1–15.

8. Lee Dyer and N. O. Heyer, "Human Resource Planning at IBM: A Field Study" (Working paper, Ithaca, N.Y.: Cornell University, 1984); James C. Rush and Laurie C. Borne, "Human Resources Planning Contributes to Corporate Planning at Ontario Hydro," *Human Resources Planning* 6, no. 4 (1983), pp. 193–207; Donald F. Parker, John A. Fossum, Jan H. Blakslee, and Anthony J. Rucci, "Human Resources Planning at American Hospital Supply," *Human Resources Planning* 6, no. 4 (1983), pp. 207–19.

9. K. M. Rowland and S. L. Summers, "Human Resources Planning: A Second Look," *Personnel Administrator*, December 1981, pp. 73–80; Thomas G. Gutteridge and Elmer H. Burack, "Industrial Manpower Planning: Rhetoric versus Reality," *California Management Review* 10, no. 3 (1978), pp. 13–22.

10. Walker, *Human Resources Planning;* also see R. B. Frantzreb, "Confessions of a Manpower Modeler," in *Manpower Planning for Canadians*, 2nd ed., ed. L. F. Moore and L. Charach (Vancouver: Institute of Industrial Relations, University of British Columbia, 1979).

11. Milkovich and Mahoney, "HRP and PAIR Policy."

12. G. Milkovich and T. Mahoney, "Human Resources Planning Models: A Perspective," *Human Resources Planning* 1, no. 1 (1978), pp. 1–27; J. Wadel and R. Bush, "Probabilistic Forecasting of Manpower Requirements," *IEEE Transactions on Engineering Management*, August 1962, pp. 136–38; N. Kwak, Walter Garrett, and S. Barone,"A Stochastic Model of Demand Forecasting for Technical Manpower Planning," *Management Science* 23, no. 10 (1977), pp. 1089–98; G. Milkovich, A. Annoni, and T. Mahoney, "The Use of Delphi Procedures in Manpower Forecasting," *Management Science*, December 1972, pp. 381–88; and A. Delbecq, A. Van de Ven, and D. Gustafson, *Group Techniques for Program Planning* (Dallas, Tex.: Scott, 1975); A. Drui, "The Use of Regression Equations to Predict Manpower Requirements," *Management Science* 9, no. 4 (1963), pp. 667–77; I. M. Gascoigne, "Manpower Planning at the Enterprise Level," *British Journal of Industrial Relations*, March 1968, pp. 94–106; Wendell W. Burton, "Manpower Planning in an Inflationary Period," *Personnel Administrator*, August 1979, pp. 33–38.

13. Burton, "Manpower Planning."

14. See Milkovich and Mahoney, "HRP and PAIR Policy."

15. Henry Dahl and K. S. Morgan, *Return on Investment in Human Resources* (Kalamazoo, Mich.: Upjohn Company Report, 1982).

16. F. A. Muckler, "Evaluating Productivity," chap. 2 in *Human Performance and Productivity*, ed. M. D. Dunnette (Hillsdale, N.J.: Lawrence Erlbaum, 1982); Committee for Economic Development, *Productivity Policy: Key to the Nation's Economic Future* (Washington, D.C.: U.S. Government Printing Office, 1983): T. K. Connellan, *How to Improve Human Performance* (New York: Harper & Row, 1981); Work in American Institute, *Productivity through Work Innovations*, 1982; D. L. Rowe, "How Westinghouse Measures White Collar Productivity," *Management Review*, November 1981, pp. 42–47; Jon English and Anthony R. Marchione, "Productivity: A New Perspective," *California Management Review* 25, no. 2 (1983), pp. 57–66; Peter F. Drucker, "Managing Productivity," (working paper, 1983).

17. *People & Productivity* (Minneapolis, Minn.: Honeywell Corporate Human Resources, 1982).

18. See S. Makridukis and S. C. Wheelwright, *Forecasting Studies in the Management Services*, vol. 12 (New York: North Holland Publishing, 1979); Edwards et al. *Manpower Planning.*

19. Vetter, *Manpower Planning;* W. Rudelius, "Lagged Manpower Relationships in Development Projects," *IEEE Transactions on Engineering Management*, December 1976, pp. 188–95.

20. Ibid.

21. *People & Productivity*, Honeywell.

22. See references no. 6, 12, and 18.

23. D. Quinn Mills, "Planning with People in Mind," *Harvard Business Review*, July–August 1985, pp. 97–105.

24. Jack Fiorito, Thomas H. Stone, and Charles R. Greer, "Factors Affecting Choice of Human Resource Forecasting Techniques," *Human Resource Planning* 8, no. 1 (1985), pp. 1–18.

25. P. F. Buller and W. R. Maki, "A Case History of a Manpower Planning Model," *Human Resource Planning* 4, no. 3 (1981), pp. 129–38.

26. Ibid.
27. Rowland and Summers, "HRP: A Second Look"; Gutteridge and Burack, "Industrial Manpower Planning"; Gascoigne, "Manpower Planning."
28. George Milkovich and D. Phillips, "Human Resources Planning at Merck: A Field Study" (Working paper, Ithaca, N.Y.: Cornell University, 1984).
29. Dahl and Morgan, *Return on Investment.*
30. L. Dyer, "Human Resource Planning," in *Personnel Management,* ed. K. Rowland and G. Ferris (Boston: Allyn & Bacon, 1982), pp. 52–77; D. M. Atwater, E. S. Bres III, R. J. Niehaus, and J. A. Sheridan, "An Application of Integrated Human Resources Planning Supply-Demand Model," *Human Resource Planning* 5, no. 1 (1982), pp. 1–15; B. W. Holz and J. M. Wroth, "Improving Strengths Forecasts: Support for Army Manpower Management," *Interfaces* 10, no. 6 (1980), pp. 37–52; and J. R. Hinrichs and R. F. Morrison, "Human Resource Planning in Support of Research and Development," *Human Resource Planning* 3, no. 4 (1980), pp. 201–10.
31. Dyer, "Human Resource Planning."
32. Berg, "The Kodak Way."
33. W. H. Mobley, R. W. Griffith, H. H. Hard, and B. M. Maglino, "Review and Conceptual Analysis of Employee Turnover Process," *Psychological Bulletin* 16, no. 3 (1979), pp. 493–522; Charles E. Michaels and Paul E. Specter, "Cause of Employee Turnover," *Journal of Applied Psychology,* 67, no. 1 (1982), pp. 53–59; James E. Rosenbaum, "Organizational Career Mobility: Promotion Choices in a Corporation during Periods of Growth and Contraction," *American Journal of Sociology* 85, no. 1 (1979), pp. 21–48.
34. R. C. Grinold and K. T. Marshall, *Manpower Planning Models* (New York: Elsevier North-Holland Publishing, 1977); W. L. Price, A. Martel and K. A. Lewis, "A Review of Mathematics Models in Human Resource Planning," *Omega,* 8, no. 6 (1980), pp. 639–45; D. J. Bartholomew and A. F. Forbes, *Statistical Techniques for Manpower Planning* (New York: John Wiley & Sons, 1979); R. J. Niehaus, *Computer-Assisted Human Resources Planning* (New York: John Wiley & Sons, 1979).
35. See, for example, Dyer, "Human Resource Planning"; Walker, *Human Resources Planning;* Milkovich, Dyer, Mahoney, "HRM Planning."
36. R. G. Murdick and F. Schuster, "Computerized Information Support for the Human Resource Function," *Human Resource Planning* 6, no. 1 (1983), pp. 25–35.
37. Walker, *Human Resources Planning.*
38. Several references exist on this subject: the advanced reader is directed to R. C. Grinold and K. T. Marshall, *Manpower Planning Models* (New York: Elsevier North-Holland Publishing, 1977); D. J. Bartholomew, *Stochastic Models for Social Processes,* 2nd ed. (New York: John Wiley & Sons, 1973); and Harrison White, *Chains of Opportunity: System Models of Mobility in Organizations* (Cambridge, Mass.: Harvard University Press, 1970). Students new to this topic are directed to Thomas A. Mahoney, George T. Milkovich, and Nan Weiner, "A Stock and Flow Model for Improved Human Resources Measurement," *Personnel,* May–June 1977, pp. 57–66; and Victor H. Vroom and K. R. MacCrimmon, "Towards a Stochastic Model of Management Careers," *Administrative Science Quarterly,* June 1968, pp. 26–46; K. M. Rowland and M. G. Sovereign, "Markov-Chain Analysis of Internal Manpower Supply," *Industrial Relations* 9, no. 1 (1969), pp. 88–

89; T. Mahoney and G. Milkovich, "Markov Chains and Manpower Forecasts," Office of Naval Research Technical Report NR 151–323–7002, 1970; and D. J. Bartholomew and A. R. Smith, eds., *Manpower and Management Science* (London: English University Press, 1970).

39. Some examples of Markov simulation applications include: S. H. Zanakis and M. W. Maret, "A Markov Application to Manpower Supply Planning," *Journal of the Operational Research Society* 31, no. 4 (1980), pp. 1095–1102; L. B. Bleau, "The Academic Flow Model: A Markov Chain Model for Faculty Planning," *Decision Sciences*, April 1981, pp. 294–309; H. L. Clark and D. R. Thurston, *Planning Your Staffing Needs* (Washington, D.C.: Bureau of Policies and Standards, U.S. Civil Service Commission, 1977); C. C. Pegels, "A Markov Application to an Engineering Manpower Policy Problem," *IEE Transactions on Engineering Management*, May 1981, pp. 39–42; J. A. Hooper and J. Catalavello, "Markov Analysis Applied to Forecasting Technical Personnel," *Human Resource Planning* 4, no. 2 (1981), pp. 41–54; Bartholomew and Forbes, *Statistical Techniques for Manpower Planning*; W. G. Piskor and R. C. Dudding, "A Computer-Assisted Manpower Planning Model," in *Manpower Planning and Organization Design*, ed. D. T. Bryant and R. J. Niehaus (New York: Plenum Press, 1978), pp. 145–54; Grinold and Marshall, *Manpower Planning Models*; E. S. Bres III, D. Burns, A Charnes, and W. W. Cooper, "A Goal Programming Model for Planning Officer Accessions," *Management Science* 26, no. 8 (1980), pp. 773–82; S. H. Zanakis and M. W. Maret, "A Markovian Goal Programming Approach to Aggregate Manpower Planning," *Journal of Operational Research* 32, no. 2 (1981), pp. 55–63.

40. See, for example, Milkovich and Phillips, "HRP at Merck"; N. Mathys and H. LaVan, "A Survey of Human Resource Information Systems (HRIS) of Major Companies," *Human Resources Planning* 5, no. 2 (1982), pp. 57–69.

41. Several examples of application have been reported in the literature. See reference 38.

42. H. G. Heneman III and M. G. Sandver, "Markov Analysis in Human Resource Administration," *Academy of Management Review* 2, no. 3 (1977), pp. 535–42.

43. Niehaus, "Computer-Assisted Manpower Planning"; Mahoney and Milkovich, "Markov Chains and Manpower Forecasts"; Jackson F. Gillespie, Wayne E. Leininger, and Harvey Kahalas, "A Human Resource Planning and Valuation Model," *Academy of Management Journal*, December 1976, pp. 650–56; E. S. Bres III, R. J. Niehaus, A. P. Schinnar, and P. Steinbuch, "Efficiency Evaluation of EEO Program Management," *Human Resource Planning* 6, no. 4 (1983), pp. 233–47; F. Krzystofiak, "Estimating EEO Liability," *Decision Sciences* 2, no. 3 (1982), pp. 10–17; J. Ledvinka and R. L. LaForge, "A Staffing Model of Affirmative Action Planning," *Human Resource Planning*, 1978, pp. 135–50; and G. Milkovich and F. Krzystofiak, "Simulation and Affirmative Action Planning," *Human Resource Planning* 2, no. 1 (1979), pp. 71–80.

44. Tom Peters, "Why a Small Staff Means High Productivity," *New York Times*, April 21, 1985, pp. 1, 14–15.

45. Larry Reirstein, "More Companies Use Free-Lancers to Avoid Cost, Trauma of Layoffs," *The Wall Street Journal*, April 18, 1986, p. 23; Amanda

Bennett and Douglas R. Sease, "To Reduce Their Costs, Big Companies Lay Off White-Collar Workers," *The Wall Street Journal*, May 22, 1986, pp. 1, 24; Lee Dyer, F. Foltman, and G. Milkovich, "Employment Stabilization" (Working paper, Cornell University, 1984); Mark Thompson, "The Permanent Employment System: Japan and Mexico," Sixth World Congress of Industrial Relations, Kyōto, Japan, March 28–31, 1983; R. Fuller, C. Jordan, and R. Anderson, "Retrenchment: Layoff Procedures in a Nonprofit Organization,"*Personnel*, November-December 1982, pp. 19–24; R. H. Ketchum, "Retrenchment: The Uses and Misuses of Life in Downsizing an Organization," *Personnel*, November-December 1982, pp. 25–30; Linda Wintner, Employee Buyouts: An Alternative to Plant Closings (New York: The Conference Board, 1983); F. Foltman, "Managing a Plant Closing: An Overview" (Working paper, ILR School, Cornell University, 1981); T. Bailey and T. Jackson, "Industrial Outplacement at Goodyear," *Personnel Administrator*, March 1980, pp. 42–48; D. L. Ward, "The $34,000 Layoff," *Human Resources Planning* 5, no. 1 (1982), pp. 35–43; Dick Schaaff, "Are You Training Yet for Outplacement and Retirement?" *Training*, May 1981, pp. 70–84; E. B. Silverman and S. D. Sass, "Outplacement," *Training and Development Journal*, February 1982, pp. 71–84; R. S. Barkhaus and Carol L. Mak, "A Practical View of Outplacement," *Personnel Administrator*, March 1982, pp. 77–85; C. H. Driessnank, "Outplacement—The New Personnel Practice," *Personnel Administrator*, October 1980, pp. 81–93; P. D. Johnston, "Personnel Planning for a Plant Shutdown," Personnel Administrator, August 1981, pp. 53–60.

46. Monsanto, "Incentives for Early Retirement Are Offered to 1900," *The Wall Street Journal*, September 22, 1982, p. 4.

47. Ibid.

48. "A Guide to Plant Closings," *Perspectives*, No. 3 (New York: The Conference Board, 1986).

49. George T. Milkovich and Jerry M. Newman, *Compensation*, 2nd ed. (Plano, Tex.: Business Publications, 1987).

50. "Employees Learn to Love Being Leased," *Fortune*, April 1, 1985, p. 80; "Tax Legislation Puts Leasing of Employees in a New Light," *The Wall Street Journal*, September 22, 1986, p. 27.

51. Bill Saporito, "Cutting Costs without Cutting People," *Fortune*, May 25, 1987, pp. 26–32.

PART TWO CASES

▶ ITHACA'S OWN
CASE 3: SETTING OBJECTIVES

This project involves setting human resource objectives for Ithaca's Own. Exhibit 8–2 on pp. 271–72 illustrates examples of objectives established by Merck.

1. Develop a recommended list of five critical human resource objectives for I-O. To do so, refresh your understanding of I-O, Case 1 (p. 228) as well as I-O's actual budget allocations (Exhibit 3) and employment plan (Exhibit 4). These exhibits are reproduced here, but be sure to reread the additional information on I-O on pages 228–231 in Case 1.
2. Recall question A-2, p. 232, in the very first Ithaca's Own case. That question asked you to make recommendations for how I-O could reallocate its human resource efforts to be more consistent with its business

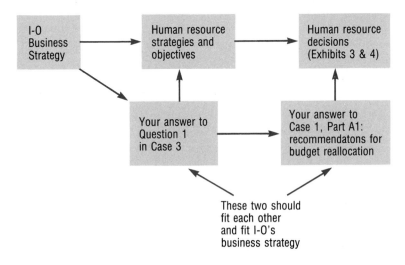

EXHIBIT 3
Human Resource Strategic Programming—Budget Allocations (percents)

		Functions		
Strategic Programming	R&D	Operations	Marketing	Administrative Services
Total of Ithaca's Own (100%)	25%	60%	10%	5%
Training and development	15	40	30	20
Managerial	5	15	10	10
Technical	10	10	10	10
Skill-Craft	—	15	10	—
Staffing	45	10	30	20
Recruiting	35	10	20	10
Succession charting	5	—	5	5
Career planning	5	—	5	5
Performance evaluation	10	15	10	20
Compensation design	10	10	10	20
Equal Employment Opportunity	10	15	10	10
New programs	10	10	10	10
	100%	100%	100%	100%

EXHIBIT 4
I-O Human Resource Requirements and Turnover

| | | Planned Year | | |
	Current Year Employment	Forecasted Requirements	Estimated Turnover	Surplus/ (Shortage)
R&D:				
Principal scientist	10	7	0	3
Associate scientist	50	43	3	4
Assistant scientist	70	65	3	2
Manager	10	10	2	(2)
Group leader	20	23	4	(7)
Technician	30	32	4	(6)
Secretary and clerical	3	2	0	1
Total	193	182	16	(5)
Operations:				
Manager	3	3	2	(2)
Supervisor	9	8	1	(0)
Foremen	35	31	2	2
Operators	60	72	10	(22)
Secretary and clerical	3	2	1	0
Total	110	116	16	(22)
Marketing and sales:				
Managers	3	5	0	(2)
R&D consultants	10	6	2	2
Account consultants	8	11	1	(4)
Professional	30	38	2	(10)
Secretary and clerical	15	17	5	(7)
Total	66	77	10	(21)
Administrative services:				
Human resource managers and director	5	5	0	0
Purchasing director	2	2	1	(1)
Finance and data processing director	3	4	2	(3)
Human resource professionals	10	10	1	(1)
Finance professionals	10	8	0	2
Secretary and clerical	11	9	4	(2)
Total	41	38	8	(5)

directions and environmental conditions. Now, compare the recommendations you made at that time to the objectives you just set for I-O. Are the budget allocations consistent with the objectives you established? If they are not consistent, what adjustments would you make? Do your objectives fit I-O's business strategy? The chart below shows how your answers should fit with each other and with I-O's business strategy.

EXHIBIT 1

Merger of Two Insurers into Cigna Corp.
Brings Discord, Layoffs, and Profit Drop

By Daniel Hertzberg

PHILADELPHIA— When Connecticut General Corp. and INA Corp. tied the knot in the nation's biggest financial-services merger last year, the two insurers vowed to live happily ever after.

But a cartoon that soon circulated around INA's headquarters here suggested a rockier marriage. It showed two armies advancing on one another. One was a disciplined phalanx of Roman legionnaires, with "CG"—for Connecticut General—on their shields. The other was a ragtag band of barbarians waving clubs and axes and led by a figure clearly resembling INA's chairman, Ralph S. Saul. One barbarian was asking another: "Isn't it time we got our act together?"

From the start, Connecticut General and INA hailed their combination, in a $4.3 billion swap of stock, as a "merger of equals." The companies were of similar size— each with revenue exceeding $5 billion—though they came from different sides of the insurance business. When the new financial-services giant named Cigna Corp. started up on March 31, 1982, the top corporate jobs were carefully apportioned, five to INA executives, four to Connecticut General's. And, in a highly unusual arrangement, "co-chief executive officers"—one from each company—were named to run Cigna.

Considerable Discord

Little more than a year later, the cartoon seems prophetic. Bliss hasn't reigned. Officials from Connecticut General's disciplined ranks have gained control of Cigna. INA's president has left, and the system of dual chief executives has been discarded. Now, there's only one, Robert D. Kilpatrick, Connecticut General's 59-year-old former president. Moreover, the announcement about two chief executives apparently was a sham; there was private agreement before the merger that Mr. Kilpatrick would lead the merged company.

Cigna's problems haven't been limited to turmoil in the executive suite. The huge insurer's earnings have been disappointing, it has ordered extensive layoffs, and its stock has taken a beating despite the bull market on Wall Street.

As much as any of the recent jumbo-sized mergers, Cigna's problems show that top executives at many companies are right in worrying that a merger may cost them their jobs, notwithstanding any fine-sounding assurances. Even when the companies are of equal size, one soon edges out the other. "There's no question that Connecticut General people have overwhelmed the INA people," says Donald E. Franz Jr., a securities analyst at Smith Barney, Harris Upham & Co.

Penchant for Planning

Cigna illustrates other difficulties. B. P. Russell, the chairman of Xerox Corp.'s Crum & Forster insurance unit, says Cigna is "a fine outfit, but they've got all sorts of problems because they're trying to put together two insurance operations, and they've got two of everything." Especially tough is melding two top managements with different styles, different "corporate cultures." To people outside the industry, all insurers may seem cut from the same gray cloth. But INA and Connecticut General were run very differently, executives at both companies agree.

At Connecticut General, a disciplined, deliberate management style is epitomized by what employees call "The Process." In this companywide planning program, man-

(continued)

EXHIBIT 1 (continued)

agers meet individually with 2,000 employees to set up specific, written goals to advance the company's master plan. Each employee is then subject to periodic review.

"The planning goes so far down in the organization that everyone can identify with their part of the plan," says an admirer at another insurer. However, an ex-executive complains that the employees "tend to put on blinders. Once you got the plan, the plan is what you achieve. You don't see other opportunities."

At INA, the style was more freewheeling. "Smart risk taking," not management skills, were at a premium, says Andrew M. Rouse, a Cigna executive vice president who came from INA. Adds one former Cigna executive: "At INA, anyone could speak his mind. When we came together with the CG people, they were accustomed to everything being within The Plan."

The differences stem partly from the two companies' different businesses. Connecticut General was a leading writer of group life and health insurance and group pensions. In life insurance, a company insider says, "you never really need to rush because things move too slowly." INA, in contrast, mainly wrote property and casualty insurance, where unpredictable events and boom-and-bust cycles prevail.

Other Differences

The two managements had other important differences. Connecticut General's top executives generally spent years rising through its ranks. Mr. Kilpatrick, its six-foot, five-inch, president, started there as a trainee in 1954. Several key INA officials, in contrast, came from outside the insurance business, arriving in the mid-1970s to revitalize the company. INA's chairman, Mr. Saul, was a former president of the American Stock Exchange, and Richard M. Burdge, another top INA executive, had been chief operating officer of the Amex.

"CG people are stayers; INA people are recent comers, and therefore goers," a Connecticut General insider says.

Even the two corporate headquarters differ. Connecticut General sits on an isolated, wooded-tract in Bloomfield, Conn., a 15-minute drive from Hartford. A paternalistic employer, it buses workers from Hartford and provides them with a store and bowling alley in Bloomfield. INA, in Philadelphia, pays less attention to corporate niceties. "In a big city, you expect people to take care of themselves," Mr. Rouse says.

The merger almost immediately got off to a rocky start. Three weeks after the start-up, Cigna's top officials warned a group of Wall Street securities analysts that their profit estimates were too high. Cigna's stock plunged, eventually dropping 40%. Operating profit in 1982 fell 26% to $490.1 million, or $6.38 a share, from $658 million, or $8.51 a share, in 1981 (calculated as if the companies were combined that year).

More Bad News

Earlier this week, there was further bad news. Cigna said it expects to report a 25% decline in operating earnings for the second quarter, and on Wednesday Cigna's stock plunged $4.75 a share on the New York Stock Exchange to $42.75, well below its all-time high of $55.375 in April 1982. The stock dropped another 50 cents.

Company officials blame the disappointment earnings on a "brutal" property-casualty insurance market—a situation, insiders note, that inevitably has reduced the influence of former INA officials. Cigna has responded to its poor earnings with tough steps. In a move that stunned the industry, it slashed 2,000 jobs from its payroll last year and vowed to drop 2,000 more by 1984 in a $100 million cost-cutting campaign.

Rumors of management tensions cropped up quickly, too. They centered on John R. Cox, the 50-year-old former president of INA, who became an executive

(continued)

EXHIBIT 1 (*continued*)

vice president and the head of Cigna's property-casualty operations, and Wilson H. Taylor, a 40-year-old former senior vice president of Connecticut General, who became Cigna's chief financial officer. In June 1982, the two men appeared together at a hastily convened securities-analyst meeting in an attempt to dispel the talk of a rift.

But by last January, the Connecticut General takeover of the executive suite had become obvious, analysts say. Cigna announced that Mr. Kilpatrick would become the sole chief executive. Mr. Saul remained chairman but relinquished both his title of co-chief executive and day-to-day control of Cigna's operations.

Necessary Maneuver?

The 60-year-old Mr. Saul says that before the merger, he told directors of both companies that he planned to withdraw from active management within two years. Agrees Mr. Kilpatrick: "There was no question who was going to be the chief executive officer." Mr. Saul defends the deceptive announcement about dual chief executives. "I don't think we could have done the merger without" it, he comments.

Once Mr. Saul reduced his role, "Kilpatrick began to set the tone for the company," says Mr. Cox, adding: "People like myself weren't accustomed to that planned, structured approach." The next month, Mr. Cox said he was leaving, and Mr. Taylor was picked to replace him as the property-casualty chief. Officials say Mr. Cox isn't suffering financially, that he held $1 million of INA stock at the time of the merger and also had a "golden parachute" with generous severance provisions.

Mr. Cox says that he wasn't fired, that indeed he turned down an offer by Mr. Kilpatrick to make him Cigna's chief financial officer. Mr. Cox explains that he didn't want the job and that the offer reflected Connecticut General's longtime practice of rotating its top officers. "When you are a senior person, and you say, 'No,' you're really saying, 'I quit,' " Mr. Cox says. Observers also speculate that he realized that he had lost out on a chance to become Cigna's chief executive.

Other Departures

There have been other departures, too. Last month, INA's Mr. Burdge said he would quit as the head of Cigna's affiliated businesses group. He was replaced by Robert E. Patricelli, a Connecticut General alumnus. Mr. Burdge said he wanted to switch to noninsurance pursuits. A few other executives from both companies have also left.

However, Mr. Kilpatrick calls reports of turmoil at Cigna exaggerated. "The coming-together of these two companies to make Cigna has been one of the most orderly mergers of its size," he contends. "The wethey attitude has disappeared entirely," and executive turnover has been "very minimal," he adds.

And in fact, INA executives now head Cigna's investment operations and run its planning and legal affairs. After some hesitation, the company also chose Philadelphia for its headquarters. But officials from Connecticut General run Cigna's biggest money-making units, including employee benefits and financial services, plus property-casualty. One INA man who left Cigna considers it inevitable "to start worrying about your career."

In light of the weak second-quarter earnings, Mr. Kilpatrick has reversed his earlier prediction of higher profits for this year; now, he expects operating earnings to be "moderately below" 1982's, a spokesman said yesterday. Some analysts believe that it may take three to five years before the full benefits of the merger are realized.

Chiding Critics

Mr. Saul chides the analysts and the press for asking too much too soon of the new company. "Here we take a very bold, long-term step," he says, "yet we're expected to produce short-term results."

(continued)

EXHIBIT 1 *(concluded)*

Cigna's future may hinge on developments in the insurance industry. Many insurers think that the workplace will become an important distribution point for property-casualty insurance. Big corporations may offer group automobile and homeowners insurance as employee benefits, much as they currently do with group life and health insurance. This blend of employee benefits and property-casualty insurance would suit Cigna remarkably well.

Meanwhile, some INA alumni say they welcome Connecticut General's disciplined management style. For example, Mr. Rouse, now a Cigna executive vice president, says a giant company like Cigna "has got to put more emphasis on what CG was stronger at"—management skills. The true picture, he adds, is a lot more complicated than Roman legions versus barbarians. "A cartoon always deals in hyperbole," he says.

3. In the chart on page 346 the arrows go from business strategy to human resource strategy to human resource decisions. Are there any situations in I-O where the arrows go in the other direction? That is, do the human resource decisions made in the past act as a constraint on possible I-O business strategies?
4. Which criteria would you use to evaluate the effectiveness of the HRM function?

▶ CIGNA

Exhibit 1 reprints a description of problems at Cigna Corporation from *The Wall Street Journal*. Use the diagnostic approach to provide a framework for examining the Cigna situation.

Discussion Questions

1. Which factors in the external environment are affecting Cigna Corporation?
2. Which factors in Connecticut General and INA Corporation's internal organization environment are important to consider?
3. What is happening here? What, if any, human resource management issues should Cigna be concerned about? If you were an outside human resource management consultant, what would you recommend? What additional data would you recommend collecting, and why?

4. What should be Cigna's objectives? How can it go about setting its objectives?

▶ STRATEGIC HUMAN RESOURCE PLANNING

Background

In Part Two we discussed business strategies and presented Miles and Snow's three strategic types: Defenders, Prospectors, and Analyzers. Two points were emphasized: first, that organization units may differ in their financial and marketing directions (i.e., strategies); and second, that different business strategies may require different human resource strategies. We have also suggested that there is no single best approach to human resource management. Rather, the best depends in part on the organization's strategies and objectives. Hence the manager must consider the strategic directions of the organization when designing human resource actions.

Strategic Grids and Screens

The use of analytical techniques to guide strategic decisions has grown rapidly over the past decade. A typical technique is the planning matrix shown as Exhibit 1. The matrix relates an *organization's strength and weakness* to certain environmental characteristics such as *industry attractiveness*, which yield opportunities and risks for the organization. For industry attractiveness, the vertical axis is determined by such factors as the size of the potential market or the growth rate in consumer demand. Organization strengths (the horizontal axis) are determined by technology, market share, financial conditions, or human resources. In the case of non-business establishments (government units, universities, United Way), the dimensions on a strategic matrix may become "strength of the demand for services provided" and "the organization's strengths and weaknesses."

Several possible states of cells emerge in the matrix. We have identified three strategic stages for illustrative purposes: Invest (grow), Evaluate (manage selectively), Disinvest (harvest). The characteristics of each stage are included in the exhibit. For example, a business unit in an invest stage is often a highly attractive business (high growth potential, profitability, or high service demand) and has a relatively high business strength (proven management, or good labor relations). According to this conventional strategic analysis, such a business unit should be considered a good risk and may receive increased deployment of resources to take advantage of the opportunity. Conversely, the disinvest stage combines a less attractive business (shrinking market or highly competitive) with low business

EXHIBIT 1

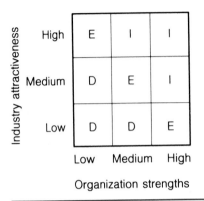

STRATEGIC PLANNING MATRIX

		Low	Medium	High
Industry attractiveness	High	E	I	I
	Medium	D	E	I
	Low	D	D	E

Organization strengths

I = Invest (emerging, growth)
  Strong revenue, market share potential
  Cash scarcity
  Individual decision makers
  Entrepreneurial managers
  Long-term orientation
  Invest for future
E = Evaluate (manage selectively)
  Revenue potential unclear
  Control expenses
  Formalizing management systems
  Intermediate to short-term orientation
D = Disinvest (harvest)
  Revenue potential weak
  Control expenses
  Formalized management systems
  Short-term orientation

strength (obsolete plant). Such a unit may be a drag on the enterprise and eliminated.

Such analysis, employed by General Electric and a host of other organizations, should help to direct the deployment of resources within the organization and to protect developing business directions. Even though there is little rigorous empirical research that supports such models, many industrial and consulting firms subscribe to some variation of the framework.

Discussion Questions

Speculate about the personnel actions that are most consistent with each business strategy. Exhibit 2 provides a framework for your comments.

1. Is planning formalized or not? Is the personnel function likely to be centralized in all strategies?
2. Which strategy is most likely to go outside for talent? Which is most likely to "grow their own"—promote from within and develop employees?
3. Which type would emphasize paying whatever is necessary to hire (competition is key)? Which would emphasize internal pay relationships? Which would focus on incentive plans?

EXHIBIT 2
Strategies

Human Resource Activities	Invest (I)	Evaluate (E)	Disinvest (D)
Planning			
Staffing			
Compensation			
Training			
Labor relations			

4. Would the types of training (e.g., technical, managerial, specific, general) emphasized differ by strategy?
5. Is the management's approach to unions at all related to the strategy it is following? How would the presence of a union affect the ability of the firm to pursue its strategy?
6. You may wish to return to this project after you have finished this book. Compare your answers now to those you give after reading the text.

Exhibit Three

THE DIAGNOSTIC MODEL

ASSESS HUMAN RESOURCE CONDITIONS	SET HUMAN RESOURCE OBJECTIVES	CHOOSE AND APPLY HUMAN RESOURCE ACTIVITIES	EVALUATE RESULTS
EXTERNAL CONDITIONS	EFFICIENCY	Planning	EFFICIENCY
Economic Conditions	Organization	**Staffing**	EQUITY
Government Regulations	Employee	Development	
Unions	EQUITY	Employee/Union Relations	
ORGANIZATIONAL CONDITIONS	Organization	Compensation	
Nature of the Organization	Employee		
Nature of the Work			
EMPLOYEE CONDITIONS			
Abilities			
Motivation			
Interests			

Part

three

Staffing

*T*he previous sections have shown how organizations assess conditions, set objectives, and use employment planning to identify and anticipate employee surpluses and shortages. Part Three discusses the third step in the diagnostic model, choosing activities. This section focuses on staffing activities.

Organizations are dynamic. Employees are constantly moving into, through, and out of them. Managing this employee movement is one of the most important human resource management activities. Even the most carefully designed organization, with precise information on the nature of its employees and the work, cannot function efficiently unless the right number and types of employees move into, through, and out of those work roles. Part Three shows how human resource activities affect which employees are chosen, how they move through the organization, and how they leave.

Definition
Staffing is the process of moving employees into, through, and out of the organization, to produce the desired quantities and types of employee assignments.

Chapter Nine described how human resource managers identify important shortages and surpluses of employees. The shortages and surpluses suggest areas where employee movement is desired. Staffing activities translate these desires into action. Staffing activities change the composition of the work force. They work to the degree that they improve the fit between the desired and actual *number* and *characteristics* of employees assigned to jobs, at the minimum cost.

Part Three examines staffing through four chapters. Chapter Ten examines recruitment, the activity that identifies and attracts candidates for employment offers. Chapter Eleven addresses external employee selection, the activity that chooses who receives an offer to join the organization. Chapter Twelve addresses external employee separation/retention, the activity that manages the pattern of employees leaving the organization. Chapter Thirteen addresses internal staffing, the activity that manages the pattern of employee movements between jobs.

chapter

ten

RECRUITMENT AND INDIVIDUAL JOB SEARCH

CHAPTER OUTLINE

Imagine applying for a job without ever touching a pen or paper. You enter the employment office, sit down at a computer terminal, respond to questions on the screen by typing your answers on a keyboard, and receive a printout of your information when you are finished. At the end of each day, electronic résumés are fed into the organization's central memory bank, where they can be quickly scanned to identify the desired number and characteristics of applicants for various jobs. This is not a futuristic description, but the actual system currently used by IBM at its Tucson, Arizona, manufacturing site. Electronic Application System for Employment (EASE) offers the advantages of speed, efficiency, accessibility, and potential cost savings to IBM. But how might it affect job applicants? Does it present a desirable high-tech image, or a feeling of being just a number in a computer? Does it provide a realistic preview of one aspect of some manufacturing jobs—responding to computer-generated instructions and status reports—or does it needlessly rebuff applicants who are apprehensive about computers or who cannot read and type well?

EASE is one of many options for identifying and attracting individuals to be job candidates. Identifying and attracting a pool of job applicants is called recruitment; it is the first step in the staffing process. The preceding questions illustrate some of the trade-offs facing human resources managers when they make decisions about recruitment.

For college students, perhaps the most visible recruiting activity occurs on college campuses. Every spring, the college placement office swells with activity. Students and recruiters are coming and going; the latter study student résumés while the former read annual reports. Most importantly, both schedule interviews. Classmates who had never been seen in a pressed shirt suddenly appear as if they have stepped out of *Dress for Success*. Stress seems to go up with the unemployment rate. The placement office becomes a labor market. Exchanges take place between buyers (employers) and sellers (students), and elaborate mechanisms develop to facilitate and regulate the exchange. Students may be required to bid for interviews with an allocated number of points. Some students may bid all their allotted points to ensure an interview with a highly desired firm. Other students try to finesse the process by calling employers directly to schedule an interview, and save their points for other firms.

Both employers and students face several important decisions. The organization must decide where to find candidates (sources), how to recruit them (methods), and how to judge the results (evaluation). Students must decide which firms to interview, how to market themselves, and (eventually) which job offer to accept. The job the student accepts largely defines immediate earnings and social status; it becomes a major source of self-identity and satisfaction/dissatisfaction in his or her life.

Definition

Recruiting activities identify and attract a pool of candidates for changes in employment status, from which some will later be selected to receive offers.

Recruiting encompasses decisions about choosing (1) communication methods, (2) recruiters, (3) recruitment messages, and (4) required applicant qualifications. Obviously, recruiting takes place both when employers search for candidates outside the organization (external recruiting) and inside the organization (internal recruiting). This chapter focuses on external recruiting, and Chapter Thirteen discusses how recruiting applies to internal staffing decisions.

A DIAGNOSTIC APPROACH TO RECRUITING

Because recruiting is often the first contact between employers and employees, and because it is a very public activity, it is affected by conditions inside and outside the organization. And it has important implications for efficiency and equity.

Assessing External Conditions

Product and Labor Markets

Conditions in the labor market are a major factor in the design of the recruiting process.[1] If an abundant supply of the skills is sought, informal recruiting will probably attract more than enough applicants. But during periods of full employment, more elaborate and prolonged recruiting may be necessary to attract promising applicants.

Classical economic theory views wage differences as the principal mechanism for allocating labor. Jobs for which there is an abundant supply of skilled labor attract many applicants, which holds down wages for those jobs. Jobs requiring skills that are less common or that require long periods to gain the necessary training and experience may need to pay relatively higher wages to attract sufficient people.[2]

In addition to wages, other factors (job security, location, the challenge of the job) influence labor force behavior. Economists combine all these factors into one concept, the "net advantage" of one job over another. People choose the employer and job with the greatest net advantage for their own circumstances.[3]

In addition to differences in "net advantage" among jobs and employers, there are also differences in labor markets. Some markets are national, some regional or local; some vary by occupation (engineers, teachers, crafts).[4] Further, labor market conditions vary over time.

Broad labor market changes created by women entering the labor force and older people working longer as well as demographics provide valuable information for planning recruiting decisions.[5] Though several authors have downplayed the role of money in determining individual's job choices, Sara Rynes argues that money can be a potent recruitment tool if managed properly.[6]

Governments and Society

Laws and regulations, especially EEO laws, are another external condition that affects recruiting decisions.[7] Governmental agencies may review recruitment sources, advertising, and applicant data to determine the organization's EEO compliance. Recruiting plays a key role in affirmative action (AA) programs that seek out new sources of qualified women and minorities. Honeywell, Inc.'s personnel managers lobbied the Transit Commission in Minneapolis to run public buses between plants and minority neighborhoods. In this case, recruiting was not only affected *by* the external environment, it affected that environment.

Recruiting messages do not affect only those who accept employment offers. They affect the perceptions of rejected applicants who may become future customers or competitors. Similar to advertising, these messages are often a source of general information about the employer for the larger community.

Unions

A union's most obvious effect on recruiting decisions is embodied in a collective bargaining agreement that stipulates hiring for certain jobs through the union hiring hall. This is a common practice in the construction and maritime industries. Then most of the recruiting decisions rest with the union. A more indirect effect may occur as applicants compare employment offers in union firms and nonunion firms. Applicant preferences for work in a unionized versus nonunionized environment may affect their choices. Moreover, collectively bargained work rules and relationships may distinguish union employers from nonunion employers.

Assessing Organization Conditions

As Chapter Nine showed, the decision to recruit springs from an anticipated or current labor shortage, which in turn reflects human resource objectives; these ultimately depend on organizational objectives. Moreover, the nature of the strategic objectives may define desired applicant characteristics. Organizations operating in a narrow, relatively stable market may seek out people with backgrounds in finance or production. Organizations seeking to exploit new products or markets may look for people with basic engineering research or marketing skills. Organizations operating in mixed markets may look for individuals with abilities in applied research, marketing, and production.[8]

Organizational culture and traditions shape recruiting decisions. Organizations such as IBM and Eastman Kodak Company embrace long-held values stressing the importance of individual dignity and lifetime employment. They believe these values distinguish them from their competitors in the labor market, making it easier to attract desired employment candidates.

Recruitment decisions depend on the nature of the tasks, responsibilities, and activities required by the jobs being staffed. As discussed in Chapter Five, job analysis information can support recruitment decisions by suggesting the individual characteristics necessary for the job. An important consideration in choosing recruitment strategies is whether applicants will be trained after hiring. Businesses require more stringent applicant requirements if little or no training is provided than if job skills can be learned after hiring. Moreover, jobs that are new and unfamiliar may require greater effort and larger recruitment budgets. Employment agencies generally supply lower-level positions while executive search firms provide upper-level managers. College recruiting frequently fills entry-level positions.[9]

Individual differences between job applicants affect recruitment because it is a process of attraction. It is not sufficient to simply let qualified individuals know that an opportunity exists. Recruitment must also ensure that candidates' interests are compatible with the job's requirements and that the job outcomes are likely to motivate them to perform effectively.

(See Chapter Six on individual differences.) Accurate communication of job specifications and the organization's strategies and objectives is helpful to applicants.[10] When candidates have a clear idea of the requirements of the job, the rewards the job offers, as well as where the organization is headed, they can more accurately assess whether or not the job offers a good match with their own personal abilities and interests.[11] This process of candidates evaluating their own interest in a job is called *self-selection*.[12]

Setting Objectives for Recruitment Activities

Recruiting activities serve three purposes in the staffing process: First, they attract the candidates who apply for employment opportunities. The size and characteristics of the candidate pool limit the extent to which the rest of the staffing activities achieve their objectives. No amount of careful choice can make up for an insufficient quantity of candidates or a candidate pool with inappropriate qualifications. Second, recruiting can affect whether candidates receiving employment offers accept them. If top candidates refuse job offers, no amount of careful choice can fill the employment openings. The third purpose of recruiting activities is to exchange information. As we discuss in the next chapter, recruiters gather some of the information used to select candidates during the recruitment process. Moreover, during recruitment activities candidates receive information that helps them decide whether this employment opportunity is right for them. Recruitment also serves a public relations function by affecting the impressions left with rejected candidates, who may be potential customers or future employees in different jobs. Finally, managers use information from recruitment to evaluate and plan other human resource activities, such as EEO targets or future labor supply forecasts.

Achieving these objectives requires understanding not only how applicants identify and choose employment offers, but also how to manage recruitment activities. Recruiting involves an interaction between "individuals and organizations attracting and selecting each other."[13]

THE APPLICANT'S SEARCH PROCESS

How Applicants Seek Employment

Job search research has focused on two variables: method and effort. A review of 22 studies on methods used by job-seekers found that much job information is acquired on an informal basis. Friends and relatives are the most frequent source, with direct application (walk-ins) a close second.[14] Methods vary by occupation, with managerial and clerical job-seekers more likely to use a private employment service than are blue-collar job-seekers.[15]

Research has found that search effort is inversely related to financial security.[16] If a person has nonwage income or unemployment benefits, fewer hours are spent each week looking for a job.[17] A study of MBAs found that those who conducted more intensive searches were more satisfied than their less informed counterparts both one and three years following the job choice.[18] However, initial postchoice dissatisfaction may occur if attractive alternatives have to be rejected. The same study also found high search effort related to higher salary increase over the three-year period.

William Glueck categorized business and engineering students according to the approach they used to search for jobs.[19]

1. *Maximizers* took as many interviews as possible, got as many offers as possible, and then rationally chose the best one, based on self-specified criteria.
2. *Satisfiers* took the first offer they got. They tended to believe that one company was about the same as any other.
3. *Validators* were in between. They would get an offer (their favorite), get one more just to see if their favorite was a good one, and then take the favorite one.

Little is known about the relationship between effort and efficiency of methods used, nor about the relationship between methods used and duration of unemployment. Some research suggests there may be differences. For example, one study found that male users of public employment services tended to remain unemployed longer than users of alternative methods.[20] It also found that those who get help from friends and relatives in obtaining jobs were more likely to experience a reduction in wage level from a previous job than were those who used alternative methods. So friends and relatives who provide job information may also apply pressure to accept a job offer, even at a lower wage, and to meet performance standards once on the job. Advice for organizations seems to also hold true for individuals—use a variety of search methods.

The perceived likelihood of receiving job offers appears to affect search behavior, especially if the costs of job pursuit are borne by the applicants. But Sara Rynes and Edward Lawler found that their subjects did not evaluate expectancies in ways directly predictable from expectancy theory.[21] Some subjects chose job interviews solely on job attractiveness (valences) and appeared to ignore likelihood of getting a job (expectancies). Others emphasized the expectancy of securing a job in a geographical location, and ignored the job attractiveness. For others, personal characteristics such as a lack of confidence or risk aversion seemed to be the source of differences in job search and choice behavior.

Choosing an Occupation

Just as organizations have ideal specifications for recruits, many recruits seem to have a set of preferences for a job. A student leaving college may want a job in San Diego, preferably close to the beach, that pays $35,000 a year and requires little or no responsibility or supervision. This recruit is unlikely to have *all* expectations fulfilled. Recruits anticipate compromises just as organizations do.

From the individual's point of view, choosing an organization is a two-step process. First, the individual makes an occupational choice—probably in high school or just after. Then that person chooses an organization to work for within the occupation.[22]

Occupational choice has been analyzed from psychological, economic, and sociological perspectives. Occupational choice is influenced by the person's psychological preferences, the realities of the labor market and the person's calculation of net advantage, and the structural limitations of an organization and the individual's socialization to it.

Psychologists analyze occupational choice as part of the person's emotional and intellectual growth. Occupational choice is influenced by the person's needs, desires, hopes, and aspirations. Economists see the occupational choice process as the way people seek to maximize the future flow of income and minimize their time and effort to obtain it. Sociologists emphasize how the family, educational system, peer group, and guidance agencies influence and constrain occupational choice.

All three approaches to understanding occupational choice are interrelated. To understand an individual's aspirations without reference to the economic and organizational limitations on them, or to study the idea of maximizing net advantages without including a persons' motivations, makes little sense.[23] To this list, reflecting on our own occupational choice, we also add chance or luck.

Choosing an Organization

We have stated that everyone makes an occupational choice, and then an organizational choice within that occupation. This is true for many persons, especially those that stay in school through high school and beyond. But some do not even complete high school. In a study of 1,600 men, Michael Ornstein found that 25 percent of American blacks and 15 percent of whites enter the job market without high school educations.[24] For these people, chances are the occupational choice is quite limited. In either case, what does the research tell us about how people make organizational choices?[25]

Compensatory Models and Reservation Wage

Most of the research on how people evaluate competing offers has concentrated on college students. The postcollege organization choice is unique for several reasons. First, it may be the only time an individual has more than one job offer to consider at a time. A person usually has only one alternative to compare to the present job. For example, a loan officer in a bank may be offered a job in the trust department for the same employer, or even for a different employer, but rarely is there more than one option to consider at a time. Second, because of the number of students/ recruiters exchanging information at the same time, most college students probably have more accurate information on labor market conditions than they will ever possess again. People who are currently employed but seeking to change jobs, or those who are unemployed, do not have the information network that provides them such data, nor may they have the option of searching until the perfect job is found. Instead, they may take the first offer that is above some minimum level. Glueck's study would classify them as satisfiers. The minimum level of pay required to make the job offer acceptable is called the *reservation wage*.[26]

In contrast to this approach is the *compensatory model*, in which trade-offs between job attributes are made. For example, low job responsibility can be offset by a promise of rapid promotion; an unattractive geographical location can be offset by high pay, or a job for a spouse, or an effective management training program. Although the compensatory model may seem logical with multiple job offers, there is more research support for noncompensatory-reservation wage strategies that take the first offer that meets minimum requirements.[27]

Research on attributes of the job itself (i.e., pay, location) generally concludes that different people respond to different attributes. C. E. Jurgensen did a study in which he asked applicants to rank their preferences among job attributes, and then asked them to rank what they felt were other people's preferences.[28] He found some interesting differences (see Exhibit 10–1), especially in the importance of pay. People agree that pay is very important to others, but are less willing to indicate that it is important to them. Why the difference? Perhaps it is considered socially unacceptable for an individual to indicate an unseemly interest in money.[29] When managed effectively as a recruiting tool, pay can affect organizational choice and enhance recruiting effectiveness.[30]

EXHIBIT 10–1
Median Ranks of 10 Job Attributes Obtained from Applicants to the Minneapolis Gas Company

| | Sex and Preference Source | | | |
| | Men | | Women | |
Attribute	Self	Others	Self	Others
Advancement	3.3	3.8	5.3	4.3
Benefits	6.8	5.2	8.0	5.9
Company	4.5	6.8	4.6	7.1
Co-workers	6.0	7.7	5.2	7.3
Hours	7.6	5.4	6.9	5.0
Pay	5.6	2.1	6.0	2.1
Security	2.5	3.6	4.9	5.4
Supervisor	6.3	7.4	5.3	7.0
Type of work	3.3	4.9	1.5	3.5
Working conditions	7.9	6.9	6.5	6.8
Number of respondents	(39,788)	(32,810)	(16,833)	(15,138)

Source: C. E. Jurgensen, "Job Preferences (What Makes a Job Good or Bad?)," *Journal of Applied Psychology,* 1978, pp. 267–76. Copyright 1978 by the American Psychological Association. Adapted by permission of the publisher and author.

Although research on job attribute importance is interesting, it may not be very helpful for decision making because it fails to tell us *how much* of a particular job attribute difference affects applicant behavior.[31] A more useful approach is illustrated by a study that asked 5,000 young men to estimate their probabilities of signing up for the armed services under present inducement levels, versus an additional $2,000, $5,000 or $8,000 sign-on bonus. The number responding they would "probably" or "definitely" join were correspondingly 1.1 percent higher, 9.7 percent higher, and 18.3 percent higher.[32]

Now that we have explored the process by which applicants identify and choose employment opportunities, we can turn to the employer's perspective, focusing on how recruiting activities are managed. Recruiting involves four choices: (1) communication methods, (2) recruiters, (3) recruitment messages, and (4) required applicant qualifications.[33]

CHOOSING RECRUITING COMMUNICATION METHODS

One of the most visible and important decisions about recruitment activities involves communication methods. Communication informs candidates of available employment opportunities and allows candidates to inform the organization of their availability and qualifications.

Employee Referrals

Present employees commonly refer candidates to the organization. Those identified through referrals seem less likely to leave the organization in the first year.[34] However, this is not true in companies with low morale or substandard working conditions.[35]

Perhaps employees giving the referral also give a realistic preview of jobs and thus ease adjustment once on the job. Or perhaps the "referrer" exerts pressure on the person referred to meet performance standards. Unfortunately, this source of applicants is often questioned by EEO officials on the grounds that it tends to perpetuate the race/sex composition of the present work force. It is also possible that this form of recruiting could have adverse consequences for social relations on the job if informal groups develop that hinder communication and cooperation. If an organization uses this form of recruiting, it must treat all applicants equitably and should provide employees with feedback regarding the status of persons they recommend to the company.

According to an American Management Associations (AMA) survey, 41 percent of respondents use in-house referrals to fill positions, with larger firms slightly more likely (47 percent) to use this method. In-house referrals were particularly likely for new and unfamiliar positions, which are frequently harder to fill. Some firms provide cash awards for referrals, with the highest awards for high-salary positions (up to $5,000), and lower rewards (sometimes less than $250) for lower-salary and entry-level positions.[36]

College Recruiting

Many of you reading this section might be interested in learning how to improve your own chances of getting a job; the appendix to this chapter provides that information. There are also numerous self-help books on the subject, and college placement services frequently provide help to student job applicants. Here, we examine college recruiting from the perspective of the employer.

College recruiting serves as a major source of talent in organizations. One survey of 230 organizations reported that they hired 50 percent of all managers and professionals with less than three years of work experience through college recruiting; thus, they recruited 37,000 individuals through this method.[37] The AMA survey found 17.3 percent of respondents used college recruiting over all positions, but this reflects frequent use for entry-level positions, and less frequent use for upper-level positions.[38]

College recruiting also represents a large investment. One estimate suggests that an average employer spends $329,925 in one year to recruit 161 college graduates, and devotes 16 percent of the personnel function budget and 17 percent of personnel headcount to college recruiting activities.[39] Though this may seem expensive, college recruiting serves many functions. Even when they have few positions to fill, organizations may feel they maintain a better image or remain more familiar to potential future customers and employees by regularly visiting campuses. The recruiting process may also keep an employer informed about labor market conditions, pay rates among competitors, and competitors' job vacancies.

Designing a college recruiting strategy involves choosing schools, attracting students, and planning site visits.[40]

Choosing Schools

Several factors affect which schools' students are targeted for recruiting. Smaller organizations may have sufficient resources to recruit only locally, while large organizations can recruit nationally. Certain professional positions such as engineers and accountants may be recruited most intensively at specialized and prestigious schools, while sales personnel or entry-level managers may be recruited more broadly. Bank of America, for example, limits the number of business schools at which it recruits future financial and trust officers. IBM recruits broadly, but designates key schools for more intensive recruiting efforts.

Fortune 1,000 firms reported recruiting at an average of 47 campuses per year, with schools generally chosen at corporate headquarters. The most important factors used in choosing schools were

Reputation in critical skill areas.

General school reputation.

Performance of previous hires from the school.

Location.

Reputation of faculty in critical skill areas.

Nearly two thirds of respondents reevaluated campus choices annually, with 20 percent of them dropping some schools for various reasons, such as lack of success in finding acceptable applicants, low job acceptance rates, and cutbacks in recruiting operation. About 14 percent of them added schools due to increased recruiting activity and new skill requirements.[41]

Attracting Applicants

Once the colleges are chosen, firms must inform students about themselves and the opportunities they offer. Companies try to attract students to sign up for interviews with their representatives. Students' decisions to interview with various organizations are probably influenced by the nature of the jobs available, the organization's image, and students' familiarity with various organizations. Fortune 1,000 companies relied most heavily on company brochures to communicate with prospective applicants. In addition, they donated money or equipment, held job fairs, advertised with the College Placement Council, sponsored college intern programs, and sent executives to visit campuses. Less frequent methods included advertising in trade journals, ambassador programs, and wine and cheese receptions.[42]

Site Visits

After interviewing applicants at the college, organizations invite promising candidates to their offices to meet, evaluate, and be evaluated by the hiring organization, as well as to receive further job information. Companies in the Rynes-Boudreau survey indicated that candidates visiting plants typically spent 57 percent of their time with potential supervisors, 24 percent with staff, and 19 percent with potential peers. The site visit often provides the final information before the applicant and organization decide whether to accept and offer employment.

Noncollege External Applicant Sources

Although college recruiting is highly visible and important for many management and professional positions, a great deal of recruiting takes place through noncollege sources as well.

Other Educational Institutions

High schools and vocational-technical schools are another major source of job applicants, depending in part on the jobs to be filled. High schools supply clerical and sales personnel as well as trainees and apprentices for many semiskilled jobs. High school recruiting is usually done through contacts with school officials and teachers, bulletin boards, part-time jobs, summer intern programs, or participation in career day programs. Vocational and technical schools supply semiskilled and skilled labor. As the number of these schools has increased, recruiting has become more formalized.

Walk-Ins

Walk-ins are simply people who come to an organization seeking employment, often in response to "help wanted" signs at work sites. This is a very inexpensive source of job applicants, especially for lower-skilled labor. When local unemployment is high, it is likely to yield the most applicants but the quality of applicants may be mixed.

Employment Agencies: Public and Private

Public employment agencies. The United States Employment Service (USES) operates over 2,400 employment agencies in the United States. These public agencies are staffed by state employees, but funds come from the federal government. Companies may use this low-cost option for some positions as frequently as they use private agencies.[43] One fifth of the AMA survey respondents used public agencies, with usage ranging from a high of 32.5 percent for human resource specialists to a low of 9.7 percent for high-level general managers. Smaller firms relied on public services to a much greater extent than large firms. The U.S. Employment Service has typically been limited to placement of clerical, unskilled laborers, production workers, and technicians. They have recently instituted innovations in test use.[44] The effectiveness of public agencies would improve if employers both demanded good service from their local agencies and supported them by giving them job requisitions for a broader range of job vacancies.

Private employment agencies. These agencies usually specialize in specific skills, ranging from accountants to executives. They are often able to meet an organization's needs more quickly than it could through its own recruiting efforts. By prescreening candidates, a good agency may save an employer both time and money for high-level jobs with infrequent vacancies.

Professional associations. Engineers, lawyers, professors, and physicians are usually members of professional associations. These associations provide opportunities to share ideas, make acquaintances, and learn about employment opportunities. Organizations often ask their own employees who are members of professional associations to recruit this way.

One fourth of the AMA survey respondents used executive search firms for higher-salary managerial positions, and private employment agencies for lower-salary and entry-level positions. Larger firms were more likely to use executive search firms for managerial talent. Hiring organizations usually expected to pay about 30 percent of the first-year's salary for candidates acquired through search firms, with private agencies commanding much smaller fees.

Advertising

Advertising is the most commonly used recruiting method. Recruiting ads should influence a variety of market segments.[45] The first and major segment is qualified applicants, that is, applicants who have the abilities and interest required to do the job. A second segment is readers who are already employed. Ads help build an organization's image, which may determine where people seek jobs in the future. The third segment is the organization's own employees, and the fourth segment includes potential customers, investors, government officials, and others. Thus, recruitment advertising can influence both the applicant pool and the organization's image to the entire public.

Advertising methods include print, radio, and TV advertising; participation in job fairs; and summer internships. Job fairs and radio and TV advertising may attract a greater number of unqualified candidates, but may be useful in specialized situations. A recent innovation is recruiting by computer.[46] Engineers, designers, and programmers can use their computer terminals to dial a telephone number which displays pertinent data on jobs available at competing employers on their screens.

The AMA report found that all firms advertised, but they spent their advertising resources differently. Larger firms depended on national advertising and spent more for every category of advertising used. More is spent advertising for high-level jobs. Of all the recruiting methods studied, advertising varied most and had the largest effect on overall costs.[47] Though most employers perceive newspaper advertising to be an effective recruiting method, several studies have found it to be worst in new hire performance and turnover.[48]

Which Recruitment Communication Methods Are Actually Used?

A survey of 450 *Personnel* magazine subscribers in August 1985 asked them to indicate the recruiting methods they used for various positions. The survey revealed that advertising was most frequently used, with preferences for other methods generally favoring lower-cost methods as Exhibit 10–2 shows.

EXHIBIT 10–2
Recruiting Communication Method Preferences

Files of previous job applicants	61.6%
Posted listing for in-house applicants	47.0
An in-house referral system	41.2
A private employment agency	39.5
An executive search firm	31.0
A public/community employment bureau	21.9
A college recruitment program	17.3
An on-site or off-site open house	4.3

Adapted by permission of the publisher from *Hiring Costs and Strategies,* an AMA Report, pp. 13, © 1986 American Management Associations, New York. All rights reserved.

Nonpermanent Employees

Employers frequently experience short-term changes in their need for workers because of seasonal fluctuations, uncertainty about the future business climate, or unusually high levels of vacations and illnesses. Carrying extra workers is costly and sufficient overtime may not be available. One tactic to increase flexibility is to tap sources of nonpermanent employees. Nonpermanent employment options include:

1. *Agency temporaries,* employed by a temporary help agency and supplied to the contracting firm (such as word processors, clerks, and accountants).
2. *Short-term hires,* hired either for a specific time or for a specific project (such as extra staff for the holiday season).
3. *On-call workers,* a pool of workers available on an as-needed basis (such as retirees who work a few days a month).
4. *Contract work,* products or services provided by a separate organization (such as cleaning, security, consulting, and food service).

Although small—representing less than 1 percent of total wage and salary employment, the temporary help industry is expected to continue to grow through the mid-1990s.[49] Between 1970 and 1986, the number of people employed by temporary help firms grew from 184,000 to 760,000.[50] Exhibit 10–3 shows the percentage of organizations using different flexible

EXHIBIT 10–3
Percent of Organizations Using Flexible Staffing Methods

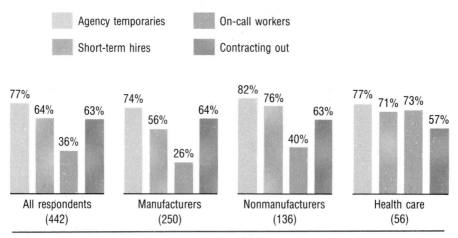

Note: Percentages are based on all usable responses, with the number of respondents shown in parentheses.

Source: The Bureau of National Affairs, Inc., *The Changing Workplace: New Directions in Staffing and Scheduling* (Washington, D.C.: The Bureau of National Affairs, Inc., 1986).

staffing methods. Such staffing methods can be less expensive than maintaining a larger full-time work force and may protect jobs for permanent employees. However, they are not as useful when jobs require extensive training or where continuity is valuable. Also, some feel they "take advantage of those who don't have jobs" by eroding permanent employment opportunities.[51] Temporary or supplemental workers who expect to be considered for permanent positions also cause difficulties.

Employee leasing involves a longer-term arrangement whereby an employer dismisses its existing employees, who are then hired by the leasing company and leased back to the original employer. The leasing firm assumes responsibility for payroll, benefits, taxes, and government-required paperwork, and then charges the subscriber a fee covering these expenses and administration. Some small organizations have used employee leasing as a way to establish a "safe harbor" whereby they pay lucrative pension plans to owners, but avoid obligations to employees by leasing them. Changes in current tax law may severely restrict this.[52]

CHOOSING RECRUITERS TO REPRESENT THE ORGANIZATION

Whose responsibility is it to recruit? Recruiters are one of the main sources of information about organizations and jobs, as well as cues about the likelihood of receiving job offers.[53] Applicants may perceive recruiters as symbols of organizational efficiency or camaraderie. These characteristics, however, cannot be known with certainty prior to accepting a site visit or a job offer.[54]

From an organization's perspective, a successful recruiter is able to accurately represent the organization in a way that kindles an applicant's enthusiasm. That person is also sensitive to the possibility of unconscious race or sex bias in evaluating recruits.[55] Even so, some research has shown that recruiters frequently project poor personalities and inadequate preparation in campus interviews.[56]

College applicants prefer recruiters who are somewhat, but not much, older than themselves;[57] female recruiters may produce lower perceptions of organizational attractiveness or lower job acceptance.[58] Research also suggests that applicants prefer certain personality traits such as warmth, enthusiasm, supportiveness, concern, and empathy in recruiters.[59] These recruiter traits seem to be associated with applicants' expectations of receiving a job offer.[60] However, the effects of such characteristics on job or organizational attractiveness to applicants and their willingness to accept job offers seem to be small. One study observed that after the campus interview the initial effects had disappeared by the time candidates visited the plants.[61] Several studies suggested that recruiters tell far less about job and organizational characteristics than applicants would like to know.[62] This lack of information has been linked to unfavorable applicant perceptions of their interview performance, lower intention to accept job offers, and lower willingness to place follow-up phone calls after interviews.[63]

Considering what employers and applicants seem to want, how do organizations determine who recruits? College recruiting managers rated several selection criteria as important, including strong interpersonal skills, enthusiasm for the company, knowledge of the company and its jobs, and credibility with students and co-workers. Formal credentials, such as recruiter training or seniority, were rated as considerably less important.[64] The AMA survey found that a recruiter's annual salary averaged $33,600, with highest-salaried recruiters used for the highest-paid jobs. Larger firms paid recruiters more but also required recruiters to be responsible for filling a larger number of vacant positions.[65]

CHOOSING RECRUITMENT MESSAGES: FLYPAPER VERSUS REALISM

One recruiting objective is to attract candidates who accept job offers. Eager to attract candidates, recruiters may use the "flypaper" approach—telling candidates only about the most attractive dimensions, getting as many people in the door as possible, and seeing who "sticks."[66] A "marketing" approach involves "determining the needs and wants of a special target group, and then presenting career opportunities that satisfy those concerns."[67] As we shall see, such behavior may reflect the goal of filling vacancies rather than attracting applicants that best match job requirements. When the applicant's inflated expectations are later unmet, dissatisfaction and low commitment may result, and the employee may leave. Chapter Twelve discusses the role of satisfaction and unmet expectations in employees' decisions to quit.

Many have recommended a different approach that gives recruits a more accurate picture of the job and the organization, including the negative aspects. This approach, called a "realistic job preview" (RJP), may reduce separations, absenteeism, or other negative work behaviors caused by unmet expectations.[68] For example, a film for potential operators at Southern Bell made it clear that the work was closely supervised, repetitive, and sometimes required dealing with rude or unpleasant customers.

By far the most frequently debated recruitment decision is whether information should provide a realistic or inflated impression.[69] Research suggests that RJPs increase employee retention.[70] Four explanations for this relationship have been offered.[71] First, accurate recruiting messages may give applicants the opportunity to drop out of the running for a job if they feel their interests and qualifications do not fit. Second, realistic pre-hire information lowers applicants' expectations, decreasing unmet expectations after hiring. Third, the realistic information may help applicants develop better strategies for coping with work problems. Fourth, applicants may simply develop more positive feelings for employers that provide complete and honest information.[72]

The *timing* of recruitment messages may also be important. If job candidates accept their first minimally satisfactory job offer, making offers as early as possible may be fruitful.[73] Long lags between recruitment procedures may cause large numbers of applicants to withdraw from the applicant pool,[74] though evidence is mixed on this point.[75]

CHOOSING REQUIRED APPLICANT QUALIFICATIONS

Should companies try for the cream of the crop by setting stringent qualification requirements and spending more resources recruiting until the best candidates can be located? Or is it better to set somewhat lower qualification standards in the interest of filling vacancies more easily? Generally, increasing required qualifications not only decreases the number of applicants, but also increases their quality.[76] One study suggested that implementing a more rigorous application process decreased the size of the applicant pool but did not change the average level of applicants' qualifications.[77] Another study found that specifying higher GPAs and specific engineering majors in recruitment advertising reduced applications from unqualified applicants.[78]

Responses to the Rynes-Boudreau survey indicated that in two thirds of the companies line managers set applicant's qualifications with guidance from the human resource department. Thirty two percent had raised qualification levels over the previous three years. They cited needs for higher levels of technical expertise, a desire for greater applicant maturity, increased needs for theoretical competencies, desires for greater work experience, and increased supplies of candidates with master's degrees. Eighteen percent lowered qualifications, citing overly high job expectations from master's degree students, higher expenses to attract and retain employees, high separations, and difficulty in attracting those with higher qualifications.[79] Disenchantment with MBAs was also reported in an earlier survey.[80]

One interesting variant on applicant qualifications is the increasing trend to seek retired workers. The number of people age 15 to 20 is dropping, and the number of people over 50 is increasing, so retired people

are being actively recruited for jobs traditionally filled by younger workers. For example, P&C, a grocery chain, recently published help-wanted
ads proclaiming, "Senior Citizens Welcome."[81]

EVALUATING RECRUITING ACTIVITIES

What difference do recruiting programs make? How do they affect organizational goal attainment? Which evaluation methods are actually used by
organizations? Now that we have explored theories about how individuals
make employment choices and examined the four recruitment decisions,
let us discuss recruitment consequences.

Efficiency

Costs

The AMA report estimated recruiting costs in several important areas for
several different jobs. Exhibit 10–4 shows the results for three representative jobs. This report also found that it took between 5½ and 10 weeks
to fill managerial positions.

EXHIBIT 10–4
Recruiting Costs by Category for Three Jobs

	Job Titles (yearly salary)		
Cost category	General Manager ($80,000)	Purchasing Director ($50,000)	Computer Programmer ($28,000)
Employment agency fee	$16,000	$ 8,000	$4,550
Search firm fee	21,200	12,150	6,650
Referral awards	1,250	200	450
Advertising			
Local	1,600	900	800
Regional	1,750	1,350	950
National	1,950	1,950	1,550
Trade	1,600	700	1,000
Travel/lodging			
Candidate	2,450	1,150	650
Recruiter	1,300	400	400
Recruiter/salary (per hire)	532	321	235
Relocation	23,200	7,000	8,900

Adapted by permission of the publisher from *Hiring Costs and Strategies,* an
AMA Report, p. 13, © 1986 American Management Associations, New York. All rights
reserved.

Productivity

In view of these substantial costs, it would seem sensible to evaluate recruitment by the returns to recruitment resource investments. One recent model focused on the productivity-related outcomes of recruitment and on the link between recruitment and selection activities. A computer simulation based on the model suggested that human resource managers can reap very large productivity benefits by integrating recruitment with other staffing activities. Thousands of dollars in increased productivity per year are possible, depending on the number of employees and years affected and on the quality of recruiting activities.[82] Different recruitment communication methods seem to affect posthire performance and turnover; however, those communication methods doing best in research are not the ones generally preferred by recruiting managers. Realistic recruitment can affect posthire retention in some situations, though the process by which this occurs is less clear. Finally, the level of required applicant qualifications and inducements can affect the quantity and quality of applicant pools.

Still, this potential for successful recruitment does not seem to be frequently realized. The AMA report found that employers were "less than optimistic" about their prospects of getting the right person the first time out. Only a third of them rated their chances as "excellent," defined as a 90 percent chance of adequately filling the position with the first selection. About half rated their chances as "good"—a 75 percent to 90 percent chance—and a tenth rated their chances as only "fair"—no better than a 75 percent chance. Moreover, respondents were less optimistic for upper-level positions, where they incur substantially greater recruiting costs. High-turnover firms were less optimistic than low-turnover firms.[83] This may be partly due to poor objective-setting and evaluation that prevents managers from seeing the link between recruitment and organizational goal attainment.

Equity

Recruitment decisions can affect perceptions of organizational fairness among government agencies, society, and employees. Recruitment activities largely determine the minority and female composition of applicant pools. Such pools often serve as the benchmarks indicating the hiring patterns of the organization. More aggressive recruitment of minorities and females is widely recognized and encouraged as a method of achieving affirmative action.[84]

The image projected by recruiting advertisements, external recruiters, and recruitment information provided to job candidates can affect public

EXHIBIT 10–5
Possible Measures to Evaluate Recruiting Activities

Attracting	*Screening*
Number of applicants	Total visits offered
Cost per applicant	$\dfrac{\text{Visits offered}}{\text{Applicants}}$
Time required to locate applicants	
	$\dfrac{\text{Qualified minorities and females}}{\text{Qualified applicants}}$
$\dfrac{\text{Qualified applicants}}{\text{Total applicants}}$	
	$\dfrac{\text{Visits offered to minorities and females}}{\text{Visits offered}}$
$\dfrac{\text{Minority and female applicants}}{\text{Total applicants}}$	
Offers and Hires	*Results*
$\dfrac{\text{Offers extended}}{\text{Visits accepted}}$	Performance rating of hires
	Tenure of hires
$\dfrac{\text{Offers extended}}{\text{Qualified applicants}}$	Costs per level of performance
	Absenteeism per hire
$\dfrac{\text{Offers accepted}}{\text{Offers extended}}$	
Costs per hire	
Time lapsed per hire	
Same ratios for minorities and females	

sentiment toward the organization favorably or unfavorably. Just consider the beneficial effects of recent advertisements by a leading chemical manufacturer emphasizing job opportunities to improve the treatment of illnesses or to help feed starving populations. Recruiter behaviors and statements to campus applicants affect the perceptions not only of those eventually hired, but also of those rejected. Recruitment activities can also affect the attitudes and equity perceptions of employees. Providing realistic job information during the recruitment process may lower unrealistically high expectations, increase perceptions of honesty, and decrease disappointment.

Recruiting Evaluation Practices

Do actual organizations carefully assess human resource conditions and evaluate outcomes in making recruiting decisions? Though studies are limited, research suggests that they do not. Although surveyed Fortune 1,000 organizations consistently indicated that objective factors, such as costs, applicant quality, new-hire performance, and retention rates, are of some importance in evaluating recruiting strategies, organizations rarely collect objective data on such factors. Filling job vacancies and following proper procedures dominate the evaluation information actually collected. Less than 30 percent of companies recorded retention rates, school-related recruiting costs, students' grade-point averages, or on-the-job-performance differences across different recruiting sources or strategies.[85] Exhibit 10–5 shows a variety of possible recruiting outcome measures.

Of course, the key to effectiveness measures is their value to decision making. Human resource managers must ask: "How would this information be used? Which decisions would it affect? Would it change decisions to make them more correct? Is the value of the more correct decisions worth the cost of the information?"

SUMMARY

This chapter examined internal and external recruiting, the human resource activity that identifies and attracts a pool of candidates for employment offers. Recruitment is a two-sided process, with both employers and candidates exchanging information. Recruitment decisions include choosing: (1) sources, (2) communication methods, (3) recruiters, (4) recruitment messages, and (5) required applicant qualifications.

By establishing the characteristics of the candidate pool, recruitment sets the limits on what subsequent selection activities can accomplish. Thus, recruitment is the first step in the external staffing process. How does the organization choose which applicants to offer employment? That is the subject of the next chapter, regarding employee selection.

APPENDIX / How to Get a Job

The recruiting process takes on special significance as you prepare to find a job. This section summarizes the important steps in this process from a student's perspective. Keep in mind, however, that most colleges have placement experts who can provide additional specialized information concerning their particular placement process.

Exhibit 10–6 lists the four major steps in job search.

Assessing Conditions

The first step is to carefully consider the conditions affecting your job search. These three major areas are yourself, the available jobs, and the external environment.

EXHIBIT 10–6
Stages in the Job Search Strategy

			Consider
Assess Conditions	*Prepare Your Case*	*Present Your Case*	*Offers*
You	Résumé	Interviews	Reply
Opportunities	Cover Letter		
Environment	Job Sources	Site Visits	Accept/Reject

Assessing Yourself

The job you get must fit you. So, the first step is to carefully consider what you need and desire from your work. For most students, the job categories they consider are largely determined by their college training. But even within fairly specialized categories such as personnel management, there is a wide variety of job types. A good match depends on how well you know what you want. Consider the following questions:

1. How hard do I like to work?
2. Do I like to be my own boss, or would I rather work for someone else?
3. Do I like to work alone, with a few others, or with large groups?
4. Do I like to work at an even pace or in bursts of energy?
5. Does location matter? Do I want to work near home? In warmer climates? In ski country? Am I willing to be mobile?
6. How much money do I want? Am I willing to work for less money but in a more interesting job?
7. Do I like to work in one place or many; indoors or outdoors?
8. How much variety do I want in work?

It is also important to consider what you want from an employer. The following questions illustrate issues to ponder:

1. Do I have a size preference?
2. Do I have a sector preference (private, not for profit, public sector)?
3. What kinds of industries interest me? (This is usually based on interests in company products or services.)
4. Have I checked to make sure that the sector or product or service has a good future and will lead to growth in opportunity?

Finally, it is important to carefully consider your own employment preparation. What do you have to offer an employer? For which jobs are your particular credentials suited? Specific areas of consideration parallel the parts of a résumé, so this process will help you prepare a résumé. At this stage it is also important to identify the job opportunities for which you are qualified.

Assess Job Opportunities

To assess the numbers and types of jobs available to you, you should use as many sources of jobs and job information as you can. The right sources for you are those best tailored to your particular job desires. Some of the sources you should consider include:

Newspapers and Professional Publications. Read the media ads for the type of job you want, and read the professional publications and newspapers in the area you have selected. *The Wall Street Journal* and the *New York Times* are examples of where to look. Respond to ads that sound interesting.

College Placement Offices. These offices have some job information, and they are the place where recruiters offer job interviews. Get to know the placement office people. Sign up for all interviews that sound interesting that you can work into your schedule.

Professional Associations. Many professional associations provide job placement services. Get your name in the placement application file. Job ads appear in their publications, too.

Private Employment Agencies and Executive Search Firms. Another source of jobs is the private employment agency. Generally, you should visit them and bring a résumé. They charge a fee, often payable by the employer, but sometimes payable by you. The fee can be as much as 15 percent of the first year's salary. Executive search firms tend to recruit middle managers and up (salaries in the $50,000 range).

Some firms also offer résumé preparation, testing services, and career counseling. They often charge up to $1,500, whether you get a job or not. Though this fee is usually paid by employers, ask about any costs that you must bear.

Personal Contacts. One of the best sources of jobs is to contact people working for the organization or who have worked there in the past. Develop your contacts from as many sources as you can: parents, relatives, friends, fraternity brothers, or sorority sisters. Some experts estimate that 80 percent of jobs are never advertised. Contacts get these jobs. You might consider conducting an "exploration interview" with someone who holds or previously held a job similar to one you are considering. Alumni from your school are often quite willing to participate in such interviews. Exhibit 10–7 lists several questions appropriate for such an interview.

Direct Mail. It is useless to mail unsolicited résumés to personnel offices without a personal approach. One way that sometimes works is to write a personalized letter to the personnel manager of the organization

EXHIBIT 10–7
Questions for a Job Exploration Interview

Personal background
1. When you were in college, what did you think your career was going to be? What was your undergraduate major field of study? What was your graduate field of study?

Preparation
1. Which credentials, educational degrees, or licenses are required for entry into this kind of work?
2. What kinds of prior experience are absolutely essential?
3. How did *you* prepare yourself for this work?

Present job
1. Describe what you do during a typical workweek.
2. Which skills or talents are most essential for effectiveness in this job?
3. What are the toughest problems with which you must deal?
4. What do you find most rewarding about the work itself, apart from external motivators, such as salary, fringe benefits, or travel?

Prior experience
1. Which of your past work experiences affect what you do now?
2. Have any of your job changes been for reasons of lifestyle?

Career future
1. If things develop as you'd like, what sort of ideal career do you see for yourself?
2. If the work you do was suddenly eliminated, which different kinds of work could you do?
3. How rapidly is your present career field growing? How would you describe or estimate future prospects?

Lifestyle
1. What obligations does your work place on you, outside the regular workweek? Do you enjoy these obligations?
2. How much flexibility do you have in dress, work hours, vacation schedules, and place of residence?

Advice
1. How well is my background suited to this job?
2. What additional educational preparation do you feel would be best?
3. Which kinds of experiences, paid employment or other, would you recommend?
4. If you were a college graduate and had it to do over again, what would you do differently?

Hiring criteria
1. If you were hiring someone to work with you today, which factors would be most important in your hiring decision and why?

Adapted from *Student Job Search* (Ithaca, N.Y.: Cornell University, Office of Career Services, NYSSILR, 1987).

explaining why you are applying to them. Find out the manager's name. Specify your preferences and advantages in the letter and tell the manager you will call in 10 days to two weeks for a job interview. Sitting back and waiting for an organization to come to you is not fruitful.

Assess Environmental Conditions

As discussed in Chapter Two, factors in the environment affect your job-seeking behavior. If jobs are scarce, you have to start looking earlier and look harder. You may need to compromise your expectations.

Prepare Your Case

With your job preferences established, and a firm grasp on the available job opportunities and what they offer, you are ready to begin preparing your case for employment.

Preparing a Résumé

A résumé is the first, and sometimes the only, glimpse a prospective employer has of a job applicant. It should present a professional, organized, competent image. Thus, it should be uncluttered, balanced, grammatical, accurate, and readable. Exhibit 10–8 contains a sample résumé for a human resource management student. Most résumés include the following information:[86]

1. Identification—name, address, and phone number.
2. Career or job objective.
3. Educational background (including directly related coursework).
4. Work experience (related to the job).
5. Activities or community involvement.
6. Interests and/or hobbies (where relevant to the job).
7. Published papers or articles.
8. A statement indicating references.

Preparing a Cover Letter

When you send your résumé to employers, include a cover letter. Your objective is to write a cover letter that will make the employer want to learn more from your résumé and, perhaps, through a subsequent job interview. Keep the following guidelines in mind:

1. Each letter should be a typed original, not a photocopy.
2. Grammar, spelling, and style should be perfect. Have someone else (preferably someone skilled in editing) proof it for you.
3. Send the letter to a *person*, not an office. If you know someone in the company, send it to them. If not, call and get the name of an executive in the area in which you want to work.
4. If someone encouraged you to apply, ask their permission to use their name in the letter.
5. Keep the letter simple. Express interest in the position. Briefly summarize your credentials, and request an interview.

EXHIBIT 10–8
Sample Résumé for a Human Resource Management Student

PROFESSIONAL OBJECTIVE:
A position in human resource management utilizing my education, training, and experience while gaining exposure to a wide range of personnel functions with particular emphasis on employee relations.

PERSONAL QUALIFICATIONS:
Excellent organizational skills, well-developed leadership abilities.
Strong academic and practical background.
Proven interpersonal skills with groups and individuals.

EDUCATION:
Cornell University, Ithaca, New York
New York State School of Industrial and Labor Relations
Bachelor of Science Degree, June 1, 1988

Bucknell University, Lewisburg, Pennsylvania
School of Arts and Sciences, September 1984–May 1985

COURSE CONCENTRATIONS:
Organizational behavior and development   Compensation administration
Labor history, law, management, and   Employee staffing and supervision
economics   Human resource economics
Psychology   Statistics
                                                                 Collective bargaining

EMPLOYMENT EXPERIENCE:
Resident Adviser (August 1987–June 1988)
Department of Residence Life, Cornell University
Responsible for directly assisting 90 college freshmen adjust to university life by coordinating educational and social programming and providing personal and academic counseling.

Labor Relations Intern (May 1987–August 1987)
Central New York Bottle Company, a Division of Philip Morris, Inc., Auburn, New York.
Administered corporate quality awareness program including a 30-day participation booster campaign, researched and compiled three-year analysis of grievances, worked with employee involvement implementation, grievance resolutions, workers' compensation, disability claims, and nonexempt attendance program maintenance.

Research Intern (January 1987)
Buffalo-Erie County Labor Management Council, Suite 407, Convention Tower, Buffalo, New York.
Developed and administered several research techniques and compiled the information into a case study of labor-management participation in an abrasives company.

Marketing/Public Relations Supervisor (May 1986–August 1986)
Darien Lake Amusement Park, Corfu, New York.
Composed and supervised the administration of consumer surveys.

Proposals Intern (January 1985)
GTE Sylvania, Mountain View, California.
Organized and revamped the entire proposals department filing system.

Restaurant Supervisor (Summers 1982–1985)
Service Systems/Darien Lake, Corfu, New York.
Sole supervisor of the largest fast-food stand in an amusement park.

ACTIVITIES:
Resident adviser
Cornell dining employee
Secretary–Treasurer, college student government
American Society of Personnel Administrators
N.Y.S. School of Industrial and Labor Relations Ambassador
N.Y.S. School of Industrial and Labor Relations Student Adviser
Volunteer at area nursing home
Traveling, skiing, socializing

REFERENCES:
Available on request

Source: *Student Job Search* (Ithaca, N.Y.: Cornell University, Office of Career Services, NYSSILR, 1986).

EXHIBIT 10–9
Example Cover Letter

725 State Street
Ithaca, NY 14850
February 8, 1988

Mr. Samuel Staples
Personnel Manager, Federal Mogul Corporation
198 Hollywood Blvd.
Los Angeles, CA 95678

Dear Mr. Staples:

I am currently a senior in the School of Industrial and Labor Relations at Cornell University and am seeking employment in the field of human resources. The Office of Career Services has informed me that your organization will be recruiting at our school this semester. I would very much like to meet with you to discuss employment opportunities at Federal Mogul. Because of the limited interviews and bidding system that further restricts the possibility of being successful in obtaining an interview, I would appreciate being included on your invitation list.

My main interest in human resources is in the areas of training and organizational development. These areas will provide me the opportunity to make a contribution in the development of an organization's human resources at both the individual and the unit levels, which I feel greatly influences operations. I plan to begin my career as a generalist or in the area of compensation to establish a solid grounding in the organization in which I am employed. Either position will provide an overall picture of an organization's human resource function as it relates to other operating functions. After reviewing the available information on the position at Federal Mogul, I believe it would provide this opportunity.

Additionally, my experience, as can be seen by my résumé, is very compatible with much of the industry in which your organization operates. Although limited, my knowledge of your firm will allow me to become a contributing member more rapidly. This knowledge has been acquired through several temporary part-time positions with Federal Mogul.

Once again, I am very interested in the opportunities at Federal Mogul. Thank you very much for your consideration. I look forward to hearing from you.

Cordially,

Source: *Student Job Search* (Ithaca, N.Y.: Cornell University, Office of Career Services, NYSSILR, 1987).

Exhibit 10–9 contains a sample cover letter for a student in human resource management.

Interview Preparation

Initial employment interviews are usually a half hour long, so it is very important that you be well prepared to present your case. Several steps will help you prepare:[87]

1. *Research the employer.* This means more than reading the promotional brochure. You can check through the *New York Times Index* or recent issues of such business publications as *The Wall Street Journal* or *Business Week* for developments related to the area in which you want to work. Placement offices often collect annual reports and employment manuals for companies who recruit on campus regularly.
2. *Know your résumé and anticipate questions.* Have a friend or instructor read your résumé and identify obvious questions. Be prepared to emphasize your strengths and to discuss areas of weakness in a way that best represents your qualifications.
3. *Have questions in mind for the interviewer,* such as: "Please describe the job duties." "Why is the position open?" "Where does it fit in the organization's hierarchy?" "What have been the best results produced by others in this job?" "What do you like most about your job and this company?"
4. *Dress neatly* in clothes similar to those expected on the job.

Present Your Case

The moment of truth arrives. You are about to enter the office and begin the interview. If you have prepared carefully, you will be ready to get the most out of the interview and provide the interviewer with information that best represents your qualifications.

Interview

Though no two interviews are the same, campus interviews typically follow this sequence:

1. *Introduction,* initiated by the interviewer, involves personal introductions, some small talk to set the applicant at ease, and perhaps a plan for the interview.
2. *Interrogation,* also initiated by the interviewer, involves questions designed to probe the candidate's strengths and weaknesses and assess problem-solving abilities.

3. *Selling*, initiated by the applicant, provides a chance to describe qualifications in more detail, ask questions about the job and company, and demonstrate interest and knowledge about the company.
4. *Conclusion*, initiated by the recruiter, involves a description of the decision-making process, dates by which the candidate can expect to hear from the company (usually two to four weeks), and the end of the interview.

Interview Follow-Up

Be sure to keep a record of your contacts. Immediately after leaving the interview make the following notations:

- The name of the interviewer.
- The type of opportunity for which you were considered.
- Location of work.
- Your reaction and possible interest.
- *Your next action.*

Answers to Invitations for Visits

If you receive an invitation for a plant visit, acknowledge it in one of three ways:

1. Accept and set the date when you will be there.
2. Indicate your desire to accept at a later date if you need more time to consider.
3. Decline for whatever honest reason you have.

Follow-Up to Site Visit

If you make a site visit, as soon as you return send a letter of thanks to the individual who issued the invitation, as well as to any others you believe should receive a special note of appreciation.

Considering Offers

With hard work and luck, your efforts will pay off with one or several employment offers. Though you may think this is the end of the process, it still requires careful handling.

Replying to an Offer

Offers of employment may be made verbally, by telegram, or by letter, the last two being the most usual means.

Again, there are innumerable ways of handling an offer. Most companies do not expect an immediate acceptance or rejection, but they do expect an acknowledgment. *Therefore, be sure to reply within three days* after receiving the offer, thanking them and stating a time when you will send definite word, provided they have not already specified a deadline date. If they have, send a letter of acknowledgment and indicate your final answer will be forthcoming by the specific date.

Delaying a Final Answer
The occasion might arise when you need an extension of time. If so, send another letter and state quite frankly your reasons and request their indulgence. Remember always to keep in mind the employer's position as well as your own.

Accepting an Offer
It is probably unnecessary to go into detail on how to accept an offer beyond the fact that an enthusiastic note of appreciation should be sent, together with an indication of when you will report for work. This latter point, of course, is developed by mutual agreement.

Rejecting an Offer
Letters of rejection should be sent just as soon as you realize you are definitely not interested in accepting. It is not necessary to state your exact reasons for turning down an offer, or to say where you expect to go, but it is courteous to express your sincere thanks for having been favorably considered. It is helpful for the organization to know what your true feelings are regarding them, such as preference for a different location, another product, or different initial training.

DISCUSSION AND REVIEW QUESTIONS

1. How are recruiting and job search related?
2. How do external conditions affect recruiting?
3. What is a realistic job preview? When is it likely to be a good idea?
4. Compare the advantages and disadvantages of various recruiting methods, such as advertising, employment agencies, personal referrals, and others.
5. How do employers recruit college students for jobs? Describe effective and ineffective recruiters.
6. Discuss the relationship between organizational and occupational choice decisions. How are they similar, and different?
7. Outline an approach to specifying the job characteristics you want prior to your job search.

NOTES AND REFERENCES

1. J. Ullman and T. G. Gutteridge, "Job Search in the Labor Market for College Graduates: A Case Study of MBA's," *Academy of Management Journal* 17, no. 2 (1974), pp. 381–86.

2. Sara Rynes, Donald Schwab, and Herbert G. Heneman III, "The Role of Pay and Market Pay Variability in Job Application Decisions," *Organizational Behavior and Human Performance* 31, no. 2 (1983), pp. 353–64.

3. Kenneth G. Wheeler, "Perceptions of Labor Market Variables by College Students in Business, Education and Psychology," *Journal of Vocational Behavior* 22, no. 1 (1983), pp. 1–11.

4. R. E. Azevedo, "Scientists, Engineers, and the Job Search Process," *California Management Review* 17, no. 1 (1974), pp. 40–49.

5. L. C. Thurow, *Generating Inequality: Mechanisms of Distribution in the United States Economy* (New York: Basic Books, 1975).

6. Sara L. Rynes, "Compensation Strategy in Recruiting," *Topics In Total Compensation* 1, no. 1 (September 1987).

7. Richard R. Reilly and Georgia T. Chao, "Validity and Fairness of Some Alternative Employee Selection Procedures," *Personnel Psychology* 35, no. 1 (1982), pp. 1–62; R. D. Arvey, *Fairness in Selecting Employees* (Reading, Mass.: Addison–Wesley Publishing, 1979).

8. Judy D. Olian and Sara L. Rynes, "Organizational Staffing: Integrating Practice with Strategy," *Industrial Relations*, Spring 1984, pp. 170–83; Raymond E. Miles and Charles C. Snow, *Organization Strategy, Structure, and Process* (New York: McGraw-Hill, 1978); C. Snow and R. E. Miles, "Organizational Strategy, Design and Human Resources Management," (paper presented at 43rd Meeting of Academy of Management, Dallas, Texas, August 1983).

9. American Management Associations, *Hiring Costs and Strategies: The AMA Report* (New York: American Management Associations, 1986).

10. Herbert E. Gerson and Louis P. Britt III, "Hiring—the Dangers of Promising Too Much," *Personnel Administrator*, March 1984, pp. 5–8, 112.

11. Sara L. Rynes, Herbert G. Heneman III, and Donald P. Schwab, "Individual Reactions to Organizational Recruiting: A Review," *Personnel Psychology*, Autumn 1980, pp. 529–42; John P. Wanous, Thomas L. Keon, and Janina Latack, "Expectancy Theory and Occupational/Organizational Choices: A Review and Test," *Organizational Behavior and Human Performances* 32, no. 1 (1983), pp. 66–86.

12. J. L. Farr, B. S. O'Leary, and C. J. Bartlett, "Effect of Work Sample Test upon Self-Selection and Turnover of Job Applicants," *Journal of Applied Psychology* 58, no. 2 (1973), pp. 283–85; D. P. Schwab, "Organizational Recruiting and the Decision to Participate, in *Personnel Management: New Perspectives*, ed. K. Rowland and G. Ferris (Boston: Allyn & Bacon, 1982).

13. L. W. Porter, E. E. Lawler III, and J. R. Hackman, *Behavior in Organizations* (New York: McGraw-Hill, 1975).

14. D. W. Stevens, "A Reexamination of What Is Known about Job-Seeking Behavior in the United States" (paper presented to the Conference on Labor Market Intermediaries, sponsored by The National Commission for Manpower Policy, November 16–17, 1977).

15. C. Rosenfeld, "Job-Seeking Methods Used by American Workers," *Monthly Labor Review*, August 1975, pp. 39–42.
16. L. D. Dyer, "Job Search Success of Middle-Aged Managers and Engineers," *Industrial and Labor Relations Review*, January 1973, pp. 969–79; J. Barron and D. W. Gilley, "The Effect of Unemployment Insurance on the Search Process," *Industrial and Labor Relations Review*, March 1979, pp. 363–66.
17. Martin Feldstein, "The Economics of the New Unemployment," *Public Interest*, Fall 1973, pp. 3–42; Ronald G. Ehrenberg and Ronald L. Oaxaca, "Unemployment Insurance, Duration of Unemployment and Subsequent Wage Gain," *American Economic Review*, December 1976, pp. 754–66; Finis Welch, "What Have We Learned from Empirical Studies of Unemployment Insurance," *Industrial and Labor Relations Review*, July 1977, pp. 451–61.
18. Thomas Gutteridge and Joseph Ullman, "On the Return to Job Search," in *Proceedings of Academy of Management*, Boston, August 1973, pp. 366–72; and J. C. Ullman and T. G. Gutteridge, "The Job Search," *Journal of College Placement* 33, no. 2 (1973), pp. 67–72.
19. William Glueck, "Decision Making: Organization Choice," *Personnel Psychology*, Spring 1974, pp. 66–93; "How Recruiters Influence Job Choices on Campus," *Personnel*, March–April 1971, pp. 46–52.
20. *Empirical Analysis of the Search Behavior of Low-Income Workers* (Menlo Park, Calif.: Stanford Research Institute, 1975); G. L. Reid, "Job Search and the Effectiveness of Job-Finding Methods," *Industrial and Labor Relations Review*, June 1972, pp. 479–95.
21. S. L. Rynes and J. Lawler, "A Policy-Capturing Investigation of the Role of Expectancies in Decisions to Pursue Job Alternatives," *Journal of Applied Psychology* 68, no. 4 (1983), pp. 620–31; J. H. Greenhaus, C. Seidel, and M. Marinis, "The Impact of Expectations and Values on Job Attitudes," *Organizational Behavior and Human Performance* 23, no. 1 (1983), pp. 3–17.
22. J. H. Greenhaus and O. C. Brenner, "How Do Job Candidates Size Up Prospective Employers?" *Personnel Administrator*, March 1982, pp. 21–25; L. W. Porter and R. M. Steers, "Organizational, Work, and Personal Factors in Employee Turnover and Absenteeism," *Psychological Bulletin* 80, no. 3 (1973), pp. 151–76; S. Rottenberg, "On Choice in the Labor Markets," *Industrial and Labor Relations Review* 9, no. 2 (1965).
23. J. F. Dillard, "An Update on the Applicability of an Occupational Goal-Expectancy Model in Professional Accounting Organizations," *Decision Sciences* 12, no. 1 (1981), pp. 32–38; N. Schmitt and L. Son, "An Evaluation of Valence Models of Motivation to Pursue Various Post High School Alternatives," *Organizational Behavior and Human Performance* 27, no. 2 (1981), pp. 135–50; V. L. Holmstrom and L. R. Beach, "Subjective Expected Utility and Career Preferences," *Organizational Behavior and Human Performance* 10, no. 3 (1973), pp. 201–7; T. R. Mitchell, "Expectancy Models of Job Satisfaction, Occupational Preference and Effort: A Theoretical, Methodological, and Empirical Appraisal," *Psychological Bulletin* 81, no. 4 (1974), pp. 1053–77; K. G. Wheeler and T. M. Mahoney, "The Expectancy Model in the Analysis of Occupational Preference and Occupa-

tional Choice," *Journal of Vocational Behavior* 19, no. 2 (1981), pp. 113–22.

24. Michael Ornstein, *Entry into the American Labor Force* (New York: Academic Press, 1976).

25. D. F. Parker and L. Dyer, "Expectancy Theory as a Within-Person Behavioral Choice Model: An Empirical Test of Some Conceptual and Methodological Refinements," *Organizational Behavior and Human Performance* 17, no. 1 (1976), pp. 97–117; A. Pecotich and G. A. Churchill, Jr., "An Examination of the Anticipated-Satisfaction Importance Valence Controversy," *Organizational Behavior and Human Performance* 27, no. 2 (1981), pp. 213–26; J. H. Greenhaus, T. Sugalski, and G. Crispin, "Relationships between Perceptions of Organizational Size and the Organizational Choice Process," *Journal of Vocational Behavior* 13, no. 1 (1978), pp. 113–25; E. E. Lawler III, W. J. Kuleck, Jr., J. G. Rhode, and J. E. Sorenson, "Job Choice and Post-Decision Dissonance," *Organizational Behavior and Human Performance* 13, no. 1 (1975), pp. 133–45.

26. George T. Milkovich and Jerry Newman, *Compensation* (Plano, Tex.: Business Publications, 1984).

27. Rynes and Lawler, "Policy-Capturing Investigation"; Wanous, Keon, and Latack, "Expectancy Theory."

28. C. E. Jurgensen, "Job Preferences (What Makes a Job Good or Bad?)," *Journal of Applied Psychology*, May 1978, pp. 267–76.

29. R. L. Opsahl and M. D. Dunnette, "The Role of Financial Compensation in Industrial Motivation," *Psychological Bulletin*, October 1966, pp. 94–118.

30. Sara L. Rynes, "Compensation Strategy in Recruiting."

31. Sara L. Rynes, "Recruitment, Organizational Entry, and Early Work Adjustment," in *Handbook of Industrial and Organizational Psychology*, 2nd ed., ed. Marvin D. Dunnette (Chicago: Rand McNally, in press).

32. David B. Balkin and S. Groeneman, "The Effect of Incentive Compensation on Recruitment: The Case of the Military," *Personnel Administrator*, January 1985, pp. 29–34.

33. John W. Boudreau and Sara L. Rynes, "Role of Recruitment in Staffing Utility Analysis," *Journal of Applied Psychology* 70, no. 2 (1986), pp. 354–66; Sara L. Rynes and John W. Boudreau, "College Recruiting in Large Organizations: Practice, Evaluation and Research Implications," *Personnel Psychology* 39 (1986), pp. 729–57.

34. J. C. Ullman, "Employee Referrals: Prime Tool for Recruiting Workers," *Personnel* 43, no. 1 (1966), pp. 30–35; D. P. Schwab, "Recruiting and Organizational Participation," in *Personnel Management*, ed. K. Rowland and G. Ferris (Boston: Allyn & Bacon, 1982); P. J. Decker and E. T. Cornelius, "A Note on Recruiting Sources and Job Survival Rates," *Journal of Applied Psychology* 64, no. 3 (1979), pp. 463–64; M. J. Gannon, "Source of Referral and Employee Turnover," *Journal of Applied Psychology* 55, no. 1 (1971), pp. 226–28.

35. R. E. Hill, "New Look at Employee Referrals as a Recruitment Channel," *Personnel Journal* 49, no. 1 (1970), pp. 144–48; D. F. Caldwell and W. A. Spivey, "The Relationship between Recruiting Source and Employee Success: An Analysis by Race," *Personnel Psychology* 36 (1983), pp. 67–72.

36. American Management Associations, "Hiring Costs and Strategies."

37. V. R. Lindquist and F. S. Endicott, *Trends in the Employment of College and University Graduates in Business and Industry* (Evanston, Ill.: Northwestern University, 1984); V. R. Lindquist and F. S. Endicott, *Trends in the Employment of College and University Graduates in Business and Industry* (Evanston, Ill.: Northwestern University, 1986).

38. American Management Associations, "Hiring Costs and Strategies."

39. Sara L. Rynes and John W. Boudreau, "College Recruiting in Large Organizations: Practice, Evaluation, and Research Implications," *Personnel Psychology* 39 (1986), pp. 729–57.

40. Ibid.

41. Rynes and Boudreau, "College Recruiting in Large Organizations."

42. Ibid.

43. American Management Associations, "Hiring Costs and Strategies."

44. Robert M. Madigan, K. Dow Scott, Diana L. Deadrick, and Jill A. Stoddard, "Employment Testing: The U.S. Job Service Is Spearheading a Revolution," *Personnel Administrator*, September 1986, pp. 62–69.

45. V. M. Evans, "Recruitment Advertising in the '80s," *Personnel Administrator*, March 1978, pp. 21–25, 30.

46. William M. Bulkeley, "Some Firms Are Recruiting by Computer," *The Wall Street Journal*, February 11, 1984, pp. 35, 40.

47. American Management Associations, "Hiring Costs and Strategies."

48. James A. Breaugh, "Relationships between Recruiting Sources and Employee Performance, Absenteeism, and Work Attitudes," *Academy of Management Journal* 24 (1981), pp. 142–47; James A. Breaugh and R. B. Mann, "Recruiting Source Effects: A Test of Two Alternative Explanations," *Journal of Occupational Psychology* 57 (1984), pp. 261–67; Martin J. Gannon, "Sources of Referral and Employee Turnover," *Journal of Applied Psychology* 55 (1971), pp. 226–28; P. J. Decker and Edwin T. Cornelius III, "A Note on Recruiting Sources and Job Survival Rates," *Journal of Applied Psychology* 64 (1979), pp. 463–64; Donald P. Schwab, "Recruiting and Organizational Participation," in *Personnel Management*, ed. K. M. Rowland and G. Ferris (Boston: Allyn & Bacon, 1982).

49. Max L. Carey and Kim L. Hazelbaker, "Employment Growth in the Temporary Help Industry," *Monthly Labor Review* 109, no. 4 (April 1986), pp. 37–44.

50. Bureau of National Affairs, *The Changing Workplace: New Directions in Staffing and Scheduling* (Washington, D.C.: Bureau of National Affairs, 1986).

51. Ibid.

52. Ibid.

53. Sara L. Rynes and Howard E. Miller, "Recruiter and Job Influences on Candidates for Employment," *Journal of Applied Psychology* 68 (1983), pp. 147–54.

54. L. V. Gerstner, "College Recruiting: Why the Good Ones Get Away," *Management Review* 55 (1966), pp. 226–28; and Rynes, Heneman and Schwab, "Individual Reactions to Organizational Recruiting."

55. Kenneth N. Wexley and W. F. Nemeroff, "Effects of Racial Prejudice, Race of Applicant, and Biographical Similarity on Interviewer Evaluations of Job Applicants," *Journal of Social and Behavioral Sciences* 20, no. 1 (1974), pp. 66–78.

56. C. W. Downs, "Perceptions of the Selection Interview," *Personnel Administration*, May–June 1969, pp. 8–23; and R. L. Hilgert and L. S. Eason, "How Students Weigh Recruiters," *Journal of College Placement* 28 (1968), pp. 99–102.

57. Hilgert and Eason, "How Students Weigh Recruiters"; B. K. Marks, "Successful Campus Recruiting," *Personnel Journal* 46 (1967), pp. 79–84; D. P. Rogers and M. Z. Sincoff, "Favorable Impression Characteristics of the Recruitment Interviewer," *Personnel Psychology* 31 (1978), pp. 495–504.

58. M. Susan Taylor and T. Bergmann, *The Relationship of Organizational Recruitment Practices to Applicants' Reactions: A Field Investigation* (Working paper, University of Maryland, 1985).

59. C. P. Alderfer and C. G. McCord, "Personal and Situational Factors in the Recruitment Interview," *Journal of Applied Psychology* 54 (1970), pp. 377–85; C. W. Downs, "Perceptions of the Selection Interview," *Personnel Administration* 32 (1969), pp. 8–23; T. J. Harn and George C. Thornton III, "Recruiter Counselling Behaviors and Applicant Impressions," *Journal of Occupational Psychology* 58 (1985), pp. 57–65; Hilgert and Eason, "How Students Weigh Recruiters"; N. Schmitt and B. Coyle, "Applicant Decisions in the Employment Interview," *Journal of Applied Psychology* 61 (1976), pp. 184–92; Taylor and Bergmann, *The Relationship of Organizational Recruitment Practices.*

60. Sara L. Rynes and Howard E. Miller, "Recruiter and Job Influences on Candidates for Employment," *Journal of Applied Psychology* 68 (1983), pp. 147–54; Schmitt and Coyle, "Applicant Decisions in the Employment Interview."

61. Taylor and Bergmann, *The Relationship of Organizational Recruitment Practices.*

62. C. W. Downs, "Perceptions of the Selection Interview"; P. Herriott and C. Rothwell, "Organizational Choice and Decision Theory: Effects of Employers' Literature and Selection Interview," *Journal of Occupational Psychology* 54 (1981), pp. 17–31; and M. Susan Taylor and Janet A. Sniezek, "The College Recruitment Interview: Topical Content and Applicant Reactions," *Journal of Occupational Psychology* 57 (1984), pp. 157–68.

63. Rynes and Miller, "Recruiter and Job Influences on Candidates for Employment"; Schmitt and Coyle, "Applicant Decisions in the Employment Interview."

64. Rynes and Boudreau, "College Recruiting in Large Organizations."

65. American Management Associations, "Hiring Costs and Strategies."

66. John P. Wanous, *Organizational Entry: Recruitment, Selection, and Socialization of Newcomers* (Reading, Mass.: Addison-Wesley Publishing, 1980).

67. K. Krett and J. F. Stright, "Using Market Research as a Recruitment Strategy," *Personnel*, November 1985, pp. 32–36; R. Stoops, "Reader Survey Supports Market Approach to Recruitment," *Personnel Journal* 63 (1984), pp. 22–24; R. Stoops, "Nursing Poor Recruitment with a Marketing Approach," *Personnel Journal* 64 (1985), pp. 92–93.

68. J. P. Wanous, "Effects of a Realistic Job Preview on Job Acceptance, Job Attitudes, and Job Survival," *Journal of Applied Psychology* 58, no. 3 (1973), pp. 327–32; D. R. Ilgen and W. Seely, "Realistic Expectations as an Aid in Reducing Voluntary Resignations," *Journal of Applied Psychology*

59, no. 4 (1974), pp. 452–55; Roger A. Dean and J. P. Wanous, "Reality Shock: When a New Employee's Expectations Don't Match Reality" (paper presented at the Academy of Management National Meeting, August 15, 1982, New York City).

69. Rynes, "Recruitment, Organizational Entry, and Early Work Adjustment."
70. R. R. Reilly, B. Brown, M. Blood, and C. Malatesta, "The Effects of Realistic Previews: A Study and Discussion of the Literature," *Personnel Psychology* 34 (1981), pp. 823–34; Glen M. McEvoy and Wayne F. Cascio, "Strategies for Reducing Employee Turnover: A Meta-Analysis," *Journal of Applied Psychology* 70 (1985), pp. 342–53; S. L. Premack and John P. Wanous, "A Meta-Analysis of Realistic Job Preview Experiments," *Journal of Applied Psychology* 70 (1985), pp. 706–19.
71. Reilly, Brown, Blood, and Malatesta, *The Effects of Realistic Previews.*"
72. Rynes, "Recruitment, Organizational Entry, and Early Work Adjustment."
73. L. G. Reynolds, *The Structure of Labor Markets* (New York: Harper & Row, 1951); H. L. Sheppard and A. H. Belitsky, *The Job Hunt* (Baltimore: The Johns Hopkins University Press, 1966).
74. Richard Arvey, J. Gordon, D. Massengill, and S. Mussio, "Differential Dropout Rates of Minority and Majority Job Candidates Due to 'Time Lags' between Selection Procedures," *Personnel Psychology* 38 (1975), pp. 175–80.
75. Taylor and Bergmann, *The Relationship of Organizational Recruitment Practices.*
76. L. V. Gerstner, "College Recruiting: Why the Good Ones Get Away," *Management Review* 55 (1966), pp. 4–12; F. T. Malm, "Hiring Procedures and Selection Standards in the San Francisco Bay Area," *Industrial and Labor Relations Review* 8 (1955), pp. 231–52; Judy D. Olian and Sara L. Rynes, "Organizational Staffing: Integrating Practice with Strategy," *Industrial Relations* 23 (1984), pp. 170–83.
77. W. F. Gerson, "The Effects of a Demanding Application Process on the Applicant Pool for Teaching Positions." (Ph.D. Dissertation, University of Pennsylvania, 1975). *Dissertation Abstracts International* 36, 7773A.
78. N. A. Mason and J. A. Belt, "Effectiveness of Specificity in Recruitment Advertising" (Presented at 45th annual meeting of the Academy of Management, San Diego, August 1985).
79. Rynes and Boudreau, "College Recruiting in Large Organizations."
80. Lindquist and Endicott, *Trends in the Employment of College and University Graduates in Business and Industry.*
81. "Recruiting the Experience of Ages," *Syracuse Herald–American*, April 5, 1987, page C-5.
82. Boudreau and Rynes, "Role of Recruitment in Staffing Utility Analysis."
83. American Management Associations, "Hiring Costs and Strategies."
84. James Ledvinka, *Federal Regulation of Personnel and Human Resource Management* (Boston: Kent Publishing, 1982).
85. Rynes and Boudreau, "College Recruiting in Large Organizations."
86. NYSSILR, Office of Career Services, *Student Job Search* (Ithaca, N.Y.: Cornell University, 1987).
87. Ibid.

chapter eleven

EMPLOYEE SELECTION

CHAPTER OUTLINE

> Using tests to help make personnel decisions is centuries old. . . . But the modern era of personnel selection had its beginning on 6 April, 1917, when the United States declared war on Germany. That evening, after a hurried meeting, Yerkes, Gingham, and Dodge drafted a letter urging all . . . psychologists to give whatever assistance they could to the war effort. . . . Within less than two years, 1,726,966 men were tested.[1]

John Welsh, chairman of General Electric Company, is reported to personally pore over thick volumes that contain detailed dossiers on prospects for top management jobs. He says that "selecting the right people is my most important job."[2] When Apple Computers, Inc. hired a high-level executive with extensive marketing experience at Pepsico, its stock prices advanced and market analysts lauded the decision.[3] Every spring companies cull through graduating students to select the most promising. These decisions are critical to the success of any organization.

Choosing which employees to hire is necessary in all organizations, and the quality of choices often affects organizations for decades. One study estimated that using an ability test instead of an interview to select computer programmers could produce a return over 100 times as high as the increased testing cost, a total return of over $54 million.[4]

Definition

External selection uses information about externally recruited applicants to choose which of them will receive employment offers. Applicant *screening* is a form of selection that uses information to identify obviously unqualified applicants before gathering additional selection information.

Ultimately, a selection decision is made about every applicant, because every applicant either receives an employment offer or not. Human resource managers determine which information is used to make these decisions. Choosing external selection activities involves deciding:

1. Which evidence to gather to justify selection techniques.
2. How to use the applicant information from the selection techniques.
3. Which selection techniques can supply job applicant information.

A DIAGNOSTIC APPROACH TO EXTERNAL SELECTION

Similar to recruiting, external selection is highly visible. It affects external, organizational, and employee considerations.

Assessing External Conditions

Because external selection draws on applicants from outside the organization and determines individual opportunities in important ways, conditions outside the organization affect it.

Labor Markets

Labor markets affect the size and quality of the applicant pool which, in turn, affects the choice of selection methods.[5] In periods of high unemployment, an organization may face a very large applicant pool containing candidates with widely varying qualifications. For example, vacancies for auto workers in the Midwest might attract several—or even several hundred—applicants for each job opening. Many have long work experience and high job qualifications; others may be just finishing high school or vocational school. During periods of low unemployment, smaller applicant pools emerge because many of the top candidates may have already found employment elsewhere.[6] One example is the shortage of computer programmers faced by high-technology manufacturing organizations. This may cause some organizations to hire virtually any applicant rather than leave vacancies unfilled. Clearly, the quality of selection decisions is much more important for the automobile manufacturer, where the organization can afford to be choosy and where the differences among applicants are large.

Governments

Equal opportunity legislation remains the most significant influence on the design of selection systems.[7] When a selection procedure has an adverse impact (e.g., a smaller proportion of female or minority applicants meet hiring standards than white male applicants), the personnel professional needs to demonstrate that the procedure is job-related. The Uniform Guidelines on Employee Selection Procedures, issued by the EEOC and OFCCP, show accepted methods for demonstrating that hiring decisions are job-related.[8] Failure to comply with these methods can have considerable financial consequences for employers. Burlington Northern, Inc. as an example, agreed to a $40 million settlement, due in large part to its inability to show that its selection standards for locomotive engineer training programs were job-related.[9] The threat of expenses like these, more than anything else, has caused employers to try to ensure that selection procedures do not cause adverse impact. Or, if they do, that they can be defended. Recent Supreme Court decisions have also upheld the right to work of people with physical or mental impairments or contagious diseases.[10]

Much has been said about how stringent, complex, and unreasonable the guidelines are. Proponents argue that "while there is some truth in the complaints, the guidelines call for little more than adequate development of selection procedures—the same sort of procedures that have been called for by industrial psychologists for decades."[11] Others contend that the "uniform guidelines are based on 'false theories' about selection research and they are unnecessary and inflationary regulations."[12]

Recent legislation reforming immigration laws have created new citizenship verification requirements for human resource managers, and new dangers of discrimination against protected groups. The Immigration Reform and Control Act of 1986 now prohibits employers from knowingly hiring, recruiting, or referring for work certain aliens. These people are not authorized to work in the United States either because they have entered the country illegally or because their immigration status does not permit employment.[13] Exhibit 11–1 summarizes the requirements and penalties under the act. Obviously, the U.S. government hopes this law will substantially change the selection practices of many employers who rely on alien workers. It remains to be seen whether such changes will occur.

Organizational Conditions

The strategies and objectives of an organization influence the selection process. For example, organization units with emerging or new products may require experienced people who possess marketing and technical skills. The focus is on product design and establishing sales in a new market. Other units, with more established product lines, face more mature markets and may try to select people with finance and manufacturing skills to control product quality and costs.[14]

It is questionable whether the research has advanced enough to prescribe the employee qualities that best match different strategies.[15] Some even question the soundness of matching strategies with different selection systems. For example, some executives seem to believe that a well-trained manager is a jack-of-all-trades who can run any unit, no matter its strategy or condition.

Dominant coalitions within an organization influence the selection process.[16] Powerful managers try to influence the selection process to

EXHIBIT 11–1
Synopsis of the Immigration Reform and Control Act of 1986

Purpose:
To curtail the flood of immigration by undocumented aliens into the United States by making the hiring of such aliens illegal for U.S. employers.

Employment eligibility verification requirements:
The law prohibits employers from knowingly hiring, recruiting, or referring for work aliens who are not authorized to work in the United States. The employer must ask for and examine evidence of prospective employees' identities and employment eligibility indicated by the following documents:

1. A United States passport.
2. A certificate of United States citizenship.
3. A certificate of naturalization.
4. An unexpired foreign passport, if the passport has an appropriate unexpired endorsement of the Attorney General authorizing the individual's employment in the United States.
5. A resident alien card or other alien registration card that contains a photograph or other personal identifying information and that is evidence of authorization for employment in the United States.

If none of the above are available, then the employer must ask for two documents, providing separate evidence of employment eligibility and identity.

Penalties for violations:
1. $250 to $2,000 for a first offense, for each alien involved.
2. $2,000 to $5,000 for a second offense, for each alien.
3. $3,000 to $10,000 for third offense, for each alien.
4. Criminal penalties of up to six months' imprisonment and/or a $3,000 fine for pattern or practice violations.
5. Civil fines of $100 to $1,000 for recordkeeping violations.

Sources: Reproduced with permission from HUMAN RESOURCES MANAGEMENT—IDEAS AND TRENDS IN PERSONNEL Issue No. 130, pages 177–178 (November 14, 1986), published and copyrighted by Commerce Clearing House, Inc., 4025 W. Peterson Avenue, Chicago, IL 60646. The Bureau of National Affairs, Inc., *Immigration Reform: A Practical Guide* (Washington, D.C.: Bureau of National Affairs, 1987).

make certain that their strategies and policies are continued. A study of hospitals found that the major source of financing influenced the selection process.[17] When a major portion of the hospital's budget came from private insurance, administrators with accounting backgrounds were selected. On the other hand, when the largest portion of the budget was derived from private donations, the managers were selected on the basis of their business or professional contacts. Selection decisions seemed to be aligned with the sources of financial power in the organization, according to this study.

Many employers also give co-workers a voice in the selection choice. Applicants are interviewed by their prospective co-workers and the workers express their preferences. University departments use this procedure in which the faculty and students express preferences about applicants. At the Lincoln Electric Company, the work group selects replacements or additions.[18]

Setting Objectives for External Selection Activities

Efficiency

Selection programs can be costly. Annual operating costs for testing large numbers of employees can range as high as $5 million, with development costs reported as high as $100,000.[19] Whether such costs pay off depends on whether the selection information improves selection choices. As Chapter Six showed, employees' motivation and capability derive from the match between individuals and jobs. External selection is the organization's initial attempt to create such a match. Although the vast majority of selection effort tries to match individual abilities and qualifications with job content, selection may also consider the match between the individual's needs or interests and the job's returns.[20] Research suggests that the returns to selection investments can be extraordinary.[21] Thus, efficient selection provides information that improves selection decisions at the minimum cost.

Equity

Selection contributes to fairness perceptions within and outside the organization. For job applicants, the selection activity often represents their first experience with the organization. Applicants have preferences for certain selection activities and form judgments about the organization based on their selection experiences.[22] Society also attends to organizational selection decisions. Organizations screening for prior drug use or using polygraph tests to detect honesty must consider the reactions of customers, unions, and the government.[23] Of course, EEO legislation is the most visible and powerful factor determining equity in selection. The EEOC threatens lawsuits or fines if selection activities reject disproportionate numbers of protected groups without demonstrating the relationships between selection and job performance. So, in addition to considering productivity and cost, selection decisions must consider these important factors in setting equity objectives.

VALIDITY INFORMATION

Every external selection decision is a prediction: Based on applicants' measured characteristics, we predict what their future behaviors will be if they are hired. Which selection information will improve these predictions?

Are selection predictions supported by evidence? These questions are addressed by gathering information to justify the selection procedures.

Definition

Validity is the degree to which predictions from selection information are supported by evidence. *Validation* is the process of gathering information about selection program validity.

Validity depends on both the selection techniques as well as the particular prediction situation to which they are applied.

Validation is important for two reasons: First, validity is necessary for selection techniques to improve decisions. If prediction information from selection techniques is not valid, decisions based on the information are no better than decisions without it. Validity evidence helps human resource managers choose selection techniques more effectively, leading to better selection decisions and a higher-quality work force. The second reason validity is important involves equity. When selection programs reject a disproportionate number of protected group members, validity evidence is a defense against charges of illegal discrimination.

A human resource manager can find out if selection inferences are justified by gathering information. This gathering process is called the *validation method*. Validation methods are chosen based on the quality of the information they produce and the decisions they affect. The closer the validation method mirrors how selection techniques are actually used, the better it predicts how the selection technique actually works. Ideally, one would validate a selection technique by applying it to every job applicant, hiring all of them, measuring their work behaviors, and then calculating the relationship between the technique's predictions and eventual employee work behaviors. Because this is obviously impractical, managers use alternative validation methods. The two general approaches to validation are criterion-related and content-based.

Criterion-Related Validation Approaches

Criterion-related methods actually measure a *predictor*, which may be the score on a selection technique such as a test. They also measure a *criterion*, which is the score on job behaviors, such as performance, absenteeism, tenure, or training success for each person in a sample. Then they compute the statistical predictor-criterion relationship. The predictor must provide information that distinguishes applicants from each other in consistent and reliable ways, based on characteristics relating to job behaviors. The criterion must also be carefully chosen to measure job behaviors or work results that are: (1) affected by individuals, rather than group or technology-determined effects; (2) relevant to organizational goals; (3) measurable at reasonable cost, with adequate quality, and in practical ways; and (4) affected by individual differences.[24] Criteria should also reflect factors that remain stable over time.[25]

Validity Coefficient

Exhibit 11–2 plots the relationship between the selection procedure and the job behavior. Figure 1 shows very little relationship between the two. Figure 2 shows a small relationship; there is a tendency for people who do well on the selection technique to also perform well. And Figure 3 shows a strong relationship between the selection procedure and subsequent job behavior. The stronger the relationship, the more "valid" the selection procedure.

All the data shown in a scatter plot can be summarized into a single index called a correlation coefficient. It is called a *validity coefficient* in selection design. Numerically, it is identified by the symbol r; the values for r range from -1.0 to $+1.0$. In Exhibit 11–2, Figure 3 has a higher r (.65) than Figure 2 ($r = .40$), and Figure 2 has a higher r than Figure 1 (.12). A validity coefficient is statistically significant if the relationship between the selection procedure and the job behavior is not due to chance.[26]

Predictive versus Concurrent Validation

Validation methods using samples of job applicants are called *predictive* validation methods, while those using samples of current employees are called *concurrent* validation methods. Exhibit 11–3 compares the two. Both involve preliminary job analyses, selection technique design, and performance measure design (steps 1 and 2). The difference is that the predictive process tests applicants, hires them, and only then measures the criterion. The concurrent process tests employees and measures their current performance at the same time.

Predictive Validation. Not all predictive validation methods are alike. Exhibit 11–4 indicates the differences between five common predictive validity designs. The Follow-Up/Random Selection design offers the greatest opportunity to reflect the full range of applicant characteristics and performance levels because it uses a random sample of actual applicants. However, hiring randomly can be costly if low-performing applicants make expensive mistakes. The Follow-Up/Present System is especially appropriate if the new selection technique is applied after applicants are screened with the present system. But it may mask the validity of the new

EXHIBIT 11–2
Validity Coefficients Corresponding to Relationships between Selection Technique Scores and Job Behavior Scores

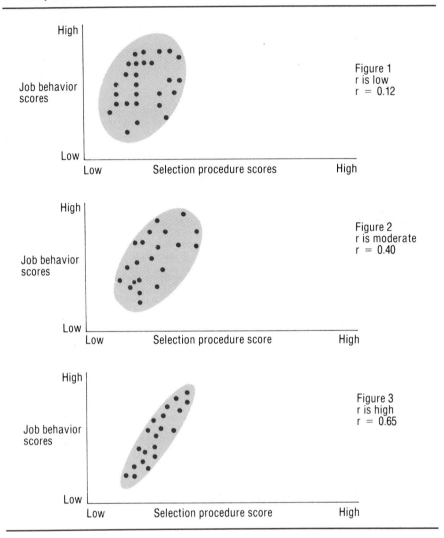

selection technique if the present system removes low-scoring applicants who would also have performed poorly. The Select-by-Predictor method guarantees that low-scoring applicants are not hired, so their criterion scores and the consequences of rejecting them are never known. The Hire and Then Test method resembles concurrent validation (discussed next). Shelf Research runs the same risks as the Follow-Up/Present design but

EXHIBIT 11–3
Predictive versus Concurrent Validation

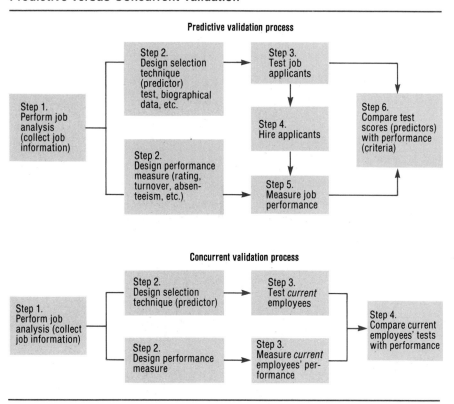

Predictive validation process

Step 1. Perform job analysis (collect job information)

Step 2. Design selection technique (predictor) test, biographical data, etc.

Step 2. Design performance measure (rating, turnover, absenteeism, etc.)

Step 3. Test job applicants

Step 4. Hire applicants

Step 5. Measure job performance

Step 6. Compare test scores (predictors) with performance (criteria)

Concurrent validation process

Step 1. Perform job analysis (collect job information)

Step 2. Design selection technique (predictor)

Step 2. Design performance measure

Step 3. Test *current* employees

Step 3. Measure *current* employees' performance

Step 4. Compare current employees' tests with performance

may be an inexpensive validation method when useful selection data already exist in organizational files.

Concurrent Validation. Predictive validation can sample only those individuals the organization hires, and involves a delay between obtaining predictor information and discovering its validity. Concurrent validation samples the entire work force, measuring each employee's predictor score and current work behaviors. Thus, it produces quicker results because predictors and criteria are measured at the same time. As with the predictive validation, the usefulness of concurrent validation depends on its ability to reflect how the predictor relates to the criterion when applied to future applicants. If current employees are less motivated than applicants to do well on the predictor (because it is not really going to affect their employment chances), or if promotions and dismissals restrict the variability among current employees on predictor and criterion scores, then a concurrent validation study may incorrectly suggest that the predictor and

EXHIBIT 11–4
Examples of Different Predictive Validity Designs

Predictive Validity Design	Description of Procedure
1. Follow-Up/Random Selection	Applicants are tested and selection is random; predictor scores are correlated with subsequently collected criterion data.
2. Follow-Up/Present System	Applicants are tested and selection is based on whatever selection procedures are already in use; predictor scores are correlated with subsequently collected criterion data.
3. Select by Predictor	Applicants are tested and selected on the basis of their predictor scores; predictor scores are correlated with subsequently collected criterion data.
4. Hire and Then Test	Applicants are hired and placed on the payroll; they are subsequently tested (e.g., during a training period) and predictor scores are correlated with criteria collected at a later time.
5. Shelf Research	Applicants are hired and their personnel records contain references to test scores or other information that might serve as predictors. At a later date, criterion data are collected. The records are searched for information that might have been used and validated had it occurred to anyone earlier to do so.

Source: Robert D. Gatewood and Hubert S. Feild, *Human Resource Selection* (New York: CBS College Publishing, 1987).

criterion are unrelated. However, research suggests that validation results for mental ability tests are similar for both concurrent and predictive methods.[27] Considering the time and resources saved, a well-conducted concurrent validation study may be preferable to a predictive study.

Other Validation Approaches

Two criterion-related validation approaches provide a means of obtaining predictive validation information while combating the effects of small samples.

Synthetic Validation. With small samples of applicants or current employees in a particular job, statistical validation is not very informative, because such a small sample may not reflect the diversity of future applicants. One way to increase the power of validity evidence is to relate predictor scores to the same job dimension across several jobs, combining the employees into a larger sample. For example, a typing ability test might be validated against typing performance not only for secretaries, but also for receptionists and clerks. This procedure is called synthetic validation.[28]

Validity Generalization. Predictive validation studies often encounter difficulties that may mask true predictor-criterion relationships. Samples of applicants may be very small, criterion measures may be error-prone, and the range of measured applicant or employee characteristics may be restricted. Differences in these factors across studies can produce varying validity results, making it appear that predictor-criterion relationships are situationally determined. For decades, this belief led managers to assume that predictors found valid in one situation might still be invalid if used in a slightly different situation. Thus, validity evidence appeared useless unless it reflected the exact situation to which a predictor would be applied.

Validity generalization opposes this "situational specificity" belief by combining the results of many validity studies, and removing the effects of these "artifacts" that mask the true predictor-criterion relationship. Applications of this technique suggest that selection processes are often equally valid in similar (but not identical) situations.[29] Using validity generalization, human resource managers may borrow validity results from similar selection situations using similar selection techniques. Thus, they can avoid the expense of conducting their own validation studies. This approach is not without controversy,[30] but it is already being used by the United States Employment Service.[31] The U.S. Department of Labor is currently exploring the EEO/AA implications of this approach.[32]

Content-Based Validation

Content-based validation involves constructing selection techniques so that they measure the knowledge, skills, and abilities (KSAs) used on the job.[33] Unlike criterion-related validation, content validation computes no predictor and criterion scores, nor a validity coefficient. Instead, it relies on judgments about the job content (usually based on job analysis) and the selection technique to determine the correspondence between them.

Perhaps the clearest example is the judgment that a typing test is appropriate for predicting future typing behaviors. Exhibit 11–5 illustrates

EXHIBIT 11–5
Content Validation for a Typist/Clerk

Example KSAs of Typist-Clerk	Example Job Tasks of Typists-Clerk		Measures of KSAs
	1. Types and proofreads business correspondence, reports, and proposals on written instruction	· · · 5. Checks and computes travel claims and expenses using a 10-key adding machine	
1. Ability to type reports and correspondence at a minimum of 50 words per minute	√		Typing test of example of business correspondence
2. Ability to read at 12th grade reading level	√		Reading test involving reports, correspondence, and proposals at 12th grade reading level
3. Ability to use basic business styles for typing of business correspondence	√		Typing test of example of business correspondence
4. Knowledge of arithmetic at 10th grade level including addition, subtraction, division, and multiplication		√	Arithmetic test requiring arithmetic calculations on business expense data using 10-key adding machine
. . .	. . .	. . .	. . .
9. Ability to operate a 10-key adding machine		√	Arithmetic test requiring arithmetic calculations on business expense data using 10-key adding machine
Percent (%) of time performed	75%	· · · 15%	

Note: A check mark indicates that a KSA is required to perform a specific job task. Measures of KSAs are those developed to assess particular KSAs.

Source: Robert Gatewood and Hubert S. Feild, *Human Resource Selection* (New York: CBS College Publishing, 1987), p. 132.

a simple approach to content validation for clerk/typists. These jobs contain two performance dimensions, typing performance and calculating performance. The top part of the exhibit gives examples of typing tasks on the left and calculating tasks on the right. In the bottom part of the exhibit, the left column lists KSA areas. Those applying to each dimension have a checkmark under the appropriate job task. The right column lists corresponding measures of those KSAs. Notice how each measure mirrors the KSA as closely as possible. Finally, at the bottom, because typing takes up 75 percent of the job, while calculating takes up 15 percent, typing performance should receive a 75 percent weight, while calculating should receive 15 percent.

Content validation alone is less appropriate when job applicants are ranked for selection, rather than setting a passing score above which all are qualified. Nor is it appropriate when highly subjective judgments identify job behaviors or predictor KSAs, when the KSAs can be learned on the job, and when the predictor task does not resemble the work task.[34] Many employers use content-based validation to construct predictors that are later validated using criterion-related methods.[35] An interesting variant on this approach involves having selection experts predict the validity coefficient of a particular predictor applied to a particular situation. One recent study found that such predictions by industrial psychologists compared favorably to the results of a typical single-organization criterion-related validation study.[36]

Extent of Test Validation

Validation does not appear to be a common practice. A Bureau of National Affairs (BNA) survey of 437 organizations found that 16 percent had validated their procedures according to the federal Uniform Guidelines on Employee Selection Procedures. Validation was more likely for firms employing over 1,000 employees than for smaller firms. Of those organizations that had validated selection procedures, the most common criteria were formal performance evaluation records, supervisory statements gathered specifically for validation, length of service, production rates, absence/tardiness, and success in training programs. Twenty-nine percent of those with validated selection procedures said they used a concurrent method and 18 percent used a predictive method. Fifty-three percent used other methods, such as private consultants or information from test publishers.[37]

Government Regulation of Validation

Validity evidence can be a defense against findings of adverse impact (an unacceptably small proportion of women or minorities meeting hiring standards, as discussed in Chapter Three), but courts look carefully at all aspects of the validation study in considering such evidence. Courts have considered:

The *predictor* (such as the adequacy of job analysis, test content, and whether companies considered less harmful alternatives).

The *criterion* (such as adequate job analysis, measurement quality, rating processes, and whether it involves training results).

The *validation procedure* (such as sample sizes, concurrent versus predictive validation strategy, and job groups).

The *data analysis* (such as the size and statistical significance of the validity coefficient, evidence of costs/benefits, setting passing scores, prediction fairness for minority groups, and validity generalization evidence).[38]

Managers are well advised to consider psychological standards when gathering validation evidence.[39]

USING SELECTION INFORMATION

No matter how valid the selection procedures, their effectiveness depends on how the employers use predictor information.

Single-Job Selection versus Classification

Selection procedures are typically evaluated for their ability to predict performance in one job. However, selection devices can also classify applicants for a variety of jobs. The largest employer using this strategy is the U.S. military, which tests thousands of applicants and assigns them to several hundred jobs based on their test scores. Using predictors for classification requires that they not only correlate with each individual job, but that decision rules also indicate what predictor scores justify classification into various jobs.[40]

Deciding Who Rates Applicants

Someone must gather and score the applicant information, unless predictor scores are computed in a completely mechanical way. One example is a typing test score based on the total words typed less errors. In the vast majority of organizations, the personnel department handles most selection procedures, though responsibility for interviews is often shared with the hiring supervisor.[41] Thus, the personnel department bears great responsibility for the accuracy and usefulness of selection information. No matter how valid or appropriate the selection technique, if decision makers ignore selection technique results or use them improperly, the consequences can be severe.[42]

Using Multiple Selection Procedures

The typical selection process includes multiple procedures to collect information about applicants. Multiple procedures allow the process to be adjusted to fit a particular situation.

Multiple Hurdles Process

In a multiple hurdles process each selection procedure serves as a screen. Each applicant must get through a screen to proceed to the next. Failure to qualify at any hurdle means rejection. A multiple hurdles process assumes that an applicant's strengths and weaknesses do not balance each other. The lack of one quality cannot be overcome by the presence of others. This makes sense for certain jobs in which a minimum level of physical or analytical skills are required. An accountant needs a certain aptitude with numbers, and an air force pilot needs a high degree of eye/hand coordination. However, a Supreme Court decision ruled that where multiple hurdles are used, every single hurdle must be job-related and free from illegal discrimination. (See *Connecticut* v. *Teal* in Chapter Three.)

Compensatory Process

Compensatory selection processes recognize that applicants' limitations on some qualifications can be counterbalanced by strengths in others. Further, an applicant is not rejected or hired until the entire process is completed. In that way, data obtained from all the selection procedures are combined to assist managers in making the decision.

Hybrid Process

A hybrid process uses both multiple hurdles and compensatory logic. Most jobs require certain minimum qualifications for successful performance. Examples include college degrees, typing speed, or "two years of experience." Because these qualifications are essential for successful performance, they become part of the hurdles. Applicants without them are rejected. Beyond these minimums, a blend of other qualifications may lead to success. Some talents compensate for others. So employers use the compensatory process. Usually the hybrid process begins with hurdles to screen out those not minimally qualified. Employers must be absolutely sure that these hurdles comply with EEO regulations, however.

CHOOSING SELECTION TECHNIQUES

A variety of selection techniques measure applicants' characteristics. These techniques include application forms, biographical information, interviews, ability tests, personality assessments, work samples, and physical/physiological characteristics.

Application Forms

The first selection information applicants usually provide is their response to an application blank or form. An application form typically consists of a series of questions about the general suitability of applicants for employment.[43] Application forms may request: name, age, race and physical characteristics, religion, gender, marital and family status, physical health, citizenship, military service, arrest and conviction records, work history, education, and credit rating.

Questions in each of these areas, however, can be legally vulnerable. If adverse impact occurs and application blank information was collected that might have contributed to it, an employer may have to defend its collection and use. Robert Gatewood and Hubert Feild suggest considering whether

1. The information could cause adverse impact if used for selection decisions.
2. The information is really needed to judge an applicant's competence.
3. The question conflicts with recent EEOC guidelines or court decisions, or with the spirit of federal and state laws.
4. The question constitutes an invasion of privacy.
5. Available information can demonstrate the question's relevance to job performance.[44]

One review of application forms from 151 Fortune 500 firms suggested rather widespread use of risky questions.[45]

Using checklists to analyze application forms can increase the consistency and possibly the validity of screening decisions. Such checklists provide a standard list of factors to consider in reviewing applications. For example, one might check to see which computers programmer applicants have used, or which word processing software and telephone systems secretarial applicants have used.

The weighted application blank (WAB) technique evaluates application blank information by scoring responses to each question, multiplying scores on each question by weights reflecting that question's importance in predicting job performance, and then adding up the weighted scores to produce a total score for each applicant.[46] The typical approach is to divide current jobholders into two or three categories (high, middle, and low), based on some success criteria such as performance as measured by production records or supervisor's evaluation, or high versus low absenteeism. Then examine the characteristics of high and low performers. On many characteristics for a particular organization and job, there may be no difference in criterion scores by age or education level, but there may be differences by years of experience, for example. A weight is assigned to the degree of differences: for no difference, 0; for some difference: ± 1; for a big difference, ± 2. Then these weights are totaled for all applicants, and the one with the highest positive score is hired. Research suggests that WABs can predict tenure and reduce separation costs.[47]

Biographical Data

Application blanks can be cursory and unsystematic in the information they gather. To combat this, experts have developed several more detailed and systematic methods of gathering and evaluating biographical information.

Biographical Information Blanks (BIBs)

Biographical information blanks ask applicants questions about their backgrounds, life experiences, attitudes, and interests. They use multiple-choice questions such as:

When you were a teenager, how often did your father help you with your schoolwork?

1. Very often
2. Often
3. Sometimes
4. Seldom
5. Never
6. Father was not at home

Employers analyze these questions statistically or with expert judgment to determine which questions best predict future work behaviors.

Training and Experience (T&E) Information

A variation of biographical data involves examining training and experience information. Research has found some support for the validity of T&E information.[48] Exhibit 11–6 provides an extract of a T&E evaluation form.

EXHIBIT 11–6
Training and Experience Evaluation Form

> Directions: Listed below are some important job tasks performed by a Personnel Research Analyst. Read each of the tasks. If you have had experience or training in performing a task, check the box marked "Yes." If you have not, then check the box marked "No." For the task(s) marked "Yes," please describe your experience and training. All of your responses are subject to review and verification.

Have you had experience or training with this task?

Task

Yes No
☐   ☐

1. Computed and monitored applicant flow statistics for nonexempt job applicants using computerized statistical packages (for example, SPSS, SAS).

Experience

Employer: _____ Title: _____
Dates of employment: From __ To __
Describe your experience with this task: _____
_____
_____

Training

Formal coursework and location: ___
_____
Training programs attended and location: _____
_____
On-the-job training: _____

☐   ☐

2. Designed and conducted test validation studies for entry-level jobs.

· · ·   · · ·

☐   ☐

3. Supervised research assistants in collecting data for human resource studies.

· · ·   · · ·

☐   ☐

4. Trained personnel assistants in the use of personnel tests (for example, typing, basic math and verbal tests) for entry-level jobs.

EXHIBIT 11–6 (concluded)

.   .
.   .
.   .

Yes   No
☐   ☐

5. Made oral presentations to line and/or upper-level managers on the results of personnel research studies.

Source: Robert D. Gatewood and Hubert S. Feild, *Human Resource Selection* (New York: CBS College Publishing, 1987).

Accomplishment Record

The accomplishment record approach is suitable for professionals who claim "my record speaks for itself." They are often unwilling to go through formal procedures such as taking tests or filling out application blanks. A government regulatory agency developed the method and applied it to attorneys. Lawyers describe their professional achievements on an accomplishment record form. It does not measure typical biographical data such as college grades, quality of schools attended, or interests. Instead, the focus is on actual legal accomplishments and critical dimensions of the attorney's jobs in the agency. Exhibit 11–7 shows the "using knowledge" dimension of the job and an applicant's response to it. Exhibit 11–8 shows the scale to score the applicant's accomplishment. This approach validly predicts attorneys' job success and has "face validity" because the attorneys using it believe it is appropriate and valid.[49]

Education

The length and type of formal education an applicant has can indicate ability or skills, work motivation, and intelligence. A recent study suggested that managerial advancement was more likely and faster for those entering an organization with a college degree.[50] One analysis suggested that educational requirements challenged in court were upheld more often when organizations asserted validity with a criterion-related validity study, had strong affirmative action programs, and applied educational requirements to highly technical jobs. Education requirements were less likely to be upheld when used simply to upgrade work force quality.[51]

Similar to the application form and reference check, biographical data relies on the assumption that past behavior can predict future behavior. Research shows that biographical data does work.[52] Responses to BIBs seem to be accurate for verifiable and moderately subjective items.[53] Research evidence suggests that biographical data require constant updating

EXHIBIT 11–7
Accomplishment Record Form for "Using Knowledge"

USING KNOWLEDGE

Interpreting and synthesizing information to form legal strategies, approaches, lines of argument, etc.; developing new configurations of knowledge, innovative approaches, solutions, strategies, etc.; selecting the proper legal theory; using appropriate lines of argument, weighing alternatives and drawing sound conclusions.

Time Period: *1974–75*

General statement of what you accomplished:

I was given the task of transferring our anti-trust investigation of . . . . . . into a coherent set of pleadings presentable to . . . . . . and the Commission for review and approval within the context of the Commission's involvement in shopping centers nationwide.

Description of exactly what you did:

I drafted the complaint and proposed order and wrote the underlying legal memo justifying all charges and proposed remedies. I wrote the memo to the Commission recommending approval of the consent agreement. For the first time, we applied anti-trust principles to this novel factual situation.

Awards or formal recognition:

none

The information verified by: *John B. Goode, Compliance*

Source: L. Hough, "Development of the Accomplishment Record Method of Selecting and Promoting Professionals," *Journal of Applied Psychology* 69, no. 1 (1984), pp. 135–46. Copyright 1984 by the American Psychological Association. Reprinted by permission of the author.

and analysis to ensure their validity.[54] Users of biographical data must be alert to possible adverse impact. Some studies have found race and sex differences in biodata scoring keys.[55]

Reference Checks

Checking references involves collecting information from people who have previous experience with the applicant. These checks verify information on application forms and other biographical forms or gather additional information for selection decisions. Reference givers can be contacted in person, by phone, or by mail. Often, reference information fails to distinguish among applicants because the comments are usually positive,

EXHIBIT 11–8
Accomplishment Record Rating Scale for "Using Knowledge"

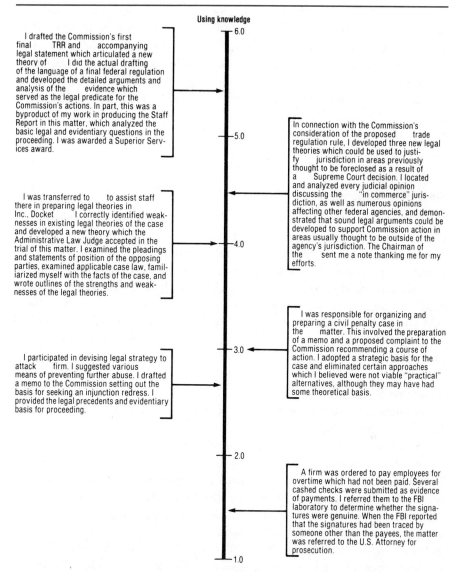

Using knowledge

— 6.0

I drafted the Commission's first final   TRR and   accompanying legal statement which articulated a new theory of   I did the actual drafting of the language of a final federal regulation and developed the detailed arguments and analysis of the   evidence which served as the legal predicate for the Commission's actions. In part, this was a byproduct of my work in producing the Staff Report in this matter, which analyzed the basic legal and evidentiary questions in the proceeding. I was awarded a Superior Services award.

— 5.0

In connection with the Commission's consideration of the proposed   trade regulation rule, I developed three new legal theories which could be used to justify   jurisdiction in areas previously thought to be foreclosed as a result of a   Supreme Court decision. I located and analyzed every judicial opinion discussing the   "in commerce" jurisdiction, as well as numerous opinions affecting other federal agencies, and demonstrated that sound legal arguments could be developed to support Commission action in areas usually thought to be outside of the agency's jurisdiction. The Chairman of the   sent me a note thanking me for my efforts.

I was transferred to   to assist staff there in preparing legal theories in Inc., Docket   I correctly identified weaknesses in existing legal theories of the case and developed a new theory which the Administrative Law Judge accepted in the trial of this matter. I examined the pleadings and statements of position of the opposing parties, examined applicable case law, familiarized myself with the facts of the case, and wrote outlines of the strengths and weaknesses of the legal theories.

— 4.0

I was responsible for organizing and preparing a civil penalty case in the   matter. This involved the preparation of a memo and a proposed complaint to the Commission recommending a course of action. I adopted a strategic basis for the case and eliminated certain approaches which I believed were not viable "practical" alternatives, although they may have had some theoretical basis.

— 3.0

I participated in devising legal strategy to attack   firm. I suggested various means of preventing further abuse. I drafted a memo to the Commission setting out the basis for seeking an injunction redress. I provided the legal precedents and evidentiary basis for proceeding.

— 2.0

A firm was ordered to pay employees for overtime which had not been paid. Several cashed checks were submitted as evidence of payments. I referred them to the FBI laboratory to determine whether the signatures were genuine. When the FBI reported that the signatures had been traced by someone other than the payees, the matter was referred to the U.S. Attorney for prosecution.

— 1.0

Source: L. Hough, "Development of the Accomplishment Record Method of Selecting and Promoting Professionals," *Journal of Applied Psychology* 69, no. 1 (1984), pp. 135–46. Copyright 1984 by the American Psychological Association. Reprinted by permission of the author.

though some research has suggested that the adjectives used or the number of words in a letter may indicate the reference giver's true intentions.[56] Moreover, because providing negative reference information may place reference givers at legal risk, many are reluctant to do more than verify employment dates and jobs held.[57] The Privacy Act of 1974 gives applicants a legal right to examine reference letters unless they explicitly waive this right. This makes it very important to ensure that questions to references are carefully constructed to provide only that information needed for the employment decision. "Personnel 'voyeurism' can only lead to possible legal liability and can endanger the legal status of the recruitment and selection process."[58]

Selection Interviews

The selection interview is virtually always part of employee selection.[59] Fifty-six percent of the participating companies in one survey stated that interviews are the most important aspect of their selection process. Ninety percent reported that they had more confidence in the interview than in any other method.[60] Several reviews of research have concluded that the evidence suggests low interview validity.[61] However, recent work suggests that interviews can demonstrate validity if conducted properly and studied carefully.[62] Several aspects of the interview have been investigated to explain this.

Interview Structure

Three different interview approaches are used—structured, semistructured, and unstructured.

Structured. In a structured interview the interviewer prepares a list of questions in advance and does not deviate from it. The interviewer uses a standard form to note the applicant's responses to the predetermined questions. It is almost similar to a biographical information blank with the interviewer filling in the answers. Many of the questions asked in a structured interview are forced choice in nature, and the interviewer need only indicate the applicant's response with a check mark on the form. The interviewer may also follow a prearranged sequence of questions. The structured interview is very restrictive, however, for the information elicited is narrow and there is little opportunity to adapt to the individual applicant. This approach is equally constraining to applicants, who are unable to qualify or elaborate their answers.[63]

Semistructured. In the semistructured interview, the interviewer prepares the major questions in advance, with some follow-up questions in areas of interest. Although this approach calls for greater interviewer preparation, it also allows for more flexibility than the structured approach. The interviewer is free to probe into those areas that seem to merit further investigation. Since these interviews have less structure, however, it is more difficult to replicate them. This approach combines enough structure to facilitate the exchange of factual information with adequate freedom to develop insights.

Unstructured. The unstructured interview involves little preparation. The interviewer prepares a list of possible topics to cover, and sometimes does not even do that. The overriding advantage of the unstructured type is the freedom it allows the interviewer to adapt to the situation and to the changing stream of applicants. Spontaneity characterizes this approach, but in the hands of an untrained interviewer, digressions, discontinuity, and eventual frustration for both parties may result. Students frequently encounter personnel recruiters whose sole contribution, other than the opening and closing pleasantries, is "Tell me about yourself."

Variables Affecting the Interview

Exhibit 11–9 summarizes the three general factors affecting interview information.

EXHIBIT 11–9
Variables Affecting the Employment Interview

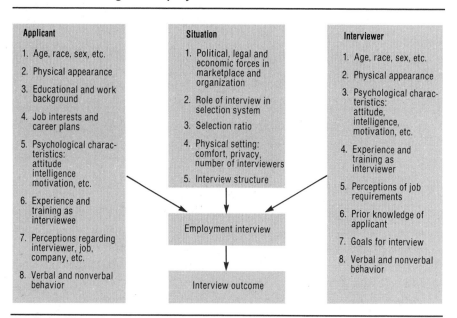

Source: Richard D. Arvey & James E. Campion, "The Employment Interview: A Summary and Review of Recent Research," *Personnel Psychology* 35, no. 3 (1982), pp. 281–322.

Applicant Factors. Applicants' qualifications and experience should, and usually do, influence the selection decision. But what about other characteristics such as applicants' sex or ethnic background? What about the topics discussed, questions asked, or the interviewer's interpretations of applicants' responses? Over 50 studies have examined the effects of applicants' sex, race, physical attractiveness, age, and marital status on the selection decision.[64] The results are mixed. One review concluded that stereotyping in the interview does exist.[65] One example: evidence showed that female applicants were generally evaluated less favorably than males, especially for jobs traditionally held by men. Yet another study found that differences in assessing males and females were not of sufficient magnitude to be significant. The latter study did find that stereotyping seems most evident when the interviewer has little data or time to collect it. Consider the typical campus interview which runs about 30 minutes. Some of that time is devoted to giving data on the job and employer. If stereotyping occurs in the college interview, it has serious consequences, since it acts as a "hurdle" that must be crossed. College interviewers become powerful "gatekeepers" to job opportunities. The validity of their decisions has not been well studied.[66]

Situation. The introduction discussed how the diagnostic model suggests that political, legal, and market forces affect selection. Interview structure also affects interview results, as discussed earlier. In addition, using panels of interviewers can help to offset individual errors or biases. Finally, we discuss the effect of the selection ratio later in the evaluation section.

Interviewer. Research suggests that interviewers follow several potentially damaging strategies in interviews such as:[67]

1. *Overemphasis on negative information*—the interview has been called a search for negative information, and often the finding of even a small amount of negative information can lead to the rejection of an interviewee.
2. *Interviewer stereotypes*—often interviewers develop a stereotype of the ideal job candidate; successful interviewees are thus not necessarily the ones best qualified, but the ones who conform to the stereotype; if different interviewers have different stereotypes, an interviewee could be evaluated positively by one and negatively by another.
3. *Job information*—lack of relevant job information can increase the use of irrelevant attributes of interviewees in decision making.
4. *Different use of cues by interviewers*—some interviewers may place more weight on certain attributes than on others, or they may combine attributes differently as they make their overall decisions.

5. *Visual cues*—interviewees' appearance and nonverbal behavior (e.g., whether they "look" interested) can influence their evaluation in an interview greatly, yet perhaps be unrelated to job success.
6. *Similarity to interviewer*—sex, race, and/or attitude similarity to interviewers may lead to favorable evaluations.
7. *Contrast effects*—the order of interviewees influences ratings; for example, strong candidates who follow weak ones look even stronger by contrast.
8. Spending too much time on nonjob-related issues.
9. Evaluating applicant acceptability early in the interview.

Although interviewing may seem like a simple process, it is actually a highly complex interaction between applicants and interviewers.

Guidelines for Better Interviewing

If, as research suggests, interviews have low validity and are prone to problems, why are they so widely used? Several answers have been suggested.[68] First, the interview assesses important interpersonal qualities, such as sociability or verbal fluency, that are not captured by other selection techniques. This is more likely when appropriate applicant characteristics have been carefully specified and interviewers are competent to assess them. Second, the interview has "face validity," in that it appears relevant to managers and applicants. Would any manager be willing to hire someone without an interview? Would you be willing to take a job without one? Probably not. Third, interviews can be a public relations tool, presenting a favorable organizational image to both job candidates and others. However, as Chapter Ten discussed, realistic job information may be more effective than a "selling" approach, and such information may be better communicated in written form. Moreover, ineptly handled interviews can do an organization's image more harm than good.[69]

Gatewood and Feild make the following recommendations for developing an interviewing program:[70]

1. Restrict the use of the interview to the most job-relevant characteristics.
2. Limit the use of preinterview data about applicants.
3. Adopt a semistructured format by predetermining the major questions.
4. Use job-related questions.
5. Use multiple questions for each characteristic.
6. Develop a formal scoring format to evaluate each applicant characteristic separately.
7. Use multiple interviewers simultaneously whenever possible.
8. Train interviewers in the processes and pitfalls of selection interviews.

EXHIBIT 11–10
Basic Interviewing Skills*

I. *Planning the interview.* Examination of the application blank, the job requirements, and also mapping out areas to be covered in the interview. Planning and organizing questions pertinent to these areas. Insuring that the interview will be held in an optimal environment, free from interruption.

II. *Getting information.* Use of appropriate questioning techniques to elicit relevant information in the same sequence over all interviewees. Probing incomplete answers and problem areas while maintaining an atmosphere of trust. Structuring the interview. Comprehensive questions and follow-up comments.

III. *Giving information.* Effectiveness in communicating appropriate and accurate information about the organization and available jobs for which the applicant would qualify, and in answering the applicant's questions. Closing the interview.

IV. *Personal impact.* The total effect the interviewer has on the applicant, both as an individual and as a representative of the organization. This includes the applicant's first impression of the interviewer, given to the applicant through the interviewer's tone of voice, eye contact, personal appearance and grooming, postures and gestures, as well as the interviewer's impact throughout the interview.

V. *Responding to the applicant.* Concern for the applicant's feelings while maintaining control over the interview. Reacting appropriately to the applicant's comments, questions, and nonverbal behaviors. Convey a feeling of interest in the applicant, encourage an atmosphere of warmth and trust, and make use of encouragement and praise.

VI. *Information processing.* Gathering, integrating, and analyzing interview information, culminating in a final placement decision. Identifying personal characteristics and judging them in the context of the job requirements. Skill in assimilating, remembering, and integrating all information relevant to the final evaluation.

* Contributed by Milton D. Hakel, Department of Psychology, Ohio State University.
Source: Richard W. Beatty and Craig Eric Schneier, *Personnel Administration: An Experiential Skill-Building Approach*, 2d ed. (Reading, Mass.: Addison-Wesley Publishing, 1981).

Milton Hakel's guidelines for interviewers appear in Exhibit 11–10, and Exhibit 11–11 contains his guidelines for interviewees.[71]

Ability and Personality Tests

The Uniform Guidelines define any systematic standardized procedure for collecting applicant information (including interviews, application blanks, and reference checks) as a test.[72] However, psychologists and managers usually consider tests to be paper and pencil instruments administered in a consistent and standardized manner to applicants. Such tests measure a wide variety of characteristics, including applicants' general and specific abilities/aptitudes, personality, and interests. Because they require professional expertise and resources to develop, tests are usually obtained from catalogues or private consultants.[73]

EXHIBIT 11–11
Effective Interviewing: Guidelines for Interviewees

Dress appropriately.

Be punctual.

Know the interviewer's name and correct pronunciation.

Make sure your "body language" communicates your interest and attentiveness.

Do some research regarding the organization and the interviewer to ask pertinent questions.

Pause briefly and pensively before answering complex questions.

Try not to discuss salary in preliminary interviews.

Be responsive to each part of each question.

Ask how any personal or potentially illegal questions are related to job performance before responding.

Bring pencil and paper in case some information (for example, a telephone number) must be recorded.

Make some notes regarding high (and low) points of interview shortly after it ends in order to follow up in subsequent interviews.

Thank the interviewer for his/her time.

Be certain that any responses on application blanks or résumés are consonant with those provided in the interview.

Contributed by Milton D. Hakel, Department of Psychology, Ohio State University.

Source: Richard W. Beatty and Craig Eric Schneier, *Personnel Administration: An Experiential Skill-Building Approach,* 2d ed. (Reading, Mass.: Addison-Wesley Publishing, 1981). © 1981 by Addison-Wesley.

Ability Tests

Ability tests assess individuals' aptitudes and achievements.[74] Achievement covers the effects of training and experience, such as the learning which occurred in apprenticeship training or an accounting course. Aptitude refers to the individual's potential to acquire a skill. Examples of aptitudes include intellectual abilities, perceptual accuracy, spatial and mechanical abilities, and motor abilities. Aptitude tests indicate what a person might be able to do, given training or experience. Exhibit 11–12 illustrates items typical of a common aptitude test of mental ability. The United States Employment Service (USES) classifies applicants for job openings using the General Aptitude Test Battery (GATB), scored for different jobs based on validity generalization findings.[75]

Recent evidence suggests that ability tests are highly valid for a wide variety of jobs. Exhibit 11–13 summarizes validity generalization evidence for several jobs and tests.

Personality Tests

Personality tests measure traits such as general activity, restraint, aggressiveness, sociability, emotional stability, objectiveness, and friendliness.[76]

EXHIBIT 11–12
Items Illustrating Mental Ability Tests

Tracing: draw a continuous line through each space without touching the lines.

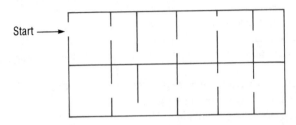

Tapping: put three dots in each triangle as quickly as you can.

Dotting: put one dot in each square as quickly as you can.

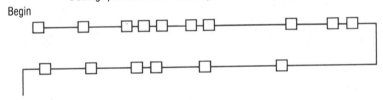

The Guilford–Zimmerman Temperament Survey items in Exhibit 11–14 are an example. Even though personality tests were not originally designed for employee selection, the notion that personality affects performance in certain jobs is widely accepted.[77] How often have you thought, "He (or she) is a perfect salesperson"? In fact, research has found that sociability and emotional stability were valid predictors of managerial performance.[78]

Interest inventories assess an applicant's preferences. For example, the Strong Vocational Interest Test asks individuals to state whether they like, are indifferent to, or dislike certain activities, school subjects, behaviors of people, and jobs.[79] By comparing their responses to those of successful people in a field, it is possible to find similar and different patterns of interest. The primary use of an interests test, however, is vocational counseling, not selection.

EXHIBIT 11–13
Validity Coefficients for Ability Tests in Various Jobs

Job	Ability	Estimated Average Validity Coefficient
First line supervisor	General mental ability	.64
	Mechanical ability	.48
	Spatial ability	.43
Mechanical Repairman	Mechanical ability	.78
Bench Worker	Finger dexterity	.39
General Clerk	General mental ability	.67
Computer Programmer	Number series	.43
	Figure analogy	.46
	Arithmetic reasoning	.57
Operator (petroleum industry)	Mechanical ability	.33
	General mental ability	.26
	Chemical comprehension	.30
Maintenance (petroleum industry)	Mechanical ability	.33
	General mental ability	.30
	Chemical comprehension	.25

Source: Robert D. Gatewood and Hubert S. Feild, *Human Resource Selection* (New York: CBS College Publishing, 1987).

EXHIBIT 11–14
Sample Items from the Guilford–Zimmerman Temperament Survey

You start to work on a new project with a great deal of enthusiasm.

In being thrown by chance with a stranger, you wait for him to introduce himself.

You avoid arguing over a price with a clerk or salesman.

You find yourself hurrying to get places even when there is plenty of time.

The thought of making a speech frightens you.

You would rather apply for a job by writing a letter than by going through with a personal interview.

You seldom give your past mistakes a second thought.

You nearly always receive all the credit that is coming to you for things you do.

Most people are paid as well as they should be for what they contribute to society.

You hesitate to tell people to mind their own business.

Most people use politeness to cover up what is really "cut-throat" competition.

If anyone steps ahead of you in line, he is likely to hear from you about it.

You would rather be a miner than a florist.

Source: J. P. Guilford and Wayne S. Zimmerman. Copyright 1949, 1976, Sheridan Psychological Services, Orange, Calif. Reprinted by permission. All rights reserved. No reproduction or use is permitted by any means without the express written consent of Sheridan Psychological Services.

Administering tests by computer is of increasing interest to companies. AT&T gives about 100,000 tests a year.[80] It is already administering tests for word processors and computer operators by computer and anticipates expanding the use of computers. Even researchers at the Education Testing Service are experimenting with computerized college admission tests.

Physical/Physiological Testing

One of the most controversial selection techniques measures applicants' physical and physiological characteristics. Such testing might include polygraphs, physical exams, drug use screening, or genetic screening. Though rarely used, such tests have generated a great deal of attention.[81]

Polygraphs, sometimes called lie detector tests, primarily help employers predict and prevent employee theft. Often companies use polygraphs in conjunction with background checks and written honesty tests. The federal government and law enforcement agencies use polygraphs more than the private sector.[82] Evidence of effectiveness is very mixed.[83] Although some employers may value such tests for quick and relatively low-cost honesty screening, state and federal legislation increasingly limits or prohibits polygraph use. In fact, proposed federal legislation may prohibit their use by all employers affecting interstate commerce. Unions may regard such tests as pseudoscientific and as a form of intimidation.[84]

Genetic screening involves identifying individuals with high susceptibility to workplace toxins and those genetically predisposed toward contracting various occupational diseases. It is presently unclear whether such characteristics are job-related, because little validity data exists.[85]

Physical ability testing involves measuring applicants' strength or endurance. One recent study found that an arm strength test for steelworkers could predict job performance and produce handsome payoffs.[86] Reynolds Metals Company uses measures of heart rate, oxygen consumption, and ventilation rate to select employees for very strenuous manufacturing jobs.[87] Physical ability tests are especially likely to produce adverse impact against females, handicapped persons, and some racial minorities, so their use should be justified with defensible validity evidence.[88]

Work Samples and Performance Tests

Work sample tests are miniature replicas of on-the-job behaviors, which collect data on applicants performing in simulated but realistic work conditions. Examples include tests of shorthand or word processing, equipment repairs, and blueprint or technical reading. Some auto plants use trial periods on the job to select manufacturing employees.[89] Such trials have exhibited high validity and freedom from discrimination.[90] They are most applicable when tasks can be completed in a relatively short time, when applicants are not expected to learn the task on the job, when inexpensive materials can be used, and when scoring procedures are highly standardized.[91]

Validity and Popularity of Selection Techniques

Exhibit 11–15 presents average validity coefficients summarizing hundreds of validity studies. Exhibit 11–16 presents the percentages of organizations using various selection techniques. The validity evidence suggests that standardized and job-related techniques such as ability tests, job tryouts, and biographical inventories appear to be most valid. Yet, usage evidence suggests that less standardized, job-related techniques such as reference checks and unstructured interviews are most popular. Some moderately valid techniques, such as work samples, have achieved good popularity. In contrast, the most valid technique (ability tests) shows rather low popularity, though such tests are used much more frequently for skilled and clerical employees.[92]

Experts attribute the unpopularity of testing to fears of regulatory scrutiny and the costs of adequately documenting test validity in cases of adverse impact. In fact, ability tests are technically no more legally vulnerable than interviews, reference checks, or application blanks.[93] The

EXHIBIT 11–15
Average Validities of Selection Techniques

Predictor	Validity
Ability composite	.53
Job tryout	.44
Biographical inventory	.37
Reference check	.26
Experience	.18
Interview	.14
Training and experience ratings	.13
Academic achievement	.11
Education	.10
Interest	.10
Age	−.01

Source: John E. Hunter and Rhonda Hunter, "The Validity and Utility of Alternative Predictors of Job Performance," *Psychological Bulletin* 96 (1984), pp. 72–98. Copyright 1984 by the American Psychological Association. Reprinted by permission of the author.

EXHIBIT 11–16
Percentage of Companies Using Selection Techniques

Reference/record check	97%
Unstructured interview	81
Skill performance test/work sample	75
Medical examination	52
Structured interview	47
Investigation by outside agency	26
Job knowledge test	22
Mental ability test	20
Weighted application blank	11
Personality test	9
Assessment center	6
Physical abilities test	6
Polygraph test/written honesty test	6
Other	3

Source: The Bureau of National Affairs, Inc., "Employee Selection Procedures," *ASPA–BNA Survey No. 45*, May 5, 1983.

popularity of the interview may be due to its ability to serve other purposes. Clearly, managers base selection program decisions on multiple objectives and pay attention to multiple constituencies. The question remains, however, do selection decisions really make any difference?

EVALUATING EXTERNAL SELECTION ACTIVITIES

Recent research has focused more attention on the costs and benefits of external selection activities than on any other human resource activity. Moreover, as we have seen, the government, unions, and communities carefully monitor the equity of external selection.

Efficiency

Selection activities work if the information they provide is used to make better hiring decisions, adding more valuable employees to the work force. Obviously more accurate predictive information enhances the value of selection. However, validity alone is not enough. Researchers have devoted great attention to identifying the factors that influence the effects of selection on the productivity and efficiency of those hired. Exhibit 11–17 lists these factors, as well as summarizing their independent effects on the efficiency impact of selection. We discuss each of these factors in turn.

EXHIBIT 11-17
Factors Affecting the Efficiency Consequences of Selection

Selection System Factor	Effect on Selection Efficiency
Validity (Correlation) Coefficient: Linear relationship between predictor and criterion scores.	Higher values (approaching 1.0) improve efficiency more and vice versa.
Base Rate: Success rate produced by selecting without the new selection procedure.	Values closer to 50 percent allow the most improvement in efficiency.
Selection Ratio: Proportion of applicants achieving a predictor score high enough to receive employment offers.	Lower values imply choosier selection systems, and improve efficiency more and vice versa.
Variability in Applicant Value: The difference between applicants in the value of their potential contributions to the organization.	Higher values imply that differences detected by selection can be more important, so selection effects on efficiency are greater, and vice versa.
Leverage: The number of selectees and time periods affected by the selection program.	Higher values imply the program affects more productivity, so selection effects on efficiency are greater and vice versa.
Program Costs: The value of resources necessary to develop and implement the selection program.	Higher values imply more resource requirements, so selection effects on efficiency are less and vice versa.

Diagram of Validity, Base Rate, and Selection Ratio

Exhibit 11–18 diagrams the first three factors (validity, base rate, and selection ratio) related to selection validity. In this exhibit, the horizontal axis represents applicants' scores on a selection device. The vertical axis represents their actual (or predicted) scores on the job behaviors used as selection criteria. The horizontal line represents the dividing point between satisfactory and unsatisfactory performance, that is, everyone performing higher than this level is satisfactory. The vertical line represents the dividing point between qualified and unqualified applicants, that is, everyone scoring higher than this level is qualified.

The diagonal dotted line represents the *prediction function*, showing the performance level we predict for each predictor score. For example, for applicants whose selection scores equal the selection cutoff, the predicted performance score is the performance cutoff. The elliptical area around the prediction function represents the region of applicant predictor-criterion score combinations. The dots represent examples of individual applicant predictor-criterion score combinations. Because predictions

EXHIBIT 11–18
Diagram of How Validity, Base Rate, and Selection Ratio Affect Selection

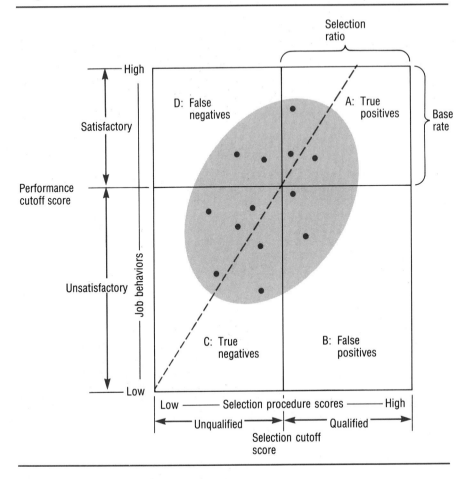

are not perfect, the points do not fall exactly on the predictor line. Some-times the predicted score is too high, and sometimes it is too low.

Regions A and C represent accurate predictions. The part of the el-lipse in region A represents "true positives"—those applicants rated as qualified, who truly perform satisfactorily. The part of the ellipse in region C represents "true negatives"—those applicants rated as unqualified who do perform unsatisfactorily. However, regions B and D represent inaccur-ate predictions. The part of the ellipse in region B represents "false posi-tives," or applicants rated as qualified who fail to perform satisfactorily. And the part in region D represents "false negatives," or applicants rated as unqualified, who would have performed satisfactorily. We estimate the position of the predictor line, the ellipse, and the size of these regions from validity studies.

Next we discuss two different ways to define selection efficiency, and how each of these factors affects them.

Selection Efficiency Defined as Prediction Success

The first model—often called the Taylor–Russell model—defines selection usefulness according to how much it improves prediction success. The "success ratio" represents the percentage of those applicants hired who eventually succeed.[94] In Exhibit 11–18, the success ratio is the proportion of applicants falling in region A, divided by the proportion of applicants falling in regions A and B. The ability of selection to improve the success ratio depends on three factors—the validity, the base rate, and the selection ratio.

Validity. Validity is the strength of the linear relationship between the predictor and criterion. In Exhibit 11–18, validity is simply how thin the ellipse is around the predictor line. Higher validity decreases the proportion of the ellipse in regions D and B. Thus, when selection raises the validity, the success ratio (region A divided by region A plus B) goes up.

Base Rate. The base rate is simply the success ratio resulting from selection without the new predictor. In Exhibit 11–18, it is the proportion of the sample falling in regions D and A. The base rate is affected by recruitment, and by the level of performance required for satisfactory job behaviors. High base rates occur when recruitment attracts a pool of highly qualified applicants. Higher base rates in Exhibit 11–18 mean that the ellipse is moved up—more applicants perform satisfactorily—and vice versa. Base rates near 50 percent provide the best opportunity for selection systems to improve the success ratio. Very low base rates mean that almost no applicants can perform satisfactorily, so there are few to select. Very high base rates mean almost everyone can perform satisfactorily, so there are few to reject.

Selection Ratio. The selection ratio reflects choosiness in selection. It is the proportion of the ellipse falling in regions A and B. The more choosy we are, the higher (farther to the right) our selection cutoff is, and the smaller is the selection ratio. With valid selection, being more choosy reduces the size of both regions A and B, but region B is reduced more, so the success ratio improves as the selection ratio falls.

Tables are available for predicting the success ratio resulting from combinations of base rates, validity levels, and selection ratios.[95] However, we really cannot determine whether to invest resources in improved selection programs using only the success ratio because it fails to reflect several factors discussed in Chapter Eight for evaluating and planning human resource programs. First, the success ratio provides no measure of the value of improved success. Avoiding selection errors may be important when mistakes are quite costly, but sometimes a few selection mistakes may be easily corrected through training or even employee dismissals. Second, the success ratio fails to tell how much the selection system affects productivity. (Will we make 10 or 1,000 selection decisions? How long will these decisions affect job behaviors?) Third, the success ratio fails to acknowledge the costs of improved selection, such as the costs of recruiting better qualified applicants, implementing a more valid selection device, and being more choosy.

Defining Selection Efficiency as Dollar-Valued Returns

A second model has been proposed to address these limitations. The Brogden-Cronbach-Gleser (BCG) model defines usefulness as the increase in dollar-valued return produced by a new selection system compared to random selection.[96] It can also compare two alternative selection techniques by taking the difference in their dollar-valued returns. This model focuses on the value of job performance differences, rather than on the proportion of correct hiring decisions. It reflects not only the validity, base rate, and selection ratio, but also the cost of the selection technique, the variability in applicant value, and the leverage (number of employees and time periods) affected by selection.

Cost. This is the value of the resources used to develop, implement, and maintain the selection technique. For a testing program, it might include the price of obtaining the test, the cost of a validation study, the clerical cost of administering and scoring the test, and the cost of managerial time spent interpreting the test results and choosing applicants. As an example, let's consider a selection program that costs $50 per applicant.[97]

Selection Ratio. As in the Taylor–Russell model, the selection ratio represents choosiness. However, instead of focusing on how choosiness affects the proportion that can pass the selection cutoff, the BCG model focuses on the increase in applicant qualifications. The more choosy the selection system (that is, the lower the selection ratio), the higher the average test score of those selected is above the average of the applicant pool.

In this model, test scores and performance scores are expressed in standard deviation units. A standard deviation is simply a statistical quantity reflecting certain assumptions. If we ranked the applicants on their predicted performance levels, it would be the difference between the average score of the group and the score of a person better than 85 percent of the group, or the difference between the average of the group and the score of a person worse than 85 percent of the group.

If we selected the top 50 percent of the applicants, this would produce an average test score among those selected that was .80 standard deviations above the test score of a randomly selected group of applicants. Of course, that means we have to test twice as many applicants as we plan to hire. So at $50 per applicant, we have to spend $100 per new hire to test enough people.

Validity. As in the Taylor–Russell model, validity reflects how closely predictor scores relate to criterion scores; that is, the thinness of the ellipse in Exhibit 11–18. By translating our predictor and criterion scores into standard deviations, validity becomes the percentage change in criterion score (job behaviors) associated with a change in predictor score (selection technique). High validity means that when we choose applicants with high predictor scores, a lot of that predictor score increase is reflected in higher performance.

Continuing our example, if the average test score of our applicants is .80 standard deviations above average, and if test validity is .60, then we would predict that applicants selected using the test will produce an average criterion score .48 (i.e., .60 × .80) standard deviations better than a randomly selected group of applicants.

Variability in Applicant Value. Knowing how many "standard deviations" better our test-selected applicants can perform compared to a randomly selected group of applicants is difficult to use in decision making. We must ask, "Is it worth $100 per applicant to get a .48 standard deviation increase in performance?" To make this information meaningful, we have to translate it into dollar units. We need to know how much a one-standard-deviation performance difference is really worth. Researchers have measured this value in many ways. All of them have some problems, and none of them claims any greater validity than another.[98] In general, however, the dollar value of performance differences should be higher in jobs where employee behaviors affect important outcomes, and where different applicants are likely to perform very differently, such as the chief executive officer of an organization.

In our example, suppose we estimated that the difference between someone performing the job better than 85 percent of the applicants and the performance of the average applicant was worth $1,000 per person, per year. Now, this model would predict that the .48 standard-deviation performance improvement produced by using the test yields a group of new hires averaging $480 per person, per year better than selecting randomly.

Leverage. To get the total benefits, we need to know how many people we select and how long they perform at this level. Assume that we select 100 persons and they stay for three years. Thus, selection affects 300 person-years of productivity. This is the "leverage" of the selection program (see Chapter Eight). If each person-year is worth an average of

$480 more than if we selected randomly, the total value of selecting one group of 100 persons is $144,000 over their three-year tenure (i.e., $480 times 300).

Computing Total Utility. Having established benefits of $144,000, we must consider the total costs of the selection system. Recall that we test 200 applicants to get our 100 new hires (a selection ratio of 50 percent), and we spend $50 per applicant. The total cost of testing 200 applicants $10,000. The total utility of the selection program is the benefits ($144,000) minus the costs ($10,000), or $134,000. This represents a return of 1,340 percent on the $10,000 investment.

Though this figure may seem quite high, it is not unusual. Several studies have estimated returns from selection programs amounting to millions of dollars.[99] This selection utility model has been enhanced to include financial investment considerations and the reapplication of selection programs to future groups of applicants. This increases the value still further because the program affects more employees.[100] Research has shown that even very large errors in estimating the variables, such as overestimating the validity or value of performance differences, or underestimating costs, generally does not alter the conclusion that valid selection pays off.[101] Decisions to adopt less valid selection techniques such as unstructured interviews may have more serious consequences for organizational efficiency than most managers realize.

Equity

Of course, selection techniques cannot be evaluated solely on their effects on productivity. As we have seen, many highly valid selection techniques may produce adverse impact, increasing the risk of illegal discrimination, possible lawsuits, and fines. Regulatory agencies monitor selection activities very closely. In fact, the infrequent use of ability tests and other scorable selection devises is often traced to the perception that they may produce adverse impact if minority-group members or women score lower.[102]

Selection also serves as one tool for advancing affirmative action goals. Enhancing recruitment efforts to reach qualified minority applicants, reducing barriers that prevent minority groups from applying (such as providing transportation or child care), and ensuring that selection systems are not unfairly biased against minority group members can all be used to increase and maintain minority-group representation.

Organizations may adopt systems using preferential treatment to advance affirmative action progress.[103] However, research suggests that selection systems designed to achieve high minority representation at the expense of selecting the most qualified candidates may reduce productivity.[104] One study estimated that setting a cutoff score equal to the average of the applicant pool produced substantial dollar-value reductions in work force productivity compared to a top-down selection strategy. Moreover, selection based on preferential treatment may cause the preferred members of minority groups to doubt their confidence to perform effectively.[105]

Finally, managers must consider the political and personal coalitions within organizations when evaluating external selection activities. No selection system can work unless decision makers are willing to apply it and use its results. Too often, elegant and complex systems may be implemented without adequately persuading decision makers of their value. For example, managers may feel that structuring interviews unnecessarily restricts their discretion. Human resource managers must be prepared to communicate the benefits and costs of external selection decisions effectively.

SUMMARY

Selecting employees to join the organization affects important human resource objectives. Selection works when it identifies differences among applicants that predict important differences in their job behaviors. The quality of selection often determines the match between individuals and jobs. Moreover, because external selection serves as the gateway into the organization, all subsequent human resource activities depend on the results of external selection.

However, selecting the best is more valuable if you can keep the best. Organizations must also manage employee separations. Separation patterns determine whom the organization keeps, rather than whom it selects. The next chapter discusses the activities and decisions affecting employee separations and work force reductions.

DISCUSSION AND REVIEW QUESTIONS

1. What is validity? Which purposes does validity evidence serve? What is a validity coefficient, and what are its characteristics?
2. What distinguishes predictive and concurrent validation? What are the advantages and disadvantages of each of the five predictive designs? When might a well-conducted concurrent validation study be preferable to a predictive validation study?
3. What does research show about the processes and results of selection interviews? If the interview has problems, why is it so widely used? What guidelines can improve interview usefulness?

4. Generally, do organizations seem to use the most valid selection techniques? Which factors other than validity might explain the popularity of selection techniques?

5. The $134,000 payoff from hiring 100 people is just an estimate. Which factors might make it higher? Which factors might make it lower?

NOTES AND REFERENCES

1. Marvin Dunnette and Walter C. Borman, "Personnel Selection and Classification Systems," *Annual Review of Psychology* 30 (1979), p. 478.
2. John Welsh, presentation to Cornell Graduate School of Business, 1984.
3. "Apple Must Rely on the MacIntosh," *The Wall Street Journal*, April 3, 1984, p. 4.
4. John Boudreau, "Effects of Employee Flows on Utility Analysis for Human Resource Productivity Improvement Programs," *Journal of Applied Psychology* 68 (1983), pp. 396–407.
5. Richard D. Arvey, *Fairness in Selecting Employees* (Reading, Mass.: Addison-Wesley Publishing, 1979).
6. Brian Becker, "Utility Analysis of Human Resource Management Programs: Some Caveats" (Unpublished manuscript, 1985).
7. Richard D. Arvey, *Fairness in Selecting Employees.*
8. U.S. Equal Employment Opportunity Commission, U.S. Civil Service Commission, U.S. Department of Labor, and U.S. Department of Justice, "Uniform Guidelines on Employee Selection Procedures," *Federal Register, 1978* 43, no. 166, pp. 38295–309; E. E. Patter, ed., *Employee Selection: Legal and Practical Alternatives to Compliance and Litigation* (Washington, D.C.: Equal Employment Advisory Council, 1983); Dale Yoder and Paul D. Staudohar, "Testing and EEO: Getting Down to Cases," *Personnel Administrator*, February 1984, pp. 67–73.
9. Personal interview with Fran Coyne, vice president, personnel, at Burlington Northern.
10. *Human Resource Management News*, March 7, 1987. Chicago, Ill.: Enterprise Publications.
11. Mary L. Tenopyr and Paul D. Oeltjen, "Personnel Selection and Classification," *Annual Review of Psychology* 33 (1982), pp. 581–618; Sheldon Zedeck and Wayne F. Cascio, "Psychological Issues in Personnel Decisions," *Annual Review of Psychology* 35 (1984), pp. 461–518.
12. Frank L. Schmidt and John E. Hunter, "Employment Testing: Old Theories and New Research Findings," *American Psychologist*, October 1981, pp. 1128–37.
13. Bureau of National Affairs, *Immigration Reform: A Practical Guide* (Washington, D.C.: Bureau of National Affairs, 1987).
14. Charles C. Snow and Raymond E. Miles, "Organizational Strategy, Design and Human Resources Management" (paper presented at Academy of Management meetings, Dallas, Tex., 1983); also see Marc Gerstein and H. Reisman, "Strategic Selection: Matching Executives to Business Conditions," *Sloan Management Review*, Winter 1983, pp. 33–43; A. D. Szil-

agy, Jr., and D. M. Schweiger, "Matching Managers to Strategies: A Review and Suggested Framework" (working paper, Houston, Tex., University of Houston, 1984).

15. Ibid.

16. Snow and Miles, *Organizational Strategy.*

17. G. R. Salancik and J. Pfeffer, "Who Gets the Power—and How They Hold On to It," *Organizational Dynamics,* Winter 1977, pp. 3–21.

18. Tenopyr and Oeltjen, "Personnel Selection."

19. Bureau of National Affairs, "Employee Selection Procedures," *ASPA–BNA Survey No. 45* (Washington, D.C.: Bureau of National Affairs, May 5, 1983).

20. Ronald A. Ash, Edward L. Levine, and Steven L. Edgell, "Exploratory Study of a Matching Approach to Personnel Selection: The Impact of Ethnicity," *Journal of Applied Psychology* 64, no. 1 (1979), pp. 35–41.

21. Joe R. Rich and John W. Boudreau, "Effects of Variability and Risk in Selection Utility: An Empirical Comparison," *Personnel Psychology* 40 (1987), pp. 55–84; Wayne F. Cascio and Val Silbey, "Utility of the Assessment Center as a Selection Device," *Journal of Applied Psychology* 64 (1979), pp. 107–18; Frank L. Schmidt, John E. Hunter, R. C. McKenzie and Tressie W. Muldrow, "Impact of Valid Selection Procedures on Work Force Productivity," *Journal of Applied Psychology* 64 (1979), pp. 609–26.

22. Sara L. Rynes, "Recruitment, Organizational Entry, and Early Work Adjustment," in *Handbook of Industrial and Organizational Psychology,* 2nd ed., ed. Marvin Dunnette (Chicago: Rand McNally, in press).

23. Bureau of National Affairs, *Polygraphs and Employment,* Special Report (Washington, D.C.: Bureau of National Affairs, 1985).

24. Robert D. Gatewood and Hubert S. Feild, *Human Resource Selection* (New York: CBS College Publishing, 1987), pp. 506–11.

25. Gerald V. Barrett, Marilyn S. Caldwell, and Ralph A. Alexander. "The Concept of Dynamic Criteria: A Critical Reanalysis," *Personnel Psychology* 38 (1985), pp. 41–56.

26. See George F. Dreher and Paul R. Sackett, *Perspectives on Employee Staffing and Selection* (Homewood, Ill.: Richard D. Irwin, 1983); Richard R. Reilly and Georgia T. Chao, "Validity and Fairness of Some Alternative Employee Selection Procedures," *Personnel Psychology* 35, no. 1 (1982), pp. 1–62.

27. Gerald V. Barrett, James S. Phillips, and Ralph A. Alexander, "Concurrent and Predictive Validity Designs: A Critical Reanalysis," *Journal of Applied Psychology* 66 (1981), pp. 1–6; Neal Schmitt, Richard Z. Gooding, Raymond A. Noe, and Michael Kirsch, "Meta-Analyses of Validity Studies Published between 1964–1982 and the Investigation of Study Characteristics," *Personnel Psychology* 37 (1984), pp. 407–22.

28. Robert M. Guion, "Synthetic Validity in a Small Company: A Demonstration," *Personnel Psychology* 18 (1965), pp. 49–63; John W. Hamilton and Terry L. Dickenson, "Comparison of Several Procedures for Generating J-Coefficients," *Journal of Applied Psychology* 72, no. 1 (1987), pp. 49–54.

29. See, for example, Frank L. Schmidt, I. Gast-Rosenberg, and John E. Hunter, "Validity Generalization Results for Computer Programmers," *Journal of Applied Psychology* 65 (1980), pp. 643–61; Frank L. Schmidt,

John E. Hunter, and Kenneth Pearlman, "Task Differences as Moderators of Aptitude Test Validity in Selection: A Red Herring," *Journal of Applied Psychology* 66 (1981), pp. 166–85; Frank L. Schmidt, John E. Hunter, Kenneth Pearlman, and G. S. Shane, "Further Tests of Schmidt-Hunter Bayesian Validity Generalization Procedure," *Personnel Psychology* 32 (1979), pp. 257–81; N. S. Raju, and Michael J. Burke, "Two New Procedures for Studying Validity Generalization," *Journal of Applied Psychology* 68 (1983), pp. 382–95; Michael J. Burke, "Validity Generalization: A Review and Critique of the Correlation Model," *Personnel Psychology* 37 (1984), pp. 93–116; Frank L. Schmidt, and John E. Hunter, "A Within-Setting Empirical Test of the Situational Specificity Hypothesis in Personnel Selection," *Personnel Psychology* 37 (1984), pp. 317–26; Frank L. Schmidt, Benjamin P. Ocasio, Joseph M. Hillery, and John E. Hunter, "Further Within-Setting Empirical Tests of the Situational Specificity Hypothesis in Personnel Selection," *Personnel Psychology* 38 (1985), pp. 509–24.

30. Frank L. Schmidt, Kenneth Pearlman, John E. Hunter, and Hannah Rothstein Hirsh, "Forty Questions about Validity Generalization and Meta-Analysis," *Personnel Psychology* 38, no. 4 (1985), pp. 697–798; Paul R. Sackett, Mary L. Tenopyr, Neal Schmitt, and Jerard Kehoe, "Commentary on Forty Questions about Validity Generalization and Meta-Analysis," *Personnel Psychology* 38, no. 4 (1985), pp. 799–801.

31. Robert M. Madigan, K. Dow Scott, Diana L. Deadrick, and Jil A. Stoddard, "Employment Testing: The U.S. Job Service Is Spearheading a Revolution," *Personnel Administrator*, September 1986, pp. 62–69.

32. Bureau of National Affairs, *Fair Employment Practices* (Washington, D.C.: Bureau of National Affairs, 1987), p. 22.

33. American Psychological Association, Division of Industrial/Organizational Psychology, *Principles for the Validation and Use of Personnel Selection Procedures* (Washington, D.C.: American Psychological Association, 1979).

34. Gatewood and Feild, *Human Resource Selection*.

35. M. D. Dunnette, *Predicting Job Performance of Electrical Power Plant Operators* (Minneapolis: Personnel Decision Research Institute, 1983).

36. Frank L. Schmidt, John E. Hunter, Paul R. Croll, and Robert C. McKenzie, "Estimation of Employment Test Validities by Expert Judgment," *Journal of Applied Psychology* 68, no. 4 (1983), pp. 590–601.

37. Bureau of National Affairs, "Employee Selection Procedures."

38. Lawrence S. Kleiman and Robert H. Faley, "The Implications of Professional and Legal Guidelines for Court Decisions Involving Criterion-Related Validity: A Review and Analysis," *Personnel Psychology* 38 (1985), pp. 803–31.

39. American Psychological Association, *Standards for Educational and Psychological Testing* (Washington, D.C.: American Psychological Association, 1985).

40. Lee J. Cronbach and Goldine C. Gleser, *Psychological Tests and Personnel Decisions*, 2nd ed. (Urbana: University of Illinois Press, 1965).

41. Bureau of National Affairs, "Employee Selection Procedures."

42. Frank L. Schmidt, Murray J. Mack, and John E. Hunter, "Selection Util-

ity in the Occupation of U.S. Park Ranger for Three Modes of Test Use," *Journal of Applied Psychology* 69, no. 3 (1984), pp. 490–97.

43. Gatewood and Feild, *Human Resource Selection*, p. 277.

44. Ibid.

45. Ernest C. Miller, "An EEO Examination of Employment Applications," *Personnel Administrator*, March 1981, pp. 63–70.

46. Allen Schuh, "Application Blank and Intelligence as Predictors of Turnover," *Personnel Psychology*, Spring 1967, pp. 59–63; Schuh, "The Predictability of Employee Tenure: A Review of the Literature," *Personnel Psychology*, Spring 1967, pp. 133–52; George W. England, *Development and Use of Weighted Application Blanks*, rev. ed., Bulletin 55 (Minneapolis: Industrial Relations Center, University of Minnesota, 1971); David Weiss, "Multivariate Procedures," in *Handbook of Industrial and Organizational Psychology*, ed. M. D. Dunnette (Chicago: Rand McNally, 1976), pp. 344–54.

47. England, *Development and Use of Weighted Application Blanks*; Raymond Lee and Jerome M. Booth, "A Utility Analysis of a Weighted Application Blank Designed to Predict Turnover for Clerical Employees," *Journal of Applied Psychology* 59 (1974), pp. 516–18.

48. Ronald A. Ash and Edward L. Levine, "Job Applicant Training and Work Experience Evaluation: An Empirical Comparison of Four Methods," *Journal of Applied Psychology* 70, no. 3 (1985), pp. 572–76.

49. Leaetta Hough, "Development and Evaluation of the Accomplishment Record Method of Selecting and Promoting Professionals," *Journal of Applied Psychology* 69, no. 1 (1984), pp. 135–46.

50. Ann Howard, "College Experiences and Managerial Performance *Journal of Applied Psychology* [Monograph] 71, no. 3 (1986), pp. 530–52.

51. Ronni Meritt-Haston and Kenneth N. Wexley, "Educational Requirements: Legality and Validity," *Personnel Psychology* 36, no. 4 (1983), pp. 743–54.

52. Terry W. Mitchell and R. J. Klimoski, "Is It Rational to Be Empirical? A Test of Methods for Scoring Biographical Data," *Journal of Applied Psychology* 67, no. 4 (1982), pp. 411–618.

53. Garnett Stokes Shaffer, Vickie Saunders, and William A. Owens, "Additional Evidence for the Accuracy of Biographical Data: Long-Term Retest and Observer Ratings," *Personnel Psychology* 39 (1986), pp. 791–809.

54. Reilly and Chao, *"Validity and Fairness"*; James J. Asher, "The Biographical Item: Can It Be Improved?" *Personnel Psychology* 25, no. 2 (1972), pp. 251–69; Aurelee Childs and Richard J. Klimoski, "Successfully Predicting Career Success: An Application of the Biographical Inventory," *Journal of Applied Psychology* 71, no. 1 (1987), pp. 3–8.

55. Reilly and Chao, "Validity and Fairness."

56. S. H. Peres and J. R. Garcia, "Validity and Dimensions of Descriptive Adjectives Used in Reference Letters for Engineering Applicants," *Personnel Psychology* 15 (1962), pp. 279–86; A. Mehrabian, "Communication Length as an Index of Communicator Attitude," *Psychological Reports* 17 (1965), pp. 519–22.

57. L. A. Wrangler, "The Employee Reference Request: A Road to Misdemeanor?" *Personnel Administrator* 18 (1973), p. 47.

58. Robert L. LoPresto, David E. Mitcham and David E. Ripley, *Reference Checking Handbook* (Alexandria, Va.: American Society for Personnel Administration, 1985), p. 17.
59. Bureau of National Affairs, "Employee Selection Procedures."
60. Milton D. Hakel, "Employment Interview," in *Personnel Management: New Perspectives*, ed. K. Rowland and G. Ferris (Boston: Allyn & Bacon, 1982).
61. Eugene Mayfield, "The Selection Interview—A Re-Evaluation of Published Research," *Personnel Psychology* 17 (1964), pp. 239–60; Neil Schmitt, "Social and Situational Determinants of Interview Decisions: Implications for the Employment Interview," *Personnel Psychology* 29 (1976), pp. 79–101.
62. Richard D. Arvey, Howard E. Miller, Richard Gould, and Phillip Burch, "Interview Validity for Selecting Sales Clerks," *Personnel Psychology* 40 (1987), pp. 1–12; D. L. Whetzel, Michael A. McDaniel, and Frank L. Schmidt, "The Validity of the Employment Interview: A Review and Meta-Analysis" (paper presented at the annual meeting of the American Psychological Association, Los Angeles, 1985).
63. Richard D. Arvey and James E. Campion, "The Employment Interview: A Summary and Review of Recent Research," *Personnel Psychology* 35 (1982), pp. 281–322.
64. R. C. Carlson et al., "Improvements in the Selection Interview," *Personnel Journal* 50 (1971), pp. 268–74; S. McIntyre, D. Moberg, and B. Pesner, "Preferential Treatment in Pre-Selections according to Sex and Race," *Academy of Management Journal* 23, no. 4 (1980), pp. 738–49; William F. Giles and H. S. Feild, "Accuracy of Interviews' Perceptions of the Importance of Intrinsic and Extrinsic Job Characteristics to Male and Female Applicants," *Academy of Management Journal* 25, no. 1 (1982), pp. 148–52; D. N. Jackson, Andrew Peacock, and R. R. Holden, "Professional Interviewers' Trait Inferential Structures for Diverse Occupational Groups," *Organizational Behavior and Human Performance* 29 (1982), pp. 1–20.
65. For a thorough review of the research in this area, see Zedeck and Cascio, "*Psychological Issues in Personnel Decisions.*"
66. Ibid.
67. N. Schmitt, "Social and Situational Determinants of Interview Decisions: Implications for the Employment Interview," *Personnel Psychology* 29, no. 1 (1976), pp. 79–101; Gatewood and Feild, *Human Resource Selection*.
68. Arvey and Campion, *The Employment Interview*.
69. Gatewood and Feild, *Human Resource Selection*.
70. Gatewood and Feild, *Human Resource Selection*, p. 366.
71. Milton D. Hakel, "Employment Interview," in *Personnel Management: New Perspectives*, ed. K. Rowland and G. Ferris (Boston: Allyn & Bacon, 1982).
72. "Uniform Guidelines on Employee Selection Procedures," *Federal Register*, August 25, 1978; A. W. Blumrosen, "Employee Selection Procedures—The Bottom Line and the Search for Alternatives: The Bottom Line after *Connecticut v. Teal*," *Employee Relations Law Journal* 8, no. 4 (1983), pp. 572–87; G. W. Florkowski, "Alternative Selection Procedures and the Uniform Guidelines: Improving the Quality of Employer Investi-

gations," *Employee Relations Law Journal* 8, no. 4 (1983), pp. 603–17; D. E. Thompson and P. S. Christiansen, "Court Acceptance of Uniform Guidelines Provisions: The Bottom Line and the Search for Alternatives," *Employee Relations Law Journal* 8, no. 4 (1983), pp. 587–602; James A. Craft, "Personnel Selection and Classification," in *Handbook of Psychological Assessment*, ed. Gerald Goldstein and Michael Herson (Elmsford, N.Y.: Pergamon Press, 1984).

73. The Pyschological Corporation, *1985 Catalogue of Tests, Products, and Services for Business, Industry, and Government* (Cleveland, Ohio: The Psychological Corporation, 1985); Science Research Associates, *SRA Test Catalogue for Business* (Chicago, Ill.: Science Research Associates, 1987).

74. Judy D. Olian and Tom C. Snyder, "The Implications of Genetic Testing," *Personnel Administrator*, January 1984, pp. 19–23; Edwin Ghiselli, *The Validity of Occupational Aptitude Tests* (New York: John Wiley & Sons, 1966); J. E. Hunter and F. Schmidt, "Ability Tests: Economic Benefits versus the Issue of Fairness," *Industrial Relations* 21 (1982), pp. 293–308.

75. Madigan, Scott, Deadrick, and Stoddard, "Employment Testing: The U.S. Job Service is Spearheading a Revolution."

76. See Tenopyr and Oeltjen, *"Personnel Selection;"* and Zedeck and Cascio, "Psychological Issues in Personnel Decisions."

77. Lee J. Cronbach and G. A. Schaeffer, *Extensions of Personnel Selection Theory to Aspects of Minority Hiring* (Stanford, Calif.: Stanford University: Institute for Research or Educational Finance and Governance, 1981).

78. J. P. Guilford and W. S. Zimmerman, *The Guilford-Zimmerman Temperament Survey* (Orange, Calif.: Sheridan Psychological Services, 1949, 1976).

79. John L. Holland, "Vocational Preferences," in *Handbook of Industrial and Organizational Psychology.*

80. R. Koenig, "Interest Rising in Testing by Computer," *The Wall Street Journal*, April 18, 1983, p. 29.

81. American Management Associations, *Hiring Costs and Strategies: The AMA Report* (New York: American Management Associations, 1986); Bureau of National Affairs, "Employee Selection Procedures."

82. Bureau of National Affairs, *Polygraphs and Employment.*

83. Norman Ansley and Marcia Garwood, *Validity and Utility of Polygraph Testing* (Washington, D.C.: Department of Defense, 1984); Paul R. Sackett and Michael M. Harris, "Honesty Testing for Personnel Selection: A Review and Critique," *Personnel Psychology* 37 (1984), pp. 221–45.

84. Bureau of National Affairs, *Polygraphs and Employment.* Daniel J. Herron, "Statutory Restrictions on Polygraph Testing in Employer-Employee Relationships," *Labor Law Journal*, September 1986, pp. 632–38.

85. Judy Olian, "Genetic Screening for Employment Purposes," *Personnel Psychology* 37 (1984), pp. 423–38.

86. J. D. Arnold, John M. Rauschenberger, W. Soubel, and Robert M. Guion, "Validation and Utility of a Strength Test for Selecting Steel Workers," *Journal of Applied Psychology* 67 (1983), pp. 588–604.

87. Commerce Clearing House, *Human Resources Management—Ideas and Trends* (Chicago: Commerce Clearing House, 1986).

88. Joyce Hogan and Ann M. Quigley, "Physical Standards for Employment and the Courts," *American Psychologist* 41, no. 11 (1986), pp. 1193–217.

89. "Job Tryouts Without Pay Get More Testing in U.S. Auto Plants," *The Wall Street Journal*, January 10, 1985.

90. Wayne Cascio and Neil Phillips, "Performance Testing: A Rose among Thorns?" *Personnel Psychology* 30 (1979), pp. 187–97.

91. Gatewood and Feild, *Human Resource Selection.*

92. Bureau of National Affairs, "Employee Selection Procedures."

93. Ibid.

94. H. C. Taylor and J. T. Russell, "The Relationship of Validity Coefficients to the Practical Effectiveness of Tests in Selection: Discussion and Tables," *Journal of Applied Psychology* 23 (1939), pp. 565–78.

95. Ibid.

96. Hubert E. Brogden, "On the Interpretation of the Correlation Coefficient as a Measure of Predictive Efficiency," *Journal of Educational Psychology* 37 (1946), pp. 65–76; Cronbach and Gleser, *Psychological Tests and Personnel Decisions.*

97. This is roughly the average cost reported in the BNA survey, "Employee Selection Procedures."

98. John W. Boudreau, "Selection Utility Analysis: A Review and Agenda for Future Research" (paper presented at the International Conference on Advances in Selection Research, University of Manchester Institute of Science and Technology, May 1987).

99. Joe R. Rich and John W. Boudreau, "Effects of Variability and Risk in Selection Utility: An Empirical Comparison," *Personnel Psychology* 40 (1987), pp. 55–84; Cascio and Silbey, "Utility of the Assessment Center as a Selection Device"; Frank L. Schmidt, John E. Hunter, R. C. McKenzie, and Tressie W. Muldrow, "Impact of Valid Selection Procedures on Work Force Productivity," *Journal of Applied Psychology* 64 (1979), pp. 609–26.

100. John W. Boudreau, "Economic Considerations in Estimating the Utility of Human Resource Productivity Improvement Programs," *Personnel Psychology* 36 (1983), pp. 551–57; John W. Boudreau, "Effects of Employee Flows on Utility Analysis of Human Resource Productivity Improvement Programs," *Journal of Applied Psychology* 68 (1983), pp. 396–407.

101. John W. Boudreau, "Decision Theory Contributions to HRM Research and Practice," *Industrial Relations* 23 (1984), pp. 198–217.

102. American Management Associations' "Hiring Costs and Strategies"; Frank L. Schmidt and John E. Hunter, "Employment Testing: Old Theories and New Research Findings," *American Psychologist*, October 1981, pp. 1128–37.

103. James Ledvinka, *Federal Regulation of Personnel and Human Resource Management* (Boston: Kent Publishing, 1982).

104. K. Galen Kroeck, Gerald V. Barrett, and Ralph A. Alexander, "Imposed Quotas and Personnel Selection: A Computer Simulation Study," *Journal of Applied Psychology* 68 (1983), pp. 123–36; Schmidt, Mack, and Hunter, "Selection Utility in the Occupation of U.S. Park Ranger."

105. Madeline E. Heilman, Michael C. Simon, and David R. Repper, "Intentionally Favored, Unintentionally Harmed? Impact of Sex-Based Preferential Selection on Self-Perceptions and Self-Evaluations," *Journal of Applied Psychology* 72, no. 1 (1987), pp. 62–68.

chapter twelve

EMPLOYEE SEPARATIONS, WORK FORCE REDUCTION, AND RETENTION

CHAPTER OUTLINE

Late in 1986, General Motors Corporation closed several plants in the Midwest, displacing thousands of manufacturing workers in an effort to cut costs and improve efficiency.[1] Forty percent of employers in a recent survey experienced a major layoff or plant closing between 1981 and 1985, with more than half occurring during 1984 and 1985.[2] And in the public sector, demonstrators in Albany, New York, protested the expected layoff of 700 state employees.[3] Though some studies showed that layoffs may cost more than they're worth,[4] experts predicted that a sluggish economy would lead to more work force reductions.[5]

In response, Congress considered several bills to require employers to provide advance notice and other assistance to employees dislocated by plant closings.[6] To avoid layoffs, IBM announced its most sweeping early retirement plan in history—a plan to lure 10,000 older and senior employees to leave the company voluntarily. Several other companies, such as Xerox Corporation and AT&T, also offered "golden handshakes."[7] Even the ability of organizations to dismiss employees for cause is being reassessed, as court cases continue to redefine and limit the employer's discretion to dismiss employees at will.[8]

Staffing is an ongoing process that does not end when employees are hired. Clearly, managing who leaves an organization is as important and controversial as managing who joins. The external selection activities we discussed in Chapter Eleven involved adding employees to the organization's work force to improve its composition and value. In this chapter we explore how human resource decisions affect who leaves and who stays.

Definition

Employee separations occur when the employment relationship is ended and employees leave the organization. Employee separations affect *work force reduction* (a decrease of employees) and *employee retention* (the characteristics of employees who are retained).

Similar to selection, separation decisions can be initiated by the employer as discharges and layoffs, but they can also be initiated by the employee as quits or retirements. This chapter discusses how human resource activities affect employee separations and how separations influence the quantity and quality of the work force. Though employee separations are often viewed as a problem to be avoided, we take a broader perspective, viewing separations as a staffing process that determines the quality of the retained work force.

A DIAGNOSTIC APPROACH TO WORK FORCE REDUCTION/RETENTION

As the preceding examples illustrate, work force reduction and retention can be highly charged issues. After all, they literally affect the livelihood of employees. They are carefully observed by organizational and external constituents interested in the equity of organization's human resource management. However, such activities are also essential to the organization's efficiency. It may do little good to invest in valid selection, improved compensation, or extra training if an organization cannot retain its employees effectively.

External Conditions

Product and Labor Markets

Market conditions affect both employees' decisions to leave and organizations' decisions to reduce their work forces. Dissatisfied employees seem reluctant to leave during times of high unemployment and more likely to leave during periods of low unemployment.[9] Economic downturns and reductions in product demand are the primary reasons organizations consider work force reductions through layoffs and other means.[10] In designing work force reduction/retention policies, human resource managers must consider market factors.

Government and Society

State and federal governments as well as the courts are concerned about work force reduction/retention from several perspectives. As we saw in Chapter Three, equal employment opportunity and affirmative action goals are often affected by layoffs, with recently hired minorities and females frequently first in line for such reductions. The importance of ensuring equity to all employees affected by layoffs has prompted several bills in Congress. Among the most controversial provisions is a requirement that employers provide advance notice of plant closings and layoffs.[11] Finally, equity in the process of dismissing or discharging employees has prompted several state courts to restrict the rights of employers to dismiss employees at will.[12] The trend is evident: Employers can expect closer scrutiny of their work force reduction/retention policies and more legislation to regulate those policies.

Unions

Organized labor's activities to shape work force reduction/retention policies include supporting federal legislation protecting American jobs, requiring advance notice of plant closings, and negotiating safety nets of benefits for dislocated employees. Unions also administer grievance systems to ensure that employee discharges are subject to proper review. Collective bargaining agreements frequently stipulate seniority-based reductions.[13]

Organizational Conditions

Clearly, organizational characteristics affect work force reduction/retention. Layoffs are much more likely in larger manufacturing firms.[14] Companies with traditions and cultures reflecting commitments to guaranteed or lifetime employment seem more likely to look for alternatives to work force reductions. Organizational strategies govern the extent of reductions, because these strategies determine how to best match existing employees' skills and abilities to emerging business directions.

The nature of the employees also has important effects. The relationship between employee characteristics (such as skills, abilities, and motivation) and the pattern of employee separations can have profound effects on organizational goals. Employee separations have quite different implications depending on whether the most valuable employees separate or the least valuable employees separate.[15] Organizations also attend to employee attitudes and equity perceptions in managing work force reduction and retention, often with stated policies to ensure consistent and fair treatment. Moreover, employees' attitudes and motivations are important factors in their decisions to leave organizations. (See Chapter Seven.)

Setting Objectives for Employee Separations, Work Force Reduction, and Retention

Similar to employee selection, employee separations affect the composition of the work force. Thus, managing employee separations, work force reduction, and retention requires paying attention to efficiency and equity.

Efficiency

Whether employee separations occur due to employee quits, retirements, layoffs, or discharges, administering the separations often incurs substantial costs.[16] Although employee separations are typically viewed as something to be avoided and reduced to lower such costs, in fact they can be beneficial.[17] Similar to employee selection, employee separations and resulting retentions can enhance work force value when the firm retains the best employees. Moreover, when separations are replaced, the interaction between the separation pattern and the quality of those acquired affects the productivity and efficiency of the work force. Therefore, organizations must base their management of employee separations, work force reductions, and employee retentions on efficiency-related objectives and information. Failure to recognize how employee separations affect organizational efficiency can lead to poor management and cause substantial negative effects on work force productivity.[18]

Equity

As noted earlier, employee separations, work force reductions, and employee retentions affect the equity perceptions of several organizational constituencies. It is not enough for management policies to ensure high organizational productivity, such policies also affect employees' attitudes and are scrutinized by legislative and regulatory bodies. Equal employment opportunity and Affirmative Action progress is affected by whether those minorities hired can be retained. Communities are rightfully concerned about large employers' plans for layoffs and plant closings. Many communities are enacting or considering laws requiring advance notice of such decisions. Several recent court cases have addressed the limits of an organization's right to terminate employees.[19] Finally, employees' equity perceptions are undoubtedly shaped, in part, by the perceived fairness and consistency of dismissals and layoffs. Therefore, managing employee separations, work force reductions, and employee retentions involves attending to equity as well as efficiency.

THE ROLE OF EMPLOYEE SEPARATIONS IN THE STAFFING PROCESS

Employee Separations/Retentions as "Reverse Selection"

The vast majority of research and professional activity treats employee separations as a negative outcome, to be reduced or avoided.[20] However, more recent research takes a broader view of employee separations, noting that they need not always be bad for organizations.[21] Most recently, employee separations have been portrayed as part of the staffing process, affecting work force composition just as employee selection does.[22] In fact many of the principles of employee selection discussed in Chapter Eleven

EXHIBIT 12–1
Comparison between Employee Selection and Retention

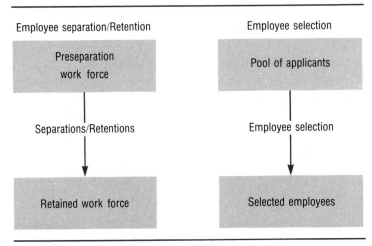

Employee separation/Retention   Employee selection

| Preseparation work force | Pool of applicants |

Separations/Retentions   Employee selection

| Retained work force | Selected employees |

apply as well to employee separations. Exhibit 12–1 illustrates the similarities.

As Chapter Eleven showed, employee selection affects the composition of the work force by choosing some of the persons in the applicant pool to receive job offers and join the organization. The effect of selection on organizational goals depends on the relationship between the employees' skills, abilities, motivation, interests, and minority status and the staffing objectives. Validity in selection refers to the degree to which the inferences about applicants' performance are supported by evidence. Selection works to the degree that the characteristics of the chosen applicants conform to the desired employee characteristics.

At first glance, employee separations may seem to be the exact opposite of employee selection. In employee selection, employees join; in separation they leave. Indeed this is the typical way of thinking about employee separations—in terms of how many employees are leaving. However, the effects of employee separations do not really occur through those who leave. The leavers are no longer members of the organization and, therefore, have little effect on it. Rather, those who are retained as a result of the separations are the ones who affect future organizational goals. As Exhibit 12–1 shows, we can think of the preseparation work force as an applicant pool. When separations occur, the organization retains some subset of the preseparation work force, and this retained group determines the effects of the separations/retentions on future organizational goals. Employee separations/retentions operate like "reverse selection" in which a subset of the existing employees remains with the organization.

The characteristics of these retained employees determine the effects of separations/retention on the organization.

Separations Initiated by Employees versus Employers

Separations are choices made by employers and/or employees to terminate the employment relationship. One way to categorize them is according to whether they are initiated by the employer or the employee.

Definition

Resignations are separation decisions initiated by the employee. They include *quits* (employee decisions to leave the organization when retirement is not a major factor) and *retirements* (employee decisions to leave the organization affected by retirement-related considerations).

Definition

Dismissals are separation decisions initiated by the employer. *Discharges* occur for individual-specific reasons such as incompetence, violation of rules, dishonesty, laziness, absenteeism, insubordination, and failure to pass the probationary period.[23] *Layoffs* occur because of the need to reduce the size of the work force.

In fact, separation decisions are seldom solely at the discretion of either the employee or the employer. In most cases, both parties can affect the decision. For example, the employer may ultimately decide whether to dismiss or lay off employees, but inducements such as severance pay and outplacement assistance may encourage some employees to leave. The decision to quit or retire ultimately rests with the employee. Human resource activities, such as compensation, benefits, and career management, however, often manage to reduce or increase the attractiveness of resignation for employees.

The Concept of Validity in Separations/Retentions

Chapter Eleven noted that the validity in selection reflects the degree to which inferences about how applicants will perform after being hired are supported by evidence. When an organization uses information with high validity to select applicants, it is more likely that the predictions about the applicants' performance will be correct. Validity is important in selection because it enhances efficiency by helping to select applicants who better contribute to productivity. Validity also affects equity by providing a rationale for selection systems should they exclude a disproportionate number of minority applicants. In addition, validity plays an important part in employee separations.

Validity Applied to Dismissals

When the organization initiates the separation decision, the information used to determine which employees leave or stay has a certain validity. The pattern of retentions affects the future productivity of the work force. Moreover, the retention pattern also affects work force characteristics related to equity, such as the minority composition of the work force.

Consider the situation shown in Exhibit 12–2, where an organization has 20 salespeople producing average yearly sales of $2,500 per person. The total yearly sales of this work force is $50,000 per year (that is, 20 times $2,500). Individual sales levels vary between $4,000 and $1,000 per

EXHIBIT 12–2
Separation/Retention Effects on a Work Force

Salesperson	Yearly Sales	Years of Seniority	Minority
Jeremy	$ 4,000	8	No
Rudolfo	4,000	8	No
Maggie	4,000	2	Yes
Manuel	4,000	6	Yes
Herbert	4,000	6	No
Karl	3,000	8	No
Donald	3,000	4	Yes
Lindsey	3,000	8	Yes
Ralph	3,000	6	No
Beuford	3,000	4	No
Arthur	2,000	8	No
Dorothy	2,000	2	Yes
James	2,000	6	No
Bertram	2,000	4	No
Jesse	2,000	4	Yes
Oliver	1,000	2	No
Anne	1,000	2	Yes
Enrique	1,000	2	Yes
Fred	1,000	6	No
Barney	1,000	4	No
Total	$50,000	100	
Average	$ 2,500	5	

person. Seniority varies between two and eight years, and averages five years. The work force currently contains eight minorities (a representation rate of 40 percent). Suppose the organization decides to lay off 25 percent of the work force, or five people. It is considering laying them off based either on past performance or on seniority.

Performance-based layoffs will remove the five poorest-performing employees (Oliver, Anne, Enrique, Fred, and Barney). This will produce a retained work force containing 15 employees averaging $3,000 in yearly sales and producing a total yearly sales level of $45,000. The minority representation rate remains unchanged under this scheme because it leaves 6 minority-group members in the 15-person retained work force. However, such a layoff scheme removes two of the senior employees (Fred and Barney).

Seniority-based layoffs will remove the five least-senior employees (Maggie, Dorothy, Oliver, Anne, and Enrique). This will produce a re-tained work force containing 15 employees all with more than two years' tenure. However, because some low-tenure employees perform well, the average yearly sales level of those retained would be $2,733.33, producing a total yearly sales level of $41,000, which is lower than when layoffs are performance-based. Moreover, because minority-group members fall pri-marily among the low-tenure employees, this scheme removes four minority salespersons, producing a representation rate of 26.6 percent (4 divided by 15), which is lower than the 40 percent representation rate in the prelayoff work force.

The same process occurs in decisions regarding discharges. With dis-charges, however, the separation decision is much more likely to be based on performance-related behaviors than seniority. Still, the consequences of dismissals for both efficiency and equity are best understood by focusing on who is retained rather than who is dismissed.

Validity Applied to Resignations

The analogies between selection and retention are readily apparent in the case of dismissals, because the organization initiates both actions. The validity concept applies as well, however, to resignations initiated by employees. Although the organization has less discretion regarding resig-nations, the quantity and pattern of resignations still affect the efficiency and equity of the retained work force.

For example, suppose that the pattern of quits among the salespersons in Exhibit 12–2 was such that the best performers tended to leave. Spe-cifically, suppose that the organization lost Maggie, Manuel, Ralph, and Beuford (a 20 percent quit rate). The retained work force of 16 employees would produce average yearly sales of $2,250, or total yearly sales of

$36,000—a substantial drop from the $50,000 total in the preseparation work force. Moreover, because two of the four separations involve minorities, the minority representation rate falls to 37.5 percent (that is, 6 divided by 16).

Now, suppose the patterns of retirements from this work force was such that the best-performing and most senior employees tended to leave. Specifically, suppose that Jeremy, Rudolfo, Karl, and Lindsey retire. This would have the same effect on productivity as the quit pattern. The retained employee group's average yearly sales would fall to $2,250, producing total yearly sales of only $36,000. Because only one of these retirements involves a minority-group member, the representation rate would actually rise to 43.75 percent among the retained employees.

The view that employee separations constitute a staffing process has only recently been developed. Unlike employee selection, there is less information about the validity of retention patterns or the ability of human resource management decisions to affect them. Separations are managed through other staffing and human resource activities, such as compensation and benefits. Therefore, our discussion focuses on the management decisions affecting each type of separation.

MANAGING RESIGNATIONS

Quits

Quits occur when employees choose to leave the organization for reasons other than retirement. Many researchers and professionals use the term *turnover* to signify employee quits. However, *turnover* is confusing because it also signifies quits and their subsequent replacements (that is, the organization "turns over" the position to a new person).[24] This chapter focuses on the separations. Quits are initiated by employees, so research has sought to explain why employees choose to separate.

The Decision to Quit

Industrial psychologists and others have studied employees' quit decisions extensively. They have proposed several models of the quit decision.[25] Exhibit 12–3 depicts a widely used model. Similar to earlier models, this one views the employee's decision to quit as a function of: (1) the relative attractiveness of the current employment relationship compared to alternatives (perceived desirability of quitting); and (2) the perceived opportunity to obtain an attractive alternative employment relationship (perceived ease of quitting). Intentions to quit precede the quit decision. These intentions result from comparing the present job to perceived alternative

EXHIBIT 12–3
A Model of the Employee Quit Decision

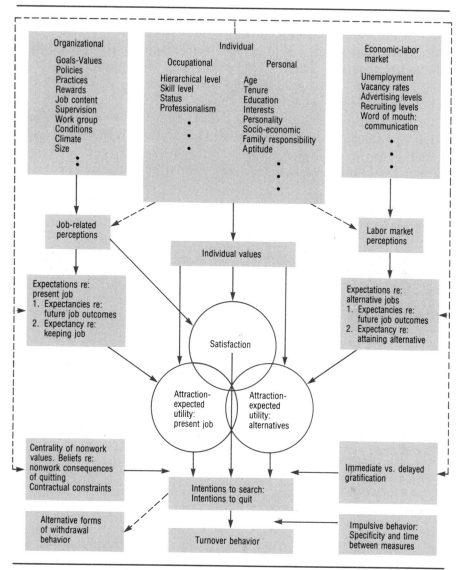

Source: William H. Mobley, *Employee Turnover: Causes, Consequences, and Control* (Reading, Mass.: Addison-Wesley Publishing, 1980).

jobs, and the dissatisfaction with the current employment relationship. Intentions are also influenced by the nonwork consequences of quitting, contractual constraints, and the need for immediate gratification. The attractiveness of the present employment relationship and alternative employment relationships in other organizations are a function of the expected future outcomes from each, and the expectancy of keeping the current job or finding an alternative job. Attractiveness of current and alternative employment relationships as well as satisfaction also result from individual values (see Chapter Six). Job and labor market perceptions affect expectations about current and alternative employment relationships. These perceptions are a function of actual aspects of the organization (e.g., policies, practices, and rewards), the labor market (e.g., unemployment and recruiting levels), and the individual.

Several aspects of the model in Exhibit 12–3 have received research support. Exhibit 12–4 shows the results of a recent review of research studies. The results generally support the decision process in Exhibit 12–3 and highlight the variety of factors affecting employee quit decisions.

EXHIBIT 12–4
Employee Quits Research

Variable Associated with Quits	Direction of Relationship	Strength of Relationship
External		
Employment perceptions	Positive	Strong
Unemployment rate	Negative	Moderate
Accession rate	Positive	Weak
Union presence	Negative	Strong
Work-Related		
Pay	Negative	Strong
Performance	Negative	Moderate
Role clarity	Negative	Moderate
Task repetitiveness	Positive	Weak
Overall satisfaction	Negative	Strong
Satisfaction with work itself	Negative	Strong
Satisfaction with supervision	Negative	Strong
Satisfaction with co-workers	Negative	Moderate
Satisfaction with promotion	Negative	Moderate
Organizational commitment	Negative	Strong
Personal		
Age	Negative	Strong
Tenure	Negative	Strong
Gender	Women positive	Strong
Biographical data		Strong
Education	Positive	Strong
Marital status	Married negative	Moderate-weak
Number of dependents	Negative	Strong
Aptitude and ability		Moderate-weak
Intelligence	None	
Behavioral intentions	Positive	Strong
Met expectations	Negative	Strong

Adapted from: John L. Cotton and Jeffrey M. Tuttle, "Employee Turnover: A Meta-Analysis and Review with Implications for Research," *Academy of Management Review* 11, no. 1 (1986), pp. 55–70.

The study also suggested that the strength of the relationships depends on the employees, industry, and employees' nationality.[26]

One explanation for the association between unions and lower quits is that unionized situations contain mechanisms for employees to express their dissatisfaction with the employment relationship without leaving. (See Chapters Sixteen and Seventeen on Labor Relations and Collective Bargaining.) Employees have a voice through grievance mechanisms, and this voice allows them to attempt to change the situation rather than leave.[27] One recent study found that a large number of voice opportunities resulted in lower quits among nurses in both unionized and nonunionized settings.[28] Thus, voicing dissatisfaction becomes a frequent alternative form of withdrawal behavior.

Implications for Managing Employee Quits

Measuring the Separation Rate. The vast majority of human resource management research and professional practice measures the quantity, or percentage, of quits with a concern for minimizing them. The Bureau of National Affairs (BNA) reports monthly turnover rates computed with the following formula:

$$\frac{\text{Number of total separations during month}}{\text{Average number of employees during month}} \times 100$$

For 1986 the average median monthly separation rate across all companies was 1 percent, implying a yearly separation rate of about 12 percent. Separation rates are higher in small companies, in nonmanufacturing industries, and in the northeast and western regions of the United States. Organizations may also attempt to distinguish unavoidable quits caused by factors beyond the organization's control from avoidable quits caused by aspects of the employment relationship, such as pay. One survey found that over 81 percent of companies compute separation rates on a regular basis, most of them on an annual or monthly basis. Seventy-seven percent compared turnover rates among organization units, while 54 percent compared them to rates from other companies. Twenty-one percent of the organizations felt they had a turnover problem.[29]

Human Resource Activities Affecting Quits. The research just cited suggests that quits result from a variety of factors reflecting individual perceptions and attitudes, organizational policies, and external factors. If the objective is to reduce the quantity of employee separations, the model and research evidence suggest several work-related factors that could be affected by human resource activities. These factors include pay, role clarity, satisfying work, improved supervision, and improved co-worker relationships. Personal factors, such as biographical data and education, that are considered in selection decisions and attempts to provide more realistic job previews (as discussed in Chapter Ten) could also affect quit decisions.

One survey found that 84 percent of companies conducted exit interviews with separating employees to discover the reasons for their separation. The survey also found that 72 percent of responding companies had made some change in human resource activities to reduce separation rates. Activity changes included:

Wage and Salary Levels (67 percent said they had made changes).

Orientation/Induction Procedures (60 percent).

Exit Interviews (57 percent).

Fringe Benefits (54 percent).

Supervisory Training (54 percent).

Selection Methods (49 percent).

Employee Training (42 percent).

Upward Communication (40 percent).[30]

Evidence on the effectiveness of such interventions is limited in part because so many factors can affect employee separations; however, one recent study examined 20 experiments using job enrichment and realistic job previews (RJPs) to reduce separation rates. Results suggested that RJPs produced an average improvement in separation rates of 9 percent, while job enrichment produced an improvement of 17 percent.[31]

Nonetheless, many factors affecting quits are not easily managed by employers. To avoid the problems associated with sudden unexpected vacancies, employers often request or require notice from employees before they quit. Eighty percent of companies responding to one survey required two weeks' notice of resignation, though 59 percent of those companies imposed no penalties if such notice was not given.[32]

Implications for Employee Retention

Attention to employee quits usually centers around the quantity (or rate) or costs incurred to separate and replace employees. However, these factors reflect only part of the issue. The pattern of quits affects the value of the retained work force. If those who quit are the most valuable future employees, even a very low quit rate may cause substantial harm. Conversely, if those who quit are the least valuable future employees, then even high quit rates may not be cause for alarm. The research evidence in Exhibit 12–4 suggests that employee performance is negatively related to the probability of quitting (that is, high performers tend to stay), but the effect is moderate and individual study results are mixed.[33] When high performance is observable by competitors and/or when alternative opportunities are attractive and easy to obtain, the potential for losing high performers is substantial. For example, large commercial banks may lose high-performing financial managers tempted by the larger bonuses available at brokerage firms. In any case, organizations would do well to consider the effects of quits not only on costs and employment levels, but also on the quality of the retained work force. Depending on who is retained, quits may often be functional rather than dysfunctional for the organization.[34]

Of course, quits also affect the minority composition of the work force. If minority-group members find the employment relationship less attractive than nonminority group members, they may leave more frequently. An organization that cannot successfully retain its minority-group members finds it much more difficult to attain EEO/AA goals, no matter how aggressively it recruits and hires minorities.

Retirements

Retirements are a special case of resignations. In many ways, they are similar to quits in that they are initiated by the employee, and thus are the product of a choice process similar to Exhibit 12–3. Until recently, some firms set mandatory retirement at age 65 and sometimes age 70, thus making retirement more similar to a dismissal than a resignation.[35] However, a 1987 change in the Age Discrimination in Employment Act prohibits discrimination on the basis of age for anyone over age 40, removing the previous upper limit of age 70. Thus, for most employees without work impairments, retirement becomes an option rather than a requirement. Still, retirements are distinct from quits because they usually occur at the end of the individual's work career. One exception is the military, where it is possible for employees in their late 40s to receive pension benefits after 25 years of service and begin new careers. Retirements are also distinct from quits because retirees collect retirement benefits. From the organization they receive pension benefits and continued insurance coverage; from the government they receive social security and medicare benefits. These latter benefits may be structured to reflect some normal retirement age such as 62 or 65 (see Chapter Twenty on benefits).

Retirement decisions are likely to reflect the same factors as employee quits shown in Exhibit 12–3, but the nature of those factors is somewhat different. Individual factors such as age, health, and family responsibilities are different for those of retirement age than for others. Organizational factors, such as increased eligibility for pension benefits or reduced future promotion opportunities, are also different for retirement-age employees.

Finally, instead of simply considering alternative employment relationships, retirees consider the alternative of an employment-free lifestyle, with its unique attractions and concerns.

Managing Employee Retirements

Similar to quits, retirements are affected by many human resource activities, including compensation, career opportunities, training, and selection. All of these activities affect the attractiveness of the current employment relationship vis-à-vis retirement. The human resource activities most directly affecting employee retirement decisions involve how retirement income and benefits are structured. Chapter Twenty discusses how to manage employee benefits and shows that retirement benefits constitute an important component of the total benefit package because they include pension income and continued medical and life insurance. In this chapter we focus on managing retirements as a work force reduction strategy by restructuring retirement benefits to make retirement attractive to more employees.

Early Retirement Incentives: An early retirement incentive, or "window," is an enhancement to the existing package of retirement benefits that increases the number of employees eligible to receive retirement benefits and/or increases the value of retirement benefits. The retirement benefits affected by the plan may include pension payments both before and after age 62 when social security payments begin, company-paid insurance premiums, and any other retirement-related benefits.

Retirement incentive programs require decisions about:

1. The extent of employee eligibility.
2. The formula to calculate early retirement benefits.
3. The specific retirement benefits affected by the incentive.
4. The length of the election period.
5. The source of funds for the additional retirement obligations.
6. Additional support activities, such as managerial training and financial counseling.

Exhibit 12–5 outlines IBM's early retirement incentive plan announced on September 18, 1986, with an election period ending on June 30, 1987. The IBM plan maintained the existing retirement benefit package and increased the pool of eligible employees by adding five years to each employee's actual age and service for retirement computations. For example, a 50-year-old employee with 10 years of service who was ineligible to receive a monthly income under the previous plan would become eligible to retire and receive a monthly pension calculated for a 55-year-

EXHIBIT 12–5
IBM's Early Retirement Incentive

Provisions of the existing retirement plan:
A. Each regular employee who retires at age 65 or older with one or more years of service, or at or after age 55 with 15 or more years of service, will receive in addition to social security benefits a monthly income for life which equals the greatest of:
  1. $18 times the number of years of service; or
  2. One-twelfth of 1.5 percent of compensation for every year of service; or
  3. A pension benefit, calculated by subtracting one twelfth of 50 percent of the estimated social security benefit, from one twelfth of 50 percent of average compensation during the last 5 years of the current 10-year base period (1977–1986) with 35 years of service, plus one twelfth of 1.5 percent of each year's compensation after 1986. An adjustment to this benefit will be made for employees who retire with fewer, or more than, 35 years of service at the end of 1986.
B. For computation purposes, annual compensation for each year of service prior to January 1, 1987, is considered to be the average compensation for the years 1977 through 1986.
C. Early retirement at reduced income is permissible at or after age 55 with 15 years of service, or at any age with 30 years of service.
D. Employees with 10 or more but less than 15 years of service have vested rights for income at or after age 62. Employees with 17 or more years of service have vested rights for income at or after age 55.

1986 early retirement incentive:
    On September 12, 1986, IBM announced the 1986 retirement incentive, an amendment to the plan which added five years of age and service to the actual age and service of employees to determine eligibility and for calculation of retirement benefits.
    On December 18, 1986, IBM announced an enhancement to the incentive: All employees who became eligible to retire under the incentive will retain such eligibility permanently and will have their retirement benefits based on service through retirement date plus five years.

Funding for the retirement incentive:
    IBM will fund the entire cost of the plan by periodic contributions to the IBM retirement plan trust funds on an actuarial basis.

Source: 1987 Proxy Statement, International Business Machines Corporation (Armonk, N.Y.: IBM Corporation, March 18, 1987).

old with 15 years of service. Retirement eligibility also includes postretirement participation in IBM's health and life insurance benefits.

For employees over 55 with more than 15 years of service who were already eligible for retirement, the incentive for early retirement is the increase in their monthly pension based on longer service and greater age. IBM also augmented its early retirement plan with training for managers to clearly and effectively communicate its implications to their subordinates, as well as company-funded financial counseling for eligible employees. After June 30, 1987, pension calculations no longer reflected the extra five years of age, though employees remain eligible for retirement and retain the extra five years of service for pension calculation purposes.

Early retirement windows were recently announced by several other prominent firms such as Xerox Corporation, International Telephone and Telegraph, Hewlett-Packard Company, and Phillips Petroleum Company.[36] Early retirement packages have also appeared in the contracts of public school teachers.[37] Legislation has even been proposed to offer "early out" options to encourage retirement among federal government employees.[38]

A recent Towers, Perrin, Forster & Crosby (TPFC) survey of 100 large employers that offered retirement incentives between January 1983 and December 1985 suggests the following characteristics of early retirement incentives: 66 of the firms undertook the incentives to reduce employment levels and costs and avoid layoffs while 20 firms desired to eliminate staff redundancy. Fifty-four employers offered open-window programs to salaried employees only, 60 employers targeted nonunion employees, and 42 companies offered the incentive to all employees. The election period ranged from 4 to 11 weeks for 60 of the employers, but was less than 4 weeks at 7 firms. The vast majority of employers (92 out of 100) did not limit the number of acceptances. About 75 of the firms provided preretirement and/or outplacement counseling to eligible employees. Sixty-five companies paid extra incentive benefits from the company's regular qualified pension plan, 13 financed the incentive through a special nonqualified pension plan, and 18 employers paid for the incentive from the company's regular severance pay plan.[39] (We describe outplacement counseling and severance pay later in this chapter.)

Early retirement incentives are not without their risks. The International Telephone and Telegraph Corp. early retirement incentive failed to achieve the 50 percent reduction—from 850 to between 350 and 400—in headquarters staff needed, forcing the company to resort to layoffs.[40] Legal risks exist as well. The Philadelphia office of the EEOC found that Du Pont's early retirement program discriminated on the basis of age because it imposed a cap of 40 years of service and 70 years of age in computing benefits. EEOC said the cap denied workers over 65 or with more than 35 years of service the right to take full advantage of the retirement inducement.[41]

Still, the limited evidence suggests that such programs have the potential to induce substantial reductions in the work force and produce consequent cost savings. For example, IBM estimated that 4,000 jobs would be eliminated when its plan was announced in September 1986.[42] However, by the first quarter of 1987 the company's chairman stated, "We now expect more than 12,000 U.S. employees to take advantage of the retirement incentive announced last year."[43] At that time, 1,000 out of an eligible 4,000 Xerox employees had accepted its early retirement offer.[44]

The TPFC survey of 100 employers found that 16 reported early retirement costs ranging between $1,000 to $300,000 with an average of $50,000. Twenty-five employers reported total first-year cost savings from early retirement incentive programs ranging between $61,000 to $60 million, with an average of $7.3 million.[45]

Implications for Employee Retention

Retirements remove senior employees, causing the organization to retain younger employees. The value of those retained depends heavily on the relationship between employee age or tenure and the employee's value to the organization. As discussed in Chapter Nine, employment planning can anticipate critical shortages due to retirements, so human resource activities can ensure that replacements exist among the retained work force. Chapter Thirteen discusses how internal staffing decisions can contribute to this process.

Though there has been a great deal of attention to the costs and cost savings resulting from early retirement incentives, we know little about the validity of early retirement incentives, that is, their effect on the value of the retained work force. Because pension benefits are calculated on the previous salary, it is possible that such incentives are most attractive to employees with the fastest-rising pay levels. Assuming these pay levels reflect employees' value, organizations may risk inducing their best senior employees to retire early, while retaining poor performers. The substantial salary and benefit cost savings produced by such incentives may be quickly offset by reductions in the value of the retained work force. On the other hand, if retirement incentives provide increased opportunities for the organization to promote talented younger employees, the productivity effects could be quite positive.[46]

MANAGING EMPLOYEE DISMISSALS

Unlike resignations, employee dismissals are initiated by the employer, and, therefore, are influenced more by the employer's choice process than by the employees'. Because they represent the most extreme employment action, literally ending the employment relationship, a great deal of human resource activity attempts to avoid them. However, they are a fact of organizational life that should be managed effectively. There are two categories of resignations, discharges and layoffs.

Discharges

Discharges terminate the employment relationship because the employee's behaviors reflect seriously harmful consequences. Among human resource managers reporting their most serious discipline problems, 60 percent cited attendance, 17 percent cited performance, and 9 percent cited alcohol or drugs.[47]

The Decision Process for Discharges

Because discharges represent the most extreme disciplinary action, they are not undertaken lightly. In the vast majority of organizations, they represent the culmination of repeated unsuccessful efforts to resolve the behavior problem or conflict. We discuss conflict resolution systems in detail in Chapter Seventeen; here, we focus on their implications for discharging employees.

Virtually all organizations responding to the BNA survey adopted some form of progressive discipline involving oral and written warnings for initial conflicts. If the conflict is not corrected, they take more stringent disciplinary actions, such as reprimands and suspension without pay, finally culminating in discharge. Discharges are rarely the only disciplinary step; however, a majority of the organizations in the BNA survey reported a one-step discharge decision for extreme infractions. These include computer fraud/security violations, falsifying work records, divulging trade secrets or proprietary information, willful damage to company property, falsifying an employment application, stealing company property, physical assault, possession of alcoholic beverages, possession of a weapon, and possession of illegal drugs.[48] Fifty-four percent of companies with nonunion work forces included counseling in the process, and 71 percent included a formal appeals procedure. Those with unionized work forces were slightly more likely to include counseling (57 percent) and much more likely to have appeals procedures (98 percent). Discharges are more likely than any other disciplinary action to require approval by one or more managers at a higher level than the supervisor.[49] Thus, discharge is reserved for only the most serious conflicts.

A recent research review suggested that discharge rates are higher during economic prosperity, perhaps because increased hiring demands lead to selection errors. This review also found that unionized employees had similar discharge rates to nonunionized firms paying equal wage levels; that discharged employees have longer, more difficult job searches; and that discharge likelihood decreases with seniority and age.[50]

The Employment-at-Will Issue

Perhaps the most controversial issue regarding employee discharges involves the limits of an employer's right to dismiss employees at will. Employment-at-will may be to the 1980s what equal employment opportunity was to the 1970s.

The Concept. When an employee is fired for cause, what constitutes sufficient or just cause? Indeed, is any "cause" required?

In early industrial England, both master and servant had obligations spelled out in law. A master could not discharge a servant unless that individual's conduct had been less than satisfactory. An employee could not quit without giving sufficient notice.

The U.S. industrial revolution modified this view, however. Rather than stressing the mutual duties of employment, the courts began to stress the right to freely choose an employer or employee. In 1910 the California Supreme Court described the employment-at-will rule:

> Precisely as may the employee cease labor at his whim or pleasure, and, whatever be his reason, good, bad, or indifferent, leave no one a legal right to complain; so, upon the other hand, may the employer discharge, and whatever be his reason, good, bad, or indifferent, no one has suffered a legal wrong.[51]

Changed Attitude toward Employment-at-Will. The employer's right to terminate at will has been steadily eroding. The 1935 Wagner Act made it illegal for employees to be fired because of union activity. Collective bargaining agreements covering approximately 20 percent of the nonagricultural United States labor force forbid firing unionized employees, except for cause. Approximately 19 percent of the U.S. work force are federal, state, or local government employees, of whom the majority are protected from arbitrary dismissal by civil service rules. Title VII of the Civil Rights Act protects employees from being fired on the basis of race, color, sex, religion, or national origin. In addition, some legislation, such as OSHA and the Clean Air Act, includes protection against retaliatory discharge for employees who report employers' violations. However, unjust dismissal remains a potential problem for the 70 million employees in the United States who are neither civil servants, union members, or members of protected classes.

In the past decade, the courts have begun to limit the application of the at-will doctrine. Still, the treatment of wrongful or abusive discharge has been uneven. The court actions have examined the at-will doctrine in two ways; as a violation of public policy and as a violation of implied contracts between the employer and employee.

In special circumstances the firing of an employee *violates public policy*.[52] However, the "interest that the employee seeks to vindicate must be public, and not personal." For example, public policy protects

1. An employee who refuses to commit an unlawful act; the court held that an employee was protected from discharge when she refused to submit false testimony at a trial and thereby commit perjury.
2. An employee who exercises the right to perform an important public policy obligation; an employee was protected from discharge when he blew the whistle on his employer's illegal conduct.
3. An employee who exercises a statutory right or privilege; an employee may sue his employer on the grounds that his filing of a workers' compensation claim resulted in a retaliatory discharge in violation of the employee's statutory right.

However, a Florida court held that an employee could not sue when he was discharged for filing a workers' compensation claim, and an Alabama employer was permitted to fire an employee who refused to falsify medical records.[53] Without a national law, consensus in the state courts eludes us thus far.

Employee discharges can *violate employment contracts*. Personnel policies and manuals have been construed as implied, enforceable contracts. In *Toussaint* v. *Blue Cross/Blue Shield of Michigan*, the court held that an employee's discharge was improper because the employer had discussed permanent employment during the interview and it was reinforced in the employee handbook.[54] So, simply referring to "permanent" employment may imply a contract, especially if the reference can be combined with statements on the application blank or oral statements during an employment interview.

Some courts have also indicated that any action must be in the context of the total employment relationship. Thus, factors such as length of service or an employee's moving the family to work for an employer may imply a contract. For example, in *Clearly* v. *American Airlines*, the court ruled that termination without legal cause after 18 years of apparently satisfactory service amounted to "bad faith," because it would deprive the employee of pension and benefit rights.[55]

Implications for Human Resource Management. As the state courts judicially redefine traditional employment-at-will, employers must become increasingly concerned about liability for wrongful discharge. Several lawyers specializing in the area have recommended the following guidelines to reduce potential liability.[56]

1. Wrongful discharge liability begins at the preemployment interview. Avoid any oral representation of permanent employment.
2. Revise employee handbooks to remove any implications that employment is other than at-will. Words such as "permanent" employee should be dropped. Include such statements as "this handbook is not a binding contract."
3. Job applications should list employer's rights and state that employment is at-will. For example, Sears Roebuck & Co. has had a clause on its employment blanks for years which reads, "my employment and compensation can be terminated, with or without cause, and with or without notice, at any time, at the option of either the Company or myself." All applicants sign this clause, which has consistently been upheld in termination and demotion lawsuits.
4. Document performance evaluations. Supervisors must be entirely truthful when they evaluate subordinates. They must document each instance of unacceptable behavior and the supervisor's response to it. Dissatisfaction must be communicated to the employees. They must be properly notified that their performance is jeopardizing their job.
5. The employer is in control of a discharge, and therefore has the time and tools to handle it carefully and properly. In planning a discharge, an employer should list all potential issues raised by the decision, any prior disciplinary action, the investigation of the employee's conduct, and carefully document the charges. The discharge should be discussed with the employee to hear the employee's interpretation of events. Discrepancies should be investigated—the employee may be right.
6. Establish a conflict resolution procedure.

These guidelines are also important to avoid legal suits by employees who were discharged in legally appropriate ways. When the reasons for discharge are not well documented, employees can sue their former employers for libel based on the former employer's statements to the employee's prospective employers about past job performance.[57]

Taking action to avoid implying an employment contract is a troublesome notion. It smacks of using a divorce lawyer as the best man or matron of honor at your wedding. If an employer repeatedly tells employees, "we may fire you at any time," it is hard to imagine employees making any personal commitment to a job or an organization. Yet employers may face considerable liability if they do not take some of the suggested actions.

Certainly this points up the need for an effective, work-related performance evaluation program.

Implications for Employee Retention

Discharges usually require substantial amounts of documented evidence.
Thus, to the extent that behaviors leading to the discharge would have
continued in the future, the organization is likely to retain more valuable
employees as a result of discharges. The progressive discipline and documentation processes necessary to ensure legal safety and perceptions of
equity may also contribute to the validity of discharge decisions. Such
processes carefully document employees' behaviors that may predict future problems. Persistent problems are likely to continue, so the discharge
may usually choose the acceptable employees to stay.

Such positive employee retention effects are compromised, however,
when the discharge decision is not based on factors relevant to employee
value. If discharge policies are not carefully administered, it is possible
that they may produce opportunities for misuse, resulting in discharges of
valuable employees because of biased decisions. Because discharges are
based on employees' behaviors, the quality of the performance assessment
process, as discussed in Chapter Seven, is a critical factor determining
whether discharges produce beneficial effects on employee retentions.

Layoffs

Work force reductions through layoffs are one response to employee surpluses. Unlike the case of discharges, employees are seldom directly responsible for the conditions leading to the surplus. The surplus is usually
caused by "economic reasons" such as poor business decisions, poorly designed products, poor marketing, or market declines not under the control
of the organization or the employees. Thus, layoffs are among the most
difficult decisions human resource managers must make.

The Decision Process for Layoffs

As with discharges, employers often go to great lengths to avoid layoffs.[58]
For example, Control Data Corporation (CDC) attempts to avoid layoffs through their Rings of Defense Strategies shown in Exhibits 12–6
and 12–7.[59]

The first defense is to cut overtime, then call back work that was subcontracted to outside vendors. Next, the company dismisses supplemental
employees and part-time employees. Finally, if the surplus still remains,
CDC turns to programs related to full-time employees—their Inner Rings
of Defense. Here programs such as hiring freezes, voluntary layoffs, dis-

EXHIBIT 12–6
Rings of Defense Strategies

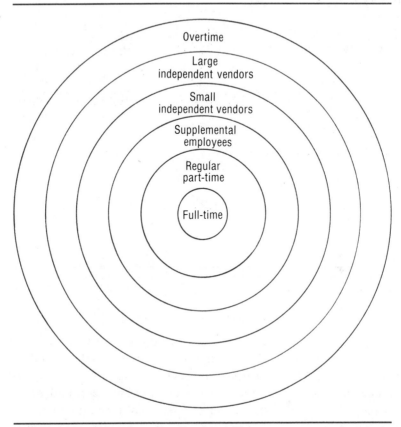

Source: Control Data Corporation, Bloomington, Minn.

missing poor performers are designed. Finally, CDC considers attempts to share work and reduce normal work hours. CDC uses all these programs before laying off full-time employees.

Many organizations have employment stabilization programs, although they may not be as elaborate as CDC's. Under such programs, organizations are committed to make every effort to provide continuous employment for employees. In fact, one of the major motivations for early retirement incentives is to accomplish work force reductions without resorting to layoffs. As discussed in Chapter Nine, when employment planning reveals current or anticipated employee surpluses, organizations have a variety of available alternatives. Many have argued the merits of job security for the organization.[60] Although employment stabilization and job

EXHIBIT 12–7
Inner Rings of Defense

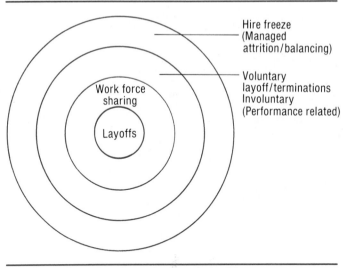

Hire freeze
(Managed
attrition/balancing)

Voluntary
layoff/terminations
Involuntary
(Performance related)

Work force
sharing

Layoffs

Source: Control Data Corporation, Bloomington, Minn.

security policies seem to be adopted with little concern for their costs,[61] layoffs can be more costly than alternatives.[62] A recent federal study found that when compared to reductions through normal attrition, the costs of reductions in force (RIFs) implemented in 1982 exceeded budgetary savings achieved in six of eight agencies. Excess costs amounted to over $1 million for three of the six agencies.[63] Thus, human resource managers would do well to consider alternatives other than "throw the crew overboard" when the organizational ship is sinking.[64]

Nonetheless, experts anticipate layoffs will continue.[65] One study reported that 59 percent of the 512 companies responding to a questionnaire experienced either substantial layoffs or a plant closure between January 1982 and January 1985.[66] Another recent study found 40 percent of respondents experiencing a major layoff or plant closing between 1981 and 1985, with more than half occurring during 1984 and 1985.[67] Many prominent organizations such as AT&T, Time Inc., Chevron Corporation, USX Corporation, General Motors Corporation, Allegis Corporation, Firestone Tire and Rubber Company, B.F. Goodrich Company, and Eastman Kodak Company have resorted to layoffs to reduce their work forces.[68] Even John Akers, president of IBM, has described IBM's tradition of no layoffs as a practice and not a policy: "You practice a practice as long as you can."[69]

Human Resource Activities for Managing Layoffs

Exhibit 12–8 lists human resource activities for managing layoffs and plant closings.

Notice of Layoff/Closing. Most companies give at least some advance notice of layoff or plant shutdown. Collective bargaining agreements often require such notice. Federal legislation requiring 90 days' advance notice was narrowly defeated in the House of Representatives in November of 1985. In 1987 such legislation existed in Massachusetts, Maine, and Wisconsin; 38 states had pending statutes.[70] One survey found that advance notice ranging from less than three months to more than one year was given in 196, or 88 percent, of the 224 plant closures reported. Organizations giving longer notice were more likely to have retraining and outplacement programs. Even though advance notice can engender feelings of goodwill and provide employees with an opportunity to search for new employment, it may run the risk of prematurely reducing the work effort between the notice date and the actual layoff or closure date.

Order of Layoff and Bumping. Layoffs usually occur based on seniority or ability. In unionized organizations, contracts may stipulate considering seniority in layoff decisions or require ability to do the work in combination with seniority. Layoffs can create legal conflicts when minority-group members have less tenure than nonminority-group members. As discussed in Chapter Three, EEO legislation suggests that any layoff system must be applied equally to members of minority and nonminority groups. When minority-group members have low seniority, however, even a neutral seniority-based system may produce a much larger proportion of minority layoffs. Recent Supreme Court decisions suggest that preferential treatment for less senior minorities in layoffs may not be an acceptable approach to maintaining affirmative action progress.[71]

Bumping occurs in situations where senior employees whose jobs have become obsolete transfer into jobs of less senior workers. Although bumping maintains jobs for long-service employees, it can cause problems if it leads to frequent job changes for a large number of employees.

EXHIBIT 12–8
Human Resource Activities for Managing Layoffs and Plant Closings

Notice of layoff/closing
Order of layoff and bumping
Income maintenance (severance pay, Supplemental Unemployment Benefits, and extension of benefits)
Job-search assistance (outplacement)

Source: Ronald E. Berenbeim, *Company Programs to Ease the Impact of Shutdowns* (New York: The Conference Board, 1986).

Income Maintenance (Severance Pay, Supplemental Unemployment Benefits, and Extended Benefits). Organizations often establish policies to maintain the income of laid-off employees for some period after the layoff. The BNA survey found that 87 percent of the responding companies paid severance benefits to laid-off or terminated employees at some time. Fifty-nine percent had formal, ongoing plans as part of their regular policies. Ninety-three percent of severance pay plans applied to dismissal for economic reasons, with 33 percent or less applying to discharges or resignations. Eligibility and the amount of severance pay are usually determined by length of service, such a one week's pay for those with two to four years with the company, two weeks' pay for four to six years, three weeks' pay for six to eight years, and four weeks' pay for over eight years. Median severance payments averaged $2,486 per recipient, with a low of $333 and a high of $25,000.[72] Supplemental Unemployment Benefits (SUB) are federal severance payments designed to supplement state unemployment insurance benefits.

Organizations may allow dismissed employees to remain eligible for employer-provided benefits such as health and life insurance. Seventy-nine percent of the companies in the Conference Board survey continued health care benefits after plant closings, with 49 percent continuing them for less than five months.[73] The BNA survey found that 54 percent of companies continued health care coverage for dismissed employees, and 32 percent continued life insurance coverage, though most of these organizations increased the workers' premiums.[74] As discussed in Chapter Twenty, the Consolidated Omnibus Budget Reconciliation Act (COBRA) dictates substantially longer extensions of health care benefits for most employee separations.

Job-Search Assistance (Outplacement). A majority of organizations offer employees assistance in locating and finding new employment. Frequent forms of assistance include individual or group counseling, recommendation letters, job market information, and secretarial and administrative support. The average median cost of outplacement assistance per recipient was $3,138, with a low of $44 and a high of $50,000.[75] These programs can be helpful when outplacement counselors are properly trained.[76] Such efforts may also be enhanced by integration with federal programs such as the Job Training Partnership Act or the United States Employment Service.[77]

Implications for Retained Employees

Layoffs frequently involve removing a larger portion of the work force than any other form of employee separations, so they can have the most profound effect on the retained work force. Clearly, whether the layoffs are based on seniority, job type, or ability affects the future work force value. Seniority-based layoffs may be beneficial if senior employees are best suited for the organization's future work requirements; however, younger workers often have the skills and flexibility needed in the future. Bumping arrangements can help to retain employees with long service, but they can also cause substantial disruptions in the retained work force. Finally, combining layoffs with human resource activities to improve work force value through retraining or redeployment to high-demand jobs for those retained enhances the retained work force's value. Clearly, layoffs can be managed as a staffing process in combination with other human resource activities.

The minority composition and attitudes of the retained work force are also likely to be affected by layoffs. Because minorities are often less senior, layoff decisions based on seniority may reduce minority representation. Moreover, retained employees' satisfaction and perceptions of equity and job security are likely to be affected by layoffs. How the layoff process is managed may determine the willingness of retained employees to support future organization initiatives.[78]

EVALUATING EMPLOYEE SEPARATIONS, WORK FORCE REDUCTIONS, AND RETENTION

Although employee separations are sometimes initiated by employees and other times by employers, managers can evaluate their effects by focusing on the retained work force. Typically, they evaluate employee separations solely by the quantity (or rate) of employees who quit, resign, are discharged, or are laid off. Such evaluation approaches are severely limited because they fail to account for the efficiency and equity consequences of employee separations.

Efficiency

Costs

Separations and programs to manage them can be costly. As we have seen, separations involve activities such as exit interviews, outplacement assistance, counseling, and severance pay, as well as requiring administrative and clerical support. Such costs can easily amount to thousands of dollars per separation.[79] Researchers cite these costs often as arguments for the harmful effects of some separations, such as quits. However, they emphasize costs less strongly in discussions of other separations. Yet, costs are clearly applicable to all separations. Although managers can reduce separation costs by more efficiently managing the separation process, they often use cost figures to argue that separations—especially quits—should always be reduced. However, this cost-based focus fails to account for separation effects on the productivity of the retained work force.

Productivity

Quits are not necessarily harmful to the organization. Quits can be functional when they improve the productivity of the work force by removing poor performers, or allow replacement of highly paid employees with newer and lower-paid employees of similar ability.[80] As we have seen, the notion that separations can improve work force productivity applies not only to quits, but to all separations. If employers manage separations so that the most valuable performers are retained, the productivity benefits can be substantial. By the same token, if the separation pattern is such that the most valuable performers leave, the potential productivity reductions are also substantial. The magnitude of these effects depends on the quality and quantity of the retained work force.[81] This perspective suggests that human resource managers would do well to look beyond simply the quantity and cost of separations, adopting an evaluation framework that encompasses productivity as well.

Equity

Employee separations are both a result and a cause of equity perceptions. Quits appear to be related to employee satisfaction and work attitudes. Moreover, the manner in which organizations dismiss, retire, and lay off employees serves as one index of their commitment to fairness and equity. Governments at the local, state, and federal levels carefully monitor the effects of separations on communities and minority group representation. Discharges are becoming more vulnerable to legal challenge as the "employment-at-will" concept is honed by state courts and governments. The decision to terminate the employment relationship is one of the most difficult facing employees and employers. Clearly, the impact of separations on the attitudes and composition of the retained work force must encompass equity as well as productivity or cost.

SUMMARY

The employer, the employee, or both can terminate the employment relationship. Employee separations have important impacts on the organization because they affect the efficiency and equity of the retained work force. Beyond their effects on the work force, however, employee separations are widely debated and closely scrutinized by governments, communities, and potential employees. The trend seems clear: Companies expect human resource managers to manage employee separations more carefully.

Such management requires a framework for objectives and evaluation that integrates employee separations/retentions into the staffing process. This chapter has proposed such a framework, demonstrating the similarities between external employee selection and employee separation/ retention. Employee separation/retention constitutes a reverse selection process through which a subset of the current employees are chosen to remain in the organization. Clearly, employee recruitment, selection, and separation/retention are an integrated set of staffing activities.[82] By understanding this fundamental similarity between employee selection and separation/retentions, human resource managers are better prepared to manage the external staffing process more effectively.

Of course, employees do not just join or leave an organization, they also move between jobs within the organization. The next chapter concludes our discussion of the staffing process by examining internal staffing.

DISCUSSION AND REVIEW QUESTIONS

1. Why can we characterize employee separations as "reverse selection"? How does the management of employee separations affect the staffing process? How does the concept of validity apply to the four types of employee separations/retentions?

2. Give three examples of managerial actions that might reduce the number of employee quits, using the model in Exhibit 12–3 and the research findings of Exhibit 12–4 as your guides. Why might human resource activities fail to affect employee quit behavior? Would a reduction in the number of quits necessarily be a good thing? Why or why not?

3. What is an early retirement incentive? Which six decisions are required for such an incentive? What are the advantages and disadvantages of such incentives for organizations?

4. Discuss why employee discharges are likely to be valid work force reduction strategies. What is the "employment-at-will" issue, and how does it affect how discharges are managed? Is it likely to affect the validity of discharges? Why or why not?

5. Discuss the four human resource activities for managing layoffs in terms of their likely effect on the efficiency and equity goals of organizations. Do these goals always coincide? Give one example where they do and one example where they do not.

NOTES AND REFERENCES

1. Bureau of National Affairs, *Daily Labor Reporter*, no. 222 (November 18, 1986).
2. Bureau of National Affairs, "Severance Benefits and Outplacement Services," *Personnel Policies Forum Survey No. 143* (Washington, D.C.: Bureau of National Affairs, 1986).
3. "NY PEF Members Demonstrate to Protest Expected Layoffs," *Bureau of National Affairs Government Employee Relations Reporter* 25, no. 1199.
4. "Retraining, Not Firing More Economical, Study Says," *Bureau of National Affairs, Daily Labor Report* no. 55 (March 24, 1987); United States General Accounting Office, "Reduction in Force Can Sometimes Be More Costly to Agencies than Attrition and Furlough," Report to the Director Office of Management and Budget (Washington, D.C.: U.S. General Accounting Office, July 24, 1985).
5. "More Layoffs Projected for 1987," *BNA's Employee Relations Weekly*, no. 47 (December 1, 1986).
6. *Bureau of National Affairs Employment and Training Reporter* 17, no. 39 (May 13, 1987).
7. *BNA Employee Relations Weekly* 5, no. 1 (January 5, 1987).
8. Daniel J. Koys, Steven Briggs, and Jay E. Grenig, "The Employment-at-Will Doctrine: A Proposal," *Loyola University of Chicago Law Journal* 17, no. 2 (Winter 1986); Daniel J. Koys, Steven Briggs, and Jay E. Grenig, "State Court Disparity on Employment-at-Will," *Personnel Psychology*, 1987.
9. Barry Gerhart, "The Prediction of Voluntary Turnover Using Behavioral Intentions, Job Satisfaction, and Area Unemployment Rates" (Academy of Management, New Orleans, 1987).
10. Bureau of National Affairs, "Employment Practices: Promotion, Transfer, Layoff, and Separation," *Personnel Management Practices*, section 207 (Washington, D.C.: Bureau of National Affairs, 1987); "Time Inc. Net Falls, Layoffs Set," *New York Times*, January 31, 1986; "Falling Prices Mean Layoffs," *New York Times*, July 21, 1986.
11. *Bureau of National Affairs, Employment and Training Reporter* 17, no. 39 (May 13, 1987).
12. Koys et al., "The Employment-at-Will Doctrine, A Proposal."
13. Bureau of National Affairs, "Policy Guide, Layoffs," *Personnel Management Practices*, no. 650, section 207 (Washington, D.C.: Bureau of National Affairs, Inc., 1987).
14. Bureau of National Affairs, "Severance Benefits and Outplacement."
15. John W. Boudreau, "Utility Analysis: A New Perspective on Human Resource Management Decisions," in *ASPA Handbook of Personnel and Industrial Relations*, vol. 1, ed. Lee D. Dyer (Washington, D.C.: Bureau of National Affairs, 1988); John W. Boudreau and Chris J. Berger, "Decision-Theoretic Utility Analysis Applied to Employee Separations and Acquisitions," *Journal of Applied Psychology* [Monograph] 70 (1985), pp. 581–612.
16. Wayne F. Cascio, *Costing Human Resources*, 2nd ed. (Boston: Kent Publishing, 1987); T. F. Cawsey and W. C. Wedley, "Labor Turnover Costs: Measurement and Control," *Personnel Journal* 2 (1979), pp. 90–95; Dan R.

Dalton, "Absenteeism and Turnover: Measures of Personnel Effectiveness," in *Applied Readings in Personnel and Human Resource Management*, ed. Randall S. Schuler, J. M. McFillen, and Dan R. Dalton (St. Paul, Minn.: West Publishing, 1981), pp. 25–42; E. A. Dyl and Timothy J. Keaveny, "Cost Minimization in Staffing," *Human Resource Planning* 6 (1983), pp. 103–13; F. J. Gaudet, *Labor Turnover: Calculation and Cost*, Research Study No. 39 (New York: American Management Associations, 1960); Eric G. Flamholtz, *Human Resource Accounting*, 2nd ed. (San Francisco: Jossey-Bass, 1985); H. L. Smith and L. E. Watkins, "Managing Manpower Turnover Costs," *Personnel Administrator* 23 (1978), pp. 46–50; Dan L. Ward, "The $34,000 Lay-Off," *Human Resource Planning* 8 (1982), pp. 35–41.

17. John W. Boudreau, "Utility Analysis: A New Perspective"; John W. Boudreau and Chris J. Berger, "Decision-Theoretic Utility Analysis Applied to Employee Separations and Acquisitions."

18. Boudreau, "Utility Analysis: A New Perspective on Human Resource Decision Making."

19. Koys, Briggs, and Grenig, "State Court Disparity on Employment-at-Will."

20. Lyman W. Porter and Richard M. Steers, "Organizational, Work, and Personal Factors in Employee Turnover and Absenteeism," *Psychological Bulletin*, 80 (1973), pp. 151–76; Victor H. Vroom, *Work and Motivation* (New York: John Wiley & Sons, 1964).

21. Barry M. Staw, "The Consequences of Turnover," *Journal of Occupational Behaviour* 1 (1980), pp. 253–73; Dan R. Dalton and William D. Todor, "Turnover: A Lucrative Hard Dollar Phenomenon," *Academy of Management Review* 7 (1982), pp. 212–18.

22. Boudreau, "Utility Analysis: A New Perspective on Human Resource Decision Making"; Boudreau and Berger, "Decision-Theoretic Utility Analysis Applied to Employee Separations and Acquisitions."

23. U.S. Bureau of Labor Statistics, *Handbook of Methods*, Bulletin 1919 (Washington, D.C.: U.S. Bureau of Labor Statistics, 1976).

24. John W. Boudreau and Chris J. Berger, "Toward a Model of Employee Movement Utility," in *Research in Personnel and Human Resources Management*, vol. 3, ed. Kendrith M. Rowland and Gerald R. Ferris (Greenwich, Conn.: JAI Press, 1985), pp. 31–54.

25. James G. March and Herbert A. Simon, *Organizations* (New York: John Wiley & Sons, 1958); James L. Price, *The Study of Turnover* (Ames: Iowa State University Press, 1977); William H. Mobley, "Intermediate Linkages in the Relationship between Job Satisfaction and Employee Turnover," *Journal of Applied Psychology* 62 (1977), pp. 237–40; William H. Mobley, R. W. Griffeth, H. H. Hand, and B. M. Meglino, "Review and Conceptual Analysis of the Employee Turnover Process," *Psychological Bulletin* 86 (1979), pp. 493–522.

26. John L. Cotton and Jeffrey M. Tuttle, "Employee Turnover: A Meta-Analysis and Review with Implications for Research," *Academy of Management Review* 11, no. 1 (1986), pp. 55–70.

27. R. B. Freeman and James L. Medoff, *What Do Unions Do?* (New York: Basic Books, 1984); A. O. Hirschman, *Exit, Voice, and Loyalty* (Cambridge, Mass.: Harvard University Press, 1970).

28. Daniel G. Spencer, "Employee Voice and Employee Retention," *Academy of Management Journal* 29, no. 3 (1986), pp. 488–502.
29. Bureau of National Affairs, "Job Absence and Turnover Control," *Personnel Policies Forum Survey No. 132* (Washington, D.C.: Bureau of National Affairs, 1981).
30. Bureau of National Affairs, "Job Absence and Turnover Control."
31. Wayne F. Cascio and Glen M. McEvoy, "Strategies for Reducing Employee Turnover: A Meta-Analysis," *Journal of Applied Psychology* 70 (1985), pp. 342–53.
32. Bureau of National Affairs, "Separation Procedures and Severance Benefits," *Personnel Policies Forum Survey No. 121* (Washington, D.C.: Bureau of National Affairs, 1978).
33. Boudreau and Berger, "Decision-Theoretic Utility Analysis Applied to Employee Separations and Acquisitions"; Ellen F. Jackofsky, "Turnover and Job Performance: An Integrated Process Model," *Academy of Management Journal* 9 (1984), pp. 74–83.
34. Dan R. Dalton and William D. Todor, "Turnover Turned Over: An Expanded and Positive Perspective," *Academy of Management Review* 4 (1979), pp. 225–35; Dan R. Dalton and William D. Todor, "Turnover: A Lucrative Hard Dollar Phenomenon"; Dan R. Dalton, David M. Krackhardt, and Lyman W. Porter, "Functional Turnover: An Empirical Assessment," *Journal of Applied Psychology* 66 (1981), pp. 716–21; Boudreau and Berger, "Decision-Theoretic Utility Analysis Applied to Employee Separations and Acquisitions"; Boudreau, "Utility Analysis: A New Perspective on Human Resource Management Decisions"; John R. Hollenbeck and Charles R. Williams, "Turnover Functionality versus Turnover Frequency: A Note on Work Attitudes and Organizational Effectiveness," *Journal of Applied Psychology* 71, no. 4 (1986), pp. 606–11; D. C. Martin and K. M. Bartol, "Managing Turnover Strategically," *Personnel Administrator* 30 (November 1985), pp. 63–73.
35. Bureau of National Affairs, "EEO Policies and Programs," *Personnel Policies Forum Survey No. 141* (Washington, D.C.: Bureau of National Affairs, 1986).
36. "Incentive Program Accepted by More than 1,000 Xerox Employees," *Bureau of National Affairs Employee Relations Weekly*, February 23, 1987, p. 230; "ITT's Early Retirement Package Fails to Achieve Needed Staff Reductions," *Bureau of National Affairs White Collar Report* 60, no. 20 (November 19, 1986); "Hewlett-Packard Retirement Plan," *New York Times*, June 13, 1986, p. D3(L); "Phillips Petroleum Retirement Offer," *New York Times*, August 3, 1985, p. 32(L).
37. "Contracts Revise Early Retirement, Pensions, Health Care," *Bureau of National Affairs Pension Reporter* 12, no. 51 (December 23, 1985), pp. 1897–98.
38. "Roth Offers 'Early Out' Bill to Encourage Federal Retirement," *Bureau of National Affairs Daily Labor Reporter*, January 9, 1987, p. 12.
39. "'Open-Window' Early Retirement Plans Seen Successful," *Bureau of National Affairs Daily Executive Report*, no. 48 (March 13, 1986).
40. "ITT's Early Retirement Package Fails to Achieve Needed Staff Reductions."

41. "Age Bias Found in Du Pont Early Retirement Program," *Washington Post*, July 17, 1986, p. A4.
42. Marilyn Harris, "A Lifetime at IBM Gets a Little Shorter for Some," *Business Week*, September 29, 1986, p. 40.
43. International Business Machines Corporation, "Stockholders' Report, First Quarter 1987" (Armonk, N.Y.: International Business Machines Corporation, 1987).
44. "Incentive Program Accepted by More than 1,000 Xerox Employees."
45. " 'Open-Window' Early Retirement Plans Seen Successful."
46. Boudreau, "Utility Analysis: A New Perspective on Human Resource Decisions."
47. Bureau of National Affairs, "Employee Discipline and Discharge," *Personnel Policies Forum Survey No. 139* (Washington, D.C.: Bureau of National Affairs, Inc., 1985).
48. Ibid.
49. Ibid.
50. Robert C. Rodgers and Jack Stieber, "Employee Discharge in the 20th Century: A Review of the Literature," *Monthly Labor Review*, September 1985, pp. 35–41.
51. *Union Labor Hospital Association* v. *Vance Redwood Lumber Co.*, 158 Cal. 551, 112, p. 886 (1910).
52. *Phillips* v. *Goodyear Tire and Rubber Company*, Ca5, No. 79–2011 (1981); *Tamory* v. *Atlantic Richfield Co.*, 27 Ca.3d 167 (1980); *Murphy* v. *City of Topeka-Shawunee County Dept. of Labor Services*, Kn Ct App. No. 57 (1981); *Palmateer* v. *International Harvester Company*, 85 Ill., 2d 124 (1981).
53. Clyde W. Summers, "The Need for A Statute," *ILR Report*, Fall 1982, pp. 8–12; Paul Salvatore, "Legislative Action and Private Initiative: A Practical Solution," *ILR Report*, Fall 1982, pp. 13–15.
54. *Toussaint* v. *Blue Cross/Blue Shield of Michigan*, 408 Mich. 579 (1980).
55. *Cleary* v. *American Airlines*, 111 Ca. App. 3d (1980).
56. Lawrence Z. Lorber, J. Robert Kirk, Kenneth H. Kirschner, and Charlene R. Handorf, *Fear of Firing* (Alexandria, Va.: ASPA Foundation, 1984); Robert H. Nichols, "Would Labor Oppose a Statute?," *ILR Report*, Fall 1982, pp. 21–23; Ira M. Shepard and Nancy L. Moran, " 'Wrongful' Discharge Litigation," *ILR Report*, Fall 1982, pp. 26–29; "Court Says At-Will Clause in Sear's Application Form Allowed Managers to Discharge, Demote without Proving 'Cause'," *Human Resources Management Ideas and Trends*, November 24, 1982, pp. 209–10; Anthony T. Oliver, Jr., "The Disappearing Right to Terminate Employees at Will," *Personnel Journal*, December 1982, pp. 910–17; "At-Will Employment," *Human Resources Management Ideas and Trends*, May 19, 1983, pp. 73–80; Robert Coulson, *The Termination Handbook* (New York: Free Press, 1981). Also, William J. Holloway and Michael J. Leech, *Employment Termination: Rights and Remedies* (Washington, D.C.: BNA Books, 1985); Jerome B. Kauff and Maureen E. McClain, *Unjust Dismissal, 1984* (New York: Practicing Law Institute, 1984); Ralph H. Baxter, Jr., and Jeffrey D. Wohl, "Wrongful Termination Lawsuits: The Employers Finally Win a Few," *Employee Relations Law Journal* 10 (1985), pp. 258–75; Koys, Briggs, and Grenig, "State Court Dis-

parity on Employment-at-Will"; Koys, Briggs, and Grenig, "The Employ-ment-at-Will Doctrine"; Sami M. Abbasi, Kenneth W. Hollman, and Joe H. Murrey, Jr., "Employment at Will: An Eroding Concept in Employment Relationships," *Labor Law Journal* 38, no. 1 (January 1987), pp. 261–79.

57. "Fired Employees Turn the Reason for Dismissal into a Legal Weapon," *The Wall Street Journal*, October 2, 1986, p. 33.

58. Lee Dyer, F. Foltman, and G. Milkovich, "Employment Stabilization" (working paper, Cornell University, 1984); Mark Thompson, "The Perma-nent Employment System: Japan and Mexico," Sixth World Congress of Industrial Relations, Kyōto, Japan, March 28–31, 1983; R. Fuller, C. Jor-dan, and R. Anderson, "Retrenchment: Layoff Procedures in a Nonprofit Organization," *Personnel*, November–December 1982, pp. 19–24; R. H. Ketchum, "Retrenchment: The Uses and Misuses of Life in Downsizing an Organization," *Personnel*, November–December 1982, pp. 25–30; Linda Wintner, *Employee Buyouts: An Alternative to Plant Closings* (New York: The Conference Board, 1983); F. Foltman, "Managing a Plant Closing: An Overview" (working paper, ILR School, Ithaca, N.Y.: Cornell University, 1981); T. Bailey and T. Jackson, "Industrial Outplacement at Goodyear," *Personnel Administrator*, March 1980, pp. 42–48; D. L. Ward, "The $34,000 Layoff," *Human Resources Planning* 5, no. 1 (1982), pp. 35–43; Dick Schaaff, "Are You Training Yet for Outplacement and Retirement?" *Training*, May 1981, pp. 70–84; E. B. Silverman and S. D. Sass, "Out-placement," *Training and Development Journal*, February 1982, pp. 71–84; R. S. Barkhaus and Carol L. Mak, "A Practical View of Outplacement," *Personnel Administrator*, March 1982, pp. 77–85; C. H. Driessnank, "Out-placement—The New Personnel Practice," *Personnel Administrator*, Octo-ber 1980, pp. 81–93; P. D. Johnston, "Personnel Planning for a Plant Shutdown," *Personnel Administrator*, August 1981, pp. 53–60.

59. Adapted from Dyer, Foltman, and Milkovich, "Employment Stabilization."

60. Ibid.; Leonard Greenhalgh, "Organizational Decline," in *The Sociology of Organizations* 2 (Greenwich, Conn.: JAI Press, 1983), pp. 231–76; James F. Bolt, "Job Security: Its Time Has Come," *Harvard Business Review*, No-vember–December 1983; Leonard Greenhalgh, Robert B. McKersie, and Roderick W. Gilkey, "Rebalancing the Work Force at IBM: A Case Study of Redeployment and Revitalization" (working paper, Sloan School of Man-agement, Massachusetts Institute of Technology, 1985); Rosalind Klein Ber-lind, "Cutting Costs without Cutting People," *Fortune*, May 25, 1987.

61. Dyer, Foltman, and Milkovich, "Employment Stabilization."

62. Work in America Institute, *The Continuous Learning/Employment Security Connection* (Scarsdale, N.Y.: Work in America Institute, 1987).

63. U.S. Government Accounting Office, "Reduction in Force."

64. Berlind, "Cutting Costs without Cutting People."

65. The Conference Board, *Human Resources Outlook, 1987* (New York: The Conference Board, 1987).

66. Ronald E, Berenbeim, *Company Programs to Ease the Impact of Shut-downs* (New York: The Conference Board, 1986).

67. Bureau of National Affairs, "Severance Benefits and Outplacement Services."

68. "AT&T to Lay Off 26,400 Employees by 1988; Union Says Announcement

Violates Understanding," *Bureau of National Affairs Daily Labor Report*, December 22, 1986; Berlind, "Cutting Costs without Cutting People"; "Exxon Work-Force Cuts Hit Home," *The Wall Street Journal*, July 9, 1986; "Time Inc. Net Falls; Layoffs Set"; "Chevron to Cut Its Staff by 12%," *New York Times*, June 13, 1986; "U.S. Steel Corp. to Reduce Staff," *The Wall Street Journal*, May 21, 1986; E. N. Berg, "Shrinking a Staff the Kodak Way," *New York Times*, September 4, 1983.

69. Harris, "A Lifetime at IBM."

70. Thomas J. Leary, "Deindustrialization, Plant Closing Laws, and the States," *State Government*, Fall 1985, pp. 113–18.

71. *Firefighters Local Union No. 1784* v. *Stotts* 467 U.S. 561 (1984); *Wygant* v. *Jackson Board of Education* 40 FEP Cases 1321 (May 19, 1986); Bureau of National Affairs, *Affirmative Action Today* (Washington, D.C.: Bureau of National Affairs, 1986).

72. Bureau of National Affairs, "Severance Benefits and Outplacement Services."

73. Berenbeim, "Company Programs to Ease the Impact of Shutdowns."

74. Bureau of National Affairs, "Severance Benefits and Outplacement Services."

75. Ibid., Berenbeim, "Company Programs to Ease the Impact of Shutdowns."

76. "Teaching the Advantages of Inside Counseling: Training for Outplacement," *Resource*, March 1986, pp. 7–10.

77. Malcolm R. Lovell, Jr., *Economic Adjustment and Worker Relocation*, Report of the Secretary of Labor's Task Force on Economic Adjustment and Worker Dislocation (Washington, D.C.: U.S. Department of Labor, 1986).

78. Berlind, "Cutting Costs without Cutting People."

79. Boudreau and Berger, "Decision-Theoretic Utility Analysis Applied to Employee Separations and Acquisitions"; Flamholtz, *Human Resource Accounting;* Dalton and Todor, "Turnover: A Lucrative Hard-Dollar Phenomenon"; Cascio, *Costing Human Resources;* Smith and Watkins, "Managing Manpower Turnover Costs"; Bureau of National Affairs, "Severance Benefits and Outplacement Assistance"; Ward, "The $34,000 Layoff"; U.S. Government Accounting Office, "Reduction in Force."

80. Martin and Bartol, "Managing Turnover Strategically"; Dalton, Krackhardt, and Porter, "Functional Turnover: An Empirical Assessment."

81. Boudreau and Berger, "Decision-Theoretic Utility Analysis Applied to Employee Separations and Acquisitions"; Boudreau and Berger, "Toward a Model of Employee Movement Utility"; Boudreau, "Utility Analysis: A New Perspective on Human Resource Management Decisions."

82. Boudreau, "Utility Analysis: A New Perspective on Human Resource Management Decisions."

thirteen

INTERNAL STAFFING

CHAPTER OUTLINE

VII. Evaluating Internal Staffing Activities
   A. Efficiency
   B. Equity
VIII. Summary

> Some employees left the predictable and found a team. Several employees went to Miami Beach. One person didn't switch and saw everything come up roses. Another did switch and, in his own words, "hasn't stopped smiling since."
>
> Who are these people and what's going on?
>
> They are, to use a term heard often in the company these days, IBM men and women who have been redeployed—who have set out with considerable optimism on what are essentially new careers in a new place."[1]

Twelve thousand employees changed jobs at IBM Corporation during 1986, and even more job changes are expected in the future. Many people changed careers, moving from areas of surplus, such as production, to areas of shortage—marketing, sales, and programming. Xerox Corporation's Reprographics Business Group retrains chemists, engineers, and other professionals to enter completely different high-demand fields such as computer science and computer engineering. Pacific Bell maintains its policy of employment security with a companywide career planning system that updates employees on declining and rising job opportunities, and trains those willing to relocate. And Hewlett-Packard Company moves production employees in surplus occupations to office jobs in high-demand areas, with a redeployment plan that includes career mentors to provide relevant on-the-job experience and conferences between supervisors from both the hiring and originating departments.[2] One recent study of population data forecast that over a quarter of all workers in the U.S. labor force will work for the same employer for 20 years or more.[3] Most of them will hold many positions in the same organization.

Staffing decisions do not just determine who enters and leaves the organization, but also how employees move between jobs within the organization. Such decisions have always been a part of human resource management, but they are becoming more important and frequent as organizations search for ways to maintain efficiency and equity in the face of rapidly changing economic conditions. Similar to external selection and reduction, such decisions can affect the organization for decades. Moreover, employee movements between jobs determine career progress, a major factor in employees' status, income level, and satisfaction with their jobs and lives. How can organizations identify internal employment candidates? Which factors affect individuals' willingness to accept certain employment opportunities, and how can they be induced to accept the changes necessary to keep the organization flexible and competitive? This chapter examines these and other issues related to the internal staffing process.

Definition

Internal staffing involves decisions to move existing employees between employment opportunities within the same organization. Those movements include promotions (movements to higher hierarchical levels), transfers (movements to similar hierarchical levels), and demotions (movements to lower hierarchical levels).

Internal staffing integrates the principles of recruiting (discussed in Chapter Ten), selection (discussed in Chapter Eleven), and separation/retention (discussed in Chapter Twelve). Internal job candidates must be identified, informed of the employment opportunities, and induced to accept them (recruiting). Candidates must be chosen to receive employment offers (selection). The movement of chosen candidates out of their original positions affects those retained (separation/retention). Thus, internal staffing encompasses important issues of work force quality and efficiency as well as individual career progress, attitudes, and motivation.

A DIAGNOSTIC APPROACH TO INTERNAL STAFFING

As we have seen in earlier chapters, effective staffing decisions require assessing conditions and establishing objectives and evaluation based on both efficiency and equity.

External Conditions

Although internal staffing decisions focus on employment opportunities within the organization, they are affected by external conditions just as external staffing decisions.

Product/Labor Markets

As discussed in Chapter Nine, internal staffing opportunities reflect current or anticipated labor shortages and surpluses partly caused by product and labor market forces. Organizations facing changing product markets often redeploy (transfer) all or part of the work force in an effort to retain employees, while preparing for the future. In areas of increasing demand, the emphasis is on getting the internal job candidates best suited to fill the vacancies. Where demand is decreasing, the emphasis is on encouraging employees to find new opportunities to reduce labor costs and streamline operations. During periods of high unemployment, organizations may find employees willing to relocate or retrain. However, it may be more difficult to find willing internal employment candidates when alternative employment opportunities are plentiful in other companies, especially if the alternative opportunities do not involve relocation.

Government

Internal staffing is subject to the same EEO legislation as external selection. Thus, internal selection procedures that produce an unacceptably small proportion of female or minority applicants accepting employment offers or represented in the job are subject to the same governmental scrutiny, legal liability, and financial penalties as the interviews or tests used to select new hires.[4] Moreover, affirmative action progress—especially in upper-level jobs—frequently depends on decisions made about internal staffing. For example, organizations with promote-from-within policies must rely on internal staffing to achieve affirmative action in upper-level positions.

In fact, recent Supreme Court decisions suggest that under certain conditions even preferential treatment of minorities and females in promotion decisions can be an acceptable mechanism for enhancing affirmative action progress.[5] In March 1987 the Supreme Court supported the legality of a temporary promotion quota requiring a 50 percent black promotion rate in the Alabama State Police after a long history of racial discrimination.[6] As described earlier, the Supreme Court also ruled that the Santa Clara (California) Transportation Agency with a voluntary affirmative action plan legally promoted Diane Joyce over Paul Johnson.[7] Both Joyce and Johnson had scored above the minimum acceptable score (70 points) on an interview, with Joyce scoring 73 and Johnson scoring 75. Though controversial, these decisions illustrate the importance of governmental and court influences in internal staffing decisions.

Unions

Collective bargaining agreements and contract administration are frequently even more concerned with internal than with external staffing. How workers become eligible for promotion and transfer opportunities is a traditional employment security issue for unions. For promotions, seniority is an eligibility factor in 82 percent of manufacturing contracts and 59 percent of nonmanufacturing contracts. Regarding transfers, 62 percent of manufacturing contracts and 37 percent of nonmanufacturing contracts stipulate that seniority be considered. Frequently, the most senior employees must receive transfer or promotion opportunities if they are qualified to perform the vacant job's duties acceptably, even if someone else could perform better. Sixty-nine percent of manufacturing industry contracts and 47 percent of nonmanufacturing contracts require that vacancies be posted for employees' notification.[8]

Organizational Conditions

The strategic product/market objectives of organizations determine the internal demand for employees and skills.[9] Obviously, organizations changing their primary product markets must think carefully about the future roles of current employees. However, even organizations attempting to survive in the same market often face changing economic conditions that affect internal staffing. Employment planning should anticipate such changes in time to put internal staffing activities in place. The organization's size also determines internal staffing activities. Smaller organizations, or organizations at an early stage of growth, may simply not have enough internal job candidates or the resources to prepare them to adequately meet future demands. Research suggests that *internal labor markets* with a few entry points at the bottom promote from within and develop organization-specific skills in response to organizational structure and job relationships.[10]

The traditions and values of the organization also shape internal staffing. The examples in the introduction illustrated that internal staffing often helps avoid work force reductions. At IBM, Eastman Kodak, and other companies with a commitment to employment security, effective internal staffing becomes a critical component of maintaining that commitment.

Employee Conditions

Employee conditions are especially relevant to internal staffing. Unlike external recruitment and selection, internal staffing deals with current employees. Thus, the skills, abilities, interests, and attitudes of the existing work force determine the success of internal staffing activities. Both the organization and the individual have a much richer variety of information about each other in the internal staffing decision than they did when the employment relationship was initiated. Moreover, with planning, the organization and the individual can prepare themselves for anticipated internal staffing opportunities if the proper climate of trust and cooperation exists. Internal staffing activities not only draw on the existing skills, motivations, and attitudes of the work force, but also help to shape these characteristics.

As discussed in Chapter Seven, employee attitudes toward future career opportunities are an important facet of their overall satisfaction with the organization. Research also suggests that satisfaction with promotion opportunities can decrease the likelihood of employee separations.

Setting Objectives for Internal Staffing

Similar to external staffing, internal staffing activities change the composition or mix of employees in the work force. They share many of the processes of recruitment, selection, and separation/retention. Managing internal staffing activities effectively requires attention to their effects on both efficiency and equity.

Efficiency

External recruiting involves advertising, travel, and administrative costs (see Chapter Ten). External selection can involve costs of selection techniques, relocation, and validation (see Chapter Eleven). Finally, managing external separations/retentions involves outplacement, exit interviews, and severance pay (see Chapter Twelve). Because internal staffing applies activities to the existing work force, internal staffing costs parallel those of external staffing. Internal staffing includes costs of notifying employees, counseling them on career choices, and preparing them for new employment opportunities. Additional costs arise from assessing current employee capabilities, relocation, validation, career counseling, and bonuses to induce career movements.

Regarding productivity, internal staffing works when it puts the right quantity and quality of current employees in the right employment opportunities at minimum cost. Internal staffing is similar to external recruitment and selection in that it attracts an applicant pool and uses information to choose candidates most likely to contribute to organizational goals. Internal staffing is also similar to employee separation/retention because the employees separate from their previous employment roles, producing consequences for the retained work force. Emerging evidence suggests that internal staffing can have profound effects on work force quality.[11]

Equity

Because internal staffing affects current employees, decisions about internal staffing activities must be as much, or more, attuned to equity perceptions than external staffing activities. EEO/AA legislation and court decisions affect both internal and external staffing activities. So managers must consider the effects of internal staffing on the minority composition of the organization.

Careers represent more than a series of employment opportunities for those who move; they are a signal to employees about the equity of organizational policies. Perceived career opportunities affect employees' attitudes and satisfaction. Because promotions often appear to be rewards, they are subject to the same equity scrutiny as pay and benefits. Moreover, employees' career decisions usually involve a concern for self-direction or control, family inputs such as two-career planning, and a desire for assistance and information from organizations in planning and directing their own careers.[12]

Finally, because internal staffing decisions have fundamental effects on the employment security and pay levels of employees, they are a basic issue in most collective bargaining agreements. Unions desire to ensure that such decisions are made in objective and fair ways.

THE ROLE OF INTERNAL MOVEMENT IN THE STAFFING PROCESS

Internal Staffing as an Integration of Recruiting, Selection, and Separation/Retention

Research on internal staffing has focused on the *individual* factors of career development, career stages, attitudes, and behaviors,[13] as well as *organizational* factors such as the patterns of movement between positions, the role of mobility in status attainment, and efficient allocation of labor resources.[14] However, very little research documents the effects of internal staffing on organizational performance or decision systems that can better link internal staffing decisions to organizational outcomes.[15] Similarly, professionals have devoted a great deal of attention to preparing job candidates and selecting them, but much less attention to the consequences of internal movement on jobs that lose employees.[16] This chapter takes a broad perspective on internal staffing, viewing it as an integrated process encompassing all of these factors. Exhibit 13–1 illustrates how internal staffing affects the work force. The left side of the exhibit depicts the effects of internal staffing on positions serving as sources of employment candidates, and the right side reflects the perspective of the destinations of the internal employment candidates.

For the jobs or positions serving as destinations for internal movements, internal staffing is very similar to recruitment and selection, except

EXHIBIT 13–1
Illustration of the Internal Staffing Process

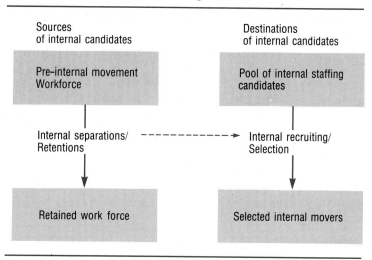

that it affects job candidates who are already employees. Just as the applicant pool established by external recruitment sets the limits of external selection, the pool of internal job candidates affects internal staffing effectiveness. Just as external selection works by using information about applicants to choose which external candidates should receive employment opportunities, internal staffing works by using information about existing employees to choose which internal candidates should receive new employment opportunities.

The effect of internal staffing on the positions that serve as sources of internal employment candidates is important and frequently overlooked. Because every internal acquisition implies moving an employee from a previous position, internal staffing affects the characteristics of the retained work force in the original position just as external separations/retentions affect the retained work force when employees leave the organization. The same employees that appear as internal staffing candidates on the right side of Exhibit 13–1 also appear as an existing work force on the left side. The same movements caused by internal recruiting/selection activities on the right side produce a corresponding pattern of employee separations from the sources of those employees on the left side (as indicated by the dotted line).

In actual organizations of any size, there are many sources and destinations of internal candidates; each position may serve as both a source and a destination. Moreover, internal staffing affects not only the number and pattern of available opportunities, but also external separations and acquisitions.[17] Chapter Nine discussed employment planning techniques for describing and forecasting these movement patterns.

The Concept of Validity in Internal Staffing

Chapter Eleven noted that validity in selection reflects the degree to which evidence supports inferences about how applicants will perform after being hired. Chapter Twelve noted that validity also applied to separations/retentions because the pattern of separations affects the characteristics of those who are retained. Internal staffing validity reflects both of these perspectives. Moreover, as with external selection and separations/retentions, validity has implications not only for organizational productivity and efficiency, but for equity as well.

An Illustration

Let us expand the example from Chapter Twelve to demonstrate how internal staffing affects the work force. Exhibit 13–2 depicts the same work force information contained in Exhibit 12–2. However, we have added a column of information—each employee's predicted performance as sales manager at this time. It is based on a scale of 2 to 10.

Suppose the organization has five sales manager vacancies and promotes solely on seniority, as is common in unionized situations. They would promote Jeremy, Rudolfo, Karl, Lindsey, and Arthur, producing an average predicted performance of 8 (out of a possible 10) points. It would achieve a 20 percent minority promotion rate (1 out of 5), and raise the minority representation rate among retained salespeople to 47 percent (7 out of 15). The 15 retained salespeople's annual sales performance would average $2,267, for a total of $34,000. Although this may seem equitable from a seniority perspective, high sales performers Maggie, Manuel, and Herbert may wonder whether it's worth working so hard or remaining with this organization if they have to wait up to six years to be promoted.

Now, suppose the organization promoted based on past performance, reasoning that high performers should be rewarded with higher status, more responsibility, and higher pay. Performance-based promotions would move Jeremy, Rudolfo, Maggie, Manuel, and Herbert up to sales manager, producing the same average predicted managerial performance level of 8. The minority promotion rate would be raised to 40 percent (that is, 2 out of 5) and the original 40 percent representation rate among salespeople is maintained in the retained group (that is, 6 out of 15 are minority-group members). However, the yearly sales level among the retained salespeople would drop to a total of $30,000 for an average of $2,000. This

EXHIBIT 13–2
Example Work Force Illustrating Internal Staffing Effects

Salesperson	Annual Sales	Years of Seniority	Minority	Predicted Managerial Performance (points)
Jeremy	$ 4,000	8	No	10
Rudolfo	4,000	8	No	6
Maggie	4,000	2	Yes	10
Manuel	4,000	6	Yes	8
Herbert	4,000	6	No	6
Karl	3,000	8	No	8
Donald	3,000	4	Yes	10
Lindsey	3,000	8	Yes	6
Ralph	3,000	6	No	10
Beuford	3,000	4	No	6
Arthur	2,000	8	No	10
Dorothy	2,000	2	Yes	4
James	2,000	6	No	8
Bertram	2,000	4	No	4
Jesse	2,000	4	Yes	4
Oliver	1,000	2	No	8
Anne	1,000	2	Yes	4
Enrique	1,000	2	Yes	6
Fred	1,000	6	No	8
Barney	1,000	4	No	4
Total	$50,000	100		
Average	$ 2,500	5		7

is far below the original average of $2,500. Moreover, as senior employees passed over for promotion, Lindsey and Arthur may wonder if they will ever get rewarded for their loyalty and long service.

Finally, suppose the organization promotes salespeople based on predicted performance as sales managers. This would promote Jeremy, Maggie, Donald, Ralph, and Arthur. They all have the highest predicted sales manager performance, so the average predicted performance rating of this promoted group is 10. This pattern achieves a 40 percent minority selection ratio (that is, 2 out of the 5 promoted employees are minority-group members), and it retains the 40 percent representation rate in the sales job (that is, 6 out of 15 retained employees are minorities). However, such a promotion pattern still removes several high-performing salespeople, leaving a retained sales work force that produces yearly total sales of $34,000, an average of $2,267 per salesperson. Moreover, it promotes two low-tenure employees (Maggie and Donald) over others with up to eight years in the sales job. It also promotes lower performers Donald, Ralph, and Arthur over top-performing Rudolfo, Manuel, and Herbert. This may not seem very fair to the high-tenure and high-performing employees, especially if those promoted end up supervising them!

Clearly, internal staffing decisions produce broad consequences, and the effects on the sources of candidates are often different from the effects on destinations. These effects have implications for both efficiency and equity. This example used promotions, but the principles apply as well to transfers or demotions. In actual decisions, multiple destinations may compete for the best candidates and multiple sources may provide candidates. Actual decision implications also depend on the validity of the selection information; that is, how accurately the predicted managerial performance scores reflect eventual managerial performance and on the willingness of salespeople to accept promotion offers.

CAREER MANAGEMENT AND CAREER PLANNING

Although it bears similarities to external staffing, internal staffing is unique because it deals with current employees. Internal recruitment locates job candidates and actively prepares employees for future internal moves. Internal selection activities not only choose the best qualified candidates, but also affect rejected candidates who remain employed. The internal selection process affects their future attitudes, motivations, and work behaviors in contrast to external selection where rejected applicants have little direct effect on organizational outcomes. Thus, in internal staffing, organizations simultaneously consider both the organization's and the individual's goals in making decisions. This dual focus of internal staffing culminates in an important aspect of internal staffing, *career development*.

Definition

Career development encompasses career management and career planning. *Career planning* is the process through which individual employees identify and implement steps to attain career goals. *Career management* is the process through which organizations select, assess, assign, and develop employees to provide a pool of qualified people to meet future needs.[18]

Employee, Managerial, and Organizational Responsibilities

Exhibit 13–3 illustrates how the processes of career planning and career management are integrated. The organization's role in career management resembles external selection, but internal staffing makes use of organization-specific information such as previous experience with the organization, training records, and past performance ratings. This may improve the validity of internal selection decisions if the information produces valid inferences about future job behaviors.

The organization's role in career planning resembles an extension of external recruiting. Even though external recruiting identifies and attracts an external applicant pool, this is usually the first contact between employer and applicant. Thus, the organization has little influence beyond attraction. In contrast, because internal staffing deals with existing employees, the pool of candidates is not only identified and attracted, but can also be prepared for future opportunities through counseling, work experiences, training, and other methods. Thus, career planning contributes to employees' career growth and improves the qualifications of employees for future employment opportunities. A variety of factors affect individuals' needs and reactions to career planning activities. These include the magnitude of career transitions, factors in their work and nonwork lives, their aspirations, their career motivation, and even whether they have an entrepreneurial tendency or not.[19] Employee career planning needs are related to career orientation and career stages.[20]

Career Orientation

Based on longitudinal study of management graduates, Edgar Schein has developed the concept of "career anchor."[21] A career anchor is a self-concept based on differing work motives and abilities that guide, stabilize, and integrate a person's work experiences. Schein identifies five different anchors.[22]

1. *Technical/functional competence.* The primary orientation of these individuals is the actual work they do, and they wish to continue using their existing skills. They avoid positions which remove them from areas of established competence or push them into general management. These people define growth as increasing skill, rather than increasing organization level. An example may be an engineer who wishes to pursue microchip design, and has no wish to supervise others.

EXHIBIT 13–3
Integration between Career Planning and Career Management

Career-Planning Activities

Employee's responsibilities:

• Self-assess abilities, interests, and values.
• Analyze career options.
• Decide on development objectives and needs.
• Communicate development preferences to manager.
• Map out mutually agreeable action plans with manager.
• Pursue agreed-on action plan.

Manager's responsibilities:

• Act as catalyst; sensitize employee to the development planning process.
• Assess realism of employee's expressed objectives and perceived development needs.
• Counsel employee and develop a mutually agreeable plan.
• Follow up and update employee's plans as appropriate.

Organization's responsibilities:

• Provide career-planning model, resources, counseling, and information needed for individualized career planning.
• Provide training in career development planning to managers and employees and career counseling to managers.
• Provide skills training programs and on-the-job development experience opportunities.

Career Management Activities

Employee's responsibilities:

• Provide accurate information to management as needed regarding skills, work experiences, interests, and career aspirations.

Manager's responsibilities:

• Validate information provided by employees.
• Provide information about vacant job positions for which the manager is responsible.
• Use all information provided by the process to: (1) identify all viable candidates for a vacant position and make a selection and (2) identify career development opportunities (job openings, training programs, rotation assignments) for employees and place them accordingly.

Organization's responsibilities:

• Provide information system and process to accommodate management's decision-making needs.
• Organize and update all information.
• Ensure effective usage of information by: (1) designing convenient methods for collecting, analyzing, interpreting, and using the information; and (2) monitoring and evaluating the effectiveness of the process.

Source: Frank J. Minor, "Computer Applications in Career Development Planning," in *Career Development in Organizations,* ed. Douglas T. Hall and Associates (San Francisco: Jossey-Bass, 1986), pp. 205–6.

2. *Managerial competence.* The primary work goal for this group is to develop the managerial abilities of *(a)* interpersonal competence, *(b)* analytical competence, and *(c)* emotional competence required at the highest levels of management.

These two career orientations were most common in Schein's sample, but even in this relatively homogenous group of management school graduates, other career anchors existed. They include:

3. *Security.* An orientation toward working for a particular organization or in a specific geographic area.
4. *Creativity.* An orientation toward creating something that is entirely their own—whether it is a product, a company, or a personal fortune.
5. *Autonomy/independence.* These persons do not adapt well to working under the constraints of organization life; many leave it to become consultants or to start their own businesses.

Career anchors, according to Schein, reflect the underlying motives and abilities that a person brings into adulthood.[23] A career anchor results from early work experiences and provides guidance as a career progresses through various stages.

Career Stages

As individuals accumulate work experience, their maturation can be considered within a biological model of growth and decay.[24] Career stage models relate maturation stages to the needs of the employee. For example, a person in an early career stage may be less concerned with pensions and vesting rights, and more concerned with upward mobility than a person in a later career stage.[25] Exhibit 13–4 shows the four career stages.

Exploration
The young adult in the exploration stage is trying to fit into the world of work. Exploration activities include trying to clarify and identify one's interests and skills, building those skills through education or training programs, dealing with constraints such as finances and parental pressure, and making initial decisions on jobs and organizations of interest. Exploration is influenced by school, family, and friends. Jobs (and roles) may be tried and rejected, false starts may occur; but throughout all these "searching" activities, the young adult is gaining knowledge and developing a self-image in terms of possible career goals and directions. Then the young adult seeks permanent employment that uses skills and meets personal needs. This leads to the second stage, establishment.

EXHIBIT 13–4
Career Stages

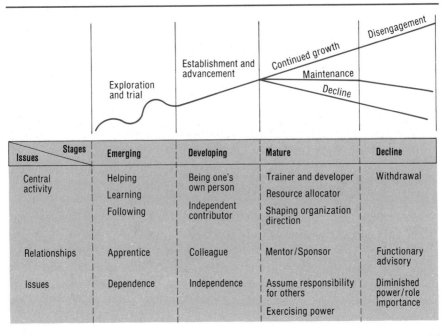

Stages Issues	Emerging	Developing	Mature	Decline
Central activity	Helping Learning Following	Being one's own person Independent contributor	Trainer and developer Resource allocator Shaping organization direction	Withdrawal
Relationships	Apprentice	Colleague	Mentor/Sponsor	Functionary advisory
Issues	Dependence	Independence	Assume responsibility for others Exercising power	Diminished power/role importance

Establishment

The establishment stage includes successful negotiation through the re-cruiting process, acceptance of a job, and orientation into the chosen or-ganization. During this early socialization into an organization, an individual develops a sense of the likely future within that organization.

Following socialization is a process of "mutual acceptance." The indi-vidual, co-workers, and supervisors must all learn the capabilities and con-straints of the others. Open exchanges of information and feedback on performance are necessary for this acceptance to occur. Such feedback pro-vides opportunities to demonstrate capabilities on both sides. In addition to fostering mutual acceptance, an individual in the establishment stage establishes a balance between responding to directives and initiating activities.

Maintenance

Here the individual has become an important member of the organization; work assignments are of a more vital nature. The organization draws on the individual's accumulated wisdom and perspective. This person is ex-pected to serve as role model and mentor for younger employees.

The maintenance stage may also be a time of midcareer crisis, which can be stimulated by these events outside the work life:

1. Family changes—children leaving home, divorce, illness, or death of parents.
2. Changed financial obligations, with resulting ability to consider options (for example, self-employment) that were previously unrealistic because of their financial risk.
3. A recognition of limits, including mortality, which may spur a reassessment of one's accomplishments and a change in goals.

Many people in midcareer, with varying degrees of apprehension and success, cycle back to the exploration stage, and make major changes in their lives at this time.

Decline

Some writers characterize the latter years of a career as a time of decline. Preparation for retirement may involve a psychological withdrawal from the organization long before physical separation occurs. A reduced role with less responsibility may be assigned; personal and work relationships may be adjusted according to their value to the individual and the amount of effort the individual is willing to expend on maintaining them.

Sociologists and psychologists may make narrower distinctions to add more stages, or integrate life and career stages; some emphasize the critical nature of the transition from one stage to the next.[26] Others postulate a "career clock," which affects the speed of movement among stages.[27] Still another postulates a concept of "career unrest," which may stem from life unrest, career self-unrest (dissatisfaction with one's personal effectiveness in one's chosen career), career content unrest (dissatisfaction with the work content of the chosen career), or job unrest (dissatisfaction with the work environment). Robert Oliver claims that career unrest diminishes an individual's ability to make a creative contribution, and so affects productivity.[28]

RECRUITMENT DECISIONS IN INTERNAL STAFFING

As Chapter Ten noted, recruitment involves identifying and attracting a pool of job candidates. Because internal staffing focuses on existing employees, internal recruitment emphasizes two-way communication and reflects an ongoing relationship between job candidates and those recruiting and selecting them.

Communicating Internal Employment Opportunities

Internal recruiting communication can emphasize either alerting employees to employment opportunities or keeping ongoing records of employees' characteristics for generating needed candidates. Job posting systems alert employees, while skills inventories and succession planning tracks the status of the internal applicant pool for decision makers.

Job Posting

In the job-posting system, the organization notifies its present employees of openings, using bulletin boards and company publications. Employees who respond to these announcements are considered for the position.

Each week Bank of America, for example, publishes a Job Opportunities Bulletin resembling the help-wanted section of a newspaper. The bulletin publishes various job openings with brief descriptions of the work involved and the qualifications required. Additionally, it lists salaries, grades, and the departments, subsidiaries, or branches offering the jobs. Copies are placed in staff lounges, hallways, and other points frequented by employees. On the back of the bulletin is an application form. Interested employees fill out forms and mail them to a coordinator to be considered.

Companies have widely adopted such systems. The preponderance use them for office, clerical, administrative, and technical positions.[29] One reason for the popularity is the implicit openness of the system, enabling all employees, including EEO-protected groups, to nominate themselves for positions for which they consider themselves qualified. Posting is also a valuable tool incorporated in many affirmative action programs and consent decrees. Job posting permits self-selection and expressions of interest by employees.

Dave Dahl and Patrick Pinto provide a useful set of guidelines for effective job-posting systems.

Post all permanent promotion and transfer opportunities.

Post the jobs for at least one week prior to recruiting outside the organization.

Clarify eligibility rules. For example, specify minimum service in the present position; state decision rules used to choose between several equally qualified applicants, if such rules will be used.

List job specifications. Make application forms available.

Tell all applicants how the job was filled.[30]

How common is job posting? A recent survey found that over all positions, 47 percent of respondents post listings for in-house applicants.

Organizations were more likely to post lower-salaried positions (such as staff accountant and human resources specialists) than high-salary positions (such as general manager and senior financial officer).[31]

Skills Inventories

As discussed in Chapter Nine, skills inventories are lists of employees and their characteristics relevant to internal employment opportunities. Thus, skills inventories represent an ongoing method through which human resource managers learn about available internal employment candidates. As with any information system, the data in such skills inventories must be tailored to organizational needs.[32] Some commonly included items are: name, employee number, present location, birthdate, employment date, current job code, prior experience, work experience with the organization, training completed, skill and knowledge ratings, education degree and major field, foreign languages spoken or written, health, professional qualifications, publications, patents, licenses, salary, and supervisory ratings of capabilities and promotability. Such inventories may also include employees' statements of career goals, geographical preferences, or anticipated retirement dates.

Managers can scan skills inventories either by computer or manually to identify sets of job candidates satisfying certain minimum requirements. Inventories also contain information for more general staffing and employment planning, as the following examples illustrate.[33]

Examples of Skills Inventories. IBM's system contains information on such data as career plans and educational goals for over 100,000 of its employees. This system allows IBM to project five-year engineering and other personnel needs for various rates of corporate growth. A monthly personnel transaction report for all divisions pinpoints possible imbalances within the total organizational system. The RCA Service Company uses its skill inventories to help management define which businesses it could be in.[34]

The U.S. Civil Service Commission has a skills inventory for all individuals above GS-14 (middle management)—about 25,000 executives.[35] This database allows the U.S. government to examine age distributions by such factors as occupation, educational attainment, mobility, and reasons for entering and leaving, and to make these data available in a usable form for analysis. Robert Smith points out several uses of such a system:

> A carefully prepared skills inventory can be used as a basis for long-range personnel planning and development by providing precise definitions of the aptitudes and abilities available and needed by the organization. It can be used to assist in the evaluation of growth potential of the present executive work force and help to identify group strengths and weaknesses for

future recruiting strategies. It may uncover interdivisional imbalances (e.g., understaffing) which could lead to future overall corporate personnel problems. Most importantly, it will serve as a motivating device by demonstrating through written feedback that the organization has a systematic approach to personal data utilization and that it is eager to develop each employee to full potential.[36]

Maintaining Skills Inventory Systems. Although designing the system is the most difficult part of developing a skills inventory, planning for the gathering, maintaining, handling, and updating of data is also important.[37] The two principal methods for gathering data are the interview and the questionnaire. Each method has unique costs and benefits. The questionnaire is faster and less expensive when many employees are involved, but inaccuracies are usually greater; people often do not spend enough time on a questionnaire. There are those who contend, therefore, that the trained interviewer can complete the reports more quickly and accurately, and this in the long run more than offsets the costs of the interviewer. Either way, managers must develop a procedure for keeping the files updated.

Computerized systems have the advantage of providing faster and more detailed information.[38] They also are useful in wider applications. Managers can project employee turnover to determine the work force required to maximize the capital investment. They can also generate a comparative analysis of employment on a time series basis on the computer; observing the changes in promotable personnel over time may provide insights into the effectiveness of recruiting and development activities. Computerized systems can analyze all the sequential events necessary in a production process. With an estimation of their associated time and cost factors, these systems can enhance accuracy of planning by defining all the necessary work activities, suggesting the latest allowable starting date for each activity, and identifying the potential costs of various courses of action.[39]

Replacement and Succession Planning

Replacement planning involves having senior executives periodically review their top executives and those in the next-lower echelon to determine two or three backups for each senior slot. They sometimes call these "truck lists" because they list replacements in case any executive is hit by a truck.[40] Succession planning not only focuses on those who might be candidates for current positions, but also attempts to plan for possible changes in those positions, as well as the promotion and development needs of subordinates.[41]

EXHIBIT 13–5
Replacement Chart

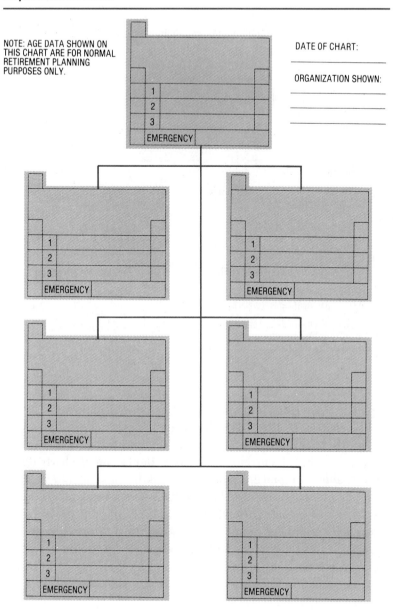

NOTE: AGE DATA SHOWN ON
THIS CHART ARE FOR NORMAL
RETIREMENT PLANNING
PURPOSES ONLY.

DATE OF CHART:

ORGANIZATION SHOWN:

EXHIBIT 13–5 *(concluded)*
Codes for Replacement Charts

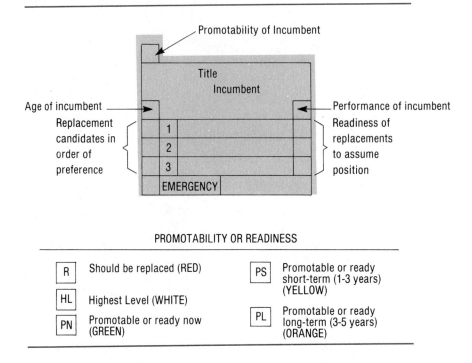

PROMOTABILITY OR READINESS

R	Should be replaced (RED)
HL	Highest Level (WHITE)
PN	Promotable or ready now (GREEN)
PS	Promotable or ready short-term (1-3 years) (YELLOW)
PL	Promotable or ready long-term (3-5 years) (ORANGE)

Typically, managers implement replacement planning by the use of charts like that in Exhibit 13–5. Based on organization charts, they provide a "snapshot" of key positions in the organization and the availability of replacements in the current work force. Replacement charts document judgments about employees' knowledge, skills, and abilities. This aids decision making when informal knowledge is less complete.

Replacement planning usually helps identify the top 10–20 percent of managers who are above standard and who can be promoted at a faster-than-average rate; the middle 60 to 80 percent who should be developed through normal position growth, and the bottom 10 to 20 percent who may not be qualified for present jobs and require some other personnel action.[42]

James Walker highlights several of the inherent shortcomings in replacement planning.[43]

- There is little consideration of the actual requirements of the positions, or of the prospective changes that occur in a job when a new person moves into it.

- Identification of backups or replacement candidates is largely subjective, based on personal knowledge of the nominating managers. There are rarely objective indicators of performance, individual capabilities, or past achievements.
- A high-potential candidate may be qualified for more than one management position, but may be "boxed in" by the vertical line-oriented replacement planning or, alternatively, may be named as a backup for several positions, giving a false impression of management depth.
- The planning is fragmented and vertically oriented; rarely is there provision for lateral or diagonal moves across organizational units.
- There is rarely any input from the individuals themselves regarding their own self-assessments and career interests.
- Most significantly, the charts rarely result in the moves planned or in other developmental activities; the process is often a static, annual paperwork exercise.

To overcome these shortcomings some employment planners have introduced succession charting.[44] According to Walker, the principal differences are that succession charting is longer range, more developmental, and offers greater flexibility.[45]

Surveys of employment planning practices show that replacement and succession planning is widely practiced. Yet we know little about the payoffs from such practices. We do know of one case where a firm's succession plans from 10 years back did not include either the current CEO or the president. Several current vice presidents had received rather lukewarm evaluations. None of these employees were earmarked on previous plans as part of the future executive team.

Exhibit 13–6 shows the framework J. Carnazza derived from analyzing the succession/replacement planning practices of 79 employers.[46] He reports that current practices tend to emphasize managers while often neglecting the nature of the work and the demand for employees. Succession planning may also overemphasize identifying replacements at the expense of integrating learning experiences relevant to future positions.[47] This can occur through a lack of specific future position requirements, a tendency to select future managers who resemble current ones, underemphasizing learning versus development, insufficient follow-up to ensure learning activities take place, and too little candidate involvement.[48]

Internal Recruiters

The process of recruiting internal job candidates is an ongoing interaction between the individuals planning their careers, their managers, and other

EXHIBIT 13–6
The Succession/Replacement Process

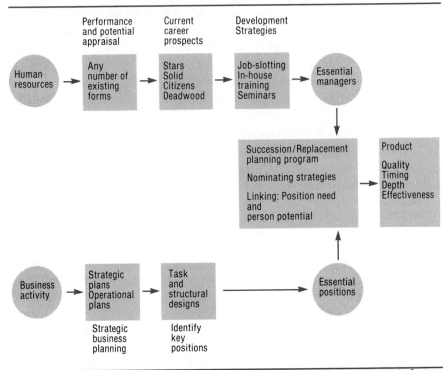

Source: J. Carnazza, *Succession/Replacement Planning: Programs & Practices* (New York: Center for Career Development, Columbia School of Business, 1982), p. 5.

support staff in the organization. Some systems emphasize nomination by employees' superiors, and others emphasize nomination by employees themselves.

Nomination by Employees' Superiors

Typically, one or more superiors plays a role in identifying the employees for internal job opportunities. This process can occur informally or formally and through a variety of mechanisms. For example, mentoring is a process through which superiors support subordinates' career advancement. The process can include such activities as sponsorship whereby the superior uses influence to open opportunities for an employee, coaching, and taking responsibility for mistakes or setbacks out of the employee's control. Mentoring also involves creating opportunities for widespread exposure; providing challenging assignments to foster learning; being a role model; counseling; providing feedback, acceptance, and friendship.[49] Though such relationships usually develop quite informally, organizations can enhance career development by formally encouraging them.[50] Thus, Frito-Lay, Inc. added quarterly manager-subordinate development conferences to its performance assessment system.[51] Hawaiian Telephone Company has employees complete a workbook to help them identify their values, interests, and decision-making styles before meeting with their supervisors to discuss career possibilities.[52] Mentoring programs carry risks of jealousy, resentment, and failure; some organizations, however, feel they are successful.[53]

Nomination by Employees Themselves

Employees play a large role in identifying career opportunities and in nominating themselves for them. They can benefit from training in these processes.[54] Career development programs are available from consulting firms, and many organizations implement their own. At 3M Company, the department of career services includes a career information center, career services orientation, career growth workshop, individual counseling, supervisory development programs, and a career development library. All of these are available to employees during working hours.[55] At Dow Jones & Company, Inc. career planning assistance has evolved into the "Druthers Program." Employees write letters to their managers in the following format: "I'd druther do that than this." The letter outlines career objectives and preparation and serves as a starting point for career development activities. The letters are kept on file for current and future job openings.[56]

SELECTION DECISIONS FOR INTERNAL STAFFING

External selection involves using information to choose which applicants to offer employment. The value and legality of external selection decisions depends, in part, on the validity of the selection information. Internal selection follows a similar process. The concept of validity plays the same role, and internal selection decisions are subject to the same EEO laws as external selection decisions. In theory, the same prediction techniques used for external selection could be used for internal selection. However, because internal selection focuses on existing employees, more information is available and the choice of predictor information is influenced by additional factors.

Experience, Past Performance, and Seniority

The nature of employees' previous experiences with the organization, their performance in previous jobs, and their seniority are important considerations in internal staffing decisions. Unions often stipulate that seniority be considered in promotion and transfer decisions.[57] Past performance is often rewarded with promotions, and employees' perceptions of the adequacy and equity of promotion opportunities influence their work attitudes and propensity to quit. Yet, evidence for the relationship between seniority and future job performance is mixed.[58] Some evidence suggests that among employees of similar age, seniority is unrelated to training time and performance in future positions; instead, the similarity between future and previous jobs, as well as past performance in previous jobs, relates to higher performance and shorter training times.[59] Thus, valid internal selection may require developing internal staffing systems that account for the similarity of jobs, the skills learned on jobs, and the total career progression of internal job candidates, not simply their seniority or past performance ratings.

Exhibit 13–7 depicts the role of career experience in developing employees for future jobs. Moving from left to right represents the career progression over time, culminating in the target job/job context. The *target job* is the position for which career progression validity is being designed or assessed. At each stage in the process, the individual brings the PCs and K & Ss they had when they entered the organization, as well as the ones they have developed through work experience (as the lines at the top of the diagram show).

Although employees always develop knowledge, skills, and personal characteristics as they progress through different positions, organizations can capitalize on this process by structuring employee work experiences to qualify them for future jobs. Experts have characterized work experiences as "*the* primary source of career learning for each individual."[60] By combining information from job analysis, career-oriented performance assessments, and information on internal career movements, organizations can provide a starting point for designing such developmental career progressions.[61]

The qualifications and background to be developed by past experience vary with the job and organization. Some have argued for matching executive characteristics to the strategic direction of the organization.[62] Research suggests that among AT&T managers, those with college degrees advanced farthest.[63] Top executives from large U.S. corporations indicated the following kinds of training or background as most important in their successors: sales and marketing (58 percent mentioned this), finance (40 percent), human resources (26 percent), legal (13 percent), data processing (12 percent), and general business (3 percent).[64] Of 93 human resource managers surveyed about their selection of first-line supervisors, over 50 percent mentioned the following factors: general competence, leadership ability, oral communication skills, human relations skills, initiative, deci-

EXHIBIT 13–7
How Person-Work Interaction Leads to Career Development

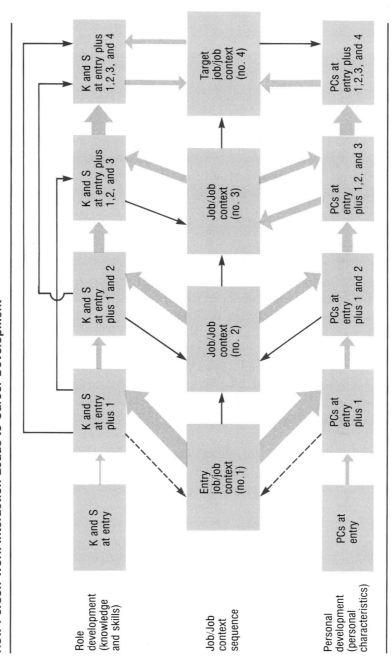

Source: Robert F. Morrison and Roger R. Hock, "Career Building: Learning from Cumulative Work Experience," in *Career Development in Organizations*, ed. Douglas T. Hall and Associates (San Francisco: Jossey-Bass, 1986), p. 241.

sion-making ability, conscientiousness, written communication skills, and ability to control.[65]

Internal Selection Procedures

Chapter Eleven noted that reference/record checks and unstructured interviews are most popular for external selection. This pattern seems even more pronounced with internal selection procedures. Exhibit 13–8 shows the use of different selection procedures for choosing promotion candidates in seven job groups. Clearly, the most common procedures across all jobs are to check organizational records, conduct an unstructured interview, and make the decision. A sizable minority of organizations conduct structured interviews and use skill tests for promotion into many office/clerical and some skilled occupations.[66] Similar results have been reported for supervisory selection.[67]

Assessment Centers

Exhibit 13–8 suggests that the assessment center is the most frequently used ability testing method for first-level and executive-level managers. Though their absolute frequency of use is still small, because many major organizations use centers, they have been the subject of a good deal of research and professional attention.[68] For instance, AT&T runs more than 40,000 people through its center each year to assess their managerial potential. JC Penney Company; Sears Roebuck & Co.; IBM Corporation; General Electric Company, and the federal government also use them. These companies use assessment center information not only to select promotion candidates, but also to identify areas for further development and training.

The basic purpose is to collect data on how people would behave if they worked on the job. The specific content of each center is tailored around the problems and situations faced in specific jobs. Exhibit 13–9 shows center activities designed to assess applicants who wish to be army recruiters. The tasks included are actual samples of the work that recruiters perform. These activities validly predict successful performance. Exhibit 13–10 lists the factors usually included in centers designed for managerial jobs.

Generally, research suggests that properly designed assessment centers are more valid predictors of future promotions than of future job performance. Critics argue that these centers may be expensive.[69] However, one study found assessment center ratings were an important factor in identifying and selecting promotion candidates.[70] Moreover, as Chapter Eleven demonstrated, even moderate validity levels can lead to large selection benefits if they affect large quantities of employees and time peri-

EXHIBIT 13–8
Selection Procedures Used for Promotion into Seven Job Groups

	Percent of Companies						
	Unskilled Semiskilled (370)	Skilled (352)	Office Clerical (436)	Professional Technical (426)	Sales (244)	First-Level Supervisor (430)	Manager Executive (433)
Background information							
Reference/record checks	56%	60%	65%	65%	60%	65%	62%
Weighted application blank	5	5	6	6	4	5	5
Investigation by outside agency	1	1	1	2	1	2	3
Interviews							
Unstructured	55	58	63	64	65	64	61
Structured	19	21	24	26	21	26	26
Ability testing							
Skill performance test/work sample	6	12	37	5	2	3	2
Mental ability test	4	5	5	4	4	3	3
Job knowledge test	3	9	8	7	3	5	3
Physical abilities test	2	2	*	1	—	—	*
Assessment center	*	1	1	3	2	5	5
Other screening techniques							
Medical examination	6	6	4	4	3	4	6
Polygraph test/written honesty test	*	*	*	*	*	*	*
Personality test	—	—	1	2	3	2	3
No answer/None used	22	17	10	11	14	10	14

Note: Percentages are based on the number of companies with employees in each job group.

*Less than 0.5 percent.

Source: The Bureau of National Affairs, Inc., "Employee Selection Procedures," ASPA-BNA Survey No. 45, May 5, 1983.

EXHIBIT 13–9
Summary of Assessment Center Program Activities

1. *Structured interview.* Assessors ask a series of questions targeted at the subject's level of achievement motivation, potential for being a "self-starter," and commitment to the Army.
2. *Cold calls.* Subject has an opportunity to learn a little about three prospects and must phone each of them for the purpose of getting them to come into the office. Assessor role players have well-defined characters (prospects) to portray.
3. *Interviews.* Two of the three cold-call prospects agree to come in for an interview. The subject's job is to follow up on what was learned in the cold-call conversations and to begin promoting Army enlistment to these people. A third "walk-in" prospect also appears for an interview with the subject.
4. *Interview with concerned parent.* Subject is asked to prepare for and conduct an interview with the father of one of the prospects he or she interviewed previously.
5. *5-minute speech about the Army.* Subject prepares a short talk about an Army career that he or she delivers to the rest of the group and to the assessors.
6. *In-basket.* Subject is given an in-basket filled with notes, phone messages, and letters on which he or she must take some action.

Source: W. C. Borman, "Validity of Behavioral Assessment for Predicting Military Recruiter Performance," *Journal of Applied Psychology* 67, no. 1 (1982), pp. 3–9. Copyright 1982 by the American Psychological Association. Reprinted by permission of the author.

ods. In fact, one study demonstrated substantial dollar payoffs from an assessment center for food and beverage salespersons.[71]

SEPARATION/RETENTION IMPLICATIONS OF INTERNAL STAFFING

The Nature of Internal Separations/Retentions

The vast majority of research and practice has focused on the effects of internal staffing on either the employees who move or the positions into which they move. Usually, companies assume that if internal staffing identifies and selects high performers for future jobs, then the internal staffing program is beneficial. However, every internal employee selection implies an internal employee separation from the employee's original position (see Exhibit 13–1). The effects of the quantity and pattern of such internal separations/retentions are expressed through their effects on the quantity and quality of the retained work force in the source positions.[72]

Though formal attention to this issue has only recently been advocated, anecdotal evidence suggests its importance. Rosabeth Moss Kanter describes one organization in which "All people hired off a campus are evaluated in terms of what kind of managers they will make," much to the

EXHIBIT 13–10
Common Dimensions Used in Managerial Assessment Centers

Oral communication skill	Effective expression in individual or group situations (includes gestures and nonverbal communications).
Oral presentation skill	Effective expression when presenting ideas or tasks to an individual or to a group when given time for preparation (includes gestures and nonverbal communication).
Written communication skill	Clear expression of ideas in writing and in good grammatical form.
Job motivation	The extent to which activities and responsibilities available in the job overlap with activities and responsibilities that result in personal satisfaction.
Initiative	Active attempts to influence events to achieve goals; self-starting rather than passive acceptance. Taking action to achieve goals beyond those called for; originating action.
Leadership	Utilization of appropriate interpersonal styles and methods in guiding individuals (subordinates, peers, superiors) or groups toward task accomplishment.
Planning and organization	Establishing a course of action for self and/or others to accomplish a specific goal; planning proper assignments of personnel and appropriate allocation of resources.
Analysis	Relating and comparing data from different sources, identifying issues, securing relevant information, and identifying relationships.
Judgment	Developing alternative courses of action and making decisions that are based on logical assumptions and reflect factual information.
Management control	Establishing procedures to monitor and/or regulate processes, tasks, or the job activities and responsibilities of subordinates. Taking action to monitor the results of delegated assignments or projects.

Source: W. C. Byham, "Starting an Assessment Center the Correct Way," *Personnel Administrator*, February 1980, pp. 27–32. Copyright 1980 by the American Society for Personnel Administration, 606 North Washington Street, Alexandria, VA 22314, $30 per year.

"annoyance of those who wanted to create a professional sales force."[73] When IBM instituted a policy to reduce the work force at its Burlington, Vermont, manufacturing plant, there was concern that Burlington might lose its most valuable employees to other plants. Therefore, although other plants were encouraged to recruit and hire Burlington workers, the corporate policy included the "10–80–10" rule: Managers could opt to retain workers in the top 10 percent, at least for six months; they cannot transfer workers in the bottom 10 percent to other sites; and the middle 80 percent are fair game.[74]

Dual-Track Career Progressions

One of the most frequent organizational dilemmas reflecting the internal separation/retention issue is that highly skilled technical employees such as engineers, research scientists, computer software designers, and salespeople often hold positions in career progressions with very "early ceilings."[75] That is, these individuals perform well and advance quickly, but they soon reach a point where further advancement requires moving out of jobs that emphasize the technical skill and into jobs of a more supervisory or managerial nature. These employees may be more interested in developing their professional expertise than in advancing through managerial positions. Promoting such employees into management positions is certain to remove top technical performers and may produce only mediocre or poor managers. Yet, employees desire advancement and it is often difficult to justify pay increases beyond certain limits without a promotion.

In an effort to retain technical experts in jobs that use their professional skills and still provide advancement and reward opportunities, organizations such as IBM; Texas Instruments, Inc.; Mobil Corporation; Union Carbide Corporation; and Westinghouse Electric Corporation have adopted "dual ladder" or "two-track" career progressions.[76] Such a system establishes two parallel career progressions: one reflecting advancement through a managerial career, and one reflecting advancement as a technical professional or staff member.[77] Movement up the managerial ladder means greater power and decision-making authority; movement up the technical ladder means greater autonomy in practicing the profession. Thus, they reflect the different career orientations of employees. Although such programs are costly and not without their risks, they reflect an awareness that filling upper-level management vacancies may be counterproductive when this means sacrificing the quality of those retained in technical and professional positions.

EVALUATING INTERNAL STAFFING ACTIVITIES

Because internal staffing combines recruitment, selection, and separation/retention activities, it has broad implications for achieving organizational efficiency and equity goals. Both external and internal staffing affect the composition of the work force. Internal staffing draws from different candidate pools, may use different selection information, and moves employees simultaneously into some positions and out of others. Its impact on organizational efficiency and equity still depends on how internal staffing affects the quantity and quality of the work force, as well as the cost of internal staffing activities.

Efficiency

Unfortunately, just as external staffing activities are often evaluated using deficient measures, such as vacancies filled, movement percentages, or program costs alone, internal staffing activities are also often evaluated deficiently and unsystematically. In fact, very little research has addressed the impact of internal staffing on organizational performance.[78] One survey of 217 companies found that none analyzed whether the performance ratings used for promotions validly predicted future performance.[79] Another survey of supervisory selection found that only 20 out of 93 respondents validated their internal selection methods.[80] Still, internal staffing has important implications for the productivity and costs of the organization, as Exhibit 13–2 demonstrated.

Costs

Internal recruiting involving job posting, computerized skill inventories, employee career counseling/training, and succession planning incurs costs of administration, materials, relocation inducements, and, probably most important, employee and managerial time. Virtually all internal selection involves some form of interview and record check, with more elaborate systems incorporating tests or assessment centers. These activities require resources to examine employee qualifications, develop and validate selection devices, and pay relocation expenses. For example, assessment center cost estimates include $3,200 in start-up costs and $600 per assessee in ongoing implementation costs.[81] Finally, internal separations/retentions may imply additional costs of selecting replacements for lost employees, overtime expenses while other workers fill in for the lost employee, and possible future training expenses to bring the retained work force up to its former productivity. However, these costs can be offset if internal staffing management enhances productivity.

Productivity

As with external recruitment, selection, and separation/retention, the effects of internal staffing on work force productivity have not been routinely evaluated. This is due not only to the complexity of their effects, but also to the lack of a framework for considering those costs and benefits.

Recently, one of the authors proposed a cost-benefit model for internal staffing based on the same principles reflected in Exhibits 13–1 and 13–2. John Boudreau proposed that the effects of internal staffing patterns are reflected in the quality and quantity of the work force in both the source and destination positions. Using a computer simulation, he explored the effects of different internal staffing parameters on work force value. His results suggest that internal staffing can have million-dollar effects on work force value when the quantity of employees and time periods, or leverage, of the programs is high. Moreover, his results suggest that the most important productivity effects of internal staffing decisions may occur through internal separation/retention in the positions serving as sources of candidates, rather than in the destinations.[82]

Clearly, evaluating efficiency by vacancies filled, or even by the validity of the internal selection process for destination positions, may omit important efficiency effects. A more complete picture of the productivity implications may emerge if we consider the effects of both internal selection and internal separation/retention.

Equity

Internal staffing activities are even more affected by equity considerations than external staffing. Governmental agencies and courts evaluate internal staffing activities and outcomes for fairness with regard to minorities and females. Internal staffing can have important effects on achieving EEO/AA goals and progress.

Unions are deeply concerned with internal staffing activities because they affect the job security and compensation levels of their members. Managers must consider collective bargaining agreements that stipulate seniority-based transfers or promotions in planning and evaluating internal staffing.

In addition, because they affect existing employees, internal staffing decisions must be even more attuned to the reactions and attitudes of employment candidates. Employees' attitudes are affected by their perceptions of the fairness of internal staffing activities. Often, employees regard promotions and transfers as rewards, recognition, and signals of their value to the organization. As Exhibit 13–2 shows, internal staffing decisions that seem fair, such as promoting the best performers, may not always satisfy organizational goals of validity and productivity in destination jobs. When employees are redeployed from surplus areas to areas of shortage, properly communicating the need for the movements and appreciation for employee sacrifices can be critical to maintaining high morale. Similarly, ongoing career counseling can help employees develop more realistic expectations and increased awareness of their career opportunities and obligations. Even the most valid and logical internal staffing system does not work if employees refuse employment offers, leave the organization, or perform poorly due to perceptions of inequity.

SUMMARY

Internal staffing activities determine how existing employees move between employment opportunities within the organization. Such movements occur constantly, and their pattern affects both the efficiency and equity of the organization, because it affects the mix of employees. Similar to external staffing activities, internal staffing involves recruiting, selecting, and separating/retaining employees. Unlike external staffing, however, not only do those selected and retained become organizational members, but those rejected also remain organizational members. Therefore, internal staffing requires an integration of recruiting, selection, and retention objectives that accounts for its effects on productivity and on the career progress and attitudes of existing employees. Used properly, internal staffing is a powerful tool for accomplishing organizational efficiency and equity objectives.

Appropriately, this chapter concludes our discussion of the staffing process, because it shows how internal recruitment, selection, and separation/retention activities are related. Of course, external recruitment, selection, and separation/retention activities are similarly related. For example, valid external selection does little good if those selected cannot be retained. Moreover, internal and external staffing are related, because the characteristics of employees who enter and leave the organization affect and are affected by the internal staffing decisions of the organization. Viewing internal and external staffing as ongoing and integrated human resource activities allows decision makers to more fully appreciate and manage their effects.

DISCUSSION AND REVIEW QUESTIONS

1. How does internal staffing integrate the processes of recruitment, selection, and separation/retention? Is it always best to promote the highest performers? Which other factors should be considered? Why must internal staffing activities be especially attuned to employee equity perceptions?
2. Distinguish between career development, career management, and career planning. How can the notions of career orientation and career stages assist employees and employers in carrying out their responsibilities with regard to these activities?
3. How are internal recruiting activities similar to external recruiting? How are they different? How would you judge the effectiveness of a job posting, skills inventory, or succession planning system? Could you use the same evaluation methods as used for external recruiting? Why or why not?

4. Which information is available for internal selection that is not available when selecting new employees? What are the advantages and disadvantages of using such internal information? How are internal and external selection procedures similar? How are they different?

5. How does internal staffing affect internal employee separations/retentions? Why is this effect often overlooked? Could this effect ever offset what appears to be a valuable internal selection process, or is the effect of internal movements on the retained work force probably not very important? How do dual-track career systems address the effects of internal separation/retention?

6. Is evaluating the rate and quantity of internal movements and the number of internal vacancies filled sufficient to tell if the system is working? Which other factors are important to a complete evaluation?

NOTES AND REFERENCES

1. Richard Bode, "Moving People to Jobs. A Big Job in Itself," *Think* 53, no. 2 (International Business Machines Corporation, 1987), p. 30.

2. Work in America Institute, Inc., *The Continuous Learning/Employment Security Connection* (Scarsdale, N.Y.: Work in America Institute, 1986), as reported in *Human Resource Management News*, February 28, 1987, p. 2.

3. R. E. Hall, "The Importance of Lifetime Jobs in the U.S. Economy," *American Economic Review*, September 1982, pp. 716–24.

4. Bureau of National Affairs, *Affirmative Action Today* (Washington, D.C.: Bureau of National Affairs, 1986).

5. *U.S.* v. *Paradise*, 43 FEP Cases 1 (1987); *Local 93, Firefighters, AFL–CIO* v. *City of Cleveland*, 41 FEP Cases 139 (1986); *Johnson* v. *Transportation Agency, Santa Clara County, California*, No. 85–1129 (1987).

6. *U.S.* v. *Paradise*.

7. *Johnson* v. *Transportation Agency, Santa Clara, California*.

8. Bureau of National Affairs, *Basic Patterns in Union Contracts*, 11th ed. (Washington, D.C.: Bureau of National Affairs, 1986).

9. Anil K. Gupta, "Matching Managers to Strategies: Point and Counterpoint," *Human Resource Management* 25, no. 2 (Summer 1986), pp. 214–34; Andrew D. Szilagyi, Jr., and David M. Schweiger, "Matching Managers to Strategies: A Review and Suggested Framework," *Academy of Management Review* 9, no. 4 (1984), pp. 626–37.

10. James N. Baron, Alison Davis-Blake, and William T. Bielby, "The Structure of Opportunity: How Promotion Ladders Vary within and among Organizations," *Administrative Science Quarterly* 31 (1986), pp. 248–73.

11. John W. Boudreau, "Utility Analysis: A New Perspective on Human Resource Management Decisions," in *ASPA Handbook of Pesonnel and Industrial Relations*, vol. 1, ed. Lee D. Dyer (Washington, D.C.: Bureau of National Affairs, 1988).

12. Douglas T. Hall and Associates, *Career Development in Organizations* (San Francisco: Jossey-Bass, 1986); "Self-Assessment Said to Be First Step in Employee Career Development Process," Bureau of National Affairs,

Employee Relations Weekly 5, no. 18 (May 4, 1987), p. 547; Richard K. Broszeit, " 'If I Had My Druthers . . .' A Career Development Program," *Personnel Journal*, October 1986, pp. 84–90.

13. Douglas T. Hall, *Careers in Organizations* (Glenview, Ill.: Scott, Foresman, 1976); Rosabeth Moss Kanter, *Men and Women of the Corporation* (New York: Basic Books, 1977); D. E. Super and Douglas T. Hall, "Career Development: Exploration and Planning," in *Annual Review of Psychology*, vol. 29, ed. M. R. Rosenzweig and Lyman W. Porter (Palo Alto, Calif.: Annual Reviews, 1978).

14. J. E. Rosenbaum, *Career Mobility in a Corporate Hierarchy* (New York: Academic Press, 1984); Shelby Stewman and Suresh L. Konda, "Careers and Organizational Labor Markets: Demographic Models of Organizational Behavior," *American Journal of Sociology* 40 (1983), pp. 298–321; Victor H. Vroom and K. R. MacCrimmon, "Toward a Stochastic Model of Managerial Careers," *Administrative Science Quarterly* 13 (1968), pp. 26–46.

15. George T. Milkovich and John C. Anderson, "Career Planning and Development Systems," in *Personnel Management*, ed. Kendrith M. Rowland and Gerald R. Ferris (Boston: Allyn & Bacon, 1982).

16. John W. Boudreau, *Utility Analysis Applied to Internal and External Employee Movement: An Integrated Theoretical Perspective* (Ithaca, N.Y.: ILR Press, forthcoming); John W. Boudreau, "Utility Analysis: A New Perspective on Human Resource Management Decisions"; John W. Boudreau, "Utility Analysis for Human Resource Management Decisions," in *Handbook of Industrial and Organizational Psychology*, 2nd ed., ed. M. D. Dunnette (Chicago: Rand McNally, in press).

17. Brian L. Steffy and Charles H. Fay, "A Methodology for Defining Structural Properties of Intraorganizational Career Mobility" (Working Paper No. 86–03, University of Minnesota Industrial Relations Center, February 1986); Shelby Stewman, "Demographic Models of Internal Labor Markets," *Administrative Science Quarterly* 31 (1986), pp. 212–47.

18. Hall and Associates, *Career Development in Organizations*, pp. 2–3.

19. Janina C. Latack, "Career Transitions within Organizations: An Exploratory Study of Work, Nonwork, and Coping Strategies," *Organizational Behavior and Human Performance* 34 (1984), pp. 296–322; Manuel London and Edward M. Mone, *Career Management and Survival in the Workplace* (San Francisco: Jossey-Bass, 1987); Thomas D. Sugalski and Jeffrey H. Greenhaus, "Career Exploration and Goal Setting among Managerial Employees," *Journal of Vocational Behavior* 29, no. 1 (August 1986), pp. 102–14; Tom Jackson and Alan Vitberg, "Career Development, Part 1: Careers and Entrepreneurship," *Personnel* 64, no. 2 (February 1987), pp. 12–17; Frank A. DeChambeau and Fredericka Mackenzie, "Intrapreneurship," *Personnel Journal*, July 1986, pp. 40–45.

20. E. Erickson, *Childhood and Society* (New York: W. W. Norton, 1950); Douglas Hall, *Careers in Organizations;* D. J. Levinson, C. Darrow, E. Klein, M. Levinson, and B. McKee, *The Seasons of a Man's Life* (New York: Alfred A. Knopf, 1978); J. Rush and A. Peacock, "A Review and Integration of Theories of Life/Career Stages" (working paper, University of Western Ontario, London, Ontario, 1980); J. Rush, A. Peacock, and G. Milkovich, "Career Stages: A Partial Test of Levinson's Model of Life/

Career Stages," *Journal of Vocational Behavior* 16 (1980), pp. 347–59; E. G. Schein, *Career Dynamics: Matching Individual and Organizational Needs* (Reading, Mass.: Addison-Wesley Publishing, 1978); John Van Maanen and Edgar Schein, "Career Development," in *Improving Life at Work*, ed. J. Richard Hackman and J. Loyd Suttle (Santa Monica, Calif.: Goodyear Publishing, 1977).

21. Schein, *Career Dynamics: Matching Individuals.*

22. Ibid.

23. Ibid.

24. Hall, *Careers in Organizations.*

25. Ibid.; also see Rush and Peacock, "A Review and Integration of Theories of Life/Career Stages"; G. W. Dalton, P. H. Thompson, and R. L. Price, "The Four Stages of Professional Careers: A New Look at Performance by Professionals," *Organizational Dynamics*, Summer 1977, pp. 19–42.

26. Manuel London and Stephen A. Stumpf, *Managing Careers* (Reading, Mass.: Addison-Wesley Publishing, 1981).

27. J. Rush, A. Peacock, and G. Milkovich, "Career Stages: A Partial Test of Levinson's Model of Life/Career Stages."

28. Robert Oliver, *Career Unrest: A Source of Creativity* (New York: Center for Research in Career Development, Columbia University, 1981).

29. J. R. Garcia, "Job Posting for Professional Staff," *Personnel Journal*, March 1984, pp. 189–92; G. A. Wallropp, "Job Posting for Nonexempt Employees: A Sample Program," *Personnel Journal*, October 1981, pp. 796–98.

30. Dave Dahl and Patrick Pinto, "Job Posting: An Industry Survey," *Personnel Journal*, January 1977, pp. 40–42.

31. American Management Associations, *Hiring Costs and Strategies: The AMA Report* (New York: American Management Associations, 1986).

32. R. G. Murdick and F. Schuster, "Computerized Information Support for the Human Resource Function," *Human Resource Planning* 6, no. 1 (1983), pp. 35–41.

33. "How Useful Are Skills Inventories?" *Personnel* 65, no. 6 (June 1986), pp. 13–19.

34. William F. Glueck, *Personnel: A Diagnostic Approach* (Plano, Tex.: Business Publications, 1982).

35. Ibid.

36. Robert Smith, "Information Systems for More Effective Use of Executive Resources," *Personnel Journal*, June 1969, pp. 452–65.

37. Robert Martin, "Skills Inventories," *Personnel Journal*, January 1967, pp. 28–30.

38. S. Simon, "The HRIS: What Capabilities Must It Have?" *Personnel*, September–October 1983, pp. 36–49; see also SKOPOS, *Personnel Data Base Systems for MICRO'S* (Los Altos, Calif., 1984), and *1st Advanced HR Systems* (Flemington, N.J.: Integral Systems); *Executrak: A Microcomputer Succession Planning System* (Fairfield, Iowa: Corporate Education Resources, 1984).

39. James W. Walker, *Human Resources Planning* (New York: McGraw-Hill, 1980).

40. Stewart D. Friedman, "Succession Systems in Large Corporations: Char-

acteristics and Correlates of Performance," *Human Resource Management* 25, no. 2 (Summer 1986), pp. 191–213.

41. Douglas T. Hall, "Dilemmas in Linking Succession Planning to Individual Executive Learning," *Human Resource Management* 25, no. 2 (Summer 1986), pp. 235–65; Gupta, "Matching Managers to Strategies."

42. Merck and Company, Inc., Rahway, N.J.: *HR Planning Portfolio*, 1984.

43. Walker, *Human Resources Planning*.

44. E. S. Brewer and W. H. Hoffman, "Multiple Career Paths: An Organization Concept," *Human Resource Planning* 5, no. 4 (1982), pp. 209–17; *Succession Planning & Management Development for the 1980's*, 21st Annual IRC Symposium in Advanced Research in Industrial Relations (New York: IR Counselors, 1983).

45. Walker, *Human Resources Planning*.

46. J. Carnazza, *Succession/Replacement Planning: Programs & Practices* (New York: Center for Career Development, Columbia Business School, 1982), p. 5.

47. Freidman, "Succession Systems in Large Corporations."

48. Hall, "Dilemmas in Linking Succession Planning to Individual Executive Learning."

49. Kathy E. Kram, "Mentoring in the Workplace," *Career Development in Organizations*, ed. Douglas T. Hall et al.; L. Phillips-Jones, *Mentors and Proteges* (New York: Arbor House, 1982).

50. Kram, "Mentoring in the Workplace."

51. "Developing Management Talent Often Difficult," *Bureau of National Affairs Employee Relations Weekly* 4, no. 38 (September 29, 1986), p. 1197.

52. "Hawaiian Telephone Co. Career Program Encourages Employee Growth," *Bureau of National Affairs Employee Relations Weekly* 4, no. 44 (November 10, 1986), p. 1406.

53. "Perspectives on Mentoring," *Bureau of National Affairs Bulletin on Training* 11, no. 6 (June 1986), p. 6.

54. John D. Drumboltz, Richard T. Kinnier, Stephanie S. Rude, Dale S. Scherba, and Daniel A. Hamel, "Teaching a Rational Approach to Career Decision Making: Who Benefits Most?" *Journal of Vocational Behavior* 29, no. 1 (August 1986), pp. 1–6.

55. "Self-Assessment Said to Be First Step in Employee Career Development Process," *Bureau of National Affairs Employee Relations Weekly* 5, no. 18 (May 4, 1987), p. 54.

56. Broszeit, "If I had My Druthers."

57. Bureau of National Affairs, *Basic Patterns in Union Contracts* (Washington, D.C.: Bureau of National Affairs, Inc., 1986); Craig A. Olson and Chris J. Berger, "The Relationship between Seniority, Ability, and the Promotion of Union and Nonunion Workers," *Advances in Industrial Relations*, vol. 1, ed. David B. Lipsky and J. M. Douglas (Greenwich, Conn.: JAI Press, 1983), pp. 91–129.

58. Michael E. Gordon and W. J. Fitzgibbons, "Empirical Test of the Validity of Seniority as a Factor in Staffing Decisions," *Journal of Applied Psychology* 67 (1982), pp. 311–19; Michael E. Gordon and W. A. Johnson, "Seniority: A Review of Its Legal and Scientific Standing," *Personnel*

Psychology 35 (1974), pp. 255–80; J. J. Mathews and B. B. Cobb, "Relationships between Age, ATC Experience, and Job Ratings of Terminal Area Traffic Controller," *Aerospace Medicine* 45 (1974), pp. 56–60.

59. Gordon and Fitzgibbons, "Empirical Test of the Validity of Seniority as a Factor in Staffing Decisions"; Michael E. Gordon, John L. Cofer, and P. Michael McCullough, "Relationships among Seniority, Past Performance, Interjob Similarity, and Trainability," *Journal of Applied Psychology* 71, no. 3 (1986), pp. 518–21.

60. Robert F. Morrison and Roger R. Hock, "Career Building: Learning from Cumulative Work Experience," *Career Development in Organizations*, p. 237.

61. Ibid.; Marvin D. Dunnette, Leaetta M. Hough, and R. L. Rosse, "Task and Job Taxonomies as a Basis for Identifying Labor Supply Sources and Evaluating Employment Qualifications," *Human Resources Planning* 2, no. 1 (1979), pp. 37–51; Donald H. Brush and Lyle F. Schoenfeldt, "Identifying Managerial Potential: An Alternative to Assessment Centers," *Personnel*, May–June 1980, pp. 68–76.

62. Anil Gupta, "Matching Managers to Strategies: Point and Counterpoint"; Andrew D. Szilagyi, Jr., and David M. Schweiger, "Matching Managers to Strategies: A Review and Suggested Framework."

63. Ann Howard, "College Experiences and Managerial Performance," *Journal of Applied Psychology* 71, no. 3 (1986), pp. 530–52.

64. Louis Harris and Associates, *Strategic Vision: A New Role for Corporate Leaders* (New York: Louis Harris and Associates, 1987).

65. "A Look at Company Supervisory Selection Systems," *Personnel* 65, no. 6 (1986), pp. 13–19.

66. Bureau of National Affairs, "Employee Selection Procedures," *ASPA–BNA Survey No. 45*, May 5, 1983.

67. "A Look at Company Supervisory Selection Systems."

68. William C. Byham, "Starting an Assessment Center the Correct Way," *Personnel Administrator*, February 1980, pp. 27–32; P. R. Sackett, "A Critical Look at Some Common Beliefs about Assessment Centers," *Public Personnel Management* 11, no. 1 (1982), pp. 140–47; Frederick D. Frank and James R. Preston, "The Validity of the Assessment Center Approach and Related Issues," *Personnel Administrator*, June 1982, p. 94; W. A. Gorham, *The Uniform Guidelines on Employee Selection Procedures: What New Impact on the Assessment Center Method?* (Washington, D.C.: U.S. Civil Service Commission, 1978), p. 78; Milan Marovee, "A Cost-Effective Career Planning Program Requires Strategy," *Personnel Administrator*, January 1982, p. 30; Anthony J. Plento, *A Review of Assessment Center Research* (U.S. Office of Personnel Management, Washington, D.C., May 1980), p. 8; Stephen L. Cohen, "The Bottom Line on Assessment Center Technology: Results of a Cost-Benefit Analysis Survey," *Personnel Administrator*, February 1980, p. 57; Task Force on Assessment Center Standards, "Standards and Ethical Considerations for Assessment Center Operations," *Personnel Administrator*, February 1980, p. 18; James C. Quick, William A. Fisher, Lawrence L. Schkade, and George W. Ayers, "Developing Administrative Personnel through the Assessment Center Technique," *Personnel Administrator*, February 1980, p. 46; Donald H.

Bush and Lyle F. Schoenfeldt, "Identifying Managerial Potential: An Alternative to Assessment Centers," *Personnel* (AMACOM), May–June 1980, p. 69; Stephen L. Cohen, "Pre-Packages vs. Tailor-Made: The Assessment Center Debate," *Personnel Journal*, December 1980, p. 989; Barry A. Friedman and Robert W. Mann, "Employee Assessment Methods Assessed," *Personnel* (AMACOM), November–December 1981, p. 70; G. L. Hart and P. H. Thompson, "Assessment Centers: For Selection or Development—IBM Workshop Experience," *Organization Dynamics*, Spring 1979, p. 63; J. T. Turnage and P. M. Muchinsky, "Transituational Variability in Human Performance within Assessment Centers," *Organizational Behavior and Human Performance* 30 (1982), pp. 174–200; D. W. Bray and D. L. Grant, "The Assessment Center in the Measurement of Potential for Business Management," *Psychological Monographs* 80, whole no. 625 (1966).

69. Paul R. Sackett and George F. Dreher, "Constructs and Assessment Center Dimensions: Some Troubling Empirical Findings," *Journal of Applied Psychology* 67, no. 4 (1982), pp. 401–10; V. R. Boehm, "Assessment Centers and Management Development," in *Personnel Management*, ed. K. Rowland and G. R. Ferris (Boston: Allyn & Bacon, 1982); Janet J. Turnage and Paul M Muchinsky, "A Comparison of the Predictive Validity of Assessment Center Evaluations versus Traditional Measures in Forecasting Supervisory Job Performance: Interpretive Implications of Criterion Distortion for the Assessment Paradigm," *Journal of Applied Psychology* 69, no. 4 (1984), pp. 595–602; George F. Dreher and Paul R. Sackett, *Perspectives on Employee Staffing and Selection* (Homewood, Ill.: Richard D. Irwin, 1983); John R. Hinrichs, "An Eight-Year Follow-Up of a Management Assessment Center," *Journal of Applied Psychology* 63 (1978), pp. 596–601; Paul R. Sackett, "Assessment Centers and Content Validity: Some Neglected Issues," *Personnel Psychology* 40 (1987), pp. 13–25.

70. Manuel London and Stephen Stumpf, "Effects of Candidate Characteristics on Management Promotion Decisions: An Experimental Study," *Personnel Psychology* 36 (1983), pp. 241–59.

71. Wayne F. Cascio and Val Silbey, "Utility of the Assessment Center as a Selection Device," *Journal of Applied Psychology* 64 (1979), pp. 107–18.

72. John W. Boudreau, "Utility Analysis Applied to Internal and External Employee Movement: An Integrated Theoretical Framework" (working paper, NYSSILR–Cornell University, 1988); John W. Boudreau, "Utility Analysis: A New Perspective on Human Resource Management Decisions."

73. Rosabeth Moss Kanter, *Men and Women of the Corporation* (New York: Basic Books, 1977), p. 130.

74. Leonard Greenhalgh, Robert B. McKersie, and Roderick W. Gilkey, "Rebalancing the Workforce at IBM: A Case Study of Redeployment and Revitalization," (working paper, Sloan School of Management, Massachusetts Institute of Technology, 1985), p. 36.

75. Milkovich and Anderson, "Career Planning and Development Systems."

76. Laurie Michael Roth, *A Critical Examination of the Dual Ladder Approach to Career Advancement* (New York: Center for Research in Career Development, Columbia University, 1982); Lisa A. Mainiero and Paul J. Upham, "Repairing a Dual-Ladder CD Program," *Training and Development Jour-*

nal 40, no. 5 (May 1986), pp. 100–105; Joseph A. Raelin, "Two-Track Plans for One-Track Careers," *Personnel Journal*, January 1987, pp. 96–101; "Dual Career Paths in Sales," *The Conference Board's Management Briefing: Human Resources* (New York: The Conference Board, 1987).

77. H. G. Kaufman, *Obsolescence and Professional Career Development* (New York: AMACOM, 1974), p. 125.

78. John W. Boudreau, "Utility Analysis Applied to Internal and External Employee Movement: An Integrated Theoretical Perspective"; Milkovich and Anderson, "Career Planning and Development Systems"; Jeffrey Pfeffer and Yinon Cohen, "Determinants of Internal Labor Markets in Organizations," *Administrative Science Quarterly* 29 (1984), pp. 550–72.

79. Robert I. Lazer, "The Discrimination Danger in Performance Appraisal," in *Contemporary Problems in Personnel*, ed. W. Clay Hammer and Frank L. Schmidt (Chicago: St. Clair Press, 1977).

80. "A Look at Company Supervisory Selection Systems."

81. Cascio and Silbey, "Utility of the Assessment Center as a Selection Device"; Wayne F. Cascio and Robert A. Ramos, "Development and Application of a New Method for Assessment Job Performance in Behavioral/Economic Terms," *Journal of Applied Psychology* 71 (1986), pp. 20–28.

82. Boudreau, "Utility Analysis Applied to Internal and External Employee Movement"; John W. Boudreau, "Utility Analysis: A New Perspective on Human Resource Management Decisions"; John W. Boudreau, "MOVUTIL: A Spreadsheet Program for Analyzing the Utility of Internal and External Employee Movement" (working paper, Cornell University, NYSSILR, 1986).

PART THREE CASES

► ITHACA'S OWN
CASE 4: EMPLOYMENT PLANNING
AND RECRUITING

Ithaca's Own has begun to enlarge its share of the "natural foods"market. Projected sales this year have increased 17 percent over the previous year, and I-O products are appearing in stores nationwide. While top management is delighted, the organization's continued success has resulted in some headaches for the Human Resource Management department.

Although a formal employment planning function does not yet exist at I-O, the Director of HRM, Mr. Wable, forecast I-O's employment requirements based on the anticipated productivity increases in each function. Wable then applied the historical rate of turnover to each position and calculated I-O's expected work force; these figures were then compared to employment requirements for the planned year. As Exhibit 1 indicates, I-O anticipates an overall shortage of 53 employees, but the employment mix within certain departments will change. For example, R&D is expected to have a net shortage of five employees, although certain positions in the department will require fewer employees in the plan year. In addition to the exhibit Mr. Wable developed, you have received a chart indicating the costs and yield ratios associated with various sources of recruitment (Exhibit 2).

Regarding internal employee movement, you have noted the following general trends: (1) Secretaries and clerical workers are seldom promoted and usually recruited externally. (2) In R&D the promotion ladder runs up the jobs listed in Exhibit 1 (that is, from technician to group leader and so on up to principal scientist). (3) In Operations the promotion ladder runs up from operator to foreman to supervisor to manager. (4) In Marketing

EXHIBIT 1
Human Resource Requirements at I-O

	Current Year Employment	− Forecast Requirements	− Estimated Turnover	= Surplus/(Shortage)
R&D:				
Principal scientist	10	7	0	3
Associate scientist	50	43	3	4
Assistant scientist	70	65	3	2
Manager	10	10	2	(2)
Group leader	20	23	4	(7)
Technician	30	32	4	(6)
Secretary and clerical	3	2	0	1
Total	193	182	16	(5)
Operations:				
Manager	3	3	2	(2)
Supervisor	9	8	1	0
Foreman	35	31	2	2
Operators	60	72	10	(22)
Secretary and clerical	3	2	1	0
Total	110	116	17	(22)
Marketing and sales:				
Managers	3	5	0	(2)
R&D consultants	10	6	2	2
Account consultants	8	11	1	(4)
Professional	30	38	2	(10)
Secretary and clerical	15	17	5	(7)
Total	66	77	10	(21)
Administrative services:				
Human resource managers and director	5	5	0	0
Purchasing director	2	2	1	(1)
Finance and data processing director	3	4	2	(3)
Human resource professionals	10	10	1	(1)
Finance professionals	10	8	0	2
Secretary and clerical	11	9	4	(2)
Total	41	38	8	(5)

and Sales professionals have been promoted either to account consultant or R&D consultant, and then to manager. (5) In Administrative Services, directors have come from several of the other three functional areas (R&D, Operations, and Marketing), but professionals are usually recruited externally.

EXHIBIT 2
Recruitment Sources, Costs, and Yields

Recruitment Source	Cost (per hire)	Yield Rate (percentage)
Agencies	$8,000	30%
Advertising	1,000	10
College recruiting	5,000	10
Unsolicited walk-ins	200	2
Employee referrals	200	8

Note: Costs are averages over all hires obtained through each method over the last two years. Yield rates are the number of applicants identified through the method divided by the number receiving job offers. For example, if advertising produced 100 applicants and 10 received offers, the yield would be 10 percent. Both costs and yield rates vary across different positions. Not all methods have been used in all positions.

Discussion Questions

1. Regarding internal staffing: For which positions are the traditional internal movement patterns likely to help alleviate these problems? For which are they likely to exacerbate the problems? Indicate the internal movement pattern you would try to induce to alleviate some of the shortages and surpluses. How might you induce movement patterns more likely to alleviate the problems?
2. Regarding external staffing: Which positions should be filled externally? Which of the four external recruitment methods are most appropriate for each externally filled position? Would you emphasize cost, yield or both in choosing recruitment methods? Justify your answer.
3. Which positions, if any, require national recruiting? Local labor market recruiting? Why? Would you recommend recruiting at additional sources to generate women and minority candidates? Give examples.
4. How would improved productivity affect the employment forecast? Which positions would be most affected? How will you handle expected surpluses in certain positions?
5. Which three additional pieces of information would be useful in preparing your report? Be specific as to how you might use these data.

▶ RALPH'S GENUINE FRENCH CUISINE

Ralph's Genuine French Cuisine is a food service company that provides regular catered meal service to organizations in western Texas and New Mexico. The bulk of their service consists of preparing and delivering lunches to office buildings. For the offices, the service is convenient and alleviates the need for a cafeteria. It is especially attractive to offices in outlying areas where a variety of food services is not available. However, many large office buildings in major cities (such as El Paso, Las Cruces, Lubbock, and Albuquerque) also use the service because it offers their employees better quality food than is available nearby, as well as the convenience of dining on-site.

Lunches consist of such delicacies as Scampi Provencale, Veal à la Ralph, and Maxime's Broccoli with Grand Marnier Sauce. Ralph's also does some limited dinner catering for organizations with two-shift schedules or employees who work longer hours.

The service is purchased by one or more organizations in a particular office building, and Ralph's agrees to deliver a specified number of catered lunches for a flat fee per month. Sales are up to $12 million per year. A key to Ralph's success is an effective sales force to communicate the benefits of the service to the purchasing managers for the companies in the office buildings.

Ralph recently hired Megan Caldwell as his new personnel director. Not long ago he called her in to discuss a problem:

"We've really got to get a handle on this turnover problem with our sales representatives, Megan. I've just reviewed the records for the last three years, and we average 30 turnovers every year. With our work force of 100 sales representatives, that means each year we have to hire and train 30 replacements, not to mention the lost productivity while the positions remain vacant. How can we get the turnover rate down?"

Caldwell verified Ralph's statistics. Thirty of the 100 sales representatives per year left for various reasons: Sometimes they got better offers— Juan's Genuine Cajun Catering is a fierce competitor. More often Ralph's sales reps discovered they didn't like the job, relocated for personal reasons, retired, or were dismissed. The average cost of separation plus recruiting, selecting, and training one replacement was $10,000.

Caldwell also gathered some sales information on the present work force and on new hires. Her data appear in Exhibits 1 and 2. Exhibit 1

EXHIBIT 1
Sales Information on
Current Work Force

Quartile	Average Sales per Year
Top 25%	$200,000
Next 25%	150,000
Next 25%	100,000
Bottom 25%	50,000

EXHIBIT 2
Sales Information on New Hires

Quartile	Year 1	Year 2	Year 3	Year 4
Top 25%	$50,000	$100,000	$175,000	$200,000
Next 25%	30,000	60,000	100,000	150,000
Next 25%	20,000	40,000	60,000	100,000
Bottom 25%	20,000	30,000	40,000	50,000

shows the sales of the existing work force by quartile. The variability in sales is rather large (the bottom 25 percent average only $50,000 per year, while the top 25 percent average $200,000 per year). Exhibit 2 shows the pattern of sales over the first four years of a sales representative's tenure. Although all sales representative's sales rise, those who turn out to be the best generally start higher and rise somewhat faster. Sales representatives are currently paid a base of $15,000, plus 8 percent commissions.

Discussion Questions

1. What is the yearly total turnover cost for the 30 separations each year? Which factors should Caldwell have included in computing her $10,000 per person turnover cost?

2. Based on the model of the Employee Quit Decision in Chapter Twelve, what are three methods Caldwell might use to reduce the turnover rate?

3. Is the 30 percent turnover rate really too high? How much could be saved in turnover costs if it were reduced to 20 percent? How much could be saved if it were reduced to 10 percent?

4. What are the sales implications if average performers separate and are replaced by average new hires (*Hint:* To compute the average of any column in Exhibits 1 and 2, just add up the figures and divide by 4). What are the sales implications for the worst possible turnover pattern? That is, the pattern where the highest-performing sales representatives leave and are replaced from the bottom 25 percent of applicants. What are the sales implications for the best possible turnover pattern? That is, the pattern where the lowest-performing sales representatives leave and are replaced from the top 25 percent of applicants.

5. Is it true that the 30 percent turnover rate is necessarily bad? How does your answer to this question suggest an integration between employee separations and external selection? List and describe three ad-

ditional pieces of information Megan could gather to properly evaluate the turnover implications.

▶ GIGANTIC AIRCRAFT COMPANY

Gigantic Aircraft Company is a large firm with a plant near Santa Barbara, California. The personnel manager has called in Joyce Piersol, a management consultant specializing in personnel, for advice on selection policies. Bill Fabris invited Piersol to come in the first thing in the morning. When Piersol arrived, Fabris said: "Joyce, I'm glad you're here. I've been having a lot of trouble in selection recently. My long suit has always been collective bargaining. I'm a lawyer by training, and I think I need help. Briefly, let me outline how we handle selection here now."

> *Blue-collar employees*—Screening interview to separate out the misfits; then a test battery—mostly abilities tests—and then interview the best of the lot. For crucial jobs, either security-wise or if the job involves expensive equipment, get two letters of reference from prior employers.
>
> *White-collar employees*—Clerical, and so forth—same as blue-collar procedures except references always are checked out.
>
> *Managerial employees*—Multiple interviews, intelligence test, personality tests, and references.

Fabris added: "I've also been making a list of what's happened in selection in the last six months since I've been in this job."

1. Our best managerial candidate was lost because she refused to take the personality test we use, the Minnesota Multiphasic Personality Inventory. She said it was an invasion of privacy.
2. For employees who handle expensive supplies, we use a polygraph test, too. We've had a few refuse to take it. Our thefts are high. We wonder if it's any good! My boss feels the polygraph is essential.
3. One man we hired is doing a good job. We accidentally found out he has a prison record. His supervisor wants to know how we missed that and wants to let him go. We have no policy on this, but I feel he's proved himself in three months on the job.
4. We're having a lot of trouble on the reference letters. When we ask people to rate the applicants on the basis of all factors, including references, we find the supervisors read different things into these letters.
5. Our turnover has been high. My boss thinks it's because we aren't matching the best people to the right jobs. I need your help.

Discussion Question

You are Joyce Piersol. Make a list of additional information necessary to help Gigantic. How would you go about acquiring the information? Based on what you know now, what are the biggest problems, and what would you do about them?

Exhibit Four

THE DIAGNOSTIC MODEL

ASSESS HUMAN RESOURCE CONDITIONS	SET HUMAN RESOURCE OBJECTIVES	CHOOSE AND APPLY HUMAN RESOURCE ACTIVITIES	EVALUATE RESULTS
EXTERNAL CONDITIONS	EFFICIENCY	Planning	EFFICIENCY
	Organization	Staffing	
Economic Conditions	Employee	**Development**	EQUITY
Government Regulations	EQUITY	Employee/Union Relations	
Unions	Organization	Compensation	
	Employee		
ORGANIZATIONAL CONDITIONS			
Nature of the Organization			
Nature of the Work			
EMPLOYEE CONDITIONS			
Abilities			
Motivation			
Interests			

Part four

Development

This part of the book explores the development of employees. The object of development activities is to provide the necessary conditions to allow individuals to perform at levels that increase their personal effectiveness as well as the organization's. As the diagnostic model shows (Exhibit Four), the process is affected by external conditions, especially labor and product market conditions, but also by governmental regulation. Within the organization, a variety of conditions affect the amount of resources the organization devotes to developing employees. Some organizations view human resources as an asset to be conserved, developed, and utilized. Other organizations view human resources more as interchangeable commodities, to be used or abandoned at the employer's discretion.

Staffing, the topic of the previous part in the book, assists managers to employ effective people in the right jobs. New employees usually require orientation and additional training, and mature or experienced employees may need retraining, as requirements change in a dynamic organization. Training (Chapter Fourteen) is one of the major activities in any organization.

chapter fourteen

TRAINING, DEVELOPMENT, AND ORIENTATION

CHAPTER OUTLINE

Training is big business, and getting bigger. Motorola, Inc. has committed itself to a training budget of 2 percent of each employee's salary. It spent $44 million in 1986 alone. Eight hundred Motorola employees have full-time training duties, while 200 training vendors (outside suppliers) and 360 in-house subject-matter experts assist. Satellite television courses through the National Technological University allow Motorola as well as other employers to offer its students a master's degree in electrical engineering. Much of its training is tied to plant and office automation and production process control techniques aimed at reducing product defects to practically zero. Motorola even trains workers for its key suppliers, many of whom lack the resources to supply training in such advanced specialties as computer-aided design and statistical defect control. Does all this training pay off? Motorola's head of training says, "We've documented the savings from the statistical process control methods and problem-solving methods we've trained our people in. We're running a rate of return of about 30 times the dollars invested—which is why we've gotten pretty good support from senior management."[1]

In California state unemployment insurance funds have been diverted to equip a $1.4 million mobile classroom trailer with computer-controlled lathes and other modern equipment. The equipment is trucked out to aerospace plants to retrain assembly workers as skilled machinists. At a cost of $2,600 per worker for 410 hours of training, the program has slashed trainees' length of unemployment and boosted their wages by an average of 55 percent. It is saving the unemployment insurance system several times its cost in reduced unemployment claims.[2]

Companies are beginning to regard training expenses as no less a part of their capital costs than plants and equipment. Just as a percentage of cost may be set aside to maintain an expensive piece of equipment, funds are now allocated to maintain the necessary skills in the work force.[3]

> **Definition**
>
> *Training* is a systematic process of changing the behavior, knowledge, and/or motivation of present employees to improve the match between employee characteristics and employment requirements.

Training is closely linked to other human resource activities. For example, employment planning identifies skills shortages. These shortages can either be filled through staffing or through strengthening those skills in the present work force. One of the main purposes of performance evaluation is to identify gaps between expected performance and actual performance—gaps that may be narrowed by training. Similarly, other personnel activities must be congruent with training. For example, newly acquired skills should be recognized with pay or promotions.

In spite of sizable budgets, good intentions, and real needs, many training programs fail to achieve lasting results. Why? Too often, it is because the purported goals of the training are vague. If we don't know where we're going, we can't tell if we got there. Nor can we tell if it's where we wanted to be (see Chapter Eight).

This chapter will discuss how the diagnostic approach can organize and improve training decisions and their results.

A DIAGNOSTIC APPROACH TO TRAINING

When we introduced the diagnostic model, we distinguished between a reactive, or problem-solving approach to human resource management, and a proactive, or forward-looking approach. Training is used in both. For example, a problem of high scrap rates or low quality on an assembly line may be attributed to employees unfamiliar with a new part. Reactive training may be offered to solve this problem. Or a group of workers may be selected for a supervisory skills class, and their potential for promotion determined in part on their performance in that class. The organization may not need additional supervisors at present, but through employment planning it knows it will need them in the future. So a proactive organization uses training both to encourage employees to invest in their own human capital as well as to solve current future problems.

External Conditions

Government

The government influences training in several ways:

1. Equal Employment Opportunity. The government influences training by exerting pressure to upgrade the skills of minorities and women; this increases the demand for training or retraining. The government also seeks to ensure that access to training is free of illegal, discriminatory restrictions. Every aspect of training—needs analysis, program design, trainee selection, and evaluation—is subject to scrutiny for disparate impact on minorities and women. For example, in *Kaiser Aluminum & Chemicals* v. *Weber,* the employer and the Steelworkers' Union voluntarily agreed to a training plan to eliminate racial imbalances. Chapter Three on equal employment opportunity discussed the need to ensure that personnel decisions are demonstrably work-related; eligibility for training and evaluation of trainees' performance are some of those personnel decisions that must comply with the EEO regulations.

2. Human Resource Policy. A second way government influences training is by funding training programs that have public policy purposes. Publicly funded job training programs have been legislated for over 20 years. They have, at various times, been designed to

> retrain the experienced labor force, to remedy the adverse effects of automation, to relieve poverty, to create jobs, to serve as a backstop for income maintenance programs, to encourage high school completion, to reduce juvenile delinquency, to convert welfare recipients into wage earners and to conserve natural resources. Virtually all worthwhile social goals have at some time been an objective.[4]

Under the 1983 Federal Job Training Partnership Act (JTPA), employers and local governments negotiate the nature of the training to be offered by employers according to their perceptions of local job vacancies and requirements. In New York City, for example, the act funded a program tailored to the financial community's need for securities clerks.[5] By selecting trainees based on a profile of requirements for entry-level jobs that was developed by the brokerage firms and banks, and tailoring the training to the job descriptions, the program has been quite successful in placing graduates. The JTPA incorporates two of the basic tenets of training, which are to identify organizations' training needs and to tailor the training to those needs.

JTPA has its critics, however. Because the programs are so tuned to business needs and select only applicants likely to be successful, they are not serving the hard-core unemployed—those adults who lack high school diplomas or are functionally illiterate tend to be chronically unemployed. Since JTPA works so closely with employers, some critics describe it as a government subsidy for training that employers would have provided anyway.[6]

The hard-core unemployed present a particular challenge to training because their expectations of success are so low.[7] In the past, they may have made efforts to find jobs or learn skills, but these efforts, for whatever reason, were not successful. They logically expect the future to be like the past, so they lack the motivation to expend the effort on training, or changing their performance. However, the Work in America Institute reports success in training people with minimal reading and computational skills by changing the instructional design. Sharply defined basic skills training is interwoven with technical skills training. They have produced cost-effective designs for training word processors, wastewater treatment plant operators, and electronic technicians.[8] The point is that government has a strong interest in training, as a way of enabling its citizens to become active participants in a healthy economy.

3. *OSHA.* As part of its efforts to ensure safe and healthful working conditions, the government sets standards authorized by the Occupational Safety and Health Act (OSHA). Employers subject to OSHA standards (see Chapter Fifteen) provide training based on identification of actual tasks performed by employees, actual and potential hazards encountered, and the equipment and practices that can minimize these hazards.

Labor/Product Markets

Labor/product markets also influence the design and administration of training programs. When necessary skills are in short supply in the external labor market, an organization may find that developing these skills among its internal labor supply is a cost-effective option. Under surplus conditions organizations may find they can readily purchase the skills and experience they need in the external market. And investing in developing their own human capital may be less attractive.[9]

Unions

Unions also play an important role in training. In the construction industry, where unions are often larger than the employers, the unions provide all or most of the training through apprenticeship programs. The U.S. Department of Labor funds apprenticeship programs in the building trades, mining, auto repair, and other fields, and issues standards and regulations governing these programs.

Organization Conditions

Some firms, such as Motorola, Inc. and General Motors Corporation, allocate a large share of their human resource budget to training; others do not. What determines this difference? The organization's business strategies, its policies toward human resources, its culture, technology as well as the nature of its employees all influence its emphasis on training.

Make or Buy Strategies

Organizations in new or emerging product markets may tend to look to hiring experienced personnel (buying talent), while those business units in more mature, stable markets may tend to invest in developing their own human resources internally (developing talent).[10] However, very little is known about why some firms expend more per employee on training than others, or the payoffs from these make-or-buy options.

Nevertheless, even in units recruiting experienced workers, some training must occur. It is not an all-or-nothing proposition. Orientation is needed for new employees, company policies and procedures must be learned, and specific tasks to be performed must be reviewed, and many jobs are unique to the organization and require special training that is not available outside the organization. The School of Veterinary Medicine at Cornell University provides an example of a unique training need. It has cows with "windows" (fistulas) in their stomachs. These cows are used in research and to teach students about the animals' digestive system. Technicians sew in these windows, clean them, care for the animals, and perform other tasks. Cornell does not expect to go into the local labor market to hire someone with experience in cow "windows." Similarly, most organizations have unique jobs that require training.

Technological Change

Continuing technological change has been the hallmark of the American economy. Although this change is more or less constant in the national economy, change within a specific organization may be discontinuous and drastic when it occurs. Also, while the overall economy gains from new technologies, workers whose jobs are substantially changed may experience economic hardship. The same holds true for professionals who fail to keep up with new technological developments; they may become obsolete. Training can help reduce some of these negative effects of change.

Obsolescence can be defined as a reduction in competence resulting from lack of knowledge of new techniques or technologies developed since completion of one's professional/job training.[11] The threat of obsolescence for professionals has long been recognized, but as the rate of change accelerates, it becomes harder to keep abreast of developments without employers' assistance. Organizations that employ large numbers of scientists or engineers cannot afford to let these expensive resources become obsolete. So organizations and individuals have a common interest in avoiding obsolescence.

Technological change is one of the most frequently cited reasons for training.[12] As the pace of change accelerates, it may become useful to think of training as a process of continuous learning. New job designs based on a work team approach can make learning an everyday part of the job and place co-workers in the role of trainers. Within the work team, the training needs are easily identified, motivation can be stronger, and learning can occur within the work setting, so there is a minimal disruption and maximal opportunity to practice the acquired skill.[13] Identifying training needs, enhancing motivation, and transferring the learned behaviors to the job are all critical issues in designing training programs.

Employee Conditions

A key criterion for selecting/designing training programs is recognition of individual differences among employees.[14] In Chapter Six, we stated that employees' performance was a function of their ability and motivation to perform. Training, as Exhibit 14–1 shows, can be designed to affect both.

Learning Ability

Individuals differ in the amount of learning that has occurred prior to training, their ability to learn, and the ways they learn.

Exhibit 14–2 shows some typical learning curves. For many individuals, rapid gains from initial practice are followed by a plateau where improvement levels off. There are many possible reasons for a plateau to occur: material to be learned may become more difficult, fatigue or boredom may inhibit performance, or individuals may have reached the upper limits of their capacity. Not every individual's learning rate plateaus at the same time, nor do all individuals learn at the same rate, as the three different curves indicate. To date it is difficult to predict with any accuracy

EXHIBIT 14–1
Effects of Training

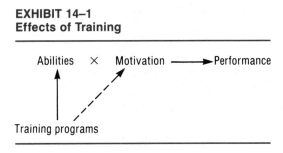

EXHIBIT 14–2

Three typical learning curves

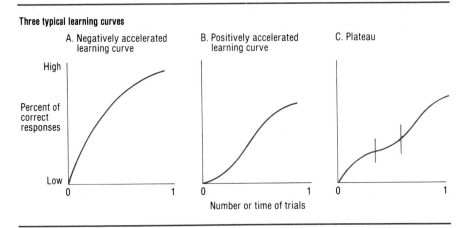

A. Negatively accelerated learning curve B. Positively accelerated learning curve C. Plateau

where a particular individual is on the learning curve. But a good trainer will use knowledge of this common learning pattern to design training programs that can be adjusted to the observed needs of the individual trainees. Changes in instructional method, additional examples, breaks to allow fatigue to dissipate, or pacing changes may be needed to reenergize learning.

Motivation

Motivation is at least as important as ability; unfortunately, it cannot be measured. It can only be inferred from behavioral observation. In Chapter Six, we discussed theories of motivation and work performance. Theories of motivation have implications for training, too.

Goal Setting. Goal setting models postulate that individuals' conscious goals or intentions regulate their behavior. The trainer's job, then, is to get the trainees to adopt or internalize the training goals of the program.[15] Kenneth Wexley and Gary Latham identify three key points in motivating trainees:

- Learning objectives of the program should be conveyed at the outset and at various strategic points throughout the program.
- Goals should be difficult enough to adequately challenge the trainees and thus allow them to derive satisfaction from achievement, but not so difficult as to be unattainable.
- The final goal of program completion should be supplemented with subgoals (periodic quizzes, work samples), to maintain feelings of accomplishment and encourage anticipation of the next hurdle.[16]

Reinforcement. Reinforcement theory says that the frequency of a behavior is influenced by its consequences. Behavior can be shaped by reinforcing progressively closer approximations to the goal behavior. Reinforcement needs to be administered as soon after the desired behavior occurs as possible. However, the same reinforcers are not effective for all people. The more familiar a trainer is with a group of trainees, the more likely it is that reinforcers can be tailored to the trainees.[17]

Expectancy Theory. Expectancy theory holds that individuals are motivated to choose a behavior alternative that is most likely to have desired consequences. There are two aspects to expectancy: First, the trainee must believe that improved skills or knowledge lead to valued outcomes, for example, increased pay, promotions, or self-esteem. Second, the trainee must believe that participating in the training program can lead to improved skills and knowledge and, therefore, to the valued outcomes. This may seem obvious, but people who have been unemployed for a long time often do not have these expectancies. They may not expect that effort expended to learn new behaviors in a training program can lead to meaningful employment. Trainers should not assume trainees have accurate perceptions of reward contingencies. Trainees must be told exactly what outcomes can be expected if the training program is successfully completed.[18]

Interaction between Motivation and Learning Ability

Exhibit 14–3 shows the interaction of motivation and learning ability. The motivation to undertake training is affected by individual characteristics, the staffing process, and reaction to the individual training needs assessment.[19] All these affect employees' motivation going into the training program. The way a trainer structures the program, including the application of learning principles, affects posttraining motivation; this, in turn, affects whether or not behavioral changes occur on the job as a result of training.

Setting Training Objectives and Planning Training Activities

Efficiency and Equity

The large monetary returns discussed in the introduction clearly show that training has great potential to affect employee productivity and organizational efficiency. Decision makers must consider whether training investments are managed to achieve the greatest return, and that requires assessing both training costs and benefits.

EXHIBIT 14–3
The Interaction of Motivation and Learning

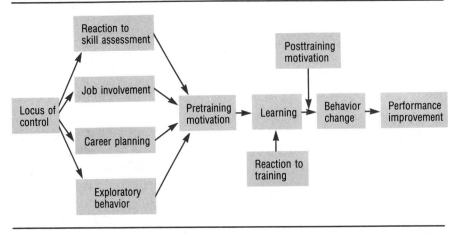

Source: Raymond A. Noe and Neal Schmitt, "The Influence of Trainee Attitudes on Training Effectiveness: Test of a Model," *Personnel Psychology* 39 (1986), pp. 497–523.

In addition, however, training affects the equity perceptions of employees and other constituents. Training is often the gateway to advancement, so the way managers allocate training opportunities can affect employees' perceptions of fairness and equity. Training can socialize or orient new employees into the organization's culture, policies, and procedures.[20] Moreover, training activities are a key tool for achieving equal employment opportunity and Affirmative Action. Finally, training activities can affect the organization's role as a good citizen, depending on whether they provide skills needed in the community. Clearly, wise decision makers will not fail to consider the equity implications of their training decisions.

Planning Training Activities

Exhibit 14–4 models the major decisions in planning training activities:

1. Determine the training needs and objectives.
2. Translate them into programs that meet the needs of the selected trainees.
3. Evaluate the results.

The rest of this chapter is organized around these three decisions.

EXHIBIT 14–4
Training Model

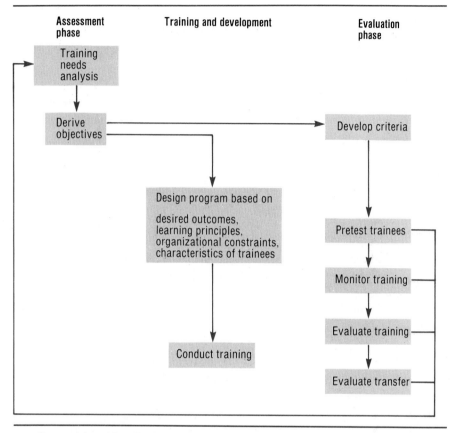

Assessment phase	Training and development	Evaluation phase

Training needs analysis

Derive objectives

Develop criteria

Design program based on desired outcomes, learning principles, organizational constraints, characteristics of trainees

Pretest trainees

Monitor training

Evaluate training

Conduct training

Evaluate transfer

Source: Adapted from *Training: Program Development and Evaluation* by I. L. Goldstein, Copyright © 1974 by Wadsworth Publishing Company, Inc. Reprinted by permission of the publisher, Brooks/Cole Publishing Company, Monterey, California.

DETERMINING TRAINING NEEDS AND OBJECTIVES

The first issue is to identify training needs relevant to the organization's objectives. This is the assessment phase shown in Exhibit 14–4. Assessing needs is important because other decisions hinge on it.[21] The content of programs, the techniques used, and even the trainees chosen depend on the objectives of the training program. Is the training for management or word processing? Are the trainees experienced? How important is this training to the organization? How much time and money are we willing to invest in it? Which payoffs can we anticipate from the training? The importance and relationship of these objectives to organizations' strategies determine the level of resources committed to training efforts.

One way to identify training needs is within a framework of three sets of analysis: organizational, job, and individual.[22]

Organizational Analysis

Organizational analysis is the process of determining where training is needed. This is a broad look at companywide needs. A thorough analysis might look at organization maintenance, efficiency, and culture.

Organizational maintenance aims at ensuring a steady supply of critical skills. If succession plans point out the need to develop managerial talent, training may include transferring high potential employees through a variety of positions and locations to ensure broad exposure to a variety of responsibilities.[23]

Organizational efficiency, a major objective in the diagnostic model, might include checking on productivity, labor costs, output quality, or various other measures. Using the diagnostic approach, managers examine the organization's strategies, the results of employment planning, and the major variances between the units' successes and failures to determine what role training could play.

Organizational culture includes the value system or philosophy of the organization. Training can be designed to impart the organization philosophy or values to employees.[24] IBM managerial training includes a large dose of the "IBM culture." Team building and quality circles also require extensive training in the philosophy and values of these approaches. When values transmitted in a training program run counter to those that prevail in the workplace, they are not maintained for long. If organizations wish the trained values to be maintained, they must be sure that the new behaviors are reinforced on the job.[25]

Finally, *specific requests for training* from operating managers provide additional inputs to training needs analysis.

Job Analysis

Analysis of the job requirements is a valuable source of data to establish training needs. Several approaches to analyzing jobs identify training needs.[26] Task analysis, work sampling, critical incident analysis, and task inventories in which employees indicate how frequently they carry out a particular activity and the importance of each activity to the job are all ways to analyze the training needs for a particular job. You may wish to refer back to Chapter Five for more detail on job analysis methods.

Employee Performance Analysis

Many employers use performance evaluation to identify developmental needs for individual employees. These needs can also be identified during career planning. Employees' abilities, knowledge, and interests are compared with the requirements of job assignments.

It makes common sense to use performance reviews and career planning to analyze training needs for an individual. Yet a number of difficulties exist. Experience suggests the managers must be willing to conduct a performance review for developmental purposes. Nonetheless, many avoid this responsibility, citing two common reasons: the frequent negative reaction of subordinates to the feedback provided, and the managers' lack of confidence or ability to carry out a developmental performance review. If managers are attempting to build cohesive workgroups, it may be counterproductive to identify a member's weaknesses, unless that interview is handled with extreme skill and tact. In an attempt to overcome these problems, some personnel professionals design systems that require subordinates and managers to prepare themselves for the review sessions. Often these self-review procedures improve employee reactions.[27]

Exhibit 14–5 evaluates a wide range of alternative methods to assess training needs. The criteria for evaluating the various methods include trainee and management involvement. Trainee involvement is desirable to provide the necessary motivation to undertake training and to use the newly trained behaviors on the job. Management involvement is necessary to provide the support and encouragement for the trainee to implement the new behaviors and provide the rewards for doing so.[28]

No one can overestimate the importance of trainee involvement and managerial support. According to the survey data reported in Exhibit 14–6, the most commonly cited reasons for training failures can include the lack of managerial support for the new behaviors and a lack of sufficient employee involvement. Thus, training decisions must consider the trainees' supervisors and co-workers, to see that the new behaviors are applied and rewarded on the job.

Although alternatives for systematic needs assessment abound, in reality it is only rarely used. L. A. Digman found that 81 percent of companies surveyed identified training needs only by reacting to problems that cropped up.[29] Fewer organizations even claim to have regular ongoing processes for defining training needs. Training needs analysis must be part of the ongoing process of managing human resources. It must be linked through the organization's human resource plans to the numbers and skills required (employment planning), to the jobs performed (job analysis), and the individual employees (career planning and performance evaluation).

EXHIBIT 14–5
Needs Assessment Methods

Technique \ Criteria	Potential Participant Involvement	Management Involvement	Time Required	Cost	Relevant Quantifiable Data
Advisory committees	Low	Moderate	Moderate	Low	Low
Assessment centers	High	Low	Low	High	High
Attitude (opinion) surveys	Moderate	Low	Moderate	Moderate	Low
Group discussions	High	Moderate	Moderate	Moderate	Moderate
Interviews with potential participants	High	Low	High	High	Moderate
Management requests	Low	High	Low	Low	Low

Observations of behavior (on the job performance)	Moderate	Low	High	High	Moderate
Performance appraisals	Moderate	High	Moderate	Low	High
Performance documents	Low	Moderate	Low	Low	Moderate
Critical incident method	High	Low	Moderate	Low	High
Questionnaire surveys and inventories (needs assessment)	High	High	Moderate	Moderate	High
Skills test	High	Low	High	High	High
Evaluations of past programs	Moderate	Low	Moderate	Low	High

Source: John Newstrom and John Lilyquist, "Selecting Needs Analysis Methods," *Training and Development Journal*, October 1979, p. 56. © 1979, *Training and Development Journal*, American Society for Training & Development. Reprinted with permission. All rights reserved.

EXHIBIT 14–6
Why Training Fails

Reason for Failure of Training Programs	Percent Who Mentioned
No on-the-job rewards for behaviors and skills learned in training	58%
Insufficient time to execute training programs	55
Work environment does not support new behaviors learned in training	53
Lack of motivation among employees	47
Inaccurate training needs analyses	40
Training needs changed after program had been implemented	35
Management does not support training program	30
Insufficient funding of training program	21

Source: The Conference Board, *Trends in Corporate Education and Training* (New York: The Conference Board, 1985).

Stating Objectives

Exhibit 14–4 shows that specific objectives must be derived from the analysis of training needs. The idea is to state the objectives so that the success or failure of the training program can be evaluated by referring to these objectives.[30] For skills training, this is straightforward; for example, the successful trainee will be expected to type 55 words per minute with two or less errors per page. But behavioral objectives can be more difficult to state. Contrast the objective

to understand that each employee is an individual

with

the supervisor develops profiles on each employee listing personnel data and comments on the specific examples of performance and reviews the employee's profile prior to any developmental meetings with the employee.[31]

There is no way to judge if the first objective has occurred. The second objective contains verifiable statements that provide a basis for evaluating whether or not the program was successful.

Stating measurable objectives is particularly difficult for programs designed to increase self-awareness, such as sensitivity training or assertiveness training. Nevertheless, clear behavioral standards of expected results are necessary so that the content of the training and the programs and techniques can be addressed specifically to these expected results. Decisions on content, potential trainees, and training method flow logically from these behavioral objectives.

LEARNING PRINCIPLES

Training endeavors to induce learning, a relatively permanent change in knowledge, skills, or behaviors. Studies of human learning suggest several principles which offer valuable guidance for designing effective training programs. These principles are: conditions of practice, knowledge of results, relevance of material, and transfer to the job.

Conditions of Practice

For maximum learning, active practice of the skill to be acquired is necessary. Practice should continue beyond the point where the task can be performed successfully several times (overlearning). Distributed practice sessions (divided into spaced segments) are more effective than massed practice, a fact often ignored in training programs for the sake of expediency. And the size of the unit to be learned at each practice session affects the learning rate.

Whether a task should be divided into subparts depends on the difficulty of the task and the degree of interrelationship between the subtasks. For example, a parts clerk would probably learn to correctly identify the stock before learning the computerized system for maintaining a parts inventory. On the other hand, a tool and die maker's tasks of feeding, aligning, and stamping are more difficult to subgroup into simpler elements without those elements becoming meaningless, and so would probably be taught as a single unit.

Knowledge of Results

Errors are eliminated faster when trainees receive feedback on how they are doing. Guidance and/or role modeling can provide this feedback, reinforce appropriate learning, and prevent inadequate behavior patterns from developing.

Relevance of Material

Material that is rich in associations for trainees is more easily understood. Meaningfulness can be enhanced by providing an overview of how the training fits with the job, how the training sequences fit together, and the anticipated consequences of applying the key behaviors on the jobs.

Transfer to the Job

How learning is transferred to the job is a most perplexing issue for every training program.[32] The traditional approach to boost transfer has been to maximize the identical elements between the training situation and the actual job. This may be feasible for training skills such as operating a cash register, but not for teaching leadership or conceptual skills. Often what is learned in a training session faces resistance back at the job. Techniques for overcoming this resistance include creating positive expectations on the part of the trainee's supervisor, creating opportunities to implement the new behavior on the job, and ensuring that the behavior is reinforced when it occurs. Commitment from top management to the training program also helps in overcoming resistance to change.

CHOOSING TRAINING PROGRAMS

After assessing conditions, setting measurable and specific objectives, and keeping learning principles in mind, the content and format of training programs are chosen.[33] Training program options can be organized by whether they focus on socialization and orientation, management training, or management development.

Orientation/Socialization

Orienting new employees has three objectives: One is simply learning job procedures. The second objective involves establishing relationships with co-workers, including subordinates and superiors, and fitting into the employer's way of doing things.[34] The purpose is to develop realistic job expectations and positive attitudes toward the employer. The third objective is to give employees a sense of belonging by showing how their job fits into the overall organization.

Transamerica Corporation recently implemented a new orientation program in their information system's group. They began by surveying a cross section of employees: managers, new hires, and people with different levels of experience. On the basis of information gathered from this group, they put together a 19-hour program. The program has proved so popular and the information presented so valuable that employees who are not new hires are signing up to attend. Among the factors they credit for their program's success:

1. Knowledgeable and enthusiastic presenters of information—the managers in charge of various areas are the presenters.
2. Top management's commitment—this motivates middle managers to participate and to send their new people to the sessions.
3. Follow up with participants to evaluate the program and revise its contents based on these evaluations.[35]

The orientation process is continuous. It does not occur at one point but is achieved more slowly and over time. Orientation usually starts *before* a person actually enters an organization with job choice, attraction to organizations, and selection. How organizations handle these activities sends signals to potential employees.[36]

As with all training, orientation involves change. It often includes the relinquishing of certain attitudes, values, and behaviors. The new recruit must learn the basic goals of the organizations, the preferred means by which those goals should be attained, the basic responsibilities of the job, the required behavior patterns for effective performance, and a set of rules. They learn many of these things from other co-workers and members of a work group or team.[37] Thus, the work group is an important part of the orientation process.

Orientation should not be expected to produce conformity to a single standard; rather, it narrows the extremes in behavior and attitudes. There is pressure *not* to hold extreme values or attitudes; there is more pressure *not* to produce extremely poorly than there is to produce at a specific level.

Nonmanagement Training

Training in nonmanagement areas is often called skills training. Skills training programs may be held on or off the job.

On-the-Job Training

A typical on-the-job training program places the trainee into the real work situation, where an experienced worker or the supervisor demonstrates the job and the tricks of the trade. On-the-job training avoids the major difficulties with off-the-job training: lack of relevance and reinforcement in the actual job situation.[38] For example, the literature offers many examples of managers who did well in formal classrooms but then made no changes in their behaviors at work. The importance of a job or task, how it fits in with other tasks and other jobs, and the consequences of improper performance are usually far easier to demonstrate to the trainee on the job.

Although on-the-job training can be inexpensive and simple, there are risks. Damaged machinery, low quality, unsatisfied customers, misfiled forms, or less than optimal performance are examples. On-the-job trainers must be well trained themselves. They should be good performers on the job; plus, they should be aware of training techniques. The Job Instruction Training approach (Exhibit 14–7) is one way to systematize the training and ensure follow-up.[39]

EXHIBIT 14–7
Job Instruction Training (JIT) Methods

First, here's what you *must do* to *get ready* to teach a job:
1. Decide what the learner must be taught in order to do the job efficiently, safely, economically, and intelligently.
2. Have the right tools, equipment, supplies, and material ready.
3. Have the workplace properly arranged, just as the worker will be expected to keep it.

Then, you should *instruct* the learner by the following *four basic steps:*

Step I—*Preparation* (of the learner)
1. Put the learner at *ease.*
2. Find out what is already known about the job.
3. Get the learner interested and desirous of learning the job.

Step II—*Presentation* (of the operations and knowledge)
1. *Tell, show, illustrate,* and *question* in order to put over the new knowledge and operations.
2. Instruct slowly, clearly, completely, and patiently, one point at a time.
3. Check, question, and repeat.
4. Make sure the learner really knows.

Step III—*Performance try-out*
1. Test by having the learner perform the job.
2. Ask questions beginning with *why, how, when* or *where.*
3. Observe performance, correct errors, and repeat instructions if necessary.
4. Continue until you *know* the learner knows.

Step IV—*Follow-up*
1. Check frequently to be sure instructions are being followed.
2. Taper off extra supervision and close follow-up until the learner is qualified to work with normal supervision.

Remember—If the learner hasn't learned, the teacher hasn't taught.

Apprenticeships

Apprentice training combines on-the-job and off-the-job training. Apprenticeships require the cooperation of the employer, schools, government agencies (which frequently subsidize the apprenticeships and set standards for them), and unions.[40]

The apprentice commits to a period of training and learning that involves both formal classroom learning and practical on-the-job experience. These periods can vary from 2 years (barber, ironworker, baker, meat cutter) through 4 or 5 years (electrician, engraver, tool and die maker, plumber) up to 10 years (steel-plate engraver). During this period, the pay is less than that for the master worker.

In the United States, the apprenticeship programs are disproportionately composed of building trades programs. Although enrollments in registered apprenticeship programs are at historic highs, the proportion of the civilian labor force participating in apprenticeship training in the United

States is extremely low—only 0.3 percent. If registered apprentices in the United States equaled the proportion of the labor force enrolled as apprentices in Austria, Germany, or Switzerland, there would currently be 7 million apprentices in the United States instead of 395,000. Apart from the requirement to conform to social policies such as affirmative action and fair labor standards, employers and unions are relatively free to organize apprenticeships to suit their own needs.

Management Development

Unlike skills training, management development often focuses on less well-defined skills, and the manager often shoulders a greater responsibility for personal development.[41] One of the most integrated management development programs exists in the Eastman Kodak Company, and is illustrated by the pyramid in Exhibit 14–8. A one-year analysis of successful managerial behavior, as well as strategic forecasts of future managerial needs, identified critical management skill dimensions shown in the bottom section of the pyramid.

These dimensions were found to apply from the first-line management job all the way to midmanagement. For example, the same problem analysis and planning skills needed by a team leader (shown in the bottom of the pyramid) would be revisited and enhanced for new supervisors, only now they would apply to unit operations instead of simple team projects. These skills are revisited again when the employee reaches second-level manager rank, but now they apply to strategic business plans, and so on.

In addition, Kodak's training organization identifies and provides tailored programs to fit specific and unique business unit needs. These tailored programs also build upon the core skills of the management education pyramid shown in the exhibit.[42]

On-the-Job Management Development

Training managers on the job typically combines two approaches: role modeling and job transfers.

Role Models. One of the best methods of developing new managers is for effective managers to teach them.[43] The role model sets a good example of how to be a manager, answers questions, and explains why things are done the way they are. It is the manager's obligation to help the manager-trainee make the proper contacts so that the job can be learned easily and performed well.[44]

Research on the role modeling approach stresses that if the trainees are to develop, the superior must delegate enough authority to let them make decisions and even mistakes.[45] A climate for learning not only pro-

EXHIBIT 14–8
Eastman Kodak Company's Planned Approach to Management Education

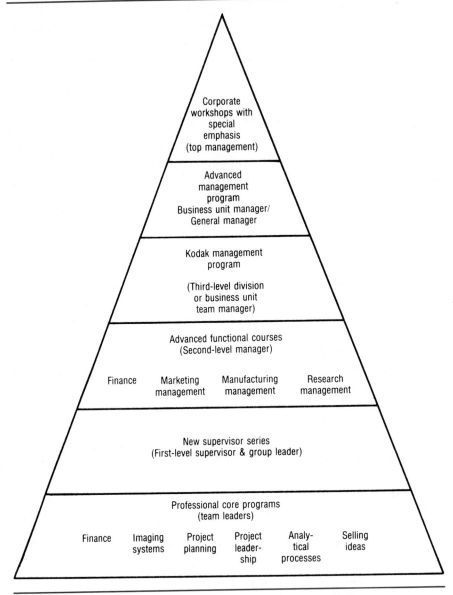

Adapted with permission from Eastman Kodak Company, Rochester, New York.

vides opportunities to learn, but also encourages a feeling of mutual confidence.

Appropriately chosen task-force and special assignments are often used as a form of coaching and counseling in the role model approach. Although most organizations use coaching and counseling by a role model, it is not without its problems. Chris Argyris points out that coaching reinforces or perpetuates current executive styles within an organization. This may not always be desirable.[46] Other problems he identifies are that too often superiors are not rewarded for providing an effective role model, and the system does not allow the subordinate to make mistakes.

Despite these difficulties, coaching and counseling by a role model are probably the most widely used management development techniques and may yield good results. However, there has been little systematic study or evaluation of these techniques, so it is difficult to demonstrate their effectiveness.

If one good role model can be useful, perhaps two or more are even better. This is part of the notion behind the second on-the-job management training approach: job transfers.

Transfers. In this approach, trainees are rotated through a series of jobs to broaden their managerial experience. The jobs typically involve exposure to a variety of functions, product lines, and geographic areas.[47]

Advocates of rotation and transfer contend that this approach broadens the manager's background, accelerates the promotion of highly competent individuals, introduces new ideas into the organization, and increases organization effectiveness.[48] However, some research evidence questions the wisdom of rotation. The organization may be moving employees before they have experienced consequences of their decisions. Without having to live with their results, trainees may be learning the wrong thing.

There is negative reaction to transfers too. Some employees maintain that IBM really means "I've Been Moved." Changing social values and the increase in dual career couples have combined with skyrocketing relocation costs to make organizations consider transfers more thoroughly than they used to.[49] Jeanne Brett and James Werbel investigated why some employees and their families are willing to move and others are not; which conditions make moving difficult; and the effects of a mobile lifestyle.[50] They concluded that employees are most willing to move when the new job promises to be a challenge and a contribution to their career development.

Plateaued Managers

Role models and transfers are useful ways of developing young managers; a more compelling problem is maintaining the commitment and productivity of middle managers. These long-term employees, who have reached their highest career levels,[51] have "plateaued" and may stay that way for another 10 to 20 years. At IBM, for instance, 80 to 90 percent of the managers are long-term employees. At General Electric Company, the problem's dimensions are huge. Of 83,000 GE managers and professionals, more than 11,000 have been with the company more than 30 years, almost 26,000 have been there more than 20 years, and more than 48,000 for more than 10 years.

One study divided 30 engineering managers into two groups: those who were actively and enthusiastically involved in the organization, and those who were passive.[52] The passive managers did not express extreme dissatisfaction, but they expressed no particular interest or enthusiasm for their jobs or the company. Both groups had 16 to 25 years of service with the employing organization. What accounted for the differences in motivation? The research is based on self-reports of what happened many years before and, therefore, may be faulty. Nonetheless, it suggests that the most important difference between the two groups was whether their early job assignments were connected to the mainstream of the company's activities. A sense of doing a task that is important to the company may carry through later career stages: early challenging positions boost confidence in ability to handle new hurdles.

The second factor affecting middle management motivation according to this study is openness and candor about a person's career prospects. Obviously, not everyone can be a general, no matter how good s/he is—there is a greater supply than demand. Supervisors can, however, skillfully provide clear and honest feedback about performance and prospects, however limited. When they do, employees are more likely to believe they have been fairly treated by the organization and maintain their commitment and productivity.

While further research is called for, it's clear that maintaining skills to avoid obsolescence, and maintaining motivation to produce, are two training issues that will only increase in importance as the U.S. work force ages.

Off-the-Job Management Development

Off-the-job programs are more common for management/professional development than they are for skills training. Development programs for professionals such as scientists and engineers usually involve their return to universities or research centers for seminars. Or, they may receive sabbaticals for work in advanced research. Colleges of business frequently offer courses aimed at practitioners, ranging from Supervision I to advanced management seminars.

Many large organizations run their own advanced management programs; examples include General Electric's Crotonville facility, IBM at Sands Point, the U.S. Army War College, and the Federal Executive Institute in Charlottesville. In other organizations, the personnel staff or consultants run programs at various work sites. Professional associations such as American Management Associations and the American Society of Personnel Administrators also run extensive training and development programs.

Motorola, however, recently cut back its training facility in Tucson, Arizona. They reasoned that spending 30 days in the desert at its renowned Motorola Executive Institute was a luxury managers no longer had in a time of rapid change in their product market.[53] Decentralized training is more cost-effective and also could be fine-tuned to training needs. Now their programs for managers emphasize clearly articulated objectives, similar to those previously recommended for skills training. For example, to "identify and understand key emerging Asian competitive threats, understand the factors in Asia that are subject to change and that may affect Motorola's business; and provide a perspective that will be helpful in the development and improvement of strategic plans in the respective business units."[54]

Off-the-Job Management Development Techniques. Exhibit 14–9 describes some techniques frequently used to develop managerial abilities in off-the-job programs.[55] Their common thread seems to be to attempt to simulate real situations and then critique the ways trainees respond to the situation.

The case method is probably the most common technique and it is briefly reviewed here. Others listed in Exhibit 14–9 are treated in detail in the references.

Argyris discussed the case method with a number of practitioners of the technique.[56] From these discussions he identified five features everyone agreed were central to the case method:

1. Use of actual problems of organizations.
2. Maximum involvement of participants in stating views, confronting other views, and making decisions.
3. Minimal dependence on faculty.
4. Rarely any right or wrong answer.
5. Create appropriate levels of drama so as to involve people.

But a study he did of executives attending a management seminar concluded that it didn't work that way. Faculty members, in fact, dominate the group interaction and do little to relate the case to situations the ex-

EXHIBIT 14—9
Off-the-Job Management Development Techniques

Technique	Description	Effectiveness
Case method	Trainees study a written description of real decision-making situations, analyze, and choose solutions.	Best if there is interaction between trainer and trainee and among trainees. Can be effective with good cases and trainees, but little research exists to evaluate this technique.
Role playing	Each participant is assigned a role and reacts to other players' role playing. Background information on other players and the situation is given, but there is no script. Can be video-taped for reanalysis.	Success depends on ability of participants to play the roles believably. Evidence on effectiveness is mixed.
In-basket	Trainee is given material which includes items from a manager's mail and telephone messages. Important and pressing matters are mixed in with routine items. Different subordinates' or supervisor's versions of a situation make solutions less clear cut. Trainee is critiqued on the number of decisions made in the allotted time period, quality of decisions, and priorities used in making them.	Some evidence that method is useful in predicting managerial success.
Management games	The operating characteristics of a company are described in the form of equations which can be manipulated in response to decisions made by a team. Each team's decisions compete with those of other teams. Results of team decision provide inputs for next round of decisions.	Advantages include integration of interacting decision makers, provision of feedback, and the requirement that decisions be made with inadequate data, which simulates reality. Disadvantages include development and administration costs and the sometimes unrealistic or limited models underlying the equations.

ecutives face on the job. Faculty members usually led the group to a "preferred" solution, thus violating most of what the same faculty members identified as central to the case method. Argyris criticizes the case method because it may facilitate learning that does not question the underlying values of participating executives or the policies of their organizations. He feels that questioning assumptions is a basic management skill to be fostered. Thus, Argyris concludes that the whole issue of applicability of material learned in case studies needs to be given more serious consideration. Many of these same criticisms would apply to other training techniques as well.[57]

Frequently training and development programs combine on-the-job and off-the-job efforts.[58] Incorporating real work situations with more formal off-the-job analysis and development minimizes the major drawbacks of each separate approach.

EVALUATING RESULTS

Evaluation is the final phase of the training. As Exhibit 14–4 suggested, methods to evaluate must be designed into the training program from the very beginning at the time the objectives are specified. Training evaluation is like brushing your teeth after every meal. Everyone advocates it, but few actively do it.

Evaluation Criteria

It is convenient to consider two criteria for evaluating the results of training: internal and external.

Internal criteria are associated with the content of the program. For example, a program offered by ComputerLand to train customers in the use of computer software could be judged on how fast and accurately the trainees can operate the programs. The criteria are found in the course content. A commonly used internal criterion is participant reaction—how the trainees feel about a specific training experience.[59] But it may not be the most relevant criterion, because it fails to address any skills, or behavioral or attitudinal changes. So even though participant reaction is useful, it is not a sufficient evaluation.

External criteria are related to the ultimate purpose of training. Possible external criteria include performance evaluation ratings, changes in sales volume, or costs. They measure some aspect of performance and try to relate changes in performance to training.[60] For example, are sales up because use of computer software permits better tracking of potential customers?

Most researchers state the need for external measures of changes in job behavior and organizational effectiveness. Some even advocate multiple behavior indexes to capture the dynamic nature of the training process, with its multiple objectives for individuals and the organization.[61]

John Newstrom lists four bases for evaluating training: (1) trainees' reaction, (2) learning that occurs, (3) behavioral changes, and (4) results of those behavioral changes, such as increased sales.[62] He demonstrates that different conclusions would be reached evaluating the same programs using only *one* of the four evaluation techniques; therefore a complete evaluation must use multiple criteria.

Other writers emphasize the importance of choosing evaluation standards before conducting the program. Unless agreed on beforehand, the selection of criteria can be merely a value judgment that leaves the training results open to attack.[63]

The matrix presented in Exhibit 14–10 illustrates these four bases for evaluating training:[64]

1. Are the trainees happy? (trainee reaction)
2. Do the materials used in the training session teach the concepts specified? (learning that occurs)
3. Are the concepts applied on the job? (behavioral changes)
4. Does the application of the concepts positively affect the organization? (results)

Note that trainees' reaction is only the first question. The effect on the organization remains the bottom line in training.

The fourth criterion is training results. Do training activities affect the organization? From a managerial perspective, an important component of this question involves whether the costs of training are offset by the training benefits.

Efficiency: Costs

The introduction suggested that training has become big business. For individual human resource managers, even more compelling evidence of training costs comes from the budget allocated to training programs. Training costs can be divided into one-time costs of development and ongoing costs of implementation. One example calculated costs of $134,000 to develop an off-site training program (including training department overhead, staff salaries, consultants, equipment, and materials) plus $16,500 to deliver one two-day meeting for 20 people (including lost work time of participants, facility costs, and transportation).[65] A more recent study calculated the costs of a supervisory skills training program applied to 62 bank employees in five sessions. One-time costs involved developing materials and videotapes ($10,000) plus salaries, benefits, and travel for trainers for five days ($2,800). Total costs over the five sessions included trainers' salaries ($3,350), equipment and materials ($755), facilities ($580), and trainees' salary costs of $17,791. Thus, the total cost to train 62 bank employees was $35,276 (that is, $569 per trainee).[66] Of course, the particular training costs differ with each training program. Exhibit 14–11 shows several training cost examples. Generally, training costs should include all resources that must be acquired or shifted from other uses to develop and conduct the program (see Chapter Eight).

The substantial budget costs of training often lead managers to see only the cost per trainee and consider cutting training programs to save costs. Although it may often be appropriate to cut ineffective training programs, it is impossible to judge effectiveness by costs alone. Very often, such shortsighted decision making may cost more in lost productivity than it saves in program expenses. Managers must pay attention to the benefits of training.

Efficiency: Benefits

Training produces many benefits for organizations. Exhibit 14–12 lists several examples of training program outcomes. Training outcomes roughly correspond to internal criteria discussed earlier, while operational outcomes correspond to external criteria, also discussed earlier. Though the internal criteria may provide useful information for monitoring how the training program is conducted or how participants react and learn from it, the external criteria are closer to organizational productivity outcomes.

However, the external criteria have two problems. First, they are hard to measure in the same tangible units as costs (that is, dollars). Second, it is often difficult to be sure that the training program is responsible for changes in these outcomes. Regarding the first problem (measurement), there is no easy answer. However, several recent authors have proposed methods for attaching dollar values to such costly individual behaviors as turnover and absenteeism (see Chapter Eight). Some have even attempted to value job performance in dollars (see Chapter Seven). Though such estimates are bound to be crude and imperfect, exact precision is often not necessary.

EXHIBIT 14–10
Evaluation Matrix*

What We Want to Know	What Might Be Measured	Measurement Dimensions	What to Look At (sources of data)	Alternative Data Gathering Method
I. Are the trainees happy? If not, why? a. Concepts not relevant b. Workshop design c. Trainees not properly positioned	Trainee reaction during workshop	Relevance Threat Ease of learning	Comments between trainees Comments to instructor Questions about exercises "Approach behavior" to exercises	Observation Interview Questionnaire
	Trainee reaction after workshop	Perceived "worth" V—Relevance; or C—Learning energy	"Approach behavior" to project Questions about project concepts	Observation Interview Questionnaire
II. Do the materials teach the concepts? If not, why not? a. Workshop structure b. Lessons —Presentation —Examples —Exercises	Trainee performance during workshop	Understanding Application	Learning time Performance on exercises Presentations	Observation Document review
	Trainee performance at end of workshop	Understanding Application Facility Articulation	Action plan for project Use of tools on exercises Presentations	Observation Document review Interview Questionnaire
III. Are the concepts used? If not, why not? a. Concepts —Not relevant —Too complex —Too sophisticated b. Inadequate tools c. Environment not supportive	Performance improvement projects	Analysis Action plan Results	Discussions Documentation Results	Observation Interview Document review Questionnaire (critical incident)
	Problem solving technique	Questions asked Action proposed Action taken	Discussions Documentation Results	Observation Interview Document review Questionnaire (critical incident)

IV. Does application of concepts positively affect the organization? If not, why not?	Ongoing management approach	Dissemination effort Language People management process	Discussions Meetings Documentation	Observation Interview Document review Questionnaire (critical incident)
	Problem solving	Problem identification Analysis Action Results	Discussions Documentation Results	Interview Document review Questionnaire (critical incident)
	Problem prediction and prevention	Potential problem identification Analysis Action	Discussions Documentation Results	Interview Document review Questionnaire (critical incident)
	Performance measures Specific to a particular workshop	Output measures Interim or diagnostic measures	Performance data	Document review

Source: K. Brethower and G. Rummler, "Evaluating Training," *Training and Development Journal*, May 1979, pp. 14–22.

EXHIBIT 14–11
Training Cost Categories and Examples

Equipment	Facilities
Training devices	Classrooms
Computer	Laboratories
Video	Offices
Trainers	Libraries/learning centers
Telecommunications	Carrels
Laboratory equipment	
Personnel	**Materials**
Instructors	Workbooks
Managers/administrators	Texts
Clerks	Slides, tapes
Programmers	Programs
Analysts/designers	Tests
Evaluators	Paper
Consultants	Film
Artists	

Source: Greg Kearsley, *Costs, Benefits, and Productivity in Training Systems* (Reading, Mass.: Addison-Wesley Publishing, 1982), p. 24.

EXHIBIT 14–12
Examples of Training Outcomes

Training Outcomes

Student throughput (number of graduates)	Achievement level (accuracy, speed)
Student completion time	Revision time
Testing time	Failure rate
Development time	Absence rate during training
Retention period	Accident rate during training
Attitude change	Amount of practice

Operational Outcomes

Production rate/quality	Quality/speed of service
Sales volume	Accident rates (on the job)
Equipment failure rates	Job proficiency
Job turnover rates	Customer or employee satisfaction

Adapted from: Greg Kearsley, *Costs, Benefits, and Productivity in Training Systems* (Reading, Mass.: Addison-Wesley Publishing, 1982), p. 60.

Regarding the second problem—establishing the program's effect—again there is no easy answer. The key here is to design training evaluation to control possible extraneous factors and isolate the effects of training.[67]

A recent statistical review of 17 studies suggested that training generally does have a positive effect on supervisors' ratings of behavior.[68] One study estimated monetary benefits from training 62 bank employees between $34,627 (assuming training effects last only one year) and $194,885 (assuming training effects last 20 years). And, this is after subtracting the $35,276 cost of training 62 employees. Thus, it is possible (though rare) for training to be evaluated rigorously. However, even these studies could not obtain perfectly precise cost and benefit estimates. Fortunately, a method is available that makes such estimate precision less necessary.

Break-Even Analysis for Training

Clearly, precise estimates of training costs and benefits are seldom, if ever, available. However, we could say the same thing about any human resource management activity. In fact, we could say the same thing about management activities in general, including marketing, finance, and production. As Chapter Eight pointed out, however, it is often not necessary to establish perfect precision to make rational managerial decisions. Let us review an example presented earlier. Exhibit 14–13 presents information on a training program's costs and benefits. This is the same information presented in Exhibit 8–5; details of the training program appear in Chapter Eight. As shown in the exhibit, total costs of the program are $1 million including first-year start-up costs of $500,000. However, the leverage of the program (the number of person-years of productivity affected by it) is 1,200 as shown in the top of the exhibit.

Rather than dwell on the imperfections of the training effectiveness measures, we can compute the minimum level of training benefits necessary to cover the training costs. This minimum return equals $833 (that is, $1 million divided by 1,200). If the increase in work force value created by the training program (per person, per year) is greater than $833, the investment pays off, and vice versa. Several studies have suggested that break-even analysis often produces break-even effect levels that are quite low.[69] When this is true, it may be possible that even imperfect training assessments based on only a portion of the possible training outcomes may be sufficient to justify the training investment. Such an approach is certainly superior to attempting to precisely measure training program effects down to the last dollar.[70]

Equity

Of course, efficiency-related criteria are hardly the sole basis on which to evaluate training. As with other human resource management activities,

EXHIBIT 14–13
Example Cost–Benefit Analysis for a Training Program

Computing Quantity/Leverage

Year	Trained Employees Added to the Work Force	Trained Employees Leaving the Work Force	Net Increase in Trained Employees in the Work Force	Total Trained Employees in the Work Force
1	200	0	200	200
2	25	5	20	220
3	25	5	20	240
4	25	5	20	260
5	25	5	20	280

Total person-years of productivity affected = 1,200

Estimating Program Quality

Supervisors were asked to estimate the dollar value of the expected increase in employee service value from the training program, on a per-person, per-year basis, less the increased service costs that would have to be incurred to maintain that increased service value. The estimates of net value ranged from a low of $1,000 to a high of $10,000 per person-year.

Computing Program Costs

Year	Start-Up Costs	Ongoing Program Costs	Total Costs
1	$500,000	$100,000	$ 600,000
2	0	100,000	100,000
3	0	100,000	100,000
4	0	100,000	100,000
5	0	100,000	100,000

Total program costs over five years = $1,000,000

Computing Total Program Returns

Total program returns = (Program quality × leverage) − Program costs

Program Quality	Leverage	Program Costs	Total Program Returns
$ 833/person-year	1,200	$1,000,000	$ 0
1,000/person-year	1,200	1,000,000	200,000
10,000/person-year	1,200	1,000,000	11,000,000

Adapted from: John W. Boudreau, "Utility Analysis: A New View of Strategic Human Resource Management," in ASPA/BNA Handbook of Human Resource Management, vol. 1, ed. Lee D. Dyer (Washington, D.C.: Bureau of National Affairs, 1988).

training can have profound effects on the equity perceptions of employees and other constituents. Training is often seen as a reward for good performance and a gateway to advancement. Training is a key tool in advancing equal employment opportunity and affirmative action programs. Finally, training can contribute to community goodwill when it provides skills for the chronically unemployed or other disadvantaged groups. Thus, while evaluating the efficiency contributions of training programs is important, the wise manager will ensure that the effects of training on equity goals are not overlooked.

SUMMARY

U.S. organizations spend at least $200 billion each year on training. While that figure is astonishing, even more astonishing is that we know so little about how to effectively manage this investment. Financial analysts and investment managers, who are responsible for the consequences of their decisions, devote considerable effort to ensure that comparable capital and financial outlays are well managed. Unfortunately, of all the activities in personnel management, training seems most subject to passing fads and fashions.

Managers need to approach training decisions more systematically. They need to assess needs and objectives, design program alternatives to meet these needs and to achieve the objectives, and conduct cost-benefit evaluations. Until they deal with these issues, managers will remain unguided in their expenditure of the billions of dollars in training. As it now stands, the state of research in the management of training offers little comparative evidence by which to evaluate the impact or generalizability of various approaches to training the work force.

It is important to call out a basic premise underlying the discussion of training in this chapter. In training today we tend to shape the individual to fit the job requirements. Perhaps training and development in the future must include managing the job design process, too. We need to study ways to design jobs differently—to build in future-needed skills in the present job so that employees can begin to prepare for future jobs. Human resource professionals need to create expectations in all employees that skills learning and change will be an ongoing process throughout their careers. Both employees and employers have responsibility to adapt to this change.

DISCUSSION AND REVIEW QUESTIONS

1. Which factors in the diagnostic model help explain why there is such a wide range among employers in what they spend on training?
2. Which organization measures indicate a need for training?
3. How do learning principles affect training?
4. Why is it difficult to evaluate training?
5. What are possible criteria for evaluating training? What are the pros and cons of each?

NOTES AND REFERENCES

1. Michael Brody, "Helping Workers to Work Smarter," *Fortune*, June 8, 1987, pp. 86–88.
2. Ibid.
3. *Serving the New Corporation* (Alexandria, Va.: American Society for Training and Development, 1986).
4. Robert Guttman, "Job Training Partnership Act: New Help for the Unemployed," *Monthly Labor Review* 106 (1983), p. 3.
5. "A Roundtable: Do Jobs Programs Work?" *New York Times*, December 12, 1982, p. E5; Damon Statson, "Classes Tailored to Business Prepare the Jobless for Jobs," *New York Times*, October 27, 1983, p. 38.
6. Karen Blumenthal, "Job-Training Effort, Critics Say, Fails Many Who Need Help Most," *The Wall Street Journal*, February 9, 1987, pp. 1, 15.
7. Eli Ginzburg, ed., *Employing the Unemployed* (New York: Basic Books, 1980).
8. Jerome Rosow and Robert Zager, *Training for New Technology, Part III: Cost-Effective Design and Delivery of Training Programs* (Scarsdale, N.Y.: Work in America Institute, 1986).
9. Lester Thurow, *Generating Inequality* (New York: Basic Books, 1975).
10. Charles Snow and Raymond Miles, "Organizational Strategy, Design, and Human Resources Management" (paper presented at 43rd meeting of the Academy of Management, Dallas, Tex., August 1983).
11. John A. Fossum, Richard D. Arvey, Carol A. Paradise, and Nancy E. Robbins, "Modelling the Skills Obsolescence Process: A Psychological/Economic Integration," *Academy of Management Review* 11, no. 2 (April 1986), pp. 362–72.
12. Pat Choate, *Retooling the American Work Force* (Washington, D.C.: Northeast-Midwest Institute, 1982); H. Allan Hunt and Timothy L. Hunt, *Human Resources Implications of Robotics* (Kalamazoo, Mich.: W. E. Upjohn Institute for Employment Research, 1982).
13. Jerome Rosow and Robert Zager, *Training for New Technology, Part II: Toward Continuous Learning* (Scarsdale, N.Y.: Work in America Institute, 1985).
14. Kenneth N. Wexley and Gary P. Latham, *Developing and Training Human Resources in Organizations* (Glenview, Ill.: Scott, Foresman, 1981), p. 112; J. Kevin Ford and Raymond A. Noe, "Self-Assessed Training Needs; The

Effects of Attitudes toward Training, Managerial Level, and Function," *Personnel Psychology* 40 (1987), pp. 39–53.

15. Dov Eden and Gad Ravid, "Pygmalion versus Self-Expectancy: Effects of Instructor- and Self-Expectancy on Trainee Performance," *Organizational Behavior and Human Performance* 30 (1982), pp. 351–64.

16. Wexley and Latham, *Developing and Training.*

17. David A. Kolb, "Experiential Learning Theory and the Learning Style Inventory: A Reply to Freedman and Stumpf," *Academy of Management Review* 6, no. 2 (1981), pp. 289–96.

18. Wexley and Latham, *Developing and Training.*

19. Raymond A. Noe and Neal Schmitt, "The Influence of Trainee Attitudes on Training Effectiveness: Test of a Model," *Personnel Psychology* 39 (1986), pp. 497–523.

20. Steven L. McShane and Trudy Baal, "Employee Socialization Practices on Canada's West Coast: A Management Report" (Burnaby, B.C.: Simon Fraser University, Faculty of Business Administration, December 1984).

21. W. McGehee and P. Thayer, *Training in Business and Industry* (New York: John Wiley & Sons, 1961).

22. M. Moore and P. Dutton, "Training Needs Analysis: Review and Critique," *Academy of Management Review* 3 (1978), pp. 532–54.

23. James Walker, *Human Resource Planning* (New York: McGraw-Hill, 1980); James Walker, "Training and Development," in *Human Resources Management in the 1980s*, ed. Stephen J. Carroll and Randall Schuler (Washington, D.C.: Bureau of National Affairs, 1983).

24. Chris Argyris, *Reasoning, Learning and Action* (San Francisco: Jossey-Bass, 1982).

25. G. P. Latham and L. M. Saari, "Application of Social Learning Theory to Training Supervisors through Behavioral Modeling," *Journal of Applied Psychology,* 61, no. 3 (1979), pp. 239–46.

26. David A. Bownas, Michael J. Bosshardt, and Laura F. Donnelly, "A Quantitative Approach to Evaluating Training Curriculum Content Sampling Adequacy," *Personnel Psychology* 38 (1985), pp. 117–31.

27. J. M. Ivancevich and S. V. Smith, "Goal Setting Interview Skills Training: Simulated and On-the-Job Analysis," *Journal of Applied Psychology* 66, no. 6 (1981), pp. 697–705.

28. James S. Russell, James R. Terborg, and Mary L. Powers, "Organizational Performance and Organizational Level Training and Support," *Personnel Psychology* 38 (1985), pp. 849–63; James S. Russell, Kenneth N. Wexley, and John E. Hunter, "Questioning the Effectiveness of Behavior Modeling Training in an Industrial Setting," *Personnel Psychology* 37 (1984), pp. 465–81.

29. L. A. Digman, "Determining Management Development Needs," *Human Resource Management*, Winter 1980, pp. 12–17.

30. E. A. Prieve and D. A. Wentorf, "Training Objectives—Philosophy or Practice?" *Personnel Journal*, March 1970, pp. 235–40; J. P. Campbell, "What We Are About: An Inquiry into the Self-Concept of Industrial and Organizational Psychology" (presidential address to Division of Industrial and Organizational Psychologists, 86th annual meeting of American Psychological Association, Toronto, 1980).

31. William McGehee, "Training and Development, Theory, Policies, and Practices," in *ASPA Handbook of Personnel and Industrial Relations*, ed. Dale Yoder and H. Heneman, Jr. (Washington, D.C.: Bureau of National Affairs, 1979), pp. 5.1–5.4.

32. Kenneth N. Wexley and Timothy T. Baldwin, "Post-Training Strategies for Facilitating Positive Transfer: An Empirical Exploration" (paper presented at national meeting of the Academy of Management, San Diego, California, 1985).

33. Irwin L. Goldstein, "Training in Work Organizations," *Annual Reviews of Psychology* (Palo Alto, Calif.: Annual Reviews, 1980).

34. Daniel C. Feldman, "A Socialization Process that Helps New Recruits Succeed," in *Current Issues in Personnel Management*, ed. K. Rowland, G. Ferris, and J. Sherman (Boston: Allyn & Bacon, 1983); David F. Jones, "Developing a New Employee Orientation Program," *Personnel Journal*, March 1984, pp. 86–87.

35. Bureau of National Affairs, "Training and Development Programs," *Personnel Policies Forum Survey No. 140* (Washington, D.C.: Bureau of National Affairs, 1985).

36. Daniel C. Feldman, "A Contingency Theory of Socialization," *Administrative Science Quarterly* 21, 2nd quarter (1976), pp. 433–52; Daniel C. Feldman, "The Role of Initiation Activities in Socialization," *Human Relations* 30, no. 4 (1977), pp. 977–90.

37. Jane S. Mouton and Robert R. Blake, *Synergogy: A New Strategy for Education, Training and Development* (San Francisco: Jossey-Bass, 1984).

38. Paul Ryan, "Job Training Employment Practices, and the Large Enterprise: The Case of Costly Transferable Skills," in *Internal Labor Markets*, ed. Paul Osterman (Cambridge, Mass.: MIT Press, 1984).

39. Fred Wickert, "The Famous JIT Card: A Basic Way to Improve It," *Training and Development Journal*, February 1974, pp. 6–9.

40. F. Foltman and V. Briggs, *Apprenticeship Research* (Ithaca, N.Y.: ILR Press, 1980); Jonathan S. Monat, Robert T. Patton, and Dean C. Elias, "Improving Management Training Using Apprenticeship Principles," *Training and Development Journal*, October 1975, pp. 20–24.

41. Douglas T. Hall and Associates, *Career Development in Organizations* (San Francisco: Jossey-Bass, 1986).

42. Personal communication with Mary Ann Williams, Director of Management Education for Eastman Kodak Company, Rochester, New York.

43. J. Sterling Livingston, "New Trends in Applied Management Development," *Training and Development Journal*, January 1983, pp. 15–24; William McGehee and William J. Tullar, "A Note on Evaluating Behavior Modification and Behavior Modeling as Industrial Training Techniques," *Personnel Psychology* 31, no. 3 (Autumn 1978), pp. 477–84.

44. Jerry I. Porras and Brad Anderson, "Improving Managerial Effectiveness through Modeling-Based Training," *Organizational Dynamics*, Spring 1981, pp. 60–77.

45. P. J. Decker, "The Enhancement of Behavior Modeling Training and Supervisory Skills by the Inclusion of Retention Processes," *Personnel Psychology* 35 (1982), pp. 323–32.

46. C. Argyris, "Some Limitations of the Case Method: Experiences in a Man-

agement Development Program," *Academy of Management Review* 5, no. 2 (1980), pp. 291–98.

47. Jeanne M. Brett and James Werbel, *The Effect of Job Transfer on Employees and Their Families* (Washington, D.C.: Employer Relocation Council, 1980); Jeanne M. Brett, "Job Transfer and Well-Being," *Journal of Applied Psychology* 67, no. 4 (1982), pp. 450–63.

48. Karen E. Debats, "The Current State of Corporate Relocation," *Personnel Journal*, September 1982, pp. 664–70.

49. Ceil Blomquist, "Study Shows Relocation Resistance Reversing," *Personnel Administrator*, December 1982, pp. 55–56.

50. Brett and Werbel, *Effect of Job Transfer.*

51. Jay W. Lorsch and Haruo Takagi, "Keeping Managers Off the Shelf," *Harvard Business Review*, July–August 1986, pp. 60–65.

52. Ibid.

53. James F. Bolt, "Tailor Executive Development to Strategy," *Harvard Business Review*, November–December 1985, pp. 168–76.

54. Ibid.

55. John Newstrom, "Evaluating the Effectiveness of Training Methods," *Personnel Administrator*, January 1980, pp. 55–60.

56. Chris Argyris, "Some Limitations of the Case Method."

57. Arch R. Dooley and Wickham Skinner, "Casing Case Method Methods," *Academy of Management Review*, April 1977, pp. 277–89; C. Argyris, "Some Limitations of the Case Method."

58. McGehee, "Training and Development."

59. D. P. Hunt, "Effects of Human Self-Assessment Responding on Learning," *Journal of Applied Psychology* 67, no. 1 (1982), pp. 75–82; B. Mezoff, "How to Get Accurate Self-Reports of Training Outcomes," *Training and Development Journal*, September 1981, pp. 56–61.

60. Kenneth N. Wexley, "A Typology to Evaluate the Effectiveness of Training Programs to Improve Productivity and Quality of Work Life" (paper presented at 42nd annual meeting of Academy of Management, Dallas, Texas, August 1982).

61. David W. Mealia, "A Macro/Micro Decision Model for the Training and Development Specialist," *Relations Industrielles* 37, no. 3 (1982), pp. 657–68.

62. John W. Newstrom, "Catch-22: The Problems of Incomplete Evaluation of Training," *Training and Development Journal*, November 1978, pp. 22–24.

63. J. P. Campbell, "What We Are About: An Inquiry into the Self-Concept of Industrial and Organizational Psychology" (presidential address to Division of Industrial and Organizational Psychologists, 86th annual meeting of American Psychological Association, Toronto, 1980).

64. Karen Brethower and Geary Rummler, "Evaluating Training," *Training and Development Journal*, May 1979, pp. 14–22.

65. W. J. McKeon, "How to Determine Off-Site Meeting Costs," *Training and Development Journal*, 1981, p. 117. Adapted in Wayne F. Cascio, *Costing Human Resources*, 2nd ed. (Boston: Kent Publishing, 1987), pp. 224–25.

66. John E. Mathieu and Russell L. Leonard, Jr., "Applying Utility Concepts to a Training Program in Supervisory Skills: A Time-Based Approach," *Academy of Management Journal* 30, no. 2 (1987), pp. 316–35.

67. T. D. Cook and Donald T. Campbell, *Quasi-Experimentation: Design and Analysis Issues for Field Settings* (Chicago: Rand McNally, 1979); Irvin L. Goldstein, *Training: Program Design and Evaluation*, 2nd ed. (Monterey, Calif.: Brooks/Cole Publishing, 1986); Jack J. Phillips, *Handbook of Training Evaluation and Measurement Methods* (Houston, Tex.: Gulf, 1983).

68. Michael J. Burke and Russell R. Day, "A Cumulative Study of the Effectiveness of Managerial Training," *Journal of Applied Psychology* 71 (1986), pp. 232–45.

69. John W. Boudreau, "Decision-Theory Contribution to HRM Research and Practice," *Industrial Relations* 23 (1984), pp. 198–217; John W. Boudreau, "Utility Analysis: A New View of Strategic Human Resource Management," in *ASPA/BNA Handbook of Human Resource Management*, vol. 1, ed. Lee D. Dyer (Washington, D.C.: Bureau of National Affairs, 1988); Beth C. Florin-Thuma and John W. Boudreau, "Effects of Performance Feedback Utility Analysis on Managerial Decision Processes," *Personnel Psychology*, in press, 1987; Joe R. Rich and John W. Boudreau, "Effects of Variability and Risk on Selection Utility Analysis: An Empirical Comparison," *Personnel Psychology* 40 (1987); John W. Boudreau, "Utility Analysis in Human Resource Management Decisions," in *Handbook of Industrial and Organizational Psychology*, 2nd ed., ed. M. D. Dunnette (Chicago: Rand McNally, in press); Mathieu and Leonard, "Applying Utility Concepts."

70. Boudreau, "Decision Theory Contributions to HRM Research and Practice."

PART FOUR CASES

► ITHACA'S OWN
CASE 5: DEVELOPING NEW MANAGERS

Human resource management at Ithaca's Own has increased requirements for competent managers to help meet the organization's objective. This coming year, I-O plans to promote 10 people to managerial jobs. None of them have had previous experience as managers. The HRM department is now faced with the challenge of helping to train the new managers.

Current Practice

As a relatively new company, I-O has not yet developed a formal training program, nor documented a policy regarding promotion to managerial status. In the past, when a managerial position was filled from within the organization, these promotions occurred on an ad hoc basis. Training is informal. It is usually on the job by an experienced manager familiar with the organization.

Top management at I-O feels that existing training practices are not appropriate to help prepare the work force for promotion to managerial jobs. In order to develop a more systematic approach to training, the CEO decided to allocate an additional $50,000 for managerial training.

Discussion Questions

Recommend a program designed to prepare employees to become managers at I-O. Your recommendations should consider four factors:

1. Program objectives, their clarity and rationale.
2. Content of the program.
3. Appropriateness of the technique(s) selected.
4. An evaluation strategy.

Based on these factors, design a development program for potential managers at I-O which includes the following concerns:

1. What are your recommended objectives for the program? Be as specific as possible.
2. What type of development experiences will these new managers need? Which training technique, or combination of techniques, would address these needs? What criteria would you use for selecting a method(s)?
3. Who should be responsible for conducting the training program? Why? Would you extend training to existing managers at I-O? Why or why not?
4. How should I-O go about evaluating the program? What information would you need to evaluate it?

▶ TRAINING COST-BENEFIT ANALYSIS AT MASSIVE MANUFACTURING CORP.

> Spend $3,333 per trainee in a fancy new training system when we could spend $1,000 and use a good old classroom system? You've got to be kidding! We're facing tight budgets and worsening foreign competition, Petrie. The time has passed when you can get support for any bells and whistles fad that comes down the pike. This company has allowed training to run unchecked for too long, and this is a perfect example of the problem.
>
> Vice President of Marketing, Carol Rose

So went the last comment about a proposed new training system for Massive Manufacturing Corp. Rob Petrie, the vice president of training, was surprised. In the past, he had enjoyed strong support from top management, but with increasing competition, his training group was asked to account for their contribution to the organization's competitive position. More and more, managers were questioning whether training was necessary. Several managers had threatened to refuse to send their employees to many of the standard training programs, claiming that competitive pressures were too tight for that luxury. This was understandable, because the managers saw training as simply an additional cost added to their budget.

However, Petrie felt his programs really were contributing. This latest proposal was an example. He had proposed delivering training to manufacturing engineers through an innovative two-way audio and one-way video system that would greatly speed training. Of course, it required funds to build the network, but the payoff could be tremendous. Clearly, however, management was not buying it on faith. He needed some hard numbers. The problem was, he did not have time for a full-blown scientific study with precise statistics and cost figures.

You were recently hired as Petrie's assistant. Petrie was impressed with your training in management and personnel, and hoped you would bring a much-needed analytical perspective to the training organization. He asked you to put together an analysis within 10 days. You had learned about break-even cost-benefit analysis in your personnel class, and knew that it could provide a quick and concise analysis in this situation. So, you gathered some information.

Exhibit 1 shows the analysis for the proposed new audio-video training program. (This analysis is the same one shown in Chapters Eight and Fourteen. Details are in those chapters.) Its large training capacity allows all 200 currently employed engineers to be trained in the first year, with 25 new engineers trained in each following year. Assuming a 5-engineer separation rate, this puts 20 new engineers into the work force after the first year, producing a leverage of 1,200 person-years (see Exhibit 1). However, this option is costly, involving a half million construction and set-up commitment before the first training program can even start, and requiring ongoing program costs of $100,000 per year. The marketing manager divided the total $1 million cost by the number of trainees over the five-year program (i.e., 300) to get the $3,333 per trainee figure. You computed an equation for total program returns as shown, and you tried out a couple of hypothetical productivity improvements ($833, $1,000, and $10,000) to see their implications. You found that to break even (that is, produce benefits that just cover costs), the audio-video training program must improve engineering performance by $833 per person-year, but that at higher productivity levels the benefits increase quickly.

Exhibit 2 shows similar information pertaining to the current classroom training program. In the top part of Exhibit 2, you see the effects of severely limited classroom space—the program can be offered only to 45 engineers per year. Thus, it trains only 225 engineers over the five-year period. However, it costs only $1,000 per trainee, or $45,000 per year, for a total cost of $225,000. The marketing manager divided this $225,000 figure by the total number of trainees (i.e., 45×5, or 225) to get her $1,000 per trainee figure). Ms. Rose, the marketing manager, insists that classroom training is as effective or maybe a little more effective than audio-video training, and its lower cost per trainee makes it the clear value. (Also, if you don't get the extra $775,000 for your project, some of it will be available for a new ad campaign featuring Rose's daughter.)

You don't have any comparative training effectiveness information, but you do know that these engineers are paid an average of $40,000 per year. They make product design decisions that affect millions of dollars in manufacturing costs and profits.

EXHIBIT 1
Cost and Leverage Information for the Audio-Video Training

Computing Quantity/Leverage

Year	Trained Employees Added to the Work Force	Trained Employees Leaving the Work Force	Net Increase in Trained Employees in the Work Force	Total Trained Employees in the Work Force
1	200	0	200	200
2	25	5	20	220
3	25	5	20	240
4	25	5	20	260
5	25	5	20	280

Total person-years of productivity affected = 1,200

Estimating Program Quality

Program effectiveness is unknown, but these engineers earn an average salary of $40,000 and make product design decisions that affect millions of dollars in production costs and profits.

Computing Program Costs

Year	Start-Up Costs	Ongoing Program Costs	Total Costs
1	$500,000	$100,000	$ 600,000
2	0	100,000	100,000
3	0	100,000	100,000
4	0	100,000	100,000
5	0	100,000	100,000

Total program costs over five years = $1,000,000

Computing Total Program Returns

Total program returns = (Program quality × leverage) − Program costs

Program Quality	Leverage	Program Costs	Total Program Returns
$ 833/person-year	1,200	$1,000,000	$ 0
1,000/person-year	1,200	1,000,000	200,000
10,000/person-year	1,200	1,000,000	11,000,000

Adapted from: John W. Boudreau, "Utility Analysis: A New View of Strategic Human Resource Management," in *ASPA/BNA Handbook of Human Resource Management*, vol. 1, ed. Lee D. Dyer (Washington, D.C.: Bureau of National Affairs, 1988).

Discussion Questions

1. Compute the leverage of the classroom training option (in Exhibit 2). Copy the information on the number of trainees from Exhibit 2, and follow the same logic developed in Chapter Eight to come up with a

EXHIBIT 2
Cost and Leverage Information for the Present Classroom Training

Computing Quantity/Leverage

Year	Trained Employees Added to the Work Force	Trained Employees Leaving the Work Force	Net increase in Trained Employees in the Work Force	Total Trained Employees in the Work Force
1	45	5		
2	45	5		
3	45	5		
4	45	5		
5	45	5		

Total person-years of productivity affected =

Estimating Program Quality

Program effectiveness is unknown, but these engineers earn an average salary of $40,000 and make product design decisions that affect millions of dollars in production costs and profits.

Computing Program Costs

Year	Start-Up Costs	Ongoing Program Costs	Total Costs
1	$0	$45,000	$ 45,000
2	0	45,000	45,000
3	0	45,000	45,000
4	0	45,000	45,000
5	0	45,000	45,000

Total program costs over five years = $225,000

   figure for the total person-years of productivity affected by filling in the blank information in Exhibit 2.

2. Compute a payoff function showing the relationship between total program returns, program leverage, and program quality. Use the symbol P2 to represent the unknown program quality per person-year from the classroom training, and follow the same logic as shown in Exhibit 1.

3. Draw a graph with total program returns on the vertical axis and dollar productivity improvement per person-year on the X axis (this is the variable left unknown in Exhibit 1). Graph the payoff function for audio-video training, and the payoff function for classroom training. For example, when both programs have zero payoff per person-year, the audio-video payoff is −$1 million and the classroom payoff is −$225,000.

4. What is the break-even point for each of the two programs (i.e., the total program cost divided by total leverage)? Where does it appear on your graph? What do the two break-even values mean?

5. Which program is the better investment if both training methods produce equal benefits and the improved productivity per person-year equals $1,000 per person-year? (*Hint:* Use the value $1,000 in each of your payoff functions and compute total program payoff for each option.) Which is better if both produce a payoff per person-year of $3,000? What if the classroom training produces a payoff per person-year of $4,000 and the audio-video training produces a payoff per person-year of only $3,000?

6. What are the implications of your analysis? Is it true that the audio-video training must be more effective in improving productivity per person-year to justify its cost? Explain your answer.

7. Name three additional factors Petrie should consider in choosing whether to present your findings to argue for support for the new program. Name three additional pieces of information you would like to have, and say how you would use them.

THE DIAGNOSTIC MODEL

ASSESS HUMAN RESOURCE CONDITIONS	SET HUMAN RESOURCE OBJECTIVES	CHOOSE AND APPLY HUMAN RESOURCE ACTIVITIES	EVALUATE RESULTS
EXTERNAL CONDITIONS Economic Conditions Government Regulations Unions ORGANIZATIONAL CONDITIONS Nature of the Organization Nature of the Work EMPLOYEE CONDITIONS Abilities Motivation Interests	EFFICIENCY Organization Employee EQUITY Organization Employee	Planning Staffing Development **Employee/Union Relations** Compensation	EFFICIENCY EQUITY

Part five

EMPLOYEE/LABOR RELATIONS

*I*n a previous part of the book we discussed the necessary conditions to encourage maximum development of employees. Another aspect of human resource management involves the daily relationship between employees and the organization. Employees may have problems, either job-related or personal, that inhibit their performance. Or managers, through their supervisory styles, may inhibit employees' creativity and contributions. Chapter Fifteen, "Employee Relations," describes ways organizations and employees might interact so that both can achieve their objectives.

Often, employees faced with unsatisfactory conditions join together in unions to collectively bargain to improve these conditions. Chapters Sixteen and Seventeen, Labor Relations and Collective Bargaining, consider the impact of unions on human resource management. Although unions themselves receive the most attention in the popular press, the influence of unions extends beyond their membership. They also affect nonunionized organizations, notably in conflict resolution and wage setting. Unions are part of the social and political fabric of the country.

Chapter Sixteen analyzes the current status of labor relations in the United States and alternative ways for organized labor and employers to interact. Chapter Seventeen examines the collective bargaining process and its impact on employers and employees.

The quality of employee/labor relations, as the diagnostic model in Exhibit Five shows, is affected by external conditions. Collective bargaining agreements are legal contracts subject to regulation. The whole unionizing and negotiating process is regulated, too, to provide some semblance of a balance of power among participants. Economic conditions affect employee/labor relations by limiting which options each side can afford to utilize. Within the organization, the culture and values set the tone about how the employee/employer relationship is viewed. Both employees and employers have rights and responsibilities. Some employers initiate systems to protect the rights of employees; others do not. Some employers view it as their responsibility to assist troubled employees or to smooth work adjustments; others do not. Some wait for unions to organize their employees to negotiate protection of rights; others do not.

The quality of the employment relationship affects both equity and efficiency. Unfortunately, this effect is unmeasurable, since it consists of trust, morale, and dignity—characteristics that cannot be quantified and, therefore, do not lend themselves to neat statistical reports. But the activities discussed in these chapters are among the most important ones for any manager.

These chapters continue the discussion of the employee development process, because they are also concerned with the conditions that allow individuals to develop their abilities and to contribute to the organization.

chapter

fifteen

EMPLOYEE RELATIONS

CHAPTER OUTLINE

Managers supervise a variety of employees as part of their jobs. Most employees perform effectively most of the time—but not always. What happens, for example, when the checkout cashier suspects he has been singled out unfairly for special scrutiny by his supervisor and the stress from this scrutiny affects his job performance? What happens if the supervisor suspects the cashier is stealing? Suppose an employee is frequently late. Is it because of difficulties with child care arrangements, or drugs? These examples illustrate a time-consuming and worrisome aspect of any manager's job—dealing fairly with troubled employees. Personal problems, both on and off the job, affect employees' work behavior. Because social as well as economic relationships are involved, an organization is frequently in the best position to motivate and provide assistance to employees at such times.

Many organizations seek to go beyond changing negative behavior or assisting troubled employees. They wish to build on strengths: to provide a work environment where employees and the organization can flourish. They also wish to tap into employees' expertise on how to assist the organization to do jobs faster, cheaper, and smarter. Employee relations activities are those whose objective is to create an atmosphere of trust, respect, and cooperation.

Definition

Employee relations activities are those which seek greater organizational effectiveness through the enhancement of human dignity and growth. They seek to establish direct, two-way communication between managers and employees to provide mutual assistance and involvement in decision making.

Employee relations permeate all other human resource activities. Job sharing, retraining and redeployment programs, preretirement counseling, and career management could all be considered employee relations activities. Thus, employee relations are not only specific activities, but also the intangible quality of management-employee relationships, part of the philosophy of the organization. The values statements of corporations pro-

EXHIBIT 15–1
Values of Borg-Warner Automotive, Ithaca Plant

A Continuing Tradition of Innovation   Our greatest tradition is innovation. We have come this far by combining the preservation of established systems with the introduction of fresh ideas, realizing that therein lies the heart of progress. We must support and encourage creativity in each other, knowing that from innovative thinking comes the concepts that will help us anticipate, respond to and bring about change. In an ever-changing world, innovation is a fundamental building block in our leadership in the automotive industry.

Taking Initiative   Each employee has the obligation to take initiative whether it be by learning to do something new or contributing an idea during a problem-solving session. Taking initiative reflects our basic drive to act on our instincts, satisfy our thirst for information and to have a hand in making a difference. Taking initiative means going beyond the expected in search of the ideal, and that's what Morse Automotive is all about.

Working Together   Teamwork is the foundation upon which our success is built. Each of us offers effort, skill and perspective; our special contribution is in blending these together as a means of achieving shared goals. Our commitment to doing individual jobs well must be matched if not exceeded by our dedication to seeking each other's input, keeping each other informed, and appreciating each other's viewpoints. Working together in this way enables us as a team to accomplish what no one could do alone.

Belonging to the Global Community   At Morse Automotive, we accept seriously and with pride our obligation to conduct ourselves responsibly, ethically and legally, in accordance with the highest standards of business practice through-out the world.

Epilogue   These values are our standards, the benchmarks by which we will measure our achievements. They define our purpose and our principles, our mission and our meaning. Each day we have the opportunity to make something happen, to urge ourselves forward. Our purpose, our mission is to seize the opportunity, to achieve our present goals and pursue the bright promise of our future. There is no doubt that we have the talents and abilities to do so. With these values to guide us, let us at Morse now make a commitment to do so, together.

Providing Quality Workmanship at a Competitive Price   Our real success is in our customer's success: our reputation is based on it; our future relies on it. To our customers, the Morse name means quality workmanship at a competitive price and our responsibility is to keep it that way. Our customers' cost competitiveness is dependent on our cost effectiveness as well as that of our suppliers. Therefore, we must seek out every opportunity to reduce our costs and give our customers the edge they require in the worldwide automotive market.

Finding the Right People for the Right Job   We are firmly committed to selecting and employing the most qualified person for every available position without regard to sex, color, creed, age or national origin. This commitment is enhanced and supported by a selection process that involves peers in interviewing and evaluating prospective employees. In this way, we strive to hire those best equipped both personally and professionally to do the job at hand.

---

vide a more concrete definition of employee relations. Exhibit 15–1 shows an example from Borg-Warner. The missions range from holding problem-solving sessions to fostering effective teamwork to involving present employees in the staffing process.

A DIAGNOSTIC APPROACH TO EMPLOYEE RELATIONS

The quality of employee relations in an organization is a function of many things. Even though organization climate and values are perhaps the most important, external factors play a role, too.

External Conditions

Economic
There is no doubt that a company making a profit and experiencing growth finds it easier to make a commitment to an open, supportive employee relations policy.[1] Flexible work hours become possible, and child care becomes affordable.

A fundamental tenet underlying sound employee relations is that employees and management must have confidence in each other's intention to be fair and equitable. Fairness and trust are harder to maintain when the pie to be divided is shrinking and cutbacks are required. So product market conditions play a significant role in setting the context for employee relations.

Government
Government plays a role, too, to a certain extent. The Occupational Safety and Health Act requires certain responses from employers. Legislation such as EEO and privacy laws regulates the actions of managers and employees.

Unions
Unions play a substantial role in shaping employee relations. They can ensure the success of a quality of work life program by their support and participation, for example. But they also play an indirect role, in that many employee relations programs are motivated by a desire to maintain a union-free status for the organization.[2] Many employers believe that they have more flexibility in the absence of a union. For example, promotions can be on the basis of merit or potential, rather than strictly on the seniority that most union contracts require.[3] People can be switched among jobs, and jobs can more easily be changed to adopt new technologies or adjust to changing market conditions. Many employers believe that the services a union may provide—job security, grievance procedures, good wages—can and should be provided by an enlightened management without the intervention of a union.[4]

Internal Conditions

Organization Culture and Values

The employee relations atmosphere reflects the values and culture of the organization. In many organizations employee relations programs emphasize safeguarding employees' rights, as well as providing a forum for their input into work and job decisions. They set up a communication system that makes employees aware of problems/objectives of the organization and makes managers aware of problems/objectives of the employees.

Some organizations committed to strong employee relations programs evaluate managers on whether discipline procedures or conflict resolution systems are fairly administered; women and minorities are given equal access to training, promotions, or other job rewards; and on the results of surveys of employees' attitudes about the organization and its management practices.

Employee Conditions

Experts often cite the rising educational level of the work force as a fundamental change in the work force. Such employees, some assert, want a greater say in work decisions and are more willing to challenge management.[5] The rising number of employees suing employers support such assertions. But this contrasts with the fact that formalized worker participation programs exist mainly in manufacturing firms where the bulk of jobs do not require high levels of education.[6] So even though we cannot say for certain what difference the educational level of employees makes, it is safe to say that some workers want to be involved in decision making, but others do not. The desires of both groups should be accommodated.

Whether or not they wish to participate in work decisions, all employees have a right to expect fair treatment from employers, and a method of recourse if treatment is perceived to be unfair. Employee relations programming provides an internal recourse, so that everyone can stay out of our already overcrowded courtrooms.

Setting Employee Relations Objectives and Strategies

Some writers have characterized employee relations as hardly more than a union avoidance strategy.[7] That is too simple a perspective. Although union avoidance can certainly be an objective of employee relations programming, many organizations in industries where the likelihood of unionization is quite low still maintain strong employee relations. Union avoidance is not the only objective; indeed, it may be nothing more than a side effect. More typically, the objective is to provide an atmosphere in which all employees can perform their jobs to the best of their abilities and contribute a creative spark to the organization.

Employee relations activities affect both efficiency and equity. They affect efficiency in that they confront the reasons for performance discrepancies and help remove them. When the problem is an individual employee's behavior, employee assistance and conflict resolution systems seek constructive solutions designed to restore individual performance. If the problem is the organization's behavior, employee-management committees can identify possible changes that increase organization efficiency.

Equity is affected in that much employee relations programming sends the message that the organization is a concerned institution, one that protects, assists, and deals fairly with all its members.

EMPLOYEE RELATIONS DECISIONS

The typical decisions managers face in designing employee relations programs include:

- Communication: How best can we convey our philosophy to employees?
- Protection: Are there aspects of the workplace that threaten the well-being of employees?
- Assistance: How shall we respond to special needs of specific employees?
- Cooperation: To what extent should decision making and control be shared?
- Discipline and conflict: How shall we deal with it?

Even though some of these topics have been touched on before, in this chapter we focus more directly on their employee relations aspects.

COMMUNICATION

The core of an employee relations program is an employee handbook.[8] The handbook sets out the rules and policies within which employees and managers must operate. Handbooks tell how the organization sets wages, allocates training and promotion opportunities, which services it provides, and what it expects from employees. Later exhibits in this chapter provide examples from various employee handbooks.

Lawyers today routinely advise employers to include a disclaimer that although general policies, rules, and regulations are specified, the handbook is not a binding employment contract. Discharged employees have successfully argued in courts that handbooks *can* imply a contract and, therefore, employees cannot be dismissed without just cause. However, interpretations vary among judicial districts.[9]

Obviously, merely writing a handbook is not enough. It must be continuously updated and publicized to employees; supervisors must also be thoroughly familiar with it. Because supervisors are the ones who translate policy into action, IBM gives all its new supervisors two weeks of intense training in implementing IBM's employee relations approach.

Communication comes up again in this chapter when we discuss conflict. For now, let's move on to the topic of protection.

PROTECTION

Every manager and employee wants a healthy and safe work environment. The issue confronting contemporary organizations is cost related: What are the trade-offs between eliminating risks at the workplace and the costs involved? What are the trade-offs between tolerating some risks to employees' health and safety and compensation to be paid because of workers' injuries and lawsuits? Is any risk acceptable?

In some organizations work environments may be so bad that improvements are required. One required response to health and safety concerns is to compensate the victims of job-related accidents with workers' compensation and similar insurance programs. This is necessary but reactive. Another response is proactive; prevention is the strategy taken by most organizations.[10]

Prevention programs take many forms; they include redesigning jobs to diminish hazardous conditions, conducting safety training programs, even offering pay bonuses for good safety records. In an attempt to prevent accidents and improve overall safety records, Kerr-McGee Corporation considers applicants' accident records in selecting miners for its uranium and potash mines.

Safety and Health Hazards

Safety hazards are those aspects of the work environment with the potential of immediate and sometimes violent harm to an employee. Examples are loss of hearing or eyesight; cuts, sprains, bruises, broken bones; burns and electric shock.

Health hazards are those aspects of the work environment which slowly and cumulatively (and often irreversibly) lead to deterioration of an employee's health. Typical causes include physical and biological hazards, toxic and cancer-causing dusts and chemicals, and stressful working conditions.

EXHIBIT 15–2
Injury Frequency Rates, Compensation Cost per Injury, and
Compensation Cost (by age and sex)

	Injury Frequency per Unit of Exposure	Compensation Cost per Injury	Compensation Cost per Unit of Exposure
Males	12.0	$1,558	$18,732
Less than 25 years old	22.3	789	17,585
25 to 44 years old	10.9	1,421	15,506
45 years old and over	10.9	2,072	22,550
Females	5.2	1,176	6,160
Less than 25 years old	4.5	557	2,501
25 to 44 years old	4.9	1,169	5,693
45 years old and over	5.8	1,379	8,057

Source: Alan E. Dillingham, "Demographic and Economic Change and the Costs of Workers' Compensation," in *Safety and the Work Force*, ed. John D. Worrall (Ithaca, N.Y.: ILR Press, 1983).

Causes of Work Accidents and Illnesses

The major causes of accidents and illnesses are the job itself, the working conditions, and the employees.[11] Accidents and illnesses are not evenly distributed among jobs. Employees facing serious health and safety dangers include firefighters, miners, construction and transportation workers, roofing and sheet metal workers, recreational vehicle manufacturers, lumber and wood workers, and blue-collar and first-line supervisors in manufacturing and agriculture. A few white-collar jobs are relatively dangerous: those of dentists and hospital operating room personnel, beauticians, and X-ray technicians.

Working conditions that cause problems include poorly designed or inadequately repaired machines, lack of protective equipment, and the presence of dangerous chemicals or gasses. Other working conditions that contribute to accidents include excessive work hours leading to employee fatigue, noise, lack of proper lighting, boredom, horseplay, and fighting at work.

Some employees seem to have more accidents than the average. For example, Exhibit 15–2 shows work injury rates by age and sex. The highest rate is for males under age 25, with a steady decline in following years. However, when older workers are injured, the costs per injury are higher. Females of all ages have substantially lower injury rates, due in large part to the differential occupational distribution of the sexes.[12]

Occupational Safety and Health Act

The Occupational Safety and Health Act (OSHA) is intended to remedy health and safety problems on the job. Its purpose is to provide employment "free from recognized hazards" to employees. To accomplish this aim, it established safety standards, defined as those "practices, means, operations, or processes, reasonably necessary to provide safe . . . employment." The standards affect any aspect of the workplace. OSHA does not try to inspect all industries equally, but creates priorities based on known hazardous occupations. Similarly, all standards do not have equal emphasis. Those dealing with most hazardous conditions get highest priority.

Unions have played a major role in lobbying the government for stricter enforcement of OSHA's regulations. This is consistent with their long history of concern for employees' safety.

Is OSHA effective? Economic studies have failed to find any statistically significant impact on national injury rates attributable to OSHA.[13] One of the worst industrial accidents ever occurred in Bhopal, India, in 1985. Over 2,000 people were killed after a Union Carbide Corporation plant released a deadly gas into the air. Even though the accident occurred outside the United States, it involved a U.S. employer who is fully aware of OSHA's requirements. The continuing problem of inadequate worker protection has several causes: First, technology is constantly introducing new chemicals, whose potential hazards may not be fully appreciated for years. Second, OSHA focuses on design standards that dictate the physical characteristics of plants and equipment. But Bhopal, Chernobyl, and Three Mile Island all have shown that human error is a common culprit in large-scale disasters. People can circumvent almost any designed-in control system.

OSHA clearly holds management completely responsible for providing adequate training in, and enforcing the use of, safe procedures. In contrast, the employee's own responsibility for personal health and safety is not presently covered in OSHA's approach. For example, if employees wish to skip medical tests to determine if they are developing an occupational disease, OSHA has ruled they may. If an employee refuses to wear safety equipment required by OSHA and an OSHA inspector sees this violation, the employer is held responsible. True, the employer can discipline or possibly fire the employee. However, it may then face challenges by unions or in the courts for unlawful discharge.

To increase employees' awareness of hazards, OSHA established a communication standard in 1986. Often referred to as "right to know," the standard is intended to protect the safety of workers by keeping them informed of the dangerous substances with which they are working, any hazards and symptoms of exposure, and the proper steps to take if they have been exposed. In addition to chemical manufacturers, manufacturers, importers, and distributors of petroleum, stone, textiles, food, and paper are covered by the standard.

Because OSHA puts full responsibility for employees' health and safety on management, many employers have begun screening people for factors that may affect health and safety on the job.[14] Screening for drug and/or alcohol use is the most common example. Medical screening is extremely controversial, for a number of reasons:[15] First, many believe it to be an invasion of privacy. Serious ethical issues arise if an employer has access to nonjob-related information about an individual's medical history: sexually transmitted diseases, family histories of alcoholism or mental disease—any illness that carries a social stigma.

This objection can be overcome if medical information is kept in the hands of the medical staff, and the employer is given only relevant data. That brings up the second objection: Is the quality of data adequate for use in selection decisions? The fallibility of drug testing has been well publicized; predictive screening for susceptibility to certain conditions is not well developed scientifically. Eliminating the hazards for everyone rather than screening for susceptibility to them seems a better approach.

Co-Worker Relations

What happens if the threat to health and safety—whether real or perceived—comes from co-workers: smokers, AIDS victims, alcohol or drug abusers, or sexual harassers? Organizations must tread a narrow line here, so as not to trammel on the rights of one employee while protecting another. Court rulings generally provide guidance as to how the employer may proceed.

AIDS

Acquired immunodeficiency syndrome (AIDS) has surpassed cancer as the disease people fear most. The fear is partly rational, because the disease thus far is always fatal, and control seems years away. But irrational fears exist, too; people sometimes refuse to work with suspected AIDS victims. Legally, AIDS is considered a handicap; therefore its victims are protected against job discrimination and cannot be fired or transferred, as long as they are able to perform their jobs.[16] But this stance does not allay co-workers' fears of contracting the disease. Even though medical experts agree that the disease is not transmissible under normal workplace conditions, managers must take a strong role in educating the work force to this fact. The San Francisco AIDS Foundation has developed written materials and a film entitled "AIDS in the Workplace: Epidemic of Fear" to assist employers in such efforts.[17]

Smoking in the Workplace

Companies' concern about employees' health or comfort and their mounting complaints about smoke have led to an increase in policies on smoking at work.[18] To date, the courts have generally rejected employees' claims to their right to a smoke-free work environment; however, a few states require organizations to have a smoking policy. An ASPA–BNA survey found that the most common employer response to complaints about smokers was to encourage employees to resolve the problem themselves. Less than 3 percent were willing to transfer either the smoker or the objecting employee.[19]

Harassment

The Supreme Court has ruled that an employer is strictly liable for allowing a "hostile environment," even if an employer is unaware of any incidents of racial or sexual harassment.[20] Because the employer alone has the power to promptly and irrevocably end harassment (through warning, transferring, demoting, or even firing the harasser), employer liability is justified. However, the employer can reduce its liability by firmly stating and publicizing its policy forbidding harassment and developing a mechanism for employee complaints. The employer should include both the policy statement and the description of complaint resolution procedures in the employee handbook. We discuss various approaches to resolving conflict later in this chapter.

Substance Abuse

Illegal drugs have become pervasive in American society. It's not surprising that they have also become an issue in the workplace. Yet alcohol abuse is still a far more common cause of impaired performance and absenteeism than abuse of illegal drugs. The difference is that the mere possession of some drugs is illegal, whether or not they are used. An increasing number of employers advocate mandatory drug testing of all employees. Such large-scale testing is not only of dubious legality, but also certainly ill-advised.[21] Testing may be justified for certain job classifications, such as bus drivers, pilots, or nuclear plant operators, where the consequences of working while impaired are severe. But for most jobs, "use of screening as a substitute for good supervision is inappropriate, if not irresponsible."[22] More productive ways to handle suspected drug and alcohol abuse are discussed in the next section.

EMPLOYEE ASSISTANCE

How does a manager respond when employees' personal problems impair their work behavior? It varies. One response is to search for ways to get rid of the troubled employee. Another is to attempt to assist employees either through internal programs or by putting employees in contact with outside professional assistance.

Various surveys report that referral to outside sources of assistance is the most common response of organizations, but some in-house counseling, especially for alcoholism, is also common.[23] Such counseling may range from a brief chat with a supervisor who warns the troubled employee that failure to seek outside help will result in dismissal, to private appointments with professional counselors at the work site.

Employer assistance with personal problems is not new. In 1917, the Ford Motor Company's Legal Aid Department assisted employees "free of charge in all matters involving legal questions, insurance, investments, settlements of disputes, purchase of real estate, and filling out and securing naturalization papers."[24] Its Medical Department had its own modern operating room and six-bed ward, and its English School taught reading, writing, and speaking simple English to thousands of employees. The bulk of these assistance programs ended in the 1920s, however, as the result of pressures accompanying the phenomenal growth of the company, the complexity and cost, and the loss of influence of top managers who supported such a benevolent approach.

In the 1970s and 1980s, assistance programs have again become popular. Today's programs are structured in large part on the basis of research into alcoholism and effective ways to deal with alcoholic employees. Two components appear to be necessary for a successful program:

1. *A written policy.* Even though many of us wish to help our friends if we become aware of a personal problem, the sad fact is that most of us are unsure of how to proceed. Our intentions are honorable, but lack of expertise limits our usefulness. We muddle through. So, too, in organizations. Co-workers and supervisors are typically the first ones aware of a problem, and they are in a position to provide the necessary emotional support and motivation to confront the problem. A written policy can guide them in how to proceed. Research has found supervisors' willingness to confront employees whose performance is impaired is highly related to a written policy outlining performance, discipline, and medical practices.[25] Exhibit 15–3 illustrates an employee assistance policy which clearly spells

EXHIBIT 15–3
A Sample Employee Assistance Program Policy

Purpose
    XYZ Corporation cares about the well-being of its employees and recognizes that a variety of personal problems can disrupt their personal and work lives. For instance, alcoholism is a treatable disease with devastating effects on one's personal health, family, and work. Drugs, family problems, and emotional distress can have similar effects. Most people solve their problems either on their own or with the advice of family and friends; however,

EXHIBIT 15–3 (concluded)

sometimes people need professional advice. XYZ Corporation, through its EAP, provides access to professional counseling services for its employees, and those in need of professional assistance are encouraged to use it. In those facilities where XYZ Corporation has union contracts, the company will conduct the EAP as a cooperative and joint venture with labor's elected representatives.

XYZ Corporation recognizes that it has no right to interfere unless employees' personal problems adversely affect their job performance. When unsatisfactory performance does occur, supervisors will encourage employees to solve their problems on their own or with the assistance of the EAP services.

Policy

The EAP operates within the following framework:

1. A wide range of problems may affect employees' job performance adversely. These include alcohol and drug addiction, marital and family difficulties, and emotional distress. The EAP will assist employees to resolve these problems and others for which employees may seek help.
2. Employees' current jobs and future advancement will not be jeopardized by using EAP services.
3. As with all health and personnel documents, EAP records will be maintained in a confidential manner.
4. When necessary, sick leave may be granted for treatment and rehabilitation on the same basis as it is granted for other health problems.
5. Employees will be responsible for complying with the EAP service's recommendations and treatment plans.
6. The EAP service will also be available to employees' families.

Procedure

1. Employees who need professional advice are encouraged to use the EAP's counseling services, and those whose personal problems adversely affect their work are encouraged to seek help voluntarily from the EAP services.
2. Supervisors are responsible for confronting employees about their unsatisfactory performance and helping them to improve their work.
   a. Supervisors bring employees' unsatisfactory work to their attention and encourage them to solve the problem on their own or with the help of the EAP counseling services. Supervisors also point out to the employees that continued unsatisfactory performance will lead to formal discipline.
   b. If performance improves, no further action will be taken.
   c. If job performance continues to be unsatisfactory, regardless of whether or not employees have accepted help, regular disciplinary procedure will be followed, up to and including discharge. At each step of the procedure, supervisors will encourage employees to seek help from the EAP counseling service.

Source: William J. Sonnenstuhl and Harrison M. Trice, *Strategies for Employee Assistance Programs: The Crucial Balance* (Ithaca, N.Y.: ILR Press, 1986).

out the supervisors' role. A written policy also demonstrates full managerial support for the policy and the options organizations will pursue if performance does not improve.

2. *A program coordinator.* A coordinator ensures that procedure and policies are known and carried out throughout the workplace. A highly visible coordinator can advise supervisors, encourage them to confront the troubled employee, and reassure employees as to the confidentiality of the service.

Approaches to Employee Assistance

When confronted with impaired job performance, an employer can either ignore it, fire the employee, or intervene to try to change the performance. There are two different approaches to intervention; most assistance programs probably contain elements of both approaches.

Constructive Confrontation

This strategy evolved as a technique for identifying employed alcoholics and for counteracting the typical responses of guilt, denial, rationalization, and manipulation.[26] Focusing solely on job performance, it documents to the employee clear instances of impaired performance. Obviously, if job performance is not impaired, then there is no situation that warrants the organization's intervention. Confrontation is best combined with a progressive discipline strategy: Continued unacceptable performance leads to progressively more severe discipline, culminating in dismissal.

That is the confrontation part of the strategy. The constructive part (1) expresses emotional support and group concern for the employee's welfare, (2) emphasizes that employment can be maintained if performance improves, and (3) suggests alternatives for the employee to regain satisfactory improvement. The support and the confrontation are offered in combination, and both focus heavily on job performance.

Counseling

Improved job performance does not necessarily mean that the underlying problems have been resolved. Additionally, job performance may not be affected until the problem has become severe. Rather than focusing on job performance, a counseling approach focuses on the cause of the problem—either in the individual or the social relationship surrounding the individual. Professionally trained psychotherapists are involved. In spite of its tantalizing promise of tackling problems before they become severe, counseling appears to be most useful when it becomes clear that problems are beyond employees' control.[27] Before then, employees fear the stigma of being labeled "mentally ill" and so avoid contacting counselors.

Which approach, confrontation or counseling, has the better track record? Research indicates that programs which maintain a balance between the two approaches have better outcomes than single-approach programs.[28] Constructive confrontation motivates employees to change their behavior, and counseling provides one means of doing so.

An Illustration: Control Data's EAR

In 1974 Control Data Corporation established an employee assistance program called Employee Advisory Resource (EAR).[29] EAR provides free 24-hour phone counseling for evaluation and referrals, as well as face-to-face sessions in several locations throughout the country.

Exhibit 15–4 shows the nine areas for assistance that employees have requested. Contacts concerning personal problems account for about 60 percent of the calls; those for work-related problems 40 percent. Exhibit 15–5 lists the work-related problem areas for which employees sought assistance.

Although these data are useful for identifying those aspects of the organization employees find troublesome, the program relies on employee-initiated contacts. Whether or not these contacts were associated with impaired job performance is not known.

EXHIBIT 15–4
Personal Problems

Category	Percentage of Calls
Financial (bankruptcy, financial difficulties relating to inflationary costs, poor financial management)	26%
Legal (most often family and tenant-landlord conflicts)	21
Chemical (10% alcohol; 3% drugs)	13
Mental health (mainly depression)	9
Familial (parent-child and parent-relative relationships)	8
Marital (difficulties with communication and problem resolution)	8
Personal (difficulties with identity, relationships, and sex)	5
Physical health	5
Miscellaneous (problems not characterized by one of the above groups)	6

Source: David J. Reed, "One Approach to Employee Assistance," *Personnel Journal,* August 1983, pp. 648–52.

EXHIBIT 15–5
Problems at Work

Category	Percentage of Calls
Compensation and benefits (sick pay, health insurance coverage, vacation, overtime, sick leave, retirement)	22%
Performance (disputes over the content of regular performance appraisals to specific disciplinary actions)	19
Transfers and promotions	7
Policies and procedures (requests for familiarization with specific written corporate policies)	14
Interpersonal relations (conflicts with supervisors or other employees)	10
Career counseling	8
Miscellaneous (including discrimination complaints, rehabilitation problems, complaints about working conditions, and other problems not characterized by another group)	20

Source: David J. Reed, "One Approach to Employee Assistance," *Personnel Journal,* August 1983, pp. 648–52.

Family-Job Conflict

Sometimes a problem lies neither in the individual nor the workplace, but in conflicting demands between family and job responsibilities. The increase in the number of women working outside the home makes it likely that a sizable percent of employees experience family-job conflict; however, such conflict is not limited to women. One study identified such conflict in nearly one third of the men in a national sample.[30]

Conflict, defined as "simultaneous occurrence of two (or more) sets of pressures such that compliance with one (role) would make more difficult compliance with the other," comes from several possible sources:

1. Time devoted to one role makes it difficult to fulfill requirements of the other.
2. Stress from participation in one role makes it difficult to fulfill requirements in the other.
3. Specific behaviors required in one setting are completely different from behaviors in the other.[31]

Even though there is little empirical evidence on this third point, an example might be conflicts between the self-reliant, aggressive behavior expected at work and the open, nurturing behavior expected of a parent.

EXHIBIT 15–6
Work Schedule Adaptions (percentage of companies by size having programs for some or all positions)

	1–500	501–1,000	1,001–2,500	2,500+	All Companies
Part-time professionals	34.3	45.8	63.3	40.0	42.3
Flextime	45.7	62.5	46.2	57.5	49.4
Job sharing	13.7	20.8	41.4	20.0	20.2
Extended summer leave	6.0	8.3	24.3	10.0	10.1

Source: Resource Survey No. 15, reported in *Resource*, June 1986, p. 2.

Handling such conflict is essentially a personal matter, but an organization's employee relations philosophy influences its response to employees experiencing such conflict.[32] A number of options exist to make work role requirements more flexible: more flexible work scheduling, providing child care assistance, and increasing employees' control over how they meet their job requirements.

Work Schedule Adaptations
From the employee's perspective, an important aspect of a job is the hours of work required, the arrangement of the hours, and freedom (or lack of it) in determining work schedules. The work schedule affects the nonwork part of a person's life: time with the family, for leisure, and for self-development.

Recent evidence shows that a sizable portion of job dissatisfaction is related to lack of control over hours of work, forced overtime, and lack of freedom to adjust hours to personal needs.[33] Exhibit 15–6 shows some recent survey data regarding the availability of work schedule adaptations. Flextime is the most common adaptation.

Flexible Hours (Flextime)
Flextime is an arrangement of working hours which provides for all employees to be present for a specified period (core time), but the rest of the required hours may be completed at their discretion within a specified period.[34]

The State Street Bank in Boston is typical of organizations that have installed flextime. The employees work a five-day week and can vary their starting times, as long as they work their full 40 hours over the week. All employees work from 11 A.M. to 2 P.M., since these are the hours with peak workloads and communications. This is also the time meetings take place and employees work together. A survey of employees indicated that:

63 percent of employees felt more satisfied with their jobs.

59 percent experienced shorter commuting time.

70 percent indicated more time for leisure or family activities.

47 percent felt they were more productive with flextime.

The majority were extremely satisfied with flextime. Advocates of flextime assert that it allows employees the same freedom to manage their own time that managers and professionals often have.

The major disadvantages with flextime include:

All employees are not present when others want them.

There may be difficulty in keeping records of hours worked for pay purposes, and this can increase costs.

Middle management may perceive a loss of control, and unions may desire fewer hours for their members, not rearranged hours.

There can be conflicts between flextime and the present wage and hours laws, especially about overtime pay and lunch breaks.

Flextime may be hard to implement in interdependent jobs. Manufacturing to inventory may be costly, and in service industries coordination may be difficult.

A recent government survey discovered that one in eight workers has the freedom to adjust his or her starting and quitting times.[35] Flextime can have a positive effect on equal employment opportunity compliance. Since working women frequently experience time conflicts resulting from family requirements, the discretion that flextime allows may help an employer attract and retain more women employees.

Part-Time Workers

About 18.6 million Americans—17.5 percent of the work force—were working part-time in 1985, according to the Bureau of Labor Statistics. Women made up two thirds of this group. Teenagers and retirees also frequently work part-time. Principal advantages to employers include flexibility in scheduling workers to meet peak demand periods, and reduction in costs of benefits and overtime.

Although part-time work has been hailed as beneficial for working parents, it has also been severely criticized by some women's organizations such as 9to5, the National Association of Working Women. Part-time work is "marginal" employment, 9to5 says, because it pays low wages and forces workers to give up benefits. A better choice, the group suggests, would be for more employers to establish family-oriented workplace policies such as parental leave, child care, and flexible scheduling, so that "parents are not forced to choose marginal jobs in order to provide care for their families."[36]

Most part-time work is concentrated in the service industries, especially education, health care, personal services (for example, beauty shops), business services such as advertising, and entertainment and recreation. The second most frequent location of part-time labor is in retail and wholesale trade, then agriculture, and finally manufacturing.

Job sharing, a special type of part-time work, occurs when a single job is divided between two workers. Because it requires schedule compatibility between the two people sharing the job, as well as roughly equivalent or complementary skills, most job sharing is initiated by the employees. More and more organizations seem willing to consider this alternative as they gain familiarity with its advantages.

Compressed Workweek

A compressed workweek is the scheduling of the normal 40 hours of weekly work in less than five days. The typical compressed workweek follows a four-day, 40-hour schedule.

Research on the effects of compressed workweeks is uneven.[37] Some studies concluded it has positive effects on productivity, absenteeism, and other behaviors. Others conclude it does not. One pattern in the negative studies suggests that positive results occur shortly after the introduction of the compressed workweek; then they decline. Individual and job differences may explain many of the contradictions in the research findings. In general, older employees seem to find a compressed workweek undesirable, especially where the work is physically or mentally taxing. Younger employees suggest it interferes with their social life. Another factor is the nature of the task involved. In general, taxing physical or mental work probably is not suitable for a compressed workweek schedule.

Home Work

With the widespread use of computer terminals and advanced telephone technology, some companies are beginning to contract out routine forms processing. For example, Blue Cross/Blue Shield pays a flat rate per claim form processed to clerks who do the processing on computer terminals in their homes. Other work that can be done this way includes processing catalog sales, transcribing tape dictation, keyboarding computer programs, or even writing software. People who have such work arrangements, mostly women, appreciate the convenience such arrangements provide. However, unions are unhappy. They argue that such arrangements weaken their organizations, erode wage standards, and open the way for worker exploitation. Present federal law bans home work in the garment industry and in several others. This ban was passed over 40 years ago to prevent companies from dodging minimum wage and child labor laws. The American Federation of Labor and Congress of Industrial Organizations (AFL-CIO) and the Service Employees International Union have proposed a new ban on "high-tech" home work, too. For the immediate future, however, the practice is expected to spread, as technological changes continue to exert influence on organizations.[38]

Ideally, these work schedule adaptations can work to the advantage of both the employer and the employee. However, many employers are reluctant to accede to employees' requests for scheduling flexibility, especially if the employees are valued professionals. They often feel that part-time professionals jeopardize project management continuity, and so give them less critical assignments. Cut off from participation in high-visibility projects of significance to the organization, part-timers frequently find their career progression stymied.

Child Care Assistance

One of the most frequently cited causes of work/family conflict is concern for adequate, affordable child care: there simply is not enough of it available. Half of all women with children under age six are in the labor force today. Many of them are principal breadwinners in their family. At the same time, almost half are in clerical and sales jobs, and only one fourth are in higher paying professional and managerial positions.[39] Corporations are beginning to provide options ranging from day care centers located at the work site to coverage of expenses as part of flexible benefits to referral services.

Which approach an organization adopts depends on its employee relations philosophy as well as the needs of its employees. One survey of 55 companies found that each employee with children under age 13 misses an average of eight working days a year due to child care problems, and 39 percent of the parents had considered leaving their jobs because of child care problems. Other studies have linked satisfactory day care with reduced absenteeism and turnover. So the presence or absence of satisfactory child care clearly affects work behavior.[40] The issue is, what role should an organization play in this area? This is a more compelling issue in organizations that employ a large proportion of young parents than in organizations with aging work forces.

IBM initially tried to address child care in its employee assistance program (EAP), but found that its more clinically oriented EAP staff was not equipped to provide child care assistance. So the organization has contracted with local referral services around the country. Employees are given the name of the referral service in their area. The referral service then tells employees which child care services are available and the costs. The referral agency must ensure that the child care providers are licensed, insured, and/or meet certain standards. Information on the referral service is mailed to the home of every IBM employee. However, IBM emphasizes that it makes referrals, not recommendations. The parent must make the final decision. IBM reports 100 percent follow-up on all referrals made to IBM parents.

On-site child care has a rather poor track record. Levi Strauss & Company provided on-site care, including an infirmary for sick children, but soon closed the child care center. Costs of downtown space, commuting patterns, and a limited number of eligible employees at a work site make this choice rarely affordable or appropriate. Many people dislike taking their children out of their home or school area. Others feel that commuting with children is too disruptive and stressful.

Exhibit 15–7 presents an optimistic picture, in that many more companies say they favor various programs to reduce family-job conflict than presently provide them. For example, while 80 percent favor a child care information service, only 30 percent presently provide it. This implies that if organizations knew how to locate and organize such information, they would be willing to provide it. Many employers are simply not aware of the extent of the need for child care.[41]

Stress

This topic is receiving a lot of attention, at least in the popular press. It is a difficult area to study, because what one person finds stressful, another may find exhilarating. For example, there is no shortage of candidates (qualifications aside) to become astronauts, television talk show hosts, or president—occupations that surely involve stress.

One view of stress relates it to control: the lack of ability to make one's own decisions at work or use a range of skills. One medical study bypassed the popular picture of the executive under stress, and found that workers in jobs that combine high psychological demand with low decision control (mail workers or telephone operators) are approximately five times more likely to develop coronary heart disease than those who have greater control over their jobs.[42] Exhibit 15–8 locates jobs along the two dimensions of psychological demand and decision control.

If an objective of employee relations is to assist employees under stress, this study is important not only for its job design implications, but

EXHIBIT 15–7
Which Programs Do Companies Favor? (comparing corporate programs of today with attitudes about tomorrow)

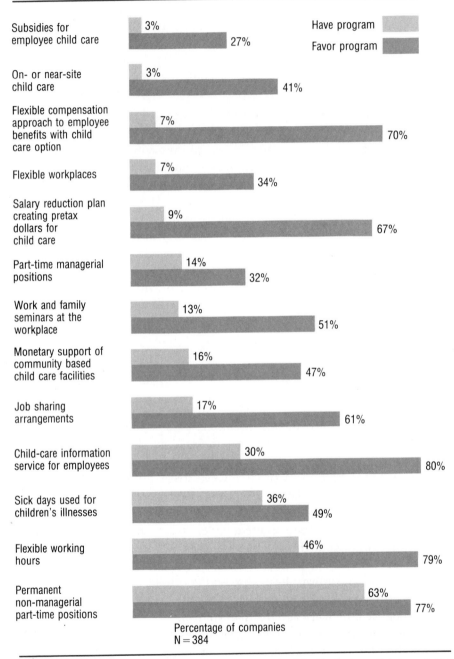

| | Have program |
| | Favor program |

Subsidies for employee child care — 3% / 27%

On- or near-site child care — 3% / 41%

Flexible compensation approach to employee benefits with child care option — 7% / 70%

Flexible workplaces — 7% / 34%

Salary reduction plan creating pretax dollars for child care — 9% / 67%

Part-time managerial positions — 14% / 32%

Work and family seminars at the workplace — 13% / 51%

Monetary support of community based child care facilities — 16% / 47%

Job sharing arrangements — 17% / 61%

Child-care information service for employees — 30% / 80%

Sick days used for children's illnesses — 36% / 49%

Flexible working hours — 46% / 79%

Permanent non-managerial part-time positions — 63% / 77%

Percentage of companies
N = 384

Source: Catalyst, 14 E. 60th St., New York, NY 10022. Published in *Business Link* 1, no. 2 (Fall 1984), p. 5 © Copyright Catalyst 1984.

EXHIBIT 15–8
Stress at Work

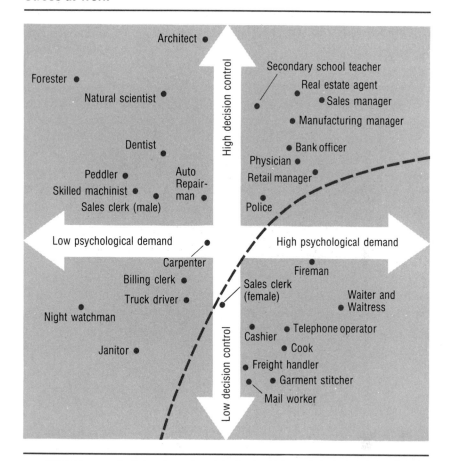

Architect •

High decision control

Secondary school teacher
Real estate agent
• Sales manager
• Manufacturing manager

Forester •

Natural scientist •

• Bank officer

Dentist •

Physician •

Retail manager •

Peddler •   Auto
Repair-
Skilled machinist •   man •

Police

Sales clerk (male)

Low psychological demand   High psychological demand

•

Carpenter

Fireman •

Billing clerk •

Sales clerk
(female)   Waiter and
• Waitress

Truck driver •

•
Night watchman

• Telephone operator
Cashier

Janitor •   • Cook

• Freight handler

Low decision control

• Garment stitcher

Mail worker

Research suggests that workers whose jobs involve high psychological strain but little decision making are more subject to cardiovascular illness. Jobs at the right of the curve are among
the top 25 percent in a combined risk factor of low control and high psychological demands.

Source: R. Karasek, J. Schwartz, C. Pieper, and C. Schafter, Department of Industrial and
Systems Engineering; University of Southern California Los Angeles.

also because it points out the importance of control as a factor related to
stress. Helping employees to identify and alter areas in which they feel a
lack of control is a major objective of employee assistance programs.

COOPERATION

The issue of control leads us directly into our next employee relations
decision: to what extent do managers yield control to cooperatively solve
workplace problems? And to what extent are employees interested in be-

coming involved in cooperative efforts? The highest degree of potential employee involvement in organizational decisions occurs when workers are also owners.[43] Workers buying plants to save their jobs is not unusual. Research has found, however, that most owner/workers view their ownership only as a financial investment, and rarely exercise their full decision-making rights. U.S. tax law currently favors Employee Stock Ownership Plans as a way to increase employees' equity in a company. (We discussed these plans in greater detail in the benefits chapter.) But even here, employee ownership does not typically alter the decision-making structure.

Encouraging employee participation is an idea everyone favors; translating the ideal into practice, however, steps on people's toes.[44] Control translates into power, and most people do not like giving it up. Managers and supervisors may feel the most efficient way to accomplish a task is to make a decision and act on it, rather than increasing the numbers of people involved in the decision process. Employees may also be wary if a managerial interest in working together does not square with past managerial behavior. Although cooperation is an appealing notion, it can be a hard sell.

Despite a great deal of overlap, there are three main thrusts in programming: quality-of-work-life programs, employee/management committees, and organization initiatives such as sociotechnical job design and gainsharing compensation whose objective, at least in part, is to increase employees' involvement.

Quality of Work Life

Quality of work life (QWL), or quality circles, stem from the recognition that the properly trained rank-and-file employee may be in the best position to identify unrecognized problems with product quality and/or how work is done. Shop-level worker committees are trained to use statistical and problem-solving analysis to improve quality and productivity in their particular work area.[45] This approach is an outgrowth of William Deming's quality control principles in Exhibit 15–9. The focus is very much on the immediate work area; organization practices are of interest only in considering how they may interfere with product quality.

A program at General Motors Corporation is fairly typical. Instituting a QWL goal at GM was a drastic change from accepted practice. First efforts were to eliminate the subtle and not so subtle barriers between workers and managers spelled out in Exhibit 15–10. No neckties and one cafeteria may seem trivial, but as signs of differential status, they were barriers to cooperative efforts. Participation is always voluntary, and the group avoids getting involved in issues covered in the union contract.

EXHIBIT 15–9
Dr. Deming's 14 Points for Management

1. Create constancy of purpose toward improvement of product and service, with a plan to become competitive and to stay in business. Decide to whom top management is responsible.
2. Adopt the new philosophy: We are in a new economic age. We can no longer live with commonly accepted levels of delays, mistakes, defective materials, and defective work.
3. Cease dependence on mass inspection. Require, instead, statistical evidence that quality is built in, to eliminate the need for inspection on a mass basis. Purchasing managers have a new job, and must learn it.
4. End the practice of awarding business on the basis of price tag. Instead, depend on meaningful measures of quality, along with price. Eliminate suppliers that cannot qualify with statistical evidence of quality.
5. Find problems. It is management's job to work continually on the system (design, incoming materials, composition of material, maintenance, improvement of machine, training, supervision, retraining).
6. Institute modern methods of training on the job.
7. Institute modern methods of supervision of production workers. The responsibility of supervisors must be changed from sheer numbers to quality. Improvement of quality will automatically improve productivity. Management must prepare to take immediate action on reports from supervisors concerning barriers such as inherited defects, machines not maintained, poor tools, or fuzzy operational definitions.
8. Drive out fear, so that everyone may work effectively for the company.
9. Break down barriers between departments. People in research, design, sales, and production must work as a team, to foresee problems of production that may be encountered with various materials and specifications.
10. Eliminate numerical goals, posters, and slogans for the work force, asking for new levels of productivity without providing methods.
11. Eliminate work standards that prescribe numerical quotas.
12. Remove barriers that stand between the hourly worker and that worker's right to pride in work.
13. Institute a vigorous program of education and retraining.
14. Create a structure in top management that will push every day on the above 13 points.

Joint employee-management teams visited other facilities using QWL techniques, including some in Japan. If this does not seem very revolutionary, remember that until 1987 salaried and hourly workers at a GM engine factory in Tonowanda, New York, could not use the same bathroom.[46]

The QWL program at the Fiero plant in Pontiac, Michigan, resulted in the complete reorganization of the managerial structure.[47] An entire level of supervision was removed. Exhibit 15–11 shows the new structure. At the lower part of the structure, the team members identify problems

EXHIBIT 15–10
Elimination of Barriers between Salaried and Hourly Personnel

Dress code	Casual dress No neckties
Parking	Executive garage closed No reserved parking Combined hourly and salaried lot
Food service	No salaried hourly distinction No private dining One cafeteria
Rest rooms	No salaried hourly distinction
Overnight drive program	Open to all employees
Committee	Open to both hourly and salaried where appropriate

and solutions. The resources to implement the solutions are provided from higher levels. For example, if a supplier's door gaskets are found to have a high rate of defects, that supplier is invited to meet with team members to discuss how this problem can be resolved. The supplier meets with the assembly line workers, not with some top manager in purchasing. Team

EXHIBIT 15–11
Revised Organization Structure at Pontiac Motor Division Car Assembly Plant

Objectives		**Activities**
Goal setting Planning Developing policy Future business: Products, facilities, resources Coordination with other PMD staffs	Administration team: Plant manager Staff Chairman	Providing overall leadership Participating in plant developmental activities Providing resources Sanctioning and developing innovations Monitoring progress Providing feedback
Coordination Developing procedures Overseeing policy and implementing procedure Performance monitoring	Business team: Superintendent Supervisors Committee members Support personnel	Developing learning curves Developing training and orientation programs Providing consultation Developing employee handbook Monitoring progress Providing feedback
Coordination Performance monitoring Providing resources Communication/Feedback Training/Teaching	Supervisor 1 Supervisor 2 Team Team Coordinators Coordinators	Participating in training programs Serving as trainers Providing technical assistance Monitoring progress
Performance objective Control Monitoring Assignments Administration	Team Coordinator / Team Members	Developing job skills Gaining team flexibility Engaging in problem-solving and decision-making activities Team building Teaching

members can recommend changing suppliers, if they feel that can solve the problem; GM purchasing power backs them up. However, approval must still come from higher levels.

Team members meet weekly for half an hour, during which time the assembly line is turned off. Attendance at team meetings is mandatory, but participation is not.

The program has had two basic thrusts: training and quality control. Workers *and* suppliers have been encouraged to enter training programs, especially those dealing with (but not limited to) electronics, robotics, or statistical quality control.

The second thrust, quality control, has required a reorganization of the inspection system. The company no longer relies on inspection of the final product. Instead, a tally sheet stays with the car from start to finish, and all workers are responsible for inspecting their own work. As each step is completed, the worker records on the tally sheet if the job was completed correctly, or if there were problems.

Even though the Fiero plan resulted in widescale organization change, many QWL issues are more mundane: "Fans and lights"—the physical aspects of the work environment are salient to the employees experiencing discomfort. How management responds to these issues may determine employees' willingness to cooperate on production and quality-related issues.

Employee-Management Committees

Employees may also get involved in issues outside their immediate work area. Joint committees with greater authority and formalized structure provide the opportunity for participation.[48] Membership on the committee is usually rotated and voluntary. A committee's written charter indicates purposes, responsibilities, and procedures. This charter specifies how the committee solicits employees' input, on what issues, and what authority it has. Equally important, it spells out issues over which it does not have jurisdiction, such as individual grievances or wages. Dealing with wages and grievances raises the possibility of violating the National Labor Relations Act by interfering with employees' rights to self-organize.

Committees can be excellent communication links; however, they require participation of committed people, both higher management and employees. Employee-management committees have operated with varying degrees of success at the national, industry, regional, community, plant, and production-unit level. Traditionally they are in unionized manufacturing plants, where they supplement collective bargaining.[49] That may account for their more highly structured, formalized nature in comparison to QWL committees.

Organization Initiatives

Commonly, management must lead the way to greater cooperation by demonstrating a willingness to share control. Many human resource activities are initiated by management, in the expectation that they may lead to increased employee involvement. Job redesign and gainsharing are two activities currently popular.

Job redesign requires restructuring the way work is done so that employees (or employee groups) have greater control over how and when it is done. Semiautonomous work groups make the bulk of decisions formerly reserved to middle layers of management; these layers can now be eliminated.

Gainsharing compensation plans are a natural complement to semiautonomous work groups, although gainsharing also has wider applications.[50] The objective of gainsharing is to return the financial results of productivity gains to the employees responsible for the increased productivity. The plans seek to boost productivity through greater employee motivation and involvement. We discuss various approaches to gainsharing in the compensation chapters in Part Six.

The best known approach is the Scanlon Plan, developed in the late 1930s.[51] The plan combines an employee suggestion program, and an employee-management committee with a bonus pay system based on the relationship between the sales value of production and labor costs. The plan recommends that workers understand why they undertake certain tasks; that a consensus exist between management, unions, and workers on common goals; that everyone have an opportunity for input; and that everyone receive full information on matters relating to the operation of the enterprise. Joint production committees, in which workers and managers develop suggestions to reduce labor costs, play an essential part in this approach to employee-management cooperation.

The plan uses historical experience in a plant to establish labor costs as a percentage of sales dollars. They determine the base ratio by dividing payroll by sales, plus or minus inventory. The company grants a bonus when labor costs are less than the base ratio in any given month.

The Scanlon Plan demonstrates that cooperative initiatives are most likely to be successful when they are part of an overall organizational thrust to go beyond an employee suggestion system and obtain employee involvement in organization decisions. Quality circles, employee-management committees, and organization initiatives may all exist in the same location and involve the same individuals.

CONFLICT

Discipline programs ensure adherence to generally accepted work rules. Exhibit 15–12 illustrates the elements of such a system. When rules are not adhered to, the organization must resolve the resulting employee-management conflict.

The first element in a discipline system is the establishment of work and behavior rules. The rules concern behavior that is directly or indirectly related to work productivity.

A second important element is the communication of the rules to all employees. The employee handbook is an appropriate forum. Unless employees are aware of the rules, it is unfair to expect them to follow them. Closely related is a willingness to accept the rules and their enforceability. Participation in the formation of rules may help ensure that rules are fair and related to organization objectives. For example, rules regarding hair length are relevant to job safety in some settings, but irrelevant in most others. Though rules are ideally kept to a minimum, periodically they may need revision to remain relevant.

The third element of the disciplinary process is an assessment mechanism. Performance evaluation typically assesses deficiencies in work behaviors at scheduled intervals; supervisors learn of rule-breaking behavior as a result of either observation or investigation, for example, investigation of theft or falsifying records.

EXHIBIT 15–12
Elements in a Disciplinary System

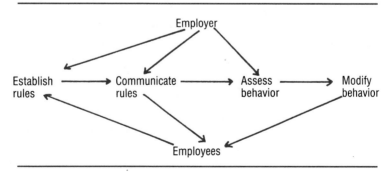

Finally, the disciplinary process includes assistance in changing behavior and administering punishment. Counseling and confrontation to motivate change may be part of the program.

Disciplinary Process

Discipline usually follows a progressive system in that companies deal with second or later infractions more harshly than first offenses. Exhibit 15–13 is a progressive employer discipline policy that follows this approach.

The first technique the manager can use is counseling; this is the most frequent method of disciplinary action. The supervisor determines if in fact a violation took place, explains to the employee why the violation significantly affects productivity, and suggests that it should not happen again. This approach works for most violations.

If a second or more serious violation takes place, the supervisor again counsels the employee, this time noting that the incident will be entered in the employee's personnel file. If the violation is sufficiently serious, the employee may also be given an oral or written warning of the consequences of a future recurrence.

When the incident concerns ineffective productivity, the employee may request transfer or be asked to transfer to another job. The employee may have been placed in the wrong job, there may be a personality conflict between the employee and the supervisor, or more training might help. In some rare cases, supervisors use demotions or downward transfers.

If counseling and warnings do not result in changed behavior, and if a transfer is not appropriate, the next step is normally a disciplinary layoff. When damage results from the deviant behavior, deductions may be made from an employee's pay over a period of time to pay for the damage. Most disciplinary action does not require this severe a step. The layoff is usually of short duration, perhaps a few days up to a week.

The next most severe form of punishment is getting an employee to quit. Getting the unsatisfactory employee to quit has many advantages over termination, for both employee and employer. Both save face. The employee finds another job and then quits, telling the peer group how much better things are at the new location. The employer is satisfied because an ineffective employee has left without recourse to firing.

Getting an employee to quit is not a forthright approach to discipline. However, many prefer it to the ultimate punishment: discharge. To many inexperienced managers, discharge is the solution to any problem with a difficult employee. Often, however, discharge is not possible, because of

EXHIBIT 15–13
Progressive Discipline Policy

In order to provide a fair method of disciplining employees, the employer has established a formal progressive discipline procedure.

A. Discipline—general guidelines
 1. Discipline may be initiated for various reasons, including but not limited to, violations of the employer's work rules, insubordination or poor job performance. The severity of the action generally depends on the nature of the offense and an employee's record, and may range from verbal counseling to immediate dismissal.
 [A portion of the sample policy is omitted here.]

B. Progressive discipline
 1. With the exception of offenses requiring more stringent action, employees will normally be counseled once verbally before receiving a written warning.
 2. In the event of another performance problem or a violation of any employer policy or rule, a written warning should ordinarily be issued.
  a. The warning should be signed and dated by the employee. If the employee refuses to sign the warning, another supervisor should be immediately brought in and asked to sign and witness that the employee has seen, but refused to sign, the warning.
  b. The warning should inform the employee of the possible consequences, including final written warning, suspension and/or discharge, should additional violations or performance problems occur.
  c. A written warning need not pertain to the same or similar offense for which the verbal counselling was given.
 3. If a third offense occurs within 12 months of the previous written warning, a final warning should be issued.
  a. The warning should be signed and dated by the employee. If the employee refuses to sign the warning, another supervisor should be immediately brought in and asked to sign and witness that the employee has seen, but refused to sign, the warning.
  b. The warning should inform the employee that termination may result if further violations or performance problems occur.
  c. A final written warning need not pertain to the same or similar offense for which any prior verbal or written warning was issued.
  d. In addition to the final written warning, the supervisor may also suspend the employee without pay or take other disciplinary action deemed appropriate.
 4. If the employee violates any policy of the employer or fails to improve his or her level of performance, termination may result.

C. The employer must, of course, reserve the right to deviate from this policy when it feels that circumstances warrant such a deviation.

Reproduced with permission from *Employee Handbook and Personnel Policies Manual* by Richard J. Simmons © 1983 Richard J. Simmons, Castle Publications, Ltd., P.O. Box 580, Van Nuys, California 91408.

seniority rules, union rules, too few replacements in the labor market, or fear of wrongful discharge lawsuits. And discharge is costly, both directly and indirectly. Direct costs include a loss of all human resource investments already made in the person: recruiting, selection, and training. Severence pay may be added. Indirect costs are the effect of the firing on other employees.[52] These may not occur if it is a blatant case of deviant behavior or severe inability, but frequently the facts are not clear, and employees may believe the action was arbitrary. If this is the case, productivity may drop, and valuable employees may leave, lest they become victims of arbitrary action, too. Thus, discharge is a final resort—when all else fails, or in very serious cases involving fraud or theft.

Documentation of actions and the behavior that precipitated them is required every step of the discipline process. This documentation may protect the employer from subsequent lawsuits accusing it of wrongful discharge, harassment, or violating employees' rights.

Conflict Resolution

Employers must handle conflict in a way that protects employees' rights. In addition to discipline issues, conflict on the job may arise for a host of reasons: sexual harassment; equal opportunity complaints; or disputes over promotions, pay, or admission to training programs. Some organizations have designed procedures for handling these conflicts. These procedures provide a mechanism for employees and managers to voice their disagreements and receive a fair hearing.

Employees who belong to a union collectively bargain some of these disputes and take others through a formal grievance procedure. We discuss these union procedures in Chapter Seventeen.

It's unclear what percentage of nonunion employees have access to conflict resolution procedures. South Carolina, for instance, has a very low rate of unionism in its work force—only 6.3 percent are unionized. Stuart Youngblood and Leonard Bierman report on that state's unique approach to providing its nonunionized employees a means of resolving conflict over unjust dismissals.[53] Within the State Department of Labor, a Division of Labor/Management Services (LMS) has been given authority to mediate dismissal cases. Almost 3,000 workers a year contact LMS because they feel they have been unjustly fired. LMS investigates and advises them. If LMS feels it is appropriate, it contacts former employers, asking them to review the case and surrounding circumstances. LMS stresses that its objective is to seek "fair and equitable treatment for employees and employers." LMS offers to mediate the issue. It enjoys a great deal of cooperation from employers. In some cases, their efforts have brought about reinstatement of dismissed workers; in other cases employers agreed to give "clean" references that would not serve as barriers from future employment for the affected employees. For example, in a "clean" reference, a supervisor might change the reason for a dismissal from "insubordination" to "personality conflict."

Although not as widely utilized outside the metropolitan Columbia area where it is located, LMS has been very successful in assisting workers who have contacted the agency. Thus, it provides another method of recourse for employees.

Resolution Systems

The system an organization uses depends on the problems it deals with as well as its compatibility with other organizational structures.

Procedures can vary on two dimensions:

1. Degree of formality. High formality means explicit statements concerning appealable issues, steps to follow, and roles and responsibilities of parties.
2. Degree of independence from management. Are workers forced to complain to their immediate superiors, or does the system use people further removed?

The most independent system would use an outside arbitrator, and may even provide independent legal counsel to employees. Even though many writers imply that the more formal and independent a process is, the more accepted it will be, in fact no research has addressed this issue.

The hierarchical system is the most formal, the least independent, and also the most common.

Hierarchical Systems

The supervisor who evaluates employees also administers discipline to most nonunion employees. When an employee is found to be ineffective, the supervisor decides what needs to be done. In the hierarchical system, a supervisor who might be arbitrary, wrong, or ineffective becomes a police officer, judge, and jury over the employee.

A person accused of speeding can have counsel in many of our courts; the judge is not the arresting officer, and the penalty may be a $50 fine. In the employment situation, where the employee has none of these safeguards, the penalty for an infraction of work rules may be loss of job and salary. Even if the employee is convicted of speeding, appeal to a higher court is possible. What can employees do if they are unfairly treated by their supervisors?

Some organizations such as IBM have several systems including "Speak Up" and "Open Door." In the former, employees may take their grievances to their immediate managers or a manager one level beyond. Emphasis is on handling conflicts informally at first, but if the employee does not feel satisfied, more formal written complaints occur. Under their "Open Door" program, employees are encouraged to write to any manager, including the chief executive. All letters are answered and responses are followed up with visits from employee relations professionals. IBM reports both systems are heavily used by employees. But an inherent limitation is that the whole value system of the hierarchy is based on support of the supervisors to build a good management team. So although the system may offer *procedural* justice in that employees are notified of an action and given the opportunity to be heard before a final decision is reached, *substantive* justice may be lacking if the system does not prevent arbitrary actions.[54] A few organizations have designed peer systems to protect employees from fear of supervisory action.

Peer Systems

In contrast to hierarchical systems where employees complain to managers, peer systems rely on independent or related peers to assess the situation and recommend action. They can be implemented in several ways.

General Electric Company's conflict system for 1,800 nonunion production workers at a Columbia, Maryland, electric-range plant uses a five-member panel, comprising the plant manager, a personnel officer, and three specially trained hourly employees. Control Data Corporation uses a similar companywide "peer review" procedure. The company uses a computer to select at random a review board including two peers of the aggrieved employee and an executive from a different division. A personnel ombudsman serves as the nonvoting chairperson.

In its first six months, the Control Data Corporation board considered four cases of discharges. In two cases, workers were reinstated with back pay. The other two were fired for just cause, the board ruled. In one of the reinstatements, the board decided a professional's personality clash with his supervisor gave him little opportunity to succeed under the difficult circumstances. Control Data is unique in that it uses its conflict resolution procedures for production workers in addition to managers and professionals.

The Adolph Coors Company originally established a peer review system to prevent unionization. But the system has additional value. It involves employees in a review of decisions and builds a sense that most disciplinary action is fair. It helps employees to realize the difficulties of the supervisor's position. And externally, it makes a difference with a court knowing that an employee with a grievance has chosen not to use the system.

Ombudsmen

Another approach to resolving conflicts is the use of an ombudsman who investigates complaints, hears all sides, and tries to help the parties arrive at a solution they all can live with. The Intercom system at Chemical Bank of New York is an example. Interested bank employees from outside the personnel office receive special training and then serve a three-year term as Intercom representatives. Representatives come from all job levels and departments of the bank. Trained Intercom representatives listen to employees and talk to them about their job concerns. Management only becomes involved at the request of employees.

To be effective, conflict resolution systems must appear more attractive than quitting or suing. John Aram and Paul Salipante conclude that this implies four criteria for evaluating such systems.[55]

1. Fairness of settlement. Employees must perceive that an organization is both capable and willing to change a situation leading to the problem.
2. Timeliness of settlement. Reducing the period of uncertainty and the loss of benefits stemming from continuance of the dispute is one of the main advantages of resolution over litigation.
3. Ease of utilization. Time and effort required to file and follow through with an appeal must be minimal.
4. Protection from recrimination. Future raises and promotions must not be perceived to be threatened by filing a grievance or complaint.

EVALUATING RESULTS

The effectiveness of employee relations lies in its efficiency and equity outcomes for employees and employers.

Efficiency

Efficiency measures of employee relations could include improved product quality (measured by reductions in reject rate), enhanced productivity (indicated by an increase in output per working hour), and reduced costs (measured in cost per unit produced). Obviously, these measures could change as a result of factors other than employee relations.

One empirical study correlated QWL programs at 18 GM plants with economic performance, such as labor costs and product quality, which could be characterized as efficiency. The study also considered industrial relations performance, such as grievance rates, absenteeism, and attitudinal climate of union/management relationship, which could be characterized as equity.[56] The authors were primarily interested in whether ongoing QWL programs could smooth collective bargaining relationships, as measured by the number of contract demands introduced in local, as opposed to national, bargaining. Despite their common technology, employer, and union, the 18 plants experienced extreme variations in grievance rates, discipline rates, and other industrial relations and economic measures.

Even though the industrial relations performance measures were strongly related to economic performance, the authors were hesitant to conclude that QWL programs caused any of these improvements, because of the short time span covered by the available data (nine years), and incompleteness in data. However, they did speculate that QWL efforts could be seen as one strategy to break out of the cycle of high conflict and low trust that can occur in a collective bargaining relationship. The key test of QWL success, they say, is whether effective collaboration can be maintained at the workplace during periods of difficult negotiations at the bargaining table.

The utility approach to evaluation can estimate the economic value of a job-based alcoholism program.[57] As you recall from Chapter Eight, the procedure is to translate the economic value of an increase (or decrease) in job performance into an estimate of the program's value. Using public health estimates that alcoholism affects around 10 percent of the labor force and managers' estimates of the costs of impairment at various organization levels, employers can calculate the value of a program to reduce impairment.

An assistance program for city employees in Phoenix, Arizona, claims a higher degree of alcoholism rehabilitation than community treatment sources, because of the added clout of threatened job loss. They estimate cost savings due to their employee assistance program at over $2 million a year.

Control Data reports that a recent study of four worker compensation cases projected a savings to the company of $705,000 through rehabilitation intervention by the EAR program. Only worktime loss was computed; the figures did not include medical expenses. So their measure was an estimate of costs not incurred.

Equity

Studies of the direct results of employee relations on employee equity are difficult because employee relations reflect an overall philosophy. It is difficult to disentangle the effects of employee relations from anything else. One study of discipline, for example, found that supervisory discipline behaviors were related to employee satisfaction with the supervisor, but the researchers were unable to link satisfaction with the supervisor to any overall job satisfaction or even grievances and absences.[58]

One way to examine those outcomes is to consider employees' options without strong employee relations. Valued employees who are disgruntled can leave an organization fairly easily and go on to other opportunities. Less valued employees have fewer options to leave, but they can reduce their commitment and motivation, or even sabotage other employees' work efforts.

A second option for disgruntled employees is to unionize to pool their efforts to change the workplace. If employees take this step, the organization loses flexibility in its human resource actions. A third option for employees is to sue the employer. More and more employees are taking this option, and it is costly. Wells Fargo & Company's cost estimates for lawsuits filed by employees who felt they were unfairly fired range up to $6 million. Avoiding even one such suit would pay for a lot of employee relations programming.

Three conditions appear necessary to introduce more cooperative approaches to organization decision making:[59] First, management must be willing to concede something of value to employees to obtain credibility. The concession may be control over physical work conditions, or it may be job security. Second, successful implementation is almost never achieved without a severe job-threatening crisis. In GM's case, the tremendous market appeal of low-priced, high-quality Japanese cars in the late 1970s provided that crisis. Third, a skilled outside adviser can help break down old patterns of behavior. Last, there must be support for the new approach at multiple levels of the organization.

With savings so difficult to document, you may ask why employers bother to offer counseling assistance, conflict resolution systems, or child care. The fact is that good intentions, a show of concern, may be all the justification that is required. Some employers may be committed to such programs, just as they are committed to the wider communities in which they are located. It is a question of responsibility to society. Effective management helps ensure that employee relations programs are well designed and that efforts are directed toward achievable, worthy objectives.

SUMMARY

Many organizations have a wide variety of activities aimed at enhancing the quality of the employment relationship. Some of the programs are formal, such as conflict resolution procedures or quality circles. Other activities are more casual, such as organizing and funding an employee picnic. Encouraging a cooperative rather than adversarial relationship is the goal. The underlying assumption is that such an atmosphere will better allow employees to perform their jobs and contribute a creative spark to the organization.

The effects of employee relations programs are difficult to assess. Most of their benefits take the form of cost-avoidance—lawsuits not filed, turnover or absenteeism that did not occur, productivity that did not decline. Additionally, many of the programs contribute to a better atmosphere. They demonstrate that the employer is committed to cooperative relationships, respects the employees, views them as a source of profitable suggestions, and will make efforts to accommodate their preferences.

Because of the difficulty in justifying these programs on a cost basis, top management's commitment to employee relations is essential. If this commitment falters (often through a change in management) it seems an easy choice to cut these programs to improve the bottom line. So the human resource manager must be in touch with employees—to be sure that programs are working effectively—and with top management—to maintain their commitment.

DISCUSSION AND REVIEW QUESTIONS

1. A Minnesota jury awarded $60,000 to a former bank teller who said she had suffered emotional damage because she had been pressed by her employer to take a polygraph, or lie-detector, test. The teller, who passed the test but had nightmares afterward, had been questioned about funds that were missing. With the advantage of hindsight, what would you advise your employer, the Suburban National Bank of Eden Prairie, Minnesota, to do when it suspects internal theft?

2. A Texas insurance company recently fired its auditor for failing to complete a timely audit. The auditor claims he could not complete the audit because his employer made claims that could not be verified and that the auditor believed were unrealistic. What would you do if you were the employer? The employee?

3. How might a successful assistance program for handling alcohol-impaired employees be structured?

4. Describe a progressive discipline system.

5. Is employee relations a good substitute for a union?

NOTES AND REFERENCES

1. Lee Dyer, Felician Foltman, and George Milkovich, "Contemporary Employment Stabilization Practices," in *Industrial Relations and Human Resource Management: Text, Readings, and Cases*, ed. T. A. Kochan and T. A. Barocci (Boston: Little, Brown, 1984).

2. Jack Fiorito and Christopher Lowman, *The Role of Employer Human Resource Policies in Union Organizing* (Iowa City: University of Iowa working paper, 1986).

3. Robert E. Allen and Timothy J. Keaveny, *Contemporary Labor Relations* (Reading, Mass.: Addison-Wesley Publishing, 1983).

4. Thomas A. Kochan, Harry Katz, and Robert McKersie, *The Transformation of American Industrial Relations* (New York: Basic Books, 1986).

5. Daniel Spencer, "Employee Voice and Employee Retention" (paper presented at 1982 Academy of Management meetings, New York City).

6. David A. Nadler and Edward E. Lawler III, "Quality of Work Life: Perspectives and Directions," *Organizational Dynamics*, Winter 1983, pp. 20–30; Edward E. Lawler III and Susan A. Mohrman, "Quality Circles After the Fad," *Harvard Business Review*, January-February 1985, pp. 65–71.

7. Kochan, Katz, and McKersie, *The Transformation of American Industrial Relations;* John P. Bucalo, "Successful Employee Relations," *Personnel Administrator*, April 1986, pp. 63–84.

8. Bucalo, "Successful Employee Relations."

9. Julius M. Steiner and Allan M. Dabrow, "The Questionable Value of the Inclusion of Language Confirming Employment-at-Will Status in Company Personnel Documents," *Labor Law Journal*, September 1986, pp. 639–45.

10. John D. Worrall, ed., *Safety and the Work Force* (Ithaca, N.Y.: ILR Press, 1983); Robert S. Smith, "Protecting Workers' Health and Safety," in *Instead of Regulation*, ed. Robert W. Poole (Lexington, Mass.: Lexington Books, 1981); R. S. Schuler, "Occupational Health in Organizations: Strategies for Personnel Effectiveness," *Personnel Administrator*, January 1982, pp. 47–56.

11. Alan Dillingham, "New Evidence on Age and Workplace Injuries," *Industrial Gerontology*, Winter 1981, pp. 1–10; Craig A. Olson, "An Analysis of Wage Differentials Received by Workers on Dangerous Jobs," *Journal of Human Resources*, Spring 1981, pp. 167–87; Donald F. Parker and Thomas DeCotiis, "Organizational Determinants of Job Stress," *Organization Behavior and Human Performance* 32 (1983), pp. 160–77; Norman Root, "Injuries at Work Are Fewer among Older Employees," *Monthly Labor Review*, March 1981, pp. 30–34.

12. Alan E. Dillingham, "Demographic and Economic Change and the Costs of Workers' Compensation," in *Safety and the Work Force*, ed. John D. Worrall (Ithaca, N.Y.: ILR Press, 1983).

13. Ann P. Bartel and Lacy Glenn Thomas, "Direct and Indirect Effects of Regulation: A New Look at OSHA's Impact," *Journal of Law and Economics*, April 1985, pp. 1–25.

14. Dale Masi, "Company Responses to Drug Abuse from AMA's Nationwide Survey," *Personnel*, March 1987, pp. 40–46; Barry A. Hartstein, "Drug Testing in the Workplace: A Primer for Employers," *Employee Relations Law Journal*, Spring 1987, pp. 577–608.

15. Judy Olian, "The Changing Structure of Employment Relations" (presentation at University of Maryland, College Park, October 1, 1985); Richard I. Lehr and David J. Middlebrooks, "Work-Place Privacy Issues and Employer Screening Policies," *Employee Relations Law Journal* 11, no. 3, Spring 1987, pp. 407–21; Mark A. Rothstein, "Screening Workers for Drugs: A Legal and Ethical Framework," *Employee Relations Law Journal*

11, no. 3, Spring 1987, pp. 422–37; Helen Axel, ed., *Corporate Strategies for Controlling Substance Abuse* (New York: The Conference Board, 1986).

16. "AIDS and Employment: News, Warnings, and Guidelines," *Fair Employment Practices*, May 1, 1986, p. 52; *Arline* v. *School Board of Nassau County*, U.S. No. 85–1277, 1987.

17. Information on the video "AIDS in the Workplace: Epidemic of Fear" can be obtained from the San Francisco AIDS Foundation, 333 Valencia St., San Francisco, CA 94103, 415–864–4376.

18. Elaine Gruenfeld, "Smoking in the Workplace," *ILR Report*, Spring 1986, pp. 9–17.

19. ASPA–BNA Survey No. 50, *Smoking in the Workplace* (Washington, D.C.: Bureau of National Affairs, 1986).

20. *Meritor Savings Bank* v. *Vinson*, U.S. Supreme Court 40 FEP Cases 1826 (1986). See Chapter Three for additional information on sexual harassment.

21. Lehr and Middlebrooks, "Work-Place Privacy Issues and Employer Screening Policies."

22. Rothstein, "Screening Workers for Drugs."

23. William J. Sonnenstuhl and Harrison M. Trice, *Strategies for Employee Assistance Programs: The Crucial Balance* (Ithaca, N.Y.: ILR Press, 1986); Bureau of National Affairs, *Alcohol and Drugs in the Workplace: Costs, Controls, and Controversies* (Washington, D.C.: Bureau of National Affairs, 1986).

24. *Essays on American Industrialism: Selected Papers of Samuel M. Levin* (Detroit, Mich.: Wayne State University, 1973).

25. Bradley Googins, "Employee Assistance Programs," *Social Work*, November 1975, pp. 464–68; Bradley Googins, "The Use and Implementation of Occupational Alcoholism Programs by Supervisors: An Analysis" (Ph.D. dissertation, Florence Heller Graduate School for Advanced Studies in Social Welfare, Brandeis University, 1978); Bradley Googins and Norman Kurtz, "Supervisory Networks: Toward an Alternative Training Model," *Labor Management Alcoholism Journal*, July-August 1979, pp. 35–40.

26. Sonnenstuhl and Trice, *Strategies for Employee Assistance Programs*.

27. Dale A. Masi, *Human Services in Industry* (Lexington, Mass.: Lexington Books, 1982); William A. Carahan, *Legal Issues Affecting Employee Assistance Programs* (Arlington, Va.: Association of Labor Management Administrators and Consultants on Alcoholism, 1984).

28. Janice Beyer and Harrison Trice, "A Field Study of the Use and Perceived Effects of Discipline in Controlling Work Performance," *Academy of Management Journal* 27 (1984), pp. 743–64.

29. Lucinda Lamont, "Control Data's Review Process," *Personnel*, February 1987, pp. 7–11.

30. R. L. Kahn, D. M. Wolfe, R. Quinn, J. D. Snoek, and R. A. Rosenthal, *Organizational Stress* (New York: John Wiley & Sons, 1964).

31. Jeffrey H. Greenhaus and Nicholas J. Beutell, "Sources of Conflict between Work and Family Roles," *Academy of Management Review* 10, no. 1 (1985), pp. 76–88.

32. C. A. Smith, D. W. Organ, and J. P. Near, "Organizational Citizenship Behavior: Its Nature and Antecedents," *Journal of Applied Psychology* 68 (1983), pp. 653–63; K. R. Knudsen, "Management Subcultures: Research and Change," *Journal of Management Development* 1, no. 4 (1982), pp. 11–

26; T. A. DeCotiis and D. J. Koys, "The Identification and Measurement of the Dimensions of Organizational Climate," *Academy of Management Proceedings,* 1980, pp. 171–75; Jon L. Pierce, "The Management-Employee Climate and Its Impact upon the Employee's Organizational Self-Esteem," 1986 ASPA/CCH Survey, *Human Resources Management,* June 13, 1986; E. Schein, "Coming to a New Awareness of Organizational Culture," *Sloan Management Review,* Winter 1984, pp. 3–16.

33. Randall Dunham and Jon L. Pierce, "Attitudes toward Work Schedules: Construct Definition, Instrument Development, and Validation," *Academy of Management Journal,* March 1986, pp. 170–82; S. D. Nollen, *New Work Schedules in Practice: Managing Time in a Changing Society* (New York: Van Nostrand Reinhold, 1983); Graham Staines and Joseph Pleck, "Non-standard Work Schedules and Family Life," *Journal of Applied Psychology* 69, no. 3 (1984), pp. 515–23; Thomas H. Patten, Jr., "Trends in Hours and Working-Time Arrangements in the United States of America, 1830–1985," (paper presented at International Industrial Relations Association, Hamburg, Germany, 1986); Paul Flaim, "Work Schedules of Americans: An Overview of New Findings," *Monthly Labor Review,* November 1986, pp. 3–6. Entire issue devoted to topic.

34. J. L. Pierce and J. W. Newstrom, "Employee Responses to Flexible Work Schedules: An Inter-Organization, Inter-System Comparison," *Journal of Management* 8, no. 1 (1982), pp. 9–25; R. B. Dunham, J. L. Pierce, and M. Castaneda, *Alternative Work Schedules: Two Field Experiments* (working paper, Graduate School of Business, University of Wisconsin, Madison, 1985); Donald J. Petersen, "Flexitime in the United States: The Lessons of Experience," *Personnel,* January-February 1980, pp. 21–31; Gretl S. Meier, *Worker Learning and Worktime Flexibility* (Kalamazoo, Mich.: W. E. Upjohn Institute for Employment Research, 1983); David A. Ralston, William P. Anthony, and David J. Gustafson, "Employees May Love Flextime, but What Does It Do to the Organization's Productivity?" *Journal of Applied Psychology* 70, no. 2 (1985), pp. 272–79.

35. Flaim, "Work Schedules of Americans."

36. "The Changing Workplace: New Directions in Staffing and Scheduling," BNA Response Center, 9435 Key West Ave., Rockville, MD 20850, 1986; Diane S. Rothberg, "Part-Time Professionals: The Flexible Work Force," *Personnel Administrator,* August 1986, pp. 27–39; Thomas J. Nardone, "Part-Time Workers: Who Are They?" *Monthly Labor Review,* February 1986, pp. 13–19.

37. J. A. Breaugh, "The 12-Hour Workday: Differing Employee Reactions," *Personnel Psychology* 36 (1983), pp. 277–88; S. Ronen and S. B. Primps, "The Compressed Work Week as Organizational Change: Behaviors and Attitudinal Outcomes," *Academy of Management Review* 6 (1981), pp. 61–74; Janina C. Latack and Lawrence W. Foster, "Implementation of Compressed Work Schedules: Participation and Job Redesign as Critical Factors for Employee Acceptance," *Personnel Psychology* 38 (1985), pp. 75–92.

38. William Atkinson, "Home/Work," *Personnel Journal,* November 1985, pp. 105–9.

39. Martin O'Connell and David Bloom, *Juggling Jobs and Babies: America's Child Care Challenge* (Washington, D.C.: Population Reference Bureau, 1987).

40. Karen Lehrman, "Firms Can't Afford to Neglect Employee Child Care," *The Wall Street Journal*, June 12, 1986, p. 35; Sara Rynes, "The Quest for Harmony between Work and Family: Whose Problem Is It?" (Presentation at Cornell University, Ithaca, New York, June 1985); Graham L. Staines, Kathleen J. Pottick, and Deborah A. Fudge, "Wives' Employment and Husbands' Attitudes toward Work and Life," *Journal of Applied Psychology* 71, no. 1 (1986), pp. 118–28; John. P. Fernandez, *Child Care and Corporate Productivity* (Lexington, Mass.: Lexington Books, 1985).

41. Dana Friedman, "Corporate Child Care," *Harvard Business Review*, July-August 1983, pp. 17–23.

42. Columbia University Department of Industrial Engineering and Operation Research reported in *New York Times*, February 21, 1987.

43. Ben Fischer, "A Skeptic Looks at Employee Buyouts," and Corey Rosen, "Growth versus Equity: The Employee Ownership Solution," *ILR Report*, Spring 1985, pp. 19–26.

44. David A. Nadler and Edward E. Lawler III, "Quality of Work Life: Perspectives and Directions," *Organizational Dynamics*, Winter 1983, pp. 20–30.

45. Mitchell Lee Marks, Philip Mirvis, Edward Hackett, and James Grady, Jr., "Employee Participation in a Quality Circle Program: Impact on Quality of Work Life, Productivity, and Absenteeism," *Journal of Applied Psychology* 71, no. 1 (1986), pp. 61–69; Janice A. Klein, "Why Supervisors Resist Employee Involvement," *Harvard Business Review*, September-October 1984, pp. 87–95; Anat Rafaeli, "Quality Circles and Employee Attitudes," *Personnel Psychology* 38 (1985), pp. 603–15.

46. "Changing Attitudes," *The Wall Street Journal*, April 6, 1987, p. 12.

47. Kochan, Katz, and McKersie, *The Transformation of American Industrial Relations*.

48. Charlotte Gold, *Labor-Management Committees: Confrontation, Cooptation, or Cooperation?* (Ithaca, N.Y.: ILR Press, 1986); Donna Sockell, "The Legality of Employee Participation Programs in Unionized Firms," *Industrial and Labor Relations Review*, July 1984, pp. 541–56; Lee P. Stepina, "No Free Lunch: Labor-Management Productivity Committees," *National Public Employment Reporter*, November 1982, pp. 5–11; Harriet Gorlin and Lawrence Schein, *Innovations in Managing Human Resources*, Report No. 849 (New York: The Conference Board, 1984).

49. Tracy H. Ferguson and John Goal, "Codetermination: A Fad or a Future in America?" *Employee Relations Law Journal* 10, no. 2 (1986), pp. 176–99.

50. Robert B. McKersie, "The Promise of Gain Sharing," *ILR Report*, Fall 1986, pp. 7–11.

51. James W. Driscoll, "A Multiple-Consistency, Control-Group Evaluation of the Scanlon Plan," (working paper, Sloan School of Management, 1982).

52. Donald F. Barkman, "Team Discipline," *Personnel Journal*, March 1987, pp. 58–63; E. C. Walterscheid, "When Employees Act Contrary to the Interests of Their Employers," *Employee Relations Law Journal*, Spring 1987, pp. 609–29; Janet P. Near and Marcia P. Miceli, "Retaliation Against Whistle Blowers: Predictors and Effects," *Journal of Applied Psychology* 71, no. 1 (1986), pp. 137–45; Cliff Roberson, *Employee Misconduct* (Lexington, Mass.: Lexington Books, 1986); Richard C. Hollinger and John P. Clark,

Theft by Employees (Lexington, Mass.: Lexington Books, 1983); Dean Tjosvold, *Managing Work Relationships* (Lexington, Mass.: Lexington Books, 1986); *Employee Discipline and Discharge* (Washington, D.C.: The Bureau of National Affairs PPF Survey No. 139, January 1985).

53. Stuart A. Youngblood and Leonard Bierman, "Due Process and Employment at Will," in *Research in Personnel and Human Resources Management*, ed. K. M. Rowland and G. R. Ferris (Greenwich, Conn.: JAI Press, 1985).

54. Alan F. Westin, "Individual Rights and Fair Procedure Systems," *ILR Report*, Fall 1982, pp. 5–8; Jerald Greenberg, "A Taxonomy of Organizational Justice Theories," *Academy of Management Review*, January 1987, pp. 9–22.

55. John D. Aram and Paul F. Salipante, Jr., "An Evaluation of Organizational Due Process in the Resolution of Employee/Employer Conflict," *Academy of Management Review* 6, no. 2 (1981), pp. 197–204.

56. Harry C. Katz, Thomas A. Kochan, and Kenneth R. Gobeille, "Industrial Relations Performance, Economic Performance, and QWL Programs: An Interplant Analysis," *Industrial and Labor Relations Review*, October 1983, pp. 3–17.

57. Janice Beyer and Harrison Trice, "The Best/Worst Technique for Measuring Work Performance in Organizational Research," *Organizational Behavior and Statistics*, May 1984, pp. 1–21.

58. Richard D. Arvey, Gregory A. Davis, and Sherry M. Nelson, "Use of Discipline in an Organization: A Field Study," *Journal of Applied Psychology* 69, no. 3 (1984), pp. 448–60.

59. Nadler and Lawler, "Quality of Work Life."

chapter

sixteen

LABOR RELATIONS

CHAPTER OUTLINE

Fourteenth-century Europe was a time and place of turmoil. Forty percent of the population had died from the Black Plague.

> The shortage of labor brought the plague's greatest social disruption: a concerted demand for higher wages. Peasants as well as artisans, craftsmen, clerks, and priests discovered the lever of their own scarcity. Within a year after the plague had passed through northern France, the textile workers of Saint Omer had gained three successive wage increases. In many guilds, artisans struck for higher pay and shorter hours. In an age where social conditions were regarded as fixed, such action was revolutionary. The response of rulers was instant repression. In the effort to hold wages at pre-plague levels, the English issued an ordinance in 1349 requiring everyone to work for the same pay as in 1347. Penalties were established for refusal to work, for leaving a place of employment to seek higher pay, and for the offer of higher pay by employers. . . . The ordinance was reissued in 1351 as the Statute of Laborers. . . . Down to the 20th century, this statute was to serve as the basis for "conspiracy" laws against labor in the long struggle to prevent unionization.[1]

Dealing with unions is frequently an emotionally charged activity. Few employers or employees get as emotionally involved over recruiting methods or selection techniques, for example, as they do over labor relations. The reason is that labor relations and collective bargaining go to the heart of employee relations problems—power. Power to hire, to pay, to judge performance, to fire, translates into power to affect significant human needs. Many employees have turned to unions as a source of strength in numbers. By acting collectively, union members hope to gain greater power to influence employers' decisions. In a nonunionized organization, management has flexibility in hiring and promoting people, establishing the nature of the work and work rules, administering pay and benefits, and in other personnel matters. Much of this changes when employees elect to join a union. Then, the union and the employer negotiate a contract which spells out details of many personnel matters. Thus, labor relations affects all other human resource management activities.

Definition

Labor relations is a continuous relationship between a defined group of employees (represented by a union or association) and an employer. The relationship includes the initial recognition of the rights and responsibilities of union and management, the negotiation of a written contract concerning wages, hours, and other conditions of employment, and the interpretation and administration of this contract over its period of coverage.

This chapter reviews the legal framework for the union movement in the United States. We also discuss why employees join unions, how unions operate, and employer and union strategies for labor relations. The next chapter discusses collective bargaining, contract negotiation and administration, and evaluating the results of labor relations activities.

A DIAGNOSTIC APPROACH TO LABOR RELATIONS

The balance of power between unions and employers has fluctuated over the years. In the 1950s and 1960s, many union members enjoyed substantial yearly pay hikes plus cost-of-living increases.[2] Exhibit 16–1 demonstrates the magnitude of the wage differential between union and nonunion workers over time. Although the size of the differential has fluctuated, it was consistently favorable to the unions in the 1950s and 1960s,

EXHIBIT 16–1
Union/Nonunion Wage Differential, 1920–1980

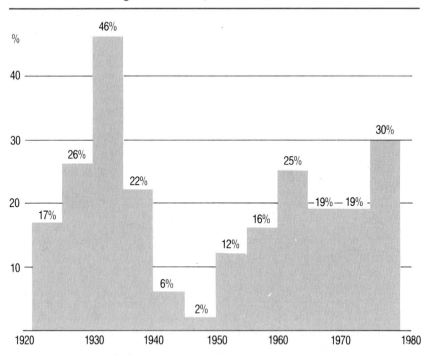

Note: Approximate percentage differentials were calculated as antilogs of estimated union coefficients in semi-log regression models.

Source: George Johnson, "Changes Over Time in the Union/Nonunion Wage Differential in the United States" (mimeographed; University of Michigan, Ann Arbor, February 1981), Table 2.

EXHIBIT 16–2
Union Membership as a Percentage of the Nonagricultural
Labor Force 1930–1984

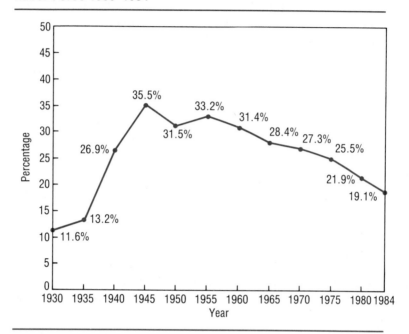

Note: The September 1984 figure is the percent of employed wage and salary workers (in all) industries, private and public, who were union members. In 1980, this figure was 23.0 percent. The 1984 figure is reported in Larry T. Adams, "Changing Employment Patterns of Organized Workers," *Monthly Labor Review* 108 (February 1985), table 1.

Source: The 1930–80 figures are from the *Handbook of Labor Statistics* (Washington, D.C.: Bureau of Labor Statistics).

which was also the period of greatest union membership. Exhibit 16–2 shows those membership figures. The chart shows a long decline that has accelerated in the 1980s. For example, in 1957, one out of every three nonagricultural workers was a union member. In 1986 the rate was close to one in six.

What has caused the decline? The diagnostic model identifies factors that affect the union/employer relationship and account for the relative strength of the parties involved.

External Conditions

Economic

Perhaps more than any other human resource activity, labor relations is affected by economic conditions on a global scale. Foreign competition in the product market has had a devastating impact on union membership, employment, and wage scales in the auto and steel industries.[3] Other industries, notably transportation and communications, have experienced the dislocations that have accompanied deregulation.[4] For example, United Parcel Service, part of the deregulated trucking industry, has negotiated a two-tier wage structure under which newly hired package loaders and sorters receive only 60 percent of what currently employed workers receive for doing the same jobs. Exhibit 16–3 lists some other concessions that have been forced on union members.

Product market conditions have similar effects on the unions and employers. Hard times for an employer constitute hard times for the union. Membership declines when declining demand for a firm's products or services reduces employment levels. In contrast, labor market conditions can affect unions and employers differently. If the labor market is tight, the union's power may be enhanced. If unemployment is high, management may have an advantage: It can sustain a strike, and perhaps even benefit economically by replacing employees with new hires at lower pay rates. Hundreds of TWA cabin attendants, Cargill salt miners, and Geo. A. Hormel & Company meatpackers found themselves without jobs when their employers filled their jobs with lower-paid replacements following unsuccessful strikes.

Government

The government creates the legal environment within which labor relations takes place. The government's attitude toward labor relations has varied over time. In the United States the legal principle which dominated labor relations laws into the 1800s was that of individual rights: Every individual was free to negotiate employment terms and to change employers at will. Unions were considered to be a criminal conspiracy that abridged the rights of individuals. The argument was that group attempts to regulate wages could have an adverse effect on not only the profits of the employer but also on free trade, the community in general, and workers who were not part of the union. This theory was invoked in almost every case of unionism. The leading case was that of the Philadelphia Cordwainers. Prior to 1805, shoe merchants set the pay rate for cordwainers (shoemakers) on the basis of how the shoes were marketed: one price for making shoes to be wholesaled, another price for shoes to be sold at the merchants' shop, and a third price for custom-ordered shoes. In 1805, the cordwainers tried to establish a standard rate for each type of shoe regardless of how the shoes were marketed. They asked all cordwainers to refuse to work except for this wage rate. But the courts declared that "the collective action of a few persons in pursuit of their selfish interests con-

EXHIBIT 16–3
Union Concessions

Industry	Company	Givebacks
Steel	Wheeling-Pittsburgh	Eliminated cost-of-living adjustment (COLA), six paid holidays, one week of vacation
	Bethlehem	Cut pay 8%; reduced premium for Sunday work
	LTV	Cut pay $1.14 per hour; reduced premium for second and third shift
Meat-packing	John Morrell	Eliminated profit sharing and implemented lower pay for new hires
	Wilson Foods	Tied pay increases solely to company's profitability
Airline	TWA	Reduced job classifications and medical benefits
	American	Instituted longer probation and eliminated medical coverage for first-year machinists and ground workers
	Eastern	Cut pay for pilots and flight attendants 20% and won two-tier pay scale for pilots
Mining	Phelps Dodge	New workers hired during strike decertified union
	Kennecott	Reduced average wage $3.22 per hour; eliminated 12 pay levels and COLA
	Pinto Valley	Cut pay 20%
Trucking	Some 110 trucking companies	Lowered starting salary 30% for new hires; cut pay 8% for supplementary workers
Grocery Store	P&C Food Markets	Eliminated COLA and reduced premium pay
	Eagle Food Stores	Reduced premium pay and number of paid personal days
	Kroger, National, and Schnuck Markets	Cut top pay rates, premium pay, and number of paid personal and sick days

Source: Data from U.S. Department of Labor.

travened the interests of citizens in general and was, hence, a criminal conspiracy."[5]

The courts continued to find collective activity illegal well into the 19th century. Employers and much of society refused to recognize unions as legitimate organizations. Even though the 1842 case *Commonwealth* v. *Hunt* allowed the association of workers, unions were legal only if their self-interest did not interfere with free market competition, and if the union did not use force against nonmembers. This interpretation still permitted judges to decide that almost any union action was an illegal interference with market competition.

Railway Labor Act. This act, passed in 1926, is the first national labor law to be found constitutional that gives employees the right to choose whether or not to be represented by a union and to engage in union activity. Additionally, it encourages the use of arbitration and mediation as dispute resolution mechanisms. Although it applies only to the railway and airline industries, many of its provisions were later extended to other industries through additional legislation.

Norris-LaGuardia Act. Severe economic disruption and massive unemployment in the 1930s aroused public sympathy to the plight of laborers and led to the passage of two important labor laws. The *Norris-LaGuardia Act*, passed in 1932, declared union membership to be a legal right of all employees. It limits the power of employers in two ways: First, it forbids "yellow dog contracts," or contracts that force employees to agree not to join a union or participate in any union activity. Second, the law forbids federal judges from issuing injunctions against lawful union activities unless there is a clear and present danger to life or property. (An injunction is a judicial order requiring or, more commonly, forbidding a specific behavior.) Unions must be given an opportunity to respond to charges before the injunction is issued, that is, to show cause why an injunction should not be issued.

The act applies to all private sector employees and unions. It does not require employees to bargain with unions, nor does it prohibit them from discriminating against employees for union activity. But it does establish employees' legal right to form a union, without reference to any public interest standard.

Wagner Act. Passed in 1935, the Wagner Act finally put labor on a more equal footing with management. It guarantees employees' rights to organize and bargain free from employers' interference. It requires employers to bargain with a union over wages, hours, and conditions of work, if a majority of employees desire such union representation. And it establishes the National Labor Relations Board (NLRB) to conduct representation elections and investigate charges of unfair labor practices. The NLRB's role in the collective bargaining process is further discussed in the next chapter.

Refusing to obey the Wagner Act, many employers simply would not allow employees to unionize until the Supreme Court upheld the law in 1937. Companies had systematically spied on union activities, infiltrated union governments, and spent millions on spying, strikebreaking, and munitions. Youngstown Sheet and Tube Company is said to have amassed 8 machine guns, 369 rifles, 190 shotguns, 450 revolvers, 109 gas guns, 3,000 rounds of gas, and almost 10,000 rounds of shotgun shells and bullets in preparation for a strike. Republic Steel Company had purchased almost $80,000 worth of repellent gases and allegedly possessed the largest private arsenal in the United States.[6]

Taft-Hartley Act. Some unions responded to this violence in kind, leading to passage of the *Taft-Hartley Act* in 1947. Technically an amendment to the Wagner Act, Taft-Hartley corrects both union and employer abuses. When faced with the threat of unionization, some employers had established their own union without consulting the majority of employees, and signed labor contracts that were very favorable toward management. These "sweetheart contracts" were outlawed by Taft-Hartley; employers are now forbidden from assisting or establishing labor organizations.

Taft-Hartley also specifies exclusive representation. When a majority of employees desires a specific union, that union represents all employees in the bargaining unit, whether or not they are union members. Exclusive representation is a major difference between unions in the United States and many other countries.

Additionally, Taft-Hartley established the Federal Mediation and Conciliation Service (FMCS), which offers assistance in contract settlement and maintains a list of arbitrators to help interpret contract language and resolve disputes.

Taft-Hartley also specifies that requiring all employees in a bargaining unit to join a union as a condition of continued employment is legal if such a stipulation is agreed to by both employer and union. This is called a *union shop*. If the collectively bargained contract does not contain such a clause, then it is illegal for an employer to either require or forbid employees' union activity, or to use union status as a promotion decision factor.

Landrum-Griffin Act. Union membership is never supposed to be a basis for a hiring decision. Such *closed shop* arrangements are illegal. However, in the construction industry, because of the relative strength of regional unions in comparison to individual employers, the bulk of hiring is done through union halls. This is legal under the *Landrum-Griffin Act* (1959), which permits union job referrals if the union agrees not to discriminate on the basis of union membership. Objective criteria such as experience and training must be used as a basis for referral. Naturally, the only way to get the experience and training is through union apprenticeship programs.

Landrum-Griffin resulted from the charges in the 1940s and 1950s of labor racketeering. It establishes a "bill of rights" for union members: the right to vote for union officers, the right to vote on dues increases, freedom of speech in union matters, and the right to sue their union. It also requires union officers to respect certain financial transactions.

In addition to this national legislation, many states have other laws which may further regulate the activities of unions or employers. One of the most common is right-to-work laws, which outlaw union shop clauses.[7]

Organization Conditions

Organizations vary in their approaches to labor relations. Their objectives can range from union suppression to union avoidance or even cooperation.

Union Suppression

Some employers view a move by workers to organize as a personal challenge. Often they see themselves as benevolent employers, betrayed by ungrateful employees. They may also believe that a union will constrain their flexibility and, thus, their ability to operate effectively. For whatever reason, murmurs of organizing became a call to battle.

Antiunion tactics include a variety of actions, not all of which are legal. The most extreme behavior is to fire employees perceived to be union activists. Even though such a move is clearly and absolutely illegal, unfortunately it continues to occur. There is even some evidence that it is becoming more common.[8] Exhibit 16–4 shows that from 1968 to 1980 the number of unfair labor practices charges against employers rose fourfold, and the number of workers awarded back pay or ordered reinstated to their jobs rose fivefold. The reason for this increase may be that the penalties for such activities are slight. If the NLRB rules that an employee was illegally fired for union activity, the employer must reinstate the worker and pay any difference between wages the worker would have earned if not fired and wages actually earned. Because the appeals process takes time, it may be several years before the union activist is back once again. This delay typically works to the employers' advantage and so may make them willing to run the risk. Thus, they view the payoffs of remaining nonunion as greater than the financial penalties of illegal behavior.

EXHIBIT 16–4
**Employer Unfair Labor Practices against Unions, and Number of
NLRB Representation Elections, 1950–1980**

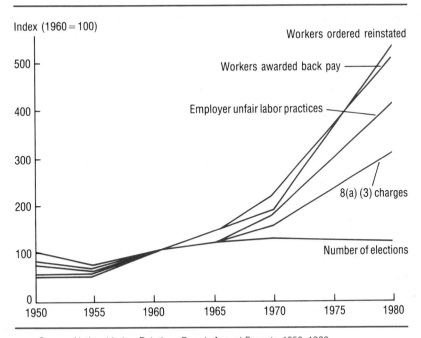

Source: National Labor Relations Board, *Annual Reports,* 1950–1980.

In addition to back wages, employers guilty of illegally firing union workers must post a notice that they will not do so again. Richard Freeman asserts that

> Such notices are jocularly referred to as "hunting licenses" which, rather than convincing workers that management will forgo such tactics in the future, warns them of how far management is willing to go to defeat unionism.[9]

There are several legal tactics employers may use to try to thwart an organizing campaign.[10] For example, they may launch heavy communication campaigns emphasizing the privileges and benefits that employees now enjoy that may be lost with union membership.

Employers seek to convince employees that not only is a union not necessary, but also it is actually harmful because of union dues, possible strikes, or subservience to union officials. It is illegal for an employer to promise future benefits in return for voting against a union or to threaten election result consequences.

In addition to communicating with employees, union opposition tactics include delaying the organizing campaign. Research shows that delaying the organizing campaign works in the employer's favor.[11] The employer may delay by objecting to the proposed makeup of the bargaining unit. For example, employers may argue that employees at multiple locations all belong in the same bargaining unit. Specifying a diverse bargaining unit increases the difficulty and expense for union organizers. It may also weaken any bond of shared experience among potential union members.

Once employees decide to join a union, some employers still refuse to accept it. Although they are legally required to bargain with union representatives, they may try to get the union decertified through another election. Currently, unions are removed in more than 75 percent of decertification elections, and the number of such elections held has doubled in the last 10 years. Or, employers may refuse to sign a labor agreement. Even though they are required to bargain in good faith, it can be a long way to a signed contract.

Union-Free Status

In the previous chapter, we discussed employee relations programs that may be motivated in part by an employer's desire to maintain a union-free environment. Such programs have the objective of demonstrating concern and respect for employees, and giving them substantial control over their work lives. The philosophy here is that "employees do not need a union, they are part of the organization which is as fair and equitable as possible."

A number of organization conditions appear to be related to whether or not a work force is unionized. Three important conditions are the location, size of the facility, and the nature of the work.

Plant Location. In the United States, union membership is concentrated geographically. New York is the most highly organized state, with almost half of its nonfarm workers in unions or associations. Michigan, West Virginia, and Pennsylvania follow. In contrast, the southern states have relatively few union members and share a strong antiunion bias. For example, union membership in South Carolina is around 6.3 percent. Southern textile companies were infamous (or famous, depending on one's perspective) for their resistance to union organizers. Within a specific geographical region, small towns or the outskirts of large cities are also viewed as less favorable for unions.

Plant Size. In response to technical and economic change, many companies are shifting from large, centralized organizations to smaller, decentralized local business units with more independence from the corporate headquarters. Organizations have done this because they feel the smaller size gives them greater flexibility in responding quickly to market changes. Smaller plants are also less likely to be unionized. Perhaps their size and multiple locations make it less cost-effective for an outside union to mount an organizing campaign.

Nature of Work. Some occupations have historically contained a high percentage of union members. Printing and truck driving are examples. Some nonunion employers subcontract their own printing and trucking to avoid having printers or truck drivers on their payroll. By doing so, these employers hope to reduce the likelihood of a union campaign. If subcontracting is not possible, some employers go to great lengths to ensure that their employees in those occupations enjoy wages, benefits, and working conditions directly comparable to those earned by union members doing the same jobs for different organizations.

In addition to occupations, union membership varies among industries. Over one third of employees in federal, state, and local government and in the transportation, communications, and public utilities industries are union members. This is twice the national average. In the services and financial industries, less than 8 percent of employees belong to unions.[12]

Cooperation

Although labor relations disputes—strikes, violence, and allegations of illegal behavior—capture the attention of the public, the vast majority of contract negotiations and day-to-day administration is done in an atmosphere of mutual respect. If not harmonious, most relationships are at least cooperative, though some employers do not become cooperative until they have exhausted all other possibilities.[13] "Resigned to the inevitable" may be more descriptive for some.

Employee Conditions

In a study of large nonunionized employers, Fred Foulkes discovered that some employers attribute their union-free status to specific worker characteristics.[14] For example, some have long perceived women to be more antiunion than men. The personnel directors interviewed by Foulkes characterized women as not wanting to get involved in the politics of a union, or as less committed to a career in the organization and, therefore, more tolerant of poor conditions. Women's increasing commitment to the labor force and unions' increasing sensitivity to issues of particular concern to many women, such as pay differentials among jobs, child care, flexible work arrangements, and parental leave, seem to have changed this perception. Recent surveys are finding that women are more interested than men in joining unions.[15] In 1986 the teamsters' union sponsored a conference on women in the workplace. According to the AFL–CIO, in 1986 one out of every three union members was a woman.

Some also perceive a high percentage of professional employees as a hindrance to unionization. Professionals have historically been less interested in unions, but similar to the attitudes of women, this, too, may be changing.

There has been a great deal of research on employee conditions and labor relations. Most of it seeks to predict who is likely, or unlikely, to be persuaded to join a union.

Why Employees Join Unions

Pragmatically, people join unions if they perceive the benefits to be greater than the costs. At the extreme, potential increases in wages must be greater than the amount of dues paid. Psychologically, however, there are additional reasons for joining. Thomas Kochan has developed the model in Exhibit 16–5; it summarizes the research on the topic. An individual's decision to join or avoid a union, according to the model, is influenced by three critical determinants:

1. *Perceptions of the work environment.* Dissatisfaction with bread-and-butter aspects of the job, such as wages and benefits, dissatisfaction with supervision, or with the treatment of one group of employees versus another, all can translate into a greater interest in unionism.

EXHIBIT 16–5
Psychological Determinants of Propensity to Unionize

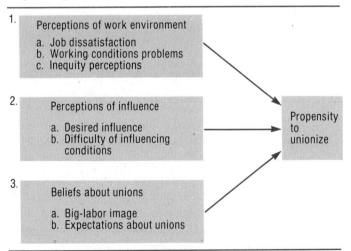

Source: Thomas Kochan, *Collective Bargaining and Industrial Relations* (Homewood, Ill.: Richard D. Irwin, 1980), p. 144.

2. *Desire to participate or influence* the job and the employment conditions surrounding the job. According to Kochan, a key here is that the lack of other effective alternatives for influence turns employees to unions.

3. *Employee beliefs about unions.* Employees who are dissatisfied have certain expectations about what a union can do for them. When organizing efforts predispose or convince them that a union can improve their situation, employees are more likely to join.

Some researchers have taken this theme a step further, and analyzed why people don't join unions. Generally there are three reasons:

1. *They identify with management.* Those who work with or are close to management tend to identify with it and consider the union as an adversary. If they experience job dissatisfaction, however, they lose this identification and consider joining a union.[16]

2. *They do not agree with the goals of unions.* Other employees may disagree with the objectives of unions politically and organizationally. For example, they may prefer merit to seniority rules, may fear union social or political power, may resent paying dues, and may feel unions interfere in free enterprise and individual initiative.[17]

3. *They see themselves as professionals and unions as inappropriate for professionals.* For years, many employees such as engineers, nurses, teachers, and others saw themselves as independent professionals working for an organization. The concepts of union member and independent professional were viewed as opposites.[18]

The overall conclusion from the research is that there are no substantial differences between people who do and do not join unions. Rather, the work situation seems to make the biggest difference. That is why union organizers sometimes say that employers' personnel practices are the unions' greatest organizing weapon.

Unions are organizations and employers, too. Once we have explored how unions operate as an organization, and their strategies, we consider the decisions involved in labor relations.

UNIONS IN THE UNITED STATES

Unions, similar to any other organizations, have objectives. Objectives may be job conscious or class conscious.[19] *Job consciousness* leads to relatively limited economic goals pursued through such mechanisms as collective bargaining. The labor movement in the United States pursues this objective.

Class consciousness, on the other hand, seeks fundamental change in the political and economic system; unions obtain such change through the political arena. Even though U.S. unions may endorse candidates and encourage their members to actively participate in the political process, their objectives still remain the economic betterment of their members. They do not seek an alternative economic or political system. However, such fundamental change may be the objective of the union movement in European or South American countries.

The Union Organization

To become a union member, a person joins one of the 60,000 or so local unions. The local is a subunit of one of the nearly 200 national unions. Most of these belong to the American Federation of Labor—Congress of Industrial Organizations (AFL–CIO). This federation represents the majority of unionized employees. The AFL–CIO provides research, education, lobbying, and public relations services.

The AFL–CIO's chief governing body is the biennial convention, which sets policy. Between conventions, the executive officers, assisted by the executive council and the general board, run the AFL–CIO. Executive officers are the president, who interprets the constitution between meetings of the executive council and heads the union staff, and the secretary-treasurer, who is responsible for financial affairs. The executive council, with 33 vice presidents, meets three times a year, and sets policy between conventions. The general board consists of the executive council and the head of each affiliated national union and department.

National headquarters provides many services to subsidiary union bodies: training for regional and local union leaders, organizing help, strike funds, and data used in negotiating contracts. Specialists available for consultation include lawyers, as well as public relations, and research personnel. Under the national union are regional groups of local unions which may provide office space and facilities for local unions.

The national unions are a varied group. Some large unions are independent of the AFL–CIO, for example, the mine workers. Very large unions which are members of the AFL–CIO are steel workers, electrical workers, carpenters, machinists, hotel and restaurant workers and the teamsters, who rejoined the AFL–CIO in 1987. The smallest national union, a unit in the printing trade, has 18 members.

The keystone of the trade union movement is the 60,000 local unions. A local represents all the union members in a geographic area for a craft union (for example, all carpenters in San Francisco) or in a plant for an industrial union (for example, UAW members at the Lansing, Michigan, Oldsmobile plant). Therefore, our major focus is on the local level.

The Local Union

In general, the local union is a branch of the national union and has little legal authority. In many unions, the local must get permission from the national union before it can strike. The national can charter or disband a local as well as suspend it or put it under national trusteeship. That is what happened in Austin, Minnesota, in 1986. Local P-9 of the United Food and Commercial Workers' union had a lengthy, bitter strike at Geo. A. Hormel & Company, the city's largest employer. After the union rejected a federal mediator's recommended settlement, Hormel resumed operations. A number of P-9 members returned to work, and additional replacements were hired. P-9 leadership continued the strike. When they refused an order from the national union to end the strike, the national union took over the local, removed the leadership, and ended the strike. The entire community was affected by the strike and hard feelings persisted for a long time.[20]

Union Leaders

Just as there is great variety in the size and power of nationals, so there is great variety in locals. They vary in size from eight or so members up to the 40,000 or so members in Local 32-B (New York City) of the Service Employees International Union. The local union elects officials such as president, secretary-treasurer, business representative, and committee chairperson. If the local is large enough, the business representative and secretary-treasurer are full-time employees. The business representative plays a crucial role in contract negotiations and grievances. The president and other officials, such as committee chairperson, hold full-time jobs in the trade or industry. Typically, they get some released time for union duties and union-connected expenses are reimbursed.

Another local union personality is the shop steward or job steward. The steward represents the union on the job site and handles grievances and disciplinary matters. Normally the steward is elected by members in the unit for a one-year term.[21]

Both employers and unions are political entities, but politics is more fundamental to unions. Union leaders, especially local union leaders, have much less power than their managerial equivalents. They are always subject to reelection, and the contracts they negotiate must be ratified by union members. Members can also keep union leaders in line by voting their union out or by engaging in wildcat strikes. Union members are typically apathetic about union affairs except in times of crisis, such as the decision to strike. Usually only 10 to 15 percent of the members attend an ordinary union meeting. This gives more freedom and power to the union leader during "normal" times.

In theory, unions are democratic; their members are supposed to influence their policies and decisions.[22] However, in the typical union an oligarchy has developed; a small percentage of members run it, and the higher the salaries of the union officials, the more this is so.

The union leader often has a strong personality and can mobilize the members against the employer. The effective union leader realizes, however, that the demands made by the union must not put the employer out of business. The union leader's job should be "to discern, reconcile, and then represent the diverse and often conflicting demands and interests of the membership."[23] This is a significant point—the membership is frequently divided about what it wants. Managers usually exaggerate the power of the local union leader and overlook the pressures members and union subordinates can apply.

In sum, there is usually more conflict and less power on the union side of the bargaining table. Conflicts on the management side are usually settled by a decision from higher up the chain of command. This is less likely in unions.

UNION STRATEGIES

Both unions and employers take internal and external actions to help them achieve their labor relations objectives. The matrix in Exhibit 16–6 categorizes these actions. External actions try to change the context in which labor relations/union organizing activity occurs. The initial context defines conditions and imposes certain limits on what is possible. Both unions and employers seek to manipulate these initial conditions in a direction more favorable to their position.[24] For example, an employer might locate new plants in rural or suburban areas with a view to reducing their attractiveness as a union target. Two unions might merge for greater financial strength, as part of an external action.

By contrast, internal actions focus on intraorganizational characteristics. An organization's internal actions may include involving employees in decisions on how jobs are to be structured. A union may try to mobilize discontent among employees as part of an internal action.

This internal/external perspective is useful in examining the current status of unions and the actions being taken to change that status. The union movement today is in trouble. In the 1980s, many unions became victims of their successes in the 1950s and 1960s. The appalling working conditions and arbitrary employer behaviors that had gained them public sympathy earlier in this century had vastly improved. Legally, they were no longer the underdog. They had negotiated generous agreements for

EXHIBIT 16–6
Internal versus External Labor Relations Actions

	Internal	External
Employers	Jobs designed around employees Equitable and competitive compensation Communication with employees Employee involvement programs Subcontract some jobs Other employee relations programs	Plant size and location Delaying tactics Outside consultants Lobby legislative and regulating bodies
Union	Help set intraorganization strategy Cooperation programs Alternate forms of representation Communication with membership	Merge with other unions Lobby legislative and regulatory bodies Political activities to support sympathetic candidates Communications with public

their members. Good times for employers meant that generous labor settlements could be passed on to consumers in the form of higher prices. A highly structured, formalized relationship between unions and management evolved. Detailed contracts were enforced through grievance procedures. But the base of the unions' power—the detailed contract, the uniformity of its administration, the narrow job rules, and the emphasis on stability—were the very factors that constrained employers' ability to respond to the economic dislocation and competition of the 1980s.[25] Formalized procedures that could only be changed through lengthy negotiation made it difficult to react fast enough to changes in external conditions.

Exhibit 16–7 shows this rigidity in structures. Comparing work practices among nonunion and union plants within the same firm, the compensation structure is vastly more flexible in new, nonunion plants. For example, the number of job classifications and wage grades is substantially lower. Having fewer job classifications increases flexibility because it is easier to move employees to other jobs within the same classification than to a job in another classification. When, for example, "maintenance" workers are separately classified as "electrical maintenance," "plumbing maintenance," or "diesel maintenance," it is more difficult to schedule work for each maintenance employee. But if most of the maintenance employees are in the same job classification, then scheduling is simplified, and em-

EXHIBIT 16–7
Comparison of Work Practices in Union and Nonunion Plants of the Same Firm

Workers Practices	New Nonunion (N = 3)	Old Nonunion (N = 2)	Union (N = 3)
Number of job classifications	6	65	96
Number of wage grades	7	11	14
Number of maintenance job classifications	1	10	11
Percent maintenance workers in a "General Maintenance" classification	75%	20%	1%
Supervisors prohibited from doing subordinates' work	No	No	Yes
Subcontracting occurs only after meeting with union employees	100%	0%	0%

Source: Anil Verma, "Union and Nonunion Industrial Relations at the Plant Level" (Ph.D. dissertation, Sloan School of Management, MIT, 1983).

ployees can be redeployed according to the demands of the work and of the individuals' skills. Although the exhibit shows the new, nonunion plant experiencing the greatest degree of flexibility, part of this may be due to plant size and age. A lot of bureaucracy builds up over time. However, even the old nonunion plant in the exhibit had more flexible practices than the union plant. So unions do appear to constrain an employer's flexibility and speed of response.

Formalized procedures not only cause a great deal of difficulty for employers; they have also hurt unions. Unions as organizations tend to be more democratic than employers, who cannot be voted out. Thus, it is not surprising that union organizations have had such a difficult time responding to the changes they have experienced. However, the outline of their response is beginning to emerge.

Changes in Internal Union Actions

We can identify three main thrusts to changes many unions are making in the way they operate.

1. Involvement in employer's strategic decisions.
2. Cooperative programs.
3. Alternative forms of representation.

Involvement in Employer's Strategic Decisions

For several years, former UAW president Douglas Fraser was on Chrysler Corporation's board of directors. This is the most vivid example of a union's participation in shaping an employer's directions. This probably was a unique case brought about by the extreme financial distress of Chrysler and the interest and capabilities of Fraser. A lot of people in and out of the labor movement in the United States are uncomfortable with such arrangements.[26] They feel they stray too far from the traditional roles of adversarial participants in a capitalistic economic system.

Another strategic involvement is through employee stock ownership.[27] By themselves, stock ownership programs may give employees equity in the company, but may not increase their role in strategic decision making. At the minimum, however, ownership provides employees the ability to vote for the board of directors.

A third way of affecting employer's strategy may also be categorized as external action. It involves enlisting outside allies to exert pressure to change or rescind a decision. There have been several instances of plant closing decisions that were successfully overturned when coalitions of union and community leaders located new buyers. In New York, professionals from Cornell's School of Industrial and Labor Relations Extension Service intervene. They assist employers and unions to change production methods, making old plants more productive and thereby reducing the decline in manufacturing jobs in the state. Sometimes, unions conduct corporate campaigns to put pressure on banks with financial ties to an employer, hoping to induce the bank to put financial pressure on targeted employers.

Cooperative Programs

Resistance to unions dies hard. Most employers, unless they have no choice, prefer to remain nonunion. If they are only partially unionized, they may try to redirect their business to favor growth in the nonunionized segments, often at the expense of unionized segments.[28] Some people allege that this is what has happened in the airline industry since deregulation. Unionized airlines have been purchased by nonunionized employers. Planes and routes of the unionized segment may then be diverted to fuel growth of the nonunionized part of the business.

Despite these suspicions, there are outstanding examples of union-management cooperation. The General Motors Corporation and UAW cooperative participation program discussed in the previous chapter provides one example; the Communications Workers of America and AT&T provide a second. They formed a private organization, the Alliance, whose executive directors are drawn equally from AT&T and CWA. The presidents of both organizations sit on the executive board. The purpose of the Alliance is to help retrain and relocate CWA members whose present jobs at AT&T are no longer needed. Relocation may be within AT&T, or it may be in other companies. The executive team goes into a site and assists the union local and company managers to design training programs and redeployment activities that fit the needs at each location. The team recently assisted in the placement of 150 out of 170 eligible long distance operators from AT&T's Springfield, Massachusetts, location.

Union-management cooperation has been the topic of a lot of recent research.[29] The conclusions are similar to those presented on participation programs in the previous chapter: after an initial rush, the high is difficult to sustain.

Alternative Forms of Representation

About 28 percent of all nonunionized workers either voted for a union in an unsuccessful organizing campaign or are former union members.[30] Hence, a large reservoir of sympathy presumably exists outside union membership. This amounts to support on which unions are currently unable to draw. Present U.S. law requires that a majority of those who vote determine the outcome for the entire bargaining unit. If those employees who wanted a union could have one, even though they constitute a minority in a bargaining unit, the decline in union membership may turn around. Such arrangements would require a change in national legislation, as the Taft-Hartley Act presently requires that a majority vote determines the outcome for the entire unit.[31] The United States is one of the few countries with such a requirement.

Another alternative would be to offer an associate membership. The purpose of this membership could be to increase awareness of the positive contributions of unions and mobilize support for its political initiatives.

Changes in External Union Actions

Externally, unions appear to be at a very low point. Many of the legislative changes they have supported have been unsuccessful, and some political candidates are ambivalent about seeking union support. A Harris poll conducted for the AFL–CIO found that the American public continues to see a need for unions. Yet a majority of nonunion workers believe unions are unable to make a significant difference in the areas of concern.[32] The one third of nonunion employees who express an interest in traditional union membership face limited prospects of achieving it on their jobs because

1. Union organizing activity currently covers less than 1 percent of those eligible to organize.[33]
2. It is unlikely that a majority of a given employee's co-workers will agree that unionization is needed, so they will vote against a union in an election.

3. Employer opposition can substantially reduce the probability of a successful union election.

So the outlook for unions is uncertain. In the early 1980s, unions appeared ready to launch a major drive to organize clerical employees, especially in the insurance and banking industries. But these efforts were remarkably unsuccessful, perhaps due to greater "preventive labor relations" on management's part.[34] Perhaps as more employees find their opportunities for advancement do not meet their expectations, they will again turn to unionism. However, as noted in the last chapter on employee relations, employees can also turn to the courts, to federal and state human rights commissions, and to state-sponsored dispute resolution procedures.

SUMMARY

Labor relations is a major activity in unionized organizations. It also is an activity of major interest in society as well. Cataclysmic events in the 1930s awoke the public to the wretched conditions faced by American workers. The public's identification with union goals led to a changed regulatory climate and phenomenal growth in union strength in the 1940s and 1950s. After that, unions began a long decline.

The industries that were most heavily unionized were typically the ones hit hardest by competitive pressures in the 1980s. Foreign competition, deregulation, and a changed climate of public opinion have severely weakened unions, to the point where in 1985, the pay increases for union members were 40 percent less than increases given to nonunion workers.[35] Union troubles eased slightly in 1986 and the wage differential again favors unions; yet, overall unemployment remains high enough to inhibit potential strikers when employers demand not only pay cutbacks but also changes in the rules that govern the way work is done.

Many people continue to blame unions themselves, or at least the collective bargaining process as it presently exists in the United States, for unions' trouble. They cite high wage settlements that drove many jobs out of the country, and contracts that built up rules that eventually interfere with productivity. These costly side effects might be justified if the outcomes of the labor relations process were more palatable to the American public. Critics, however, say that unions that win the biggest settlements are not the ones whose members are "most deserving." Rather, they are the ones with the most effective bargaining power. They are less likely to be the $4-an-hour textile workers than $20-an-hour auto workers.

On the other side of the coin, management historically has exhibited trouble maintaining the discipline and foresight to deal directly and fairly with employees. Commitment to employees can be difficult to maintain when economic conditions change. History is not on the side of the employer. Without unions, government and the courts will be asked to increase their intervention in the workplace.

Many people feel that collective bargaining offers a superior approach. Creative agreements may be tailored to unique circumstances. The next chapter discusses the specifics of the collective bargaining process.

DISCUSSION AND REVIEW QUESTIONS

1. Why do people join unions?
2. What role does the government play in labor relations?
3. Describe the various organization approaches to dealing with unions.
4. Which factors have contributed to the past success of unions in the United States?
5. Which factors have contributed to the recent decline in union membership in the United States?

NOTES AND REFERENCES

1. Barbara W. Tuchman, *A Distant Mirror: The Calamitous Fourteenth Century* (New York: Alfred A. Knopf, Inc., 1978). Reprinted by permission.
2. Matthew Rothschild, "Rank-and-File Blues," *The Progressive*, August 1983, pp. 25–27.
3. Harry C. Katz and Charles F. Sabel, "Industrial Relations and Industrial Adjustment in the Car Industry," *Industrial Relations*, Fall 1985, pp. 295–315.
4. Peter Cappelli, "Competitive Pressures and Labor Relations in the Airline Industry," *Industrial Relations*, Fall 1985, pp. 316–38.
5. John Fossum, *Labor Relations*, 3rd ed. (Plano, Tex.: Business Publications, 1985).
6. Ibid.
7. William J. Moore and Robert J. Newman, "The Effects of Right-to-Work Laws," *Industrial and Labor Relations Review*, July 1985, pp. 571–85.
8. Paul Weiler, "Promises to Keep: Securing Workers' Rights to Self-Organize under the NLRB," *Harvard Law Review*, June 1983, p. 1769; William N. Cooke, "The Rising Toll of Discrimination against Union Activists," *Industrial Relations*, Fall 1985, pp. 421–42; Richard B. Freeman, "Why Are Unions Faring Poorly in NLRB Representation Elections?" in *Challenges and Choices Facing American Labor*, ed. T. Kochan (Cambridge, Mass.: The MIT Press, 1985).
9. Freeman, "Why Are Unions Faring Poorly," p. 55.

10. John Chalykoff and Peter Cappelli, "Union Avoidance: Management's New Industrial Relations Strategy" (paper presented at the thirty-eighth annual meeting of the Industrial Relations Research Association, December 1985, New York); Jack Fiorito and Christopher Lowman, "The Role of Employer Human Resource Policies in Union Organizing," (working paper, University of Iowa, February 1986).

11. Janice A. Klein and E. David Wanger, "The Legal Setting for the Emergence of the Union Avoidance Strategy," in *Challenges and Choices Facing American Labor.*

12. Larry T. Adams, "Union Membership of Wage and Salary Employees in 1986," *Current Wage Developments*, February 1987, pp. 3–8.

13. Michael Schuster, "Models of Cooperation and Change in Union Settings," *Industrial Relations*, Fall 1985, pp. 382–94.

14. Fred K. Foulkes, *Personnel Policies in Large Nonunion Companies* (Englewood Cliffs, N.J.: Prentice-Hall, 1980); John G. Kilgour, *Preventive Labor Relations* (New York: AMACOM, a division of American Management Associations, 1981).

15. Kay Deaux and Joseph C. Ullman, *Women of Steel: Female Blue-Collar Workers in the Basic Steel Industry* (New York: Praeger Publishers, 1983); Richard Freeman and Jonathan S. Leonard, "Union Maids: Unions and the Female Work Force" (working paper, Cambridge: NBER, June 1985); Richard Moore and Elizabeth Marsis, "Will Unions Work for Women?" *The Progressive*, August 1983, pp. 28–30.

16. Michele M. Hayman and Lamont Stallworth, "Participation in Local Unions: A Comparison of Black and White Members," *Industrial and Labor Relations Review*, April 1987, pp. 323–35.

17. James E. Martin, "Employee Characteristics and Representation Election Outcomes," *Industrial and Labor Relations Review*, April 1985, pp. 365–76.

18. Robert L. Aronson, "Unionism among Professional Employees in the Private Sector," *Industrial and Labor Relations Review*, April 1985, pp. 352–64.

19. Selig Perlman, "Labor and Capitalism in America," in *The Collective Bargaining Process*, ed. Jean A. Baderschneider, Richard N. Block, and John A. Fossum (Plano, Tex.: Business Publications, 1983).

20. Jeremy Main, "The Labor Rebel Leading the Hormel Strike," *Fortune*, June 9, 1986, pp. 105–10.

21. Alex Kotlowitz, "Job of Shop Steward Has New Frustrations in Era of Payroll Cuts," *The Wall Street Journal*, April 1, 1987, pp. 1, 23.

22. A. H. Raskin, "Big Labor Tries to End Its Nightmare," *New York Times*, May 4, 1986, 1F, 8F.

23. George Taylor, "The Role of Unions in a Democratic Society," in *Government Regulation of Internal Union Affairs Affecting the Rights of Members* (Washington, D.C.: U.S. Government Printing Office, 1958), p. 19.

24. John J. Lawler and Robin West, "Impact of Union Avoidance Strategy in Representation Elections," *Industrial Relations*, Fall 1985, pp. 406–420.

25. Thomas A. Kochan, Harry C. Katz, and Robert B. McKersie, *The Transformation of American Industrial Relations* (New York: Basic Books, 1986).

26. Peter Cappelli and Robert B. McKersie, "Labor and the Crisis in Collec-

tive Bargaining," in *Challenges and Choices Facing American Labor* (Cambridge, Mass.: MIT Press, 1985).

27. Corey Rosen, "Growth versus Equity: The Employee Ownership Solution," *ILR Report,* Spring 1985, pp. 19–25.

28. Anil Verma, "Relative Flow of Capital to Union and Nonunion Plants within a Firm," *Industrial Relations,* Fall 1985, pp. 395–405.

29. Schuster, "Models of Cooperation and Change"; Paula B. Voos, "Cooperative Labor Relations and the Collective Bargaining Environment" (paper presented at the thirty-eighth annual meeting of the Industrial Relations Research Association, December 1985, New York); John Joyce, "Codetermination, Collective Bargaining, and Worker Participation in the Construction Industry," in *Challenges and Choices Facing American Labor,* ed. T. Kochan; Paula B. Voos, "Managerial Perceptions of the Economic Impact of Labor Relations Programs," *Industrial and Labor Relations Review,* January 1987, pp. 195–208; Mitchell Lee Marks, Philip H. Mirvis, Edward J. Hackett, and James F. Grady, "Employee Participation in a Quality Circle Program," *Journal of Applied Psychology* 71, no. 1 (1986), pp. 61–69.

30. *The Changing Situation of Workers and Their Unions,* Report of the AFL–CIO Evolution of Work Committee (Washington, D.C.: AFL–CIO, 1985).

31. U.S. Department of Labor, *U.S. Labor Law and the Future of Labor-Management Cooperation* (Washington, D.C.: U.S. Government Printing Office, 1986).

32. *The Changing Situation of Workers and Their Unions.*

33. Ibid.

34. John C. Kilgour, "White-Collar Organizing: A Reappraisal," *Personnel,* August 1986, pp. 14–19.

35. "Troubles of U.S. Labor Unions Eased in 1986," *New York Times,* February 15, 1987, p. 16.

chapter seventeen

COLLECTIVE BARGAINING

CHAPTER OUTLINE

If the famous movie of the 1960s, *The Graduate*, were to be remade today, the buzz word whispered by the successful manager to Dustin Hoffman as the magical key to future happiness would be "flexibility." Students have the luxury of hearing, over and over again, of the need for flexible career plans, flexible organizations, even a "high-flex society."[1]

At the same time, the American press provides a constant barrage of details of the "inflexibility" of the labor relations system in the United States: national unions that force plants to close rather than reduce health insurance; union members under two-tier wage systems who permit new hires to receive substantially lower wages for doing the same work rather than accept pay cuts themselves; auto makers' buying off workers with ever higher wages while they do nothing about the boring, mindless, enervating nature of the jobs they defend their right to manage.[2]

For most Americans, what they read in the newspaper is as close as they ever get to a union. The dramatic events that receive press coverage shape their opinion, rightly or wrongly, of the nature of collective bargaining in the U.S. today. That is unfortunate, because they probably miss the flexibility that is inherent in the collective bargaining process. The outcome of the process is a contract that governs daily work relationships and has the beauty of renegotiation on a regularly scheduled basis—potential flexibility built right in. So, for example, in 1986 the United Steelworkers union negotiated child care agreements with two big steel companies, in the face of tough bargaining pressures.[3] In 1984 General Motors Corporation, Ford Motor Company, and Chrysler Corporation negotiated the Job Opportunity Bank program with the United Auto Workers. Each of the auto companies contributes funds to provide income and training for workers with a year or more of seniority who lose their jobs as a result of changes in work rules, technology, or buying components from outside sources rather than making them. In exchange, management gets flexibility in assigning such workers.

At Ford's Rawsonville, Michigan, parts plant, management started a pilot employment guarantee program in exchange for a reduction in trades classifications. Less skilled workers may handle routine maintenance and repair, while tradesmen operate in broadly skilled teams. Under the terms of this program, workers with at least one year's seniority cannot be laid off during the life of the agreement. In 1987, guaranteed employment was part of the national Ford-UAW agreement. Layoffs are disallowed for any reason except a decline in sales. Ford is obligated to find new jobs for union members if required employment levels at a location decline.[4]

So flexibility does exist in collective bargaining. Unions and management have wide latitude in what they negotiate. Union members are typically willing to demonstrate their flexibility if they believe management will do the same. The key to understanding collective bargaining is to realize that there are multiple parties to agreements, and that agreements that govern daily work change regularly through the negotiation process.

The previous chapter examined the employer and the union as organizations that participate in collective bargaining, the diagnostic factors that influence them, and the objectives and strategies that employers and unions may adopt. This chapter looks at the collective bargaining process and evaluates its effects on the objectives of efficiency and equity. To begin the bargaining process, the first step is the organizing campaign.

THE ORGANIZING CAMPAIGN

When employees are not represented by a union, either the employees themselves or a union can initiate unionization. In some cases, when employees are quite dissatisfied, they can take the initiative and invite a union in to begin organizing their employer. Exhibit 17–1 is an example of the kind of material a union might use to mobilize employee discontent with employment conditions and steer them toward union formation as a solution.

Whether the employees or the union take the initiative, next comes a time of high drama: the organizing campaign itself.

Authorization Cards

Union organizers try to get the employees to sign cards which authorize that union to represent them in collective bargaining. In the United States, 30 percent of the employees must sign cards before the union can call for a representation election. In most Canadian provinces, if 60 percent of the workers sign authorization cards, the union is certified without a representation election. There is no "campaign" on either side. This may be one reason why union membership in Canada is increasing, while in the United States it is not.

In general, the union tries to keep the initial stages of the campaign secret so it can get up momentum before management can mount a counteroffensive. During the organizing period, unions and management pur-

EXHIBIT 17–1
Union Organizing Material

Why Unionize?

Though many people face employment problems, or witness the problems of co-workers, they wonder whether a union can really help. Some see unions as just another institution.

But unions are what the members make them. Many of the myths about unions come from misinformation or lack of information altogether. What can unionizing do for you?

A union gives you the legal right to negotiate with your employer. Though different people may have individual problems the source is the same—the lack of representation in decision making.

We're not talking about just a lack of communication. Many employers institute new channels for suggestions. But who decides whether to implement these suggestions?

A union guarantees the right to participate in decision making. Once the union is voted in it must be consulted by the employer on any issue concerning working conditions and wages. Employees are informed of proposed changes, and in many cases must agree before changes are made.

Salaries and benefits are almost always improved. For instance, unionized clerical workers earn 32 percent more than nonunionized clericals, according to the U.S. Department of Labor.

The contract is decided on by the members at your workplace. You write in the issues that concern you, and then negotiate with your employer.

Many people fear that when the union comes in, flexibility goes out. Does a union mean time-clocks, limited wage scales, and rigid working conditions? No. In fact, it can mean the opposite. Your contract can call for the maintenance of current employment practices, including flexibility.

Will a union destroy the friendly atmosphere that may exist in the office? To make any change in conditions you'll have to apply pressure. Management will be pressuring your supervisor too—to keep things as they have always been.

Once you have unionized, though, your employer will have a new respect for the organized power your union represents, clearing the way for even better working relations.

How to Do It

1. Organizing committee. A group of employees who want to unionize call in an organizer and form a committee. They coordinate the drive—provide information, learn the concerns of co-workers, and know who is interested and why others are not.

2. Card-signing. The Organizing Committee gets "authorization cards" signed by employees. The cards authorize the union to bargain with management for wages, benefits and working conditions.

The card is confidential. Your employer will not see it.

3. Calling for the election. In order to call for an election you only need 30 percent of the eligible employees to sign cards. However, it may be wiser to wait until a majority supports the union.

4. Who can vote. The bargaining unit represents a community of interest. It could include all employees in one department, one job category throughout the company, or all employees. It could include one location or several

EXHIBIT 17–1 (concluded)

locations. The final determination is made by the National Labor Relations Board (NLRB).

5. Winning the election.   A secret ballot election is conducted by the NLRB. It takes a simple majority of the people voting to win the election.

6. The contract.   Once the election is won, your legal relationship with management is dramatically changed and you are placed on an equal basis for deciding wages, hours, and other working conditions.

Management is bound by law to "bargain in good faith." That means that they have to be willing to give and take. They cannot go in with a no-compromise attitude.

The employees can meet to decide what should go into the contract and select representatives to negotiate with management.

7. Will we have to strike?   Probably not. 95 percent of contracts are settled through discussion.

8. Dues.   Dues vary depending on the union. Dues will provide experienced staff, legal assistance, researchers, and other resources.

Published by Working Women, 1224 Huron Road, Cleveland, OH 44115.

---

sue campaigns to affect employee attitudes toward unionization. Typically, the union stresses how it can improve the workers' lot in terms of compensation, benefits, working conditions, and increased influence and control over decisions related to their jobs.[5] Management mounts a countercampaign stressing how well off the employees are already and the cost of union membership in dollars and "loss of freedom."[6] It is illegal for either side, in mass meetings, literature, or individual meetings, to threaten employees with discharge or violence. Both sides must be truthful, or the procedure can be set aside.

Hearings

After the authorization, the NLRB holds a hearing to decide if there is enough evidence to hold an election. The NLRB seeks to determine two things:

1. *Valid signatures.* Do the people who signed authorization cards actually work there, and do they constitute 30 percent of employees?
2. *Appropriate bargaining unit.* A bargaining unit delineates which group of employees will be involved in the representation election; for example, all employees in technician job categories at a particular plant location or all nonexempt employees at multiple locations.[7]

Typically, a union proposes a bargaining unit. The NLRB must determine if this unit is "appropriate," using two criteria: Will it ensure employees freedom of choice, and does it foster "industrial peace and stability"? It is not the NLRB's role to choose the "best" bargaining unit, only an "appropriate" unit. Employers frequently challenge the union's specification of a unit to influence which employees are eligible to vote in the election or just to delay the procedure.

Holding the Election

After determining that all requirements are met, the NLRB examiner schedules an election. The NLRB provides ballot boxes, counts the votes, and certifies the election. The union becomes the employees' representative if it wins the election.

To win an election, 50 percent plus 1 of the people who vote in the election must vote for the union. Occasionally there may be more than one union on the ballot. If this is the case, they hold a runoff election between the two top choices; for example, either between the two unions, or between no union and the more popular union. When a union wins an election, the NLRB certifies that union's exclusive right to represent everyone in the bargaining unit. No other union may represent employees in the unit, and all employees in the unit are represented, whether or not they join the union.

Researchers have spent a great deal of effort trying to specify what factors affect the outcomes of union elections.[8] First, employees are more likely to unionize if an employer is perceived to have demanded different behavior than was expected, or failed to provide rewards expected. Second, an individual must believe that there is little likelihood of changing conditions except through collective bargaining. Third, some critical mass of like-minded activists is necessary to begin the unionizing attempt. Fourth, unionization by this activist coalition depends on their understanding of how collective bargaining works and their belief that the likely benefits of organizing outweigh the drawbacks.

Most union elections are very close. One study found that a shift of eight votes would have changed the outcome of the average election.[9] So it is no wonder that participation rates are high—typically 90 percent—compared to roughly 50 percent in major political elections. Employees accurately perceive that their vote *can* make a difference.

Success of Campaign Tactics

In the 1980s, employers have become increasingly aggressive in their communication campaigns and in their use of outside consultants to advise them.[10] Exhibit 17–2 presents the relative frequency of various employer

EXHIBIT 17–2
Frequency Distribution of Reported Employer
Campaign Activities (N = 175)

Campaign Activity	Relative Frequency
Captive audience speeches	65%
Small group meetings	36
Supervisor training	38
Literature distribution	70
Employee surveillance	34
Excelsior-list irregularities	11
Administration of surveys	11
Employment discrimination	24
Wage increases during campaign	16
Threats of reprisal	10
Promises of gain/inducements	4
Directed election	22
Management consultant used	20

Source: John J. Lawler and Robin West, "Impact of Union-Avoidance Strategy in Representation Elections," *Industrial Relations*, Fall 1985, pp. 406–20.

activities, as reported by union organizers. How successful are such tactics? It is hard to say. Economists who analyze aggregated data conclude that:

1. The amount of company communication influences election results, with unions winning most elections in which management opposition is light, but less than half of those in which opposition is severe.
2. Union success is lower the longer the delay between the initial petition and the actual election.
3. Elections in which companies readily agree to the bargaining unit proposed by the union produce greater chances of wins than elections in which the NLRB stipulates the unit and, therefore, who can and cannot vote.[11]
4. From one quarter to a half of the decline in union election success results from management opposition to organizing campaigns.

The problem with these conclusions is that they are based on nationwide data and do not consider what affects a particular election result. At the level of the individual union election, most employers' strategies have a relatively weak effect; however, their effects may be cumulative, and it may be that a weak effect is sufficient to change an election outcome.

Hiring an outside consultant appears to be the employer strategy that has the most strongly negative impact on union organizing success.[12] However, there is also some evidence that an overly aggressive employer campaign can backfire and enhance the chances of union victory. Perhaps the most potent employer tactic is fair and effective human resource management not only by the personnel department but also by each manager in the organization.

Decertification

Once a union, not necessarily always a union. The same group of employees who vote in a union can vote one out, using much the same procedure as in certification. An election, supervised by the NLRB, can be called for by either the employees in the unit involved or a labor organization acting on their behalf. Whoever requests the election must provide evidence that at least 30 percent of the employees want a decertification election. A petition signed by a majority of the bargaining unit employees is the most common evidence.

A decertification election cannot be held within 12 months of the certification election or while a labor contract is in effect. Decertification elections have doubled in the last 10 years, and unions have been losing three fourths of them, as Exhibit 17–3 shows.[13]

EXHIBIT 17–3
Increases in Decertification Elections

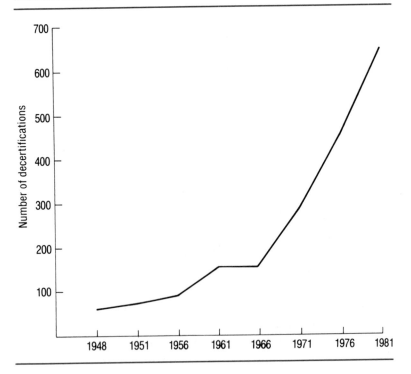

NEGOTIATING A CONTRACT

Once a union is recognized as the bargaining representative for a group of employees, its officials are authorized to negotiate an employment contract. This contract differs in several important ways from a typical legal contract. It is unusual because:

1. So many people are bound by it. If you buy a car, you may feel a lot of people are involved; the salesperson, perhaps the salesperson's supervisor, the loan processor, and the license bureau. But a union contract involves all the people who are employed in the bargaining unit. This number may run into the hundreds.
2. The contract is not strictly voluntary, in that neither side can walk away from it. Workers are already employed, the union cannot say "I'll go get another employer," and the employer is legally required to bargain.
3. Most contracts specify all details of a one-time event. By contrast, the collective bargaining agreement governs a day-to-day relationship, but may be incomplete and purposely vague. If there is no meeting of the minds, a statement of general principle may be given. For example, a statement supporting worker participation plans was contained in GM–UAW contracts for years before any programs actually began.

Preparation

Preparation for negotiation is an area in which little research has been done, mainly because the parties to the negotiation prefer secrecy. The more complex the bargaining, the further ahead preparations begin.

The beginning part of the preparation analyzes problems in contract administration and possible changes in contract language. If management or the union wishes to make changes in a contract, it must notify the other party and the Federal Mediation and Conciliation Service (FMCS) in writing of their desire to terminate or modify the contract at least 60 days before the contract expires. This notification also should include an offer to meet with the other side to discuss the issue.

Probably since the signing of the last contract, both sides have been compiling lists of issues to be brought up the next time. Management has asked its supervisors how they would like the contract modified to avoid problem areas. The industrial relations department has been studying patterns in grievances to identify problems. Management has examined the contract to identify undesirable sections, especially those that restrict its rights.

Based on these data, both sides gather statistical information and prepare bargaining positions. For example, management seeks information on economic conditions affecting the job (e.g., wage rates, productivity) from its staff, industry data, and published sources. Management also attempts to determine the cost of each likely union demand. Computer simulation can help here. Preliminary trade-offs are thought through.

Often there are differences within management groups over bargaining objectives. A common complaint is: "I'm having more trouble with my company than I am with the union." When these management differences are worked out before the negotiations start, the bargaining process is more effective. If an employer negotiates with more than one union, for example, different unions representing various bargaining units within the employer, careful preparation is essential, for what is negotiated with one union is brought up by the others. Typically, a careful balance of wage, benefit, and status differentials is maintained among unions.

The union also prepares for negotiations by preparing lists of problems with the contract. It, too, gathers statistical information, studies the issues likely to be raised, and coordinates with any other unions involved. Unions may also have internal differences, usually over what the bargaining objectives are; for example, younger workers may want job security, while older workers favor better pensions.[14]

Negotiation Issues

Any labor contract can have a large number of clauses; studies show that the number of items an employer must bargain over is increasing. They fall into five groups:

1. Union Security. This is usually the first bargaining issue for a union. Most unions prefer a *union shop clause:* When workers take jobs in this bargaining unit, they must join the union after a certain time period. Union membership is a condition for continued employment. A union shop clause is legal. A *closed shop*, where union membership is a condition of hiring, is illegal.

If a union shop clause cannot be won, a union may settle for an *agency shop:* Even if workers do not join, they must still pay the equivalent of dues to the union. Exhibit 17–4 shows the agency shop clause from an agreement between TRW Inc. and the Globe Industries Employees' Independent Union.

Another option is a *maintenance of membership clause:* Workers may or may not join the union, but once they join, they must maintain (continue) their membership for the duration of the contract. Membership can only be dropped within 30 days of contract expiration. A maintenance of membership clause guarantees stability in numbers for a union.

EXHIBIT 17–4
Labor Contract: Agency Shop Clause

Section 1:   Agency shop
  A.   Membership in the union is not compulsory. However, membership in the
       union is distinct from the assumption of equal financial obligations to all
       represented employees. Therefore, all represented employees, as a
       condition of employment, no later than ninety (90) calendar days after
       the beginning of their employment or the date of this Agreement,
       whichever is later, either become and remain members of the union in
       good standing or make payments to the union in an amount equal to the
       initiation fees and membership dues uniformly required by the union of
       its members.

Section 2:   Checkoff
  A.   The company agrees to deduct from the wages of those employees who
       so authorize by written assignment (on mutually agreed upon forms)
       regular monthly union membership dues and initiation fees or payments
       in lieu thereof.

---

   2. Contract Administration. The contract specifies its duration, commonly two to three years, and procedures to ensure that it is applied/
enforced as intended. Exhibit 17–5 shows part of the administrative details
of the TRW contract. We return to contract administration later in this
chapter.

   3. Compensation and Working Conditions. All contracts stipulate
compensation and working conditions, such as direct compensation rates,
benefits, and hours of work. Issues concern whether overtime should be
voluntary, and the size of cost-of-living adjustments. Unions may bargain
about not only payments for pensions but also the details of early retirement provisions, for example.

   One wage clause that has generated a great deal of controversy is the
two-tier wage structure, in which the top rate of pay for new employees
is substantially lower than that for previously hired employees. Exhibit
17–6 shows the size of these differentials in a TRW contract. The new
employees may earn less than half as much as the previous employees on
the same job.

   Because employees with identical job titles, duties, responsibilities,
and performance receive substantially different pay rates, two-tier structures seem particularly hard to reconcile with the objective of equity.[15]
Fortunately, most such plans phase new employees into the higher rates
after several years, so eventually the differential disappears. But pending
renegotiation, about one third of such clauses specify permanent differentials. Current trends in contract negotiations indicate that both unions and

EXHIBIT 17–5
Labor Contract: Administrative Details

ARTICLE II

Section 1:   Strikes and Lockouts
  A.   The union agrees that there shall be no strikes, picketing, boycotts, interruptions of work, or any other interferences directly or indirectly, with the operation of the plant so long as the grievance procedure under this Agreement is followed by the company.
  B.   The company agrees that there shall be no lockouts, so long as the grievance procedure under this Agreement is followed by the union.
  C.   Any violation of this Article, by any employee, shall constitute cause for immediate discipline and/or discharge.

ARTICLE III

Section 1:   Grievance Procedure
  A.   All differences, disputes and grievances that may arise between the union and the company out of this contract shall be taken up immediately under this grievance procedure.
       Any employee who has a complaint over the interpretation or application of this Agreement shall discuss the alleged complaint with his supervisor in an attempt to settle the alleged complaint. Any such complaint not so settled shall be processed according to the grievance procedure specified in this contract.

EXHIBIT 17–6
Labor Contract: A Two-Tier Wage Structure

Job	Pay Rate for Employees Hired on or After March 3, 1986	Pay Rate for Employees Hired Before March 3, 1986
CNC chucker	$6.00	$12.00
CNC mill	6.00	12.00
Plating/painting technician	5.50	11.65
Punch press operator	5.00	12.44
Special machine operator	5.00	11.49

management are having second thoughts about two-tier arrangements. Equity issues among employees and membership pressures on union officials raise serious concerns about two-tier clauses.

   4. Employee Security and Seniority. Seniority is continuous service in a work unit, plant, or organization. Unions feel that seniority should be the determining factor in promotions, layoffs, and recalls. Management claims its right to make these decisions on the basis of job performance.

Many contracts stipulate that in cases of promotion and layoff, when efficiency and ability are substantially equal, the most senior employees shall be favored. Exhibit 17–7 shows part of the seniority clause from TRW's contract.

Seniority is an area of unresolved conflict between some union supporters and some EEO advocates. The Supreme Court has upheld the legality of seniority systems as long as the original intent of the system was not to discriminate.[16] Because minorities and women are more likely to have low seniority, layoffs on a seniority basis hurt them disproportionately.

5. Management Rights. This issue usually presents an especially difficult set of problems. Management lists certain areas or decisions as management rights or prerogatives, which are thus excluded from bargaining. Management tries to make these lists long, and unions try to chip away at

EXHIBIT 17–7
Labor Contract: Seniority Clause

ARTICLE VII

Section 1:   Seniority Recognition
  A.   Seniority is defined as length of service within the bargaining unit from the most recent date of hire. Length of service is defined as the length of employment with the company from the most recent date of hire.
  B.   An employee shall be considered probationary during the first ninety (90) working days of employment. Such period may be extended for thirty (30) additional working days for illness only, by endorsement of the employee's work record and notification to the union of such extension. During the period of probationary employment, the company shall be the sole judge of the employee's qualification for continued employment without recourse to the grievance and arbitration procedure under this Agreement. Upon successful completion of the probationary period, the employee's seniority shall date back to the most recent date of hire.

Section 2:   Promotion
  A.   All job vacancies as indicated on the promotional chart will be posted on the bulletin boards, and any employee may apply for a job vacancy, as defined in paragraph B of this Section.
  B.   There are three (3) types of job vacancies.

  "Type A"—Job will be awarded to the most qualified of the four (4) most senior applicants from the work group who are willing to accept the job.

  "Type B"—Job will be awarded to the most qualified of the two (2) most senior applicants from the work group who are willing to accept the job.

  "Type C"—Jobs in the Miscellaneous Work Group and entry level jobs will be awarded to the most senior bidding employee.

  Before a Type A or Type B job is posted for bid, employees with recall rights to such jobs must be recalled. This includes internal displacement as well as actual recall from layoff.

---

them. In many cases, the wage concessions that unions made in the early 1980s were in exchange for reduction in the items of management's sole discretion.

Refusal to Bargain

What happens if an employer disagrees with the bargaining unit specified by the NLRB, or simply refuses to abide by the election results? The union can file a charge of unfair labor practice with the NLRB, which enforces labor law. If the NLRB finds a violation, it can issue a "cease and desist" order to the employer. Continuing refusal to obey results in the NLRB taking the employer to federal court to enforce the order.

In spite of the legal requirement to bargain in good faith, a lot of newly certified unions are unable to negotiate a contract. One study reports that in a survey of 2,656 union representation elections held in 1970, nearly a quarter of the units where unions were certified did not have a contract when contacted five years later.[17] Some units had decertified their union, some employers had gone out of business, and other unions had simply become inactive. Most of the unsuccessful unions in this study were small (fewer than 100 members). Another study restricted to larger-size bargaining units (over 100 employees) found that 63 percent obtained contracts within three years after the election, but only 56 percent were able to get a second contract.[18] Again, firms move or go out of business, unions get decertified or simply lapse into inactivity.

Bargaining Structures

In Chapter Sixteen, we saw how a local union may be part of a national or even international union, which may be part of the AFL–CIO. There are also employer organizations. Thus, the parties negotiating a contract may not be single employers or single unions. For example, an *employer group*, such as the Bituminous Coal Owners Association, may negotiate with a single union, such as the United Mine Workers, or with several unions—United Mine Workers and Union Operating Engineers. *Multiemployer bargaining* is common in industries such as construction, trucking, and garment manufacturing where large national unions face many small employers. *Coalition bargaining* involves several unions negotiating with a single employer. For example, the International Union of Electrical, Radio and Machine Workers (IUE), the United Auto Workers (UAW), and the United Electricians (UE) negotiate as a coalition with General Electric Company. These alternative structures result from one or the other parties to the negotiation trying to gain an advantage over the other.

Another way of gaining advantage is by *pattern bargaining*. Pattern bargaining is the use of a settlement in one setting as the "target" in another setting. Pattern bargaining was common into the 1970s, but it has declined in the 1980s, as local bargaining issues or problems have gained in importance over national agendas. However, Ford Motor Company may have been willing to guarantee job security in 1987 negotiations because it knew the UAW would demand similar guarantees from Ford's financially weaker competitors. So bargaining structures may even be factored into an organization's business strategy.

Formalizing the Contract

An agreement comes about when both sides feel they have produced the best contract they can. Their perceptions are influenced by the negotiations, their relative power at the time, and other factors. Power factors such as a weak union or a strong employer are very important in the settlement of the contract.

After the two sides have tentatively agreed, the union leadership must receive the membership's support. The members must ratify the contract. Ratification is not automatic and union negotiators must keep an eye toward membership ratifications or the negotiation process will have to be repeated.[19]

The agreement or contract sets out the rules of the job for the contract period. It restricts some behavior and requires other behavior. Proper wording of the agreement can prevent future difficulties in interpretation. Both sides should thoroughly discuss the meaning of each clause to prevent misunderstanding, if possible.

Even if the contract is accepted at one level, it may require adjustments at other levels. For example, when Ford Motor Company signs a contract with the UAW at the national level, local plants must then settle disputes on work rules and other issues at each plant. Only when these are settled is the contract negotiation process over for a while.

IMPASSES IN COLLECTIVE BARGAINING

The description of contract negotiation above suggests a smooth flow, from presentation of demands to settlement. This flow is not always so smooth; impasses may develop that do not allow one or both sides to keep the process moving. Three things can happen when an impasse develops: conciliation or mediation, a strike or lockout, or arbitration.

Conciliation and Mediation

Definition

Conciliation or *mediation* is the process by which a professional, neutral third party is invited in by both parties to help remove an impasse to the contract negotiations.

All experts agree that it is better for the two parties to negotiate alone. When it appears this process has broken down, however, they can invite in a mediator, usually a government mediator such as those provided by the Federal Mediation and Conciliation Service (FMCS). Some states also offer mediation services to both sides. FMCS offers such services as developing factual data if the two sides disagree, setting up joint study committees on difficult points, or trying to help the two sides find common grounds for further bilateral negotiations. Instead of waiting until an impasse, the FMCS also offers preventive mediation when the two parties anticipate serious problems prior to deadlines for strikes.

In general, fact-finding appears to work best when the negotiators are inexperienced and to be least effective when major differences exist between the expectations of each party to the dispute.

Mediators have no power to compel the two sides to reach an agreement. Instead, they seek to persuade employers and unions that it is in their best interests to reach an agreement without resorting to a strike.

Strikes and Lockouts

If an impasse in negotiations is quite serious, a strike or lockout can take place. A strike is a refusal by employees to work. A lockout is a refusal by management to allow employees to work.

Strikes can be categorized by the objectives they seek. A *contract* strike occurs when management and the union cannot agree on terms of a new contract. More than 90 percent of strikes are contract strikes.

A *grievance* strike occurs when the union disagrees on how management is interpreting the contract or handling day-to-day problems such as discipline. Strikes over grievances are prohibited in about 95 percent of contracts, but they occur fairly frequently in mining, transportation, and construction industries.

A *jurisdictional* strike takes place when two or more unions disagree on which jobs should be organized by each union. The Taft-Hartley Act gives the NLRB the power to settle these issues, and unions also have internal methods for settling them.

About 1 percent of strikes are *recognition* strikes. These occur as a strategy to force an employer to accept the union. *Political* strikes take place to influence government policy and are extremely rare in the United States.

Strikes differ, too, in the percentage of employees who refuse to work. A *total* strike takes place when all unionized employees walk out; if only a percentage of the workers does so, the result may be a partial strike, semi-strike, or slowdown. In a *slowdown*, all employees come to work but they do little work; the union insists on all work rules being followed to the letter, with the result that output slows down. This is also called "working to the contract." This old tactic is being used with increasing frequency, as an alternative to a total strike, because many employers are simply replacing striking workers with new hires.[20] In a *partial strike*, many employees strike but others come to work. This type is especially prevalent in the public sector so that essential services can be continued.

Public employees in the federal sector and in almost half of the states do not have the right to strike. Instead, impasses in negotiating contracts that cannot be resolved through mediation go to arbitration. However, arbitration is rarely used in negotiations in the private sector in the United States, although it is part of the contract administration process. Some countries do not make this sharp distinction between contract negotiation and contract administration. Their laws specify arbitration rather than strikes as the way to resolve any breakdowns in negotiations.

Anatomy of a Strike. For a strike to take place, both sides must make decisions. Management must decide it can afford to "take a strike"; that is, it has built up its inventories, has sufficient financial resources, feels it will not lose too many customers during a strike, and believes it can win. The union must believe it will win more than it loses, that the employer will not go out of business, and that management will not replace the union employees with strikebreakers. The union members must be willing to live with hardships and worries about no paychecks and be willing to give the union a strike vote. When members give the union the authority to strike, its bargaining hand is strengthened, and it can time the strike to occur when it will hurt management the most.

During the strike, the union sets up the legally allowed number of pickets at the plants and tries to mobilize support among allies in other unions and the public.

What does management do if there is a strike?[21] Lockouts are rarely used. In general, it tries to encourage the workers to return to work by advertising circulars, phone calls, and so on. The longer the strike, the harder it is on the strikers. If the union has only limited strike funds and workers' savings run out, a back-to-work movement can cause the strike to collapse. In recent years, management has tended to play a defensive "wait them out" game and to keep operating during a strike. Nonunionized employees such as white-collar workers and managers may try to keep things going, and if management goes on the offensive, it can hire strike-breakers or threaten to close the plant. A strike ends when both sides return to the bargaining table, or the weaker side gives in.[22]

Strikes or the threat of strikes do put added pressure on both sides to settle their differences. Most strikes do not seriously affect the public welfare, but if it appears this is the case, the Taft-Hartley Act allows the president to appoint a board of inquiry and issue an injunction for an 80-day cooling-off period. During this period, the employees are polled by secret ballot to see if they will accept the employer's latest offer.[23]

Who Strikes—and Why?

The threat of a strike is a powerful weapon. Managers need to assess the likelihood of a strike occurring. While only a small proportion of scheduled negotiations end in strikes, several factors correlate with the likelihood of a strike. Research shows that a strike is most likely if both sides are perceived to have equal strength, or that both sides will be hurt equally by a strike.[24] If the sides are not equal, the weaker side is forced to submit to the demands of the other, so no strike will occur. If an industry is booming, an employer gives in to union demands rather than losing production during a strike. If a local geographic area is booming (a tight local labor market), strikes increase because workers know they cannot be easily replaced, yet they may be able to pick up other jobs themselves. So economically it is a question of one side having more to lose than the other.

Organization conditions have a tremendous effect on the likelihood of a strike. Interestingly, the *variability* of the employer's profitability, rather than the *level* of profitability, affects strike activity.[25] If profit levels are volatile, both the incidence and duration of strikes increase. Perhaps this is because the uncertainty of the profit picture makes management less willing to make concessions and makes employees less confident in the competence of management.

The organization condition that appears to make the biggest difference in strike frequency is, not surprisingly, the quality of employee relations.[26] Employee relations is not only for nonunion employees. Dealing with union leadership is not the same as dealing with employees. Many employers learn this lesson the hard way. For example, the Timken Company negotiated a contract with United Steelworkers of America leadership in the fall of 1981. Union leaders confidently made many concessions in return for which the company pledged to build its new $500 million steel plant in Canton, Ohio, rather than in the Sunbelt. But the union failed to present the pact effectively and its membership rejected the contract.

Then Timken mounted a communications program aimed at rank-and-file members and their families. They held face-to-face meetings and also used newspapers and radio talk shows. The company encouraged employees and their spouses to ask questions and even set up an information hotline. The original proposal was resubmitted to the membership several weeks later, and this time it was ratified by a 10-to-1 vote.

One study compared differences between 28 companies that had experienced strikes and 28 unionized similar "nonstrike" companies.[27] In the strike companies, supervisors made no effort to resolve problems before they blossomed into formal grievances that took a long time to settle. Although both strike and nonstrike plants used overtime, the strike plants made overtime compulsory and made little effort to assist employees with the attendant family and job conflicts that inevitably resulted. In contrast, the nonstrike plants attempted to mitigate the unpleasant aspects of working long hours and management and union leadership met periodically but informally. The study concluded that "most strikes have little to do with money or benefits. Workers vote for a strike only when they are frustrated because their needs, wants, and ideas go unheard, unheeded, or unanswered." Nonstrike plants established a quality of trust through demonstration of good intentions. Unfortunately, trust does not lend itself to statistical reports. Therefore, it is easy for managers to place more emphasis on labor costs or hours worked when analyzing human resources, because these factors are readily quantifiable. The identifiable factors are too easily overlooked.

CONTRACT ADMINISTRATION

The labor contract governs the day-to-day employment relationships; it is a living document. The union steward and the supervisor are the principal interpreters and enforcers of the contract. Differences in interpretation are resolved through the grievance process. The grievance process is a mechanism for employees to voice their disagreement with the way the contract is administered; hence it is a key part of administering the contract.

Definition

A *grievance* is a formal dispute between an employee and management on the conditions of employment.

Grievances arise because of (1) differing interpretations of the contract by employees, stewards, and management; (2) a violation of a contract provision; (3) violation of law; (4) a violation of work procedures or other precedents; or (5) perceived unfair treatment of an employee by management. The rate of grievances may increase when employees are dissatisfied or frustrated on their jobs or they resent the supervisory style, or because the union is using grievances as a tactic against management.[28] Grievances may also be due to unclear contractual language or employees with personal problems or who are otherwise "difficult."

The U.S. Department of Labor has found that the most frequent incidents to lead to the filing of a grievance are employee discipline, seniority decisions at promotion or layoff time, work assignment, management rights, and compensation and benefits.[29]

The grievance process has at least three purposes and consequences. First, by settling smaller problems early, it may prevent larger problems from occurring in the future. Second, properly analyzed, grievances serve as a source of data to focus the attention of the two parties on ambiguities in the contract for negotiation at a future date. Finally, the grievance process is an effective communication channel from employees to management.[30]

Steps in the Grievance Process

The employee grievance process involves a systematic set of steps for handling an employee complaint. Most union contracts provide the channels and mechanisms for processing these grievances, though the process varies with the contract.

1. Initiation of the Formal Grievance. An employee who feels mistreated or believes that some action or application of policy violates rights in the contract files a grievance with the supervisor. It can be done in writing or (at least initially) orally. The grievance can be formulated with the help and support of the union steward. By far most of the grievances are settled at this level among the steward, the employee, and the supervisor.

The supervisor must attempt to accurately determine the reason for the grievance. The effective approach is to try to solve the problem, rather than assess blame or find excuses. The supervisor should consider what the contract says as modified by the employer's policies and past precedents in such cases. When the supervisor has a good working relationship with the steward, they can work together to settle the problem at that level.

2. Department Head or Unit Manager. If the steward, supervisor, and employee together cannot solve the grievance, it goes to the next level in the hierarchy. At this point, the grievance must be presented in writing, and both sides must document their cases.

3. Arbitration. If the grievance cannot be settled at this intervening step (or steps), an independent arbitrator may be called in to settle the issue.

Arbitration

Definition

Arbitration is the process by which two parties to a dispute agree in advance of the hearing to abide by the decision of an independent quasijudge called an arbitrator. In the United States, arbitration is typically used to settle grievance issues arising from contract *administration*.

No other topic in labor relations has more confusing jargon and labels. Arbitration refers to a process which ends in a decision, not a recommendation. Exhibit 17–8 shows Thomas Kochan's clarification of the different forms of arbitration. Under voluntary arbitration, the parties agree to submit their differences to arbitration, whereas under compulsory arbitration the law requires the parties' impasses to be submitted to arbitration. Compulsory arbitration in the United States is common only in the public sector, where employees may be legally forbidden to strike. Australia and some other countries specify compulsory arbitration for all labor disputes; no one has the right to strike. In these circumstances arbitration resolves disputes arising from contract administration *and* contract negotiation.

Under conventional arbitration, the arbitrator is free to generate any resolution that seems appropriate. Final-offer arbitration requires the arbitrator to choose either the employer's or the union's last proposal. Arbitrators may deal with a single issue or the total contract, and it may be done by a single individual or by a panel of arbitrators.

After hearing all the evidence, the arbitrator writes the arbitration award which is binding on both parties. The award normally reviews the facts in the case prior to stating the decision and usually is presented within 30 days of the hearing. The arbitrator writes the award in language understandable to all parties concerned, including the employee involved in a grievance. The award attempts to clarify the situation to prevent fu-

EXHIBIT 17–8
The Terminology of Alternative Forms of Arbitration

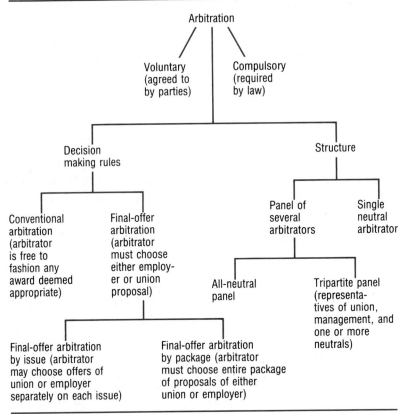

Source: Adapted from Thomas Kochan, *Collective Bargaining and Industrial Relations* (Homewood, Ill.: Richard D. Irwin, 1980), p. 290.

ture problems from arising. The arbitrator usually looks over previous arbitration awards in similar cases but need not be bound by them.

More than 75 percent of grievances are settled at the first step and another 20 percent are settled at the second.[31] Only about 1 percent go to arbitration. Studies of the personal characteristics of those who have filed grievances, as contrasted with those who have not, revealed some differences. In general, those who filed grievances were younger, had more formal education, and got more wage increases.[32] One study found gender differences in the handling of grievances: female employees are more likely to have disciplinary actions overturned than are males.[33] Of course, all these characteristics are probably secondary to the role of the union steward. The steward functions as a "gatekeeper" who can either encourage employees to file grievances (or even file in their behalf). Or the steward can seek to resolve problems informally, in consultation with management.

Handling grievances is time-consuming and expensive for both unions and management. A study of 15 grievances that went to arbitration and 15 that were taken only to informal mediation found that management and the union spent only a third as much money on mediation as on arbitration, and both spent less time in preparation for mediation.[34] Neither side showed a high level of dissatisfaction with mediation, though the two sides reported differing levels of satisfaction: The employee who filed the grievance and the union representatives were more satisfied with mediation than were the management representatives. Mediation resolved 11 of the 15 grievances. Those that were unresolved proceeded to binding arbitration, as specified in the union contract. So the sooner and more informally grievances or just complaints or inquiries can be handled, the better.

THE PUBLIC SECTOR

Public sector unions in the United States are relatively recent, although many other countries have had a long experience with them.[35] President John F. Kennedy granted modified rights to unionize and bargain over nonwage items in 1962. Since then unionization has spread to the majority of public employees. Even though subsequent presidential orders and legislation have extended bargaining rights, they still do not have the right to strike or bargain over wages. In 1981 the Professional Air Traffic Controllers Organization (PATCO) called a strike after negotiations broke down. Within hours, President Ronald W. Reagan appeared on national television and gave the workers 48 hours to return to work or be dismissed. About 11,400 of the strikers were dismissed, and PATCO's right to represent them was terminated, because it is also illegal to advocate a work stoppage among federal employees. In 1987, the air traffic controllers formed a new union with new leadership.

State and Local Employees

Almost all states have passed legislation providing state and local government employees the right to organize and bargain collectively. States with public sector laws tend to be those with a high percentage of unionized private-sector employees.[36] States with lower wages and weak organized labor have yet to pass similar laws.

EVALUATING THE EFFECTS OF LABOR RELATIONS ACTIVITIES

Labor relations and collective bargaining affect both efficiency and equity either positively or negatively. Economic theory depicts unions as a constraint on the organization.[37] In a competitive market, unions attempt to obtain monopolistic control over the supply of labor to raise wages above the market-determined rate. Moreover, as unions are likely to attempt to establish restrictive work rules to protect their members, productivity is likely to fall. Consequently, people frequently view unions as promoting inefficiency and inequality in society. Is that view accurate? Let us examine the research on the impact of unions.

Efficiency: Union Impact on Wages

Does the presence of a union in an organization raise the level of wages for workers above what it would be if the company was not unionized? The commonly held belief among workers is that unions do have a wage impact. Over 80 percent of the respondents to a Quality of Employment Survey conducted by the Survey Research Center of the University of Michigan believed that unions improve the wages of workers.[38] Efforts to determine if this perception is accurate have been a focus on research for at least 40 years.

Part of the reason for the continuing interest in this area is that the question of union impact on wages has not been totally resolved. Efforts to determine union impact on wages run into several measurement problems. The ideal situation would compare numerous organizations which were identical except for the presence or absence of a union.[39] Any wage differences among these organizations could then be attributed to the unionization. Unfortunately, few such situations exist. But even if they did, one could make the case that employers pay nonunionized employees wages close to those paid to union members to reduce the attractiveness of unions to employees. This union influence on nonunion wages and benefits is called a *spillover* effect.

Nevertheless, the best evidence we have suggests that unions do make a positive difference in wage levels, and the extent of the union effect varies over time.[40] During the 1932–33 period, union presence may have meant more than 25 percent higher wages for union versus nonunion workers. As the Great Depression receded in the late 1930s, the differential reached a low of 2 percent in the late 1940s.

The 1940s were also a period of government-imposed wage and price controls, which undoubtedly helped narrow the wage gap. The estimates do not include the value of fringe benefits, which got a big boost in the 1940s in unionized industries. So if wages and benefits were lumped together, the gap would, perhaps, be even wider.

The wage impact of unionization in the public sector appears to be smaller.[41] A summary of 13 public sector union studies concludes that the average wage effect of public sector unions is approximately +5 percent. This wage differential is smaller than typically assumed, and certainly smaller than the estimate for the private sector. The largest gains for public sector employees are reported for firefighters, with some studies reporting as much as an 18 percent wage differential attributable to the presence of a union. At the other extreme, however, teachers (primarily affiliates of the National Education Association and the American Federation of Teachers) have not fared as well, with reported wage impact of unionization generally in the range of 1 percent to 4 percent.

What Determines Union Wage Levels?

Our discussion here touches solely on the level of wages in unionized firms in comparison to the level of wages in nonunionized firms. Among the most important factors affecting wage levels in unionized organizations are the ability of an employer to pay, productivity, and changes in the cost of living.

Changes in Employer's Ability to Pay

In profitable years unions reason that part of the profits should accrue to the work force responsible for much of the organization's success. And in extremely unprofitable years, unions even offer wage concessions.[42] However, economists frequently describe wages as "sticky"; that is, they do not rise and fall readily in response to changes in economic conditions.[43] Because of the time lag built into labor contracts, wages do not rise as fast as profits do, nor fall as fast. So changes in wages typically lag behind changes in an employer's ability to pay.

Changes in the Cost of Living

A second factor affecting wage levels in unionized organizations is the linkage of wages to the change in cost of living. Intent on maintaining and improving the buying power of membership, unions made a strong drive for wage escalator clauses during the 1970s. Cost of Living Adjustments (COLA) automatically increase wages during the life of the contract as a function of changes in the consumer price index. By 1977, 61 percent of the workers covered by major bargaining agreements had COLAs in their contracts. Since then, the percentage has declined, partly because employment has been shrinking in some of the major unionized industries that have COLA clauses, and also because some unions have agreed to remove such clauses, in light of moderating increases in living costs.

Efficiency: Union Impact on Productivity

The model in Exhibit 17–9 indicates that unions can have a positive or negative effect on productivity. Which it will be depends on how management responds.[44] The model suggests some specific ways that union and employer behavior can affect productivity. Based on their analysis of the research, Richard Freeman and James Medoff conclude that "with management and unions working together to produce a bigger 'pie' as well as fighting over the size of their slices, productivity is likely to be higher under unionism. If industrial relations are poor, with management and labor ignoring common goals to battle one another, productivity is likely to be lower under unionism."[45]

Although the United States has the highest per worker productivity of any country in the world, yearly increases in productivity have lagged far behind most other industrial countries over the past decade.[46] Its productivity advantage is rapidly eroding. Many industries, most notably the steel industry, have already experienced huge losses in market share traceable in large part to poor improvements, or actual declines, in productiv-

EXHIBIT 17–9
Unionism and Productivity

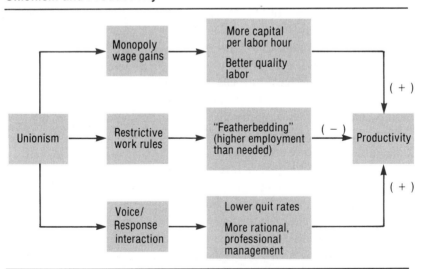

Source: Richard Freeman and James Medoff, *What Do Unions Do?* (New York: Basic Books, 1984). © 1984 by Basic Books, Inc., Publishers. Reprinted by permission of the publisher.

ity. This has led to an increasing effort to tie wage increases to productivity increases.[47] Incentive systems, profit-sharing plans, merit-based pay plans are all examples of efforts to make this productivity–wage link stronger. Even productivity bargaining and quality control circles show an increasing emphasis on the level of productivity in unionized and nonunionized organizations alike.

Equity: Union Impact on Employees' Voice

In addition to its effect on members' wages, the other positive effect claimed for unionism is that it provides workers a collective voice on subjects affecting their work.[48] By providing workers with a voice in work-related decisions, unions are likely to have a number of positive effects for both employees and organizations. First, unions act as *information collectors* for organizations, obtaining a clearer picture of the preferences of all employees rather than just new entrants to or leavers from organizations. As a result, employers are able to develop better personnel practices which reflect the needs of the existing work force. Second, unions are likely to *increase worker satisfaction by reducing inequality* among workers and guaranteeing some degree of due process in organizational decision making. Researchers, for example, discovered that unions have a significant positive effect on employees' satisfaction with pay.[49] However, job dissatisfaction appears to be higher among union members than nonunion members.[50] Steven Allen found substantially higher absenteeism rates among union members, too.[51] Since absenteeism can be interpreted as an expression of job dissatisfaction, it may be that any voice the union provides has only limited effect on job satisfaction.

Various writers have suggested that by providing workers with a voice to change organizational conditions, the probability of turnover is likely reduced. Freeman and Medoff found consistent evidence that union membership increased tenure and decreased turnover.[52] Some studies find turnover reductions as high as 50 percent attributable to the presence of a union.[53]

SUMMARY

Although it does not always live up to its potential, collective bargaining can provide the forum for a tremendous flexibility in labor-management relations. Contracts are revised on a regular schedule, and employees and employers can structure the contract to suit their particular objectives.

Although few employers invite a union to organize workers, most labor-management relationships evolve to a position of mutual respect.

However, managers have become more active and successful in resisting union organizing activities lately; in fact, their resistance is sometimes seen as a major factor in the decline in union membership.

If a union is certified, then union and management representatives begin the collective bargaining process. Collective bargaining involves both contract negotiation and administration. If the parties disagree during the negotiations, mediation may help them. If not, a strike or lockout may result. If the parties disagree about contract administration, the arbitration process provides a means to resolve the issue.

Unions affect both efficiency and equity because an effective union can provide employees a voice to change organization conditions and enhance equitable treatment of unionized employees. Efficiency is affected if having a more satisfied, stable, unionized work force results in higher productivity for the employer. However, unions can have a negative effect on productivity if work rules hinder performance. Whether or not the effect on productivity is positive depends on the quality of the employer-employee relationship.

DISCUSSION AND REVIEW QUESTIONS

1. Which factors seem to influence the outcome of a union certification election?
2. Contrast different methods of dispute settlement.
3. How do unions differ in the public sector?
4. How do unions affect productivity?
5. How do unions affect wages?

NOTES AND REFERENCES

1. Pat Choate and J. Linder, *The High-Flex Society* (New York: Alfred A. Knopf, 1986).
2. William Serrin, "AFL–CIO, Conceding Some of Labor's Problems, Offers Some Solutions," *New York Times*, February 22, 1985, p. A10.
3. Cathy Trost, "Three Labor Activists Lead a Growing Drive to Sign Up Women," *The Wall Street Journal*, January 29, 1985, pp. 1, 16.
4. Daniel D. Luria, "New Labor-Management Models from Detroit?" *Harvard Business Review*, September–October 1986, pp. 22–32; David P. Swinehart and Mitchell A. Sherr, "A Systems Model for Labor-Management Cooperation," *Personnel Administrator*, April 1986, pp. 87–98; M. Schuster, "The Impact of Union-Management Cooperation on Productivity and Employment," *Industrial and Labor Relations Review* 36, no. 3 (1983), pp

415–30; M. Schuster, *Union–Management Cooperation: Structure, Process and Implementation* (Kalamazoo, Mich.: W. E. Upjohn Institute for Employment Research, 1984).

5. Julius G. Getman, Stephen B. Goldberg, and Jeanne B. Herman, *Union Representation Elections: Law and Reality* (New York: Russell Sage Foundation, 1976); *Strike Preparation Manual* (Berea, Ohio: American Society for Personnel Administration, 1983).

6. Getman, et al., Union Elections.

7. John E. Abodeely, Randi C. Hammer, and Andrew L. Sandler, *The NLRB and the Appropriate Bargaining Unit* (Philadelphia: Industrial Research Unit, University of Pennsylvania, 1981).

8. Jeanne M. Brett, "Why Employees Want Unions," *Organizational Dynamics*, Spring 1980, pp. 316–32; Cynthia Fukami and Erik W. Larson, "Commitment to Company and Union: Parallel Models," *Journal of Applied Psychology* 69, no. 3 (1984), pp. 367–71; Mary D. Zalesny, "Comparison of Economic and Noneconomic Factors in Predicting Faculty Note Preference in a Union Representation Election," *Journal of Applied Psychology* 70, no. 2 (1985), pp. 243–56; H. G. Heneman III and Marcus H. Sandver, "Predicting the Outcome of Union Certification Elections," *Industrial and Labor Relations* 36 (1983), pp. 537–59.

9. William T. Dickens and Jonathan S. Leonard, "Accounting for the Decline in Union Membership," 1984, National Bureau of Economic Research, 1050 Massachusetts Ave., Cambridge, Mass. 02138.

10. John J. Lawler and Robin West, "Impact of Union Avoidance Strategy in Representation Elections," *Industrial Relations*, Fall 1985, pp. 406–20.

11. Richard B. Freeman, "The Effect of the Union Wage Differential on Management Opposition and Union Organizing Success," *American Economics Association Papers and Proceedings*, May 1986, pp. 92–108; Barry T. Hirsch and John T. Addison, *Economic Analysis of Labor Unions—New Approaches and Evidence* (Boston: George Allen and Unwin, 1986).

12. Lawler and West, "Impact of Union Avoidance Strategy."

13. Ellen R. Pierce and Richard Blackburn, "The Union Decertification Process: Employer Dos and Don'ts," *Employee Relations Law Journal* 12, no. 2 (1986), pp. 205–20; William J. Bigoness and Henry L. Tosi, "Correlates of Voting Behavior in a Union Decertification Election" (working paper, University of North Carolina, 1985); John Kilgour, "Decertifying a Union: A Matter of Choice," *Personnel Administrator*, July 1987, pp. 42–51.

14. Sanford M. Jacoby and Daniel J. B. Mitchell, "Development of Contractual Features of the Union-Management Relationship," *Proceedings of the Industrial Relations Research Association, Spring Meeting*, April 28–30, 1982, pp. 512–17; Carl Gersuny, "Origins of Seniority Provisions in Collective Bargaining," *Proceedings of the Industrial Relations Research Association, Spring Meeting*, April 28–30, 1982, pp. 518–23.

15. Lee Balliet, "Labor Solidarity and the Two-Tier Collective Bargaining Agreement" (paper presented at the IRRA Meetings, Dallas, Texas, December 30, 1984); James E. Martin and Melanie M. Peterson, "Two-Tier Wage Structures: Implications for Equity Theory," *Academy of Management Jour-*

nal, June 1987, pp. 297–315; Sanford Jacoby and Dan J. B. Mitchell, "Management Attitudes toward Two-Tier Pay Plans," *Journal of Labor Research* 7 (1986), pp. 221–37.

16. *Teamsters v. United States,* 431 U.S., 324 (1977); *Memphis Fire Department v. Stotts,* No. 82–206 (Decided June 12, 1984). For a discussion of seniority and affirmative action, see Louis P. Britt III, "Affirmative Action: Is There Life After *Stotts?" Personnel Administrator,* September 1984, pp. 96–100; and Lawrence Z. Lorber, "Employers Should Not Take Precipitous Action in Affirmative Action Cases," *Personnel Administrator,* September 1984, pp. 101–2.

17. Richard Prosten, "The Longest Season: Union Organizing in the Last Decade," *Proceedings of the Industrial Relations Research Association,* Winter 1979, pp. 240–49.

18. Charles McDonald, "Study of the Success in Obtaining Contracts after Winning an NLRB Election and after Obtaining a Bargaining Order," memorandum to the National Organizing Committee of the AFL–CIO, February 18, 1983. The study covered elections conducted in April 1979 through March 1981.

19. Peter F. Drucker, "Are Unions Becoming Irrelevant?" *The Wall Street Journal,* September 22, 1982, p. 34.

20. Alex Kotlowiz, "Finding Strikes Harder to Win, More Unions Turn to Slowdowns," *The Wall Street Journal,* May 22, 1987, pp. 1, 8.

21. *Strike Preparation Manual;* John P. Kohl and David B. Stephens, "Replacement Workers during Strikes," *Personnel Journal,* April 1986, pp. 93–98.

22. P. K. Edwards, *Strikes in the United States 1881–1974* (New York: St. Martin's Press, 1981); Charles R. Perry, Andrew M. Kramer, and Thomas J. Schneider, *Operating during Strikes* (Philadelphia: the Wharton School of Industrial Research Unit, February 1982); Sanford M. Jacoby, "Union-Management Cooperation in the United States: Lessons from the 1920s," *Industrial and Labor Relations Review,* October 1983, pp. 18–33; Herbert R. Northrup, "The New Employee-Relations Climate in Airlines," *Industrial and Labor Relations Review,* January 1983, pp. 167–81.

23. U.S. Bureau of Labor Statistics, *Work Stoppages, 1980* (Washington, D.C.: U.S. Government Printing Office, 1981); Robert H. Zieger, "Industrial Relations and Labor History in the Eighties," *Industrial Relations,* Winter 1983, pp. 58–70.

24. Bruce E. Kaufman, "Interindustry Trends in Strike Activity," *Industrial Relations,* Winter 1983, pp. 45–57; Sean Flaherty, "Contract Status and the Economic Determinants of Strike Activity," *Industrial Relations,* Winter 1983, pp. 20–33; J. Paul Leigh, "Risk Preference and the Interindustry Propensity to Strike," *Industrial and Labor Relations Review,* January 1983, pp. 271–85; and Margaret A. Neale and Max H. Bagerman, "The Effects of Framing and Negotiator Overconfidence on Bargaining Behaviors and Outcomes," *Academy of Management Journal* 28, no. 1 (1985), pp. 34–49.

25. Joseph S. Tracy, "An Investigation into the Determinants of U.S. Strike Activity," *The American Economics Review,* June 1986, pp. 423–36.

26. Tom Kochan, Robert McKersie, and Harry Katz, *The Transformation of American Industrial Relations* (New York: Basic Books, 1986); Dennis

Maki, "The Effect of the Cost of Strikes on the Volume of Strike Activity," *Industrial and Labor Relations Review*, July 1986, pp. 552–63.

27. Woodruff Imberman, "Who Strikes—And Why?" *Harvard Business Review*, November–December 1983, pp. 18–24.

28. Thomas A. Kochan, Mordechai Mironi, Ronald G. Ehrenberg, Jean Baderschneider, and Todd Jick, *Dispute Resolution under Factfinding and Arbitration: An Empirical Analysis* (New York: American Arbitration Association, 1979); Stephen B. Goldberg and Jeanne M. Brett, "An Experiment in the Mediation of Grievances," *Monthly Labor Review*, March 1983, pp. 23–30.

29. *Federal Mediation and Conciliation Service, Thirty-Sixth Annual Report, Fiscal Year 1983* (Washington, D.C.: U.S. Government Printing Office, 1984).

30. "Avoiding the Arbitrator: Some New Alternatives to the Grievance Procedure," *Proceedings, 30th Annual Meeting Washington, D.C.: National Academy of Arbitrators*, 1977; Steven Briggs, "Beyond the Grievance Procedure: Factfinding in Employee Complaint Resolution," *Proceedings of the Industrial Relations Research Association Spring Meeting*, April 1982, pp. 454–58; Mollie H. Bowers, Ronald L. Seeber, and Lamont E. Stallworth, "Grievance Mediation: A Route to Resolution for the Cost-Conscious 1980s," *Proceedings of the Industrial Relations Research Association, Spring Meeting*, April 1982, pp. 459–63.

31. Dan R. Dalton and William D. Todor, "Antecedents of Grievance Filing Behavior: Attitude/Behavioral Consistency and the Union Steward," *Academy of Management Journal* 25, no. 1 (1982), pp. 158–60.

32. Arnold M. Zack, "Suggested New Approaches to Grievance Arbitration," *Proceedings of the 30th Annual Meeting National Academy of Arbitrators* (Washington, D.C.: Bureau of National Affairs, 1978), pp. 105–20; Mollie H. Bowers, "Grievance Mediation: Settle Now, Don't Pay Later," *Federal Service Labor Relations Review 3*, Spring 1981, pp. 25–35; Marcus Sandver, Harry Blaine, and Mark Woyar, "Time and Cost Savings though Expedited Arbitration Procedures: Evidence from Five Industrial Settings," *Arbitration Journal*, December 1981, pp. 11–20; Thomas R. Knight, "Feedback and Grievance Resolution," *Industrial and Labor Relations Review*, July 1986, pp. 585–98.

33. Dan R. Dalton and William D. Todor, "Gender and Workplace Justice: A Field Assessment," *Personnel Psychology* 38 (1985), pp. 133–51; Dan R. Dalton and William D. Todor, "Composition of Dyads as a Factor in the Outcomes of Workplace Justice: Two Field Assessments," *Academy of Management Journal* 28, no. 3 (1985), pp. 704–12.

34. Sylvia Skratek, *Grievance Mediation of Contractual Disputes in Washington State Public Education* (Federal Way, Wash.: Washington Education Association, 1986).

35. John Fossum, *Labor Relations*, 3rd ed. (Plano, Tex.: Business Publications, 1985).

36. Thomas A. Kochan, "Correlates of State Public Employee Bargaining Laws," *Industrial Relations*, October 1973, pp. 322–37; Craig A. Olson, "The Use of the Legal Right to Strike in the Public Sector," *Proceedings of the Industrial Relations Research Association Spring Meeting*, April 1982,

pp. 494–500; Douglas M. McCabe, "Problems in Federal Sector Labor-Management Relations under Title VII of the Civil Service Reform Act of 1978," *Proceedings of the Industrial Relations Research Association Spring Meeting*, April 1982, pp. 560–64; Craig Olson, "Strikes, Strike Penalties, and Arbitration in Six States," *Industrial and Labor Relations Review*, July 1986, pp. 539–51; James E. Martin, "A Framework for Analyzing Public-Sector Union–Management Relations: An Exploration with Six Cases," *Quarterly Review of Economics and Business*, Spring 1980, pp. 49–62; James E. Martin, "Federal Union-Management Relations: A Longitudinal Study," *Public Administration Review*, September–October 1980, pp. 434–42; Henry S. Farber, *Right-to-Work Laws and the Extent of Unionization* (Cambridge, Mass.: National Bureau of Economic Research working paper no. 1136, 1983).

37. Robert J. Flanagan, Robert S. Smith, and Ronald G. Ehrenberg, *Labor Economics and Labor Relations* (Glenview, Ill.: Scott, Foresman, 1984); Milton Friedman and Rose Friedman, *Free to Choose* (New York: Harcourt Brace Jovanovich, 1980); Edward P. Lazear, "A Competitive Theory of Monopoly Unionism," *The American Economic Review*, September 1983, pp. 631–41.

38. Thomas A. Kochan, "How American Workers View Labor Unions," *Monthly Labor Review*, April 1979, pp. 23–31.

39. Fossum, *Labor Relations;* James E. Long and Albert N. Link, "The Impact of Market Structure on Wages, Fringe Benefits, and Turnover," *Industrial and Labor Relations Review*, January 1983, pp. 239–50.

40. Peter Linneman and Michael L. Wachter, "Rising Union Premiums and the Declining Boundaries among Noncompeting Groups," *AEA Papers and Proceedings*, May 1986, pp. 103–7; George Johnson, "Changes over Time in the Union/Nonunion Wage Differential in the United States" (mimeographed, Ann Arbor: University of Michigan, February 1981); Richard B. Freeman and James L. Medoff, "The Impact of Collective Bargaining: Illusion or Reality," in *U.S. Industrial Relations 1950–1980: A Critical Assessment*, ed. J. Steiber, R. B. McKersie, D. Q. Mills (Madison, Wisc.: Industrial Relations Research Association Series, 1981), pp. 47–98; H. Gregg Lewis, "Union Relative Wage Effects: A Survey of Macro Estimates," *Journal of Labor Economics*, January 1983, pp. 1–27; G. G. Cain, B. E. Becker, C. G. McLaughlin, and A. E. Schwenk, "The Effect of Unions on Wages in Hospitals," *Research in Labor Economics* 4 (1981), pp. 191–320; B. T. Hirsch, "The Inter-Industry Structure of Unionism, Earnings, and Earnings Dispersion," *Industrial and Labor Relations Review*, October 1982, pp. 22–39; Mark R. Killingsworth, "Union-Nonunion Wage Differentials: Estimates from a New Industry Cross-Section" (mimeographed, New Brunswick, N.J.: Rutgers University, 1981); Jacob Miner, *Union Effects: Wages, Turnover, and Job Training* (New York: Columbia University Press, 1981); Wallace E. Hendricks and Lawrence M. Kahn, "The Determinants of Bargaining Structure in U.S. Manufacturing Industries," *Industrial and Labor Relations Review*, January 1982, pp. 181–95.

41. David Lewin, "Public Sector Labor Relations: A Review Essay," in *Public Sector Labor Relations: Analysis and Readings*, ed. D. Lewin, P. Feuille, and T. Kochan (Glen Ridge, N.Y.: Thomas Horton and Daughters, 1977).

42. Sar Levitan and Clifford M. Johnson, "Labor and Management: The Illusion of Cooperation," *Harvard Business Review*, September–October 1983, pp. 8–16; D. Quinn Mills, "When Employees Make Concessions," *Harvard Business Review*, May–June 1983, pp. 103–13; John B. Taylor, *Union Settlements during a Disinflation*," *American Economic Review*, December 1983, pp. 981–93; Thomas Kochan and Peter Cappelli, "The Transformation of the Industrial Relations and Personnel Function" (working paper, Sloan School of Management, 1983).

43. Freeman and Medoff, "Impact of Collective Bargaining."

44. A. C. Brown and J. Medoff, "Trade Unions in the Production Process," *Journal of Political Economy*, June 1978, pp. 355–78; J. Frantz, *The Impact of Trade Unions on Productivity in the Wood Household Furniture Industry* (undergraduate thesis, Cambridge, Mass.: Harvard University, 1976); S. Allen, "Unionized Construction Workers Are More Productive" (mimeographed, Greensboro: North Carolina State University, 1981); K. Clark, "The Impact of Unionization on Productivity: A Case Study," *Industrial and Labor Relations Review*, July 1980; M. Connerton, R. B. Freeman, and J. L. Medoff, "Industrial Relations and Productivity: A Study of the U.S. Bituminous Coal Industry" (1983 revision, mimeographed, Cambridge, Mass.: Harvard University).

45. Richard B. Freeman and James L. Medoff, *What Do Unions Do?* (New York: Basic Books, 1984), p. 165.

46. D. Quinn Mills, "Reforming the U.S. System of Collective Bargaining," *Monthly Labor Review*, March 1983, pp. 18–22; Robert Guenther, "Plan for Construction Productivity Stirs Industry, Takes Aim at Unions," *The Wall Street Journal*, April 21, 1983, p. 35.

47. Robert B. McKersie and Lawrence C. Hunter, *Pay, Productivity, and Collective Bargaining* (New York: St. Martin's Press, 1973); William F. Maloney, *Productivity Bargaining: A Study in Contract Construction* (Ph.D. dissertation, Ann Arbor: University of Michigan, 1976); Michael Schuster, *Labor-Management Productivity Programs: Their Operation and Effect on Employment and Productivity* (Syracuse, N.Y.: School of Management, Syracuse University, 1980); Kim B. Clark, *Unionization and Firm Performance: The Impact on Profits, Growth, and Productivity* (Cambridge, Mass.: National Bureau of Economic Research working paper No. 990, 1982).

48. Albert O. Hirschman, *Exit, Voice, and Loyalty* (Cambridge, Mass.: Harvard University Press, 1971); Richard B. Freeman and James L. Medoff, "The Two Faces of Unionism," *The Public Interest*, Fall 1979, pp. 69–93; R. B. Freeman, "The Exit–Voice Trade-Off in the Labor Market: Unionism, Job Tenure, Quits, and Separations," *Quarterly Journal of Economics* 94 (1980), pp. 6433–74; Francine Blau and Lawrence Kahn, "The Exit–Voice Model of Unionism: Some Further Evidence on Layoffs" (paper, Champaign, University of Illinois, 1980).

49. Chris J. Berger, Craig A. Olson, and John W. Boudreau, "Effects of Unions on Job Satisfaction: The Role of Work-Related Values and Perceived Rewards" (working paper, Krannert Graduate School of Management, Purdue University, 1983).

50. Michael E. Gordon, Laura L. Beauvais, and Robert T. Ladd, "The Job Satisfaction and Union Commitment of Unionized Engineers," *Industrial*

and Labor Relations Review, April 1984, pp. 359–71; Michael E. Gordon and Sandra J. Miller, "Grievances: A Review of Research and Practice," *Personnel Psychology,* Spring 1984, pp. 117–46.

51. Steven G. Allen, "Trade Unions, Absenteeism, and Exit–Voice," *Industrial and Labor Relations Review,* April 1984, pp. 331–45.

52. Freeman and Medoff, *What Do Unions Do?*

53. Francine D. Blau and Lawrence M. Kahn, "Unionism, Seniority, and Turnover," *Industrial Relations,* Fall 1983, pp. 362–73.

PART FIVE CASES

▶ ITHACA'S OWN
Case 6 THE JACK FREELANCE AFFAIR

The director of human resource management is seeking your recommendation on what everybody in the office is calling the "Jack Freelance Affair." The director gave you the assignment late Friday afternoon and asked you to have a recommendation on his desk first thing Monday morning. All the data on the affair is in the materials which follow. Unfortunately, you will not be able to contact any of the parties involved over the weekend.

There are five pieces of information in the file the director gave you.

1. Case background.
2. Jack Freelance Case Review (prepared by a HR staff person).
3. March 15, 1988, memo to file from M. Hill (Freelance's manager).
4. April 20, 1988, memo to file from M. Hill.
5. May 6, 1988, memo to the HR Director from M. Hill, Manager of R&D.

Discussion Questions

You are to read the following case file and prepare a recommendation for the director. During your review, consider the following.
1. How fairly was Jack Freelance treated?
2. What steps for "due process" should be followed?
3. Which options in addition to termination are open to Ithaca's Own?
4. What are potential consequences if Jack is not terminated, as M. Hill recommends?
5. What are potential consequences if Jack is terminated?
6. What is your specific recommendation? (Choose one and support your decision.)

a. Terminate now.

b. Add supportive data to the file and then terminate.

c. Demote.

d. Reassign.

e. Investigate more extensively (be very specific about how long you would investigate and what data you would collect).

f. Suspension (how long?).

7. What procedures should I-O consider putting in place to help handle situations like this in the future?

Case Background

Jack Freelance is an associate scientist who has worked at I-O for four years. During this time, he worked for the same manager and received consistently "good" ratings each year. One year ago a new manager was assigned to supervise Jack. Due to changing I-O strategies and goals, the new manager decided to review and revise the department's objectives. The new manager noticed that all of his staff, with the exception of Jack, were relatively new in their jobs. In fact, all except Jack had less than one year's experience. Considering this experience, he felt Jack should perform at a higher level. He met with Jack at the beginning of the year and agreed to change the expected number of projects completed from 8 for the year to 12 in order to achieve a good rating. The rest of the staff, based on experience level, was kept at around 8 projects.

About halfway through the year, Jack and he met again to review how things were going. Jack was well behind the agreed-upon target. So the manager counseled him and made suggestions as to how the performance might be improved. An agreement was made to check progress three months later.

At this progress review, the performance was still less than the expected level. When questioned about the matter, Jack responded by saying, "Why should I be expected to complete 12 projects when everyone else only has to finish 8?" The manager responded by saying, "As we agreed at the beginning of the year, your experience and contacts in this area should enable you to perform at a higher standard." The entire meeting was documented, and Jack was warned that he must bring his performance up to standard by year's end. He was given written notice of his performance problem and the potential consequences of it, that is, conditional performance rating and possible dismissal.

At the year-end performance review, Jack's performance level still did not meet the supervisor's expectation. He received a conditional rating. Prior to meeting with Jack, his supervisor consulted with the human resources manager. It was decided to tell Jack that he had 60 days to correct his performance. If it did not improve, a recommendation for termination would be made. In the meeting, Jack was given final counseling, clearly stating the problems, and steps to resolve the issue. The meeting was documented, and although the documentation was reviewed by Jack, he refused to sign it as he felt the manager had set too high a standard for evaluation.

It is now 50 days into the 60 day period, and the manager has asked the director of human resources to agree with a recommendation for dismissal.

Jack Freelance Case Review

Jack Freelance is a white male, age 46, with a heart condition (angina pectoris—a condition marked by recurrent pains in the chest and left arm, caused by sudden decrease of blood supply to the heart). Medication required, nitroglycerin tablets.

Married, with three children, ages 18, 16, and 12.

Education
BS in chemistry from Rutgers University. Two years ago he began taking courses at Cornell University for a master's degree in chemistry, but stopped midway through his second semester.

Past Employment
Jack was first employed as a laboratory technician at Downstate Medical Center for three years while completing his BS degree. Upon completion of his degree he moved to Rochester and worked in New Product Technology at Kodak for 10 years. Jack supervised eight employees in the department while at Kodak. He later joined the R&D group in Corning Glass as an associate researcher, where he remained for the nine years prior to coming with Ithaca's Own. At the time he was hired as an assistant scientist at I-O, Jack received excellent recommendations from former employers.

Employment History with Ithaca's Own
Jack has been employed with the organization for four years and six months. He was originally hired as an assistant scientist at I-O, and was promoted to associate scientist two and a half years ago. His performance history has been good. Jack is currently the senior associate scientist in the R&D department. Although his actual job duties do not include supervision of other scientists, Jack assisted in training new recruits in the department and informally directs less-experienced scientists on projects.

Memo to File: Counseling Session with Jack Freelance

On March 15, 1988, Jack Freelance was counseled by me regarding his job responsibilities as an Associate Scientist at I-O. Specifically, he was told that his behavior of March 14, not informing me that he was leaving for the remainder of the day, was conduct not appropriate for his level and would not be tolerated.

Jack was informed that if he demonstrated this type of behavior again, it could possibly result in termination.

Jack was asked for his comments. He stated that the action being taken against him was extremely unfair and that he thought it was happening not because he left for the day without informing me, but because I suspected that he had informed OSHA of the violation.

I stressed to Jack that he was being counseled for leaving for the day without informing me of his whereabouts and the session ended.

_____

Jane Johnson, Human Resource Manager, R&D

_____

M. Hill, Manager, R&D

_____

Jack Freelance, Assoc. Sci., R&D

Two months after his promotion to associate scientist and prior to the new manager taking over, Jack was reprimanded for leaving hazardous chemicals at his work station after closing. This was discussed with him and he was told that it was not to happen again.

Seven months after the incident, his manager changed, as did the focus of his job. More emphasis was placed on individual project work as opposed to training and assisting other scientists. Everyone felt that he

Memo to File: Counseling Session with Jack Freelance
April 20, 1988

    Jack Freelance was again counseled regarding his responsibilities as an Associate Scientist at I-O. Jack did not adhere to proper operational procedures. Specifically, he had neglected to follow through on a product-testing project assigned to him and instead delegated the project to another Associate Scientist. Four days after the situation was brought to his attention, Jack had not yet approached the other scientist regarding his intention to resume the project. This type of neglect is intolerable in light of the stringent deadlines for completion of each project. In addition, Jack admitted that he had not assumed nor assisted in another project since his disposal of the product-testing project.

    I further advised Jack that as a result of his negligence of April 20, if another infraction of any kind occurred, I would have no other alternative but to recommend his termination. Jack was given an opportunity to comment and he indicated that he had none.

                               Jane Johnson

Mervin Hill

                               Jack Freelance

had the background and experience to continue in a largely self-directed, highly technical position. It was also decided that there was no need to write a job description, since this was merely a change in priorities.

When the new manager assumed responsibility, Jack informed him of a safety problem in the facility. Specifically, the building was old and it had a deteriorating asbestos ceiling about which Jack claimed he received

May 6, 1988

TO: Director of Human Resources
FROM: M. Hill, Manager R&D

Jack Freelance was counseled today as he again did not adhere to proper operational procedures. Jack committed a serious infraction by signing the results of a product-safety testing project, implying that he was responsible for the results, while another scientist had in fact completed the project. Due to the emphasis on integrity in research at I-O, Jack knew this was an infraction which could have very serious consequences.

I had previously informed him that if another problem of any kind occurred, I would recommend termination. Jack was asked if he had any comments and he responded:

"I have personal knowledge that it is not uncommon for experienced scientists to delegate the final stage of a project to a co-worker in order to begin a new project. Principal Scientists do this from time to time and are still employed at I-O."

I informed Jack that these Principal Scientists were not in my realm of responsibility, but he was, and although this is unfortunate, he did violate I-O procedures and demonstrated conduct and poor judgment not appropriate to his level. Therefore, my decision to terminate him stands.

Jack was told that if he wished, he could contact higher authority or the human resource manager of R&D.

several complaints from fellow employees. Jack further stated that he had reported this problem to his previous supervisor on several occasions and nothing had been done.

The new manager told him to ignore the complaints as no problems had resulted thus far. It seemed like a minor detail at the time.

About two weeks later, an OSHA representative formally investigated an anonymous complaint and determined that the ceiling was in fact made of asbestos, was in a deteriorating condition and constituted a serious health hazard. OSHA ordered immediate correction of the problem, which required implementing $150,000 worth of repairs to the ceiling. The new management wasn't sure that Jack had informed OSHA of the problem, but very strongly suspected that he had.

When the facility reopened, Jack was directly accused by his manager of informing OSHA of the safety violation. Jack became so upset over the accusation that he had to take his angina medication and he left the facility without informing his supervisor. Upon his return the next day, he was immediately counseled by his supervisor. At the close of the counseling session, his manager stated that it had come to his attention that Jack was on medication for a heart condition. It was further stated that this was of concern as the job is changing and the job is going to become more stressful.

One month later it was discovered that Jack had neglected to finish a project involving product safety testing and he had instead turned it over to a fellow associate scientist for completion. The incident was brought to the attention of Jack's manager who instructed Jack to resume the project himself and complete it within the three-week deadline. Both Jack and the manager agreed that the situation had been a misunderstanding caused by some ambiguity in the division of work assignments.

Four days later, however, the manager learned that Jack had not contacted the other scientist with regard to the safety testing project, nor had he begun the preliminary research for the next project. Jack again was counseled regarding the incident.

Three weeks later Jack's manager received the product safety testing project with Jack's signature on the final results, but soon discovered that the other associate scientist, not Jack, had actually completed it. Jack was again counseled and the incident was documented. Jack's manager then called R&D's manager of human resources, informed him of the last incident and requested termination.

▶ TYLER MANUFACTURING COMPANY

Tyler Manufacturing Company is a medium-sized firm producing parts for the auto industry. The firm fabricates major metal subassemblies for autos and sells its products on contract to such firms as General Motors, Ford, Chrysler. Tyler's main plant is located in the Detroit, Michigan, area, but it has a branch plant in California and another in the East.

Tyler has always had good employee relations. Their wages and benefits have always exceeded the industry's. Tyler has a company union. Recently the union leadership asked to see the vice president, Vance Henry. The union leader, Peter Vuychich, said: "Mr. Henry, at our most recent get-together, someone brought up the subject of the four-day week. As you know, the *Detroit Free Press* carried an article on this and the TV has played it up some. Some of the workers have boats and others like to hunt. This appeals to them since they could take longer breaks that way. We'd like to give it a try."

Vance said: "Well, Peter, it's a big step. Let me give it some thought." After checking around with other personnel people and reading up on the topic, Vance decided to experiment with it, but in the Detroit plant only. He asked Peter to come in again. After a brief discussion of the Lions game the previous weekend, he said: "Look, Peter, about your request on the four-day week. You know we've always gone along with what the employees want. I'm willing to try it and the president, Archibald Seeley, says he is too, if the employees want it. Take a mail poll and let me know how it comes out."

The union polled the workers and 85 percent favored the move. The new arrangement called for work on Monday through Thursday, 7 A.M. to 6 P.M., with a half hour for lunch and a 15-minute break midmorning and midafternoon.

About a month after the experiment started, a rush order came in from General Motors. This required some overtime work. There was a lot of grumbling about Friday and Saturday work. A typical comment was found in the suggestion box: "You'll kill us with this pace—six-day 60-hour weeks—leaves us no time for our families."

Vance and Richard Peterson, operations manager at the plant, looked over the productivity figures. They found that quality had dropped (reject rates went up 10 percent from inspectors) and output rate had dropped 5 percent. This upset them both a great deal. Richard said: "You know, Vance, this is all due to your damn experiment. You never asked me about it before you started, but I knew it would never work. I'll bet those last couple of hours per day are killing us. I'll get some data on productivity per half day and check it out."

Three weeks later, Richard returned with the data. During these weeks, two weeks had had no overtime, one had overtime. The productivity data were worked up to compare an "average" week before the change with these weeks (see Exhibit 1).

Richard said, "Vance, as you can see, this experiment is a disaster. We talked to the employees about the productivity drop, emphasizing that if they wanted to keep the experiment going, they'd have to get production up. As you see, on some of the days, they did. But the later in the week

EXHIBIT 1
Productivity Data for Tyler Manufacturing: Four-Day Week and Overtime Week Compared to Previous Five-Day-Week Figures

	Monday	Tuesday	Wednesday	Thursday	Friday	Saturday
Week 1						
Morning	Same	Same	−1%	−2%		
Afternoon	Same	Same	−1%	−2%		
Week 2						
Morning	+2%	+1%	Same	Same	−1%	−2%
Afternoon	Same	Same	−1%	−2%	−2%	−3%
Week 3						
Morning	+2%	+1%	Same	−2%		
Afternoon	Same	Same	−1%	−2%		

it got, the worse things were. And quality figures parallel these quantity figures. The work is just too heavy for these hours."

Vance agreed something had to be done. He called Peter in, explained the situation, and said: "I'm thinking of dropping the four-day week. My bet is that people have lost some of their enthusiasm too. Let's see."

The poll results came in: 65 percent said they'd like to continue the experiment, 35 percent wanted to revert. Vance is wondering how to handle the situation now.

Discussion Questions

1. You are Vance. How do you handle the situation?
2. What do the statistics prove about the productivity or unproductivity of the employees?
3. What part should the union play in the decision?

▶ FLINT MEMORIAL HOSPITAL*

Flint Memorial is a large proprietary hospital. It is located in a growing, progressive city. Originally built about 20 years ago, it is now in the midst of a large expansion program. Soon the original 250-bed capacity will have been enlarged to accommodate about 800 beds. The hospital has enjoyed increasingly good public relations recently because of good patient service

---

*Note: This case is from Richard P. Calhoun, *Cases in Personnel Management and Supervision,* © 1966, pp. 17–20. Reprinted by permission of Prentice-Hall, Inc., Englewood Cliffs, New Jersey.

EXHIBIT 1
Organization Chart: Flint Memorial Hospital

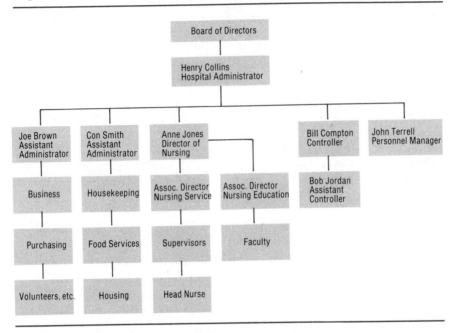

and a fine school of nursing. An organization chart showing hospital administration is shown in Exhibit 1.

Many changes have taken place in the administrative staff during the past two years. A new, well-qualified hospital administrator was employed. About the time he arrived, several members of the staff left. Anne Jones, the director of nursing, was employed to replace the former director. This position involved both nursing service and nursing education. An experienced nursing administrator, Miss Jones held an MS degree in nursing from a well-known university.

The morale of the nursing staff and faculty had been affected adversely by years of inadequate leadership. Henry Collins, the new administrator, was anxious to do something about this morale problem. When he told Miss Jones that she had been employed to meet the growing needs of the hospital and that he expected changes to be made, Miss Jones replied that she intended to make haste slowly. Each agreed that too much change might be even more detrimental to morale during this period of adjustment. Collins delegated responsibility readily. Conditions seemed to improve gradually.

Miss Jones surveyed her staff and concluded that it was above average. The members of the staff with whom she had held discussions seemed friendly and willing to cooperate. The supervisors and faculty members seemed to accept her readily. In reviewing the personnel policies that affected her employees she realized that no policy changes had been made in years; she was anxious to begin making some necessary revisions. Soon she began holding meetings with the staff to find areas of weakness and of strength.

New problems arose daily, now in nursing service, now in nursing education. Miss Jones and the faculty reviewed the rules and regulations for the student nurses and revised these in the light of present-day democratic principles. Revision was time-consuming and left little time to work on the problems of the staff of nursing service; this was the most pressing need of the moment.

John Terrell, the personnel manager, had been employed about four months after Miss Jones, to head a newly established personnel department. Miss Jones worked cooperatively with the personnel department, transferring records, putting in job requisitions, and exchanging information. The associate director of nursing service and Miss Jones's secretary were less willing to delegate responsibility to the new personnel department, but after some persuasion they began to realize that this would lighten their workload.

Mr. Terrell had previously been employed as an administrative assistant in a small hospital. Because he was apparently insecure at first, Miss Jones tried to cooperate and support him in his efforts. She had several years' experience in hospital personnel management and made available to him the literature and information she had.

Several times Joe Brown, an assistant administrator, remarked about Mr. Terrell's practice of reporting every trivial incident to Mr. Collins; Miss Jones felt Mr. Terrell might just be following directions.

Mr. Terrell and Miss Jones had discussed several times the need to revise and implement the personnel policies. After six months on the job, Mr. Terrell told Miss Jones he was revising the policies and would like her to read them over before he presented them to his committee on personnel policies. She indicated that she was very interested and wished to see them even though reorganization and the daily stress of the many disciplines and personalities in the hospital organization kept her busy.

One Tuesday morning Mr. Terrell called Miss Jones to ask when he could see her to discuss the new personnel policies. Consulting her desk calendar, she suggested Friday morning.

Mr. Terrell: But that's too late! My meeting is Thursday afternoon at 5 P.M.

Miss Jones: In that case bring them down and I'll go over them at home—I certainly want to see them.

Mr. Terrell's secretary brought the suggested policies to Miss Jones's office later that morning. Tuesday evening and Wednesday evening she read the new policy changes; she fumed inwardly. She could see the results of her efforts toward morale and cooperation evaporating. She wrote notes and recommended changes on the margin; she suggested additional policies. On Thursday morning Miss Jones called on Mr. Terrell in his office.

Miss Jones: Terrell, you can't take things away from people and expect a satisfied staff. One of your policies reduces some of the supervisors' vacation period by a week. I have 450 employees in my department. I can see nothing but hostility arising from many of these changes. Here are *my* suggestions—in writing!

Mr. Terrell: I'll look over them before the meeting this afternoon.

Miss Jones: I've been around hospitals too long to be sensitive, and as I've said, most of the employees in this institution are under Nursing. I intend to be at your meeting this afternoon, invited or not.

Miss Jones then angrily left Mr. Terrell's office.

That afternoon she attended the Personnel Policy Committee meeting. Copies of the suggested policies were passed out. Miss Jones asked for the copy on which she had noted her suggestions. Mr. Terrell, looking pained, said he had made her suggested changes. On glancing through her copy, she realized he had. Miss Jones was appeased.

Matters went along smoothly for a while after that; the combination of new-old policies was approved. One of the new personnel policies stated: "Those employees who have been employed over five years and are no longer receiving periodic increment salary raises will have their records reviewed on the anniversary of employment date; merit raises will be given consistent with performance appraisal by the supervisor."

Bob Jordan, one of the assistants to the controller, called Miss Jones about a month after the policy had gone into effect and asked if he could see her for a minute.

Mr. Jordan: This guy Terrell is getting into everyone's hair. I thought you might be interested in these.

Mr. Jordan had two authorization slips for merit raises for two of Miss Jones's supervisors. She had signed these herself, and they had been countersigned by Mr. Brown, the assistant administrator. Mr. Terrell had canceled the authorization.

Miss Jones took the authorization slips and went to Mr. Brown's office. After he read them, the two of them appeared at Mr. Collins's office and requested a short conference.

Discussion Questions

1. What is happening here?
2. Whose responsibility is it that this situation exists?
3. Could Miss Jones have helped Mr. Terrell?
4. Should this matter of merit raises have been taken up with Mr. Terrell—or had it gone too far?
5. How should Miss Jones approach Mr. Collins?
6. How should Mr. Collins handle the interview with Miss Jones and Mr. Brown?
7. What should Mr. Collins do in his subsequent interview with Mr. Terrell?

▶ LEESBURG POLICE DEPARTMENT*

From 1964 to 1984 the police of the Town of Leesburg were represented by the Leesburg Police Relief Association as their bargaining agent. During this period, the association had some limited success in obtaining wage increases and fringe benefits.

By 1984 many younger officers who had been union members in their previous jobs had joined the Leesburg force. These younger officers began to influence the association. Under the supervision of the state labor board an election was held to select a new union to represent the police officers. The International Public Employees Association (IPEA) was chosen to represent all officers up to the rank of lieutenant.

At approximately the same time, the city engaged a well-known labor attorney and also created a position of personnel director for the city. The person chosen for this position was a former local industrial union president.

The first contract obtained by the IPEA provided the police officers with a wage increase of approximately $1,000 over an 18-month period. In addition, they negotiated for a four-and-two schedule, that is, four days on and two days off, and incentive pay for college credits.

On January 1, 1987, the new mayor took office, following a campaign pledging fiscal austerity. This had been the mode of operation in two previous terms as mayor.

---

*Note: This case was prepared by Richard M. Ayres, FBI Academy, and Thomas L. Wheelen, McIntire School of Commerce, University of Virginia, as the basis for class discussion. Copyright © 1975 by Thomas L. Wheelen and Richard M. Ayres.

Presented at a case workshop and distributed by Intercollegiate Case Clearing House, Soldiers Field, Boston, Mass. 02163. All rights reserved to the contributors.

The police contract had expired on December 31, 1986, at which time the outgoing mayor, who had lost the election, declined to start new negotiations. The new mayor stalled negotiations until the city budget had been adopted.

A few token meetings between police and the city took place, but no settlement was reached. All negotiations finally terminated in late April, with the city taking the position that no part of the previous contract was binding. The chief then initiated rotating shifts for the department, which would commence on June 8, 1987. The union interpreted this action as a means by the city to force the IPEA back to the negotiating table. At the first meeting the city agreed to settle the wage issue but refused to negotiate on the rotating shifts.

The IPEA then sought a court injunction to enjoin the chief of police from initiating the rotating shifts on the date planned, June 8, 1987. The chief had wanted rotating shifts because it was felt that it would increase the efficiency of the department, and it would afford the younger officers opportunities to experience all phases of police work on all three shifts. The IPEA argument was that this system did not recognize seniority.

At the same time, the IPEA members and their spouses, children, and friends began to picket city hall during working hours. Both young and older members of the force joined the picket line. This lasted for one month. During this time, the mayor and the chief received many telephoned threats, and their homes were subject to acts of vandalism. The issue of picketing and vandalism received a great deal of local media coverage.

The police then devised a new picketing technique, that of asking the public to"honk" their car horn to show support for their police as they drove past City Hall. The picketers carried signs asking the public to participate in this program. Many complaints began to pour in from merchants, employees in the city hall, and adjoining buildings. Also, the city had an anti-noise law which outlawed "honking" horns unless emergency conditions existed.

Many acts of vandalism continued and resulted in further damage to city property. At this point, the city filed an unfair labor practice against the IPEA before the state labor board. The court turned down the IPEA's request to enjoin the chief on the rotating shift issue.

The union's next move was to place advertisements in the local paper to solicit support from the local merchants to force the mayor back to the bargaining table. This campaign was unsuccessful, and the IPEA then announced a citywide boycott of all local merchants. Police officers and their spouses were put on buses and taken to the next city to do their shopping.

Pictures of this action were in the local paper, and local merchants were enraged.

Picket lines began to thin after Memorial Day. There was a great deal of dissatisfaction within the union and its leadership. It was the younger members who developed the strike tactics. The sick list began to grow, and many of the officers eligible for retirement applied for it, rather than go on the rotating shifts. On June 9, the mayor fired five probationary police officers for violations of department rules and regulations. The probationary period for these five officers expired on June 20, 1987. The IPEA quickly claimed that these officers were fired because of their union involvement, and filed an unfair labor practice claim against the city.

The vandalism and phone threats continued. On June 19, two local adults were arrested, tried, and convicted in the district court for vandalism and sentenced with orders to make restitution. The two individuals declined to implicate any members of the police department. The city again initiated an unfair labor action against the IPEA.

Discussion Questions

1. Were there any unfair labor practices committed by either the city of Leesburg or the IPEA?
2. Did the IPEA evaluate the negative impact the tactic of boycotting the local merchants might have on their objectives?
3. Does the union have a responsibility to prevent acts of vandalism or to take appropriate action to deter future incidents?
4. How did the relationship between the IPEA and the city management contribute to the labor conflict?

Exhibit Six

THE DIAGNOSTIC MODEL

ASSESS HUMAN RESOURCE CONDITIONS	SET HUMAN RESOURCE OBJECTIVES	CHOOSE AND APPLY HUMAN RESOURCE ACTIVITIES	EVALUATE RESULTS
EXTERNAL CONDITIONS Economic Conditions Government Regulations Unions ORGANIZATIONAL CONDITIONS Nature of the Organization Nature of the Work EMPLOYEE CONDITIONS Abilities Motivation Interests	EFFICIENCY Organization Employee EQUITY Organization Employee	Planning Staffing Development Employee/Union Relations **Compensation**	EFFICIENCY EQUITY

Compensation

A paycheck is wonderfully straightforward. The numbers are so neatly exact. All the calculations behind the numbers are shown on the stub: deductions for health insurance, income taxes, social security, and pensions. Additions for regular hours, time-and-a-half for overtime, perhaps a bonus. These figures are the final result of a great number of compensation decisions, which we discuss in the next three chapters. Pay is one of the most important means employers have to attract, retain, and motivate employees. Since the pay is also a major cost of doing business, it requires careful management. When making compensation decisions, managers need to recognize that it is both an instrumental device that affects employees' work behaviors and economic well-being as well as a major expense item that affects the financial well-being of the organization.

To an increased extent, traditional approaches for determining compensation are being challenged. These challenges are from managers under increased competitive pressure and concerned about quality and unit labor costs; they are questioning whether the pay system aids them in achieving their objectives. When employees observe the large bonuses received by executives and the differences in earnings between men and women, they are challenging the equity of the entire system of pay determination. Finally, stockholders who own shares of corporations are questioning whether the compensation paid to employees in any way reflects

701

the increased (decreased) value of their shares. All these pressures from the various stakeholders are causing the traditional, often bureaucratic, pay systems to be reexamined.

The three chapters in Part Six explore compensation; Chapters Eighteen and Nineteen examine the decisions related to cash compensation; benefits decisions are the subject of Chapter Twenty.

chapter eighteen

COMPETITIVENESS AND CONSISTENCY

CHAPTER OUTLINE

Exxon Corporation is one of the world's largest firms. It employs a chief executive officer, chemical engineers, plant managers, nurses, market analysts, laboratory technicians, financial planners, hydraulic mechanics, accountants, guards, oil tanker captains, sailors, word processors, and so on. How is pay for these different jobs determined? Is the financial planner worth more than the accountant, or the mechanic more than the word processor? How much more? Which procedures are used to set pay rates and who does it? How important are the characteristics of the employee— knowledge, skills, abilities, or experience? How important are the characteristics of the work, the conditions under which it is done, or the value of what is produced? Do the procedures differ according to an employer's business strategies and its financial condition? What role do unions play?

The next two chapters address these questions. In this chapter we discuss the external and organizational conditions assessed, compensation objectives and strategies, and the four basic decisions made when managing compensation. In this and the next chapter we describe the major techniques to determine employees' pay.

A DIAGNOSTIC APPROACH TO PAY ADMINISTRATION

Compensation means different things to different people; it depends on a person's perspective. As employees, we may think of our own compensation as a return for our efforts or a reward for satisfactory or outstanding work. It may indicate the value the employer attaches to our skills and abilities—the return on our investment in education and training. For most of us, the pay we receive for the work we perform is the major source of personal wealth; hence, it is an important determinant of our economic and social well-being.

Managers have two views of compensation. First and foremost, pay is a major operating expense. Labor costs in many organizations account for more than 50 percent of total operational expenses. For this reason alone, pay requires sound administration. In addition to being an expense, pay can influence employees' work behaviors and attitudes. It may affect their decision to apply for a job, remain with an employer, work more productively, or undertake more training to be eligible for a higher-paying job. If managed inequitably, pay may cause employees to diminish their efforts, to search for alternative employment and/or to form a union. This potential to influence employees' work attitudes and behaviors is another compelling reason for ensuring that pay systems are designed and administered fairly and equitably.

Forms of Pay

> ### Definition
> *Compensation* refers to all forms of financial returns, tangible services, and benefits employees receive as part of an employment relationship.

Exhibit 18–1 shows the variety of forms compensation can take. It may be received directly in the form of cash (e.g., wages, bonus, incentives) or indirectly through services and benefits (e.g., pensions, health insurance, vacations).

This definition excludes other forms of rewards and returns that employees may receive such as promotions, recognition for outstanding work, feelings of accomplishment, choice office locations, and the like. Such factors may be thought of as part of an organization's total reward system. The administration of all these rewards should be coordinated with compensation, whenever possible.

EXHIBIT 18–1
Forms of Compensation

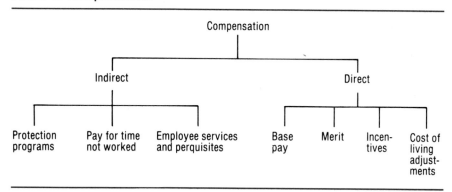

Source: George T. Milkovich and Jerry M. Newman, *Compensation*, 2nd ed. (Plano, Tex.: Business Publications, 1987).

External Influences on Pay

As Exhibit 18–2 shows, pay decisions may be affected by the economic conditions facing the firm in which a person is employed, the firm's policies and practices, its relations with unions, the types of people employed, and even pay discrimination. Important external influences that must be assessed when administering pay include the economy, government regulations, and unions' interests and power.

Economy: Product and Labor Markets

Although some may feel that people should not be subject to forces of supply and demand, they are.[1] During times of expanding demand for products and services, job opportunities expand and employers are more willing and able to increase pay to attract and retain employees with the needed skills and experience. Often increased wages may be translated into increased costs of production. Organizations that face greater costs as a result of pay increases may try to pass them on to consumers in the form of higher prices. Passing costs on is easier during periods of strong demand for products or services. Even public sector employers such as states or universities attempt to pass on their increased labor costs in the form of increased taxes or tuition.

EXHIBIT 18–2
Possible Determinants of Pay Decisions

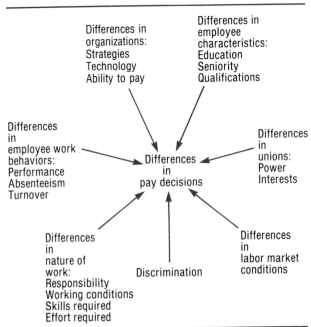

Increased competition also affects pay decisions. Managers faced with increased competition from foreign producers, surplus inventories, and the like, seek to control costs. A major line item in the budget is labor costs. And compensation decisions in large part determine labor costs. So it is not too surprising that increased competition in product markets causes managers to think twice about the amount of pay to offer.

Labor market conditions directly affect pay decisions. During periods of shortages of qualified employees, pay tends to increase at a faster rate to help attract and retain needed workers. In recessions, or when surpluses of qualified employees are available, rates of pay increases are slowed; pay may even decrease.

Government Regulations

The government influences pay both directly through laws, regulations, and controls, and indirectly through its socioeconomic policies. For example, governments' fiscal and monetary policies directly affect demand for goods and services, and subsequently the employer's demand for employees. These actions create economic forces which affect pay.

The government more directly affects compensation through wage controls and guidelines, which limit increases in compensation for certain workers at certain times, and laws that establish minimum wage rates, wage and hour regulations, and prevent discrimination.

Wage Controls and Guidelines

Several times in the past quarter century or so, the federal government has established wage freezes and guidelines. Wage freezes are government orders which permit no wage increases; wage controls limit the size of wage increases. Wage guidelines are similar to wage controls, but they are voluntary rather than legally required restrictions.[2]

Economists differ on the usefulness of wage and price freezes. Critics argue that the controls are an administrative nightmare, that they seriously disrupt the effective resource allocation by market forces, and lead to frustration and strikes.[3] Even the critics admit, however, that during times of national emergencies, and for relatively brief periods, the controls might help slow (but not indefinitely postpone) inflation.[4] The important point for us is that managers must adjust their compensation decisions to fit any governmental wage guidelines or controls.

Wage and Hour Regulations

The Fair Labor Standards Act of 1938 is the basic labor act in the United States. It has been amended many times. This law has a number of provisions, including the following:

Minimum Wages. All employers covered by the law must pay an employee at least a minimum wage per hour. In 1938 the minimum wage was

25 cents per hour. In 1988 pressures were mounting in Congress to increase it from $3.35. A number of economists questioned the desirability of increasing the minimum wage, arguing that adjusting it prices workers out of jobs.[5] All did not agree, however. Some proposed a two-tier minimum wage for trainees and younger employees to help reduce the unemployment problems among minority youth. When an increase comes, fast-food and retail firms that pay employees at or near the minimum wage are likely to be most affected. Hence their managers need to keep track of proposals to change the law and lobby the political process. Others, such as the auto and aerospace companies, pay few if any employees at the minimum wage, so their need to assess these developments is less.

Overtime Pay. An employee covered by the law who works more than 40 hours per week must be paid one and one half times the base wage.

Child Labor Prohibition. The law prohibits employing persons between 16 and 18 in hazardous jobs, such as meatpacking and logging. Persons under 16 cannot be employed in jobs in interstate commerce except for nonhazardous work for a parent or guardian. However, there are exceptions and limitations to the law.

Prevailing Wage Laws

Several laws, most notably the Davis-Bacon Act of 1931 and the Walsh-Healey Act of 1936 require that workers on covered projects receive at least a government-defined prevailing wage in an area. Covered projects include government-financed construction costing over $2,000 (Davis-Bacon) and production or supply contracts for government purchases over $10,000 (Walsh-Healey). The government theoretically surveys wages in the area and then sets the "prevailing rate" as the minimum to be paid on the government project. In practice, it takes the union rates in an area.[6] So a government-set prevailing rate may correspond to the actual rate of only a minority of an area's laborers.

Antidiscrimination Laws

The Equal Pay Act of 1963, the Civil Rights Act of 1964, the Age Discrimination Act of 1968, and their amendments ensure that all persons of similar ability, seniority, and qualifications receive the same pay for the same work. These laws were discussed in Chapter Three on equal employment opportunity. We discuss another EEO pay issue, comparable worth, later in this chapter.

Union Influences

Unions are another important external influence on employers' compensation decisions.[7] Although only less than one in five workers is a union member, it would be a mistake to conclude that their impact on pay is

EXHIBIT 18-3
Seniority as Pay Basis in a Collective Bargaining Agreement

Labor Grade	Minimum	Yr. 1	Yr. 2	Yr. 3	Yr. 4	Yr. 5	Yr. 6	Maximum
				Seniority				
A-2	$7.18	$7.23	$7.28	$7.33	$7.38	$7.43	$7.48	$7.53
A-1	6.82	6.87	6.92	6.97	7.02	7.07	7.22	7.17
1	6.45	6.50	6.59	6.60	6.65	6.70	6.75	6.80
2	6.11	6.16	6.21	6.26	6.31	6.36	6.41	6.46
3	5.81	5.86	5.91	5.96	6.02	6.06		6.11
4	5.56	5.61	5.66	5.71	5.76			5.81
5	5.36	5.41	5.46					5.51
6	5.15	5.20						5.25
7	4.87	4.92						4.97
8	4.72							4.77
9	4.56							4.61
10	4.51							4.56

minor. Frequently the real or perceived threat of becoming unionized encourages managers to improve wages and other conditions of employment.[8]

The vast majority of collective bargaining contracts specify seniority as a basis of pay increases. Exhibit 18-3 is fairly typical. We discussed the effects of unions on all human resource programs, including pay, in Chapter Seventeen.

Organization Influences on Pay

Several organization factors need to be assessed before making pay decisions. Among these are the firm's objectives and strategies, its policies and culture, the type of work which must be performed, the skills required to perform the work, and preferences of employees.[9]

Organization Strategies

All pay systems have a purpose. Answer the question—for what do we want to pay?—and you will begin to specify the objectives of the pay system. Some objectives are clearly identified; others are implied. But the pay system objectives should support the organization's strategies.[10]

Strategy refers to the fundamental direction of the organization.[11] Strategies guide the deployment of all resources, including compensation. An example is JC Penney Company signing a contract to market the Halston product line. Historically, Penney's worked hard to establish a reputation for providing good value for the price of its merchandise. This strategy was aimed at "middle America." But a new strategy sought to adjust Penney's image and attract a more affluent shopper. The Halston contract was part of that strategy. It reflects a fundamental change in directions. The organization deployed its resources—financial, capital, and human resources—in a manner consistent with these new directions. As part of this effort, Penney's designed pay incentives tied to sales targets to try to assure a maximum return on its investment in Halston. Under the incentive program, stores' sales personnel received significant payment for increased sales.

Exhibit 18–4 depicts the idea that compensation decisions are contingent on the organization and its environment. Compensation decisions that "fit" or support the firm's strategies and account for environmental pressures are more likely to contribute to the desired employee behaviors and organization performance.[12] The logic is that compensation contributes to an organization's success by signaling and rewarding behaviors consistent with the organization's objectives. The better the fit, the better the performance. Compensation decisions made in an ad hoc manner, without regard to organization and environment conditions are more likely to send mixed signals and less likely to support desired behaviors and performance.

Strategic Stages and Pay. Pay decisions can be guided by an organization's strategic stage.[13] Exhibit 18–5 shows six strategic stages ranging from start-up through decline and renewal. It also shows hypothetical examples of the pay tailored to each state. Business units just starting up

EXHIBIT 18–4
Compensation Decisions Fit the Organization and Its Environment

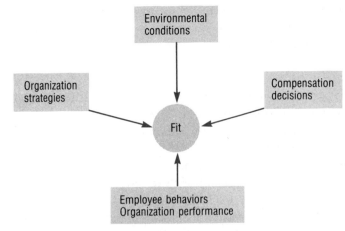

EXHIBIT 18–5
An Example of Pay Tailored to Strategic Stages of a Product or Unit

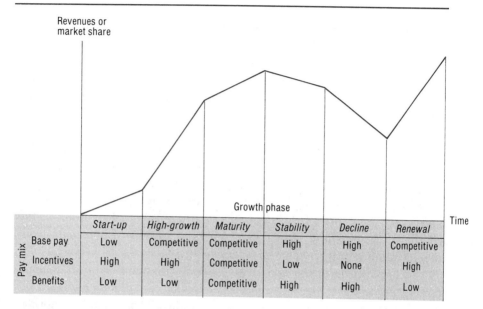

Pay mix	Start-up	High-growth	Maturity	Stability	Decline	Renewal
Base pay	Low	Competitive	Competitive	High	High	Competitive
Incentives	High	High	Competitive	Low	None	High
Benefits	Low	Low	Competitive	High	High	Low

Source: George T. Milkovich and Jerry M. Newman, *Compensation,* 2nd ed. (Plano, Tex.: Business Publications, 1987).

usually have a limited, closely related set of products and are exploring their markets. Cash-flow problems are common at this stage, but employees are confident of the future success of the business. The pay in the example includes relatively low base pay (to conserve cash), and strong emphasis on incentive pay (to emphasize unit and individual performance and to share the results of growth). Benefits may be kept low to control costs, unless the organization is competing for scarce labor; then benefits may have to be set to meet those offered by competitors. Declining business units or products may have high fixed costs, including base pay and benefits. Incentives may be restricted to encourage phase-out, or reintroduced to encourage renewal.

Exhibit 18–5 oversimplifies the real world.[14] All business units do not go through all stages. Units may be divested, others acquired. Labor market competition may preclude offering low benefits or base salaries. A variety of reasons make it difficult to characterize any single organization as being in any one stage.

The important point is that organizations can tailor pay systems to fit their overall strategies and the environment. In highly decentralized organizations, this can even mean that different business units adopt different pay systems.

Organization Culture and Values

Not only can pay programs be tailored to organization strategies and objectives, but they can also be congruent with the organization's culture and values. The notions of culture and values are complex. Pay is just one of the many systems that make up an organization; its design must be partially influenced by how it fits with the other structures and systems in the organization.[15] A highly centralized and confidential pay system, controlled by a few people in a corporate unit, does not, according to this view, operate effectively in a highly decentralized and open organization. Unfortunately, little research has been done directly on the relationship between pay systems and the culture and values of organizations. Consequently, the influence of such factors as the degree of centralization, the decision-making style of management, or the maturity of the union-management relationship, is not well understood.

The importance of the congruency of pay programs with other management processes is perhaps most clear in the case of other human resource management programs, such as recruiting, hiring, and promoting. The pay tied to a job offer or a promotion must be consistent with other systems. Some employers do not maintain significant pay differences between manufacturing workers (such as assemblers or inspectors) and their first-line supervisors. This diminishes the incentive to acquire the training required to be a supervisor or to accept the promotion to supervisor. The situation is reversed for many engineering and research jobs, where the pay for managerial positions induces people to leave engineering and research positions. Pay coexists with other structures in the organization. An effective pay system cannot be designed without taking the nature of the organization and its culture and values into consideration.

Employee Needs

Within some legally imposed limits, firms deliver compensation to employees in the various forms already identified in Exhibit 18–1. The allocation of compensation among these pay forms to emphasize performance, seniority, entitlements, or the long versus short term should be tailored to the pay objectives of the organization. It should also be tailored to the needs of the individual employees.[16]

The simple fact that employees differ is too easily and too often overlooked in designing pay systems. Individual employees join the organization, make investment decisions, design new products, assemble components, and judge the quality of results. Individual employees receive the pay. A major limitation of contemporary pay systems is the degree to which individual attitudes and preferences are ignored. For example, older, highly paid workers may wish to defer taxes by putting their pay into retirement funds, while younger employees may have high cash needs to buy a house, support a family, or finance an education. Dual-career couples who are overinsured medically may prefer to use more of their combined pay for child care, automobile insurance, financial counseling, or other benefits.[17]

Increasingly compensation decisions include the following four concerns for employers:

1. How to provide employees with choices in their pay and benefits.
2. How to keep employees informed about their compensation (increased communications).
3. How to offer employees the opportunity to participate in decision making (increased involvement).
4. How to provide employees with a voice or dispute resolution procedure.

So a wide variety of external organizational and employee conditions need to be assessed to establish compensation objectives and to design compensation systems.

SETTING COMPENSATION OBJECTIVES

A Pay Model

The pay model in Exhibit 18–6 contains three basic parts: (1) the *policies* that form the foundations of the pay system, (2) the *techniques* that make up much of the mechanics of compensation management, and (3) the *compensation objectives*, or desired results. We discuss these components and their interrelationships next, beginning with the objectives and policy options.

Compensation Objectives

As shown at the right side of the model, pay systems achieve certain objectives including efficiency and equity. These objectives are broadly conceived. *Efficiency* is typically defined more specifically as (1) improving productivity and (2) controlling labor costs. Often these two can be found in an employer's statement of pay objectives, such as "to facilitate organi-

EXHIBIT 18–6
A Pay Model

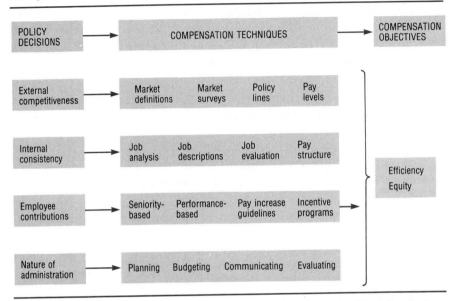

Source: George T. Milkovich and Jerry M. Newman, *Compensation,* 2nd ed. (Plano, Tex.: Business Publications, 1987).

zation performance, to control labor costs, to attract and retain competent employees, and to reward employee contributions and performance."

Equity is a fundamental objective in pay systems. Statements such as "fair treatment for all employees" or "a fair day's pay for a fair day's work" reflect a concern for equity. Thus, the equity objective attempts to ensure fair pay treatment for all participants in the employment relationships. The equity objective focuses on pay decisions recognizing both employee contributions (e.g., offering higher pay for greater performance or greater experiences or training) and employee needs (e.g., providing a "living wage," or health care insurance).

Procedural equity, often overlooked by compensation managers, is concerned with the processes used to make decisions about pay.[18] It suggests that the way a pay decision is made may be as important to employees as are the results of the decision. As an objective for a pay system, procedural equity helps ensure that employees, managers, and other relevant parties have a voice in the design of pay plans and an opportunity to voice any dissatisfaction with the pay received.

Compliance is part of the equity objective and involves conforming to various federal and state compensation laws and regulations. As these laws and regulations change, pay decisions often need to be adjusted to ensure continued compliance.

EXHIBIT 18–7
Comparison of Pay System Objectives

Hewlett-Packard Company

At Hewlett-Packard, our pay program is designed to be innovative, competitive, and equitable so that H-P will continue to attract and retain creative and enthusiastic people who will contribute to H-P's continuing success.

  Your pay has been established to reflect the company's policy of "paying among the leaders."
  Your pay will accurately reflect your sustained relative contribution to your unit, division, and H-P.
  Your pay system will be open and understandable. You are encouraged to discuss the pay process with your supervisor.

Honeywell, Inc.

To attract the best person available for each Honeywell job.
To encourage growth both on an individual basis and as a participant on a work team.
To recognize the importance of high-quality work performance and to reward it accordingly.
To encourage a career-long commitment to Honeywell.

Multiple Objective Statements

There are probably as many statements of pay objectives as there are employers. In fact, some highly diversified firms, such as TRW, Inc. and Dart-Kraft Industries, which compete in multiple lines of businesses, have different pay objectives for different business units. Exhibit 18–7 shows examples of Honeywell's and Hewlett-Packard's pay objectives. Both sets of objectives emphasize high-quality and innovative performance (productivity), competitiveness (costs), ability to attract and retain quality people (productivity), and equity (employee communications, openness, and understanding).

Basic Policy Decisions

The pay model in Exhibit 18–6 rests on four basic policies that any employer must consider in compensation management. The policy decisions shown on the left side of the pay model include (1) external competitiveness, (2) internal consistency, (3) individual contributions, and (4) the nature of the administration of the pay system. These policies form the four building blocks, the foundation on which pay systems are designed and administered. These policies also serve as guidelines within which pay is managed to accomplish the system's objectives.

External Competitiveness. External competitiveness refers to how an employer positions its pay relative to what competitors are paying. How much do other employers pay accountants, and how much does a firm wish to pay accountants in comparison to what other employers would pay them? All employers make decisions regarding external competitiveness, and in doing so they have several policy options. Some employers may set their pay levels higher than their competition, hoping to attract the best applicants. Of course, this assumes that someone is able to identify and hire the best from the pool of applicants. Another employer may offer lower base pay but a greater opportunity to work overtime, better benefits, or a better incentive plan than those offered by other employers. Or, pay and benefits may be lower, but job security may be higher.

Internal Consistency. Internal consistency, often called internal equity, refers to comparisons among jobs or skill levels inside a single organization. Pay relationships that are internally consistent are based on the content of the work or skills required and the relative contribution of the work to the organization's overall objectives. How, for example, does the work of a word processor compare with the work of a computer operator, programmer, and systems analyst? Does one job require more skill or experience than another? Is the output from one job valued more than the output from another? Internal consistency becomes a factor in determining the pay rates both for employees doing equal work and for those doing dissimilar work. In fact, determining what is an equitable difference in pay for people performing different work is one of the key issues in compensation management.

Employee Contributions. The policy on employee contributions refers to the relative emphasis placed on the performance and/or seniority of people doing the same job or possessing the same job skills. Should all such employees receive the same pay? Or should one programmer be paid more than another if one has better performance and/or greater seniority? Should managerial pay increases be based on the performance of the total corporation or the subunit they manage? On long-term or short-term results?

Nature of Administration. Although it is possible to design a system that incorporates internal consistency, external competitiveness, and employee contributions, the system cannot achieve its objectives unless it is administered properly. The greatest system design in the world is useless without competent administration. Administration involves planning the elements of pay that should be included in the pay system (e.g., base pay, short-term and long-term incentives), evaluating how the pay system is operating, communicating with employees, and judging whether the system is achieving its objectives. Are we able to attract skilled workers? Can we keep them? Do our employees feel our system is fair? Do they understand which factors are considered in setting their pay? Do employees have channels for raising questions and voicing complaints about their pay? How do the better performing firms, with better financial returns and larger shares of the market, pay their employees? Such information is necessary to evaluate or redesign the system, to adjust to changes, and to highlight potential areas for further investigation.

Balancing Consistency, Competitiveness, Contributions, and Administration

The balance or relative emphasis among the four basic policies is also a key decision in any employer's compensation strategy. Does it ever make sense to emphasize one policy concern over another? For example, many high-technology firms grant sizable salary increases to match outside offers from competing employers (an external competitiveness issue). Sometimes it makes sense to emphasize external competitiveness, because the relationship of an employer's pay level to a competitor's pay level directly affects the ability to attract a competent work force, to control labor costs, and hence to compete with products or services. Yet ignoring internal consistency and employee contributions may increase an employer's vulnerability to lawsuits, as well as increase employees' dissatisfaction. Employees believe if the workers next to them are doing the same job, but paid more, there had better be a good reason for this differential. Internal pay differences can affect employees' willingness to accept promotions, pay satisfaction, absenteeism, turnover, and unionization activity.

Thus, all four policy decisions—competitiveness, consistency, contributions, and administrative style—are critical in the management of pay systems. Achieving the desired balance among them is part of making pay decisions.

PAY TECHNIQUES

The remaining portion of the model in Exhibit 18–6 lists various pay techniques. These techniques link the policy decisions to the objectives. Uncounted variations in techniques exist; some of the most common ones are examined in this and the next two chapters.

EXTERNAL COMPETITIVENESS: PAY LEVEL

External competitiveness refers to the pay relationships among organizations. It focuses attention on how one firm's pay rates compare to the rates paid by its competitors. In practice, external competitiveness gets translated into decisions about the pay level.

Pay level refers to an average of the rates paid by an employer. There are three "pure" alternatives in setting a pay level—to set average pay so it (1) leads competition, (2) matches competition, or (3) follows what others are paying. Of the choice to match, lead, or lag, evidence suggests that the most common policy is to match what is paid by competition.

Pay Level Effects

What difference does the pay level make? Exhibit 18–8 illustrates the potential effects on compensation objectives.

Match Competition. By setting the pay level to match competition, organizations try to ensure that their labor costs are approximately equal to the labor costs of competitors. Equal labor costs help place competing employers on an equal footing in their ability to attract and maintain a qualified work force.[19]

Lead. Employers who offer higher pay rates than their competitors seek to maximize their ability to attract and retain quality employees and to minimize employee dissatisfaction with pay. The idea is that higher pay increases the number of applicants. A larger applicant pool permits the selection process, properly designed, to skim the cream of the applicants. And these higher-quality employees should exhibit greater productivity, thereby offsetting the higher wages. However, little research has been reported to support (or refute) these contentions. Some industries (e.g., pharmaceuticals) do pay higher rates for similar skills (e.g., MBAs or accountants) than other industries, but this may be because they can pass these rates on to consumers and because labor costs are not a significant portion of total operating costs in these industries.

EXHIBIT 18–8
Probable Relationships between Pay Level Policies and Objectives

Policy	Compensation Objectives				
	Ability to Attract	Ability to Retain	Contain Labor Costs	Reduce Pay Dissat-isfaction	Increase Produc-tivity
Pay above market (lead)	+	+	?	+	?
Pay with market (match)	=	=	=	=	?
Pay below market (lag)	−	?	+	−	?

Source: George T. Milkovich and Jerry M. Newman, *Compensation*, 2nd. ed. (Plano, Tex.: Business Publications, 1987).

Lag. Setting pay rates below competitors' rates may hinder an employer's ability to attract or retain employees. However, the opportunity to work overtime, to secure promotions and avoid layoffs, or a secure friendly work environment, may offset lower pay rates for many potential employees.[20]

No matter which pay level option an employer selects, it needs to be translated into practice. This is usually done by surveying relevant external labor markets and establishing the pay policy line.

Market Surveys

Wage surveys reveal what other employers are paying for similar jobs and skills.

Exhibit 18–9 shows the results of a market survey. It reports the rates paid for a lead word processing operator by selected electronics firms in Dallas. A brief description of the job duties is given with the survey data. This aids survey users to match their jobs to the job in the survey. The survey also collects the minimum, mid (50th percentile or median), maxi-

EXHIBIT 18–9
Salary Survey Results

Word Processing Operator, Lead

Duties

Assumes responsibility for directing work flow through the word processing center or cluster and provides administrative support to principals to improve overall productivity. Uses word processor to type high priority and confidential work.

High school graduate or equivalent, plus 3 years of processing (mag card/tape/diskette) experience required.

Job title: Word Process Operator III	Company Code	Minimum Rate	Mid Rate	Maximum Rate	Average Rate	Employee Population
	D	$8.34	$9.71	$11.07	$9.40	10
	Y	7.35	8.65	9.95	9.40	4
	E	7.62	8.99	10.36	9.08	3
	YY	7.78	9.05	10.32	8.94	7
	B	6.84	8.56	10.26	8.37	2
	N	6.87	8.59	10.31	8.37	14
	W	5.96	8.99	10.28	8.08	3
	XX	6.89	8.10	9.72	8.05	12
	OO	5.53	7.19	8.84	7.65	2
	Q	6.45	8.60	10.23	7.58	3
	MM	5.70	7.13	8.56	7.40	2
	G	5.48	6.78	8.08	7.36	6
	R	6.20	7.63	9.05	7.36	3

Source: Dallas Area Electronics Survey, Winter 1982. Survey sponsors: Recognition Equipment, Rockwell International, Collins Radio Group, and Texas Instruments, Inc.

mum, and average rates paid from each participating firm. This provides a sense of the distribution of rates paid for the job by each employer.

Several features of the data are worth noting. First, there is no "going rate" in Dallas for word processors—a whole range of rates are paid. The rates paid by firms included in this survey vary from $5.48 per hour to $11.07 per hour. Differences in these rates may be attributable to differences in seniority or experience, but it also may reflect different pay level decisions by the employers to lead, lag, or match competition.

Survey data can be collected in considerably greater detail. Exhibit 18–10 shows the results of a survey of computer programmer rates and a summary of those rates as 90th through 10th percentiles. Pay surveys such as these are conducted by employers, either individually or in associations, by consulting firms, and by government agencies.

EXHIBIT 18–10
Maturity Curves Based on Scatterplot for Computer Programmers (10th through 90th percentiles)

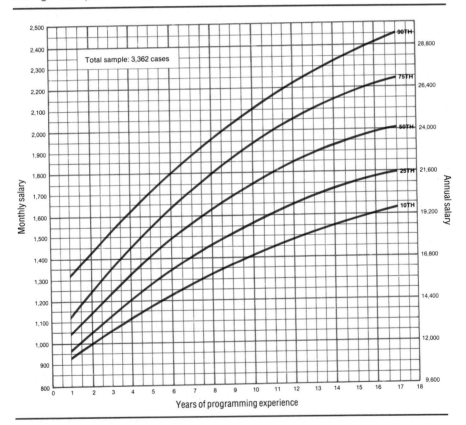

Source: Organization Resources Counselors, Inc.

Survey Decisions

How are these surveys done? One method is the personal interview, which develops the most accurate responses but is also the most expensive. Mailed questionnaires are probably the most frequently used method, because it is cheapest. The jobs being surveyed by mail must be clearly defined, or the data may be suspect. Later telephone inquiries can follow up the mailed questionnaires or gather additional data.

There are a number of critical features of surveys which can be used to evaluate their usefulness: the employers included, the jobs covered, the method used in gathering the data, the age of the data, and its accuracy are examples.

Key Jobs

In practice, employers do not seek market data for all jobs. Rather, only selected jobs, called *key* or *benchmark* jobs, are included in the survey.

EXHIBIT 18–11
Survey Rates: Rates Paid by Competitors; Pay Policy Line: Match Competition

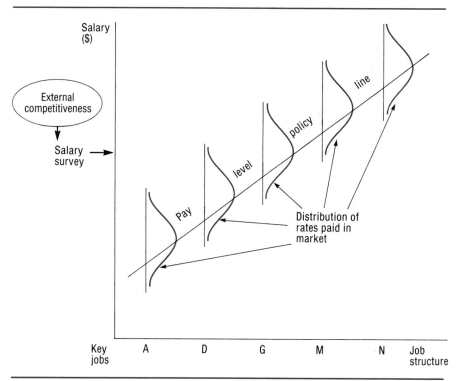

Source: George T. Milkovich and Jerry M. Newman, *Compensation*, 2nd ed. (Plano, Tex.: Business Publications, 1987).

Key jobs have the following characteristics: the work content is relatively stable over time, a large number of employees hold them, they are free of discriminatory employment patterns, and are not subject to recent shortages or surpluses in the marketplace.

Survey Results

The results gained from a survey are a distribution of rates paid by competitors for similar jobs. Exhibit 18–11 illustrates a set of hypothetical distributions for five key jobs (A, D, G, M, and N). In the illustration, the pay level policy line has been set to equal the average paid by the competition for each of the key jobs: a matching-competition policy. We could establish a lead or lag policy by simply shifting the pay level policy line up or down. Thus, market survey data help translate the concept of external competitiveness into actual pay-setting practice.

Once pay level has been determined, we turn to internal consistency.

INTERNAL CONSISTENCY: PAY STRUCTURES

The nature of the internal pay structure is another basic policy decision managers must make in designing pay systems. It typically refers to the distribution of pay rates or internal pay differentials.

Pay structures are designed to be internally equitable by paying more for certain work, such as that requiring greater knowledge or qualifications to perform, that performed under less desirable conditions, and/or whose output is more valued.

Pay Structure Effects

Pay structures focus attention on the link between employee perceptions and their work behaviors. Many compensation experts argue that equitable pay structures are related to everything from employee performance to strikes. Exhibit 18–12 shows some of the potential effects of fair pay structures. Important among them are employees' decisions to join, to stay, or to leave the organization, and to invest in the additional training required for promotions or new assignments. Pay differences influence these decisions. Consequently, equitable pay structures can be a very important management tool.

Levels and Size of Pay Differences

Pay structures differ widely across organizations.[21] Relatively flat structures (e.g., fewer levels, smaller pay differentials) tend to obscure differ-

EXHIBIT 18–12
Some Consequences of Equitable Pay Structures

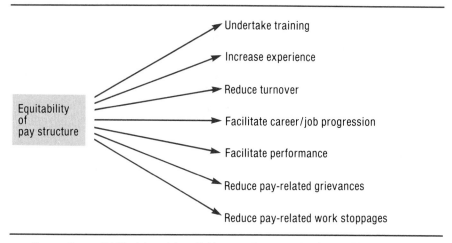

Source: George T. Milkovich and Jerry M. Newman, *Compensation,* 2nd ed. (Plano, Tex.: Business Publications, 1987).

ences in work assignments. For example, rather than designating several levels of financial, marketing, and production analysts, a single broad title, management analyst, may be used. Such broadly drawn work assignments afford flexibility to deploy the work force to specific assignments without requiring changes in titles or pay. On the other hand, broadly drawn titles often permit inequitable assignments. And if dissatisfaction rises employee turnover, reduced performance, and increased interest in unions occur. Steeper structures suggest more detailed specification of work rules and may require more frequent pay adjustments.

Considering their importance, it is surprising that so little is known about employees' perception of what constitutes fair or equitable pay differences among jobs. A study of business school students and compensation administrators concluded that a compensation differential of approximately 30 percent is considered appropriate for the higher of two (adjacent) managerial levels. Little is known about whether different employee groups (older versus younger, women versus men, office versus production workers, engineers versus accountants) hold different ideas about what constitutes fair pay differences among jobs. Yet the number of lawsuits over equal pay and pay discrimination seems to indicate that substantial disagreement exists over what constitutes equitable pay differences among different jobs.

Structure Criteria

Exhibit 18–13 pictures the hypothetical pay structure within a single organization. Each career path, or grouping of jobs, has a set of pay differentials, allowing comparison of the differences in pay among career paths. In the example, the average pay for managerial work exceeds that for work in the technical-research career path.

Two criteria that commonly establish internally consistent pay structures are the attributes of the individuals and the attributes of the jobs.

EXHIBIT 18–13
Hypothetical Job Structure with Four Occupation/Skill Groups

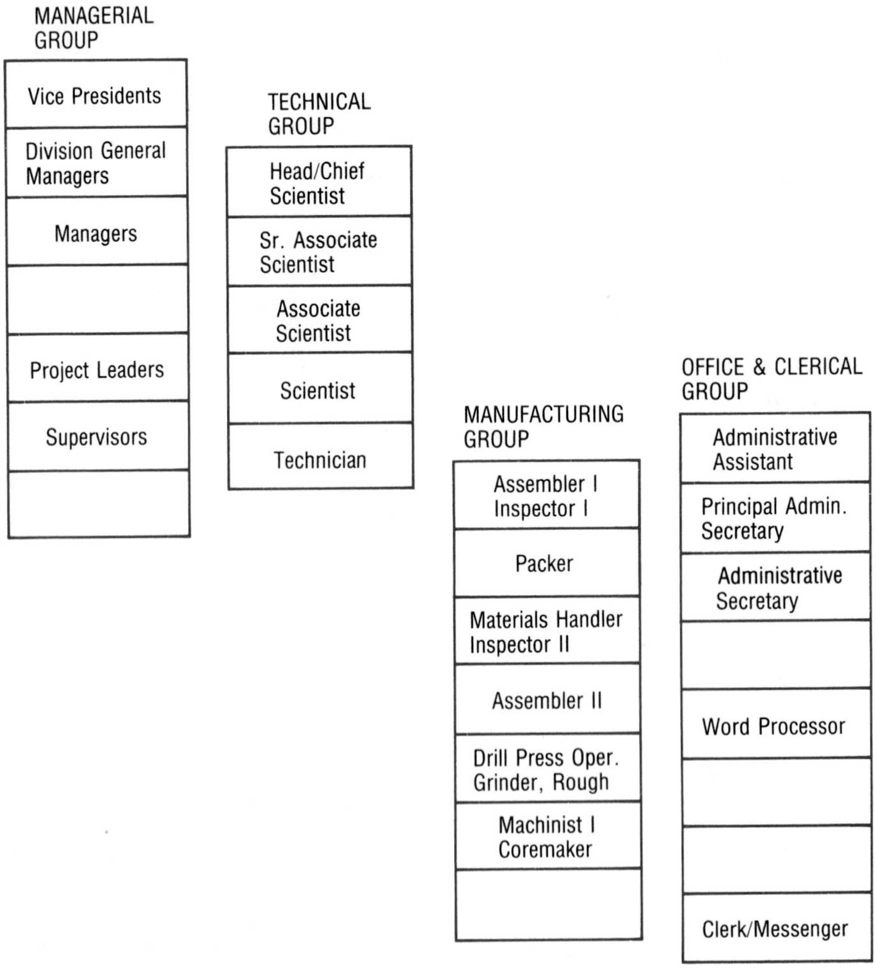

Structures Based on Attributes of Employees

Basing pay differences on individual employees' attributes rather than attributes of the jobs is not new, though it is receiving more attention.[22] Characteristics such as the skills, knowledge, and experience or seniority are commonly used. Other individual characteristics, such as minority status or sex, are illegal to use as a basis for pay differences.

Knowledge-Based Pay Systems

Under knowledge-based pay systems, individual employees are paid for the work-related skills they possess rather than for the specific job they are performing.[23] Knowledge-based pay is also referred to as skill-based pay. Under such a system at a Borg-Warner Corporation facility, an employee may be qualified to operate both a complex auto transmission chain assembly machine and a forklift. If the plant manager needs the forklift operated, the employee is assigned to drive it but is paid at the higher assembly operator rate. Under this plan, a starting rate is typically set below the starting rate paid by other employers in the area. Pay increases are earned by learning and demonstrating mastery of various work-related skills. Once a skill is mastered, pay is immediately increased, and the employee may be rotated to jobs requiring that skill when necessary.

Exhibit 18–14 contrasts job- versus knowledge-based systems. Under a knowledge-based approach, pay is based on the highest work-related skills employees possess (e.g., what they *can* do) rather than on the specific job performed (e.g., what they *are* doing). Under the job-based approach, the wage is assigned to the job, and employees move in and out

EXHIBIT 18–14
Knowledge-Based Compared to Job-Based Compensation Plans

	Job Based	Knowledge Based
Pay structure	Based on job performed	Based on skills possessed by the employee
Managers' focus	Job carries wage Employee linked to job	Employee carries wage Employee linked to skill
Employee focus	Job promotion to earn greater pay	Skill acquisition to earn greater pay
Procedures required	Assess job content Value jobs	Assess skills Value skills
Advantages	Pay based on value of work performed	Flexibility Reduced work force
Limitations	Potential personnel bureaucracy Inflexibilities	Potential personnel bureaucracy Cost controls

of the job. Under a knowledge-based approach, the wage is assigned to an employee regardless of the job performed. Hence, managers focus on controlling the pay rates assigned to jobs and on the need to allocate employees among various jobs. In contrast, under a knowledge-based plan, employees carry both the wage and a set of skills. The manager has the flexibility to reassign individual employees to any tasks as long as the employees have the required skills and are paid at the rate of the highest skill possessed. Pay increases are earned by demonstrating mastery of additional skills rather than by getting promoted to a higher pay job. Knowledge-based systems reward acquisition of additional work-related skills, whether or not those skills are used on the present job.

Advocates point to more flexible and better trained work forces as one of the key advantages of knowledge-based plans.[24] For them, knowledge-based pay is part of a philosophy of managing human resources that emphasizes teamwork and flexibility. Many plant managers also claim that the ability to freely reassign employees within the plant substantially reduces the number of employees required. Even though the facility's average wage will increase as more workers qualify for highest paid skills, the smaller work force required more than offsets the higher average wage.

Beyond advocates' testimonials and claims from plant managers, more rigorous examination of the effects of knowledge-based pay is required. Greater flexibility can be achieved by other actions. And all pay schemes, including those based on skills, can become bureaucratic burdens. Examples include the craft's master-journeyman-apprentice system or the elementary-secondary schoolteachers' pay plans (both knowledge-based schemes). Both have become heavily procedure ridden and inflexible. The recent knowledge-based plans are not inherently free of "creeping" bureaucracy. Some plans now have instituted "holding rates" for employees that have demonstrated mastery of a high paying skill for which there is no vacancy. Other plans have begun to develop elaborate peer review boards to assess skill mastery. Finally, it is feasible that two employees doing equal work could be earning different pay due to differences in their skill levels. Undoubtedly some employees and their lawyers will want to test the legality of that practice if women or minorities receive the lower pay.

Job-Based Structures

Jobs are the most common unit of analysis for determining the internally equitable pay structure, particularly for managerial and professional, office and clerical, but even for manufacturing jobs.[25] Managerial choices among various job analysis and job evaluation techniques help shape these structures.

Job analysis is a systematic process for collecting information about jobs, as explained in Chapter Five. Managers summarize the collected information as job descriptions that serve as input into the job evaluation process. Appendix A in Chapter Five contains examples of job descriptions that could be used in the compensation system.

Job evaluation involves the systematic evaluation of the job descriptions. It helps develop and maintain pay structures by comparing the relative similarities and differences in the content and value of jobs. When properly designed and administered, job evaluation can also help ensure that the pay structures are internally equitable and acceptable to the employer and employee.

Definitions of job evaluation are as diverse as the blind men's elephant. There are four common views.

1. Job evaluation is a device to classify or group jobs based on similarities and differences in their work content.[26]
2. Beyond simply classifying, it may help establish a job hierarchy based on relative value of the jobs.[27]
3. Job evaluation is an administrative procedure whose fundamental purpose is to link internal job content with external market rates.[28]
4. Job evaluation may simultaneously include the trappings of measurement (objective, numerical, documentable, reliable) and negotiations over the pay rates for jobs.[29]

All these views may be accurate, depending on how job evaluation is designed and administered.

Job Evaluation Decisions

Some of the major decisions involved in job evaluation include (1) determining its purpose(s), (2) ensuring involvement of relevant parties, (3) choosing among alternative methods.

Purposes. Job evaluation emphasizes a systematic, rational assessment of jobs as a basis for deciding pay. But there may be disagreement over what job evaluation can do. Experience suggests that specifying and understanding what purpose(s) we want job evaluation to serve influence its design and use. The plan that is designed should reflect the purpose of the plan. Because varying perspectives on job evaluation have led to controversy over its role in setting pay differentials among jobs, the purpose of the evaluation should be clearly specified.

Who to Involve in Job Evaluation?

If job evaluation is really an aid to managers and if gaining employees' understanding and acceptance of the pay structure is an important objective, then these groups need to be included in its design and administration. One common approach to gaining acceptance, understanding, and valuable ideas from managers and employees is through the use of compensation committees. Through these committees key managers and non-managerial employees advise compensation professionals about job evaluation results and also broader pay issues.

Researchers have made several case studies of employee participation in the design and administration of pay systems. For example, one reported on a plan designed with the assistance of a committee of employees and managers.[30] Within six months after the system went into effect, they reported significant improvements in turnover and satisfaction with pay.

To what extent should unions be involved in the design and administration of job evaluation? Management probably will find it advantageous to include union officials as a source of ideas and to help gain acceptance of the results. At AT&T, union-management task forces are working to design a new job evaluation plan. Their role is one of mutual problem solving. Other union leaders feel that philosophical differences prevent their active participation. In 1971 and again in 1978, researchers surveyed the leaders of 38 unions representing more than 7.2 million workers.[31] In 1971 the leadership viewed job evaluation as a threat to collective bargaining; by 1978 researchers observed a trend toward acceptance of it.

Job Evaluation Methods

The four fundamental job evaluation methods are ranking, classification, factor comparison, and point method. They can be distinguished by looking at (1) whether the evaluation is based on the whole job or specific factors, (2) whether jobs are evaluated against some standard or against each other, and (3) whether the process is qualitative or quantitative. A key feature is the degree of specificity with which the jobs are compared. To what extent are the particular characteristics for comparison called out? Imagine a continuum of specificity from ranking to classification to factor comparison to point methods. In ranking, a whole job is compared against other whole jobs on some general concept of value or job content. In classification, the job content and value are divided into categories or classes, and jobs are slotted into them. In factor comparison and point methods, content and value are broken down into factors and jobs are evaluated by the degree of each factor the job possesses. In addition to these four basic methods, uncounted variations exist. The following section offers some examples.

EXHIBIT 18–15
Typical Steps in Ranking

1. Determine jobs and units to be included.
2. Obtain job descriptions.
3. Select evaluators.
4. Define contribution or value.
5. Rank: Alternation ranking.
        Paired comparison.
6. Merge unit rankings.

Source: George T. Milkovich and Jerry M. Newman, *Compensation*, 2nd ed. (Plano, Tex.: Business Publications, 1987).

Ranking the jobs according to relative value is the simplest, fastest, easiest to understand, and the least expensive job evaluation method. Exhibit 18–15 lists the typical steps involved. However, ranking is seldom the recommended approach. There are several reasons for this. The criteria on which jobs are ranked are usually so crudely defined that the results are subjective opinions, difficult to explain or justify. Furthermore, ranking requires that users be knowledgeable about every single job under study. In larger, changing organizations this becomes a formidable task. Finally, even though ranking is simple, fast, and inexpensive, in the long term it may be more costly. Since the results are difficult to explain and defend, costly solutions are often required to overcome problems the ranking method creates.

Classification involves slotting job descriptions into a series of classes or grades covering the range of jobs in the organization. Exhibit 18–16 lists the typical steps in this method. Exhibit 18–17 illustrates class definitions with examples of typical jobs in each class. This method is widely

EXHIBIT 18–16
Typical Steps in Classification System

1. Determine jobs/units to be included in study.
2. Conduct job analysis/prepare job descriptions.
3. Select evaluators.
4. Define classes.
5. Identify and slot benchmarks.
6. Prepare classification manual.
7. Apply system to nonbenchmark jobs.

Source: George T. Milkovich and Jerry M. Newman, *Compensation*, 2nd ed. (Plano, Tex.: Business Publications, 1987).

EXHIBIT 18–17
Illustration: Class Definitions and Benchmarks

Class II

Ability to perform unskilled routine jobs which are almost entirely manual, requiring the use of simple tools or equipment.

Jobs usually do not require a knowledge of company methods or the exercise of judgment and decision. Versatility may be the prime characteristic and assignments will coincide with ability to assume tasks dependent on training and skill. Work performed under direct or limited supervision.

Benchmarks

Casual plant and field labor | Guard
Car and truck loaders | Janitor
Apprentice factory | Apprentice machine
mechanic | operator

Class IV

Ability to perform work of a skilled or specialized nature. Mechanically must have the ability to set up repair, overhaul, and maintain machinery and mechanical equipment without being subject to further check. Must have ability to read blueprints, material specifications and the use of basic shop mathematics or comparable experience with the company layout to offset these requirements.

Work may be specialized or a nonmechanical nature requiring the ability to plan and perform work where only general operations methods are available and requires the making of decisions involving the use of considerable ingenuity, initiative, and judgment. Work under limited supervision.

Benchmarks

Skilled machinist | Packaging supervisor
Skilled electrician | Shipping supervisor
Skilled mechanic

Class III

Ability to perform tasks of a semiskilled nature, either manual or nonmanual. Mechanically must have ability to operate or to examine machines for defects, dismantle, reassemble, and adjust for efficient operation without direct or constant supervision.

May have ability to perform work of nonmechanical status, but work which requires the making of some general decisions as to quality, quantity, operations, and the exercising of independent judgment.

Benchmarks

Stockroom clerk | General truck operator
Semiskilled mechanic | Research technician
Semiskilled machine
operator

Class V

Ability to perform work of the highest level in a trade or craft. This skill may be recognized with a license or other certification after formal apprenticeship training; or, after a considerable period of formal on-the-job training by demonstrated competence to perform equivalent level of skill.

Other employees to be considered for classification into grade V must regularly supervise others in the technical and other aspects of the work, perform other supervisory functions and may, in addition, perform work of a nonsupervisory nature.

Benchmarks

Master electrician | Factory supervisor
Master (chief) me- | Maintenance planner
chanic
Power plant—chief engi-
neer

used in the public sector. The General Schedule in the federal government is an example.[32] It is also commonly used for managerial and engineering/scientific jobs in the private sector.[33]

In practice, the most troublesome feature of the classification method is the need to describe each class properly. The description must be general enough to cause little difficulty in slotting jobs. Yet it must capture sufficient detail of the work to have meaning. Questions about how many classes, who defines them, and the like must also be answered.

Factor comparison involves evaluating jobs on the basis of two criteria: (1) a set of compensable factors, and (2) wages or points for a selected set of jobs. The method is more complex than either ranking or classification.[34] This complexity seems to limit its usefulness. Several versions exist; a typical example includes the following five steps.

1. Choose the key jobs to be evaluated. These jobs are well known in the organization and, in the opinion of the evaluators, are properly paid at present.
2. Rank the key jobs on important factors. Mental requirements, skills requirements, physical requirements, responsibility, and working conditions are some factors commonly used.
3. Divide up the current pay among the factors. If the job pays $3.75 per hour, how much of the $3.75 is for mental requirements? How much for skill requirements?
4. Reconcile the differences in ranking found in steps 1 and 2.
5. Place the key jobs on a scale for each factor. This becomes the basis for evaluating nonkey jobs in the structure. An example is given in Exhibit 18–18.

EXHIBIT 18–18
Factor Comparison Method Ranking Benchmark Jobs
by Compensable Factor

Benchmark Jobs	Mental Require- ments	Experience/ Skills	Physical Factors	Super- vision	Other Responsi- bilities
A. Punch press operator	6	5	2	4	4
B. Parts attendant	5	3	3	6	1
C. Riveter	4	6	1	1	3
D. Truck operator	3	1	6	5	6
E. Machine operator	2	2	4	2	5
F. Parts inspector	1	3	5	3	2

Note: Rank of 1 is high.

Source: George T. Milkovich and Jerry M. Newman, *Compensation*, 2nd ed. (Plano, Tex.: Business Publications, 1987).

According to Allan Nash and Stephen Carroll, only about 10 percent of employers that do a formal job evaluation use the factor comparison method.[35] The complexity of the preceding explanation demonstrates why. Some job evaluation methods seem so difficult to explain that their use to justify a pay structure becomes very limited.

Point method, like factor comparison, is rather complex. Once designed, however, it is relatively simple to understand and administer. Point methods have three common features (1) compensable factors, (2) factor degrees numerically scaled, and (3) weights reflecting the relative importance of each factor.

Exhibit 18–19 illustrates the steps in the design of a point plan. In point methods, each job's relative value and hence its location in the pay structure is determined by the total points assigned to it. A job's total point value is the sum of the numerical degree values for each compensable factor the job possesses. In Exhibit 18–20 the point plan has four factors: skills required, effort required, responsibility, and working conditions. Each factor has a possible five degrees. According to the weights, skills required carries more value than the other factors (40 percent of the total possible points). For example, a job's 240 total points may result from two degrees of skills required ($2 \times 40 = 80$), three degrees each of effort required ($3 \times 30 = 90$) and responsibility ($3 \times 20 = 60$), and one degree of working conditions ($1 \times 10 = 10$); ($80 + 90 + 60 + 10 = 240$).

Once the total points for all jobs are computed and a hierarchy established, the jobs are compared to each other to make certain that their relative place in the hierarchy makes sense.

The Hay Guide Chart-Profile Method, used by 5,000 employers worldwide, is perhaps the most widely used job evaluation plan. It uses Hay factors—know how, problem solving, and accountability.[36] The Ap-

---

EXHIBIT 18–19
Steps in Design of Point
Job Evaluation

---

1. Conduct job analysis.
2. Choose compensable factors.
3. Establish factor scales.
4. Derive factor weights.
5. Prepare evaluation manual.
6. Apply to nonbenchmark jobs.

Source: George T. Milkovich and Jerry M. Newman, *Compensation,* 2nd ed. (Plano, Tex.: Business Publications, 1987).

EXHIBIT 18–20
Characteristics of the Point Job Evaluation Method: Factors, Scaled Degrees, and Weights

Weights	Factors	Degrees				
40%	Skills required	1	2	3	4	5
30	Effort required	1	2	3	4	5
20	Responsibility	1	2	3	4	5
10	Working conditions	1	2	3	4	5

Source: George T. Milkovich and Jerry M. Newman, *Compensation*, 2nd ed. (Plano, Tex.: Business Publications, 1987).

pendix to this chapter contains a point plan designed for evaluating manufacturing jobs. It uses eight compensable factors.

Results of Job Evaluation

After considering job evaluation, some readers may be left with an overwhelming sense of bureaucracy run amok. There seem to be two overriding reactions. One is, why bother with it? Why not simply set wages based on what competitors are paying in the market? Another reaction is a sense of building fences around employees in a way that limits the employee and organization flexibility so necessary in dynamic, adaptive organizations. Let's look at both of these arguments.

Why Not Simply Pay Market Rates?

Job evaluation is based on the need to develop an equitable pay structure. We said in our earlier discussion of external competitiveness that certain jobs—key jobs—are comparable across several firms in the market. However, all jobs are not key jobs—all jobs are not similar across firms. It becomes difficult if not impossible to set pay rates for dissimilar jobs based solely on market data. The solution is to set the pay rates for key jobs based on what other employers are paying and set pay rates for all other jobs by slotting them around these key job rates. This slotting is accomplished via job evaluation.

AN ILLUSTRATION

In Exhibit 18–21 we have reproduced the pay level decision made earlier. Recall that this decision was based on market data and the organization's policy decision to lead, lag, or meet competition. This permits us to set pay rates for the five key jobs, A, D, G, M, and N. What about all the other jobs? Enter job evaluation. Let's assume a point job evaluation

EXHIBIT 18–21
Establishing a Pay Structure via Job Evaluation

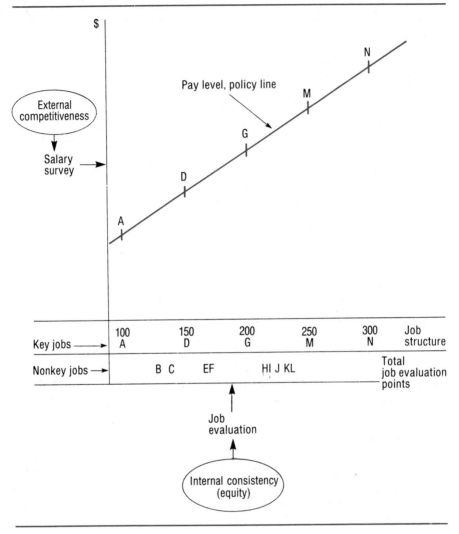

method is in use. Evaluating all jobs (A through M) establishes a job structure or hierarchy (horizontal axis). Each job is assigned job evaluation
points. The hierarchy represents the similarities and differences among
jobs based on content (compensable factors) and other variables (factor
weights). Based on this hierarchy, it is now possible to place each nonkey
job into the appropriate place on the pay level line. In the example, key

jobs A (100 pts), D (150 pts), G (200 pts), M (250 pts), and N (300 pts) and nonkey jobs B (130 pts), C (140 pts), E (165 pts), F (170 pts), H (210 pts), I (210 pts), J (230 pts), K (240 pts), and L (240 pts) are the total point results. Based on these point totals the nonkey jobs are placed into the structure. Their place in the structure is based on the market rates (reflected in the pay level line and rates for key jobs) plus the content of the work and compensable factors (reflected in the job evaluation process). Hence job evaluation links internal and external market factors. Through job evaluation, employers determine pay rates for nonkey jobs.

Obviously a point method of job evaluation is not required. Any of the job evaluation methods could be substituted to achieve a pay structure. The key is to ensure that whatever method is used is demonstrably work-related, and understood and acceptable to managers and employees.

Building Fences

The other criticism of job evaluation is that it builds fences. During a project involving the design of a job evaluation system at 3M Company, several operating managers became concerned about the effects of job evaluation on creative, committed employees. "It places them in neat, bureaucratic boxes." "It will inhibit them from going beyond their normal job, to adapt to changing and unanticipated events," were some typical comments. There is a danger that job evaluation can become a hindrance rather than a tool for more effective management of human resources. At its worst, job evaluation becomes an end unto itself; specialists become more concerned with the rules and regulations of the process than with the original purpose of attracting, retaining, or motivating employees.

Think back to the basic issue involved: building a fair and equitable pay structure that helps achieve certain objectives. To achieve such a structure, some way must be devised to set pay equal for similar jobs and to ensure that differences in pay for dissimilar jobs are equitable. Setting equitable pay differences is the real issue. With them we can encourage employees to invest in training and to seek greater responsibility, thus maintaining an experienced work force. If differences in pay are not grounded in work and business-related factors, then we run the risk of disgruntled employees, undesired turnover, grievances, strikes, and possible lawsuits.

Properly designed and administered, either skill based or job evaluation based systems can provide equitable pay structures. The challenge is to be sure that it does not inhibit creative and productive employees. In the next chapter we examine some approaches to compensation designed to reward such valued employees.

SUMMARY

A premise of this chapter is that no single best pay program exists. Rather, the design and administration of pay programs are contingent on the organizational and environmental context in which they must operate.

Within this context, there are several basic concepts and issues of concern. This chapter examined two of them. One was to establish external competitiveness by setting the pay level. This was accomplished through market surveys and determining the pay policy line. The other is to establish internal consistency in the pay structure. The structure, usually designed with the aid of job analysis and job evaluation, focuses on pay differentials.

We have begun to develop the pay system. In the next chapter, we develop it further to pay employees. We discuss employee contributions and individual pay, along with several alternative methods of paying employees. Merit pay, gainsharing, and lump sums are some major concerns in pay administration and pay discrimination that we discuss.

APPENDIX / A Skill-Based Job Evaluation Plan for Manufacturing Jobs: Factor Definitions and Points

Factor 1: Basic Knowledge

1st Degree (22 points)
Ability to read, write, add and subtract basic mathematics, interpret and complete simple instructions.

2nd Degree (47 points)
Knowledge of higher mathematical calculations such as basic decimal and fractional equations, ability to read and follow semicomplicated written instructions and to use basic measuring equipment.

3rd Degree (72 points)
Knowledge of a variety of manufacturing skills, specific training, work experience equivalent to trade school or high school, ability to read semicomplicated measuring equipment, graphics, technical or written reports.

4th Degree (111 points)
Extensive specific skills training in a specialized field; equivalent to one–two years of college or vocational (technical) training or master trade certificate.

Factor 2: Electrical/Electronic Skills

Application of the principles of electricity, electronics, electronic logic, and integrated transmission technologies such as lasers. This includes understanding of circuits, their component parts, and how they work together.

1st Degree (7 points)
Operational knowledge of electrical/electronic equipment without understanding the electrical/electronic principles on which the equipment operates.

2nd Degree (15 points)
Operational knowledge of electrical/electronic equipment with understanding the electrical/electronic principles on which the equipment operates.

3rd Degree (23 points)
Application of principles of electronic circuitry and appropriate wiring procedures.

4th Degree (37 points)
Application of principles of miniaturized electronic circuits and digital and analog transmission concepts.

Factor 3: Mechanical Skills

The application of mechanical knowledge of how/why mechanical equipment works. It includes the operation, repair, or maintenance of machinery/mechanical systems.

1st Degree (5 points)
This includes the use of basic mechanical ability to operate/adjust single or multiple pieces of mechanical or electromechanical equipment. It includes, but is not limited to, such elements as clearing jams and setting feed speeds and/or pressure changes.

2nd Degree (12 points)
This includes all elements of 1st Degree basic mechanical ability, with the additions that the incumbent is required to have the skills to perform preventive maintenance, disassemble/reassemble specific components, change tools, and the like.

3rd Degree (25 points)

Perform servicing and procedural repair activities on mechanical systems/machinery as the primary function.

4th Degree (31 points)

Apply advanced principles of mechanical skills to repair, rebuild, service to a close tolerance level of fit.

5th Degree (37 points)

Perform sophisticated diagnostic and repair activities on complex mechanical or electromechanical machinery/systems.

Factor 4: Graphics

Reading, interpreting, and/or preparing graphic representations of information, such as maps, plans, drawings, blueprints, diagrams, schematics, and timing/flowcharts.

1st Degree (5 points)

Understand basic blueprints and/or prepare rough sketches.

2nd Degree (12 points)

Understand more complex blueprints and/or prepare simple graphic information.

3rd Degree (25 points)

Understand complex, technical graphic representations of information and/or prepare technical graphics.

4th Degree (31 points)

Prepare and/or interpret complex, technical graphic representations of a wide range of information.

5th Degree (37 points)

Develop, prepare, and/or interpret highly complex, sophisticated graphic representations.

Factor 5: Mathematical Skills

The selection and application of mathematical methods or procedures to solve problems or to achieve desired results.

1st Degree (8 points)

Simple arithmetic computations involving addition, subtraction, multiplication, or division.

2nd Degree (15 points)

Computations involving decimals, percentages, fractions, and/or basic statistics.

3rd Degree (23 points)

Computations involving algebra (e.g., solving for an unknown) or geometry (e.g., areas, volumes).

4th Degree (38 points)

Computations involving the use of trigonometry (properties of triangles and circles including sine, cosine, and tangent functions), logarithms and exponents, and advanced statistics.

Factor 6: Communication/Interpersonal Skills

This factor measures the scope and nature of relationships with others.

1st Degree (28 points)

Little or no contact with others. Relationships involve providing and/or receiving information or documents.

2nd Degree (56 points)

Some contact with others. Relationships often require explanation or interpretation of information.

3rd Degree (84 points)

Substantial contact with others. Relationships usually involve discussions with stakeholders or recommendations on issues regarding policies, programs, and so on. Impact is considerable and may be limited to individual departments/programs.

4th Degree (140 points)

Extensive contact with others. Relationships usually include decisions in a broad sense and will affect several areas within the manufacturing unit.

Factor 7: Safety Skills

This factor measures the requirements for adherence to prescribed safety and personal security practices in the performance of required tasks.

These safety and personal security practices are generally required to minimize exposure to hazard or risk in the work environment.

1st Degree (10 points)
Perform work in accordance with a few simple safety procedures to minimize potential for injury.

2nd Degree (40 points)
Perform work in accordance with several specific safety procedures to minimize potential for injury.

3rd Degree (80 points)
Perform work in accordance with a wide range of safety procedures to minimize some potential for injury.

4th Degree (100 points)
Perform work in a highly variable environment where safety principles and procedures need to be tailored to deal with unforeseen hazards to minimize high potential for serious injury.

Factor 8: Decision Making/Supervision Required

This factor measures the degree of decision making required without being checked by others, and the degree to which immediate supervisor is required to outline the procedures to be followed and/or the results to be attained on the job.

1st Degree (36 points)
Limited decision making by the incumbent. Progress of work is checked by others most of the time, and/or 60–90 percent of activities are defined by other than the incumbent.

2nd Degree (89 points)
Routine decision making based on specific criteria. Progress of work is often checked by others, and/or 40–60 percent of activities are defined by other than the incumbent.

3rd Degree (112 points)
Significant decision making based on established guidelines and experience. Progress of work is checked by others some of the time, and /or 25–40 percent of activities are defined by other than the incumbent.

4th Degree (180 points)

Extensive decision making based on broad policies, procedures, and guidelines. Progress of work is seldom checked by others, and/or less than 25 percent of activities are defined by other than the incumbent.

DISCUSSION AND REVIEW QUESTIONS

1. How will strategic stages of an organization relate to pay?
2. Distinguish among the four policy decisions contained in the pay model presented in this chapter. Give examples where organizations may adopt different policies depending on the environmental and organization conditions they face.
3. What is a key job?
4. What is a pay structure? How do you construct one?
5. What are the four main job evaluation methods? What is the major advantage and disadvantage of each?

NOTES AND REFERENCES

1. See any basic text in labor economics, for example, R. Ehrenberg and R. S. Smith, *Modern Labor Economics* (Glenview, Ill.: Scott, Foresman, 1982).
2. Daniel J. B. Mitchell and Ross E. Azevedo, *Wage-Price Controls and Labor Market Distortions* (Los Angeles: Institute of Industrial Relations, University of California, 1976).
3. George P. Schultz and Kenneth W. Dam, "Reflections of Wage and Price Controls," *Industrial and Labor Relations Review,* January 1977, pp. 139–51.
4. Arnold R. Weber and Daniel J. B. Mitchell, "Further Reflections on Wage Controls: Comment," *Industrial and Labor Relations Review,* January 1978, pp. 149–58.
5. Donald O. Parsons, *Poverty and the Minimum Wage* (Washington, D.C.: American Enterprise Institute, 1980); Lester Thurow, *Youth Unemployment* (New York: The Rockefeller Foundation, 1977).
6. F. Ray Marshall, Allan M. Cartter, and Allen G. King, *Labor Economics* (Homewood, Ill.: Richard D. Irwin, 1976), p. 240.
7. R. B. Freeman and J. L. Medoff, *What Do Unions Do?* (New York: Basic Books, 1984).
8. Fred K. Foulkes, *Personnel Policies in Large Nonunion Companies* (Englewood Cliffs, N.J.: Prentice-Hall, 1980).
9. Edward E. Lawler III, *Pay and Organization Development* (Reading, Mass.: Addision-Wesley Publishing, 1981).
10. George T. Milkovich, "A Strategic Perspective to Compensation Management," in *Research in Human Resources Management,* ed. K. Rowland and G. Ferris (Greenwich, Conn.: JAI Press, 1988); R. F. Broderick, "Pay Pol-

icy, Organization Strategy, and Structure: A Question of Fit" (paper for the Research Symposium of the Human Resource Planning Society, presented at Wharton School of Management, University of Pennsylvania, 1985); D. Balkin and L. Gomez-Mejia, "Determinants of R & D Compensation Strategies in the High Tech Industry," *Personnel Psychology* 37 (1984), pp. 635–50; S. Carroll, "Business Strategies and Compensation Systems," in *New Perspectives in Compensation*, ed. D. B. Balkin and L. R. Gomez-Mejia (Englewood Cliffs, N.J.: Prentice-Hall, 1987), pp. 343–55.

11. Lee Dyer, "Strategic Human Resources Management and Planning," in *Research in Personnel and Human Resources Management*, vol. 3, ed. K. Rowland and G. Ferris (Greenwich, Conn.: JAI Press, 1985).

12. J. L. Kerr, "Diversification Strategies and Managerial Rewards: An Empirical Study," *Academy of Management Journal* 28 (1985), pp. 155–79; L. Gomez-Mejia, "The Relationship between Organizational Strategy, Pay Strategy, and Compensation Effectiveness: An Exploratory Study" (working paper, College of Business, University of Colorado, 1987); N. K. Napier and M. Smith, "Product Diversification, Performance Criteria and Compensation at the Corporate Manager Level" (paper presented at the fourth annual Strategic Management Conference, Philadelphia, 1984); J. Newman, "Pay Strategies for Declining Firms" (paper presented at National Academy of Management Meetings, August 1987, New Orleans).

13. Bruce Ellig, *Executive Compensation—A Total Pay Perspective* (New York: McGraw-Hill, 1982); Jude T. Rich, "Strategic Incentives," in *1980 National Conference Proceedings* (Scottsdale, Ariz.: American Compensation Association, 1981).

14. G. T. Milkovich, "Compensation Systems in High Technology Companies," in *Human Resource Management in High Technology Firms*, ed. A Kleingartner and C. S. Anderson (Lexington, Mass.: Lexington Books, 1987), pp. 103–14.

15. Edward E. Lawler III, *Pay and Organization Development* (Reading, Mass.: Addision-Wesley Publishing, 1981); Ellen M. Hufnagel, "Developing Strategic Compensation Plans," *Human Resource Management*, Spring 1987, pp. 93–108; P. J. Stonich, "Using Rewards in Implementing Strategy," *Strategic Management Journal* 2, no. 4 (1981), pp. 345–52; M. A. Von Glinow, "Reward Strategies for Attracting, Evaluating, and Retaining Professionals, *Human Resource Management* 24, no. 2 (1985), pp. 191–206.

16. R. L. Opsahl and M. D. Dunnette, "The Role of Financial Compensation in Industrial Motivation," *Psychological Bulletin* 66 (1966), pp. 94–118.

17. Richard E. Johnson, "Flexible Benefit Plans," *Employee Benefits Journal*, September 1986, pp. 2–7.

18. Jerald Greenberg and Ronald L. Cohen, eds., *Equity and Justice in Social Behavior* (New York: Academic Press, 1982); Robert Folger and Jerald Greenberg, "Procedural Justice: An Interpretive Analysis of Personnel Systems," in *Research in Personnel and Human Resources Management*, vol. 3, ed. K. Rowland and G. Ferris (Greenwich, Conn.: JAI Press, 1985), pp. 141–83; Jerald Greenberg, "Reactions to Procedural Injustice in Payment Distributions: Do the Ends Justify the Means?" *Journal of Applied Psychology* 72, no. 1 (1987), pp. 55–61.

19. Lester C. Thurow, *Generating Inequality: Mechanisms of Distribution in the U.S. Economy* (New York: Basic Books, 1975); Sara L. Rynes, D. P. Schwab, and H. G. Heneman III, "The Role of Pay and Market Pay Variability in Job Application Decisions," *Organizational Behavior and Human Performance* 31 (1983), pp. 353–64; Kenneth G. Wheeler, "Perceptions of Labor Market Variables by College Students in Business, Education, and Psychology," *Journal of Vocational Behavior* 22 (1983), pp. 1–11; Erica Groshen, "Sources of Wage Dispersion: How Much Do Employers Matter?" (working paper, Department of Economics, Harvard University, December 1985); Ronald G. Ehrenberg and George T. Milkovich, "Compensation and Firm Performance," (Working paper No. 2145, National Bureau of Economic Research, Inc., February 1987).

20. Thomas A. Mahoney, *Compensation and Reward Perspectives* (Homewood, Ill.: Richard D. Irwin, 1979); Kenneth E. Foster, "An Anatomy of Company Pay Practices," *Personnel*, September 1985, pp. 67–71; John Barron, John Bishop, and William Dunkelberg, "Employer Search: The Interviewing and Hiring of New Employees," *The Review of Economics and Statistics*, 1986, pp. 43–52; Charles Brown and James Medoff, "The Employer Size Wage Effect" (mimeo, November 1985).

21. E. Robert Livernash, "The Internal Wage Structure," in *New Concepts in Wage Determination*, ed. G. W. Taylor and Frank C. Pierson (New York: McGraw-Hill, 1957); also see Ehrenberg and Milkovich, "Compensation and Firm Performance"; Herbert A. Simon, "The Compensation of Executives," *Sociometry* 20 (1957), pp. 32–35.

22. Thomas A. Mahoney, "Organizational Hierarchy and Position Worth," *Academy of Management Journal*, December 1979, pp. 726–37.

23. George Milkovich and Jerry Newman, *Compensation*, 2nd ed. (Plano, Tex.: Business Publications, 1987).

24. G. Douglas Jenkins, Jr., and Nina Gupta, "The Payoffs of Paying for Knowledge," *Labor-Management Cooperation Brief* (Washington, D.C.: Department of Labor, August 1985); Henry Tosi and Lisa Tosi, "Knowledge-Based Pay: Some Propositions and Guides to Effective Use" (working paper, University of Florida, Gainesville, Fla., 1984); and Edward E. Lawler and Gerald E. Ledford, Jr., "Skill-Based Pay: A Concept That's Catching On," *Compensation and Benefits Review*, January-February 1986, pp. 54–61; Ian Ziskin, "Knowledge-Based Pay: A Strategic Analysis," *ILR Report*, Fall 1986, pp. 16–22. Also see the U.S. Department of Labor, *Exploratory Investigations of Pay-For-Knowledge Systems* (Washington, D.C.: U.S. Government Printing Office, 1986).

25. Edward E. Lawler III, "The New Pay," in *Current Issues in Human Resource Management*, ed. Sara L. Rynes and George T. Milkovich (Plano, Tex.: Business Publications, 1986); N. Gupta, G. D. Jenkins, Jr., and W. P. Curington, "Paying for Knowledge: Myths and Realities," *National Productivity Review*, Spring 1986, pp. 107–23.

26. Milkovich and Newman, *Compensation*.

27. Harold Suskin, ed., *Job Evaluation and Pay Administration in the Public Sector* (Chicago: International Personnel Management Association, 1977).

28. David A. Pierson, Karen S. Koziara, and Russell E. Johannesson, "Equal

Pay for Jobs of Comparable Worth: A Quantified Job Content Approach"
(Philadelphia: Department of Industrial Relations and Organizational Behavior, Temple University, 1981).

29. Donald P. Schwab, "Job Evaluation and Pay Setting: Concepts and Practices," in *Comparable Worth: Issues and Alternatives,* ed. E. Robert Livernash (Washington, D.C.: Equal Employment Advisory Council, 1980,
pp. 49–77).

30. George T. Milkovich and Charles J. Cogill, "Measurement as an Issue in
Job Analysis and Job Evaluation," in *Handbook of Wage and Salary Administration,* ed. Milton Rock (New York: McGraw-Hill, 1984).

31. E. E. Lawler III and G. D. Jenkins, "Employee Participation in Pay Plan
Development" (technical report to Department of Labor, Ann Arbor,
Mich., 1976).

32. Mike Burns, *Understanding Job Evaluation* (London: Institute of Personnel Management, 1978); Harold D. Janes, "Union Views on Job Evaluation,
1971 versus 1978," *Personnel Journal,* February 1979, pp. 80–85.

33. Suskin, *Job Evaluation and Pay Administration.*

34. Milton Rock, ed., *Handbook of Wage and Salary Administration* (New
York: McGraw-Hill, 1984).

35. Allan N. Nash and Stephen J. Carroll, Jr., *The Management of Compensation* (Belmont, Calif.: Wadsworth Publishing, 1975).

36. For a copy of the Hay Guide Charts and a detailed description of their use,
see Al Bellak, "Specific Job Evaluation Systems: The Hay Guide Chart-
Profile Method," in *Handbook of Wage and Salary Administration,* ed. Milton L. Rock (New York: McGraw-Hill, 1984), pp. 15/1–16.

chapter

nineteen

PAY, EMPLOYEE CONTRIBUTIONS, AND ADMINISTRATION

CHAPTER OUTLINE

The most important pay question for most of us is, how much of it do we get? The topics discussed in the previous chapter—external competitiveness and internal consistency (equity), pay levels and structures—seem abstract in comparison. This chapter examines various approaches to paying individual employees. It also considers a variety of issues associated with administering the entire pay system. These include budgeting, communication, pay discrimination, and paying special groups of employees.

How much should one employee be paid relative to another when both hold the same job in the same organization? For example, should all first-line supervisors working at Exxon Chemical's Baytown, Texas, facilities receive the same pay? Or should those with better performance and/ or seniority receive more? Should the pay increase employees receive be based on their individual performance, the performance of a team to which they belong, or the plant or corporate performance?

Employee contributions, the third basic policy decision in the pay model presented in Exhibit 18–6, helps us to answer these questions. Policies on employee contributions refer to the pay relationships between workers doing the same work within a single organization. The policy is translated into practice through a series of techniques which include pay ranges, pay increase guidelines, individual incentives, and gainsharing programs.

EMPLOYEE CONTRIBUTIONS: INDIVIDUALS' PAY

Several decisions go into determining the pay for individual employees. Two basic ones are:

1. Should different employees holding the same job or possessing the same skills be paid the same—or should managers be able to pay them differently?
2. Which factors should be used to recognize differences in employees; that is, should differences in pay be contingent on performance, seniority, or some combination of the two?

RECOGNIZING EMPLOYEE DIFFERENCES WITH PAY

Many employers do pay different rates to employees in the same job. The rates of the Dallas word processors in the last chapter (Exhibit 18–9) are an example. These differences reflect external labor market pressures and organization policies.[1] Two external influences are:

1. Variations in the quality (skills, abilities, experience) among applicants in the external market.
2. Recognition that employers place differing values on these variations in quality.

Differences in rates paid to employees on the same job also occur in response to the following organization factors:

1. Policies to recognize individual differences in experience, skill, and performance with pay.
2. Employees' expectations that longer seniority and/or higher performance deserve greater pay.

So pay differences permit managers to recognize differences among employees.

INDIVIDUAL PAY TECHNIQUES

Employers use a wide array of techniques to determine the pay of individual employees. These include *flat rates*, which are used when the policy is to not use pay to recognize individual differences. Techniques designed to give managers discretion in making pay decisions about individuals include ranges, pay increase guidelines, and individual and group incentives.

Flat Rates

In cases where wages are established by collective bargaining, single flat rates, rather than different rates, are common.[2] An example might be if all senior machinists II receive $9.50 per hour, regardless of performance or seniority. This flat rate is often set to correspond to some midpoint on a market survey for that job. Or it may simply reflect the results of the patterns established across various union-employer negotiations.

Existence of a flat rate does not mean that performance or experience variations do not exist. It means that the parties choose not to recognize these variations with pay. There may be several reasons for ignoring performance differences. Unions may argue that performance measures are biased; or the jobs may be designed in a manner that requires cooperative group effort. Different individual pay rates may hinder cooperation. Some organizations may pay a flat rate for a job and then attach a bonus or incentive to recognize performance variations. Gainsharing incentive systems follow this logic. Under these systems, differences in group or team performance rather than individual differences are recognized with pay.

Pay Ranges

Ranges set limits on the rates an employer pays for a particular job. Exhibit 19–1 shows pay ranges constructed for the pay level and structure designed in the last chapter. Five pay ranges, one for each key job (A, D, G, M, and N), have been established. Designing ranges is relatively simple. Lacking a "best" approach, designing ranges typically involves two basic steps:[3]

1. Develop Classes or Grades. In Exhibit 19–1, the horizontal axis is the job structure generated through job evaluation. A grade or class is a grouping of different jobs; thus, each grade may be made up of a number of jobs. There are five grades (I–V) in Exhibit 19–1; Grade I has one job (A) in it, Grade II has jobs B, C, D, E, and F, and so on. The jobs in each grade are considered substantially similar for pay purposes. They may have approximately the same job evaluation points (e.g., within 30 or 50 points in a 700-point job evaluation plan).

Each grade has its own pay range and all the jobs within the grade also have that same range. Jobs within a grade (e.g., jobs K, L, and M in

EXHIBIT 19–1
Establishing Ranges

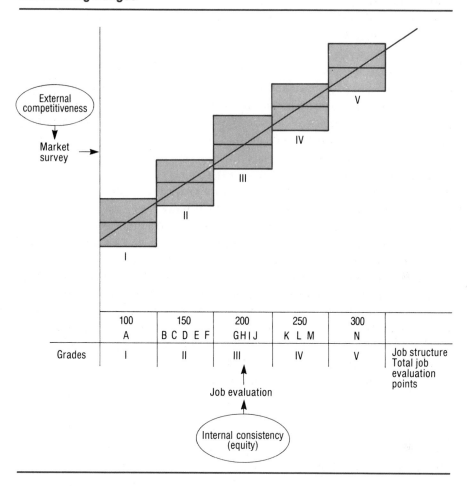

Grade IV) should be dissimilar from jobs in other grades (e.g., jobs G, H, I, and J) and have a different pay range.

What is the correct number of job grades? It simply depends on the circumstances. Designing the grade structure that "fits" each organization involves trial and error until one seems to fit the best without too many problems. The use of grades recognizes the imprecision in job evaluation. Some consulting firms, professing a high degree of confidence in their job evaluation system's ability to generate precise measurements, argue that grades are meaningless.[4] They state that each job evaluation point has a dollar value, and each job with its own point total should have its own range. Thus, they would say that the number of ranges should equal the number of jobs.

2. Set Midpoints, Maximums, and Minimums. Exhibit 19–2 shows a typical pay range with a maximum, midpoint, and minimum. Ranges permit managers to pay on the basis of employee experience or performance. The pay range for any job should approximate the range of differences in performance and/or experience that managers wish to recognize. For example, a job of plant manager accommodates a wide variation in performance level and experience, so the pay range for this job may be quite large. But there is less latitude in the job of insurance claims processor, and consequently a narrower pay range for processors. Ranges also act as control devices. A range maximum sets the lid on what the employer is willing to pay for the job; the range minimum sets the floor.

The midpoint rates for each range are usually set to correspond to the employer's pay policy line. The policy line represents the organization's pay level policy relative to what competition pays for similar jobs. The maximums and minimums (the range width or spread) are usually based on a combination of what other employers are doing and some judgment about what makes sense for a particular organization. Surveys usually provide data on both the actual maximum and minimum rates paid, as well as the established ranges (turn back to the previous chapter for examples).[5] Some compensation professionals use the actual rates paid, particularly the 75th and 25th percentiles (if available) to establish the maximum and minimum; others use the average of the established ranges reported in the survey as a starting point to design the ranges. The range spread can vary from 10 percent to 50 percent on either side of the midpoint with

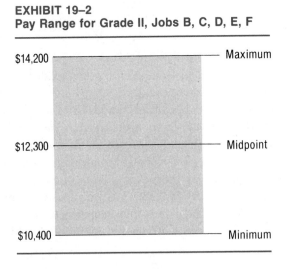

EXHIBIT 19–2
Pay Range for Grade II, Jobs B, C, D, E, F

$14,200 ——————————————— Maximum

$12,300 ——————————————— Midpoint

$10,400 ——————————————— Minimum

±20 to 30 percent of the midpoint most common. Wider range spreads, ±30 to 50 percent are common for managerial/professional/technical jobs, whereas ±10 to 20 percent are common in office/clerical/production jobs.[6]

Progression through Ranges

Once ranges are established, the next issue is to decide how employees should move through the range. Two criteria are commonly used, seniority and merit.

Seniority pay increases are based on experience or seniority on the job. Seniority-based pay increases recognize the value of an experienced, stable work force. However, as the work force grows older on the job, it also grows more expensive. So without turnover or productivity increases, unit labor costs increase under seniority-based systems.

Merit pay increases link pay to employee job performance. We discuss merit pay—pay for performance—in more detail later. If pay is tied to productivity increases, then unit labor costs are less likely to increase than they are in seniority-based systems.

The choice of which criteria to use—merit, seniority, or some combination of the two—depends on the objectives of the pay system. If managers want to try to reinforce performance improvements with pay, then some part of pay must be linked to performance. If they also wish to ensure a stable, experienced work force, then seniority needs to be included, too.

Pay Increase Guidelines

Most employees have come to expect annual pay increases. A variety of pay increase guidelines exist.[7] One, the *general increase*, typically is found in unionized firms. A contract is negotiated that specifies an across-the-board (equal for all employees) increase for each year the contract is in effect. Another, similar, increase method is based on *cost-of-living adjustments* (COLA). Under it, increases are triggered by changes in the consumer price index (CPI).[8] Exhibit 19–3 shows a typical COLA clause.

Another increase guideline, the automatic, or *seniority*, increase, was discussed earlier. For example, a pay range might be divided into 10 equal steps and employees moved to higher steps based on their longevity or seniority on the job.

By far the most common pay increase guideline for managerial and professional employees (about 97 percent are covered by it) is one based on merit.[9] Exhibit 19–4 shows an example of *merit increase* guidelines used by the Bank of America. The bank calculates pay ranges and the appropriate pay increase corresponding to each performance level. Lower

EXHIBIT 19–3
Cost-of-Living Adjustments Clause

Annual adjustments of 1 cent or .25 mills per mile for each 0.3 point CPI rise
Based upon the Difference between the
Index of January 1987 and the Indices for
the Months set Forth Below, Giving Full
Credit for All Prior Cost-of-Living
Adjustments (including amounts allocated
to Health & Welfare and Pension fund
contribution increases) Which Are Paid
Under This Agreement*

Effective Date of Adjustments

April 1, 1988	January 1988 (Published February 1988)
April 1, 1989	January 1989 (Published February 1989)
April 1, 1990	January 1990 (Published February 1990)

* For example, the April 1, 1989, adjustment will be calculated by the difference between the January 1987 Index and the January 1989 Index, subtracting therefrom the amount of the cost-of-living adjustments paid on April 1, 1989.

The Base Index figure shall be the figure for January 1987 (published February 1987) of 282.1. The cost-of-living increases shall be calculated as follows:

For every .3 point increase in the Index, there shall be a one cent (1¢) per hour or .25 mills per mile increase in the wage rates as indicated in the table below:

	Allowance	
Index Value	*Per Hour*	*Per Mile*
282.1—282.3	0	0
282.4—282.6	1¢	.25 mill
282.7—282.9	2	.50
283.0—283.2	3	.75
283.3—283.5	4	1.00
283.6—283.8	5	1.25
283.9—284.1	6	1.50
284.2—284.4	7	1.75
284.5—284.7	8	2.00
284.8—285.0	9	2.25
285.1—285.3	10	2.50

And so forth with each additional .3 point increase in the index there is a 1¢ per hour or .25 mills per mile increase in the wage rates.

Source: National Master Freight and Teamsters Agreement.

EXHIBIT 19–4
Illustration of Merit Increase Approach at Bank of America: Pay for Performance

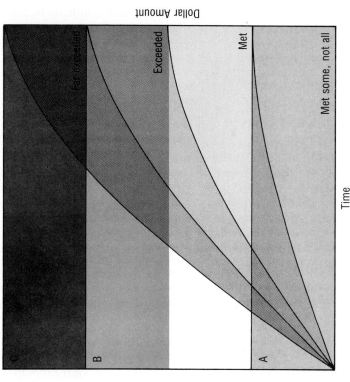

Your performance affects your pay in two ways.

First, it affects the size of the raise you receive. For example, if two employees started in the same job at the same time, at the same salary, over time the salary level of the one whose performance far exceeds will be greater than the salary level of the employee whose performance is rated as only having "met" his or her acceptable level of results. So, the better you do your job, the higher your salary can grow.

Second, the timing of your salary increase will be based on your performance and your position in your salary range. If two employees are in the same sector of their salary range, the better performer can expect to receive his or her increase sooner than the employee performing at a lower level. Thus, your performance determines how much of an increase you receive, as well as when you receive it.

Your pay is based on performance.

The better you do your job, the higher your pay can grow.

performance rates are tied to lower pay increases, and higher rates get the largest increases. In many firms, the poorest performers may receive no pay increases under a pay-for-performance guideline.

Merit Awards

Several employers, AT&T and General Motors Corporation among others, have turned to merit awards (contrasted with merit increases just discussed). Merit awards are pay increases that do not become part of an employee's base salary each year. Merit increases, on the other hand, do become part of employees' base pay. Several arguments have been advanced in favor of merit awards.[10] They are said to offer management greater flexibility and to reflect employees' performance more accurately.

Despite all the pay for performance rhetoric associated with merit awards, they are primarily cost control devices. Recall our discussion on employment planning; we discussed options for reducing labor costs by making a portion of compensation cost variable. Merit awards do this, thus offering financial flexibility. Most firms that adopt them are facing severe competitive pressures and are attempting to reduce labor costs.

Lump Sum Payments

Several employers use a variation of merit awards called lump sum payments. A quote from one company's manual illustrates this policy:

> The Lump Sum Increase Program (LSIP) is a payment option offering you the flexibility to tailor part of your total compensation to your specific needs. Under this program you can elect to receive all or part of any salary increase—whether merit, promotional, or a special adjustment—in the form of one lump sum payment (less a small discount for payment in advance). By making the full amount of your increase available as soon as it is effective, LSIP allows you to plan realistically for large expenditures without using retail credit plans having high interest rates.[11]

To date, no research evidence has reported how effective LSIP is. Smith estimated that 40 to 95 percent of eligible employees take advantage of LSIP when given the opportunity. Lawler argues "a lump sum program represents one way in which employees are treated more as individuals by the organizations that employ them and, as such, it improves the quality of work life." He goes on to state that "there are some reasons to believe the lump sum increases can also contribute to organizational effectiveness."[12] Yet, the effects of merit and awards of LSIP remain unknown; only research can tell whether this program affects employees' work behaviors or organizational effectiveness.

INCENTIVES

The technique of basing pay increases on improvement in performance is old and well-established.[13] Hundreds of different formulas exist for calculating payments to employees based on performance.[14] Incentives can be based on an individual's performance or on the operating results of a work team, plant, or even the entire corporation.

Individual Incentives

Perhaps the oldest form of compensation is the individual incentive plan, in which the employee is paid for units produced. Today the individual incentive plan takes several forms: piecework, production bonus, and commissions.

Piecework and Production Bonus

In piecework, an employee is guaranteed an hourly rate (probably the minimum wage) for performing an expected minimum output (the standard). For production over the standard, the employer pays so much per piece produced. The standard is set through work measurement studies and collective bargaining. The base rate and piece rates may be developed by surveys of compensation practices and financial analysis of revenues and expenses.

A variation of the straight piece rate is the differential piece rate. In this plan, the employer pays a smaller piece rate up to standard and then a higher piece rate above the standard.

Commissions

Commissions, another variation of individual incentives, are commonly used in sales jobs.[15] Straight commission is the equivalent of straight piecework and is typically a percentage of the price of the item. A variation is to pay the salesperson a small salary and commission or bonus when the budgeted sales goal is exceeded. JC Penney Company, Nieman-Marcus Company, and other retailers make wide use of sales incentive schemes for their store sales forces.[16]

Individual incentives are more frequent in some industries (retail, mining, textiles) than in others (lumber, steel, autos) and more in some jobs (sales, production) than in others (managerial, clerical).

Results

The research results on the effectiveness of individual incentives are mixed; most studies indicate they do increase productivity, but some question this outcome. Although production increases, other aspects decline.

For example, in sales, straight commissions can lead to less attention being paid to servicing accounts. There is also evidence that there are individual differences in the effect of incentives on performance; some employees are more inclined to perform better than others. This should not be a surprise, since theories of motivation indicate that people have varying motivations to work (see Chapter Six).

Incentive systems may be designed to affect outputs other than performance; for example, employers may use them to try to improve quality (reduce rejects) and lower absenteeism. Some incentive schemes have been designed to induce early retirement of older workers. Others are designed to reduce turnover of highly skilled workers.[17]

EXHIBIT 19–5
Factors Influencing whether to Use Individual or Group Incentives

Characteristic	Individual Level of Incentives Appropriate	Group Level of Incentives (Unit, Department, Organization) Appropriate
Performance measurement	Good measures of individual performance exist. Task accomplishment not dependent on performance of others.	Output is group collaborative effort. Individual contributions to output cannot be assessed.
Organizational adaptability	Individual performance standards are stable. Production methods and labor mix relatively constant.	Performance standards for individuals change to meet environmental pressures on relatively constant organizational objectives. Production methods and labor mix must adapt to meet changing pressures.
Organizational commitment	Commitment strongest to individual's profession or superior. Supervisor viewed as unbiased and performance standards readily apparent.	High commitment to organization built upon sound communication of organizational objectives and performance standards.
Union status	Nonunion. Unions promote equal treatment. Competition between individuals inhibits "fraternal" spirit.	Union or nonunion. Unions less opposed to plans which foster cohesiveness of bargaining unit and which distribute rewards evenly across group.

Source: George T. Milkovich and Jerry Newman, *Compensation*, 2nd ed. (Plano, Tex.: Business Publications, 1987).

Group Incentives

Employers also pay incentives to groups of employees.[18] Exhibit 19–5 shows several factors influencing whether to use individual or group incentives. Group incentives are useful when it is difficult to measure each individual employee's output and when teamwork is important. The performance of an entire team of employees, or the entire plant, determines pay increases. Examples of this include production of fiberglass insulation at Johns-Mansville Corporation plants or manufacture of electronic components by Honeywell, Inc.

Over the years several group incentive schemes have been used. Some focus on cost savings, others on quantity of production, and still others emphasize quality of the units produced. The basic premise underlying these plans is to share the gains with employees.[19] In the past few years the use of these gainsharing plans has been increasing.

Gainsharing

According to its advocates, gainsharing is more than a group incentive scheme.[20] It is part of a total management approach or philosophy. Exhibit 19–6 lists the organizational characteristics favoring a gainsharing plan. Key characteristics include small size operation, production and costs under employee control, an open, trusting participative relationship between managers and employees, and a technically competent work force. Experience suggests that a plant manager totally committed to making the incentive plan work is also required.

Gainsharing plans can be tailored to the situation, or older standard plans may be employed.

An Illustration: The Scanlon Plan

The Scanlon Plan is undoubtedly the best-known group (plant or companywide) gainsharing plan.[21] Joseph Scanlon, a union leader in the steel industry in the 1930s, developed the plan.

The Scanlon Plan includes a philosophy of management that is participatory and involves using pay incentives and a suggestion system. Each unit in the plant has a production committee made up of supervisors and employee representatives.

The committee screens the improvement suggestions made by employees and managers. If accepted, the gains (e.g., cost savings value of improved production) are shared with the work group, not just the individual who suggested it.

EXHIBIT 19–6
Conditions Favoring Gainsharing Plans

Organizational Characteristic	Favorable Condition
Size	Small unit, usually less than 500 employees
Age	Old enough so that learning curve has flattened and standards can be set based on performance history
Financial measures	Simple, with a good history
Market for output	Good, can absorb additional production
Product costs	Controllable by employees
Organizational climate	Open, high level of trust
Style of management	Participative
Union status	No union, or one that is favorable to a cooperative effort
Overtime history	Limited to no use of overtime in the past
Seasonal nature of business	Relatively stable across time
Work floor interdependence	High to moderate interdependence
Capital investment plans	Little investment planned
Product stability	Few product changes
Comptroller/Chief financial officer	Trusted, able to explain financial measures
Communication policy	Open, willing to share financial results
Plant manager	Trusted, committed to plan, able to articulate goals and ideals of plan
Management	Technically competent, supportive of participative management style, good communications skills, able to deal with suggestions and new ideas
Corporate position (if part of larger organization)	Favorable to plan
Work force	Technically knowledgeable, interested in participation and higher pay, financially knowledgeable and/or interested
Plant support services	Maintenance and engineering groups competent, willing, and able to respond to increased demands

Source: Edward E. Lawler III, *Pay and Organization Development* (Reading, Mass.: Addison-Wesley Publishing, 1981), p. 144.

Companies using the Scanlon Plan use widely varying formulas for calculating the amount of bonuses employees receive (usually a percentage of their pay). For example, some base the bonus on a ratio of total sales volume to total payroll expenses. This measure reflects labor cost changes (if corrected for inflation). Others focus on payroll costs for each type of product.

The main concept underlying the Scanlon Plan and all gainsharing plans is to use pay to help tie the goals of individuals to the goals of the organization. This is accomplished by sharing the gains from employee suggestions and technological improvements with the employees.

Profit Sharing

Profit sharing may be considered a form of gainsharing and group incentive.[22] Essentially, it is the payment of a regular share of company profits to employees as a supplement to their normal compensation. The plans must be approved by the Internal Revenue Service, which issues "model plans" to fit tax laws.

Profit-sharing plans divide a set percentage of net profit among employees. The percentage varies, but 25 percent is common. The profit share can be paid often (such as quarterly) or deferred until retirement.

The assumption underlying profit sharing is that employees who have profit-sharing plans identify more closely with the company and its profit goal and thus reduce waste and increase productivity.

But there are problems with profit sharing. First, an organization cannot share what it does not have; and in bad years there are no profits to share. The employees may have cut costs and worked hard, but perhaps a recession slowed sales and thus profits, or management chose an expensive but ineffective marketing program. Often, even in good years, it is difficult for the employee to see any connection between extra work and a share of profits received a year away, or worse, at retirement 40 years later.

Profit sharing is probably more successful in smaller firms where the employees can see the relationship between their productivity and company profits more easily. Plans restricted to executives have been more successful, as discussed later in the chapter.

Other forms of pay, such as stock ownership, are discussed in the next chapter describing benefits.[23]

COMPETITIVENESS, CONSISTENCY, AND CONTRIBUTIONS

At this point, we have covered three major policy decisions of the pay model introduced in the last chapter. We translated external competitiveness through market surveys into the pay policy line. It established the firm's pay position relative to its competitors for human resources in the labor market. Next, we translated internal consistency (equity) through knowledge-based pay systems and/or job analysis and evaluation into the pay structure. Internal consistency addresses the differences in pay among dissimilar jobs and skills and the equality of pay among substantially equal jobs and skills. Employers determine individual employee's pay through flat rates or pay differences (e.g., ranges) for those working on the same jobs. Ranges permit pay to be used to recognize differences in seniority and/or performance. Finally, employers determine pay increases through a variety of techniques designed to translate the pay policy regarding employee contribution into practice. These include general and merit increases, merit awards and lump sums, and individual and group incentives.

EVALUATING THE RESULTS OF PAY FOR PERFORMANCE SYSTEMS

From a decision-making perspective, companies evaluate pay for performance systems in terms of their objectives—efficiency and equity.

Efficiency: Pay for Performance

Can the performance of employees and organizations be affected by properly designed and managed pay programs? One way to answer this question is to consider three subquestions: (1) Is pay important to employees? (2) Should pay increases be based on performance? (3) Does tying pay increases to performance affect employee and organization performance?

Is Money Important?

From the motivational theories discussed in Chapter Six, it is apparent there is no instinctive or basic need for money. Money becomes important insofar as it can satisfy recognized needs. Research suggests that money is capable of satisfying physiological, security, and esteem needs. If these needs are satisfied by other means, or if they are not currently prepotent (e.g., other needs are greater), then money is seen as having lower instrumental value and is not particularly useful in motivating performance or any other behavior.[24]

If different needs are, in fact, of varying importance across individuals, this information could be used to design a pay-for-performance system. Edward Lawler argues for a two-step sequential process: (1) identify groups for which differential need strength is evident, and (2) devise selection programs that identify those individuals who have needs that can be satisfied through a pay system tied to performance.[25] Such a program, if successful, would permit organizations that subscribe to a pay-for-performance philosophy to implement a pay system designed to use pay for improved performance.

There is some evidence that organizations may be experiencing problems by assuming that employees place a high value on monetary rewards. One study suggests that managers overestimate the importance of pay to subordinates.[26] Given a belief that pay can motivate performance, supervisors become disillusioned when improved performance does not result from pay increases. This failure results in a general condemnation of pay as a motivator. In reality, however, it may be more advantageous not to view money as the supreme motivator, but rather as one of the numerous factors in the work environment that affects employee motivation.

Should Pay Increases Be Based on Performance?

Given that money can satisfy at least a subset of basic needs, the question now becomes *should* salary increases be based on level of performance? Substantial evidence exists that management and workers alike believe pay *should* be tied to performance.

One study asked 180 managers from 72 different companies to rate 9 possible factors in terms of the importance they should receive in determining the size of salary increases.[27] As Exhibit 19–7 indicates, workers believed the most important factor for salary increases should be job performance. Following close behind is a factor that presumably would be picked up in job evaluation (2, nature of job) and a motivational variable (3, amount of effort expended). However, a recent study reports that substantial differences were found among individual managers in the importance they said they attached to factors used in determining pay increases.[28]

EXHIBIT 19–7
Mean Ratings of Criteria that *Should Be* Used to Determine Size of Salary Increases

Criteria	Mean Rating
1. Level of job performance	6.23
2. Nature of job	5.91
3. Amount of effort expenditure	5.56
4. Cost of living	5.21
5. Training and experience	5.15
6. Increases outside organization	4.64
7. Budgetary considerations	4.53
8. Increases inside organization	3.69
9. Length of service	3.31

Source: L. Dyer, D. P. Schwab, and R. D. Theriault, "Managerial Perceptions Regarding Salary Increase Criteria," *Personnel Psychology* 29 (1976), pp. 233–42.

The role that performance levels should assume in determining pay increases is also less clear-cut for blue-collar workers. As an illustration, consider the frequent opposition to compensation plans based on performance, such as incentive piece-rate systems. Actually much of the discontent with performance-based plans is a reaction to the specific plan and the way it is administered. Lawler notes that "in many situations opposition to incentive pay comes about because the employees feel they cannot trust the company to administer incentive schemes properly."[29] From this data it appears there is some belief among employees that pay should be based on performance, particularly if the company can be trusted to administer the performance-based plan effectively.

Are Pay Increases Related to Performance?

Whether due to blind faith, belief in expert testimony, or positive review of existing research, many companies claim that they base pay on performance. In a Conference Board study of 500 companies in a variety of industries, 95 percent indicated they base increases on individual performance.[30] And some 82 percent of these companies claim their pay for performance programs are successful. Another 18 percent claim either the programs are a failure or are too new to evaluate. Perhaps the most disquieting conclusion of this study was—"there were no apparent differences in the features of the plans between those who claimed their plans were 'very successful' and those claiming theirs to be a 'failure.' "

The comparative payoffs of individual versus group (gainsharing) incentive plans have rarely been studied. One study reports that group incentives tend to compress the productivity distribution of workers. This is because the relative performance of the most productive workers tends to fall, and the most and least productive workers have higher quit rates when workers are paid on group incentives.[31]

The most positive results of pay influencing performance have been reported in the executive compensation literature. Firms' stock value and indexes of financial performance seemed to be positively related to greater emphasis on performance-based pay schemes.[32]

Negative Evidence

Most of the evidence arguing against a pay-for-performance system is based on problems encountered in implementing the system. The Civil Service Reform Act (1978) mandated that 50 percent of any pay increase for covered federal government employees be automatic (seniority based) and the other 50 percent must be performance based. One study of managers in the Social Security Administration found merit pay had no effect on organizational performance. The study measured organization perform-ance using both objective (e.g., average number of days to pay a claim) and subjective performance appraisals. The authors note, however, that the plan was not trusted by employees because they challenged it in court and its implementation was hamstrung by Congress and poor administra-tion.[33] Perhaps the best summary of these problems is offered by Clay Hamner. He lists four problems that make it difficult to implement a per-formance-contingent pay system.

1. *Pay is not perceived as contingent on performance.* Many employ-ers adopt a policy of secrecy in their pay administration practices. The secrecy surrounding pay increases may lead employees to believe that there is no direct relationship between pay and performance. In fact it may lead to beliefs that administrators are trying to hide bad pay practices under a cloak of secrecy.

2. *Performance evaluations are viewed as biased.* If performance eval-uations are based on subjective judgments by supervisors, and not on ob-jective criteria (e.g., units produced) many employees feel that ratings have the potential to be biased. Substantial evidence exists to support this position. At least one study suggests that this problem can be overcome, however, if performance criteria are carefully defined so that raters under-stand fully the different work behaviors being tapped.[34]

When performance evaluations are viewed as biased, then the pay-performance link is particularly difficult to establish. If employees view the evaluations they receive as arbitrary, little incentive exists to improve performance.

3. *Rewards are not viewed as rewards.* Assume, for the moment, that pay is supposed to be based on performance in Company A. It would be expected that A's employees compare the pay increase they receive with that of other employees in Company A. What happens if employees have an inflated view of their own performance relative to others in the com-pany? They conclude that pay is not tied to performance; otherwise their pay would be higher.

This is exactly the problem that Herbert Meyer uncovered in a study of several occupational groups in a number of companies.[35] People were asked to rate themselves on job performance relative to other employees doing similar work. Across all occupational groups, in excess of 95 percent of the employees rate themselves above average. For each of the groups, at least 68 percent of the employees thought they were in the top 25 percent of all similarly situated employees in performance. This is statis-tically impossible. But the important point is that these employees expect a pay increase commensurate with their perceived performance, and do not receive it, even though the employer thinks it was given.

4. Organizations fail to recognize sources of motivation other than money. One of the difficulties faced in compensation is the belief that money is a general panacea, capable of compensating for all other organizational problems. If one thing has been learned from the problems with poor productivity, absenteeism, and sabotage in the automobile industry, it is that money may attract workers to unsatisfying jobs; it may also help to retain workers, at least in the short run. But the ability of money to motivate under conditions where numerous other factors work in opposition is limited at best. Money can be a motivator, but not to the exclusion of other factors, including the job itself. A pay system must complement a well-designed job, rather than compensate for one that is poorly designed.

Equity: Pay Satisfaction

Besides performance, pay is presumed to affect employees' attitudes toward work.[36] Particularly important is satisfaction and dissatisfaction, since certain employee behaviors may be related to these attitudes. Lawler derived the model in Exhibit 19–8, based on his review of pay satisfaction and dissatisfaction research. A review of the research supports the following findings:

1. Satisfaction with pay is a function of how much is received, how much others are perceived to receive, and perceptions of what should have been received.

EXHIBIT 19–8
Consequences of Pay Dissatisfaction

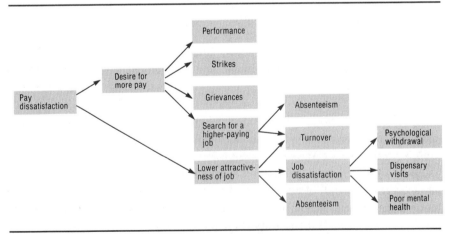

Source: E. Lawler, *Pay and Organizational Effectiveness* (New York: McGraw-Hill, 1971), p. 233.

2. Satisfaction with pay can influence overall job satisfaction as well as absenteeism, recruitment, and turnover.
3. The evidence generally supports the view that pay dissatisfaction is related to turnover. It clearly indicates, however, that the two are not always highly related. The relationship seems to be strongly affected by the importance the employee attaches to pay.
4. The stronger causal tendency is *that performance causes pay satisfaction rather than pay satisfaction causing performance.* Interestingly, pay satisfaction appears to be related to performance only when pay is based on employees' performance.
5. The evidence quite clearly shows that pay dissatisfaction can lead employees to join unions, go on strike, and file grievances.[37]

Pay dissatisfaction can be quite costly to organizations. It erodes commitment to work and may lead to absenteeism, turnover, and even lower productivity.

But what does the pay satisfaction/dissatisfaction research tell us about designing fair and equitable pay systems? The answer is, not much. Most of the studies fail to distinguish among internal pay comparisons, external market comparisons, individual pay, the mix of different pay forms, or how pay is administered.[38]

In sum, there is evidence to support the premise that pay is linked to employees' performance and satisfaction. However, in the case of the pay and performance relationship, certain potential problems often make it difficult to design a pay-for-performance system. The relationship between certain aspects of pay (level, structure, amount, and form) and satisfaction needs further research.[39]

PAY ADMINISTRATION

The fundamental tenet of this book is that any human resource management system, including compensation, implies objective-directed behavior. In the diagnostic approach, these objectives are efficiency and equity. Properly designed and administered pay techniques help managers better achieve these objectives.

Rather than goal-directed tools, however, pay systems often degenerate into bureaucratic burdens. The techniques become ends in themselves rather than focusing on objectives. Operating managers may complain that pay techniques are more a hindrance than a help, and these managers are often correct. So any discussion of compensation must consider the administration of the system.

Managers must make decisions on at least four administrative issues: (1) cost controls, (2) communication, (3) participation, and (4) special groups.

Cost Controls

One of the key reasons for being systematic about pay decisions is to control costs. Pay systems have two basic approaches that do this: (1) those inherent in the design of the techniques, and (2) the formal budgeting process.

Inherent Controls

Think back to the several techniques already discussed: job analysis and evaluation, pay policy lines, ranges, and pay increase guidelines. In addition to their primary purposes, they also regulate managers' pay decisions. Controls are embedded in the design of these techniques. A few examples illustrate the point.

Range maximums and minimums set the limits on the rates to be paid for each job. The maximum is an important cost control. It represents the top value the organization places on the output of the job. The skills and abilities a particular employee possesses may have greater potential value than the range maximum, but in a particular job for a particular employer it is the work output that is valued and paid. Presumably, some employees in this job may be qualified for other, higher-paying jobs. However, their extraneous qualifications do not affect the value of their present job. In other words, balancing a ledger has a certain value for an employer, whether it is done by a high school graduate or a certified public accountant. Range maximums and minimums are tied to the value of the work and the skills used to perform that work.

Budgeting

Budgeting, as part of the pay system, helps to coordinate and control future expenditures. Exhibit 19–9 shows an example of a budgeting process.

The cycle involves instructing managers in the use of compensation policies and techniques. Pay increase guidelines help managers to forecast their employees' anticipated pay rates for the next year. Then they review and summarize forecasts; eventually the pay budget for next year emerges.

Another approach to pay budgeting is to calculate the percentage increase in labor costs that the employer is willing (and able) to pay. This percentage increase may be influenced by factors such as changes in the economy, the cost of living, and the firm's ability to attract and retain its employees. Once this percentage increase is determined, it is allocated to the various units in the organization.

EXHIBIT 19–9
An Example of Compensation Forecasting and Cycle

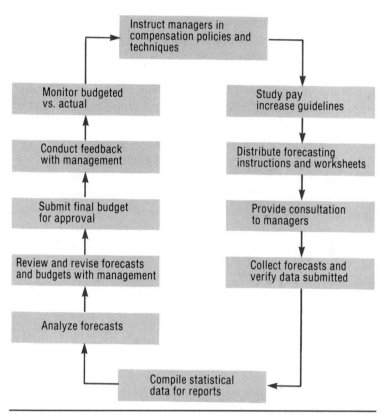

Source: George T. Milkovich and Jerry Newman, *Compensation*, 2nd ed. (Plano, Tex.: Business Publications, 1987).

Budgeting enables managers to foresee the financial impact of pay expenditures on the organization's performance. This encourages them to better manage the expenditure and distribution of compensation dollars.[40]

Communication

The literature on pay administration usually exhorts employers to communicate pay information.[41] Two reasons are usually given. One is that according to some research, employees seem to misperceive the pay system.[42] For example, they tend to overestimate the pay of those with lower-level jobs and to underestimate the pay of those in higher-level jobs. In other words, they tend to think that the pay structure is more compressed than it actually is. What difference does that make? It is important because pay differentials were designed to encourage employees to seek promotions, to undertake added training, and gain experience required for higher-level positions. Furthermore, there is even some evidence to suggest that the good will engendered by the act of being open about pay also affects employees' satisfaction with pay.[43]

The danger in pay communications should be obvious. If the pay system is not based on work-related or business-related logic, the wisest course may be to avoid formal, detailed communication. Nevertheless, employees are constantly getting intended and unintended messages through the pay increase they receive and the gossip floating among co-workers.

Some managers take a proactive approach. They reason that a pay system, properly designed, is intended to influence employees' attitudes and behaviors. To help accomplish these objectives, employee perceptions of the pay system need to be influenced. Hence, actively telling employees about the system, its techniques, and rationale is in order.

Participation

Lawler argues persuasively that employee participation can make a difference in the success of a pay system.[44] He cites two work groups doing the same kinds of jobs and operating under similar pay plans. One group had high productivity that continued to increase; the other had low and stable productivity. The first had a long history of participation in decision making; the second had the pay plan imposed by management.[45]

According to Lawler, a design process that includes employees can be successful in overcoming resistance to change.[46] Employees are more likely to be committed to the system if they have some control over what happens.

All-Salaried Work Force

The all-salaried work force, an old concept, is often considered as part of a strategy to increase employees' involvement and commitment. The all-salaried concept includes removing all time clocks, equalizing benefits and services for all employees, and converting hourly pay to biweekly rates. The objective is to improve employees' commitment to the organization by adopting a more egalitarian approach to pay practices.

During a study, TRW, Inc. emphasized that their all-salaried programs are part of a participative employee relations philosophy.[47] Such a philosophy goes beyond the pay system and involves the entire human resource management system. The fact that all employees are paid by the same method is not the critical variable—rather, what is important is the climate of respect, trust, and confidence.

Special Groups

Every organization has special groups of employees in unique circumstances. Often they are special because of the nature of the work performed. Examples include research scientists at Bell Labs, field sales jobs at Upjohn, or international assignments for any major employer.[48] The unique external and organizational conditions facing these employees often require that the pay system for them also be unique. Probably the most obvious one is the pay system for executives. Executive pay illustrates how pay systems are tailored for special groups of employees. The point is that firms typically have several pay systems, not just a single system.

EXECUTIVE PAY

For purposes of compensation, an executive is usually defined as any individual in a managerial position in the highest levels (e.g., top 5 percent) of the entire organization. A typical executive team appears in Exhibit 19–10.[49] Since executives are responsible for the direction of the organization, it is crucial that their compensation program link their actions to the organization's performance.

EXHIBIT 19–10
Typical Organization Structure of Top Management

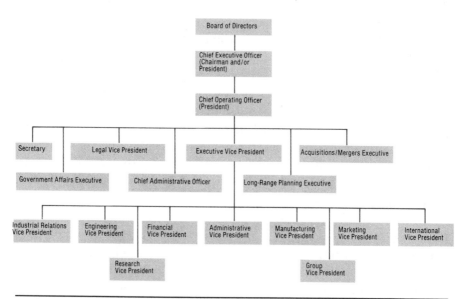

Source: Dartnell Institute of Financial Research, *Executive Compensation*, Dartnell's 14th biennial survey (Chicago: The Dartnell Corporation, 1983).

Compensation Decisions

Designers of executive pay packages typically face some of the same issues discussed earlier. Only the answers may differ because the external and organization conditions differ. (1) What competitive pay level (external competitiveness) should be set? (2) What should the pay structure (internal equity) be? (3) How much should each individual be paid (employee contributions)? and (4) What forms should compensation take (cash, benefits, etc.)?

Pay Level

Several surveys comparing different executive pay practices are available.[50] The surveys usually analyze the total compensation by executive officer title and industry subgroup. Also, the analysis is often performed on bonus- and nonbonus-paying firms.

Pay typically increases as sales volume increases. One explanation for this relationship is that sales volume is often seen as a measure of "organization size."[51] Therefore the larger the firm, the greater the responsibilities of the executive, and pay should be commensurate. To answer the pay level question—how should we set our executive pay compared to other firms—a policy decision must be made. Once the decision to lead, to meet, or to lag competition is made, then companies face the other pay issues.

Pay Structure

Pay structure for executives usually involves the pay relationships among executive officers. External surveys play a large role, as well as the simple ranking of executives in the relative importance of their responsibilities.[52]

Individual Pay and Pay Form

At the executive level the issue of how much to pay each individual executive and what form that compensation should take become intertwined. Usually specific financial performance of the firm plays a heavy role in determining the amount paid. But the form of the compensation also reflects the overall strategy of the firm and often the personal circumstances of the executive. The following section describes a few typical methods of payment.

Bonuses

Short-term incentives, or bonuses, reward the extent of financial accomplishment over a short-term (normally 1–2 years). Typically the amount of payment goes up and down each year in relation to performance. It supplements salary and can be paid in the present or in the future, in which case it is called a *deferred* bonus.[53]

Bonus plans range from being highly individualistic rewards to sophisticated plans with emphasis on corporate or unit performance.

Capital Accumulation

Long-term incentives are similar to short-term incentives in objective, except these are multiyear (3–5 years) rewards.[54] The incentive awards by definition mean the executive has a portion of compensation placed at risk with the degree of attainment of these objectives. The use of long-term incentives as part of the executive compensation package has grown in the past few years. This is in part due to the criticism that U.S. firms have been too shortsighted in their decision making as compared to their foreign competitors.

The most common forms of capital accumulation are stock options and performance share/unit plans.

Stock options give the executive the right to purchase a fixed number of the company's shares at a fixed price (exercise price) by a fixed time in the future. The executive gains as long as the stock price increases in the future. For example: The chief executive officer of a company is given the right to purchase (this is an option, not an obligation) 10,000 shares at $50 share within the next five years. If the market price of the common stock of the company increases to $65 an executive choosing to exercise the option gains $150,000 [($65 — $50) x $10,000].

Many types of stock options exist. Options are attractive to both executives and shareholders for the following reasons:

1. Executives must put up some of their own money as do the shareholders.
2. The value, the same as that of the shareholders' stock, is at risk with the price of the company stock.
3. Options are a form of profit sharing which links the executive's financial success to that of the shareholders.

Performance share units are another major long-term incentive plan. A performance share plan provides stock awards in return for meeting specific long-term financial performance targets.[55] Companies grant contingent share units at the start of each performance period, which is usually 3–5 years. At the end of the period, they convert the units into stock to the extent the financial targets are met. Usually executives must meet a minimum in performance before any award is made.

Benefits and Perquisites

Benefits are a major proportion of all employee compensation; as a result, they are a major expense to the employer. The next chapter examines them in detail. Here we consider a few of the unique perquisites (perks) available for some executives. Similar to benefits, perquisites have a low risk factor, since the degree of participation does not vary with the level of performance.

Many perks simply supplement the basic benefit package offered all employers. Some of the more valuable ones include financial counseling, low-interest loans, and tax assistance.

The employment contract, sometimes called a "golden parachute," is a perk which has grown in popularity and notoriety. The typical contract specifies a time period for which it is in effect, what constitutes acceptable performance, and the conditions of termination. These contracts are called "golden parachutes" because of the broad-based protections they offer executives in the event of a change in corporate control due to a merger or acquisition.

The most intriguing part of employment contracts is that some guarantee salaries and bonuses for the executives. This could have a negative effect on motivation and ultimately firm performance. The lesson to be learned is that employment agreements, as any other elements of executive pay, should motivate behavior directed toward the organization's objectives and strategies.

The Critics

Critics of executive pay are easy to locate.[56] Typically they report the salaries of the top paid executives, and then ask whether the executives are worth it.

We can do the same thing. Exhibit 19–11 presents a scatter diagram comparing executive pay and return on equity, a common financial measure of corporate performance. The two figures do not appear to be correlated. Others argue that such comparisons are too simple-minded, that effectiveness of executive performance shows up in later corporate results, that shareholders are satisfied, or the corporate performance is more complex than a few financial indexes. Some more rigorous research on these issues is under way, and the interested reader is urged to dig into the references.

The point to remember about special group compensation is that the basic issue faced in the design and administration of compensation plans must be readdressed in each application to each special group.

EXHIBIT 19–11
Executive Pay and Corporate Financial Performance

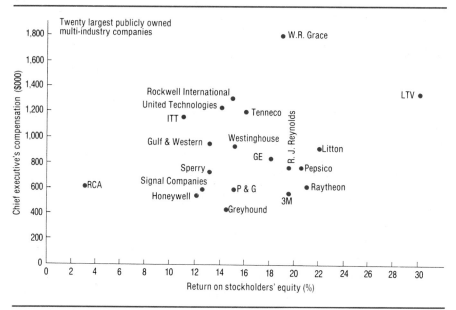

Source: *Fortune,* July 12, 1982, p. 47.

One final issue needs to be considered before bringing this discussion of pay administration to an end: pay discrimination, and in particular, comparable worth.

COMPARABLE WORTH

Where we discussed equal employment opportunity and pay discrimination, as promised in Chapter Three, in this section we tackle the minefield of comparable worth. Basically, the Equal Pay Act and the Civil Rights Act embody the principle of "equal pay for equal work." Equal work involves four factors: (1) equal skills, (2) equal effort, (3) equal responsibility, and (4) equal working conditions. These are strikingly similar to the compensable factors found in most job evaluation plans.

Differences in pay for equal work are permitted if they result from (1) differences in seniority, (2) differences in quality of performance, (3) differences in quantity and quality of production (incentives), or (4) some factor other than sex or race (e.g., premiums for night hours).

Earnings Gap

Pay decisions and administration are under challenge, due in part to the persistent earnings gap between men and women. A significant national debate over the causes of the earnings gap and how to define and subsequently eliminate pay discrimination is under way. The debate is not over whether all employees should be paid equally when they are doing the same jobs. That is required by the Equal Pay Act and the Civil Rights Act. What is at issue is pay differences for *dissimilar jobs*. Should jobs that are dissimilar in content but "of comparable value" be paid the same? For example, should nurses be paid equally with plumbers, or office clerks equally with assemblers or carpenters? The question was so interesting to Mary Lemons, a nurse for the city of Denver, that she took her employer to court.[57] She felt that nurses (mostly women) should be paid equally to tree trimmers (mostly men and unionized).

Several basic issues underlie the controversy:

1. Is the persistent gap in earnings between men and women (the average earnings of fully employed women is approximately 65 percent of the earnings of fully employed men) due to pay discrimination, or is it due to productivity-related factors (nature of the jobs, seniority, continuity of employment) and/or the collective bargaining process?
2. Should the currently accepted standard for pay determination (equal pay for equal or "substantially equal" work) be replaced with another standard—equal pay for work of comparable worth or value? (See the Equal Pay Act in Chapter Three.)
3. What is comparable worth and can it be assessed?
4. What are the consequences of adopting comparable worth as the standard for pay determination? Will the earnings gap between men and women be reduced? What will be the effects of adjusting the pay structure—on inflation, labor costs, or individual career decisions?

A Definition

Comparable worth, the principal mechanism suggested to reduce the earnings gap, has been defined as "jobs that require comparable (not identical) skill, responsibility, and effort."[58] It focuses on pay differences among occupations. However, several state and local governments have developed approaches to establishing comparable worth.[59] The Appendix to this chapter describes the steps the American Federation of State, County, and Municipal Employees (AFSCME) recommends for establishing comparable worth.[60] Basically the approach involves equal pay for all jobs with the same total job evaluation points. Thus, internal equity would dominate external market concerns. In the states of Washington and Minnesota, for example, jobs such as public health nurse and secretary received the same job evaluation points as carpenters and other craft jobs. Therefore, the rates paid to nurses and secretaries were raised to match those paid to crafts. Under this approach, the labor market forces for the nursing jobs are ignored. Rather, nurses are assumed to be operating in the same markets and represented by the same unions as craft workers.

An Application

Consider Exhibit 19–12. The black dots represent jobs held predominantly by women (i.e., female representation greater than or equal to 70 percent). The circles are jobs held predominantly by men (i.e., greater than or equal to 70 percent men). The policy line (solid) for the women's jobs is below and less than the policy line for male jobs (dotted line). A comparable worth policy would use the results of the single job evaluation plan (x axis) and price all jobs as if they were male-dominated jobs. Thus all

EXHIBIT 19–12
Job Evaluation Points and Salary

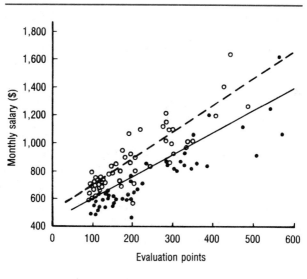

• Female-dominated jobs.
○ Male-dominated jobs.

jobs with 100 job points would receive $700, all those with 200 points would receive $800, and so on. So comparable worth is technically feasible.

Critics, Politics, and Costs

Comparable worth is, first and foremost, a political issue.[61] People who share a set of beliefs about how pay should be determined in society wish to convince a sufficient number of others that their approach is "fairer" or more "equitable." The courts do not seem inclined to interpret present laws in a manner that encompasses comparable worth. Consequently, comparable worth proponents continue to lobby for either new legislation or voluntary action supporting the comparable worth standard on the part of employers.

Since past pay legislation has outlawed lowering any wage to make pay equal, a comparable worth policy may require employers to pay all employees at the highest market line. This translates into the rate paid for jobs held predominantly by men.

Al Bellak raises a host of issues about such an arrangement:

- Would the unions give up their right to negotiate contracts independent of the pay arrangements in the other segments of the organization (i.e., would unions B, C, D, E, etc., have to agree to the same point/dollar relationship as union A, which signed the first agreement)?
- If the individual unions negotiated jointly for the same point/pay relationship, would there be any need for more than one union?
- How would an organization entice people into jobs where there were shortages because of distasteful work, if there were not premium pay for the same points?
- If one unit in a firm pays only base salary, will it have to increase its compensation level if another unit in the same firm introduces an incentive plan suitable for the business sector in which it competes?
- Must a state pay the same dollars for the same points to employees who work and live in a low-cost rural area as they do to employees in the high-cost large cities?
- Must a high-tech company raise the pay of its accountants (male-dominated) to equal the pay of its engineers (also male-dominated) for the same points?[62]

Underlying Bellak's points is a more basic one, which is whether legally mandating a job evaluation approach is defensible. Many employers do not use job evaluation at all. A mandated job evaluation approach simply does not fit all circumstances.

Opposition to comparable worth legislation is almost a reflex action for many employers. Legislation constrains their ability to act, to redesign pay systems, and to meet changing conditions. In addition, legislation usually translates into increased costs. Nevertheless, some employers that oppose a mandated approach to comparable worth are investigating how it could be implemented and its expected costs.

Some cost data are publicly available. A study in Pennsylvania reports "the average difference between existing wages for female jobs and predicted wages for female jobs based on wages for male jobs was $1.10 per hour," or $2,228 annually per affected employee.[63] Minnesota's Department of Employment Relations estimated the administrative cost of installing that state's comparable worth system at $85,000. Minnesota's actual wage adjustment allocation was $21.8 million to provide increases to 8,225 workers in female-dominated occupations over a two-year period. They estimate costs eventually at 4 percent of payroll. Other states have spent varying amounts on studies of their pay systems. North Carolina's study cost $650,000; New York's, $500,000. Note that these are only study costs. Implementing the concept is much more expensive. The state of Washington is implementing a comparable worth plan expected to cost $482 million even though the courts held it was not legally required to do so.[64]

How generalizable are these figures? Alice Cook estimated costs at .7 percent to 5 percent of the payroll.[65] A 5 percent increase in total wage costs may not be too high a price for some employers—those that can pass the costs on in the form of higher prices or increased taxes, or those whose overall labor costs are a very small portion of total costs (e.g., petroleum firms). Conversely, those employers facing greater competition and with a higher percentage of employees receiving adjustments will find a 5 percent increase in their wage costs intolerable.

Several other countries have adopted "comparable worth" as the standard for pay determination, but none have operationalized it. In fact, most countries, other than the United States and Canada, are still working to eliminate pay differentials for men and women on identical jobs.[66]

The problem of making global assessments of a position's overall contribution to organization objectives cannot be underestimated. "As work increases in complexity and interdependence, it becomes progressively more difficult to define a common criteria of worth and to assess the unique contribution of any given position to the organization.[67]

SUMMARY

The last two chapters have examined the basic pay issues and illustrated alternative techniques designed to aid managers facing these issues. It is important to place compensation in perspective. It is only one, albeit an important one, of the human resource management activities. However, it does represent a major portion of the expense budget for most managers. Consequently, the systems used to determine and administer pay must be well designed. Unfortunately, much of contemporary compensation administration is bureaucratic and technique-oriented. The concepts and objectives are often replaced with forms and paperwork. But change is in the wind. Challenged by increased economic competition, managers are beginning to manage pay. Similarly, challenges from employees and comparable-worth advocates are also causing some of the current practices to be reexamined.

The next chapter examines a major form of compensation that has long been ignored: benefits. Rising costs, concerns about their tax-free status, and questions about their value have caused personnel professionals to reexamine the management of employee benefits.

APPENDIX / A Working Woman's Guide to Pay Equity

YOU'VE COME A LONG WAY—MAYBE: A WORKING WOMAN'S GUIDE TO PAY EQUITY*

The popular cigarette ad shows a beautiful, well-dressed woman basking in her new-found liberation. Apparently she's "come a long way."

Many of the magazines where we see this ad support the idea that nothing stands in the way of a bright, well-educated, savvy woman in today's work force. It seems all she need do is dress for success.

In the real world there are a few problems, unfortunately. For example, according to the U. S. Department of Labor:

- On average, a woman with four years of college can expect to earn about the same salary as a man who never finished high school.
- Despite the ads displaying women doctors, pilots, and scientists, women are still concentrated in low-paying, dead-end jobs. Eighty percent of working women are employed in only 20 out of 427 occupations listed by the Census Bureau.

---

*Source: American Federation of State, County, and Municipal Employees, AFL–CIO.

- The proportion of poor families headed by women is steadily increasing.

Women have been streaming into the work force over the last 10 years—and where they have organized to fight for fair pay and better jobs, they *have* come a long way. But for all working women, there's still a long way to go.

HOW TO GET THE REST OF THE WAY

What can you do about low pay, lack of promotion, and wage discrimination?

For starters, maybe you should think about joining a union. In today's world it's unions that are looking out for the rights of employees in all sorts of jobs.

AFSCME, the American Federation of State, County, and Municipal Employees, is a labor union representing a million state and local government workers all over the country. Nearly half of those members are women. More than 200,000 of those women are clerical workers; the remainder work primarily in other jobs traditionally held by women.

For decades, AFSCME has been fighting for promotions, better wages and working conditions, child care, and an end to sexual harassment and discrimination. And AFSCME is the nation's leader when it comes to fighting for pay equity. In fact, AFSCME believes pay equity is the issue of the 80s when it comes to women's rights.

Pay Equity

Pay equity is basic to real progress for working women. It's a concept you'll want to become familiar with; after all, the battleground for women's equality is the workplace.

Pay equity is *not* "equal pay for equal work." It is equal pay for work of comparable value.

That means female-dominated jobs—secretary, nurse, librarian, for example—should be paid comparably to male-dominated jobs that the employer has deemed to be of comparable worth.

How does the employer determine that? It's not complicated. Most agencies and companies have personnel plans and job descriptions that enabled them to set salaries in the first place. A pay-equity study involves grading those job descriptions according to the skill, effort, and responsibility required; the education required; the hazards involved; and other factors.

These factors are rated for each job to come up with a job evaluation point total. Then jobs can be compared. If, say, a "secretary I" has the same number of points as a landscape maintenance person, the two jobs should be paid comparably. If a nurse has the same number of points as a mechanic, they should be paid comparably.

Do you think they are? Not likely. But you can find out for yourself how your own employer measures up. Use the pay equity study guide that follows.

START YOUR OWN PAY EQUITY STUDY

1. Gather Information on the Work Force. What follows is a list of information that a union or an individual can request from an employer to discover whether his or her pay practices are discriminatory.

- The number of male and female employees in each classification and the wage rate for each classification.
- The number of males and females hired in each classification during the previous 12 months.
- The number of promotional examinations taken and the number of examinations passed during the past 12 months broken down by sex and the number of males and females that were actually promoted.
- Copies of any job evaluation studies done in the last five years.
- A copy of the employer's affirmative action plan and most recent EEO-4 reports.

In the case of a government agency, the information should be available under either the state's Freedom of Information Act or the State Public Employment Relations Law.

Your employer won't be delighted to turn over this information, and may make it hard for you to obtain it. He or she might claim the information isn't available in the form you want it, or you may be charged for the computer run. It may be necessary for you to make some accommodations, but if your employer is unreasonable you can pursue legal avenues to get the information.

2. Analyze the Work Force.

- Of the total number of employees, compute the number and percentage that are male and the number and percentage that are female.
- Of the total number of position classifications, compute the number and percentage that are sex segregated (that is, 70 percent and above of the incumbents in a position are of one sex). Of the classifications

that are sex segregated, compute the number and percentage that are male and the number and percentage that are female.

- Compute the average salary of the total work force, the average salary of all males, and the average salary of all females. Compute the average salary of all sex-segregated classifications, the average salary of male-dominated classifications, and the average salary of female-dominated classifications.
- To show salary range distribution, list the number and percentage of males and females for each job classification in descending salary range order.

3. Select Representative Jobs (Benchmark Jobs).

- Include "male jobs" and "female jobs."
- Include jobs with a large number of incumbents.
- Include jobs that represent a range of wage levels.

4. Get Job Descriptions for Benchmark Jobs.

- Make certain that descriptions are detailed, accurate, and current.

5. Identify from Each Job Description the Qualifications Required to Be Hired for the Position.

- Education
- Experience
- Skills or knowledge
- Training

6. Group Jobs by Similarity of Qualifications.   Sample groupings:

- No educational requirement, no experience required.
- High school diploma (or equivalent), no experience.
- High school diploma, specific skill training, no experience.
- High school diploma, specific skill training, experience.
- College degree, no experience.
- College degree, experience.
- College degree, graduate degree in specific discipline(s).

7. Within Each Qualification Grouping, Separate the "Male" Jobs and "Female" Jobs and Calculate an Average Salary for Each Sex.

8. Compare Averages of Pay for "Male" and "Female" Jobs that Require Similar Qualifications.

9. Summarize the Findings. A pay equity problem exists if:

A pattern of sex-segregated jobs and departments is found.

Average pay is lower for women than men.

"Women's" jobs are paid lower than "men's" jobs.

When salaries for "women's" jobs which require similar qualifications to "men's" jobs are compared, the women are paid less.

10. Prepare a Concise Report to Highlight the Results of the Preliminary Study. The report that results from the above analysis should be used to advance the overall strategy you or your union use to work toward pay equity.

PUT YOUR PAY EQUITY STUDY TO WORK

Once you have documented sex-based wage disparities, the next step is to convince your employer to correct them.

Your employer might be willing to upgrade the pay and classifications of the jobs filled primarily by women—especially if there are relatively few employees and job classifications where you work.

However, most employers who are willing to address the issue will want to do a job evaluation study to determine more precisely the extent and nature of the pay inequities. Many public employers have already completed and implemented such studies and many more are in the process of doing them.

AFSCME recommends that such studies be done either by an outside consultant or jointly by the union and the employer. Studies done solely by the employer run the risk of being biased in favor of the status quo.

No matter how the study is done, it is important that the union or employees' group be involved throughout the process. In most cases a steering committee composed of labor and employer representatives oversees the study.

Technical assistance on job evaluation is available from AFSCME.

An employer refusing to take steps to correct the pay inequities you uncover in your preliminary analysis can be charged with violation of Title VII of the Civil Rights Act.

That's a serious charge. In the fall of 1983 AFSCME won over $500 million for underpaid state workers in female-dominated jobs in the State of Washington.

It was a landmark pay equity case in which the state was found guilty of violating the U.S. Civil Rights Act because it operates a sex-segregated work force in which female-dominated jobs are underpaid, according to the state's own job evaluation studies.

The ruling in *AFSCME* v. *the State of Washington* stands to break the pattern of sex-based wage discrimination in this country.

Pay equity is achievable. Thousands of employees represented by AFSCME—in San Jose, California; Spokane, Washington; the State of Minnesota and elsewhere—have already negotiated contracts providing pay equity increases. Many other public employers are in various stages of doing pay equity job evaluation studies.

Having pioneered the drive for pay equity, AFSCME intends to keep up the momentum. We have to. The battle for women's rights is now in the workplace and pay equity is fundamental to workplace justice.

DISCUSSION AND REVIEW QUESTIONS

1. In which circumstances may an employer wish to pay individuals on the same job different wages? In what circumstances may an employer wish to pay all individuals on the same job the same wages?
2. When would you use group versus individual pay incentives? What are the advantages and disadvantages of each?
3. What are "inherent controls?" Give an example.
4. Which employee groups might need a separate pay system? Why?
5. What is comparable worth, and how does it differ from equal pay? What is legally required? What are some approaches to operationalizing comparable worth?

NOTES AND REFERENCES

1. Walter A. Fogel, "Job Rate Ranges: A Theoretical and Empirical Analysis," *Industrial and Labor Relations Review*, July 1964, pp. 584–97; W. A. Fogel, "Wage Administration and Job Rate Ranges," *California Management Review*, Spring 1965, pp. 77–84; George T. Milkovich and Jerry M. Newman, *Compensation*, 2nd ed. (Plano, Tex.: Business Publications, 1987).
2. John A. Fossum, *Labor Relations* (Plano, Tex.: Business Publications, 1982), p. 192.
3. Compensation texts that the reader may find useful include David W. Belcher and Tom Atchison, *Compensation Administration* (Englewood Cliffs, N.J.: 1987); Richard I. Henderson, *Compensation Management* (Reston, Va.: Reston Publishing, 1984); Milton L. Rock, ed., *Handbook of Wage and Salary Administration* (New York: McGraw-Hill, 1984); Thomas Patton, *Pay, Employee Compensation, and Incentive Plans* (New York: Free Press, 1977); or Frederick S. Hills, *Compensation Decision Making* (Hinsdale, Ill.: Dryden Press, 1987).
4. Hay Associates make this argument that each job has its own evaluation point total and its own range. That is, each job evaluation point has a dollar value.
5. Milkovich and Newman, *Compensation*, Business Publications, 1987.
6. Belcher and Atchison, *Compensation Administration*.

7. Ibid.; Milkovich and Newman, *Compensation;* Charles Peck, *Pay and Performance: The Interaction of Compensation and Performance Appraisal* (New York: The Conference Board, 1984).

8. For example, see the discussion of COLAs in Milkovich and Newman, *Compensation;* also see Janet L. Norwood, "Two Consumer Price Index Issues," *Monthly Labor Review,* March 1981, pp. 58–61.

9. R. L. Heneman, *Pay and Performance: Exploring the Merit System* (New York: Pergamon Press, 1984); Peck, *Pay and Performance.*

10. Carla O'Dell, *Major Findings from People, Performance, and Pay* (Houston, Tex.: American Productivity Center, 1986); Andrew Weiss, "Incentives and Worker Behavior: Some Evidence" (Working paper No. 2194, National Bureau of Economic Research, Inc., March 1987).

11. C. A. Smith, "Lump Sum Increases—A Creditable Change Strategy," *Personnel* 56 (1979), pp. 59–63.

12. Edward E. Lawler III, *Pay and Organization Development* (Reading, Mass.: Addison-Wesley Publishing, 1981).

13. James Lincoln, *Incentive Management* (Cleveland, Ohio: Lincoln Electric Co., 1969).

14. Max Bazerman and Brian Graham-Moore, "PG Formulas: Developing a Reward Structure to Achieve Organizational Goals," in *Productivity Gainsharing,* ed. Brian Graham-Moore and Timothy Ross (Englewood Cliffs, N.J.: Prentice-Hall, 1983); D. Rowland and B. Greene, "Incentive Pay: Productivity's Own Reward," *Personnel Journal,* March 1987, pp. 49–57.

15. C. F. Schultz, *Compensating the Sales Professional* (New York: Towers, Perrin, Forster, and Crosby, 1985); N. Ford, O. Walker, and G. Churchill, "Differences in the Attractiveness of Alternative Rewards among Industrial Salespeople: Additional Evidence," *Sales Force Performance* (Lexington, Mass.: D. C. Heath, 1985).

16. John K. Moynahan, *Designing an Effective Sales Compensation Program* (New York: AMACOM, 1980).

17. Weiss, "Incentives and Worker Behavior."

18. *Gainsharing: A Collection of Papers* (Norcross, Ga.: Institute of Industrial Engineers, 1983); Lawler, *Pay and Organization Development,* p. 144.

19. O'Dell, *Major Findings;* Martin Weitzman, *The Share Economy: Conquering Stagflation* (Cambridge, Mass.: Harvard University Press, 1984).

20. Robert B. McKersie, "The Promise of Gainsharing," *ILR Report,* Fall 1986, pp. 7–11; O'Dell, *Major Findings;* Lawler, *Pay and Organization Development.*

21. Fred Lesieur and Elbridge Puckett, "The Scanlon Plan Has Proved Itself," *Harvard Business Review,* September–October 1969, pp. 109–18; A. J. Geare, "Productivity from Scanlon-Type Plans," *Academy of Management Review,* July 1976, pp. 99–108; George Schultz and Robert McKersie, "Participation-Achievement-Reward Systems," *Journal of Management Studies,* May 1973, pp. 141–61; Brian Moore, "The Scanlon Plant-Wide Incentive Plan," *Training and Development Journal,* February 1976, pp. 50–53; George Sherman, "The Scanlon Plan: Its Capabilities for Productivity Improvement," *Personnel Administrator,* July 1976, pp. 17–20; T. Gilson and M. Lefcowitz, "A Plant-Wide Productivity Bonus in a Small Factory," *Industrial Labor Relations Review* 10, no. 3 (1957), pp. 284–96.

22. Domenico Mario Nuti, "Profit-Sharing and Employment: Claims and Overclaims," *Industrial Relations*, Winter 1987, pp. 18–29.

23. Katherine J. Klein, "Employee Stock Ownership and Employee Attitudes: A Test of Three Models," *Journal of Applied Psychology*, May 1987, pp. 319–32; Cory Rosen, Katherine J. Klein, and K. M. Young, *Employee Ownership in the United States: The Equity Solution* (Lexington, Mass.: Lexington Books, 1986).

24. A. Maslow, *Motivation and Personality* (New York: Harper & Row, 1954).

25. E. E. Lawler III, *Pay and Organization Effectiveness* (New York: McGraw-Hill, 1971).

26. F. A. Heller and L. W. Porter, "Perceptions of Managerial Needs and Skills in Two National Samples," *Occupational Psychology* 40, no. 1 (1966), pp. 1–13.

27. L. Dyer, D. P. Schwab, and R. D. Theriault, "Managerial Perceptions Regarding Salary Increase Criteria," *Personnel Psychology* 29, no. 2 (1976), pp. 233–42.

28. Peter D. Sherer, D. P. Schwab, and H. G. Heneman III, "Managerial Salary-Raise Decisions: A Policy-Capturing Approach," *Personnel Psychology*, Spring 1987, pp. 27–38.

29. E. E. Lawler III, "Managers' Attitudes toward How Their Pay Is and Should Be Determined," *Journal of Applied Psychology* 50 (1966), pp. 273–79. E. E. Lawler III and E. Levin, "Union Officer's Perceptions of Members Pay Preferences," *Industrial and Labor Relations Review* 21, no. 4 (1968), pp. 509–17.

30. Peck, *Pay and Performance.*

31. Weiss, "Incentives and Worker Behavior."

32. Kevin J. Murphy, "Corporate Performance and Managerial Remuneration: An Empirical Analysis," *Journal of Accounting and Economics*, April 1985, pp. 11–42; D. F. Larcker, "The Association between Performance Plan Adoption and Corporate Capital Investments," *Journal of Accounting and Economics* 5 (1983), pp. 3–30.

33. Jane L. Pearce and James L. Perry, "Federal Merit Pay: A Longitudinal Analysis," *Public Administration Review*, July–August 1983, pp. 315–25.

34. Clay W. Hamner, "How to Ruin Motivation with Pay," *Compensation Review*, Third Quarter 1975, pp. 88–98; Herbert H. Meyer, "Pay for Performance Dilemma," *Organizational Dynamics*, Winter 1975, pp. 71–78.

35. Herbert H. Meyer, "The Pay-for-Performance Dilemma," *Organizational Dynamics*, Winter 1975, pp. 71–78.

36. Herbert G. Heneman III, "Pay Satisfaction," in *Research in Personnel and Human Resources Management*, vol. 3, ed. K. M. Rowland and G. R. Ferris (Greenwich, Conn.: JAI Press, 1985).

37. Heneman, "Pay Satisfaction"; Lawler, *Pay and Organization Development;* also see Stephan J. Motowidlo, "Relationship between Self-Rated Performance and Pay Satisfaction among Sales Representatives," *Journal of Applied Psychology* 67, no. 2 (1982), pp. 209–13.

38. Heneman, "Pay Satisfaction."

39. Chris Berger, "The Effects of Pay Levels, Pay Values and Employee Benefits on Pay Satisfaction" (working paper, Purdue University Graduate School of Business, 1984); Carla O'Dell, *Gainsharing Involvement, Incen-*

tives, and Productivity (New York: American Management Associations, 1981).

40. Persons interested in more detail on compensation budgeting and planning may read Milkovich and Newman, *Compensation.*

41. Dartnell Institute of Financial Research, "Executive Compensation: Dartnell's 14th biennial survey" (Chicago: The Dartnell Corp., 1982); American Management Associations, "Executive Compensation Service: Top Management Report: 33rd ed." (New York: AMA, 1982); Bruce Ellig, *Executive Compensation: A Total Pay Perspective* (New York: McGraw-Hill, 1982); James E. Cheeks, *How to Compensate Executives* (Homewood, Ill.: Dow Jones-Irwin, 1982).

42. E. E. Lawler III, "Secrecy and the Need to Know," in *Managerial Motivation and Compensation,* ed. Henry Tosi, Robert House, and M. Dunnette (East Lansing: Michigan State University Press, 1972).

43. Ibid.; also see T. A. Mahoney and W. Weitzel, "Secrecy and Managerial Compensation," *Industrial Relations* 17, no. 2 (1978), pp. 245–51.

44. Lawler, *Pay and Organization Development;* G. Douglas Jenkins, Jr., and E. E. Lawler III, "Impact of Employee Participation in Pay Plan Development," *Organization Behavior and Human Performance* 28, no. 2 (1981), pp. 111–28.

45. Jenkins and Lawler, "Impact."

46. Ibid.

47. Ian Ziskin, *The All-Salaried Work Force* (report to Corporate Compensation Department, TRW, Cleveland, Ohio, 1982).

48. Milkovich and Newman, *Compensation,* chap. 15; Belcher and Atchison, *Compensation Administration;* Rock, *Handbook.*

49. Ellig, *Executive Compensation.*

50. Ibid.; Fred Foulkes, *Handbook of Executive Compensation* (Cambridge, Mass.: Harvard University Press, 1988).

51. L. Gomez-Mejia, H. Tosi, and T. Hinkin, "Managerial Control, Performance, and Executive Compensation," *Academy of Management Journal,* March 1987, pp. 51–70; J. Deckop, "Top Executive Compensation and the Pay-for-Performance Issue," in *New Perspectives in Compensation,* ed. D. Balkin and L. Gomez-Mejia (Englewood Cliffs, N.J.: Prentice-Hall, 1987); N. Agarwal, "Determinants of Executive Compensation," *Industrial Relations* 20, no. 1 (1981), pp. 36–46; E. T. Redling, "Myth versus Reality: The Relationship between Top Executive Pay and Corporate Performance," *Compensation Review* 13, no. 4 (1981), pp. 16–24.

52. Ron Ehrenberg and George Milkovich, "Compensation and Firm Performance" (Working paper No. 2145, National Bureau of Economic Research, February 1987); Herbert A. Simon, "The Compensation of Executives," *Sociometry* 20 (1957), pp. 32–35.

53. Ellig, *Executive Compensation;* Gomez-Mejia, Tosi, and Hinkin, "Managerial Control."

54. J. T. Rich and J. A. Larson, "Why Some Long-Term Incentives Fail," *Compensation Review* 16, no. 1 (1984), pp. 26–37; A. Rappaport, "Executive Incentives versus Corporate Growth," *Harvard Business Review* 56, no. 4 (1978), pp. 81–88.

55. Ellig, *Executive Compensation.*

56. J. Dunlop, "Executive Compensation and Public Policy," in *Handbook on Executive Compensation*, ed. Fred Foulkes (Cambridge, Mass.: Harvard University Press, 1988).

57. *Lemons v. City and County of Denver* 620 F.2d, 228 (1980).

58. D. J. Treiman and H. Hartman, *Women, Work and Wages: Equal Pay for Equal Value* (Washington, D.C.: National Academy Press, 1981), p. 9.

59. Helen Remick, ed., *Comparable Worth and Wage Discrimination* (Philadelphia: Temple University Press, 1984); George Milkovich, *The Nature of the Earnings Gap* (New York: The Conference Board, 1987); General Accounting Office, "Pay Equity: Status of State Activities," (Washington, D.C.: U. S. General Accounting Office, September 1986).

60. *You've Come a Long Way—Maybe: A Working Woman's Guide to Pay Equity* (Washington, D.C.: American Federation of State, County, and Municipal Employees, 1984).

61. Milkovich, "Nature of the Earnings Gap"; Henry J. Aaron and Cameron M. Lougy, *The Comparable Worth Controversy* (Washington, D.C.: Brookings Institution, 1986); W. Y. Oi, "Neglected Women and Other Implications of Comparable Worth," *Contemporary Policy Issues* 4, no. 2 (1986), pp. 24–37; J. O'Neill, "Issues Surrounding Comparable Worth," *Contemporary Policy Issues* 4, no. 2 (1986), pp. 38–47; J. Roback, *A Matter of Choice: A Critique of Comparable Worth by a Skeptical Feminist* (New York: Priority Press, 1986).

62. Al Bellak, "Comparable Worth: A Practitioner's View," in *Comparable Worth: Issue for the 80s*, vol. 1 (Washington, D.C.: U. S. Civil Rights Commission, 1985).

63. David A. Pierson and Karen S. Koziara, *Study of Equal Wages for Jobs of Comparable Worth* (Philadelphia: Center for Labor and Human Resource Studies, 1981).

64. Nina Rothchild, "Overview of Pay Initiatives, 1974–1984," in *Comparable Worth: Issue for the 80s*, vol. 1.

65. Alice Cook, "Comparable Worth: Recent Developments in Selected States," *Proceedings of the 1983 Spring Meeting of the Industrial Relations Research Association*, Honolulu, March 1983, pp. 494–504. Some economists are beginning to model the costs and effects of comparable worth at an aggregated level, including Mark Killingsworth, "The Economics of Comparable Worth: Analytical, Empirical, and Policy Questions," in *Comparable Worth*, ed. H. I. Hartmann (Washington, D.C.: National Academy Press, 1985), pp. 86–115. See also Sandra E. Gleason and Collette Mosher, "Some Neglected Policy Implications of Comparable Worth," *Policy Studies Review*, May 1985, pp. 595–600.

66. Eric Cousineau, "Comparable Worth: A List of Readings" mimeo series 23, Industrial Relations Centre, Queen's University at Kingston, Ontario, Canada, 1987.

67. Benson Rosen, Thomas Mahoney, and Sara Rynes, "Compensation, Jobs, and Gender," *Harvard Business Review*, July 1983, pp. 170–90.

chapter

twenty

BENEFITS

CHAPTER OUTLINE

AT&T pays about $1.5 billion a year on its employees' health care and those costs have grown about 17 percent annually for the past five years. Once called fringe benefits, employee benefits are no longer "fringes." They constitute a major portion of labor costs. In 1929 benefits amounted to only 3 percent of total payroll; by 1969 they were 31 percent; in 1980 they topped 40 percent.[1] Exhibit 20-1 depicts this growth.

As employees' average income increased 90 percent from 1960 to 1985, the value of employee benefits increased almost 400 percent. The 1980s have witnessed a slight decline to a stable level of about 36 percent. The decline is attributed to two factors: First, inflation rates declined and economic expansion slowed. Second, and perhaps more important, a change occurred in the approach to managing benefits. The mismanage-

EXHIBIT 20–1
Benefits as Percent of Payroll

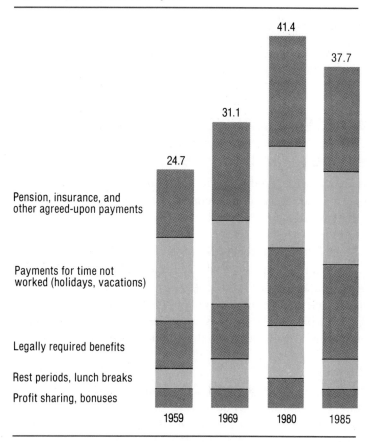

Source: Adapted from *Employee Benefits 1985* (Washington, D.C.: U.S. Chamber of Commerce, 1986).

ment of benefits in the 70s has given way in the 80s to an overriding concern for controlling the costs of benefits.[2] The emphasis shifted from "more is better" to cost containment.

Definition

Employee benefits are the indirect form of the total compensation; they include paid time away from work, insurance and health protection, employee services, and retirement income.

Up to this point we have examined decisions including direct or cash compensation, external competitiveness (pay levels), internal hierarchies (pay structure), relative mix (pay forms), and individual employee's pay. This chapter addresses the basic decisions managers make in the design and administration of benefits programs. We consider the conditions affecting benefits decisions, discuss the objectives managers try to achieve with benefits, examine the alternative forms benefits take, and then highlight what is known about their effects.

A DIAGNOSTIC APPROACH TO BENEFITS

Assessing External Influences

Your familiarity with the diagnostic model has probably already led you to anticipate the factors affecting benefits. Once again government policies and regulations are the key.

Government Policies and Regulations

The major government policies which influence benefits are fourfold: wage controls, tax policies, civil rights legislation, and specific benefit laws. The first three focus on the broader effects of government regulation on the entire benefits package; we discuss these next. The laws dealing with specific benefits are woven throughout the chapter.

Wage Controls

The War of Independence was barely over when Albert Gallatin established the first recorded profit-sharing plan in the United States at his Pennsylvania glass works. In spite of this long history, the big push for increasing benefits occurred during World War II, when the federal government imposed wage controls on employers.[3] Wartime needs created serious shortages of workers. Because increases in wages were controlled, employers and unions came up with new ways to attract and retain employees. Managers began to offer inducements not subject to government controls. If the government would not permit managers to offer greater wages to entice workers, then managers would offer to pay medical bills, provide life insurance, and subsidize cafeterias instead.

Tax Policies

If wage controls were the impetus for the use of benefits, tax policies encouraged their growth. Most benefits are nontaxable income to employees and deductible expenses to employers.[4]

In addition to encouraging the expanded use of benefits, public policy also affects their coverage by ensuring that benefits are nondiscriminatory.[5] Here discriminatory does not refer to gender or race discrimination. It means that some benefits must be available to a large portion of the work force to qualify for favorable tax treatment. For example, very specific financial rules regulate any capital accumulation plan offered by employers (pensions, stock ownership, and savings plans). The purpose of these regulations is to prevent the bulk of such nontaxable benefits being given to only a narrow group of employees—"highly compensated participants,"—typically executives and/or shareholders. In a sense, encouraging wider employee participation in benefits plans requires managers to make benefits more equitable.

Civil Rights Laws

Three laws, Title VII of the Civil Rights Act, the Age Discrimination in Employment Act (ADEA), and the Pregnancy Discrimination Act, are particularly important.

Title VII of the Civil Rights Act. Title VII prohibits discrimination in the terms, benefits, and conditions of employment based on race, color, religion, sex, or national origin. Sex discrimination existed in two types of pension plans.[6]

1. Plans that require women to contribute a higher premium than men to receive the same benefits as men, other things being equal.
2. Plans that require women to contribute the same amount but pay them smaller benefits than men, other things being equal.

The insurance industry justified such differences based on the fact that women as a class live about five years longer than men; therefore, the pension cost to the employer for the average retired woman was greater than the cost for the average retired man. But the Supreme Court rejected this position.[7] The court agreed that actuarial tables show that women live longer than men. But in many *individual* cases, women live shorter lives than men. The court ruled that Title VII of the Civil Rights Act applies to individuals, not classes. Because not all individual women live longer than all individual men, differential payments illegally discriminate against those women required to pay more. Therefore, differential payments are illegal.

In addition to paying the same premium, women must also receive the same pensions.[8] The Court found that paying lower benefits to female than male retirees, when both made the same contributions, is illegal.

Thus, actuarial tables used to determine the cost of employer-provided insurance must be based on the combined illness, accident, and death rates for both men and women. Using separate experience ratings for men and women is illegal if the employer provides the insurance. Differential ratings are still permissible if individuals buy the insurance directly from an insurance agent. Exhibit 20-2 shows how much more women pay for insurance ($15,732 over a lifetime) than men when sex-based actuarial tables are used.

EXHIBIT 20–2
How Much More Women Pay for Insurance than Men

Coverage	Lifetime Cost Differential for Women (dollars)
Typical hospital-surgical policy from State Farm Mutual for years 25 to 64. $100 daily room and board; $2,000 surgical. Includes pregnancy complications. Excludes normal pregnancy, childbirth.	+6,862
Typical disability policy for years 25 to 64 from Allstate Life. $700/month base benefit. Excludes pregnancy, childbirth, miscarriage, abortion. Includes complications and nonelective caesarean section.	+4,854
Typical policy for age 65 retirement from Minnesota Mutual. Life insurance before age 65, $100,000. Monthly pension starting at age 65, $1,000. Pay premiums for years 35 to 54. Dividends estimated by company deducted.	+5,856
Typical liability and physical damage policy, using factors rated by Insurance Services Office. Primary classifications: youthful operator; good student; unmarried; owner or principal operator; drive to work or business use, medium-size town. For years 17 to 24.	−1,840
Total difference	$15,732

Source: National Organization for Women.

Age Discrimination in Employment Act (ADEA). The Age Discrimination in Employment Act prohibits job-related discrimination against workers between the ages of 40 and 70. This law has a threefold effect on benefits:

1. Pensions: After 65, workers need not be permitted to accrue service credits (and hence greater benefits) for their pensions. In other words, after 65 a pension can be "frozen" at whatever level employees would have received had they retired at 65.
2. Life Insurance: Coverage cannot be eliminated after age 65. However, reduction in the amount is permitted if an employer can demonstrate that continuing benefit coverage at the pre-65 age level results in higher costs.
3. Health Care: Total health benefits cannot be reduced between the ages 65–70. The employer may only reduce health insurance by the amount of medicare coverage available.

Pregnancy Discrimination Act. Should women be permitted health, disability, and/or sick leave benefits because of pregnancy? The Supreme Court held that an insurance benefit that exempts pregnancy from disability coverage did not constitute sex discrimination under Title VII.[9] Reasoning that men and women were covered equally except for one condition, pregnancy, the court ruled no insurance plan must be all-inclusive.

This decision met with sufficient opposition from women's organizations, unions, civil rights groups, and sympathetic legislators to be overturned by law in 1978. The Pregnancy Discrimination Act "prohibits the denial of health, disability or sick leave benefits to pregnant women temporarily disabled by childbirth itself or by a medical condition incurred before or after childbirth if such coverage is provided for nonpregnancy-related conditions." Such coverage only applies if a valid benefit plan is already in effect. It does not require an employer to offer a medical benefit program. But if a program is offered to employees, pregnancy must be treated the same as any other medical condition.

In 1983 the Supreme Court applied the act to pregnancy benefits received by spouses of employees. The Newport News Shipbuilding Company set a limit on maternity benefits for spouses of male employees. The limit did not apply to maternity benefits for female employees, nor was there a limit on any other medical condition for spouses of female employees. The court ruled that continuing this differential was discriminatory. Benefits that distinguish in coverage between employees and dependents are legal, but dependent coverage must be the same for all dependents, regardless of sex. An employer may not pay a lesser share of maternity costs than is paid for other medical conditions, no matter if those benefits go to an employee or a dependent.

Unions

In addition to government policies, unions have been a dominant force to improve benefits.[10] In the 1960s and 1970s, a major thrust of unions' bargaining strategy was for increased levels and new forms of benefits. Group auto insurance, dental care, eyeglasses, and prepaid legal fees became common issues at the bargaining table. Unions' success at the bargaining table has a spillover effect on nonunionized employees in the same facility. One study found evidence that benefits for nonunion employees improved 15 to 50 percent when blue-collar employees in that facility belonged to unions.[11]

Witness the Chrysler Corporation experience (Exhibit 20–3). Chrysler pays all health care insurance premiums for its workers and retirees, their dependents, and survivors. Those who are covered by the premiums pay nothing. The policy covers the entire cost of their hospitalization and medical tests, and almost all of the cost of outpatient dental, psychiatric, vision, and hearing care. For retired workers and their surviving spouses, the insurance pays nearly everything that medicare does not. Workers who are laid off their jobs get full coverage for a year. The result is that for every vehicle Chrysler produces, health insurance premiums cost more than the window glass.[12]

Unions have played a major role in employers' efforts to control health care costs.[13] Since most benefits are a form of tax-free income to their members, unions actively opposed congressional efforts to tax benefits, particularly health insurance. And unions have actively worked with management in seeking approaches to contain rising health care costs, since many members view health care coverage as important as pay increases. Exhibit 20–4 lists some of the ways unions are helping to cut health care costs. Seeking second opinions before surgery and auditing the doctor's bills were the most effective cost reducers. General Motors Corporation claims that its health care bill fell by about 10 percent last year—to $2.1 billion. The savings are traced to the steps taken with the United Auto Workers. The reversal came after annual increases of 14 percent since 1973. Thus, the cost of GM's health benefits added to the price of each car dropped from $400 to $300.[14]

Economic

Competitive pressures impact benefit decisions in conflicting ways. Struggling to achieve competitive prices for their products and services, managers look to reduce, or at least curtail, increases in labor costs.[15] At 36 percent of labor costs, benefits capture a manager's attention. Approaches to reduce or manage these expenses more efficiently have high priority.

EXHIBIT 20–3
Health Care Costs at Chrysler Corporation

	Insurance Premiums*	Premiums per Hour Worked	Hourly Wage	Premiums per Vehicle Produced
1970	$ 81	$ .31	$4.27	$ 55
1973	141	.45	5.25	73
1976	230	.80	7.00	127
1979	350	1.93	9.81	287
1982	331	3.30	11.13	458
1983	364	2.74	10.47	346

Insurance premiums per active employee

Company pays full benefits for active and retired employees
$295

Drug plan added
$482

Dental plan added $1,157

Vision and hearing plans added; dental plan to retirees
$2,044

Benefits improved; vision plan to retirees
$3,154

Rapid health care inflation
Smaller work force
More retirees
$6,000

1964   1969   1974   1977   1979 1983

*In $ millions.

Note: Hourly wages of Chrysler assemblers in December of each year from United Automobile Workers. Other data from Chrysler Corporation.

On the other hand, competition in labor markets to attract and retain productive employees creates pressure to match the benefits offered by others. When others include dental insurance and recreational facilities in their offer, employers who do not may be at a disadvantage.

Assessing Internal Influences

Organization Strategies and Objectives

Organization strategies and objectives shape the benefit decisions managers make.[16] A large, well-established employer in a growing or mature industry, for example, may offer a relatively generous benefit package. But a smaller, newly formed, emerging firm may find that the high fixed costs attached to many benefits, particularly pensions, entail too great a finan-

EXHIBIT 20–4
Some of the Ways Unions Are Helping to Cut Health Care Costs

Second opinions: Require members to seek them before surgery.
Audits: Encourage workers—often with financial rewards—to check their hospital and doctor bills.
Pretesting: Encourage medical tests prior to hospital admissions.
Precertification: Set up a review board to determine on a case-by-case basis whether hospitalization is necessary—and for how long.
Outpatient surgery: Provide incentives for doctors to perform some simple operations in their offices or clinics rather than in the hospital.
Treatment review: Monitor present and past treatments to ensure that they are both appropriate and needed.
Insurance checks: Cross-check policies to stop payments of the same bill by different carriers.

cial risk. Instead, such firms often emphasize incentive pay or profit sharing, where costs vary with the firm's profitability, and de-emphasize insurance programs or other fixed cost benefits. For example, Rolm Corporation, a midsized computer firm, did not provide pensions for its employees. Rather, all employees belonged to stock option programs and a profit-sharing plan designed to provide economic security. When IBM acquired Rolm, it phased the stock option plan into the IBM pension system. As an independent firm, Rolm was not financially able to undertake the fixed costs of pension plans. Additionally, some Rolm executives felt that stock options and profit sharing supported the firm's entrepreneurial strategy better than pensions, which focus on retirement rather than firm performance.

Employee Preferences and Demographics

The preferences and demographics of the particular employees in an organization also affect benefits.[17] On the face of it, the fact that benefits are tax-free to employees would seem to make them very attractive. Yet we really do not know whether employees prefer tax-free benefits over pay in the form of cash that is taxed. It seems to depend in part on income level. A few studies found that employees at higher income levels preferred more benefits to cash, but the majority of employees prefer cash.[18] For lower-paid employees, fewer tax advantages exist, or perhaps these employees may have more immediate needs that only cash can satisfy.

Employees do have preferences among different forms of benefits. Studies suggest that most preferences vary widely, depending on employee demographics. And these preferences change over time.[19]

Employee demographics refers to the makeup of the work force (e.g., their age, sex, working spouses, number of dependents, income level, time until retirement). Employees close to retirement or with college age children clearly have different benefit preferences than newly hired employees with working spouses and preschool children. Beyond preferences, the demographics of the work force affect costs. Exhibit 20–5 shows the age profile of Ford Motor Company workers. Based on the aging of its work force, Ford expects its health care costs just for the company's hourly retirees and their spouses to jump to $300 million by 1990 from $160 million in 1984, since older workers on average have substantially higher medical expenses.[20] Work force age profiles also affect pension funding, vacation time, and other benefits.

Other demographic factors, such as the increasing proportion of women and dual-career families in an organization's work force, probably increase employees' interest in child care and flexible benefit programs to avoid duplicate coverages.[21]

Cafeteria or flexible benefit plans take differences in employee preferences into account. Under such arrangements employees choose among alternative benefit coverages. Flexi-benefit plans are covered in detail in a later section. Next we turn to setting benefit strategies and objectives.

EXHIBIT 20–5
Average Age of Ford's U.S. Hourly Workers
(in years)

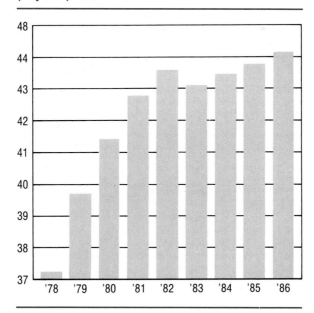

Source: John Bussey, "An Older Work Force Burdens Big Producers in the Basic Industries," *The Wall Street Journal*, March 8, 1987, pp. 1, 21.

Setting Benefit Objectives and Strategies

This book defines efficiency in productivity and cost terms and equity in fairness and justice to employees. It defines employees' behaviors by their performance, absenteeism, decisions to join, to accept promotions, or to leave. The specific objectives employers set for their benefits reflect to some extent these more generic objectives. Exhibit 20–6 shows JC Penney Company's benefits objectives. Typically benefits accomplish four objectives: (1) fostering external competitiveness, (2) increasing cost effectiveness, (3) meeting individual employee's needs and preferences, and (4) complying with legal regulations. They relate more to costs (competitiveness, cost effectiveness, and compliance) and perhaps less to equity and fairness. The connections to productivity and specific employee behaviors are more tenuous.[22] The reason is that benefits were intended to help protect employees' physical well-being and help provide for retirement. They were not intended to be tied to an individual's performance.

Integrate with Human Resource Objectives

As part of the total compensation system, benefits are also linked to the overall human resource strategies and objectives. Previous chapters discussed the decisions regarding the overall mix among pay forms—the portion of compensation allocated to base pay, merit, gainsharing, and benefits. Decisions on the various forms of benefits are necessary, too. As with all forms of compensation, the benefits offered need to be consistent with and support the organization's objectives and strategies. For example, benefits may be designed with emphasis on the short term. Health insurance, generous vacation plans, or recreational facilities may be offered to help a growth-oriented employer attract new employees. Or the emphasis may be on long-term benefits that emphasize job security and

EXHIBIT 20–6
Benefit Objectives

To Our Penney Partners:

Teamwork, sharing, and mutual support—the same kind of cooperative effort that provides outstanding value and service for our customers—are all part of our benefits philosophy. Associates in the Penney family support one another's benefits during our active careers and in retirement. The Company shares in this team effort by contributing financial support where benefits help is most needed. Too, part of this help is by creating new plans responsive to associate needs such as tax-deferred savings and the Penney Stock Ownership Plan (PenSOP). The result . . . a strong, vital program that gives substantial financial security—providing the greatest amount of protection at least cost to you.

encourage a stable, committed work force.[23] More money may be put into pension funds or tax-reduction strategies to reward employees for years of service to the organization. The configuration of the benefits package should be consistent with the strategy of the overall compensation system and help achieve the organization's objectives.

Benefit Strategies: Entitlements versus Contributions

The specific benefit decisions managers make mirror benefit strategies. Overemphasizing to illustrate the point, some organizations may foster a sense of caring and belonging as part of a family; it follows that all employees are entitled to benefits that help maintain their economic and physical well-being. Other employers pursue a more performance-driven strategy; their compensation programs, including some benefits, are linked to the performance of the firm and individual employees. In reality, many firms probably use a combination of these two extremes.

James O'Toole draws out the implications of the two extreme strategies. He argues that as benefits increase, contribution, responsibility, and initiative are less and less linked to compensation and rewards.

> Workers have an expanding sense of what is due them as rights of employment. From pension, health care, long vacations to a high standard of living, the perception by workers of what constitutes their rights is inexorably being enlarged. Concomitant with the spiraling sense of rights has been a declining sense of responsibility.[24]

O'Toole offers the following example:

> the largest single item in the Los Angeles City operating budget: Pensions for police and firefighters. It accounts for about 50 percent of all property tax revenues. The pension fund has an uncapped cost-of-living adjustment and is based on the salary of the worker on the last day before retirement—thus encouraging last minute promotions to captain shortly before "retirement" at age 38.[25]

Consequently, O'Toole sees a basic trade-off when facing benefit decisions: entitlements versus contributions. The trade-off is between the proportion of total compensation received in the form of benefits (entitlements) for simply holding a job or belonging to the organization, versus the proportion allocated to increasing unit productivity, superior performance, innovation, and risk taking (contributions).[26]

A countervailing argument to O'Toole's is that secure, committed employees are more likely to adapt and accept changes required for the organization to be competitive. Further, employees are entitled to basic benefits as part of their employment relationship.

A Benefits Gap

A related position is that all members of society have certain rights, including the right to adequate health care and freedom from poverty. Is it the government's responsibility to provide these things to every citizen, whether through welfare programs or through mandated employer-provided programs?[27] For those in society who are employed, employer-financed insurance and pensions provide a convenient method to ensure these things. For those not employed or employed in part-time jobs or in very small organizations, a benefit gap exists between the haves and the have-nots. Some in society believe that employees should not be forced to choose between job and health, or between job and family. Therefore, society's best interests are served if parental leave, child care, health care, and other benefits are available to all employees who require them. Accordingly, a minimal level of benefits should be part of any compensation system. The countervailing argument is that many small employers cannot afford a benefit program, and that any mandated program prohibits changes in response to changed economic or social conditions.

Obviously, this is a political issue that deserves public debate and dialogue. Equally apparent is that the benefit decisions managers make reflect the strategies and values of an organization.

BASIC BENEFIT DECISIONS

The typical decisions managers face in the design and management of benefit plans include:

- Competitiveness: How should our benefits compare to our competitors'?
- Coverage and Forms: Which benefits should we offer?
  Which employees should be eligible for each type?
- Communications: How can we best inform employees about their benefits?
- Choice: What degree of choice or flexibility can we include?
  How can we accommodate employees' interests and concerns?

Ideally, these decisions get made with some specific objectives and strategies in mind. Unfortunately, until the recent concerns over the uncontrolled costs of benefits, benefit decision making seemed to reflect more of a "monkey see—monkey do" policy than a "strategy and objective-driven" approach.

We now turn to consider these decisions and the alternatives available.

COMPETITIVENESS

Just as with cash compensation, an employer adopts a policy to position its total compensation, including benefits, in the marketplace. More often than not, benefits are designed to meet those offered by competitors.[28] By offering employees choices among various benefits, firms such as TRW, Honeywell, and others are attempting to emphasize a unique competitive posture regarding benefits. Even though the array of benefits offered matches competitors' offerings, the opportunity for employees to tailor benefits to their personal circumstances is relatively unique. As Exhibit 20–7 reveals, over 500 firms have installed these plans.

Assessing external competitors' benefits is accomplished through market surveys. Conducted by consultants and professional associations, these surveys provide data on the different benefits offered, their coverage, eligibility, and costs. The data allow employers to assess the competitiveness of their benefits and costs with those offered by others.

Costs are often compared on four bases:

1. Total cost of benefits annually for all employees.
2. Cost per employee per year: Item (1) divided by number of employees.
3. Percentage of payroll: Item (1) divided by annual payroll.
4. Cost per employee per hour: Item (2) divided by employee hours worked.

EXHIBIT 20–7
Flexible Benefits Plans Are Spreading

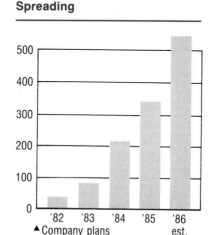

Source: Data, Hewitt Associates.

Bruce Ellig suggests these data be examined in the following manner:

1. Examine the internal cost to the company of all benefits and services, by payroll classification, by profit center.
2. Compare the company's costs for benefits to external norms. For example, compare its costs to average costs, averages by industry, and so on, for the package as a whole and for each benefit.
3. Prepare a report for the decision maker, contrasting steps 1 and 2 and highlighting major variances.
4. Analyze the costs of the program to employees. Determine what each employee is paying for benefits, totally and by benefit.
5. Compare the data in step 4 with external survey data.
6. Analyze how satisfied the individual is with the employer's program, and as compared to competitor's programs.[29]

The preceding steps place emphasis on what benefits cost an employer. The assumption is that if an organization is spending the same amount on benefits as its competitors are, then its benefits package must be competitive. Jerry Rosenbloom and Victor Hallman suggest another approach. They propose using *actuarial valuations* to assess competitiveness.[30] Using the employer's actual employee population (or targeted subpopulation), they apply a standard set of actuarial assumptions (e.g., likelihood of death or disability, need for medical care), and calculate the value to the employees of a specific benefit package under these conditions. Then they compare this value to the value of various competitors' plans under the same conditions. The object here is to compare values of plans, rather than their costs to the employers. Exhibit 20–8 illustrates the approach. In the survey the average value of all benefits of all employers is equal to 100. Then the values assigned to individual employers are graphed. For example, if the average value of benefits to an employee in a participating company is $100, the value of your benefits package is $174.80, or about 75 percent higher than the average value of survey participants.

A further external comparison is the configuration of the benefits offered. Exhibit 20–9 illustrates this. The top circle shows the percentage of the actuarial value of benefits allotted to various categories of benefits; for example, for this employer, 26 percent of the total actuarial value of its benefits is in the form of vacations and holidays. The bottom circle shows that vacations and holidays on average account for 30 percent of the value of benefits among employers included in the survey. Even though such data may not convince an employer to increase vacation pay, it does provide information on how others are allocating their benefits expenditures.

EXHIBIT 20–8
Illustration of Actuarial Benefit Value Comparisons—Pension and Profit–Sharing Plans

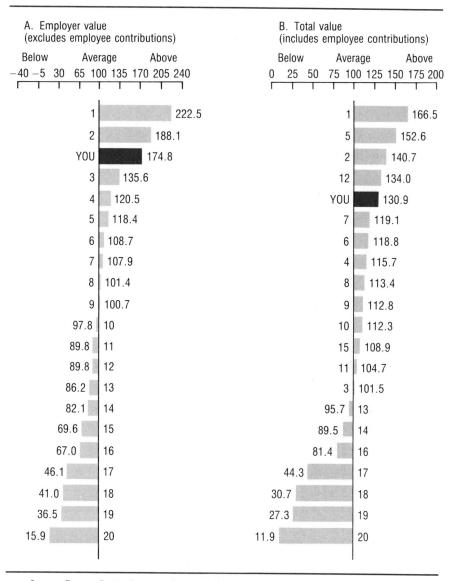

A. Employer value
(excludes employee contributions)

Below	Average	Above
−40 −5 30 65 100 135 170 205 240		

1	222.5
2	188.1
YOU	174.8
3	135.6
4	120.5
5	118.4
6	108.7
7	107.9
8	101.4
9	100.7
97.8	10
89.8	11
89.8	12
86.2	13
82.1	14
69.6	15
67.0	16
46.1	17
41.0	18
36.5	19
15.9	20

B. Total value
(includes employee contributions)

Below	Average	Above
0 25 50 75 100 125 150 175 200		

1	166.5
5	152.6
2	140.7
12	134.0
YOU	130.9
7	119.1
6	118.8
4	115.7
8	113.4
9	112.8
10	112.3
15	108.9
11	104.7
3	101.5
95.7	13
89.5	14
81.4	16
44.3	17
30.7	18
27.3	19
11.9	20

Source: Towers, Perrin, Forster & Crosby (TPF&C).

This actuarial valuation is an improvement over comparing employers' costs of benefits; however, there are some drawbacks. The approach is complex and therefore expensive to prepare and update. Additionally, all the caveats that apply to salary surveys apply here as well, for instance,

EXHIBIT 20–9
Illustrations of Actuarial Benefit Value Comparisons
—Total Value of Benefits

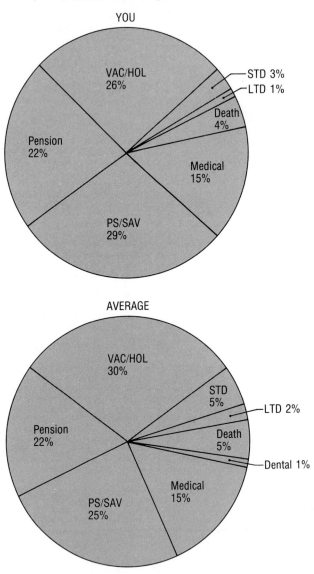

Component Plan Values As Percentages
of Overall Benefit Program

YOU

VAC/HOL 26%
STD 3%
LTD 1%
Death 4%
Pension 22%
Medical 15%
PS/SAV 29%

AVERAGE

VAC/HOL 30%
STD 5%
LTD 2%
Pension 22%
Death 5%
Dental 1%
Medical 15%
PS/SAV 25%

Source: Towers, Perrin, Forster & Crosby (TPF&C).

relevance of comparisons and accuracy of data provided.[31] There is the further issue of appropriateness: What competitors offer may not be appropriate for a particular employer. For example, with Ford's aging work force (Exhibit 20–5), an education reimbursement plan may not be suitable. Ford may be further ahead offering Medicare supplements, no matter what its competitors do. In spite of these limitations, external comparisons are necessary to assess the adequacy of benefits as well as the entire compensation package.

COVERAGE: ALTERNATIVE FORMS OF COMMON PLANS

Four benefits are typically provided employees: paid time away from work, employer-purchased insurance, employee services, and retirement income. Some benefits are legally mandated; these include unemployment insurance, workers' compensation, and social security.

Paid Time Away from Work

A paid holiday or vacation with pay did not always exist. People used to work 12 hours a day, 6 days a week, 52 weeks a year.[32] Now most employers compensate employees for some time that they have not worked, such as lunch and rest periods or coffee breaks. Employers also pay employees when they are not actually at work—holidays, vacations, or sick leave. Most organizations offer vacations with pay after a certain minimum period of employment. Exhibit 20–10 shows the service requirements for paid time off stipulated in a United Auto Workers contract. Many employers offer additional paid personal days off, to be taken at the convenience of the employee.

EXHIBIT 20–10
UAW Contract Yearly Benefits Service Requirements

Category	Seniority Requirement	Level
1. Vacation	Less than 5 years	5 days
	5 years to less than 10 years	10 days
	Greater than 10 years	15 days
2. Paid personal holiday	None	8 days
3. Sick leave	None	5 days
4. Holidays	None	9+

Source: George T. Milkovich and Jerry Newman, *Compensation*, 2nd ed. (Plano, Tex: Business Publications, 1987).

Employer-Purchased Insurance

The expenses associated with risks encountered throughout life—illness, accident, and early death, among others—can be diminished by pooling the risk through buying insurance. In addition to the tax advantage of employer-purchased insurance, many employers can buy insurance cheaper than their employees because the rate is based upon group risk rather than individual risk. The employer may provide it free to the employee (noncontributory) or the employee may pay a share of the premium (contributory). Three major forms of insurance are common: health, disability-accident, and life.

Health insurance is one of the most costly kinds of insurance, but it is extremely popular with employees.[33] Coverage often includes prescription drugs, mental health services, and dental care. As Exhibit 20–11 shows, health care costs have gone up far faster than other costs in each of the past five years.[34] This is in spite of employer and government watchdog efforts. Concerted efforts by employers and unions had slowed the rate of increase from an alarming 11.6 percent in 1982; yet in 1986 the discrepancy between the overall Consumer Price Index and the medical care component widened enormously. The Consolidated Omnibus Reconciliation Act (COBRA), passed in 1986, boosted the cost of health plans.[35] Employers are required to continue coverage for employees and their dependents after employees have lost their jobs through layoffs. Periods can range from 18 to 36 months.

EXHIBIT 20–11
Health Care Inflation

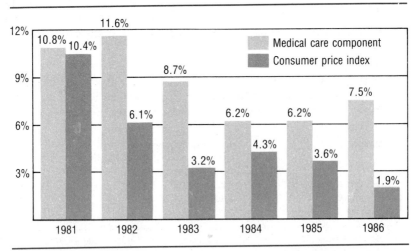

Source: *Monthly Labor Review*, U.S. Department of Labor, Bureau of Labor Statistics, 110, no. 2, February 1987, p. 79

Group life insurance is one of the oldest and most widely available employee benefits. Yet surveys show that employee preference for group life insurance is not high. In a typical program, the amount of insurance provided by the plan increases as salary increases. Continued life insurance coverage after retirement, in a reduced amount, is provided by most large companies.

Long-term sickness and accident/disability insurance protects employees who have accidents at work leaving them temporarily or permanently unable to work. Workers' compensation pays a very small part of these costs, since it is designed primarily to take care of short-term disability problems. Employer-funded long-term disability insurance supplements the benefits from workers' compensation, social security, and other agencies. About 75 percent of employers provide such coverage.

Employee Services

Services is something of a catch-all category of voluntary benefits. Included are all other benefits provided by employers such as cafeterias, saunas and gyms, free parking lots, commuter vans, infirmaries, discounts on company products, financial counseling, and child care assistance.

Educational Programs.   Many organizations provide off-the-job general educational support for their employees. The nature of the education may vary from basic reading skills programs for illiterate workers, to tuition-refund programs for managers, to scholarship and loan plans for employees' children.[36] Companies often use such plans as part of their employee development programs.

Social and Recreational Programs.   Many organizations provide recreation facilities for employees, on or off the job. Studies of the preferences of employees indicate that recreational services are the least preferred of all benefits and services offered. However, the new emphasis on controlling health care costs has increased employers' interest in healthy lifestyles. The level and rate of increase in health care costs provide a strong incentive for employers to provide wellness programs.[37]

Child Care.   The entry of record numbers of women into the labor force has dramatically increased the demand for quality child care centers. Many employees and employers feel the logical place for such centers is at the work site. Working parents frequently list adequate child care as the most important problem they face.[38]

Day care can provide a powerful recruiting tool. Applicants at a Burger King franchise, for example, reported to the manager that between 50 and 75 percent of their weekly pay went for child care expenses.[39] A child care worker offered by the employer provided an extra recruitment advantage over nearby competitors who offered higher wages. Workers bring in a weekly receipt from their sitter or child care center, and they are reimbursed for their total child care expense. The restaurant manager issues the child care payments directly from the petty cash fund to expedite workers' receipt of the payment, and the restaurant is reimbursed later by the company's head office.

Parental Leave. This benefit is another response to women's entry into the labor force. Even though few employers presently offer it, bills have been introduced in Congress for several years in a row mandating up to 18 weeks of unpaid parental leave. Many states are considering similar legislation. California's maternal leave law was upheld by the Supreme Court in 1987.[40]

Retirement Income

Employees' retirement income comes from four sources—social security benefits, private pensions, asset income, and earnings. As Exhibit 20–12 demonstrates, these sources do not provide an equal amount of income—social security is the largest source by almost two to one. But social security has gone through a series of financial crises, necessitating two major pieces of social security legislation during the past decade, both of which have increased the taxes and reduced the growth of future benefits. Financially, social security will play a smaller role in providing retirement income in the future. Some even predict that eventually it will be replaced as the major source of retirement income for the aged.

EXHIBIT 20–12
Sources of Income for the Aged (current)

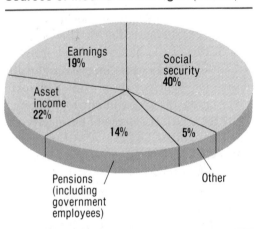

Source: Social Security Administration.

Asset Income

Asset income is money generated by personal savings and investments. The decreased role of social security retirement income in the future will be taken up by asset income—particularly through capital accumulation plans such as individual retirement accounts (IRAs) and deferred compensation plans.[41] Deferred compensation plans such as 401(k) plans (named for the section of the Internal Revenue Code that authorizes them) permit employees to postpone income taxes on a portion of salary if that salary is contributed by the employer to a qualified plan.[42] Frequently an employer matches an employee's contribution to a plan, typically on a 50 cent per $1 rate.

A number of compensation-deferral plans exist. Basically, all of them have the similar strategy of shifting income to postretirement years to capitalize on presumably lower income tax rates. However, the Tax Reform Act of 1986 reduced the attractiveness of compensation deferral plans, because many employees will always be in the top tax bracket even in retirement. (The 33 percent tax rate for the top bracket currently applies to income over $29,750).[43] The attractiveness of such plans now depends on the rate of return they offer. The Tax Reform Act also drastically cut the amount of income that can be deferred through IRAs and 401(k)s from $30,000 to $7,000, tightened restrictions on participants' borrowing against their deferred compensation accounts, and specified tests for nondiscrimination. Now, specific requirements must be met for a plan to qualify for favorable tax treatment.

Employee Stock Ownership Plans

Employee stock ownership plans are another approach to asset accumulation. Under these plans, employers make payments to a trust, which purchases the employer's stock for the benefit of employees. Employers get a tax deduction for the contribution, and employees accumulate equity in the organization. Laws regarding tax treatment and requirements for such plans are periodically revised. Thus, ESOPs (employee stock ownership plans) preceded TRASOPs (tax reduction act stock ownership plan), which preceded PAYSOPs (so named because they are tied to the company's payroll, in order to provide greater benefits to labor-intensive industries). The 1986 Tax Reform Act freed ESOPs from some restrictions placed on other capital accumulation plans. This flexibility encouraged corporations to use ESOPs to raise capital as well as transfer ownership to employees.

Employee ownership theoretically has the potential to "improve corporate performance, create a more equitable distribution of wealth, and build a society in which enriching one group will not automatically mean taking something away from another group."[44] However, the success of

ESOPs in accomplishing these objectives depends on the health of the organization before the transfer of ownership. What is needed is clear identification of an organization's particular problems, objectives, and solutions. Employee ownership does not eliminate all the problems that may exist.[45] But it does represent another retirement income option for employees and managers to consider.

In addition to stock ownership, incentive stock options (ISOs) are frequently used for executives in companies whose stock is likely to increase in value.[46] All of these variations on employee ownership are the result of legislation intended to accommodate a particular social goal or curb a particular abuse. Thus, further revisions can be anticipated.

Private Pensions

Many employers provide pension funds to retired employees, with the amount usually based on years of service and income level while employed. There is an astounding variety in pensions. While only about half of all U.S. employees are covered by private pension plans, the federal government offers pensions that are double the rate of those in private industry.[47]

Private pension plans ran into serious criticism in the recession in the 1970s. Many people who thought they were covered were not because of complicated rules, insufficient funding, mismanagement, and bankruptcies. These problems lead to the Employee Retirement Income Security Act (ERISA) passed in 1974, and the Retirement Equity Act of 1984 which amended it. ERISA was designed to regulate the approximately 400,000 private pension plans; it does not, however, require employers to provide pension plans.[48] If one is offered, then it must conform to ERISA regulations. There are five main regulations.

1. Eligibility: All employee earnings from age 21 must be included; only 1,000 hours of work are required during a year to be eligible. Many part-time employees are now covered.
2. Vesting and portability: Full vesting means employees own the pension benefits if they leave the employer prior to retirement. Prior to ERISA, employees could lose all pension rights if they left (or were terminated) before retirement. Employees can choose from three vesting alternatives: (a) 100 percent vested at 10 years of service with the employer; (b) 25 percent vested at 5 years, 50 percent at 10 years, and fully vested at 15 years; (c) vesting levels based on the combination of age and years of service with the employer.

   Portability is related to vesting. It refers to the employee's right to transfer vested pension funds from one employer to another when changing jobs. ERISA does not mandate portability.

3. Funding: The financial mismanagement of pension plans was the primary impetus for the passage of ERISA. Now, once an employer decides to offer a pension, it must conform to rigorous funding and reporting guidelines. Plans that were not funded adequately were required to become so within 10 years. Some research suggests that this funding provision has had two unanticipated effects: One is that many employers, particularly smaller and emerging ones, are not able to afford the fixed costs required. The other is that fully funded pensions represent a significant financial asset and may increase the likelihood of a merger or acquisition. Usually pension assets are not available for corporate purposes unless the plan is terminated and a new one created. One takeover attempt of USX offered $31 a share for the company's assets—over $10 a share in assets was available in the USX pension fund.[49]

4. Fiduciary liabilities: Pension fund administrators have increased legal and financial obligations under ERISA. Pension funds are to be managed solely for the participating employees and their beneficiaries.

5. Termination responsibilities: The Pension Benefit Guaranty Corporation, a nonprofit agency, was formed to protect employees whose employers failed to provide intended benefits. To cover these cases, ERISA established a reserve fund created by yearly payments from employers for each covered employee.

Mandated Benefits

Employers are legally required to offer certain programs to employees. These mandated benefits are social security, unemployment compensation, and workers' compensation.

Social Security

Established in 1935, the social security system provides some income protection to employees who have retired or are disabled, as well as to the survivors of deceased workers. Both employees and employers pay social security taxes. Exhibit 20–13 shows the current tax rates and base income. In 1987 employees paid 7.15 percent on incomes up to $42,600, for a maximum tax of $3,046. Employers paid an equal amount. When the system first started, workers lived only a few years after retirement. In 1935, 150 workers supported each retiree; in 1950 the ratio was 14 to 1, and by 1990 it will be 2 to 1. With longer life expectancies, increased benefits, and a declining number of young workers entering the work force, social security no longer replaces workers' income at the level it did previously. Currently, a covered employee receives full benefits at age 65 and reduced benefits are available at age 62. By the year 2027, many students reading

EXHIBIT 20–13
Tax Rates, Maximum Earnings Base, and Maximum Social Security Tax

Year	Taxation Rate on Covered Earnings		Total × Maximum Earnings Base		Maximum Social Security Tax (dollars)
	For Retirement Survivors and Disability Insurance (percent)	For Hospital Insurance (percent)	(percent)	(dollars)	
1978	5.05%	1.00%	6.05% ×	$17,700	$1,070.85
1979	5.08	1.05	6.13 ×	22,900	1,403.77
1980	5.08	1.05	6.13 ×	25,900	1,587.67
1981	5.35	1.30	6.65 ×	29,700	1,975.05
1982	5.40	1.30	6.70 ×	32,400	2,170.80
1983	5.40	1.30	6.70 ×	35,700	2,391.90
1984	5.40	1.30	7.0 ×	37,800	2,646.00
1985	5.70	1.35	7.05 ×	39,600	2,791.80
1986	5.70	1.45	7.15 ×	42,000	3,003.00
1987	5.70	1.45	7.15 ×	*	—
1990	6.2	1.45	7.65 ×	*	—
2000	6.2	1.45	7.65 ×	*	—

*Automatic adjustments based on average earnings level.
Source: Social Security Administration (SSA) Bulletin No. 79–10044, 1979, and Annual Statistical Supplement, 1984–85.

this book will have to wait until age 67 to receive full benefits. Finally, the benefits one receives depend on past earnings and length of work experience.

Social security provides income protection beyond pensions, including survivor benefits for children under age 18, benefits for totally disabled employees, and medicare health coverage for those beyond 65.

Unemployment Compensation

Unemployment compensation (UC) was set up as part of the Social Security Act of 1935. It is designed to provide a subsistence payment for employees between jobs. The employer pays into the UC fund at a rate based on the average number of former employees who have drawn benefits from the fund.

To be eligible for compensation, the employee must have worked a minimum number of weeks, be without a job, and be willing to accept a suitable position offered through the State Unemployment Compensation Commission. Court decisions have supported state laws denying compensation to employees on strike, although some state laws do permit payments to strikers.

To fund unemployment compensation, the employer pays a tax to the state and federal government on total wages paid. Currently the tax is 3.4 percent of the first $6,000 earned by each worker. However, if an organization has laid off very few employees, it may qualify for a lower tax rate. State unemployment commissions receive the bulk of the funds. The federal government keeps a small percentage for administrative expenses and to repay federal loans made to states that have depleted their own funds because of extended unemployment.

Each state has its own set of interpretations and payments. Payments by employers and to employees vary because the benefits may vary, experience ratings of employers may vary, and some states are much more efficient in administering the program than others.

Workers' Compensation

Workers' compensation is an employer-paid insurance program designed to compensate an employee for the expenses sustained from a work-related injury. An injury is compensable if it is the result of an accident that occurred in the course of employment. Diseases that result from occupations (e.g., black lung disease in miners) are also compensable.

The compensation comes in two forms: monetary reimbursement for disability or death and payment of medical expenses. Medical benefits account for over 30 percent of the benefits paid. Fixed schedules of minimum and maximum payments regulate the amount of compensation. The agency calculates disability payments based on formulas that take into account the employee's earnings, number of dependents, and other factors. Employers must submit detailed accident and death records.

Workers' compensation laws exist in every state, and each is different. Some states require that employers obtain insurance for workers' compensation through a private carrier; in other states, companies may participate in a state fund. Larger employers who can prove their financial ability to carry their own risk may self-insure. Improvement of safety conditions at the work site can lead to lower insurance costs if accidents decline as a result.

Some states provide a "second injury" fund in conjunction with workers' compensation. These funds relieve the liability of an employer when a preemployment condition combines with a current work-related injury to produce disability greater than caused by the latter alone. An example might be if a person with a preexisting heart condition breaks an arm in a fall that resulted from a heart attack. The broken arm is covered by worker's compensation; the heart condition is not.

Because each state offers its own program, the levels of protection, and consequently associated costs, differ considerably.[50] For example, some California lawyers advertise that they specialize in disability claims resulting from job stress. In some states, workers' compensation costs employers more than state income tax does. South Dakota publicizes its substantially lower workers' compensation rates as part of its border war to lure businesses from neighboring Minnesota. Thus, workers' compensation often becomes a litmus test of how hospitable a specific state is to business or labor, because the state sets the level of benefits and, therefore, the costs.

COMMUNICATION

Writer after writer bemoans the fact that employees do not appreciate or value their benefits, largely because they are unaware of them. But given the frequency of uncoordinated, haphazard administration, many employers seem equally unaware of them. Except for costs. Too many benefit departments are the purview of the Bob Cratchits, who may be very good at managing forms, but lack either the talent or the authority to boost their effectiveness. Researchers have found that when employees know more about their benefits, they become more satisfied.[51] So perhaps some training in effective communication should be a prerequisite for benefits administrators.

Some employers do design programs to inform employees about their benefits. Some employers even send employees copies of bills paid by the company for medical expenses on their behalf. ERISA requires employers to communicate with employees by sending them an annual report on their pension plan and basic information on their pensions.

CHOICE: FLEXI-BENEFITS

Communication is not a one-way process. A basic premise underlying benefits management is that employees need to be involved in choosing benefits; if some choice is available, then the chances are that employees will (1) understand their benefits, and (2) be more satisfied with benefits. However, the reverse is also plausible. Familiarity and understanding may breed dissatisfaction if the benefits program does not satisfy employees' needs. Yet the increased participation and involvement of employees should help ensure that benefits decisions are more responsive to their needs.

The degree of choice firms offer employees varies. Most firms allow employees to specify whether or not they wish health insurance to cover their dependents, and to designate their insurance beneficiaries. Even more choice is offered to those employees covered by collective bargaining agreements, although it is a group choice reflecting negotiators' agreements. The greatest choice in contemporary systems is in flexible benefit plans.

How Flexi-Benefits Work

Although there are various benefits programs, the *core cafeteria plan* is the most common.[52] Under its provisions, employees have identical minimum levels of benefits for health and life insurance and pensions. They may then choose whichever benefits they prefer: additional life insurance, more vacation time, better health insurance coverage, dependent health insurance, long-term disability, dental coverage, or child care services. Employees purchase these choices by using benefit credits designed into the plan. Different options require different levels of credits. Exhibit 20–14 illustrates Primerica Corporation's flexi-benefits plan. Employees periodically recertify or revise their choices. In this way changes in employees' needs are recognized.

Advantages

The basic advantage of flexi-benefits is that they are designed to meet employees' preferences. If employees' benefit preferences are satisfied, they may be less likely to be absent and more reluctant to quit.

Disadvantages

For a long time, the most serious disadvantage of flexible benefit plans for employers was uncertain treatment by the IRS.[53] In 1984 just as flexible plans were becoming widely adopted, the IRS ruled that those plans allowing employees to take out any portion of their allocation as cash forfeited their tax-exempt status. So a plan may let the employee direct how the benefits budget is allocated, but the entire budget must be allocated to benefits, not given as cash. The 1986 Tax Reform Act reduced employer uncertainty by clarifying the criteria for a tax-exempt benefit plan, including the standards for nondiscrimination.[54]

Another concern is the significant administrative effort required to maintain a flexible benefits program. Administration includes extensive communications policies, employee counseling services regarding available choices, and sophisticated record-keeping and accounting systems. Computerized human resource information systems simplify these tasks.[55]

Also related to costs is the problem of "adverse selection." Employees may choose or alter their benefits to cover the costs of extensive perceived

EXHIBIT 20–14
Flexible Benefits at Primerica Corporation

The
concept

The idea behind flexible benefits is very simple. It reflects our belief that each individual should have the ability to choose the benefits that are most meaningful to him or her. Under flexible benefits, you'll have a basic foundation — or core — of coverage and an allowance to use in putting together your own benefit program around that core.

The Development of Flexible Benefits

Think of our pre-flexible benefit program (the program we had before flexible benefits) as a circle divided into five parts — medical benefits, life insurance benefits, vacation, disability, and retirement and capital accumulation benefits. Over the past few decades, we worked hard to build a benefit program that stands among the best available in industry today. The trouble is, no one program — however rich — can ever meet everyone's needs equally well. People are too different for that.

Now picture an inner circle of benefits which we'll call the core. This core area represents fundamental protection that can't be changed under the flexible benefits system. It's a basic foundation of security for all employees — security no one can opt out of.

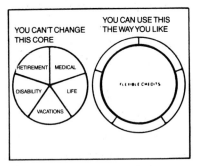

How Flexible Credits are Figured

The difference between the core and your pre-flexible benefits is transformed by insurance and actuarial calculations into flexible credits which are allocated to you in dollars. You can then use those dollars for benefit options. With them, you can build your own benefit program around the core. The amount of flexible credits you are allotted will vary from year to year. That's because they depend on your particular age, pay, family status, and years of service with the company. You'll be given your flexible credit allowance on the form you use to make your benefit option decisions. This same principle holds even if you joined us without having ever been covered by the pre-flexible program. Your flexible credit allowance will be figured the same way.

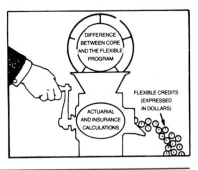

needs. For example, employees may take extensive dental coverage in one year, then opt out of dental coverage the following year. For the next few years they may pay for routine dental care themselves and then opt back into the dental care program when major work is again needed. This results in erratic cost patterns for the company, as premiums increase according to the use or overuse of the provision, and curtails its ability to spread a risk over a large group. In addition, the job of administration becomes increasingly difficult as employees opt in and out of various benefit options.

Employees also can face some disadvantages under flexible plans; namely, they can cost more. Flexible plans can mean:

1. Higher copayments. When they introduce new plans, many companies also raise the copayments and deductibles paid by employees.
2. Less protection from inflation. Many plans require employers to pay part of any increases in health care premiums.
3. Fewer cross-subsidies. Young, single employees, who tend to be light users of medical care, have traditionally partly subsidized heavier users, such as families or older employees.
4. Skewed options. By pricing some benefits higher than others, a company can steer employees toward cheaper choices. For example, complete dental coverage might be priced to cost the employee much more, proportionately, than partial coverage.[56]

Flexible Benefits as a Cost Reduction Strategy

Some claim that flexible benefits significantly lower the costs of introducing new forms of benefits. To illustrate, it may be that a company has a group insurance plan with liberal life insurance and hospital/medical benefits. The company has no dental plan. By adopting a flexible approach, the company offers a dental plan at no additional expense to the company. Employees pay the cost by reducing other personal benefit coverages. Thus, employees satisfy their needs while the employer does not increase the costs of providing an additional benefit.

Many employers use the introduction of flexi-benefit plans as an opportunity to raise employees' contributions and deductibles. For example, PepsiCo put in a flexible system for 35,000 employees. And they required employees to pay half the increase in medical costs. As costs go up, the employer and employee share them. Xerox Corporation's 55,000 employees also pay 1 percent of their annual earnings to help cover health care.[57]

Additionally, flexible benefits can address unique concerns. For example, including child care services as part of a flexible benefits package permits employees who need the service to select it. At the same time, the employer avoids the appearance of favoring one group of employees—those who require child care services—over other employees who have no use for it. Flexible benefits permit a wider variety of benefits and a greater degree of employee choice than may otherwise be affordable.

EVALUATING THE RESULTS OF BENEFIT DECISIONS

The previous section discussed the basic decisions managers face in the design and administration of benefits. These include competitiveness, coverage, communication, and choice. Certainly managers do not make these decisions unilaterally. The government, employees, and their unions are very concerned with and often very involved in the process. The costs involved make these decisions salient to all parties. Given their relevance and costs, evaluating the results of benefits decisions deserves special attention.

From a decision-making perspective, managers evaluate benefits by their objectives. Three objectives deserve special attention: The first is the cost effectiveness of benefit decisions. A second is their impact on employees' work behaviors, and the third is the fairness or equity with which employees view them.

Unfortunately much of the discussion that follows is drawn from conventional wisdom and beliefs. The lack of objective evidence to support these beliefs is disquieting, in light of the costs associated with benefit programs.

Effects on Costs

Clearly, benefit decisions influence labor costs. The first paragraph of this chapter reported the latest cost estimates; the average annual cost of employer-paid benefits is $7,580 per employee. Employers, in response to the mounting costs, have launched a variety of efforts to control costs.

Controlling Costs

Because health care costs have experienced the greatest growth, increasing almost three times faster than overall price increases in the economy (Exhibit 20–11), they have received most of the attention. Tactics for controlling costs include changing employees' consumption patterns, changing financing methods, and coordinating or managing benefits more efficiently.[58]

Changing Consumption Patterns

Copaid benefit plans require that employees pay a share of costs. For example, employees may be required to pay a share of medical insurance premiums (deductibles), or they may be required to pay a part of total medical expenses (copayments). In 1981, less than a third of medical plans required employees to pay any deductible. By 1986, two thirds of plans required deductibles. By requiring employees to pay a portion of costs, employers hope to heighten cost awareness and increase selectivity in using services. Although this is currently one of the most popular cost containment strategies, it has the potential to backfire. Without effective communication, employees may see copayment and increased deductibles as cutbacks in benefit levels. Health insurance may symbolize security—a defense against a financially and psychologically devastating crisis. Thus, many employees are more willing to take a pay cut than reduce health care coverage.[59] A strategy to overcome this problem may be to reinvest the savings that result from a copayment system in a longer-term cost-prevention program that is clearly perceived by employees to improve their health.

Requiring second opinions or preauthorization before covering certain medical expenses are other ways employers hope to motivate employees to be more selective in using medical services.

Changing Financing Methods

For employees whose health insurance premiums are based on community wide claim experience, as little as 50 percent of the premium may go to pay providers of health care. Larger companies can often afford to set up a fund internally to cover health care claims. Expenses are then paid out of this fund, rather than by an insurance company. Because of the large number of employees involved, companies can predict the risk factors from actuarial tables and anticipate and budget expenses. The advantage of self-insured employers is increased control, and if actual expenses come in under budget, the savings go to the employer rather than an insurance company. The downside of self-insurance is administrative problems and expenses, but much of this can be subcontracted to consulting firms.

Processing costs for self-insurance have been reported to be around 3 percent.[60] Thus, 97 percent goes to pay providers of care as compared to the 50–50 ratio under some insurance policies. Additionally, better coordination of benefits and elimination of state taxes and insurance company charges can boost savings an additional 10 to 20 percent. Employees can obtain better data on cost patterns, which permits better management of expenses.

So the savings from self-insurance can be substantial. However, self-insurers must have adequate numbers of covered employees to spread the risk, plus handle the added risk of similar exposure characteristics of certain occupations. For example, Boise Cascade Corporation employs loggers, an occupation that has one of the highest rates of industrial accidents in the United States. Boise may not have sufficient numbers of low-risk employees to offset the loggers, so it may be better off spreading risk among other insurance company clients.

Another way to change financing methods is to negotiate expenses. Kaiser Corporation provides the classic example of negotiating expenses. To control hospital expenses, Kaiser built its own hospital for employees and hired its own doctors. Few employers go to this extreme, although health maintenance organizations (HMOs), in which all medical services are provided for a flat monthly rate, have often been started at employers' instigation.

More and more employers are negotiating discounts with hospitals, laboratory services, and druggists.[61] Sometimes these special rates are in exchange for a certain volume of business. Many employers have enjoyed corporate rates at hotels and motels for years. They are now demanding similar breaks in medical care.

Jerry Newman recommends a "cost-centered" approach to benefits management.[62] If future costs of a benefit cannot be ascertained, he recommends that employers only offer it on a cost-sharing basis. An employer would determine a percent of the cost it was willing to bear and share all cost data with employees. The employees then choose if the benefit is worth the costs to them. Newman advocates negotiating all benefits directly with individual employees, rather than providing a package that has been determined by a benefits manager and/or union negotiator.

Improving Coordination

Often benefits are not well managed. Many employers view them almost as a "fixed cost" and take them for granted, much the same as do employees. But closer scrutiny and coordination can reduce costs. For example, two thirds of all employers do not coordinate pension levels with social security.[63] Yet it is cost effective to do so. Within plans, employers rarely analyze coverage to see that it is internally consistent.[64] Gross deficiencies as well as overlaps can occur if benefit plans are not well coordinated.

Effects on Employees' Behavior

The literature on benefits is rife with lists of employees' behavior that different forms of benefits are assumed to affect.[65] These include inducing applicants to join, reducing absenteeism, maintaining loyal, committed employees, and improving performance. There is some evidence that vesting provisions in pensions and health insurance curtail turnover and absenteeism.[66] General Motors and the UAW linked absenteeism with reduced benefits.[67] Under their scheme, employees who were absent more than 20 percent of their scheduled work time during the first six months of the contract were offered counseling. If they exceeded the 20 percent rate during the second six months of the contract their benefits were cut equal to their absence rates. Cuts occurred in paid holidays, jury duty pay, and sickness and accident benefits. They reported an 11 percent drop in "controllable" absences the first year and 10 percent and 9 percent in subsequent years of the contract.

Modified benefit programs are also helpful during periods of work force reduction, or when a socially acceptable and graceful exit is desirable for specific employees.[68] Often in these situations, health and disability insurance is extended beyond the period of employment, or retirement provisions are sweetened. In one example mentioned earlier, IBM used a 1986 Retirement Incentive. This amendment to their retirement plan added five years of age and service to employees' actual age and service for calculating retirement benefits. IBM tried to make retirement more attractive and reduce their headcount while avoiding layoffs.

Benefits' effects on other behaviors, such as applicants' decisions to join an employer, are less well researched. Some benefit terms may, at best, have an indirect effect on performance. The argument in support of an indirect effect is that unhealthy, worried, or troubled employees are not likely to perform at their best. Attention wanes, absenteeism increases, sustained effort at the job simply cannot be maintained. All of these work to lower productivity. Consequently, benefits designed to assist employees to maintain their health (health insurance), financial well-being (pensions), and personal emotional stability (drug counseling, child care, legal assistance) help avoid these problems. Certain forms of retirement benefits, particularly ESOPs, are also thought to affect productivity. Researchers believe owning shares of their employer positively affects employees' motivation and performance. Here again these suppositions are based more on belief than analysis.

Effects On Equity

Employees' perceptions of fairness and adequacy of benefits are also an important objective. Research does show that the overall level of benefits is positively related to employees' satisfaction with their benefits. And there is also some support for the proposition that increased communication and choice increase employees' satisfaction with their benefits.[69]

More work is required here. We need a better understanding of employees' reactions to various coverages and types of benefits and to the opportunity to choose among various coverages. The Opinion Research Corporation found a sharp drop in the satisfaction with benefits over the past decade.[70] Theirs was a nationwide sample of employees. They attribute this drop to a failure to restructure benefits in response to the changing demographics of the labor force which we discussed in Chapter Two.

SUMMARY

Benefits account for over one third of payroll costs. The average employer pays $7,580 a year per employee for benefits. In spite of the hefty price tag, it has only been in the last few years that managing benefits has had a high priority for employers.

Not only are benefits expensive, but they aren't always the benefits that employees want. Satisfaction with benefits has slipped dramatically in the last 10 years. Benefits have not kept step with changes in the demographics of the workplace.

This chapter has described the major benefits decisions: competitiveness, alternate coverage, communication, and choice. Competitiveness refers to structuring one's benefit package in relationship to one's competitors'. Some of the issues here are identical to those discussed in the previous chapter on external competitiveness.

Some benefits are required by law: unemployment compensation, government pensions, and workers' compensation. In addition, most employers offer additional benefits, such as compensation for time off (holidays, vacations), employer-purchased insurance (health, life, and disability), private pensions, and other services such as prepaid legal services, health club memberships, or child care centers.

Communication to employees about their benefit coverage deserves greater attention than most organizations give it. Research shows that communication tends to increase employees' satisfaction with benefits. This may occur because employees typically underestimate the value of their benefits.

One innovative approach to tuning benefits to individual preferences, as well as control costs, is flexible benefits. Under these plans, employees are given a core group of benefits, plus credits for additional benefit coverage, that they may allocate in any way they choose. The Internal Revenue Service has a number of requirements that must be met for such plans. Nevertheless, flexible benefit plans are becoming increasingly popular.

Although managers can easily calculate the effects of benefits on costs, their effects on employees' behaviors and on equity are less easily documented. Benefits may even be dysfunctional, since few of them are tied to performance. Rather, they are entitlements—given to employees as part of the conditions of employment. On the one hand, benefits provide a social good. But by steadily increasing them, fewer dollars remain to reward the risk-taking behavior or performance levels required for an organization to maintain its competitive edge and/or profitability.

DISCUSSION AND REVIEW QUESTIONS

1. Why do employers provide benefit plans?
2. How and why can benefits be tailored to individual needs?
3. Why are copayment strategies not always successful?
4. What effect does communication have on the various benefit objectives?
5. What effect will changes in society (demographic, expectations, values) have on benefits? How can an employer capitalize on such changes?

NOTES AND REFERENCES

1. U.S. Chamber of Commerce, *Employee Benefits 1985* (Washington, D.C.: Chamber of Commerce, 1986).
2. R. E. Allen and T. J. Keaveny, "Costing Out a Wage and Benefit Package," *Compensation Review* 15, no. 2 (1983), pp. 27–37; Philip Kienast, "The Modern Way to Redesign Compensation Packages," *Personnel Administrator*, June 1983, pp. 127–33; Regina E. Herzlinger and Jeffrey Schwartz, "How Companies Tackle Health Care Costs: Part I," *Harvard Business Review*, July–August 1985, pp. 69–81; R. E. Herzlinger, "How Companies Tackle Health Care Costs, Part II," *Harvard Business Review*, September–October 1985, 108–120; and R. E. Herzlinger and David Calkins, "How Companies Tackle Health Care Costs: Part III," *Harvard Business Review*, January–February 1986, pp. 70–80.
3. William J. Cohen, "The Evolution and Growth of Social Security," in *Federal Policies and Worker Status since the Thirties*, ed. J. P. Goldberg, E. Ahern, W. Haber, and R. A. Oswald (Madison, Wisc.: Industrial Relations Research Association, 1976).
4. Robert M. McCaffery, *Managing the Employee Benefits Program* (New York: American Management Associations, 1983).
5. Jerry Rosenbloom and G. Victor Hallman, *Employee Benefit Planning* (Englewood Cliffs, N.J.: Prentice-Hall, 1981).
6. Paul Schultz and Cheryl Fells, "Current Development in Employee Benefits: Meeting the Unisex Challenge," *Employee Relations Law Journal* 9, no. 4 (1984), pp. 694–704.
7. *Los Angeles Dept. of Water and Power v. Manhart*, 435 U.S. 702 (1978).
8. *Arizona Governing Committee v. Norris* 32 Fair Empl. Prac. Cas. 233 (1983).
9. *Gilbert v. General Electric Company* 429 U.S. 125 (1976); Geraldine Leshin, *EEO Law: Impact on Fringe Benefits* (Los Angeles: University of California, Institute of Industrial Relations, 1979).

10. Richard Freeman and James Medoff, *What Do Union Do?* (New York: Basic Books, 1984); James E. Long and Albert N. Link, "The Impact of Market Structure on Wages, Fringe Benefits and Turnover," *Industrial and Labor Relations Review,* January 1983, pp. 239–50; Joanne S. Lublin, "Moves to Cut Health-Care Benefits Meet Stiff Opposition from Unions," *Wall Street Journal,* October 26, 1983, p. 33.

11. Loren Solnick, "The Effect of Blue-Collar Unions on White-Collar Wages and Fringe Benefits," *Industrial and Labor Relations Review,* January 1985, pp. 236–43; and Richard B. Freeman, "The Effect of Unionism on Fringe Benefits," *Industrial and Labor Relations Review,* July 1981, pp. 506–7.

12. David E. Rosenbaum, "Chrysler, Hit Hard by Costs, Studies Health Care System," *New York Times,* pp. 1, B8.

13. "Chopping Health Care Costs: Labor Picks Up an Ax," *Business Week,* March 31, 1986, pp. 78–79.

14. Ibid., p. 78.

15. Peter Cappelli, "Concession Bargaining and the National Economy," in *Proceedings of the Thirty-Fifth Annual Meeting of the Industrial Relations Research Association,* 1982 (Madison, Wisc.: Industrial Relations Research Association, 1983), pp. 362–71; and Robert S. Gay, "Union Settlements and Aggregate Wage Behavior in the 1980s," *Federal Reserve Bulletin* 70 (1984), pp. 843–56.

16. Michael F. Carter and Kenneth P. Shapiro, "Develop a Proactive Approach to Employee Benefits Planning," *Personnel Journal,* July 1983, pp. 562–66; Diana Chapman Walsh, Sharon G. Henze, and Susan E. Kelleher, *Designing Cost-Effective Employee Health Plans* (New York: Pergamon Press, 1982).

17. Robert C. Wender and Ronald L. Sladky, "Flexible Benefit Opportunities for the Small Employer," *Personnel Administrator,* December 1984, pp. 111–18.

18. Albert R. Cole, "Flexible Benefits Are a Key to Better Employee Relations," *Personnel Journal,* January 1983, p. 51; McCaffery, *Managing Benefits.*

19. Richard E. Johnson, "Flexible Benefit Plans," *Employee Benefits Journal,* September 1986, pp. 2–7.

20. John Bussey, "An Older Work Force Burdens Big Producers in the Basic Industries," *The Wall Street Journal,* March 8, 1987, pp. 1, 21.

21. S. J. Carroll and R. S. Schuler, "Professional HRM: Changing Functions and Problems," in *Human Resources Management in the 1980s,* ed. S. J. Carroll and R. S. Schuler (Washington, D.C.: Bureau of National Affairs, 1983).

22. G. P. Brunker, "The Potential for Performance-Based Benefit Plans," *Compensation Review* 14, no. 3 (1982), pp. 23–32.

23. Olivia S. Mitchell, "Fringe Benefits and the Cost of Changing Jobs," *Industrial and Labor Relations Review,* October 1983, pp 70–78.

24. James O'Toole, "The Irresponsible Society," in *Working in the 21st Century,* ed. C. Stewart Sheppard and Donald C. Carroll (New York: John Wiley & Sons, 1980), p. 156.

25. Ibid., p. 163.

26. George T. Milkovich and Jerry M. Newman, *Compensation*, 2nd ed. (Plano, Tex.: Business Publications, 1987).

27. Linda Demkovich, "Covering Options through Mandated Benefits," *Business and Health*, January–February 1986, pp. 2–6.

28. Thomas Paine, "The Emphasis in Benefits Design Has Shifted from Enriching the Competitive Package to Cost Containment" (speech given March 29, 1984, to Employee Benefits Conference sponsored by The Conference Board).

29. Bruce Ellig, *Executive Compensation—A Total Pay Perspective* (New York: McGraw-Hill, 1982).

30. Rosenbloom and Hallman, *Employee Benefit Planning*.

31. Milkovich and Newman, *Compensation*, chap. 7.

32. Edwin Markham, Benjamin Lindsey, and George Creel, *Children in Bondage* (New York: Hearst's International Library Company, 1914).

33. Kermit Davis, William Giles, and Hubert Feild, "Compensation and Fringe Benefits: How Recruiters View New College Graduates' Preferences," *Personnel Administrator*, January 1985, pp. 43–50.

34. "Cost Containment," *Medical Benefits*, April 15, 1986, pp. 1–3.

35. Sidney Simon, "Benefits Administration that Complies with COBRA," *Personnel Journal*, March 1987, pp. 44–46.

36. Irwin Ross, "Corporations Take Aim at Illiteracy," *Fortune*, September 29, 1986, pp. 48–54.

37. *Company Practices in Health Care Management* (Lincolnshire, Ill.: Hewitt Associates, 1985); Herzlinger and Calkins, "How Companies Tackle Health Care Costs"; Gary T. McIlroy, "Health Care Costs Containment in the 1980s," *Compensation Review*, Fourth Quarter 1983, pp. 15–31.

38. Oscar Ornato and Carol Buckham, "Day Care: Still Waiting Its Turn as a Standard Benefit," *Management Review*, May 1983, pp. 57–62; Sheilia B. Kamerman, "Child-Care Services: A National Picture," *Monthly Labor Review*, December 1983, pp. 35–39.

39. Sandra L. Burud et al., *Child Care: The New Business Tool* (Pasadena, Calif.: National Employer Supported Child Care Project, 1983).

40. *California Federal Savings and Loan Association v. Guerra*, 107 S. Ct. 683 (1987).

41. Jon Sutcliffe and Jay Schuster, "Benefits Revisited, Benefits Predicted," *Personnel Journal*, September 1985, pp. 62–68; Gary S. Fields and Olivia S. Mitchell, "Earnings, Pensions, Social Security, and Retirement" (Working paper No. 44, Cornell University, 1983).

42. *Tax Aspects of 401(k) Plans: Information for Employers and Employees* (Chicago: Commerce Clearing House, 1983); Karen Ferguson, "How 401(k)s Hurt Lower-Paid Workers," *New York Times*, April 27, 1986, p. 2F.

43. Carson Beadle, "Taxing Employee Benefits: The Impact on Employers and Employees," *Compensation Review* 17, no 2 (1985), pp. 12–19.

44. Corey Rosen, "Growth versus Equity: The Employee Ownership Solution," *ILR Report*, Spring 1985, pp. 19–22; Polly Taplin, "ESOPs Meet the Needs of a Variety of Companies," *Employee Benefit Plan Review*, June 1983, pp. 10–14.

45. Ben Fischer, "A Skeptic Looks at Employee Buyouts," *ILR Report*, Spring 1985, pp. 23–26.

46. Bruce Ellig, "Stock Option Design Consideration," *Compensation Review,* First Quarter 1983, pp. 13–24; G. E. Ray and W. N. Bret, Jr., *Financial Incentives for Corporate Executives: Wealth-Building Programs and Techniques* (Englewood Cliffs, N.J.: Prentice Hall, 1976).

47. James Bovard, "Trim the Civil-Service Pension Bonanza," *The Wall Street Journal,* February 14, 1985, p. 36.

48. *Pension and Retirement Plans: Issues and Strategies* (Greenvale, N.Y.: Panel Publishers, 1986).

49. "Fat Pension Funds Can Make Companies Tempting Targets," *Business Week,* November 10, 1986, pp. 106–8.

50. U.S. Chamber of Commerce, *Analysis of Workers' Compensation Laws, 1985* (Washington, D.C.: Chamber of Commerce, 1985), Publication no. 6803.

51. Lance D. Tane, "The Three Levels of Benefits Communication," *Personnel Journal,* March 1987, pp. 92–102.

52. *Flexible Benefits: Will They Work for You?* (Chicago Commerce Clearing House, May 19, 1983); S. Sherwood, "Flexible Benefits Can Reduce Costs over the Long Term," *Business Insurance,* December 14, 1981, pp. 2–12.

53. James H. Shea, "Cautions about Cafeteria-Style Benefit Plans," *Personnel Journal,* January 1981, pp. 37–39; S. Sherwood, "Employers Not Ready to Bet on Flexible Benefits," *Business Insurance,* June 7, 1983, pp. 11–20.

54. "Viewpoint, Tax Reform: A Green Light for Flexible Programs," in *On Flexible Compensation*, October 1986, monthly newsletter published by Hewitt Associates, Lincolnshire, Illinois.

55. Simon, "Benefits Administration"; Lance Tane, "Guidelines to Successful Flex Plans: Four Companies' Experiences," *Compensation and Benefits Review,* July–August 1985, pp. 38–45.

56. "Benefits Are Getting More Flexible—But *Caveat Emptor,*" *Business Week,* September 8, 1986, pp. 64–66.

57. Ibid., p. 64.

58. Robert Becker, "Utilization Review" (speech given October 7, 1986, Lake Tahoe Health Care Cost Containment Seminar, sponsored by International Foundation of Employee Benefit Plans, Brookfield, Wisconsin). Also see numerous other references listed in this chapter.

59. David Lyle and John Willard, "Employee Involvement in Health Care Cost Management," *Employee Benefits Journal,* December 1984, pp. 9–17; Steven Greenhouse, "Health Plans Are Feeling a Little Peaked," *New York Times,* August 24, 1986, p. 5.

60. C. Bradford, "Self-Funded Trusts: An Answer to Rising Benefit Costs," *Financial Executive,* July 1981, pp. 24–26; J.C. Milligan, "Firms Foresee Higher Costs, Move toward Self-Insurance," Business Insurance, March 22, 1982, pp. 3–10.

61. Ronald Dervan, "Laying the Groundwork with Total Benefits Planning—Part I," *Pension World,* September 1981, pp. 104–6; Ronald Dervan, "Planning and Implementing Flexible Benefits Plans," *Pension World,* October 1981, pp. 23–26.

62. Milkovich and Newman, *Compensation,* chap. 12.

63. T. N. Fannin and T. A. Fannin, "Coordination of Benefits Uncovering Buried Treasure," *Personnel Journal,* May 1983, pp. 386–91; Marian Extejt,

"Who Gets the Benefits after a Divorce?" *Personnel Journal,* October 1983, pp. 790–94.

64. William J. Wiatrowski, "Employee Income Protection against Short-Term Disabilities," *Monthly Labor Review,* February 1985, pp. 32–38; Rosenbloom and Hallman, *Employee Benefit Planning.*

65. Milkovich and Newman, *Compensation;* Freeman and Medoff, *What Do Unions Do?;* Long and Link, "Impact of Market Structure on Wages."

66. Mitchell, "Fringe Benefits."

67. George Ruben, "GM's Plan to Combat Absenteeism Successfully," *Monthly Labor Review,* September 1983, pp. 36–37.

68. Scott Macey, "Reductions in Force and Employee Benefits Considerations" (paper presented at Age Discrimination and Retirement Benefits Law Conference, November 21–22, 1985, Palm Springs, California).

69. Marie Wilson, Gregory Northcraft, and Margaret Neale, "The Perceived Value of Fringe Benefits," *Personnel Psychology* 38 (1985), pp. 309–20.

70. Reported in *The Wall Street Journal,* April 30, 1985, p. 1.

PART SIX CASES

▶ ITHACA'S OWN
CASE 7 COMPRESSION AND EXTERNAL
EXPERIENCED HIRING

Ithaca's Own is committed to significantly increasing the staff levels in research and development, and sales. Finding the talent that I-O is seeking is a difficult task; paying them appropriately without causing serious internal equity concerns is even more difficult. The point is illustrated in the following example:

Internal Comparisons

	Salary after Fiscal Year 1988 Increase	Degree	Years Experience	Last Performance Rating
Manager 1	$60,876	MS	12	Very good
Manager 2	60,974	BS	7.5	Very good
Manager 3	57,132	MS	11	Very good
Manager 4	59,251	BS	8	Fully qua
Manager 5	61,302	BS	7	Outstanding
Manager 6	60,910	BS	7	Outstanding

External Offer

Outside Hire 1	64,500	BS	8	—

This scenario is repeated in nearly all external experienced offers that we make. What alternatives does I-O have to fix the problem, and what are the optimal solutions given its strategy and business conditions?

▶ ITHACA'S OWN
CASE 8 SALARY BUDGETS AND PAY INCREASES

Gordon Wable, the director of human resource management at I-O, has been notified by the CEO that he will receive a salary increase budget of 12 percent for the planned year (the amount is 12 percent of current total salaries). The increase is to be divided among the four human resource managers described below.

Assignment

Prepare a report recommending a salary increase program for Wable. Keep in mind that it is I-O's policy to compensate employees on a pay-for-performance basis. The report should include specific salary recommendations for each person, plus an analysis of current and past practices, as well as a detailed discussion of the rationale for your salary increase program. In addition, discuss three pieces of additional information I-O should start collecting to improve next year's decisions. Explain how these data will be used.

Able Lee

Able Lee has been with Ithaca's Own since the establishment of the human resource management function two years ago. As human resource manager for Operations, Able serves all facets of that department's human resource needs. In addition to his generalist duties, Able played a key role in the development of I-O's current recruiting program and currently coordinates annual college recruiting across departments. Four of the 10 professionals who service the human resource function report directly to him. Before joining Ithaca's Own, Able spent 10 years as a generalist at IBM and three years as director of college relations at General Electric. Able Lee's current performance rating is "excellent," his potential rating is "qualified." Four years ago he received an MBA degree. His current salary is $67,500; last year's increase was $4,615; the previous year's, $4,460.

Jane Johnson

Jane Johnson, also a generalist by training, services the R&D department. She is highly regarded ("excellent" performer, "promotable" potential rating), and joined I-O directly from the college campus where she received an MBA. Prior to returning for the MBA, she worked as a generalist for one of Eli Lilly's production facilities in North Carolina for six years. In addition to her current responsibilities, Jane has been asked by the director of HRM to review I-O's status concerning compliance with OSHA standards. She is responsible for two human resource professionals. Her current salary is $52,600; her last increase was $4,200 and before that it was $3,950.

Sarah Newburg

Sarah Newburg joined I-O one and a half years ago, after spending four years as a training program consultant to various manufacturing organizations. She was responsible for fine-tuning the newly developed training program to address the needs of I-O's new managers. Sarah is currently the human resource manager serving Marketing and Sales but occasionally assists other departments with their training programs. She received an MS degree seven years ago. Three professionals report directly to her. Her performance rating is "excellent," and has a "qualified" potential rating. Sarah's current salary is $40,500. Her last year's increase was $3,300.

John Dibble

John, an industrial psychologist by training, has been with Ithaca's Own for two years. Prior to joining I-O he worked for five years at Westinghouse, supervising their Quality Work Life program. John has expressed an interest in establishing an outplacement counseling service for I-O's employees but no funds have been allocated for the project yet. John services the Administrative Service department and is responsible for one human resource professional. His performance is "satisfactory" and his potential rating is "qualified." Currently his salary is $36,000; the last two increases have been $2,760 and $2,400.

▶ STATE GOVERNMENT

Shirley Fleenor is responsible for personnel for a state in the western United States. An official in the state government has a problem.

State Senator Roger McAreavy, a Republican, had just made a fiery speech on the floor of the Senate. He was attacking inefficient and ineffective government. In his speech, which was widely covered throughout the state, he said:

> I suppose that a simple businessman like myself just can't comprehend really complex matters like state government. But I'll tell you that any

business which had the record this administration does would be bankrupt by now. If Republicans were running the state, it would be run on a businesslike basis. Instead, we have the wholesale incompetence and waste of this Shaw administration which I'm sure when the people wake up will be thrown unceremoniously out the front door of the statehouse and the governor's mansion. Until that happy day, I guess the people will have to swallow hard and pay higher taxes for the incompetence in Capital City.

Even the TV picked it up. Rarely does the electronic media give much play to state government administration.

The facts the esteemed senator cited were excerpted from the recently published report by the Good Government League. Normally, these reports are filed in libraries without much comment. But this is an election year—three months from the primaries and six months from the election. Governor Shaw has announced that he will run for reelection. Senator McAreavy is running unopposed in the Republican primary.

The Good Government League's report covered many aspects of the state administration. That part that the senator cited was on page 10. It criticized the state administration for having the worst employee turnover in the area. The report showed that this state had a higher turnover than the other nine western states. It compared the state to *overall* turnover and in each category of employment as well. The report said:

> It is distressing to learn that our beloved state finishes absolute last in every category of employment turnover. Turnover is important because it is expensive and leads to gross ineffectiveness. It is expensive because every time an employee leaves, the state must incur recruiting costs, selection costs, and training costs. It is ineffective because everyone knows that there is a period during which all new employees have not reached their peak effectiveness. During that time, the employee make mistakes. Something *must* be done to stop this waste of the taxpayer's money!

About an hour after the speech was on TV, the governor's office called, and the governor's administrative assistant requested that Fleenor be in the governor's office at 7:30 A.M. the next morning to brief the governor prior to his regular Wednesday press conference. Governor Shaw knows he will get a question about McAreavy's speech, and he wants to be ready.

That's why Fleenor is still at her desk at 10 P.M. Tuesday trying to prepare a briefing for the governor.

The trouble is that the figures are true. The state has had terrible turnover. Why? Well, the pay the state government offers has been poor for years. Often, what happens is that the government winds up with those employees who cannot get employment elsewhere. This may be so because they had a bad work record or because they are not adequately trained. Once they are trained, they leave for better jobs, or the less desirable employees get fired.

One supervisor in the conservation department has characterized his plight this way. "They send us people who come into my office and say 'Oh! What is that machine there?' I reply that it is a typewriter. As soon as they are adequately trained for clerk typists, they go cross-town to the mining company or the lumber company at a 33⅓ percent raise."

The state has always had this problem, but it has gotten worse in the last few years. For one thing, more industry has come into Capital City. Second, the older industry has expanded. Since the population hasn't increased that much, the salary structure of private industry has risen to attract the people. The legislature was made aware of this, but in the spirit of "economy in government" did not raise the salary scale enough.

What the state does have is a very generous benefit plan. Most of the items in the plan are nontaxable income. In fact, the state's plan is more generous than most of the industry in the area. Too often, state employees have left for a raise in industry but fewer benefits, so that they are really behind after taxes. But that is a hard message to get across to large numbers of employees.

Fleenor has run a series of articles about the matter in the house organ, *The Stater*, but readership studies of the magazine are depressing. Most people don't read it. She has encouraged supervisors to discuss this, but follow-up studies find that most supervisors don't do it. Their excuse is that the benefits are complicated and hard to explain to employees, many of whom are not interested.

Fleenor wonders what to tell Governor Shaw in the morning.

Discussion Question

1. You are Shirley Fleenor. Prepare the brief for Governor Shaw. Prepare a program to improve the turnover situation. Assume for Plan 1 that the legislature refuses to increase wages; for Plan 2, that it raises them one half of the difference between the present salaries and salaries for comparable jobs in private industry. Include in your program a plan for taking better advantage of your benefits plan.

▶ RSO PROGRAM

Computer General makes a significant use of stock, perhaps more so than any other nonstart-up company in our industry. They use it to:

1. Reward significant contributions.
2. Retain key performers.
3. Attract management talent.

There is little communication, however, about the worth of stock to employees. Thus, much of the value of the program is lost. In addition, they do not use stock to attract entry-level people. Computer General could use stock to attract the R&D, sales, and systems talent that they desire, yet they do not make effective use of this.

What can be done to make our stock program the tool it is intended to be? How might the program be altered to gain greater productivity, attraction, and retention?

name index

subject index